THE OLD TESTAMENT:
ITS FORMATION
AND DEVELOPMENT

THE OLD TESTAMENT:
ITS FORMATION
AND DEVELOPMENT

Artur Weiser

ASSOCIATION PRESS

New York

ASSOCIATION PRESS
291 BROADWAY
NEW YORK, N. Y.

TRANSLATED BY DOROTHEA M. BARTON, M.A.

Published in England under the title

INTRODUCTION TO THE OLD TESTAMENT

© *Darton, Longman & Todd Ltd., 1961*
First Printing November 1961
Second Printing January 1963
Third Printing September 1964
Fourth Printing September 1966
Fifth Printing November 1968

This is a translation of Artur Weiser's EINLEITUNG IN DAS
ALTE TESTAMENT, which was first published by Messrs.
Vandenhoeck and Ruprecht, Göttingen, in 1948. The text used is
that of the Fourth Edition, 1957, with some minor revisions by the
author.

Publisher's stock number: 1464
Library of Congress catalog card number: 61-14178
Printed in the United States of America

CONTENTS

INTRODUCTION

1. Name and Subject Matter, History and Literature   *page* 1
2. Arrangement   7

FIRST PART

The formation of the writings of the Old Testament

SECTION I
Prolegomena

3. Historical and cultural background   11
4. The roots of the literary tradition of the OT   16

SECTION II
The pre-literary development, forms and types   21

A. POETRY

5. The Poetic Structure   23
6. Songs   25
7. Sayings   39

B. PROSE

8. Laws and Records   54
9. Narratives   56

SECTION III
The formation of the individual books of the Old Testament   69

A. THE TORAH (THE PENTATEUCH)

10. Name and contents   70
11. The tradition concerning the composition of the Pentateuch and the internal evidence   71
12. The history of Pentateuchal criticism   74

ix

13. How the sources of the Pentateuch were formed   *page* 81
14. The Yahwist strand   99
15. The Elohist strand   111
16. Deuteronomy   125
17. The Priestly Writing   135

B. THE FORMER PROPHETS

18. The Book of Joshua   143
19. The Book of Judges   147
20. The Books of Samuel   157
21. The Books of Kings   170

C. THE LATTER PROPHETS

22. Isaiah   183
23. Deutero–Isaiah (Is. 40–55)   197
24. Isaiah 56–66   205
25. Jeremiah   208
26. Ezekiel   222
27. The Book of the Twelve Prophets   230
28. Hosea   232
29. Joel   238
30. Amos   241
31. Obadiah   247
32. Jonah   249
33. Micah   252
34. Nahum   256
35. Habakkuk   258
36. Zephaniah   264
37. Haggai   267
38. Zechariah 1–8   268
39. Zechariah 9–14   272
40. Malachi   275

D. THE WRITINGS

41. The Psalms   278
42. The book of Job   287
43. The Proverbs   295
44. The Song of Songs   299

45. The book of Ruth   *page* 302
46. Lamentations   305
47. Ecclesiastes   307
48. The book of Esther   310
49. Daniel   313
50. Ezra and Nehemiah   317
51. The books of Chronicles   323

SECOND PART

The collection of the Sacred Writings and the formation of the Canon

52. The tradition concerning the formation of the Old Testament Canon   331
53. The formation of the Old Testament as a collection of Holy Scriptures   333
54. The development of the Jewish conception of the Canon and the closing of the Canon   342
55. The Canon of the Old Testament in the Christian Church   345

THIRD PART

The Text of the Old Testament

A. THE HEBREW TEXT

56. The outward form in which the text was handed down (writing and books)   351
57. The Massoretic Text   357
58. The Samaritan Pentateuch   366

B. THE VERSIONS

59. The Greek versions (Septuagint and daughter versions)   368
60. The Targumim   380
61. The Peshitta   381
62. The Vulgate   383
63. The Polyglot Bibles   385

FOURTH PART

The Apocrypha and Pseudepigrapha of the Old Testament

A. THE APOCRYPHA

64. 1 Esdras *page* 389
65. The first book of Maccabees 391
66. The second book of Maccabees 393
67. The third book of Maccabees 395
68. The book of Tobit 397
69. The book of Judith 399
70. The Prayer of Manasses 401
71. The Rest of Daniel 402
72. The Rest of Esther 404
73. The book of Baruch 405
74. The Epistle of Jeremiah 406
75. Ecclesiasticus 407
76. The Wisdom of Solomon 409

B. PSEUDEPIGRAPHA

77. The Letter of Aristeas 413
78. The book of Jubilees 415
79. The Martyrdom and Ascension of Isaiah (*Martyrium* 418
    et ascensio Isaiae)
80. The Psalms of Solomon 420
81. The fourth book of Maccabees 422
82. The Sibylline Oracles 423
83. The Ethiopic book of Enoch 425
84. The Slavonic book of Enoch 430
85. The Assumption of Moses (*Assumptio Mosis*) 431
86. 2 Esdras (4 Ezra) 433
87. The Syriac Apocalypse of Baruch 437
88. The Greek Apocalypse of Baruch 440
89. The Testaments of the 12 Patriarchs 442
90. The life of Adam and Eve (*Vita Adae et Evae. Apoca-* 445
    lypsis Mosis)

C. THE DISCOVERIES IN THE JUDEAN DESERT

page

91. Sites and Discoveries. The archaeological exploration 450
92. Biblical Manuscripts and Commentaries 454
93. Non-biblical manuscripts 459
    I. *The Manual of Discipline* 460
    II. *The Zadokite Document* 462
    III. *The War of the Sons of Light and the Sons of Darkness* 466
    IV. *Hymns and Psalms* 470
94. The Sect of Qumran 473

Index of Biblical and Post-Biblical Passages 477
General Index 485
Abbreviations 489

Preface to the Second Edition

The distressing state of learning and of economic affairs in Germany presented various difficulties which had to be overcome before this book, long since out of print, could appear again in a second edition. Its purpose is to do its part in supplying the want of textbooks felt most of all by students. All those whose kind help contributed to its appearance deserve the thanks of the readers and the author.

Unfortunately a large part of the literature which has appeared since the war in other countries cannot be embodied in it owing to the circumstances of the time. The publications so far as they were made known to me—mainly through the kind help of the English colleagues and friends to whom this book is dedicated—have been named in the bibliographies. Those works not accessible to me have been marked with an asterisk in the hope that in time they will be within the reach of interested readers in Germany also.

In response to numerous requests the Apocrypha and the most important Pseudepigrapha have now been treated in a newly added fourth part. As regards the rest, hardly a paragraph has remained unchanged.

The nature of a textbook demands that many a detailed discussion must be omitted in favour of concentration on all the problems, and that to a certain extent personal opinions should give place to the generally agreed views in the Introductory Studies of the Old Testament. It was only in the case of the question as to how the Pentateuchal sources arose (section 13), so important for the broad understanding of a great part of the OT writings, that a closer argument could not be avoided in order to state my own views on the earlier formulations of the points at issue. Yet I hope by this means to have worked out the actual problem more clearly, without exceeding the limits of the textbook.

A. WEISER

Tübingen, July 1948

Preface to the Fourth Edition

The progressive development of Old Testament studies in recent years made it necessary to revise afresh every part of the third unaltered interim edition of this book. In this revision attention has been paid to the results of research as well as to the formulation of new questions which still await solution. This provides the student with the opportunity not only to acquire a sound stock of learning, but also to be introduced into the active progress of scientific studies which will lead him on to ponder the problems critically on his own account.

For this purpose I have enlarged the bibliographies and made full use of the most recent publications, including in particular those which have appeared in other countries and which were available to me for the last editions only to a limited extent owing to the circumstances of that time. It goes without saying that in consequence the research of others, as well as my own, has altered the picture with regard to several matters to no small extent compared with earlier editions.

The discovery of manuscripts in the Judean desert has opened up new perspectives. Their significance for the history of the script and of the transmission of the text and for the history of literature has been assessed in the appropriate places. These sensational discoveries have given rise to a number of publications from many quarters which are not all of the same value and which it is hardly possible to survey. It therefore seemed necessary to put in a special section at the end of the book a comprehensive summary of the discoveries and of their interpretations which may not be unwelcome to the reader as an introduction to the most unsettled problems.

A. WEISER

Tübingen, Autumn 1956

Introduction

1. Name and Subject Matter, History and Literature

Hupfeld, *Über Begriff und Methode der sog. biblischen Einleitung.* 1844 und ThStKr 1861, p. 3 ff.; Gunkel, *Reden und Aufsätze*, 1913, p. 29–38; R. Kittel, 'Die Zukunft der alttestamentlichen Wissenschaft', ZAW 1921, pp. 84–99; Baumgartner, 'Alttestamentliche Einleitung und Literaturgeschichte'. ThR. 1936, pp. 179–222.

The Introduction to the Old Testament deals with the problem of the formation of the OT. It includes the history of the formation of its individual books, and of their collection, the formation of the canon and the history of the text. The *title* 'Introduction to the OT' occurs for the first time in the monk *Adrianus* (ob. 440) as εἰσαγωγὴ εἰς τὰς θείας γραφάς; in German theological literature it has been in use since J. D. Michaelis, 1750.

(1) The *Early Church* possessed no comprehensive introductory work; individual subjects in this field, dealing with the language, the history, the geography and especially the interpretation (questions of exegesis) were discussed in other works: *Jerome* in the introductions to his translations of the books of the OT (405); Augustine, *De doctrina christiana* (426); Junilius Africanus, *Instituta regularia divinae legis* (550). In the *Middle Ages*, which continued to depend on the above-named scholars, importance was attached to Nicholas of Lyra (ob. 1340) and to the works of the Jewish scholars Rashi (ob. 1105) and Ibn Ezra (ob. 1167), who already made occasional critical comments. But the conception of verbal inspiration taken over from Judaism stood in the way of a scientific criticism of introductory questions.

(2) *Humanism* and *the Reformation* prepared the ground for the growth of the Science of Introductory Studies. Humanism opened the door to the Hebrew language (Reuchlin) and to the basic text. The Reformation by its textual approach to the Scriptures relied on the original text instead of on the Vulgate, and in its controversy about the dogma and the tradition of the Jewish and Catholic Churches stood for a direct theological concern with the scriptures. Some beginnings of criticism in matters of authorship and of the canon are made in Luther's *Prefaces* and in Karlstadt,

De canonicis scripturis, 1520. The first works of introduction were: Sixtus Senensis (R.C.), *Bibliotheca sancta*(1566); Rivetus (Reformed), *Isagoge*, 1627; Walther (Lutheran), *Officina biblica noviter adaperta*, 1636.

(3) It was not until the age of Enlightenment and *Rationalism* that the really scientific treatment of the introductory problems was undertaken. Thomas Hobbes, *Leviathan*, 1651, III, 33, claimed that the date of composition of the OT books should be ascertained without reference to the tradition, and Spinoza, *Tractatus theologico politicus*, 1670, chapters 7–10 drew attention to problems and objectives, some of which won recognition only much later by other paths: for instance, that the historical work from Genesis to 2 Kings is a single work of Ezra, put together out of older, partly contradictory sources. These beginnings developed fully only when the theory of verbal inspiration, which obstructed all scientific investigation, was overthrown by the pressure of rationalistic criticism. The way was opened up when rationalism proposed to study Holy Scripture on the same critical principles as other literary works, a method employed by Semler in his *Essays on the unrestricted examination of the Canon*, 1771–1775 and in the *Apparatus ad liberalem VT interpretationem*, 1773. On the artistic side Herder broke fresh ground for securing a novel appraisal of the OT in his works: *Älteste Urkunde des Menschengeschlechts*, 1774–1776; *Salomons Lieder der Liebe*, 1778; *Vom Geist der hebräischen Poesie*, 1782. Eichhorn, 'the father of the modern science of introductory studies' then worked out scientifically the suggestions of Herder in the five volumes of his *Introduction to the OT*, 1780–1783 and thereby confined this branch of knowledge to three fields which in essentials still form its subject-matter today: the history of the formation of the individual writings, of the canon and of the text. The subsequent *Introductions* of Jahn, 1793; Bauer, 1795; Augusti, 1806; Berthold, 1812; are based on Eichhorn's labours and do not go substantially beyond them.

(4) De Wette, in his contributions of 1806 to OT introductory studies (to a less extent in his *Introduction* of 1817) gave prominence to *historical criticisms* and to those of the history of religion. These influenced Vatke to produce a Biblical Theology, which presents the development of the OT literature against a background of the history of religion. They influenced also the writ-

ings of Ewald, *Dichter des Alten Bundes*, 1835 ff., *Propheten des Alten Bundes*, 1840 f. and *Geschichte des Volkes Israel*, 1843 ff.

(5) In contrast with this criticism which had become partly bogged down in negations, Hengstenberg's *Beiträge zur Einleitung ins A T*, 1831 ff., produced a reaction in apologetics towards the tradition of the synagogue and the church (authenticity of the Pentateuch, of the book of Daniel, unity of the book of Zechariah). This was carried further by Haevernick, *Handbuch der historich–kritischen Einleitung in das A T*, 1836 ff., and by Keil, *Lehrbuch der historisch–kritischen Einleitung in die kanonischen und apokryphischen Schriften des A T*, 1833; it has been taken up again recently by Möller, *Einleitung in das A T*, 1934, and by E. J. Young, *An Introduction to the OT*, 1949.

(6) In the second half of the nineteenth century the scientific study of the OT received an impetus which carried the critical science of introductory studies also to victory through the *modern school of criticism* attached to the name of Wellhausen. This school, using the same methods, continued to build on what had been won by the scholars named in paragraphs 3 and 4, but as regards the content it based itself on a new picture of the history of Israel and its religion, which has become authoritative for the subsequent period. The works of Graf, *Die geschichtlichen Bücher des A T*, 1866; of Kuenen, *Historisch-kritische Einleitung in die Bücher des A T* (German by Weber and Müller, 1887 ff.) and especially of Wellhausen, *Geschichte Israels*, I, 1878 (after 1883 *Prolegomena zur Geschichte Israels*), have influenced the science of introductory studies persistently up to the present. This was the direction followed by Wellhausen's revision of Bleek, 1878; by Stade, *Geschichte des Volkes Israel*, 1881 ff., with a detailed treatment of questions of literary history; by S. R. Driver, *Introduction to the Literature of the OT*, 1891 (in German by Rothstein, 1896); W. Robertson Smith, *The OT in the Jewish Church*, 1881, [2]1892, Cornill; *Einleitung in das A T*, 1891, [7]1913, and the comprehensive *Lehrbuch der Einleiting in das A T*, by Steuernagel, 1912, which, more or less, brings to an end the 'Period of literary criticism'.

The opponents of Wellhausen's school have also discussed the questions he raised and learned from him; on the basis of the same method they reached results which, more or less, approximated to the tradition of the Jews and of the Church. In this connexion must be named the *Introductions to the OT* by Riehm, ed. by Brandt, 1889 f.; by Strack, 1883; ⁶1906, by König, 1893; by Baudissin, *Einleitung in die Bücher des A T*, 1901 and also Sellin, *Einleitung in das A T*, 1910; ⁸revised by Rost, 1950; ⁹1959.

(7) The results won in the science of introductory studies by critical analysis were mostly presented as analyses of the individual books of the OT. The attempt was also made to go further and passing beyond analysis to reach a composite presentation of the history of the formation of the OT which does not deal with the separate books in their canonical sequence but places them in the order of their historical formation and of the history of ideas. Efforts in this direction were made by Reuss, *Die Geschichte der hl. Schrift A Ts*, 1881; Wildeboer, *Die Literatur des A T*, in German, 1895, Kautzsch, *Abriss der Geschichte des alttestamentlichen Schrifttums*, 1897; Budde, *Geschichte der althebräischen Literatur*, 1906; Bewer, *The Literature of the Old Testament in its historical Development*, New York, 1922, ²1933; Meinhold, *Einführung in das A T*, 1919; ³1932 also in a certain sense belongs here. These attempts are still far from the aim of a history of literature which was to give a general picture of the literary developments from the beginnings up to Roman times. The canonical scheme for the arrangement of the OT writings was indeed replaced by a chronological framework; nevertheless the presentation itself hardly got beyond the old problems and the analysis.

(8) The scientific study of the literary history was substantially enriched by the research into comparative literature after archaeology and oriental studies had given a clearer insight into the broader relationship between the literature of the OT and those of the ancient Near East. The merely critical interest in the literature gave way before the problems of the *history of the literary forms and types* and before the history of the *themes* worked up by the biblical authors, which were pursued back to the pre-literary (oral) stage of the tradition. By this extension of the subject-matter to the *history of forms and themes*, the science of introductory studies was led to include within its scope a general history of Hebrew literature reaching out far beyond the biblical framework. This movement was initiated by Gunkel in connexion with similar efforts of classical and German philology (*Reden und Aufsätze*, 29 ff.)

and was developed by him himself into a sketch of the literary types in Israel (*Die israelitische Literatur*, Hinneberg, *Kultur der Gegenwart*, Part V, Section VII, 1906, 51–102). Gunkel gave too great prominence to what is general usage in the moulding of the form, to what is typical and impersonal in literary styles. This overshadows what is personal and unique, the significance of which in the development of the OT literature he undervalues. Since research into types directed its attention to the small literary units (isolated stories and isolated sayings) Gunkel did not always do justice to the method of compilation of the OT writings as a whole. These usually came into being not by collecting and mechanically stringing together smaller units, but by combining and developing them into larger significant compositions, the nature of which can be understood only as a whole by taking account of the personalities of the writers and especially by considering the relations of the Holy Scriptures to the cult.

(9) The latest works continue to build on the foundations laid by Gunkel: Hempel, *Althebräische Literatur und ihr hellenistisch–jüdisches Nachleben*, 1930–34, which describes not only the historical development of the literary forms, but also the connexions of the literature with the history of ideas and of religion and attaches greater importance to the personal factors; Eissfeldt, *Einleitung in das A T*, 1934, [2]1956. In this book he places a description of the pre-literary development of the oral tradition and of the early literary history of the OT books in front of the analysis of the individual OT writings and thus, to a certain degree, unites research into the literary history with an analytic 'Introduction' (similarly Rost). Oesterley and Robinson's *Introduction*, 1934, takes account at least in the Psalms, the Proverbs and the prophetic writings of the work on the literary history alongside the usual introductory questions. Cook, *The Old Testament*, 1936, goes his own way as regards method. Roman Catholic scholars, too, occupy themselves with the newer problems of the science of introductory studies in so far as it is possible within the dogmatic framework of their church; the *Introduction to the OT* by Goettsberger, 1928, offers gratifying evidence for this; also Coppens, *Introduction à l'étude historique de l'Ancien Testament* I, [3]1942, II, 1950, III, [2]1950, and Höpfl, *Introductio speciales in Vetus Testamentum*,[5] revised by Miller, O.S.B. and Metzinger, O.S.B., Rome,

1946. Amongst the recent works by non-German scholars the most important are Pfeiffer, *Introduction to the OT*, [2]1948, London 1953, Bentzen, *Inleding til det Gamle Testamente*, 3 vols., 1941, in English [2]1952, in which special attention is paid to the literary forms and cult-types of the OT; Lods, *Histoire de la littérature hébraïque et juive des origines à la ruine de l'état juive*, Paris, 1950, who under the influence of Wellhausen deals with the literary monuments of the OT in the historical sequence of their production. Engnell, *Gamla Testamentet, en traditions–historisk inledning*, I, 1945, has written an Introduction which does not seek to give a fresh description of the literary history so much as of the relationship between the oral and written tradition in the OT, taking into consideration its connexion with the cult. A short survey is offered in books intended for a wider circle of readers by Thomsen, *Das AT, seine Entstehung und seine Geschichte* (Aus Natur und Geisteswelt, 1918) told on Wellhausen's lines, and by Staerk, *Die Entstehung des AT* (Göschen, 1905, [2]1918) the second edition of which reveals the retrogressive movement which has started recently in OT studies against the results and methods of literary criticism; also Rowley, *The Growth of the OT*, 1950; Balscheit, *Der Gottesbund, Einführung in das AT*, Zürich, 1943, is a short summary with a practical theological bias. A good detailed review taking account of the latest researches is provided by Kuhl, *Die Entstehung des AT* (Sammlung Dalp), 1953.

The present task of the science of OT introductory studies is to combine analysis and synthesis. A general survey of the formation of the OT from the point of view of its literary history cannot do without a basic critical analysis of the individual writings any more than contrariwise can analysis attain its goal unless its individual conclusions allow themselves to be fitted into the general process of historical development and receive from it their place in history and their significance in life. The much-discussed question cannot be: '*Either* the literary history of the OT *or* an Introduction' in the sense of a contrast between two different disciplines, of which literary history would have a more profane, an introduction a more theological, character; instead there is 'An Introduction *and* a literary history', two legitimate methods of research side by side, which differ as regards their points of departure and the direction to which they look, but which have become indispensable to each other, side by side, for mutual support and fertilization. The presentation will resemble an 'Introduction' or 'a history of literature' according to the stress laid upon analysis or synthesis. But with all this, the fact must never be left out of sight that it is the religious use of the OT scriptures as the basis of faith for the congregation which assigns to the history of the OT literature and to the Introduction to the OT, their place in theological studies. As a theological discipline, these studies must see to it that the relationship with religion of the OT scriptures, which values them as the record of and witness to the divine revelation, is honoured as it deserves.

2. Arrangement

(1) The distinction between Old and New Testament and consequently the name Old *Testament* (testamentum, in Hebrew בְּרִית), in Greek διαθήκη=an arrangement, disposition (of property), covenant, in Greek also, last will and testament (cf. ThWB II, 106 ff.) originates in biblical usage. In Jer. 31: 31 ff. mention is made of the new covenant which Yahweh will conclude with Israel and Judah and which is to be distinguished from the covenant with their fathers. In the NT, especially in 2 Cor. 3: 6–18, this new covenant is explained as referring to its fulfilment by Christ (cf. Heb. 9: 1–14) and the designation 'old covenant' was applied already by Paul to the *Scriptures* which treat of this covenant. This accounts for the name, used first to denote the old and the new covenant and then also the holy scriptures of the old and new covenant.

(2) The OT contains the sacred literature of the Jewish religious community. The individual writings are arranged in the Hebrew canon in three parts, 'law, prophets and writings'. This division into three parts reflects something of the historical development of the collection. The OT canon represents only a part of the Israelite-Jewish literature, which was brought together and selected according to the religious and the liturgical and dogmatic standpoints. (See Second Part, The formation of the canon.) The history of the OT literature extends over a period of a thousand years with its manifold external and internal developments, which have left clear traces of themselves in the OT. The formation of

the individual writings, their collection as a sacred literature and their framing into a canon are processes which are to be distinguished from each other and were initiated in each case by different historical motives; they must, therefore, be dealt with separately. At the same time the problem of their transmission needs a special discussion in the history of the text. Thus we have a division into three parts: I. The formation of the writings of the OT; II. The collection of the sacred literature and the formation of the canon; III. The text of the OT and its transmission.

FIRST PART

The formation of the writings of the Old Testament

Prolegomena

3. Historical and cultural background

History of the people of Israel by Guthe [3]1914; by Rud. Kittel I[5]. [6]1923; by Sellin I 1924; by Jirku, 1931; by Robinson and Oesterley, 1932; by Noth,[2] 1954,[4] 1959; by Ricciotti, in German by Faschiane, 1953; Auerbach, *Wüste und gelobtes Land* I, 1932, II, 1936; Albright, *From the Stone Age to Christianity*,[2] 1946; *History of Israelite Civiliza-tion* by Bertholet, 1919; Alt. *Die Landnahme der Israeliten in Palästina*, 1925=Alt. I. 89 ff.; idem, 'Völker und Staaten Syriens im frühen Altertum', A O 1936: idem, 'Erwägungen über die Landnahme der Israeliten in Palästina', P J B 35, 1939, 8 ff.= Alt. I. 126 ff.; Noth, *Die Welt des Alten Testaments*, 1940, [3]1956; H. Wheeler Robin-son, *The history of Israel, its facts and factors*, 1941; Helling, *Die Frühgeschichte des jüdischen Volkes*, 1947; Baumgartner, 'Ras Schamra und das Alte Testament', Th. R. 1941, I ff., 85 ff., 157 ff., more literature named there; De Langhe, *Les textes de Ras Shamra-Ugarit et leurs rapports avec le Milieu Biblique de l'Ancient Testament*, 2 vols. 1945; Gordon, *Ugaritic Handbook*, Rome, 1947; idem, *Ugaritic Literature*, 1949; idem, *Ugaritic Manual*, 1955; Gressmann, *Altorientalische Texte zum Alten Testament*,[2]1926; idem, *Altorientalische Bilder zum Alten Testament*, [2]1926; Galling, *Textbuch zur Ge-schichte Israels*, 1950; Pritchard, *Ancient Near-Eastern Texts relating to the Old Testa-ment*, 1950, [2]1955; idem, *The Ancient Near-East Pictures relating to the Old Testament*, 1954; Thomsen, 'Palästina und seine Kultur in fünf Jahrtausenden'. A O 30, 1931, Watzinger, *Denkmäler Palästinas*. I. 1933, II, 1935; Albright, *The Archaeology of Palestine*, [2]1951; Jirku, *Die Ausgrabungen in Palästina und Syrien*, 1956.

(1) The history and civilization of Palestine are largely deter-mined by the fact that the country forms the bridge connecting Asia and Africa; Palestine and its inhabitants were drawn into the political and cultural struggles of the great powers on the Euph-rates, in Asia Minor and on the Nile. Even in the third millennium B.C., on which the first clear light of history falls, the dominating power over Palestine of the land of the two rivers can be descried. The second millennium is marked by the foreign rule of Egypt which was interrupted during its first half by the invasion of the Hyksos (eighteenth-sixteenth centuries). This seems to be the origin of the peculiar social and political structure of the country which maintained itself until the entry of the Hebrew tribes: the land was broken up into numerous small urban and district prin-cipalities, the rulers of which belonged to an alien military aris-tocracy with whose help the Hyksos ruled the native popula-

tion. It was only in the less populous hill country of Samaria and Galilee that larger territories could hold out.

Also, when in the second half of the second millennium the Egyptian claims to power had been maintained in Palestine against the advance of the Hittites from Asia Minor, there was no material change in the method by which the country was governed. The letters of Amarna (about 400 letters from the Near Eastern princes and Palestinian and Syrian vassals to the Egyptian kings Amenophis III and IV (*c.* 1400–1350), found in the year 1887 at El Amarna in Upper Egypt and translated by Knudtzon (*Die El-Amarna Tafeln*, 1915), are one of the most valuable documents for information about conditions in Palestine immediately before the entry of the Israelites. They afford a clear picture showing how a class of alien rulers superimposed on the population made it impossible for an independent historical activity and an individual political and cultural life to come into being. The history of Palestine in the second millennium is, so to speak, merely a section out of the history of the great empires which ruled the country.

(2) It was only when their power lapsed at the end of the second millennium that a change came about. It was caused in part by the so-called Aramaic migration, a movement of peoples starting in the first half of the second millennium from the lands of the Euphrates; in its course wandering semi-nomads with no property in land penetrated into Asia Minor and Palestine. It is still under discussion whether these have any connexion, and if so, of what kind, with the Habiru, = in Hebrew, עִבְרִים, known through the Amarna letters, the Hittite texts and documents from Mari (on the middle Euphrates) and Nuzu (in the land east of the Tigris). Amongst these there will have been tribes and groups of tribes who came to be the subsequent people of Israel. By different ways, in the first place mainly by the peaceful method of change of pasturage, and in several advances, they break into Palestine, and in the fourteenth and thirteenth centuries, as the Amarna letters testify, they threaten the existing structure of government. So we must assume contrary to the description in the book of Joshua that already before the time of Moses 'Hebrew' tribes settled in Palestine and, without ever having left the land again, joined with other tribes (the tribes of Joseph), who entered in the period after Moses, to become the people of Israel. This

holds good e.g. for the tribe of Benjamin (cf. Alt, 'Josua' BZAW 66, 1936, 13 ff.); perhaps also for the southern tribes, who according to Judges 1 conquered the land independently from the rest. The fate of the other tribes is still obscure. At any rate it is amongst these groups that the historical background of a large part of the stories in Genesis about the patriarchs is to be sought.

The decisive event for the course of history as well as for the fashioning of the OT literature did not occur till the entry of those tribes who, through their common experience of the exodus from Egypt, the deliverance at the Red Sea and the revelation of God at Sinai, had grown together under the leadership of Moses into a religious and national unity, and who gave the impulse in Palestine to the formation of 'the people of Israel' and of its religious and national tradition. Towards the end of the thirteenth century these tribes of Joseph pushed their way into just those parts of the middle highlands of Palestine occupied by one of those larger continuous territories which was not overlaid by the political state-system of the Hyksos. Because of its weaker organization this district could offer relatively the least resistance on the political and cultural side to the penetration of the Israelites. So it was just here, apart from the civilizing and economic centres of the cities, that Israel could first unfold the strength of its own national life and that it advanced slowly from the way of life of semi-nomads into that of Canaanite peasantry.

(3) For as the history of Palestine in the second millennium can be understood only as a section out of the history of the early Near-Eastern empires, so the Canaanite culture of that period has no character of its own and can only be understood as a part of the early Near-Eastern civilization. Thus civilizing influences were brought to bear on Canaan from different sides corresponding to the dominion claimed over it by various great powers; the picture of the Canaanite civilization into which Israel entered at the conquest is that of a definitely *hybrid culture*. A significant example may be seen in the signet-cylinder of Atanachili from the beginning of the second millennium (AOB, ill. 577), found in Taanach; it begins with the name of the owner 'Atanachili, son of Chabsi(m), servant of Nergal' (Babylonian god of pestilences) in Babylonian cuneiform writing beside Egyptian hieroglyphic signs and a picture (of a god) drawn from an early Babylonian type. In

still earlier times Palestine seems to have been under the influence
of the *Aegean pre-Greek Mediterranean civilization*, the effect of which
was still seen during the OT period in the worship of trees and
stones (see Hempel, 'Westliche Kultureinflüsse auf das älteste
Palästina,' PJB 1927, 52 ff.) and which remained active with
Egypt as an intermediary in several spheres (cf. also Beer, *Die
Bedeutung des Ariertums für die israelitisch-jüdische Kultur*, 1922).

The strength of the *Babylonian influence* on Canaan since the time
of Hammurabi can be seen, in addition to the dependence of
Canaanite on Babylonian jurisprudence, in the fact which we
learn from the El Amarna tablets and the discoveries in Palestine
of cuneiform writings, that the *Babylonian script* and the Accadian
language was still used in regions under Egyptian rule for official
diplomatic and business correspondence (letters, treaties, com-
mercial contracts, lists, etc.) at the time of the downfall of Babylonian power. The care of these official documents lay in the
hands of professional scribes, who, as the recent discoveries in
Ras Shamra (Ugarit) in Phoenicia have shown, enjoyed a comprehensive, including a linguistic, training. The schools for
scribes were the centres of education; the scribes, mostly in a
powerful position politically, were in charge of the 'wisdom' and
of the transmission of the cultural and literary traditions. The
discovery of tablets with cuneiform writing in Gezer, Taanach,
Shechem, etc.—in Jericho twenty-two unused clay tablets were
found—throws light on the great demand for writing material
and the lively written intercourse between the Palestinian cities.
Originally the art of writing was thought to be secret knowledge,
the characters to be magical beings; the early Egyptian hiero-
glyphics are called by the word for 'gods'. In the OT the writing
engraved on stone or clay is still reckoned to be 'the writing of
God' (Exod. 31: 18; 32: 16). Records and laws are deposited in
the sanctuary (1 Sam. 10: 25, cf. Deut. 31: 26) and this leads to the
conclusion that the art of writing was also practised in priestly
circles.

The invention of the alphabetic script which was cradled in
Palestine and Syria was an event of outstanding importance in the
history of civilization for this region and beyond it. Here from the
middle of the second millennium, a consonantal writing came into
use, in various more or less concurrent attempts, beside the

cuneiform writing and gradually drove it out. The phonetic alphabetical script was more than a match for that using words and
syllables, owing to its ingenious simplicity and the ease of learning it. This brought about its victory and universal diffusion. The
alphabetic script which at last attained absolute supremacy, was
taken over in about the ninth century B.C., with the Phoenicians
as intermediaries, by the Greeks, who enriched it with signs for
the vowels. It is the origin of our alphabet also. How far the
literary culture had spread in Palestine is shown by the lively
trade in papyrus from Egypt to the city of Byblos in Phoenicia
from which the book derived its Greek name βίβλος. In the
account of his journey the Egyptian Wen Amon (1100 B.C.; see
AOT, p. 229) relates that he brought 500 rolls of papyrus as
writing material to Byblos. And in the south Kiriath-sepher (or
sopher?)=the city of the book (or the scribe) (Jos. 15: 15 f.; Jgs.
1: 11 f.) to judge by its name seems to have been a nursery for
writing and the culture arising out of it. Egyptian influence on
Canaan extends even further. Beside the El Amarna letters, it is in
particular the remains of Egyptian temples and buildings, and
also the discovery of numerous terracottas, amulets and scarabs
which prove that together with the forms of Egyptian art and
styles Egyptian civilization and religion, above all the lower
types of popular religion, made their way into Canaan. Thus at
the period of the conquest by Israel, Palestine stands at the cross-
roads of the civilizations of the early Near-Eastern worlds, and of
these the influence of Babylon and Asia Minor may have been
stronger in the north, that of Egypt in the south.

(4) When the tribes of Israel set their feet on Palestinian soil,
they entered upon the heritage of this history and civilization.
The mixed culture of Canaan with the more developed forms of its
legal and economic systems and manner of life was superior to the
civilization of the invaders. Nevertheless, in spite of the con-
tinuance of external connexions, Israel did not simply become
merged in the foreign civilization and this it owes to the forces in
its own life. The building up of a *nation*, coalescing on the basis
of its own historical experience, and the dominating strength of
its *religion* arising from and as a result of its own history, did not
only form a rampart protecting it against foreign influence. It
enabled the people of Israel to absorb and transform alien ele-

ments in such a way as to produce something new and completely individual. It is true that Israel did not create any fresh patterns of civilization, but it filled with a fresh content of its own the old pattern it took over. The religious permeation of the cultural heritage of antiquity with the inherent creative forces of its religious faith, that is Israel's contribution to the civilization of the world.

4. The roots of the literary tradition of the Old Testament

The literature of the OT also can be understood only by taking account of the two roots which were determining factors for the history and civilization of Israel. It is on the one hand a part of the early oriental literature showing its dependence on the cultural heritage of Canaan's Near-Eastern hybrid civilization, especially as regards forms and types, but also as regards the matter it accepts; on the other hand it draws upon the sources of its own tradition. Here it is above all the vital force of the OT Yahweh-religion, which brought about an inner unity of diverging traditions by absorbing them and shaping to its own pattern even the foreign themes it took over.

(1) In addition to the types of early oriental literature, it is especially the local *legends* which were adopted through the agency of Canaanite culture; these had attached themselves to the national sanctuaries, such as Bethel, Shechem, Mamre, Beersheba, and were only subsequently transferred to Yahweh and shaped into the Israelite patriarchal legend. The local legend of Penuel which has been preserved in Gen. 32 and Hos. 12 in two differing forms is a similar case. The Palestinian background of the Yahwist history of the creation in Gen. 2 enables the Canaanite prototype to peep through. The story of Hagar in Gen. 16 and 21 has been transplanted in different ways from its native Ishmaelite soil and fitted into the Israelite legend of the patriarchs. The basic poetical form of *Parallelismus membrorum*, which we meet also in Babylon and Egypt, seems, like certain forms in the Psalms (cf. Jirku, JBL 1933, 108 ff.; Coppens, 'Les Parallèles du Psautier avec les Textes de Ras Shamra-Ugarit', (*Bulletin de l'Histoire et d'Exégèse de l'Ancien Testament*, No. 18, Séminaire Biblique, Louvain 1946) to have been brought into Israelite literature through Canaanite

mediation, and this has now been confirmed for the hymn-form by the discoveries of Ras Shamra. The *myths* point to their foreign origin, since their original character as stories about the gods shows that they arose in polytheism; it was only after they had been vigorously reshaped on monotheistic lines and shortened, that they were admitted by Israel into the stock of their own tradition, especially into that of the primeval history and the last days (cf. Gunkel, *Schöpfung und Chaos in Urzeit und Endzeit*, 1895). There is evidence for the Babylonian source of the story of the flood, the Babylonian original of which is preserved for us in the Gilgamesh epic; the Babylonian myth of Adapa which was used by the Egyptian scribes in the Amarna letters for language study has left traces in some themes in the OT. *Egyptian influence* is seen especially in the 'Wisdom literature'. The 'Wisdom of Amen-em-ope' (*c.* ninth–sixth century B.C.) has found its way in part verbatim into the Book of Proverbs. The affinity has been remarked between the Book of Job and a polemical pamphlet of the time of Ramses II (middle of thirteenth century B.C.). The connexions between Akhnaton's hymn to the sun and Psalm 104 are well known. The legal rules of the case-law of the lay jurisdiction placed in the hands of the elders of the family belong to the cultural stock of the Canaanites which Israel took over (Alt, 'Die Ursprünge des israelitischen Rechts', *Berichte über die Verhandlungen der sächs. Akademie der Wissenschaften, Phil.-hist. Klasse*, Vol. 86, 1934, No. 1; *Kleine Schriften zur Geschichte des Volkes Israel*, Vol. 1, pp. 278 ff.); these rules for their part refer back to Babylonian and Hittite parallels. The same applies to the style of Lamentations. It is thought that *Aegean* and *Arian* connexions might be established with the early legends.

This foreign matter entered into the Israelite tradition in various ways. In addition to the contacts of daily life, the circles of the scribes especially no doubt played their part as regards *literary transmission* in preserving and working out the traditions, as we learn from the Ugaritic finds. The conquest of the Canaanite cities led to the culture of their scribes being adopted as well, and when David appoints an official scribe to his court (2 Sam. 8: 17), he is adopting a well-established custom which the people no longer feel to be an innovation. *Oral traditions* seem to have been spread by wandering minstrels and story-tellers, who, amongst

B

other peoples too, performed in early days the task which belongs today to the press and the radio. But above all, it was in the cult taken over from the natives at the sanctuaries (especially those on the borders) with their feasts, songs and liturgies, whence a large part of the foreign tradition and its ideology found its way to the Israelite people. In this matter we must not undervalue the meeting at the feasts of pilgrims of the most varied origin and the role of the priesthood in transmitting the traditions of the cult and in assimilating alien religious material and forms.

(2) But the individuality of the OT literature does not lie in that which lives on in its books as the heritage of older civilizations. Its distinctive character is determined much more by what Israel had drawn and shaped out of its own history and tradition. A crucial place in the Israelite tradition, forming its mainstay, sometimes pushed expressly into the foreground, sometimes supporting it dimly in the background, is occupied by the traditions of the Mosaic period. These include the exodus from Egypt, the sojourn in the wilderness and the religious union in the covenant at Sinai, the conquest of Palestine, the awakening of both a religious and a national consciousness through the experience of their own history. The diverse features of the portrait of Moses, who is presented as a man of God, a magician, a leader of the people in their wanderings and their battles, a founder of their religion, a priest and judge, a prophet and mediator between God and the people, all show the manifold forms in which the Mosaic tradition was reflected by the different groups (cf. Volz, *Mose und sein Werk*, [2]1932, pp. 8, 140 f.). The state of this tradition no longer allows us to sift out with certainty all that reaches back into the period in the wilderness; in addition to the rudiments of the decalogue and the precepts allied with it, it seems that Miriam's hymn of victory in Exod. 15: 20 f., the battle-oath beside the throne (?) of Yahweh in the war against the Amalekites in Exod. 17: 16 and the oracles at the ark in Num. 10: 35 f. go back to the actual time of Moses. Other parts of the Mosaic tradition, such as the story of the Exodus, the traditions concerning Sinai and Kadesh, all bear the impress of a later stamp; but the roots of these traditions form the focal point at which they were shaped and where their most varied emanations—alien and innate—cross each other. In the course of a process of adoption and adjustment, lasting for cen-

turies, the most diverse items were selected, probably within the framework of a cult-tradition with a continuously active life, and were subordinated and assimilated to the combined religious and national conception of the historical Mosaic religion. With the Mosaic tradition as a centre, traditional material already at hand and concerned with earlier and later events was crystallized, and thus acquired an internal homogeneity, which is a characteristic also of Israel's literary gift of composition.

Some of the early isolated stories attached to the figures of Jacob, Isaac and Abraham, must also be attributed to the Israelites' own stock of tradition. They probably represent the originally separate, special property of different clans and tribal groups who came to Canaan in pre-Israelite times, gained a footing there (cf. Jacob in the land east of the Jordan and in central Palestine, Isaac and Abraham in the south) and adopted local Canaanite traditions (cf. Weiser, *Religion und Sittlichkeit der Genesis*, 1928. pp. 11 f.; Alt, *Der Gott der Väter*, 1929 = Alt I, 1 ff.; Noth, *Überlieferungsgeschichte des Pentateuch*, 1948). In the same way there are reflected in the popular stories of the Jacob-Laban circle the relations of the semi-nomadic immigrants with their Aramaic neighbours and in the tribal legends of the Jacob-Esau circles the situation existing between the East-Jordanian shepherds and hunters, later between Israel and Edom. Early traditions of individual tribes are found in the legend of Dinah and Tamar in Gen. 34; 38 concerning the tribes Simeon-Levi and Judah, in the stories told in Jos. 1–11, most of which contain special material concerning the Benjamites, and in the early isolated stories of the Book of Judges. The fact that these stories are fitted in different ways into the literary tradition of the OT of the pre- and post-Mosaic period is explained partly by their having retained a separate existence for a long time, partly in the case of the stories in the books of Joshua and Judges because they were drawn into the national religious conception of the unity of the great combined Israelite people, based on the Mosaic foundation and fostered in the sacral union of the twelve tribes.

(3) At first traditions such as these existed independently in *oral tradition*; this provides the explanation for variant stories and for the transference of the same theme to different figures. The legal texts seem to have been the first to assume a written form.

The closer the separate tribes grew together in common political undertakings and in the sacral fellowship of their covenant, the tighter became the bond which held their different traditions together. The same internal forces were at work both in the political and the literary process. The special vitality of the worship of Yahweh, which was the determining factor for their national union, resulted also in directing the different Israelite traditions uniformly towards the combined religious and national conception of a Greater Israel and bound firmly together the centrifugal elements from the Song of Deborah right up to the prophetic reflections on history and hopes for the future. The same forces too were at work in adopting and shaping foreign traditions. It was due to the religion of Yahweh that a *modus vivendi* was reached with what had been taken up into the traditional stock of the Israelite tribes through Canaanite mediation. The religious and national forces of Israel were strong enough to absorb alien cultural and literary material and to fit it into their own tradition. What was repugnant to the monotheistic tendencies of the faith of Yahweh (myths, foreign traditions of worship, etc.) was gradually eliminated, given a new direction or recast by a long process on which the history of the material and the tradition may occasionally be able to throw some light. Thus these elements were incorporated into the Israelite history and religion in such a way that in their proper place they no longer disturbed the homogeneous religious appeal and relevance of the OT literature, but indeed were able to deepen them. Even in spite of the political disruption of the two fraternal kingdoms this inner homogeneity of the literary tradition remained strong. This is explained by the fact that the mainstay of the tradition, the sacral union of the tribes, probably outlasted the political separation of the kingdoms. Supported by the regular cult-festivals, it fostered the proclamation of the tradition of salvation-history of the religion of Yahweh and kept it alive. It is on this soil and in this framework that there arose, and was developed that kerygmatic quality of religious literature frequently to be observed in the OT, which offered a religious presentation of history having peculiar relevance to the present with practical exhortation appropriate to the religious community. This quality has been preserved in varying forms as far as late Judaism and even in the Christian church.

The Pre-literary Development

van der Ploeg, 'Le rôle de la tradition orale dans la transmission du texte de l'Ancien Testament', RB 54 (1947), 5 ff.; Ringgren, 'Oral and written transmission in the Old Testament', *Studia Theologica*, Lund 3 (1950–51), 34 ff.; Nielsen, *Oral Tradition, a Modern Problem in O.T. Introduction* (Studies in Biblical Theology, No. 11, 1954).

Forms and Types

In the case of a people who, like Israel, from having been semi-nomads grew only gradually into a civilized way of life, it may be assumed from the start that the rise of their literature was preceded by a period when their existing or newly adopted traditions were transmitted orally. The primitive view of the might of the spoken word and the amazingly developed power of memory in circles without widespread written culture played an important part in fostering and preserving early traditions by its transmission from mouth to mouth. Even the rise of written literature did not prevent tales, proverbs and songs from continuing to be kept alive among the common people. As literary culture advanced, the oral tradition was hemmed in more and more; nevertheless—and this is confirmed for a later age by the spoken word of the prophets and the orally transmitted proverb, and the cult, in particular, has always been the place where the sacred tradition was recited and handed down by word of mouth—the course of literary fixation evolved again and again afresh out of the pre-literary stage when tradition was being fashioned out of verbal transmission. This process can be traced right down to the latest OT times.

In this way the literature remained closely bound up with the life of the people. In consequence, its forms were tied down to the traditional laws of style and forms which each had its particular 'place in the life of the people': (*Sitz im Leben des Volkes*) e.g. the priest proclaims the 'Torah', the prophet the 'word of prophecy', the judge founds his judicial verdict on the 'statutes'; the chorus of women receive the returning warrior with the 'Song of victory'. Thus it is natural when describing the pre-literary development to start from the individual types and their relationship to the life of the people.

A. POETRY

5. The Poetic Structure

Lowth, *De sacra poesi Hebraeorum*, 1753; Ley, *Grundzüge des Rhythmus, des Vers-und Strophenbaus in der hebräischen Poesie*, 1875; id., *Leitfaden der Metrik der hebräischen Poesie*, 1887; Bickell, *Carmina VT metrice*, 1882; id., *Dichtungen der Hebräer zum ersten Male nach den Versmassen des Urtexts übersetzt*, 1882 f.; Budde, 'Das hebräische Klagelied', ZAW 1882, p. 1 ff.; Sievers, *Metrische Studien* I–III, 1901–07; Rothstein, *Grundzüge des hebräischen Rhythmus*, 1909; Staerk, 'Ein Hauptproblem der hebräischen Metrik', *Festschrift für R. Kittel*, 1913, 193 ff.; König, *Hebräische Rhythmik*, 1914; Gray, *The Forms of Hebrew Poetry*, 1915, Hölscher, Elemente arabischer, syrischer und hebräischer Metrik, *Buddefestschrift*, 1920, 93 ff.; Begrich, 'Zur hebräischen Metrik', ThR 1932, 67 ff.; further literature listed there; T. H. Robinson, 'Anacrusis in Hebrew Poetry', BZAW 66, 1936, 37 ff.; id., ZAW 1936, 28 ff.; id., *VT Suppl.* I, 1953, 128 ff.; Mowinckel, 'Zum Problem der hebräischen Metrik', *Bertholetfestschrift*, 1950, 379 ff.; 'Der metrische Aufbau von Jes. 62: 1–12', ZAW 1953, 167 ff.; Fohrer, 'Die Hauptprobleme des Buches Ezechiel', BZAW 72 (1952), 60 ff.; Horst, 'Die Kennzeichen der hebräischen Poesie', ThR 1953, 97 ff.; Segert, 'Vorarbeiten zur hebräischen Metrik, *Archiv Orientální*, XXI (1953) 481 ff.; Muilenburg, 'A Study in Hebrew Rhetoric: Repetition and Style', *VT Suppl.* I (1953), 97 ff.; Fohrer, 'Über den Kurzvers', ZAW 66 (1954) 199 ff.; Mowinckel, Die Metrik bei Jesus Sirach, *Studia Theologica* IX 2 (1955), 137 ff.

As with all peoples, Hebrew poetry is older than the prose-types of their literature. According to primitive ideas the fixed formula, determined according to the wording, the sound and the rhythm, had ascribed to it a special power and effective force which the simple word did not possess. The ability to grapple successfully with certain situations in life depended on the knowledge of the right formula, the correct pronunciation of the *verba certa*, the 'set words'; this is one of the main roots of all poetic tradition. The first beginnings of Hebrew poetry too go back to this dynamic root. Although it is not possible to draw a sharp line everywhere in the OT between prosaic and poetic types, yet differences in *style* and *rhythm*, occasionally also in choice of subject, may be considered criteria of poetry.

(1) The stylistic characteristic which Hebrew poetry shares with that of Babylon, Egypt and Canaan is the so-called *Parallelismus membrorum* which probably grew out of antiphonal singing. By that is meant the style, which has long been known, but was examined in detail by Lowth, and in which the 'verse' usually consists of two parts clearly marked off from each other, bearing a definite logical relationship to each other as regards their con-

tent: (*a*) either the same idea is expressed in different phrases in the two parallel parts (hence the name synonymous parallelism); (*b*) or the idea in the first part is brought out more clearly in the second part by contrast (antithetic parallelism), (*c*) or the second part carries on the idea of the first (synthetic parallelism). The *Parallelismus membrorum* gives the style a certain terseness and allows full play to the vividness and versatility of the picture language.

(2) The method of writing OT and non-Israelite texts, by which the division into separate members is emphasized by the way they are written, supplies us with clear evidence of this characteristic of their style. Yet the old tradition of a *rhythmic arrangement* was completely lost; for the remarks of Josephus speaking of hexameters in Hebrew poetry do not rest on old tradition, but are due to his intention to give this poetry an equal rank beside that of Greece and Rome. The statements that songs were sung by choirs to the accompaniment of music and dances (Exod. 15: 30 f., 1 Sam. 18: 6 f.) make it clear that Hebrew poetry was arranged rhythmically. Our ignorance of the old pronunciation and the partially defective transmission of the text impede the research into Hebrew rhythm. We may take it as certain that Hebrew metre does not consist of a system measuring quantities and reckoning in long and short syllables, like that of Greece and Rome, but is one of *accentuation*, built up on stressed and unstressed syllables. The attempt of Bickell to work out a system of metres, based on *counting the syllables*, according to the Syrian pattern, was taken up again by Hölscher and Mowinckel who propose an alternating metric system of trochees and iambics, whilst Segert attempts to find in the earlier poetry a system of accentuation, and in the later one of alternation. But apart from the fact that nothing can be achieved without textual emendations, the iambic-trochaic metre is incompatible with the characteristic structure of Hebrew sentences which corresponds rather with the anapaestic rhythm. This is brought out especially in the attempts proposed by Ley and Sievers (similarly Rothstein) to place the stress at the end of the *verse member* which usually consists of two unstressed syllables and one stressed one, so that the accent on the verse member and the grammatical accent on the word coincide. The metric unit next in size is the *line* (half-verse or *stichos*) with two, three or four

beats or accented syllables (verse-members); the *verse* (period) is composed of these 'lines'. Amongst the regular verses the double three (3 + 3 beats) is the one most in use; amongst the irregular ones the one with five beats (3 + 2 beats) which since Budde is generally called—not quite accurately—the Qinah, the verse of the dirge (e.g. Amos 5: 2:

nāpᵉlāh lō' tôsîp qûm / btûlat yiśrā'ēl).

Yet these attempts, none of which have gone beyond the initial stages, have not been able to solve the following dilemma: if a strictly observed metric system is proposed, emendations of the text become necessary; if with Staerk and others the mixed metre is considered to be the normal thing, then there can no longer be a question of a real metrical system.

(3) If we ask whether Hebrew poetry recognizes units larger than a verse, it can up till now only be said that the use of the refrain (Ps. 42: 6, 12; 43: 5; 46: 8, 12) and the alphabetic songs, in which the letters with which each verse begins are arranged in alphabetical order (e.g. Ps. 9 f., 25, 37, 111, 112, 119, 145), points indeed to a formal and in part probably also to a logical grouping of small units; but for the present, there cannot yet be shown to exist a *structure of stanzas* written throughout in the same metre (for the study of stanzas cf. D. H. Müller, *Die Propheten in ihrer ursprünglichen Form*, 1896; idem, 'Strophenbau der Psalmen', ZAW 50, 1932, 240 ff.).

6. Songs

Budde, 'Das Volkslied Israels im Munde der Propheten', *Preuss. Jahrb.*, 1893, 460 ff.; 1895, 491 ff.; G. A. Smith, *The early Poetry of Israel in its physical and social Aspects*, ³1910; Eissfeldt, 'Der Maschal im Alten Testament', BZAW, 1913; Gunkel, Die israelitische Literatur (*Kultur der Gegenwart* I, Sec. VII, 58 ff.); Causse, 'Les Origines de la Poésie hébraïque', RHPhR, 1924, 393 ff.; 1925, 1 ff.; id. *Les Plus Vieux Chants de la Bible*, 1926; Jahnow, 'Das hebräische Leichenlied im Rahmen der Völkerdichtung', BZAW, 1923; Hempel, *Althebräische Literatur*, 19 ff.; id., *The Forms of Oral Tradition, Record and Revelation*, ed. by Wheeler Robinson, 1938, 28 ff.; id., 'The Contents of the Literature', op. cit., p. 45 ff.; Eissfeldt, *Einleitung in das AT* 100 ff.

Israel was a song-loving people. The passionate trait in its nature, its feeling for the pathos of life, prefers the stirring energy of a lively outlook and of a spontaneous frame of mind to the cool sobriety of a logical view of life; this renders it likely from the outset that such a people made extensive use, in the most varied situations, of the power of poetically fashioned sayings and songs. It appears too from what the OT itself tells us that secular and religious songs played an important role in Israel, in fun and in earnest, in public and private life. Songs ring out at work (Ecclus. 38: 25), there was singing at the harvest, the vintage, the wine-press (Jgs. 9: 27; Isa. 16: 10; Jer. 25: 30); feasts and drinking-bouts were seasoned with song and dance accompanied by the zither and the harp (Jgs. 21: 21; Amos 6: 4 ff., 5: 23; Is. 5: 11 f.). Love and death, marriages and funerals were the deep-seated cause for song, as with other peoples, so also in Israel.

(a) Profane Songs

Comparatively little by way of profane songs has been preserved for us within the books of the OT, and that little partly in a form which does not enable its original secular character to be recognized at once. The reason for this is not only that in the case of the peoples of antiquity their whole life was set more firmly in a religious framework than is done in modern largely secularized civilizations. It is also connected with the characteristic of the OT literature and its tradition, which transmits what is secular in a religious context; for instance, particularly the prophets used the worldly song as a means of proclaiming a religious message and thus still afford us a glimpse into the wealth of this literature.

(1) A short *drinking song* of care-free, ungodly gluttons is quoted in Is. 22: 13: 'Let us eat and drink, for tomorrow we shall die.' There is a similar one in Is. 56: 12. On occasion the prophets clothed their tidings of judgment in the form of a *taunt-song*, Is. 23: 15 f.; Jer. 22: 14 f. This may have been meant originally to reduce the power of the enemy not only in thought and word, but in fact (in the Greenland 'singing contest' lawsuits are decided by the plaintiff and defendant singing satirical songs alternately), and the use of the taunt-song by the prophets points in the same direction; only here it is the power of the *divine word* which comes into play as an effective agent usually when *threatening foreign nations* (Is. 37: 22–29 against Sennacherib; Is. 47 against Babylon). The use of taunt-song themes in the song of Deborah in verse 28 ff. against the retinue of the enemy's commander suggests that this type of

song had been practised for some time in ancient Israel; indeed in Num. 21: 27–30 there seems to have been preserved a pre-Israelite Amorite taunt-song about the siege of a Moabite king by Sihon, king of the Amorites (yet cf. p. 117). The Song of the Well in Num. 21: 17 f. is probably a *working song*, sung when digging a well and intended to help the work forward by means of the magic power dwelling in its words; it is now inserted into a quite definite situation in Israel's account of its history, as applying to the city of Beer east of the Jordan, and has thus been preserved for posterity. Hölscher interprets Neh. 4: 4 as a *'strikers' song'*; an ironically humorous *song of a watchman* is to be found in Is. 21: 11 f. Old *songs of the harvest and the wine-press* have not been transmitted, perhaps because they bore too deep a stamp of their origin in the Canaanite fertility religion, as is indicated probably by the customary shout of joy 'hêdād' (Is. 16: 10; Jer. 25: 30; 48: 33; 51: 14). On the other hand it is significant that a survival in the OT of the harvest song is to be found in the psalms of thanksgiving, which praise Yahweh as the giver (Pss. 65, 67 etc.).

(2) A collection of *love-songs* of different kinds has been preserved in the Song of Songs owing to the fact that these songs, some of which used to be sung at wedding feasts, were given a new religious interpretation, applying them to the relationship of Yahweh to his people; a precedent for this is already shown in Is. 5: 1–7, who clothes the doctrine of election in the form of a playful love-song with a frightening ending.

(3) The *Funeral Song* grew out of associations with foreign religions and was never assimilated to the religion of Yahweh; its cultic origin is still visible in the dirge for the dead performed according to the ritual by women and men versed in lamentation (Amos 5: 16; Jer. 9: 16). The customary wailing in the dirge and the comment in Zech. 12: 10 ff., where the 'mourning for his only son' is compared with 'the mourning of Hadadrimmon in the valley of Megiddo', has led to the conclusion that the Funeral Song is related to the ancient oriental cult of the gods of vegetation who died and rose again (Tamuz, Adonis, etc.) and this is now attested in the case of Ras Shamra. The dirge for the dead in which the deeds and virtues of the deceased were celebrated (elsewhere the bold deeds of the dead men were reproduced in funeral games) originally had the purpose of perpetuating the

power of the deceased as a blessing for his survivors by 'reproducing' it in speech. The religion of Yahweh with its exclusive claim rejected these associations with foreign religions and caused the dirge to become more and more secularized in Israel. The two laments of David which have been handed down, on Saul and Jonathan in 2 Sam. 1: 19–27 and on Abner in 2 Sam. 3: 33 f., are already quite secular in character and their shape presupposes a long previous history. The transference of the dirge to the political field freed the lament somewhat from the shackles of its form, as those on the fall of Jerusalem show (cf. Lam. 1, 2, 4). The use of the *lament for the dead collectively* originated with the prophets who used this type as a lament over the future downfall of the nation, to strengthen the religious sternness of their prophecies of judgment (cf. Amos 5: 2; Jer. 9: 10 ff.), whilst in the *mocking dirge* mainly directed against foreign foes they expressed powerfully and impressively the sublime superiority of their God (Is. 14: 4–21 against the king of Babylon or Assyria?; Ez. 27: 2 ff.; 28: 11 ff. against Tyre; 32: 2–16 against Egypt; 19: 2–14 against kings of Judah; cf. also Nahum. 3: 7, 18 f.; Hab. 2: 6 ff.).

(4) In a certain manner the *royal song* also belongs to political poetry. Although not to the same extent as in Babylon, Assyria and Egypt, yet it was the custom also at the royal court in Israel that the king and his deeds should be extolled by the singing men and women appointed to his court (2 Sam. 19: 35); it was in this sense that e.g. David was considered 'the sweet psalmist of Israel (2 Sam. 23: 1). But it is not a matter of chance that no such purely secular-political song in praise of the king is preserved in the OT. For it lies in the nature of the OT kingship that the king withdraws behind the God to whom he owes his authority. This is made just as clear in the two royal psalms, 2 and 110, which belonged to the ritual of the king's enthronement as in the royal proclamation in psalm 101 which was probably composed for a similar occasion and in the cultic song of the ark, Ps. 132. The Israelite song of enthronement is indeed dependent as regards its form on the style of ancient oriental courts, which has the domination of the world in view and is suited only to the great kings of the East; it is strangely incongruous when applied to the narrowly limited political possibilities of Israel. But the subordination of the king in the OT to the world-embracing conception of God

enables the song of the king to become a stirring confession of the world power of God, which by its living religious force stands out in contrast to the monotonous formality of the Egyptian royal songs. The king is Yahweh's king: his victory and renown are in the first place the doing of God (Ps. 18: 20 f.); to submit to the divine will by an exemplary mode of life is the ideal of the righteous temporal ruler (Ps. 101). This explains too the fact that the enthronement ritual of the king is analogous to that of Yahweh's ascent of his throne (see below (b) p. 32) and that the royal song continued to exert an influence right down to the shaping of messianic prophecy. Lately the 'Swedish School' (Widengren, Engnell, Bentzen, cf. the bibliography for (b)) in particular, has drawn attention to the connexion between the sacral character of kingship and the kingship of God in the cult-poetry of the ancient East, so that the question might be put the other way round, namely whether the OT ritual for the king and the royal songs might not have been rooted originally in the cult and were derived from God's ascending his throne. The individual problems, above all the question, how far this foreign group of conceptions, for which there is evidence also in the Canaanite religion, influenced the cult of Yahweh and the OT poetry, are still under discussion.

The Israelite king does not stand in the centre of the worship, as does e.g. the Egyptian king; and when in the OT intercessions are offered for him (Pss. 20, 72) this is done subject to the distance between God and man being clearly preserved. Even there where the secular character of the royal song is preserved most fully, as in the marriage song, Ps. 45, this religious emphasis is not lacking. Yet this psalm was probably taken into the psalter only after it had been interpreted anew as referring to the relationship between Yahweh and his congregation, as we can observe in the similar case of the Song of Songs.

(5) The great national happenings in battle and victory gave a vigorous stimulus to poetry in Israel as among other peoples. By the potency of its words, the *battle-song*, like the battle ecstasy, was intended to increase the enthusiasm and fighting strength. With an oath at the throne (?) of Yahweh, the Israelite army stormed into the battle (Exod. 17: 16); the adjuration to Yahweh to rise up for the fight probably also belongs to this category (Num.

10: 35). When the battle was won, the *song of victory* resounded, sung at the triumph by the choir of girls and women (Exod. 15: 20 f.; Jgs. 11: 34; 1 Sam. 18: 6 f.); it celebrated the renown of the hero and was intended to keep alive the memory of the mighty event and his successes by making a graphic representation of them as a lasting blessing. It was by thus actually reliving again and again what had happened that the *historical tradition* of the OT came into being. The short songs of victory in Exod. 15: 21 'Sing ye to the Lord, for he hath triumphed gloriously; the horse and his rider hath he thrown into the sea' and in 1 Sam. 18: 7 'Saul hath slain his thousands, and David his ten thousands' must be imagined as being sung with constant reiteration and increasing effect; besides these, fragments of such songs have been preserved for us in Num. 21: 14 f. and Jos. 10: 12. Usually up till now there has been included amongst the songs of victory also the 'Song of Deborah' (Jgs. 5), one of the oldest and most significant monuments of all the Israelite poetry. Yet it is not an actual song of victory, but a liturgical composition which presumably had its place in the framework of a cultic celebration by the tribal union after a victory and it must be understood in this context (cf. Weiser, ZAW 71 [1959] 67 ff.). With dramatic vivacity and lively alternation of voices and scenes it glorifies the God who appeared from Sinai; it outlines the circumstances before the decisive battle; it is addressed to those who were present at the celebration; it remembers those tribes who were not there as well as those who took part in the struggle; it represents the battle as the judgment of God on the enemies; it demands a curse on the city of Merom because it did not honour its obligation to help in the fight, and a blessing on the woman who struck down the hostile general, and it casts a triumphant and derisive glance across to the women who are awaiting anxiously and hopefully the foe who has been slain. Summing up the events described the ending draws the immediate and lasting religious conclusion for the present and the future: 'So let all thine enemies perish, O Lord: but let them that love him be as the sun when he goeth forth in his might'. From the point of view of the history of the form, this song comprising several types, such as the hymn, the taunt song, the song of praise, curse and blessing, presupposes a lengthy development. In verse 11 it itself recalls the Hebrew custom of 'rehearsing the righteous acts of the Lord'. The mention of this as well as its own structure, built up on the hymn to Yahweh (cf. Exod. 15: 21) and ending on a sonorous religious note, indicates the nature of the specific individuality of Hebrew poetry and of the OT formation of the tradition of salvation history which drew strength and content from its faith in the God of Sinai. At the same time we see here clearly, what can be said also of the development of the songs as a whole, namely why it is no longer possible in most cases to draw a clear distinction between secular and religious literature. The common types of secular songs were embedded in a historical tradition which was elucidated by, and interpreted in accordance with, its faith in God. Traditions such as these were rooted in the cult, and finally the prophets employed the song in the service of their message. These were the stages by which the religion of Yahweh, to an increasing degree, took possession of their form and content and gave them the characteristic OT stamp.

(6) The information about one of the earliest Israelite *collections of song*, no longer preserved, points in the same direction. In Num. 21: 14 there is a mention of 'the book of the Wars of the Lord', from which in fact only the song in Num. 21: 14 is quoted, but which no doubt contained a collection of battle-songs from old times; its title expresses clearly the fact that the historical tradition is brought into relation with religion in connexion with the idea of the holy war (cf. 1 Sam. 18: 17; 25: 28), an idea which has its home in the sacral union of the tribes. Besides this there was at least one other collection which is called in Jos. 10: 13 and 2 Sam. 1: 18 'the Book of the Upright' (*sēper hayyāshār*). It can no longer be determined whether the Book of Songs (*sēper hashshîr*) the mention of which in 1 Kgs. 8: 53 has been transmitted only by the Septuagint, is meant to be the same collection; if so, '*shîr*' may have been written by mistake for *yāshār*; if not, this passage may refer to another song collection. Since none of the songs spoken of in these books is earlier than the time of Solomon, it may be conjectured, owing to the lively concern for literature of that time, that the collection originated then.

(b) Cultic Songs

Balla, 'Das Ich der Psalmen', FRLANT 1912. H. Schmidt, *Die religiöse Lyrik im AT*, 1912; Baumgartner, 'Die Klagegedichte des Jeremia', BZAW 1917; Mowinckel, *Psalmenstudien I–VI*, 1921–1924; Stummer, *Sumerisch akkadische Parallelen zum Aufbau alttestamentlicher Psalmen*, 1922; Quell, 'Das kultische Problem der Psalmen', BWAT, 1926; Causse, *L'ancienne Poésie cultuelle d'Israël et les Origines du Psautier*, RHPhR, 1926; Driver, *The Psalms in the Light of Babylonian Research*; Blackman, 'The Psalms in the Light of Egyptian Research' (Simpson, *The Psalmists*, 1926); Hans Schmidt, *Die Thronfahrt Jahwes am Fest der Jahreswende im alten Israel*, 1927; idem, 'Das Gebet der Angeklagten im Alten Testament', BZAW 1928; Haller, 'Ein Jahrzehnt Psalmforschung', ThR 1929, 377 ff.; Gunkel, *Einleitung in die Psalmen*, ed. by Begrich 1933; Widengren, *Psalm 110 och det sakrala Kungadömet i Israel*, 1941; Patton, *Canaanite Parallels in the Book of the Psalms*, 1944; Bentzen, *Det sakrale Kongedømme*, 1945; Christoph Barth, *Die Errettung vom Tode in den individuellen Klage=und Dankliedern des AT*, 1947; Weiser, 'Psalm 77, ein Beitrag zur Frage nach dem Verhältnis von Kult und Heilsgeschichte', ThLZ 1947, col. 133 ff.; Weiser, Zur Frage nach den Beziehungen der Psalmen zum Kult, *Bertholet=Festschrift* 1950, 513 ff.; Weiser, 'Die Psalmen'[4] ATD 14–15, 1955, 14–68; Stamm, 'Ein Vierteljahrhundert Psalmenforschung', ThR 23 (1955) 1–68; Mowinckel, *Offersang og Sangoffer, Salmediktning i Bibelen*, 1951; Mowinckel, *Religion und Kultus*, 1953; Westermann, *Das Loben Gottes in den Psalmen*, 1954; idem, 'Struktur und Geschichte der Klage im Alten Testament', ZAW 66 (1954) 44 ff.

It is characteristic of the OT that a larger number of definitely religious songs are attested than of secular ones.

(1) One of the most widespread types of religious song is the *hymn*, the song in praise of God. The composition of hymns, the form of which Israel had taken over from the world around it, is associated with the history of OT religion from its beginnings (cf. Miriam's song of victory, Exod. 15: 20 f. and the introduction to Deborah's song, Jgs. 5: 3 f.) right up to the NT Magnificat, Luke 1: 46 ff. and the Benedictus, Luke 1: 68ff. The fact that the Jewish community designates the whole Psalter by the Hebrew word for hymn *tᵉ hillîm* shows the importance and wide distribution of this type. The original home of the hymn is the cult. When sung during the worship it was in its original form itself a cultic *act*, a part of the sacred action like the performance of the sacrifice. According to the earliest beliefs, the word in honour of the deity effected by its indwelling power the strengthening of God (cf. the OT expression 'to bless Yahweh') and the cultic re-invigoration of that which was praised. In the OT too the significance of the hymn is to bring about the presence of God by the cultic act; but it arises no longer out of the magical self-consciousness of man, but out of the self-sacrificing enthusiasm, the reverentially humble worship and adoration of God; frequently the hymn is the

response of the congregation to the revelation of God and of his salvation celebrated in the cult. Hence in the OT the petitions which are often attached to the hymn in the Babylonian model give way to a confession before God (in the shape of a prayer) and before the congregation (in the shape of a story), devoted to God alone and praising his power and greatness in creation, nature and history. The OT poetry by admitting sacred historical tradition into hymns struck out on a line of its own. This development can already be observed in the songs of Miriam and Deborah. It is probably connected with the fact that the specifically OT transmission of salvation-history had its home in the cult of the festival of the Yahvist covenant-community (cf. e.g. Ps. 44: 2 ff.) and this exercised a lasting influence on the form and content of the hymn. Old forms such as e.g. the self-affirmations of the deity were thus filled with a new meaning. The universal background of the hymn in the OT, that all peoples and even inanimate nature praise God's glory, and its eschatological extension, hoping for the final dominion of God as the fulfilment of salvation history and celebrating its completion, are based on the fundamental conceptions of the covenant-cult; and the polarity of judgment and mercy in the presentation of God in the hymns has the same origin. The prophets too, especially Deutero-Isaiah, used the hymn for proclaiming their message and deepened and developed the content of its conceptions derived from the cult. It was, perhaps, due to the influence of the prophetic ways of thought that in the so-called *Songs of Zion*, a class of hymn-like poems (e.g. Pss. 46, 48, 76), the original reference to the local cult is overlaid by a stronger emphasis on the theocentric outlook and on the eschatological bias of OT piety. In the adoration of the hymns the pious man of the OT—as an individual also—experienced the past and the future as an actually present happening for his own salvation. Psalm 103 shows what scope was provided by hymns for deep personal piety. The *form* of the hymn is usually constructed on the following pattern: 1. Introduction in the shape of an invitation (to oneself) to praise God. 2. The actual praise of God in the form of affirmations (using attributes, participial forms, relative or causal sentences with 'for') in which God's nature and operations are confessed and worked out in adoration and description, sometimes also the worshipper's own relation to God is included. 3. The conclusion which often leads back to the introductory formula.

(2) Analogous to the hymns are the songs of Yahweh's enthronement (e.g. Pss. 47, 93, 96–99). It is uncertain whether, and how far, these were used at an annual enthronement festival of Yahweh, which has to be postulated, and which, as in Babylonia, was celebrated at the turn of the year; their origin in the cult is probable. It is hardly still open to discussion that a considerable part of the psalms are explained basically by the nature of the festival cult, in which, beside other ideas, that of God's rule as king played a part; however, perhaps Mowinckel assigns to the theme of Yahweh's enthronement at the autumn festival too much space and significance, and the number of actual Enthronement songs may be appreciably smaller than he assumes. The cultic act of Yahweh's enthronement will probably have been only one part in the whole liturgy of the feast of the covenant celebrated in the autumn.*

The enthronement songs are akin to the royal songs as regards their style, but, under the influence of the OT conception of God, which transferred them to the spiritual and universal sphere, their content was deepened and broadened and this can be seen in the moral and religious nobility of their view of history and the end of history.

(3) The *dirge* occupies a large space in OT literature. Nearly a third of the psalms must be included in this class. Both its forms, the *dirge for the people* and the *dirge for the individual* grew alike out of cultic roots. This is confirmed by the customary linking of lament and vow (cf. 1 Sam. 1: 10 ff.) and the use of cultic phrases in personal prayers of lament, which like e.g. those of Jeremiah (11: 18–23; 12: 1–6; 15: 10–12, 15–21; 17: 14–18; 18: 18–23; 20: 7, 9, 10–12, 14–18) are not of direct cultic origin, but yet reveal their connexion with the cult. Many a graphic or picturesque phrase in the dirges may reveal the influence of the cult myth, telling of the gods who die and rise again, which was spread throughout the whole ancient East. Yet there is no proof that this range of conceptions possessed any kind of living reality in OT cultic poetry, even though the thought that the sick man when

---

* Since this was written Mowinckel has made a similar qualification for his earlier thesis (*Offersang og Sangoffer*, p. 128; *Religion und Kultur*, p. 76).

praying sees himself transferred to the underworld is used occasionally as a vivid picture for that stage of the illness in which he feels himself to be near death. It has been conjectured that the earliest source of the dirge, namely the power exercised by ancient magic, might be the exorcism of witches and demons which was thought of as a counter-spell against hostile powers. But only remnants of the magical formulae for this are preserved in the OT; and even where these are still used, importance is no longer attached to the magically independent power of the words, but only to man's subjection to God which his lament and supplication reveal. For it is to God that the manifold troubles without and within are referred and traced back. Joel 1–2 affords an insight into a national day of lamentation on the occasion of a plague of locusts and a famine. The people's songs of lament in the prophets, e.g. Jer. 14: 7–10; 14: 19–15: 4, point to a day of penitence in times of drought and bad harvests. The dirges in Hos. 6: 1–6; 14: 3–9; Lam. 5, come to us out of times of general political and religious distress. The most important components of the dirge which are found also in the non-Israelite literature of psalms are: invocation, lament, petition, reasoning and vow; their sequence is not everywhere the same nor complete. The many forms taken by public misfortunes, such as dearth, pestilence, foes, and by private trouble, such as illness, persecution, scorn, doubt, guilt, received an inner unity from the fact that the laments in the OT are directed to God. It is, indeed, possible that the Babylonian use in public worship of forms of lament into which only the name had to be inserted, had so far an influence on similar prayers in the OT that the 'lament' is usually kept to general terms, which make it impossible to discover the concrete external circumstances of the petitioner (H. Schmidt has tried to explain some prayers as the prayers of defendants in interrogations connected with the cult). Probably the incorporation of psalms of lament, supplication and thanks into the general act of salvation in the festival-cult favoured the tendency to make their modes of expression of more general application; besides, this characteristic may also be partly due to the fact that the inner need of the petitioner takes precedence over his external danger. The separation from God and the longing to recover the lost contact with him by experiencing his mercy and help is the real central problem of most of the personal laments. Here we can recognize the deep significance of the meeting with God and of his nearness also within the framework of the OT cult, which is not affected by the strictures of the prophets. The faith of the OT refers all suffering to God: in times of mortal peril any direct threat to the corporate life is felt to be due to God and conversely the only possible means of existence is recognized to be a life in fellowship with God. Thus the customary forms are filled with a deepened and spiritualized content. By this road some writers of psalms of lament have attained to the blessed certainty, won amid the severest inner struggles, that by their indestructible permanent relationship to God and by their completely self-sacrificing joy in him they possess the only blessing which will relieve them even of the fear of dying, and will help them in spite of much suffering to vanquish death in their hearts (Ps. 16: 10 f.; 73: 23 ff.). Very deep problems are broached here and final decisions are wrung out in prayer. In the OT psalms of lament the age-old and yet eternally new question dealing with the connexions between God and fate, between fate and sin returns in manifold variations and is answered in different ways. These begin with a massive belief in retribution and grow to a profound knowledge concerning the reality of human sinfulness and the actuality of divine mercy, which alone can overcome it, an attitude which by its genuine depth of feeling bursts the bonds of all set forms of penitence (Ps. 51). At the point where, in the Babylonian dirges, the attempt is made to obtain the intervention of the god on behalf of the petitioner by piling up flattering attributes, the OT introduces the theme of confidence as a confession of what God means to the petitioner as a reality and at the same time as a basis for the certainty that the prayer will be heard (e.g. Ps. 3: 5 ff.; 5: 13; 27: 13; 42: 5, 6, 12; 130: 5, 7). This trustful assurance has created in the OT a great wealth of expressions, such as 'salvation, life, redeemer, rock, castle, shield,' etc. In some cases, when the prayer was tied to the cult, the 'certainty that the prayer will be heard' may have been mediated through an oracular saying communicated by the priest (cf. e.g. Ps. 12: 6). But often for the individual petitioner the certainty of his being heard will have been derived from his general assurance of salvation won by a theophany and a meeting with God. In other laments (unconnected with the cult) the change-over to assurance, which is frequently to be observed, may have taken place during the prayer itself; thus Jeremiah's prayer becomes a dialogue between God and man. It is the prophetic attitude of faith which resulted in such an intensification of prayer-life and its release from external cultic ties, so that cultic things become the symbol and image of a spiritual partnership (Pss. 51, 23). The upward-surging abundant life of the OT faith in the end broke through the old set prayers of lament and created for itself new forms of expression by admitting themes from other types of religious poetry. The 'hybrid poem', seen from the point of view of the history of types, represents a phenomenon of decadence, since it is a dissolution of the old forms; but as regards its religious content, it must be considered mainly as the expression of a particularly lively faith, a sign that the estimation of literature considered from the stand-point of aesthetics and the history of the form by no means coincides with that of theology. In the 'Songs of Confidence' which belong to the most fervent products of the OT literature, the creative powers of the religion of the OT have brought into being out of the themes of the dirge what amounts to a new type of religious poetry all its own (Pss. 4, 11, 16, 27: 1–6, 121, 125, 131).

(4) The *song of thanksgiving* stands in close relation to the dirge, and also to the hymn. This can be seen in its formal construction, which like the hymn; begins with an invitation (to oneself) and an invocation of Yahweh and passes on to the main section, the 'narrative', in which the worshipper confesses his gratitude for God's saving rule which he has enjoyed. In common with the hymn and the dirge the song of thanksgiving uses the third person for the alternating invocation to God and the narrative; it is at the same time prayer and confession, the former addressed to God, the latter to the congregation. Sometimes we find the song of thanksgiving linked with a vow of a thank-offering with which it shares its name (*tôḏāh*, actually = confession). At times the song of thanksgiving itself replaces the sacrifice (40: 2 ff.; 50: 14 f.; 69: 31 f.). Its original position in the festival-cult is the thank-offering. Performed to the accompaniment of music (Ps. 43: 4), probably in the presence of the congregation at the feast (e.g. Ps. 118), it has more frequently still an external and internal connexion with the dirge which here undertakes the function of the

'narrative'. Thus both together appear as a personal confession testifying to God's saving activity, made in the presence of the congregation within the framework of the general 'salvation-history' (e.g. 6: 13; 22: 23 ff.; 28, 30, 31, 41, 54, 56, 69, and *passim*). Ps. 102 (title and verse 19) show that songs which had been written down and handed to the shrine in the manner of a votive gift served as a formula for future use. As in the case of the dirge, the songs of individuals outnumber here, too, the collective songs of thanksgiving. The form borrowed from foreign sources is filled in the OT with confessions of confidence, fortified by various experiences, in the God who has shown himself to his own as a strong helper and merciful deliverer out of all trouble. In this type, too, the breaking-up of the traditional form evident in the mixture of styles is in inverse proportion to the religious depth of personal piety.

(5) The type called *pilgrimage songs* were sung on the occasion of the regular visit to the sanctuary, in later times to the temple at Jerusalem, demanded already in early times from each Israelite (Exod. 23: 17; 34: 23; Deut. 16: 16). In these too a similar development can be observed from the congregational song (cf. Amos 4: 4 f.; Is. 2: 3; Jer. 31: 6) to the song of the individual (cf. Pss. 122: 1, 8 f.; 84: 3 ff.). In the latter the positive side of the shared experience at the divine service is clearly seen in the longing for the sanctuary and the joy of the hours spent there close to God as the source of personal piety.

Looked at as a whole, the songs developed as regards their outward form in the direction of their becoming detached from their native soil in the cult. Their strict subordination to form was weakened and broken up and they became the spiritual songs of personal piety, the character of which is a *mixture of styles*. This bursting of the bonds of external form and turning towards a more individual shaping of the material runs hand in hand with a widening, deepening and intensifying of their religious content, and in this the influence of prophetic religion no doubt played its part. The theocentric outlook on life, starting from the genuine Yahweh tradition and developed further out of the prophets' experience of God, draws together the OT poetry of religious song into a great unity which in spite of its outward variety is yet inwardly homogeneous and which compared with its early oriental prototypes has a definite character of its own. Besides this, the deepening and spiritualization of the OT religion initiated by the prophets was encouraged by the exile where in the growing custom of the divine service of the synagogue the word took the place of the cultic ceremonial, which had become impossible away from home. This also kept open in the post-exilic days the way to a further characteristic growth beside the priestly cult-religion of the second temple and its traditions, and brought it about that in Judaism, too, part of the treasure of songs was reserved as a living inheritance.

7. Sayings

Meinhold, *Die Weisheit Israels*, 1908; Eissfeldt, 'Der Maschal im AT', BZAW, 1913; Gressman, *Israels Spruchweisheit im Zusammenhang der Weltliteratur*, 1925; Humbert, *Recherches sur les Sources Égyptiennes de la Littérature Sapientale d'Israël*, 1929; Fichtner, 'Die altorientalische Weisheit in ihrer israelitisch-jüdischen Ausprägung', BZAW, 1933; Baumgartner, *Israelitische und altorientalische Weisheit*, 1933; idem, Die israelitische Weisheitsliteratur', ThR 1933, 254 ff.; more bibliography there; Zimmerli, 'Zur Struktur der alttestamentlichen Weisheit', ZAW 1933, 177 ff.; Causse, 'La sagesse et la propagande juive à l'époque perse et hellénistique', BZAW 66, 1936, 148 ff., Du Toit, *Bybelse en Babilonies-Assiriese Spreuke*, Johannesburg 1942; Rankin, *Israel's Wisdom Literature*, 1936, ²1954; Drubbel, 'Le conflit entre la sagesse profane et la sagesse réligieuse', *Biblica* 1936, 407 ff.; J. Schmidt, 'Studien zur Stilistik der alttestamentlichen Spruchliteratur', *Alttestamentl Abhedlgen* 13, 1936, 1; Dubarle, *Les Sages d'Israël*, 1946; Gese, *Lehre und Wirklichkeit in der alten Weisheit*, 1958; Hempel, 'Die israelitischen Anschauungen von Segen und Fluch im Lichte altorientalischer Parallelen', ZDMG, 1925, 20 ff.; Mowinckel, *Psalmenstudien* V, 1924; idem, *Le Décalogue*, 1927; idem, '*Zur Geschichte der Dekaloge*'; ZAW 1937, 218 ff.; Küchler, 'Das priesterliche Orakel in Israel und Juda', BZAW, 1918; Begrich, 'Die priesterliche Tora', BZAW 66, 1936, 63 ff.; Östborn, *Tora in the Old Testament*, 1945; Hölscher, *Die Profeten*, 1914; Gunkel, *Die Propheten*, 1917; Hänel, 'Das Erkennen Gottes bei den Schriftpropheten', BWAT 1923; Lindblom, *Die literarische Gattung der prophetischen Literatur*, 1924; Th. H. Robinson, 'Neuere Prophetenforschung', ThR, 1931 279 ff.; Lods, 'Recherches récentes sur le prophétisme israélite', RHR 1931, 279 ff.; Jepsen, *Nabi*, 1934; Alt, *Die Ursprünge des israelitischen Rechts*, 1934=Alt I, 278-332; Rowley, 'Moses and the Decalogue', BJRL 34, 1951; Baumgartner, 'The Wisdom Literature', OTMSt (1951), 210 ff.; Alt, 'Die Weisheit Salomos', ThLZ 76 (1951) col. 139 ff.=Alt II, 90 ff.; Fohrer, 'Neuere Literatur zur atl. Prophetie', ThR 1951, 276 ff.; 1952, 193 ff.; *Rowley-Festschrift*, 'Wisdom in Israel and in the Ancient Near East', VT Suppl. Vol. III. 1953. (See also bibliography for section 43.)

The boundary between song and saying cannot everywhere be sharply drawn. In general the saying is a shorter, more compact unit and the primitive magical element of its original form stands out more definitely than in the case of the song. Its natural purpose is to win recognition for a truth, a striking state of affairs, or an impulse of the will by a strongly expressed, powerful word. The name *māshāl* (perhaps = word of power) used for the proverb and for the taunt-song and sprung from the soil of magic points to its dynamic root.

(1) The *proverb*, the outcome of the practical experience of life, is timeless, and with its reflexions on the connexions in universal human affairs is in international use. The relationship of the Israelite proverb with the stock of non-Israelite sayings must be understood with the basis of its broad humanity in mind, and when they are in accord, there is no need to point each time to direct dependence. The proverb, since it has grown right out of the life of people, is not at first constructed metrically. Its characteristic quality is a terse vividness in illustration or comparison; e.g. Jer. 23: 28 'What is the straw to the wheat?'; 1 Kgs. 20: 11 'Let not him that girdeth on his armour boast himself as he that putteth it off'. Yet the *Parallelismus membrorum* is found already in early days. The prophets often made use of the popular proverb in their preaching and so, as all life became permeated with faith in Yahweh, it acquired a stronger religious colouring and served rather to throw light on spiritual and religious associations in life: e.g. 1 Sam 16: 7 'for man looketh on the outward appearance, but the Lord looketh on the heart'; Is. 10: 15 'Shall the axe boast itself against him that heweth therewith? Shall the saw magnify itself against him that shaketh it?' (cf. the common use of the illustration of the clay and the potter for the same idea) (Is. 29: 16; 45: 9; Jer. 18: 1 ff.; Rom. 9: 20 f.). Akin to the proverb is the *riddle* (*ḥîdāh*) (cf. the parallel use of *ḥîdāh* and *māshāl* in Prov. 1: 6). Riddles of this kind have been handed down to us in Jgs. 14: 12–18 where they are applied to the experiences of Samson. Originally the riddle was not attached to a person or a historical event; but in this case history has taken possession of it.

(2) The *Wisdom saying* developed out of the popular proverb and riddle by being worked up into a larger, more artistic unit.

This development began already in early times. There are indications of it in Solomon's cultivation of wisdom in 1 Kgs. 5: 9 ff.; in the existence of the sayings of the kings in Prov. 16: 10; 22: 29; 25: 2, 4 f., and *passim*, as well as in the production of a collection of sayings under Hezekiah (Prov. 25: 1). In the early days of Israel there certainly were, as Alt has rendered plausible from

1 Kgs. 5: 13, encyclopaedic lists of nature knowledge similar to those in Babylonia and Egypt, which have been preserved in the numerical sayings (Prov. 30: 15 f., 18 ff., 24 ff., 29 ff.) and which later influenced Job 38 ff. and Ps. 148. Yet this kind of theoretical natural science was pushed into the background by that other kind of 'wisdom' which grew out of the daily needs of human life. The wisdom-saying deals with practical wisdom for living, not with theoretical knowledge. It seems to have been cultivated among the 'wise' $h^a k\bar{a}m\hat{i}m$, who formed a special class beside the priests and the prophets (Jer. 18: 18; Is. 29: 14) and in whose hands, to begin with, as in Egypt and Babylonia, lay the training of officials and scribes (Jer. 8: 8 f.). These educated circles are the explanation of the lively interchange with non-Israelite wisdom (1 Kgs. 10: 1 ff.; Prov. 30: 1; 31: 1) which can be traced down to Hellenistic times, and of the influx of foreign linguistic material which is most clearly exemplified by the admission of the collection of sayings in Prov. 22: 17–23: 12, out of the Egyptian 'Wisdom of Amen-em-ope' (c. ninth–sixth century B.C.). In contrast with Egypt, where owing to the difficulty of learning the script the cultivation of the wisdom literature remained tied to the professional training of the scribe-class, the basis of Hebrew literature was broadened and its study was enlarged to include a general knowledge of life. This was brought about by the wisdom-schools extending their teaching of practical wisdom for living to the education of youth and by 'wisdom' becoming in the Diaspora an important means of Jewish propaganda. When used in teaching the wisdom-saying was intended to be learned by heart and this can still occasionally be recognized by the educational form and arrangement and by the use of a mnemonic style. A further stage of development is seen in the *Wisdom song* and the *Wisdom speech* in poetic form, both artistic creations, which have been admitted beside the wisdom-saying into the book of Proverbs and Ecclesiasticus. The well-known praise of the virtuous housewife in Prov. 31: 10–31, and also songs, such as Pss. 1, 127, 128, 133 and 2 Sam. 23 belong to the type of Wisdom songs. The fact that the themes of Wisdom penetrated into liturgical poetry, which can also be observed in the hortatory sections of the thanksgiving psalms, is presumably to be explained by the association of the schools for scribes with the temple, where wisdom was cultivated,

and this may have facilitated the reception of 'Wisdom' into the canonical literature of the OT.*

The content of the literature of Sayings must be judged from the point of view of its use in education. Beside the simple statement of facts drawn from experience of life, there are counsels for sensible conduct and moral exhortations. What is reasonable, and can be taught and learned, is placed in the forefront; the irrational side of life and also of the conception of God retreats into the background. This is the subject of the kindred *didactic poem* (Pss. 37, 49) in which an attempt is made to master the problem of the suffering of the righteous by demonstrating the reasonableness of the belief in requital. It is proof of the vital nearness and strength of the OT faith in God that the unreasonableness of this problem is in the last resort not solved by thought, but is recognized and overcome in practice by faith (Ps. 73). As compared with the early oriental parallels, the OT Wisdom sayings are marked by the stronger religious basis of their ethos, which tends to restrict the external standard for success and the eudaemonist conception of rewards inherent in this whole class. The fear of God takes the place of reason, as the foundation (principle) of 'Wisdom'. (Ps. 111: 10; Job 28: 28) and gives it a firmer inner support against demoralizing doubts. Through this permeation by religion of daily life derived indirectly from the prophetic preaching a 'religion for every day' developed beside the cultic piety of Judaism and this gives a colouring of its own to the Wisdom of the OT.

(3) *Blessings and curses.* The roots of the sayings containing blessings and curses also reach down into magic. The power inherent in the word itself, and also persons endowed with particular power or charisma, such as kings (2 Sam. 6: 18; 1 Kgs. 8: 14, 55), men of God (1 Sam. 9: 13; Num. 22: 6), priests (Num, 6: 23 ff.), dying persons (Gen. 27: 27 ff., 48: 14 ff.) are able, according to early ways of thinking, to bring into active operation beneficial or harmful forces by means of a solemnly composed blessing or curse, sometimes with an action to correspond (touching, laying on hands). A remainder of this conception of power lies at the root of the aetiological use of blessings and curses, which explains present circumstances as the effects of words of blessing or cursing

* cf. Mowinckel, Psalms and Wisdom, *VT Suppl.* III (1955), 205 ff.

spoken over their primeval ancestors (cf. Gen. 9: 25 ff.); it is also at the root of the conviction that a blessing once pronounced can never be revoked (Gen. 27: 37). The influence of the religion of Yahweh and the admission of blessing and curse into Yahweh's cult in which they became a cultic act (cf. Jgs. 5: 23 f.; Num. 6: 24–26; Deut. 27: 11 ff.) had already in early times resulted in their being reshaped theistically so that the actual power of blessing and cursing was reserved to the deity alone; this led through the use of the formula 'blessed by Yahweh' or through calling down blessings (*'ashʳê*) and woes (*'ôy*), also employed apart from the cult in the Wisdom and prophetic literature especially, to prayers of intercession and vengeance. The case is similar with regard to the wishes for blessings given to the bride on her journey as she leaves her father's house (Gen. 24: 60) and the words with which a mother greets her child at its birth (Gen. 29: 31–30: 24). The same tendency shows itself in the variation of the benediction for the deity to whom alone by the formula 'blessed be Yahweh' all the powers of blessing are finally ascribed, a development which ends up in the hymn. It is characteristic that, when the magical conceptions of blessing and cursing weaken and they become re-oriented theocentrically, the religious use of the curse in the OT recedes; in Ps. 10: 7 cursing is the mark of a sinner; also in the case of an oath which is originally a cursing of oneself, the curse-formula is merely paraphrased in words giving an intimation: 'God do this and that to me, and even more if...' or is even omitted altogether. When the prophets gave the OT religion greater depth and intensity, the words of benediction too received a special stamp. The conditions for divine blessing are a moral, pious behaviour and amongst the actual blessings prayed for the spiritual values in life receive increasing prominence.

From the same root as blessings and curses spring *taunts* and *boasts* (cf. Jer. 24: 9). In battles and disputes, the taunt is intended to lower and reduce the power of the opponent, the boast on the contrary to increase one's own strength and sense of power. The battle of words preceding David's victory over Goliath, reminiscent of the war-speeches of Homeric heroes (1 Sam. 17: 42 ff.), affords an insight into the use of taunt and boast and their final associations with blessing and cursing; at the same time, they

illustrate by David's retort the forces at work in the OT developing and transforming these types. In the taunt song (see section
6a 1) which arose out of the taunt saying, submission to the
divine power results in God's judgment being drawn into the
prophetic preaching, whilst the style of self-affirmation in the
boast is finally reserved for the hymn, as the expression of
Yahweh's proclamation of his uniqueness. A comparison of the
profane boast-song of Lamech (Gen. 4: 23 f.) in which the hero
extols the cruelty of his vengeance with the hymns of Deutero-
Isaiah (cf. e.g. Is. 44: 6 ff.) makes it possible to measure what the
spirit of the OT has made of this type; the self-glorification of
man has waned before the exclusive glorification of God.

A variety of *tribal sayings*, found collected in the blessings of the
dying Jacob (Gen. 49) and of Moses (Deut. 33) arranged according to the twelve-tribe pattern dates from the time of the still
relatively independent life of the tribes. Their incorporation into
their present literary and historical framework is secondary. The
separate sayings characterize the individualities of the tribes one
by one, some in a descriptive form looking back over the past
(Gen. 49: 14 f.), some in the shape of a promise by combining a
prophecy and a blessing (Gen. 49: 8 ff., 22) or of a reproach and a
curse (Gen. 49: 7). In the same class must be included also the
earlier Oracles of Balaam (Num. 24: 3-9, 15-19), poems worked up
into songs, which probably came into being in the time of David
and Solomon, as they presuppose the undivided kingdom of
Israel and were only subsequently linked with the legend of
Balaam. Their original setting in the life (*Sitz im Leben*) of the
people seems to have been the national cult-festival which we
must postulate for the tribal union at the sanctuary of the covenant. The sayings of praise and blame in Deborah's song (Jgs.
5: 15-18, 23), which presumably sprang out of a cultic victory-
celebration after the battle won by the union of the Israelite
tribes, enable us to picture such an occasion for reciting sayings
about the tribes; in this way their nature as *vaticinia ex eventu* becomes intelligible. It is uncertain how far the present collections
of tribal sayings go back to earlier isolated sayings and smaller
groups; a tribal saying originally existing by itself is woven in
Gen. 16: 10 f. into the birth story of Ishmael.

(4) *The Prophetic Saying.* The prophetic saying must be under-

stood by reference to the nature of the OT prophetic movement. Prophecy, the most important phenomenon in the shaping of the OT, developed during the OT period from various roots to become a thing of independent and unparalleled magnitude. On the one hand it goes back to ecstatic possession, a form of religion known to us in the world of the Aegean and Asia Minor and in the pre-Israelite era in Canaan. In the Samuel-Saul tradition we meet for the first time in Israel bands of ecstatic fanatics who transport themselves by music and dance into a state of raving excitement often heightened into complete unconsciousness (1 Sam. 10: 5ff.; 19: 24). In Elisha's time they still lived in monastic communities and seem originally to have had a connexion with the sanctuaries. The fact that they were possessed by spirits felt by the people at first to be unfamiliar and hence contemptible (cf. 1 Sam. 10: 11; Hos. 9: 7; 2 Kgs. 9: 11) was considered to be an effect of divine power and an enhancement of their strength which was probably turned to account in warlike undertakings together with the fighters' frenzy (cf. 1 Sam. 11: 6 ff.; 1 Kgs. 22: 10). This kind of enthusiastic piety based on experience still retains a strong element of vigorous action which was preserved also in the classical prophets who had grown far beyond the limits of ecstatic nabi-ism and in part stood in the sharpest contrast to it.

The accounts in the OT lead us also to a second line of ancestry out of which the OT prophetic movement grew up. It stands in very close connexion with the seers known probably already to the pre-Canaanite Hebrews. The man of God was considered to be a seer or soothsayer, one who by virtue of special faculties or with the help of a certain technique could obtain possession of secret lore hidden from the ordinary person. Thus in the popular tradition (1 Sam. 9: 6 ff.) Samuel appears as a seer from whom e.g. information about the whereabouts of stray asses was obtained in return for payment. We can no longer distinguish clearly what role the independent seer played in ancient Israel beside the oracle of priestly divination attested particularly in the tradition of Saul and David, since even in the early accounts the distinctions have been obliterated owing to the later combination of the two different types of seer and prophet. Thus, for example, the portrait of Balaam, the earliest figure of a seer in the OT is compounded of different features, those of a seer, a magician, an exorcist and a

prophet. Nevertheless we may conclude from the remark in
1 Sam. 9: 9, according to which the earlier designation 'seer' was
replaced later by the name 'prophet', that two lines of development were combined in the OT prophets. Moreover, it seems as if
this fusion of seer with the forms of prophetic experience took
place in the time of Samuel, perhaps under his direct influence.
At any rate in the Samuel tradition these two factors join forces.
The features of the seer, the priest and the prophet are united in
his portrait and he is considered to be carrying on the prophetic
tradition. It may be attributed to Samuel's efforts that the Nabi-
movement was not incorporated into the religion of Yahweh
without an inner transformation. The powerful impetus of the
prophet's experience allies itself with the more intellectual form
of the seer's practice of oracles and thus creates the peculiar
quality of OT prophecy, which at one and the same time announces and brings to pass what God wills and determines.

The spiritual power at work in the OT prophetic movement
produced a literature of high religious and poetical quality to
which no other religious poetry has attained. Its point of departure and foundation and at the same time its significant characteristic is the sense of being personally possessed by God, shown
in the most varied forms, including even the symptoms of paralysis of Ezekiel. As he stands under the coercive dominion of God,
the prophet feels that what he does is done by a compulsion from
above from which he is not able to escape (Am. 3: 8; Jer. 20: 9).
Therefore, *the experience of being called* has its particular place in the
prophetic message and when reduced to writing (Is. 6: 1 ff.; Jer.
1: 4 ff.; Ezek. 1: 4 ff.; Am. 7–9, sometimes at the beginning of the
original writings of the prophets) it rings through again and again
as the prophet's justification to himself and to his hearers. Probably the Hebrew designation of the prophet as *nābî'* means much
the same as 'he who is called'. Besides this, the prophetic literature
contains descriptions of other experiences, not as a continuous
autobiography or with the details fully worked out, but usually
only in so far as they are required to understand the divine
commission or word connected with the experience; moreover,
what the prophet has himself experienced is not for himself, it
took place to serve the prophetic task demanded from him by
God (cf. e.g. Jer. 16: 1 ff.; 19 and especially Ezekiel).

This foundation of prophecy on experience suggests a comparison with the revelation literature of the circles of mysticism (Lindblom) and receives its particular form from the fact that the prophets often speak of their private experiences as *reports of what they have seen and heard.** This visionary experience, into which the Oracles of Balaam and Job 4: 12 ff. give an insight, is related to that of dreams. Linked up with the sight of everyday things or mysterious images and associations, often introduced by the formula 'thus Yahweh let me see', the vision usually demands an 'interpretation', either in the form of a divine revelation or based on the prophet's own meditation. In the latter lies a danger recognized by Jeremiah in 23: 25 ff., when he sharply rejects the dreams of the nebiim as deceit of their own devising and differentiates them from the truth and power of the authentic word of God. But that does not exclude the fact that even in the case of the 'writing' prophets the individual peculiarity of their thoughts, of their personal spiritual and intellectual nature, determined decisively the mode of expression and the thought-content of their message, as a comparison between Isaiah and Jeremiah or between Amos and Hosea teaches. The stronger the basis of their experience, the more does the content of the prophet's word override the constraint of the form. Under the influence of increasing meditation the prophetic allegory gradually evolved out of the story of the vision. The imitation of a description of a vision, as a pure matter of style, without any underlying experience, such as we can observe in later times, is a sign that genuine prophecy has become extinct.

A still greater significance is attached to what is heard. The word of God, received and considered effective because of the speaker, forms the core of the prophetic message in the OT. This makes it clear that the spoken public exposition of the divine word belongs to the essence of OT prophecy. No long speeches or sermons, but a short oracular messenger's saying,† a pithy

---

* It results from what has been said that the account in the first person singular of the prophet's story of his vision is not to be included in the class of actual historical writing, as Rost (Introduction, p. 19) thinks.

† For the 'messenger's saying' attested in the Mari-texts of the eighteenth century cf. de Liagre-Böhl, 'Voorloopers der Profeten sedert 1700 v. Chr.' (*Nederlands Theologisch Tijdschrift* IV, 1949, pp. 81–91); Lods, 'Une tablette inédite de Mari, intéressante pour l'histoire du prophétisme sémitique, *Studies in OT Prophecy*, ed. by Rowley 1950, pp. 103–110; Noth, 'Geschichte und Gotteswort im AT' (*Bonner Akad.*

word addressed to a quite concrete situation, often introduced
with a formalized announcement, 'thus saith Yahweh' or, marked
as a revelation by the formula, *nᵉʾūm Yahweh* (thus whispereth
Yahweh) in the middle or at the end; it is this manner of speaking
which produces the fundamental uniformity of the prophetic
style, and it is often easy to recognize it in its original form by its
opening and concluding formula. The 'I' style of the divine
speaker suits the form of God's message; the frequent alternation
of the 'I' and the 'He' styles is a sign of the active interchange of
the 'I' of God and of the prophet, as well as of the part played by
the prophet's own thoughts when he receives the revelation. In its
essence the prophet's word is 'forth-telling', meaning that it does
not only announce what will happen, but that as an effectively
powerful word of God 'which shall not return void' (cf. Jer.
23: 29; Is. 55: 11) it will also bring about what it tells. The
dynamically active character of the prophetic saying in which the
'powerful impetus' of the earliest ecstatic prophecy lives on in a
purified form can also be seen in the fact that it is occasionally
accompanied by '*signs*' and *symbolic* efficacious *actions* (Is. 7: 10 ff.;
Jer. 27: 2 ff.; 44: 29 f.). Prophecy is divided into two kinds according to its contents: the *denunciation*, which announces disaster, and
the *promise*, which includes a prophecy of salvation. In the pre-
exilic prophecy, denunciations predominate; Jeremiah (28: 8)
bases himself on a tradition of prophesying calamities. Beside
these we find in the prophets, corresponding to the OT conception of God, which knows Yahweh as the God who expresses his
will and makes claims, two other basic forms of the types of
prophetic sayings: the *reproach* (e.g. Hos. 4: 1 ff.) usually associated
with a threat which it justifies and the *exhortation* (e.g. Is. 1: 16 f.)
occasionally issuing into a promise. In these, and in the more
fully elaborated speeches of judgment and exhortation, there
appears more clearly than in the denunciation and the promise the
individual thought and sense of responsibility of the prophets
who know themselves called to be also the critics and leaders of
their people. These types are already fully shaped in the earliest

---

Reden 3), 1950=BJRL 32, 2 (1950), pp. 194–206; W. von Soden, 'Verkündigung des
Gotteswillens durch prophetisches Wort in den altbabylonischen Briefen aus Mari',
Die Welt des Orients I 1950, pp. 397–403.
    The form of the 'messenger's saying' is related to the epistolary style and probably
borrowed from it.

writing prophets; they must, therefore, have behind them a long development, perhaps intimately associated with the cult.

Besides these four basic types of short sayings, there are also longer poetic units. We have the poem in Am. 1: 3–2: 16, with regularly constructed stanzas against the foreign nations serving as a preparation and a background for the saying against Israel itself, the visions in Am. 7–9 which originally belonged together and are worked up similarly to an oratorical climax and the poem about the plagues of Yahweh (Am. 4: 6–12) the stanzas of which are separated by a refrain (cf. Is. 2: 7 ff.; 9: 7 ff.). All these, to judge by their rhetorical character appear to have had already their present form when delivered by word of mouth; whilst the freer composition of the woes (Is. 5: 8 ff.; Am. 5: 7 ff. where the earlier arrangement is disturbed) was probably first put together when it was written down.

But the wealth of form used by the prophets is still not exhausted. The close touch with life of the prophets' preaching and their passionate tendency to permeate all life with religion is mirrored in their use of numerous other types of literature. The dirge (Am. 5: 1 f.; Is. 14: 4–23) and the national lament (Hos. 6: 1 ff.), the taunt-song (Is. 37: 22 ff.), the drinking song (Is. 22: 13) and the love-song (Is. 5: 1 ff.) are used by the prophets in the service of their message; proverbs (Am. 6: 12), the herald's cry (Am. 3: 9), an imitation of the priest's torah (Is. 1: 10 ff.; Mic. 6: 6 f.) and the pilgrim song (Am. 4: 4 f.) help to arrest the attention of the listener; the metaphor of the law suit (Hos. 4: 1 ff.; Mic. 6: 1 ff.; Is. 1: 2; 41: 1 ff.), the contentious remarks arising out of the previous argument (Am. 3: 3–8, 12) reveal the lively versatility of the prophetic style. The hymn (Is. 42: 10 ff.) becomes the expression of the prophets' exalted view of God, the prayer (Jer. 15: 10 ff.) the moving witness to their personal struggle for faith. The attempt has been made to explain Is. 33, Mic. 7: 7–20, Hab. 1–3 and Joel as 'prophetic liturgies' originating in the framework of the cult. The prophets' meditations on history and the contemporaneous diminution of the charismatic forms of experience and expression developed into the sermon-like discourse in prose in which hortatory conclusions are drawn from the historical retrospect. This type, probably connected with the tradition of salvation history in the Yahweh cult, is met with already in

C

Jos. 24 and 1 Sam. 12, and also in Jer. and Ez. and in the introductory discourses of Deut. The use of cultic forms of style in the
prophetic literature has led us recently to recognize that there was
a more positive association of the prophets with the cult of
Yahweh and its traditions and has enabled us to see in the relationship between priest and prophet that which unites rather than that
which separates them.*

The reasons for which the prophet's words which had formerly
been spoken were committed to writing varied in each case.
According to Is. 8: 1 ff.; 30: 8 f.; Hab. 2: 2, the prophetic sayings
were written down in an attempt to preserve them as a witness to
later times in proof of their truth; in the case of Jer. 36: 1 ff., and
probably also in that of Amos's vision the written composition is
an expedient because the prophet is prevented from speaking his
message. To begin with, small collections of sayings (e.g. Is. 6–9)
formed the core of the prophetic writings which were only put
together and worked up by later hands to form the present prophetic books. As the prophetic movement developed further, the
written composition of the message occupies a more prominent
place; the imitation of the prophetic manner (e.g. in the visions of
Zech. 1–8; Dan. 7–12 with its strikingly full description of the
details) and the interpretation of history in the form of *vaticinia ex
eventu*, point the way from expiring prophecy to apocalyptic; both
are a proof how deeply the two basic lines of OT prophecy, the
nature of the experience and the prophets' religious meditation on
history, influenced the literature and life of post-prophetic times.

(5) *Cultic sayings*. A number of the types already discussed
show connexions with the cult. Here we will only mention those
sayings which have their roots in the cult and their place in the
priestly tradition. In early days it was part of the priest's task to
deliver oracles, i.e. to announce the divine will for certain individual cases. The accounts of the period of Saul and David tell of
the *priestly oracle by lot* and ephod with urim and thummim, which
presupposes a definite oracular technique and a fixed form of
question offering an alternative which was answered with 'yes' or
'no' ('ûrîm = cursed?, tummîm = favourable?) (1 Sam. 14: 18 f.,

---

* cf. Welch, *Prophet and Priest in Old Israel*, 1936; Johnson, *The Cultic Prophet in
Ancient Israel*, 1944; Würthwein, *Der Ursprung der prophetischen Gerichtsrede'*, ZThK
49 (1952) 31 ff.; Weiser, 'Jeremia', ATD 21 (1955) 468 ff.

41; 23: 9 ff.) Yet in other passages (1 Sam. 30: 7; Jgs. 20: 28 f.; 2 Sam. 5: 23 f.) prophecies are made which go beyond the simple yes or no; thus when the priest delivers an oracle, beside the purely technical handling of the lots, a more charismatic activity comes into play which reveals here the relationship of the priest with the seer and the prophet. Accordingly the priest also is an announcer of the divine word. When a petition is made at the sanctuary, he promises that God will grant it (1 Sam. 1: 17). On particularly solemn occasions and for important oracles the priest's saying was probably given in poetic metre (cf. Gen. 25: 23).

Beside these more occasional utterances of the divine will transmitted to an individual, it seems that when the people came together for regularly recurring cultic purposes at the sanctuary of the covenant, the priest recited a proclamation of the divine will summarized in general terms as a fundamental ordinance of the covenant to which the people pledged themselves. This is the place for the sacral recital and the oral tradition of a brief compilation of regulations and lists of prohibitions collected in groups of ten or twelve commandments, partly for the purpose of impressing them on the memory; we can see in these the authentically Israelite root out of which the OT law was fashioned. Fragments of this kind, although revised in some degree, are to be found in Exod. 21: 12, 15–17; Lev. 18: 7–17; Deut. 27: 15–26 and in the decalogue in Exod. 20: 2 ff.; Deut. 5: 6 ff. By their content which deals with sacral, ethical and legal relationships in life, they show the close connexion between the cult of Yahweh, the nationhood and the law (see below). In the case of the decalogue, the announcement of God's will was given importance and a background by an introductory revelation of God's nature in the so-called epiphany-formula which has the form of a divine self-affirmation.* In an abbreviated and altered shape we meet this in Lev. 19: 2, 'Ye shall be holy; for I, Yahweh your God, am holy'; and standing by itself in Exod. 33: 19; 34: 6 f. In this connexion we must mention also the description of God's theophany in the

---

* The fact that the commandments of the decalogues are formulated in the indicative still points to Yahweh's announcement of his will belonging to and corresponding with that of his nature; in this form it is the divine proclamation of the *nature* of God's people who are set in contrast to their surroundings by the negative way of expressing prohibitions.

introductions to the Song of Deborah and to Moses' blessing (Deut. 33) and in the Psalms (18: 7–15; 50: 2 ff.; 68: 2 ff.; 77: 17 ff.; 97: 3–6)* which are associated with the tribal union's celebration of the covenant (see above). This description for its part fits into the broader canvas of the tradition of salvation history, the recital of which during the cultic festival of the covenant was also part of the priest's duty (see below section 13).

The *priest's torah* is the teaching given by the priest about intercourse with the deity. Its purpose is practical instruction how to distinguish sacred from profane, clean from unclean, which played a role not to be underrated, especially in the encounter of the Yahweh religion with the forms of the Canaanite religion and in the controversy between them. In its original aspect the torah consisted of the words of Yahweh recited as commands or prohibitions by the priest commissioned by God; this can still be traced in the use of the torah by the prophets (Is. 1: 10 ff.), in this case filled with prophetic content. Side by side with this we find a second kind of torah consisting of the priests' answers to questions put by the laity. This is preserved for us—again with a strong prophetic colouring—in Mic. 6: 6 ff.; Is. 33: 14 ff.; Hag. 2: 10 ff. and in the two liturgical songs of the torah, Pss. 15 and 24: 3–6. Finally the priests' torah expands into the tradition of casuistic, priestly lore, elaborated theologically and including the individual operations of the cult; thus it leads, as its forms alter, to small written collections of the torah (Lev. 6: 2, 7, 18; 7: 1, 11 and *passim*) which are on the road linking torah and law and thus mark the way along which Judaism travelled to become the 'religion of the law'.

(6) *The statutes* (for the literature see section 8). Israelite law sprang from two different sources, the one their own, the other a foreign one. Their own way of framing the law has already been mentioned; its roots seem to reach right back to the earliest days of the nation and it consists of compressed, regularly constructed legal sayings, categorically formulated and expressed metrically so as to be recited impressively, e.g. 'He that smiteth a man, so that he die, shall surely be put to death, (Exod. 21: 12; cf. Gen. 9: 6). The form and content of these rules, usually strung together in short series, express the absolute character of the divine

* cf. Weiser, *Bertholet-Festschrift*, 1950, pp. 513 ff.

authority behind them, which in the case of Israelite law as contrasted with the foreign legal codes determines the organic connexion between religion and law. The home of this type of saying
is not the practice of the normal administration of justice by the
local judicial authority, but the recital within the sacral environment of the regularly recurring cultic festival of the people meeting at the covenant-shrine as a religious congregation and as a
nation, the purpose of this recital being to inculcate the combined
religious and legal foundation of the ordinances of the covenant.
These circumstances explain the endeavour to gather together
general series of rules and prohibitions, uniform in style and
metre and easily remembered (Exod. 21: 12, 15, 17; 22: 18 f.;
31: 14 f.; Lev. 20: 2, 27; 24: 16 (crimes worthy of death); Deut.
27: 15–26 (crimes worthy of a curse). In the case of the decalogue
we see the tendency to embrace as wide a sphere as possible of
divine demands with ever greater forcefulness (direct speech with
'thou' cf. Lev. 18: 7–17) though this was only achieved by giving
up the symmetrical construction of the sentences; but as the form
became less harsh, so its combined religious and ethical content
became more forceful and more profound and it is just this to
which the decalogue owes its lasting universal significance. The
greater vitality of the OT religion asserted itself in the process by
which Israel's own legal system with its religious demands
claimed for its law ever larger areas and assimilated into itself
what had originally been of foreign origin and type.

8. Laws and Records

Jirku, *Das weltliche Recht im AT*, 1927; Hempel, 'Gottesgedanken und Rechtsgestaltung in Altisrael', ZSTh, 1930, 377 ff.; L. Köhler, 'Die hebräische Rechtsgemeinde (*Jahresbericht der Univ. Zürich* 1930–31); Noth, Das Amt des 'Richters Israels', *Bertholet-Festschrift* 1950, 404 ff.; Alt, *Die Ursprünge des israelitischen Rechts*, 1934=Alt I, 278 ff.; Noth, 'Die Gesetze im Pentateuch', *Schriften der Königsberger Gelehrten Gesellschaft*, Geisteswissenschaftl. Kl. 17. Jahrg. Vol. 2, 1940=Gesammelte Studien zum AT, 9 ff.; Rabast, *Das apodiktische Recht im Deuteronomium und Heiligkeitsgesetz*, 1949; Goetze, *Sumer*, IV 1948, 63 ff.; Schmökel, *Ur, Assur und Babylon*, 1955, 81 f.; Beer, 'Zur israelitischen—jüdischen Briefliteratur', *Kittel-Festschrift*, BWAT, 1913, 20 ff.; Alt, 'Israels Gaue unter Salomo', loc. cit., 1 ff.=Alt II, 76 ff.; idem, 'Israels Gaue unter Josia', PJB, 1925, 100 ff.=Alt II, 276 ff.; idem, 'Eine galiläische Ortsliste in Jos. 9', ZAW 1927, 59 ff.; Elliger, 'Die dreissig Helden Davids', PJB, 1935, 29 ff.; idem, 'Die Nordgrenze des Reiches Davids', PJB, 1936, 34 ff.

In several passages of the poetic type we have had to notice transitions from poetry to prose, as for example in the prophetic literature, the priests' torah and especially the statutes. Here we shall speak of those types which are stamped from the first by their nature as prose literature.

(1) *Laws*. Beside the above-named apodictic legal sayings recited in the sacral environment of the assembly of the covenant, the legal rules used for ascertaining the verdict when passing sentence, which represented the second source in the formation of Israelite law, were from their origin prosaic in form. Like our laws they are formulated as *case-law* and seek by the appropriate use of 'if' to describe and define the legal case as clearly as possible in order to state the legal deduction in the principal clause. This usually results in a ponderous, long-winded stylistic arrangement e.g. 'If men contend, and one smiteth the other with a stone or . . . and (the smitten one) die not, but keep his bed:—if he rise again, and walk abroad upon his staff, then shall he that smote him be quit; only he shall pay for his sitting and shall cause him to be thoroughly healed' (Exod. 21: 18 f.). Such passages or corpora of case-law have been admitted into the Book of the Covenant and Deuteronomy, (Exod. 21: 2–22: 16; Deut. 15: 12–18; 22: 18–29). Their subject matter includes the laws concerning slaves, homicide, personal injury, damage to cattle and fields, misappropriation of deposits and marriage law. Since these display no obligation to

Yahweh nor any idea of a common nationhood, we may infer a foreign origin for these laws. Indeed the legal system which had become indigenous in Canaan since the Hyksos period, and which for its part reveals a relationship with other early oriental legal codes (Sumerian legal ordinances of Ur, Eshnunna and Isin, the code of Hammurabi, Assyrian and Hittite law) is probably that which seems to have been taken over by the Israelites at the conquest together with the Canaanite civilization, and to have been adopted, at first as an oral tradition, into the local jurisdiction administered by the elders of the clan and the free men of the local community.

As the state developed its organization so that a part of the administration of justice in Israel passed to the king (2 Sam. 14: 1 ff.; 15: 2 ff.) and to an official judiciary, the oral tradition of law was probably committed to writing in small corpora of law, such as are found in the Book of the Covenant and in Deuteronomy beside the legal forms of authentic Israelite origin. The greater strength of Israel's characteristic way of life made itself felt by its penetration also into the casuistic law and its forms; as regards the content, this trend can be observed in the combined religious and ethical motivation which in comparison with early oriental legal codes, is more far-reaching and in certain matters more strict. The changes in the priests' torah and law and its fusion with the legal elements of the Pentateuch afford a proof of the predominantly religious tendencies which shaped the OT law.

(2) *Records, letters and lists.* The OT reports a number of covenants both political and private (in 1 Kgs. 5: 2 ff. the covenant between Solomon and Hiram of Tyre; in 2 Sam. 5: 3 between David and the elders of Israel; in Gen. 23 that of Abraham with the owner of the cave of Machpelah and the deed of purchase in Jer. 32); yet in striking contrast to the large quantity of such documents excavated in Mesopotamia and Egypt, apart from the revised document in Neh. 10 containing the pledge of the covenant, the first one of which we possess the wording is that of Judas with the Romans from the Maccabean period (1 Macc. 8: 22 ff.) We have more information in the OT about *letters*, the forms of which are derived from the Babylonian epistolary style (cf. also the tablets of El Amarna and Taanach, the letters of Lachish and

Elephantiné). In addition to important extracts from letters (e.g. the letter concerning Uriah in 2 Sam. 11: 15 and the letters of Jehu to the rulers of Samaria in 2 Kgs. 10: 1 ff.) there are preserved e.g. the letter of Jeremiah to the exiles (Jer. 29: 1–23) and in Ezr. 4 ff. letters from the diplomatic correspondence with the Great King of Persia and official documents from the reign of Cyrus, Darius I and Artaxerxes I. The number of lists handed down in the OT is still greater. In Jgs. 10: 1–5; 12: 7–15 we find in a stereotyped form a list of the so-called lesser judges of the period before the Kingdom. From David's first period we have the list of his body-guard of thirty heroes (2 Sam. 23: 24 ff.); the list of Solomon's district officers in 1 Kgs. 4: 7–19 is a contemporary document. Also in the case of the lists of places and districts used in Jos. 15–19 we have to do with official registers, even though they do not date historically from the period to which their present literary context assigns them, but probably only came into being in the seventh century.* Besides these there are genealogical lists (especially in 1 Chron. 1–9), inventories of votive offerings (Exod 35: 21 ff.) and lists of booty (Num. 31: 32 ff.), the authenticity of which as documents is doubtful in spite of analogies outside the OT. Considered as a whole the OT lacks the sense of documentary accuracy. This explains why even genuine documents such as e.g. those in the book of Ezra-Nehemiah were re-shaped and it gave no offence when for instance the edict of Cyrus was presented in two different versions (Ezr. 1: 2 ff.; 6: 3 ff.); this is the reason too for its insertion into different historical contexts.

9. Narratives

Gunkel, *Schöpfung und Chaos in Urzeit und Endzeit*, 1895; Gressmann, 'Sage und Geschichte in den Patriarchenerzählungen, ZAW, 1910, 1 ff.; Bethe, *Mythus, Sage, Märchen*, 1922; Eissfeldt, 'Stammessage und Novelle in den Geschichten von Jakob und seinen Söhnen, FRLANT 1922, I, 56 ff.; Gunkel, 'Mythus und Mythologie im AT', RGG² IV, 1930, col. 381 ff.; idem, 'Sagen und Legenden im AT', RGG² V, 1931, col. 49 ff.; Baumgartner, 'Märchen in der Bibel', RGG² III, 1929, col. 1829 ff.; Weiser, 'Glaube und Geschichte im AT', BWAT, 1931. R. Kittel, *Die Anfänge der hebräischen Geschichtsschreibung in AT* (Rektoratsrede an der Univ. Breslau), 1896; H. Duhm, 'Zur Geschichte der alttestamentlichen Geschichtsschreibung, *Plüss-*

---

* Thus Alt and Noth; yet cf. the critical opinion of Mowinckel, *Zur Frage nach den dokumentarischen Quellen in Josua 13–19*, 1946; and Kaufmann, *The Biblical Account of the Conquest of Palestine*, 1953, who considers the lists of places to be the product of historical writing.

festschrift, 1905, 118 ff.; H. Schmidt, *Die Geschichtsschreibung im AT*, 1911; Rost, 'Die Überlieferung von der Thronnachfolge Davids', BWAT, 1926; Alt, *Die Staatenbildung der Israeliten in Palästina*, 1930=Alt II, 1 ff.; ed. Meyer, *Die kulturelle, literarische und religiöse Entwicklung des israelitischen Volkes in der älteren Königszeit*, 1930; Hölscher, 'Die Anfänge der hebräischen Geschichtsschreibung', *Sitzungsberichte der Heidelberger Akademie der Wissenschaften*, phil. hist. Kl. 1942; von Rad, 'Der Anfang der Geschichtsschreibung im AT', *Archiv für Kulturgeschichte*, 32 (1944), 1–42; Noth, 'Überlieferungsgeschichtliche Studien I,' *Schriften der Königsberger Gelehrten Gesellschaft*, 18th annual set, Geisteswiss. Kl. Heft. 2, 1943, ²1957; Jacob, *La tradition historique en Israël*, Faculté de Théologie Protestante, Montpellier, 1946; Eissfeldt, *Geschichtsschreibung im Altern Testament*, 1948; Noth *Überlieferungsgeschichte des Pentateuchs*, 1948; Hölscher, 'Geschichtsschreibung in Israel, Untersuchungen zum Jahvisten und Elohisten', *Acta Reg. Soc. Hum. Litt. Lundensis* 1952.

(a) Poetic Narratives

The poetic narrative springs from the endeavour to give to life and experience a 'form' by means of the word. Therefore it stands nearer to the dynamic forces of life than the historical narrative which in its more objective contemplative way holds itself somewhat aloof from that which has been. The poetic narrative is the popular form of comment on what has happened, kept alive in oral tradition; the writing of history is from the start a type of written literature, cultivated in circles of learned scribes and intended for those in whom a corresponding amount of education and well-informed interest can be presumed. The OT narrative-literature reveals the wealth of early oriental cultural influences as much as Israel's own power of shaping them. With few exceptions the prose-narratives of the OT were gathered into larger units at the time and fitted into the framework of comprehensive accounts. Nevertheless, their original form was the self-contained, short, clear, isolated narrative which for a long time had led an independent existence in the oral tradition.

(1) *Myth.* Although no complete myth has been handed down in the OT, yet the contact with the rich tradition of early oriental myths has deeply influenced Israelite literature. The myth is originally connected with the ritual; it is the shaping of a mighty event into a kind of 'celebration in words'. The myth represents a typical event repeating itself again and again as a unique happening, very often in primeval times. It usually arises in the soil of natural religion in which those processes of nature which are impressive by their regular recurrence or their peculiarity are explained by means of personifying them and representing them

as the fortunes of gods. Therefore the nature myth is most clearly defined against the background of the idea of the cycle, a characteristic of the early oriental world-view, which developed from observing the influences of portents in the skies (astral religion) and of the changing seasons on the shaping of cultural life. Consequently polytheism is the cradle of the myth. Ignoring the fetters of space and time, its nature is to gaze into the widest vistas and to launch out into the exalted and immense.

The presuppositions for forming myths are lacking in the soil of the OT religion. Its monotheistic tendency and its organic connexion with history which stands in a certain tension with natural religion prevent Israel from creating myths of its own. They also subject the admission of foreign myths to a thorough transformation, so that we can identify in the OT only the remains of faded myths or mythological themes.* The basic conception controlling Israelite religion, namely the unique pre-eminence of Yahweh, brought it about that the OT knows no theogony and that the myths concerning the creation of the universe are subordinated everywhere to the biblical conception of creation, robbed of their own content of nature-mythology and turned into the opening bars of a *history* in which Yahweh's nature and rule proclaims itself. The specifically OT way to assimilate mythological themes to the religion of Yahweh has been to *turn the myth into history*. The original gods become creatures of Yahweh (e.g. the serpent in the story of Paradise in Gen. 3: 1, once a mythological figure); the stories of gods become the fate of men, as is shown by using as an introduction to the story of the flood (Gen. 6: 1–4) the tradition of the birth of giants from the union of the sons of God with the daughters of men, which is probably handed down only as a torso as being far too mythological. The cosmic and cultic myth of the building of the tower of Babel is in the OT torn from the soil in which it was originally rooted and has become associated with the history of the nations as the motive for their spread over the earth and their different languages. The mythological theme of the battle of the deity with the dragon of chaos (cf. Job 40: 15–41: 26) has been brought into the description

---

* I am doubtful whether, and how far, the representations of theophanies, characteristic of the OT (Exod. 19, 33; 19 ff.; Jgs. 5 : 4 f.) contain allusions to foreign myths (thus Rost).

of the catastrophe at the Red Sea and has thus been included in the history of Israel (Is. 51: 9 f.; Ps. 89: 10 ff.; 74: 13 ff.; 114). In other passages it is used to depict Israel's hopes for the future, in the course of which the battle of the deity with the monster of the chaos is transformed into Yahweh's battle with the historical enemies of Israel (Is. 17: 12 ff.; 30: 7; Ps. 87: 4; 46: 3 ff.; 47: 4). When in the OT the mythological theme is transferred from primeval times to the last age, that too is connected with the turning of myth into history; here it is the OT conception of history completing itself in eschatology which permits the entry of the most varied mythological imagery and makes it serve the faith in Yahweh. The mythical conception of the Mountain of God as the centre of the world (cf. Is. 14: 13 f.; Ez. 28: 14 ff.) to which the peoples shall flow is transferred in Is. 2: 1 ff. and Mic. 4: 1 ff. to the Mount of Zion and its temple; the battle of the deity with the dragon (Is. 27: 1; 44: 27; 50: 2), the destruction of the old world and the creation of a new heaven and a new earth (Is. 51: 6; 65: 17), the blessed peace between men and animals (Is. 2: 4; 11: 6 ff.; Hos. 2: 20, etc.) and the picture of fertility as in Paradise (Am. 9: 13; Joel 4: 18; Is. 55: 13), all these are examples of primeval times corresponding with the final era which originated in the mythology of the early oriental conception of a cycle, and have become in the OT the means with which the idea of the divine completion of history is elaborated; they play a significant part in Apocalyptic as well. But nowhere in the OT is the myth introduced for its own sake. Everywhere it serves to illustrate the surpassing greatness of the divine power. In the prophets the mythological theme together with the anthropomorphic forms of speech often becomes a poetical metaphor for the power of the sublime reality of God pressing forward in person. This method, by which the OT appropriated the material of myths and made use of it, indicates at the same time its inner victory over mythological thinking.

(2) *Sagas.* Next to the myth in OT narrative we must consider the saga which is more strongly represented. It owes its existence to the combination of poetical and historical material. It shows itself to be akin, on the one hand to historical writing, on the other to folk tales whose essentially floating themes appear in the legend attached to place and time, to a historical figure or a historical event. The saga is characterized by the popular manner of

story-telling. In the OT it is recognized by the subjects it describes. These are not the great political sequences of events, but the significant isolated features of what has happened, striking natural processes, conspicuous traits of character of the heroes for which the saga searches in their private lives and in their family circle and which it treats with love and reverence or with scorn and abhorrence. The OT has preserved a great variety of *aetiological sagas* which attempt to explain a contemporary situation by a happening in the past, a kind of popular awakening and expression of the scientific urge. Thus the *etymological saga* wishes to interpret the origin of a name; it does this in a naïve manner, as e.g. in Gen. 11 by deriving the foreign name Babel from the Hebrew root *bālal* (= to confuse) in connexion with the tale of the confusion of languages at the building of the tower of Babel. A *local nature saga* is contained in the story of Sodom in Gen. 19 which relates the origin of the Dead Sea and in the scene of Lot's wife the presence in that region of a pillar of salt; narratives with a geographical interest such as e.g. in Exod. 15: 22 ff.; 17: 7 naturally originated in and belong to the places of which they tell. The history of the tribe and the nation is mirrored in the *ethnological saga*; in the fate and the character of the ancestor it displays the typical features and the fortunes of its own tribe or nation (Cain—Kenites. Gen. 4). The narrative of Hagar and Ishmael (Gen. 16: 4 ff.; 21: 8 ff.) goes back to an Ishmaelite tribal saga; and large parts of the history of the patriarchs are founded on legendary themes concerning the history of the nation and the tribe. *Cultic sagas* too which deal with the origin of sacred customs and festivals, as e.g. Exod. 12: 1–17 explaining the introduction of, and the 'historical' reason for, the passover, must be mentioned here beside the legends of the foundation of the sanctuaries and their cult; amongst these the ἱερὸς λόγος of Bethel in Gen. 28 and that of Jerusalem in 2 Sam. 24 are preserved, both probably of Canaanite origin, but in their present form they have been historicised by being built into the framework of Israelite history. Something similar can be said of the kindred local cultic legend in Gen. 22 (see especially v. 14). To judge by their subject these cultic traditions can be classed with legends (see below); the place where they belong and were fostered must be sought in the priestly circles. In accordance with the predominance and the significance of the religious tradition of the OT, the *heroic saga* in the OT is closely associated with the legend which deals with religious matters. Even where the saga of heroes from the period of war-like activities and the awakening of the national consciousness was admitted into the OT, namely in the books of Joshua and Judges, and in a part of the history of Saul and David, it is interwoven with elements of the legend and thus receives a more or less strong emphasis on edification. The story of David's victory over Goliath (1 Sam. 17) may be named as an example of a heroic saga worked up in the manner of a legend.

Where the saga is extended to sacred persons, sacred places, sacred times, customs and institutions, they are usually designated *legends*. The OT knows, for instance, three different traditions (Exod. 4: 24 ff.; Jos. 5: 2 f.; Gen. 17) concerning the introduction of the rite of circumcision. The legend in Num. 21: 4 ff. gives an account of the 'serpent of brass' which was kept in the temple of Jerusalem right up to the time of king Hezekiah (2 Kgs. 18: 4). The tradition from the circle of the priests of the ark preserved in 1 Sam. 4–6 and 2 Sam. 6 deals with the sacred ark. The preponderance of the worship of Yahweh at the central shrine of the tribal union and since Solomon's time the preponderance of the temple of Jerusalem seems to be the reason why comparatively few cultic sagas concerning the foundation of the national shrines, numerous in early days, were kept alive. The strongest stimulus to produce OT legends was given by the great figures of the Israelite religion. Religious heroes such as above all Moses, Samuel and the prophets were the occasion for shaping a tradition which resembled the heroic saga as much as the legend. In the narrative concerning Moses and Elijah there are early attempts to describe the heroes' inner struggles for faith and to give him a character of his own which shatter the mould of the legend. The influence of the theme of a foreign folktale is shown in the story of the exposure and rescue of the child Moses, which is similar to one told of King Sargon of Akkad (2600 B.C.). The account of Samuel's childhood is developed into an idyll, into which has been admitted an aetiological theme of a narrative which probably originally referred to Saul (1 Sam. 1: 27 f.) The veneration felt for the greatness of the man of God is reflected above all in the stories of miracles of which the tradition of Elisha offers the most striking example showing how popular legends were formed. A comparison of 1 Kgs. 17: 17 ff. with 2 Kgs. 4: 8 ff. (the awakening of a dead boy) teaches how the same legend wanders from one person to another. This transference of themes, observable elsewhere, arises in the case of the cycle of Elijah and Elisha legends, handed down by the prophets' disciples, from their endeavour to draw the master and his disciple as closely together as possible. A feature running through all the OT legends of the prophets is the tendency founded on historic fact to throw into prominence the sacred person of the man of God as contrasted with the representative of worldly power (1 Sam. 15; 2 Sam. 12; 1 Kgs. 18); the ascendancy of the divine will standing behind the prophet is thereby palpably exhibited. In this way the depth of the OT conception of God, especially in the stories of the great figures in its religion like Moses, Samuel, Nathan, Elijah, creates for itself in the legend a mode of expression which as regards religion and ethics is remarkable in comparison with other literature. A later offshoot of the OT formation of legends are the *legends of martyrs* e.g. 2 Macc. 6, 7. These are composed with a view to edifying exhortation, to urge in times of distress and persecution loyalty and constancy to the faith of their fathers. The same purpose is served by the legends concerning the miraculous deliverance of Daniel when persecuted for his fidelity to his religion (Dan. 3, 6). The introduction of the historical style, which dates the events with precision and refers to documents (Dan. 6: 1; 6: 29; 3: 31; 6: 26 ff.) proves that from the viewpoint of the history of the form we have here too a late version of the legend.

Israel has also had a share in the store of international *folk tales*. It created none itself, so far as we can see. As in the case of the myth, nowhere in the OT is a folk-story preserved in a pure form; themes drawn from them are found scattered in the sagas and historical narratives, in legends and in the prophets. Everywhere in the OT the folk-tale has been turned into history, i.e. has been attached to definite historical places or persons. This means to begin with a modification of the original tale. For the folktale, which lives in a world of magic, in a belief in spirits and ghosts, is by its nature, like the myth, a floating thing, tied neither to space nor time, nor to the laws of what happens in our experience; it knows no dividing line between men and animals and no gulf between the fashionings of the imagination and sober reality. Talking animals like the serpent in Paradise and Balaam's ass (Num. 22: 28), the cruse of oil and barrel of meal which are never empty (1 Kgs. 17: 7 ff.), in fact the magical miracle is essential in these tales which were probably handed down by local tradition in Israel too by professional story-tellers. We find in the OT the kind of 'good luck' folktale about the youngest son on whom the great prize is bestowed (1 Sam. 16: 1 ff.) or about the farmer's son who sets out to seek his father's straying ass and finds a kingdom (1 Sam. 9: 1 ff.); there, too, in the story of Joseph and Potiphar's wife is the international one concerning the temptation of a youth by a bad woman, whilst the story of the judgment of Solomon is akin to an Indian fairy-tale. The characteristic use by the OT of these stories lies in their being inserted into history in order to provide it with vividness and colour, and in their being subordinated to religious faith with the intention of illustrating the power and nature of God. The magic of things becomes God's miracle. The features of the folk-tale worked into the Jonah legend serve to bring out God's mercy (see section 32). Thus in the OT the folk-tale has lost its independent position and has become a means by which the actuality of history and the actuality of God who stands behind it is expressed.

The *fable*, a relation of the folk-tale, is also represented in the OT. But just as in the case of the latter no complete fable about animals or plants has been preserved for its own sake. It serves rather as an illustration and elucidation within wider contexts, so that its original meaning became modified in the course of the active history of its transmission in Israel. The poetically-shaped fable of Jotham (Jgs. 9: 8 ff.), dealing with the trees' choice of a king and from the very beginning scoffing at kingship as such, but used in its present context as a warning against Abimelech, enables us to see that the fable had received in course of time another meaning. Similarly the short fable of the thorn's marriage proposal (2 Kgs. 14: 9), 'applied' in this place to the discussion between Amaziah, king of Judah, and Jehoahaz, king of Israel, is 'historicised' for a particular historical case. The prophets, too, did not disdain to use the fable in their preaching. The parable in Isaiah's song of the vineyard (Is. 5: 1 ff.) is based on the theme in a fable of a man's lawsuit against his vineyard. In the same way the allegories of Ezekiel, e.g. of the eagle, the cedar and the vine (Ez. 17: 3 ff.) and the mythically coloured story of the presumptuous world-wide tree and its downfall (Ez. 31) seem to have originated in fables. The fable has forfeited in the OT its independent significance. Like the folk-tale, it too has been taken into the service of history and of the witness of God.

To have recognized the different literary forms which have been interwoven to make up the OT narrative does not mean that it has become harder to understand them from the religious point of view, still less that their religious content is disparaged. On the contrary, it makes it possible to grasp more completely the religious aspect of the OT literature. For only with this history of the types as a background can we see clearly the new and characteristic things created by the authors of the OT out of the types and subject-matter of popular tradition which they found in existence and largely took over. Only thus can we see too where are the real biblical emphases and ideas which raise the OT above the level of the contemporary literature. It is the pervasive peculiarity of the OT tradition that the narrative types have no longer an independent significance, but are used as illustrations and themes for larger historical and theological compositions. The working up of isolated narratives of popular origin into groups of narratives and connected stories, their extension into larger works with a predominant religious individual content by authors of marked personality shaping their material consciously, this was the really creative act in the history of OT literature and the one which was significant for giving the OT its meaning.

(b) Narratives in prose

As contrasted with the narratives in poetry, a strong realistic impulse underlies the prose narrative. This impulse brings to the forefront the internal historical connexions of what has happened. The historical narrative in prose differs from the popular tale in presupposing a higher degree of intellectual capacity; as it is intended by its nature to be handed down in writing, its origin must be sought amongst the scribes, and its readers in a definite educated upper class. A kind of official writing of history for which the Babylonian and Assyrian practice of compiling records provided a model, seems to have been carried on at the royal court in the form of annals. Yet apart from the lists mentioned on page 56, hardly any piece of writing of this kind has been handed down. Although the book of the acts of Solomon mentioned in the book of Kings (1 Kgs. 11: 41) and the books of the chronicles of the Kings of Israel (or Judah), (1 Kgs. 14: 19, 29 and elsewhere) still bear the official title of such annals, they are probably not to be regarded as official historical accounts. On the other hand the account of the building of the Jerusalem temple (1 Kgs. 6–8) and of the reforms of Josiah (2 Kgs. 22 f.) seem to have been produced by the official activity of the temple scribes and to have been handed down amongst the priests as temple annals.

A larger amount of independent historical writing has been transmitted in the OT. What Israel created in this field represents in part a quite outstanding achievement which can show itself beside the best productions of ancient historical writing in general. Israel's writing of history began with the isolated narrative, complete in itself. To this type belong the story of Abimelech's kingdom in Shechem (Jgs. 9), written from the point of view of the democratic rejection of the form of government connected with the Canaanite city kingdoms, and the description, resembling the popular heroic saga, of Saul's relieving the city of Jabesh in Gilead besieged by the Ammonites (1 Sam. 11). In the accounts of Saul's battles with the Philistines in 1 Sam. 13–14, we can recognize a first collection of anecdotal stories told amongst the soldiers. With the awakening of Israel's national consciousness which was powerfully strengthened by the success of David's policy, the interest in history increased and the development of historical writing was brought to its highest pitch. No wonder that the figure and fate of David provided the occasion for the first descriptions in longer historical sequences. Fitted together out of isolated stories, but welded into a single and, specially towards the end, a well-rounded whole by the internal objective blending of its material and by its purposive arrangement, the story of David's rise (1 Sam. 16: 4–2 Sam. 5: 25) probably sprang from the endeavour to provide a historical justification for the transfer of the kingship from Saul to David. The history of David's reign (2 Sam. 7: 9–20; 1 Kgs. 1–2) is a masterpiece, both as regards the skill in narrative learned from the saga, and also the subordination of the parts to the one great controlling object in view, thus revealing a genuine historical sense; for its purpose is to exhibit the intricate internal and external connexions and events which finally resulted in Solomon becoming king. The altogether life-like description does indeed reduce the religious element outwardly, but yet below the surface lies the dominating idea that Yahweh invisibly determines the course of things behind and in all human affairs (2 Sam. 11: 27; 12: 24; 15: 25 f.; 17: 14; 1 Kgs. 2: 44 f.). At the same time the narrator who stood close to the events shows a remarkable inner detachment from them, which stamps his work as an outstanding historical source for David's period. The OT has also handed down a comprehensive account of Solomon's reign (1 Kgs. 3–11). It is derived in part from documents containing annals and statistical material, but no longer possesses the same private independence of judgment which distinguishes the narrative of David's reign. We cannot fail to note the transition from the rapid blossoming of a free historical presentation under David to the courtly writing of history under Solomon centred round the royal prestige.

Beside the great men in politics the prophetic figures have also stimulated prose narrative. In Am. 7: 10–17 we possess an account by a friend's hand of the prophet's expulsion from the national sanctuary at Bethel; it describes with short strokes the dramatic and significant scene when priest and prophet met and seizes in an accurate manner on the unique quality and also on the essentials of that historic moment and of the actors in it. Here lie the roots of the biographies of the prophets. We owe to Baruch's loyalty and devotion to his master and friend his biographical account of the fortunes and sufferings of Jeremiah (Jer. 19: 14–20: 6; 26; 27–29; 34; 36–45; 51: 59 ff.); it was born out of their common experience of the same fate and out of their faith in the divine mission of the prophet whose words Baruch handed down as a sacred legacy to posterity; it is both a witness to the outspoken courage of faith and a beautiful memorial of a friend's true loyalty.

We first meet an actual autobiography in the memoirs of Nehemiah, a work which—though not without some complacency—seems to have been intended by the author as a votive offering to God and reveals a tendency towards 'confessions'

(Neh. 5: 19; 13: 14, 22, 29, 31). The golden age of prose literature coincides in Israel with the golden age of the national state. The OT narratives are distinguished by a sound sense for the political necessities and relationships combined with the power of religious historical thought which, in a sober and realistic presentation, does not fail to see the inner connexions and the relationship to God of what takes place.

We must include in the pre-literary development also the manner by which the different transmitted records of historical events were appropriated, collected and interpreted, and which led to the formation of the OT tradition distinguished by its common religious orientation. This side of the history of the OT transmission took place within the sphere of the sacral institution of a religious community. As it met regularly at the cultic festival, it knew itself to be the bearer and guardian of the tradition relating to Yahweh in which it understood itself to be the 'people of Yahweh' chosen and claimed by him. Here there ensued that transmuting of the different historical traditions into 'salvation history', that form typical of the OT, in which history is not presented as an end in itself but as the testimony to God's saving activity in mercy and judgment. In the context of the thought and action at the cult this evidence served to bring home the salvation which at times took real shape. To this extent the different forms of contemplating and presenting history as 'salvation history', to be found also outside the so-called historical books in the prophetic literature (e.g. Am. 4: 6 ff.; Hos. 11: 1 ff.; 12: 1 ff.; Jer. 2: 1 ff.) and in the liturgical poetry (e.g. Pss. 78, 105, 106, 135, 136), deserve to be regarded as a special type which grew out of what was originally oral preaching (see section 4). From this association there developed at that time also the *liturgical speech*, shaped like a sermon, edifying and hortatory in tone, which, in the book of Deuteronomy (cf. Breit, *Die Predigt des Deuteronomisten*, 1937), in Jos. 24; in 1 Sam. 7, 12; and in Jeremiah (7: 1 ff.; 8: 4 ff.; 10: 1 ff.; 11: 1 ff.; 16: 1 ff.; 17: 19 ff.; 18: 1 ff.)* enables its roots in the divine service still to be recognized.

This, for its part, served as a pattern for the so-called *Deuteronomistic writing of history*, which is particularly evident in the books of Judges and Kings. On the strength of the impression made by

---

* cf. with this Weiser, *Jeremia*, p. 482.

the national collapse and the religious crisis connected with it, it attempts to make the historical tradition fruitful for its day as a divine measure of education, by setting up the rational pattern of retribution as the dominant point of view and sacrificing the variety of historical events and personalities to a theological pragmatism, though this resulted in restricting and paralysing the descriptive skill as seen by the literary historian. The situation is the same in the case of the historical book of the Chronicles, which sprang from the post-exilic cultic piety; its levitical liturgical interests and its rejection of secular material increased the importance of the religious outlook on history and brought it into the foreground. Yet we are indebted just to this circumstance that the OT historical tradition was not completely forgotten. Nevertheless under the dominant theological rationalism of such a view of history there was lost that inner unconstrained vision into the depths and therewith that sense of religious realities which distinguishes the pre-exhilic historical works and the prophetic interpretation of history in the OT.

The Formation of the Individual Books of the Old Testament

A. THE TORAH
The Pentateuch

Commentaries: KeH: Dillmann, Gen.[6] 1892, Num. 1886. Deut. 1886; Dillmann –Ryssel, Exod.–Lev.[3] 1897.–SZ: Strack, Gen. [2] 1905; Exod.–Num. 1894; Öttli, Deut. 1893.–HK: Gunkel, Gen.[3] 1910, [5]1922; Baentsch, Exod.–Num. 1903; Steuernagel, Deut. [2]1923.–KHC: Holzinger, Gen. 1898, Exod. 1900, Num. 1903; Bertholet, Lev 1901, Dt. 1899.–KAT: Procksch. Gen. [2-3]1923; König, Deut. 1917.–ICC: Skinner, Gen.[2] 1930 (1951); Gray, Num. [2]1912 (1955); Driver, Deut. [4]1952.–W.C.: Driver. Gen.[12] 1926; McNeile. Exod. 1908; Binns, Num. 1927.–HSAT: Holzinger, Gen.– Num.; Marti, Deut.–SAT: Gunkel, Gen. [2]1921; Gressman, Exod.–Deut.[2] 1922.– TU: Böhl. Gen.[2] 1930, Exod. 1928; De Wilde, Lev. 1937; Edelkoort, Num. 1930.– HS: Heinisch, Gen. 1930; idem, Exod. 1934; Lev. Num. 1936; Junker, Deut. 1933. –HAT: Beer, Exod. 1939; Delitzsch, Gen. 1887.–König, Gen. [2-3] 1925; Frey (Gen.) 4 vols. 1938–40; Zimmerli, I Mose. 1–11 (Prophezei) 2 vols. 1944;–EB: Junker, Gen.; Schneider, Exod.–Num.; Junker, Deut. [2]1955.–ATD: von Rad, Gen. [4]1956.– HBK: Kalt, Gen.–Lev.; Kramer, Num.–Deut. 1955–LStB: de Vaux, Gen. 1951.– Couroyer, Exod. 1952; Cazelles, Lev. 1951; Num. 1952, Deut. 1950.–LSt.B (Clamer): Gen. 1953, Lev. Num. Deut. 1946; IB: Simpson, Bowie, Gen.; Rylaardsdam, Park, Exod. 1952; Micklem, Lev.; Marsh, Butzer, Num.; Wright, Shires, Parker, Deut. 1953.–HSC: Greenstone, Num. 1938.–SBB: Freedman, Gen., Rabinowitz, Exod., Lehrmann, Lev., Fisch, Num. Deut. [2]1950.–TBC: Richardson, Gen. 1–11 1953. Cassuto, *La questione della genesi*, 1934; Allis, *Five Books of Moses*, 1944; Wellhausen, *Die Komposition des Hexateuchs und der historischen Bücher*[2] 1889; Holzinger, *Einleitung in den Hexateuch*, 1893; Steuernagel, *Allgemeine Einleitung in den Hexateuch*, Handkommentar zum AT 1.3. 1900, 249 ff.; Klostermann, *Der Pentateuch*, 1893, 1907; Merx, 'Die Bücher Moses und Josua', RV II[3], 1907; Eerdmanns, *Alttestamentlische Studien I*, 1908, *III*, 1910, *IV*, 1912; Dahse, *Textkritische Materialien zur Hexateuchfrage I*, 1912; Smend, *Die Erzählung des Hexateuchs auf ihre Quellen untersucht*, 1912; Eichrodt, *Die Quellen der Genesis von neuem untersucht*, 1916; Eissfeldt, *Hexateuchsynopse*, 1922; Löhr. *Untersuchungen zum Hexateuchproblem I*, 1924, *II*, 1925; Stärk, 'Zur alttestamentlichen Literarkritik', ZAW 1924, 34 ff.; McQueen Gray, *OT criticism, its Rise and Progress*, 1923; Simpson, *Pentateuchal Criticism*,[2] 1924; J. Morgenstern, 'The oldest Document of the Hexateuch', HUCA 4 (1927), 1–138; Yahuda, *Die Sprache des Pentateuch in ihren Beziehungen zum Ägyptischen*, 1929; König, *Ist die moderne Pentateuchkritik auf Tatsachen begründet?* 1933; Volz-Rudolph, 'Der Elohist als Erzähler? Ein Irrweg der Pentateuchkritik', BZAW 1933; Humbert, 'Die neuere Genesisforschung', ThR 1934, 147 ff.; Mowinckel, 'Hat es ein israelitisches Nationalepos gegeben? ZAW 1935, 130 ff.; Bea, *De Pentateucho*,[2] 1933; idem, 'Der heutige Stand der Pentateuchfrage', *Biblica* 1935, 175 ff.; Battersby-Harford, 'Problems of the Pentateuch', *Expository Times* 1935–6, 488 ff.; Mowinckel, *The two sources of the pre-deuteronomic primeval history (JE) in Gen.* 1–11, Oslo 1937; Rudolph, 'Der Elohist von Exodus bis Josua,' BZAW 1938; von Rad, 'Das formgeschichtliche Problem des Hexateuchs', BWAT 1938; Eissfeldt, 'Die Komposition von Exod. 1–12', ThBl

1939, col. 224 ff.; idem, 'Die Komposition der Bileamerzählung, ZAW 1939, 212 ff.;
Eissfeldt 'Die Geschichtswerke des AT'; ThLZ 1947, col. 71 ff.; Simpson, *The early
traditions of Israel, a critical analysis of the predeuteronomic narrative of the Hexateuch*, 1948;
Eissfeldt, 'Die ältesten Traditionen Israels', BZAW 71, 1950; Noth, *Überlieferungsgeschichte des Pentateuchs*, 1948; Coppens, A. von Hoonacker, *De Compositione Litteraria
et de Origine Mosaica Hexateuchi. Disquisitio Historico-Critica*, 1949; North, 'Pentateuchal Criticism', OTMSt (1951) 48 ff.; Coppens, Chronique de l'Ancien Testament.
'Le problème de l'Hexateuque' (*Analecta Lovaniensia Biblica et Orientalia* 2. ser. No.
38) 1953; Jepsen, 'Zur Überlieferungsgeschichte der Vätergestalten', *Wiss. Ztschr.
d. Karl-Marx-Univ.*, Leipzig; 3. Jhrg. 1953–4, 265 ff.; Steinmann, *Les plus anciennes
Traditions du Pentateuque*, 1954; Levy, *The Growth of the Pentateuch*, 1955; Rost, 'Zum
geschichtlichen Ort der Pentateuchquellen', ThLZ 53 (1956), 1 ff.

10. Name and contents

1. The five books of Moses form the most important part of
the Jewish canon. From the law contained in them the Jews
called them 'the Law' (Torah), 'the Law of Moses', 'the Book of
Moses' (Ezr. 6: 18 and elsewhere) or some similar name. Originally the name applied only to those parts dealing with the law
(2 Kgs. 14: 6; 2 Chron. 30: 16; Ezr. 10: 3), but later it was extended
to the whole work (Mt. 5: 17 'the law and the prophets'; Mk.
12: 26 'the book of Moses'). The division into five books, already
customary at the time of the Septuagint, led to the work being
designated in Greek as ἡ πεντάτευχος (βίβλος)=the book of the
five scrolls, attested first in Tertullian, put into Latin as *pentateu-
chus* (*liber*), whence is derived the name 'the Pentateuch' in current
use amongst scholars. The designation 'Hexateuch', widespread
in modern research, is based on the assumption that the book of
Joshua was originally part of the whole work. When the books of
Judges, Samuel (and Kings) are added to make one large historical
work (Budde, Eissfeldt, Hölscher) the names Octateuch, or
Enneateuch are also occasionally used. On the other hand those
who consider Deuteronomy to be the beginning of an independent historical work extending as far as to the books of the Kings
(Noth, Engnell) had better employ the name 'Tetrateuch'. In the
Hebrew Bible the individual books are called after their first word
(the first book of Moses: bᵉrē'shît, etc.), in the Greek and Latin
translations and in scientific usage their designation is derived
from their main contents: Genesis (beginning), Exodus (going
out), Leviticus (the levitical law), Numbers (ἀριθμοί=numbering
of the people), Deuteronomy (second law).

2. The work, after placing the creation of the world in a univer-

sal setting, describes how Israel came into being and presents the fundamental traditions of the history of salvation as far as the death of Moses before the entry into the land of Canaan. The contents of the individual books may be summarized in rough outline as follows: Gen. 1–11 primeval history; 12–50 history of the patriarchs (12–25 Abraham; 25, 26 Isaac; 25–36 Jacob; 37–50 Joseph). Exod. 1–19 Israel's oppression and exodus from Egypt as far as Sinai; 20–24 the decalogue, the Book of the Covenant, the making of the covenant; 25–31 laws about the tabernacle and the Aaronic priesthood; 32–34 the breaking of the covenant and the new law; 35–40 the carrying out of the law concerning the tabernacle. Lev. 1–7 the Torah concerning offerings; 8–10 the consecration of the priests and the first offerings; 11–15 the laws of cleanness. 16 the day of atonement; 17–26 the Holiness Code; 27 vows and tithes; Num. 1–9 numberings and laws; 10–20 departure from Sinai to Kadesh; 20–36 journeyings to Moab. Deut. 1–4 Moses' first speech, historical retrospect to the time in the wilderness; 5–11 Moses' second speech, hortatory introduction; 12–26 statutes and rights, Deuteronomic laws; 27–30 cursing and blessing; 31–34 conclusion, Moses hands his office over to Joshua, Moses' song (32) and blessing (33), Moses' death (34). Genesis and Deuteronomy stand out by themselves; as regards the others the divisions of the books do not correspond with the structure of the material. This would rather require more definite breaks at Exod. 19 and Num. 10 which would divide up the contents into the history as far as Sinai, the revelation at Sinai and the departure from Sinai into the land of Moab.

The literature of the world contains no book to equal the Pentateuch in its importance and its effect (Merx, p. 7 ff.); its influence extends to the religion and culture of Jewry and of the Christian and Islamic peoples.

11. The tradition concerning the authorship of the Pentateuch and the internal evidence

1. The Pentateuch is an anonymous book; there is no indication anywhere in it that the whole of its contents go back to Moses. On the other hand in various places it is said that particular passages are written by Moses: in Exod. 17: 14 a report of the

victorious battle against the Amalekites, in 24: 4 the Book of the Covenant; in 34: 27 another collection of laws; in Num. 33: 2 a list of the halting places; also the book of Deuteronomy (Deut. 1: 5; 4: 45; 31: 9, 24) and the song of Moses in 31: 19, 30. Whilst in the pre-exilic prophets there is no tradition of a Mosaic law, in the later literature of the Old Testament Moses is considered to be the transmitter and probably also the author of the law in Mal. 3: 22; 2 Chron. 25: 4; 35: 12 and *passim*; Ezr. 3: 2; 7: 6 and *passim*. That Moses composed the whole Pentateuch is first explicitly asserted in the works of Philo and Josephus and in the Talmud. This view is presupposed also in the New Testament in Mt. 19: 7 f.; Mk. 12: 26; Jn. 5: 46 f.; Acts 15: 21; Rom. 10: 5. With a few exceptions it has remained the prevailing tradition of the Christian Church unchallenged up to the seventeenth century.

2. Whilst the internal evidence, by designating Moses as the author of individual passages in the Pentateuch, points indirectly to the fact that the rest of the book cannot claim to have sprung from him, a number of reasons exclude Moses directly as the author. In many places the *post-Mosaic origin* is evident: Gen. 12: 6; 13: 7 'and the Canaanite was then in the land' presupposes the conquest of Canaan just as much as the designation of Canaan as the 'land of the Hebrews' in Gen. 40: 15 (cf. Exod. 15: 15 ff.; Lev. 18: 24 ff.; Deut. 2: 12). The interval between the time of Moses and the author is shown in the oft-recurring formula 'unto this day' in Gen. 32: 33; Deut. 3: 14; 34: 6 and is clearly seen in the remark in Deut. 34: 10 'there hath not arisen a prophet since in Israel like unto Moses'. The use of the name Dan in Gen. 14: 14 and Deut. 34: 1, first adopted in the time of the judges (Jgs. 18:29), cannot have originated with Moses. The note in Gen. 36: 31, speaking of the kings of Edom 'before there reigned any king over the children of Israel', and the law about a king in Deut. 17: 14 ff. cannot have been written before the time of the kings of Israel. Moreover, most of the legal passages assume an agricultural population settled in Canaan and therefore cannot have been composed by Moses. In many places the geographical standpoint is clearly not that of Moses, as for instance when the country east of the Jordan is described simply as 'beyond Jordan' in Gen. 50: 10 f.; Num. 22: 1; Deut. 1: 1, 5.

In addition to this it is evident that the Pentateuch cannot be the continuous work of a single author. This is shown by the existence of *two differing accounts* (doublets) of the same event: thus e.g. the story of the creation in Gen. 1 and 2; 4 ff., the call of Moses in Exod. 3 and 6, the sending away of Hagar in Gen. 16 and 21 are told twice over, and in Gen. 21: 22 ff. and 26: 26 ff. the origin and interpretation of the name Beer-sheba are recorded twice; the account of the danger which befell their ancestress recurs three times, in Gen. 12, 20 and 26. Besides this, *discrepancies* can be observed just in these parallel passages we have named. Gen. 1 represents a view of the primeval condition of the world before the creation different from that of Gen. 2. In the former chaos is pictured as a sea, in the latter as a desert. In Gen 1 the order of the works of creation is plants, beasts, man; in Gen. 2 the man, plants, beasts. In Gen. 1 man and wife are created at the same time, in Gen. 2 at quite different times. In the story of the flood the contradictions have even been kept in, although in this case the two stories have been worked up into a single continuous account. According to one version in Gen. 7: 12 the flood was caused by forty days and nights of rain, according to the other in Gen. 7: 11 by the breaking in of a second chaos; similarly the flood is said to have lasted for different periods: in 7: 12 and 8: 6–13b for 40+21 days; in 7: 11, and 8: 14 for 12 months+10 days. In 7: 2 we are told that Noah takes seven pairs of each of the clean beasts and one pair of each of the unclean ones with him into the ark; in 6: 19 he takes only one pair of each sort of living thing. Such examples can easily be multiplied. For further details see Holzinger, section 5.

At times the thread of the story is broken off or is taken up again at an impossible place, as in Gen. 7: 11–13; Gen. 37–39. This fact which is especially noticeable in the stories relating to Sinai induced Goethe to speak of 'extremely poor and incomprehensible editing'. Moreover, we find *different styles and linguistic usages*. The difference leaps to the eye at once between the description of the creation in Gen. 1 which proceeds with the solemn symmetry of recurring stereotyped phrases and that in Gen. 2: 4 ff. which tells the story in lively and vivid fashion. Here and in the account of the flood one strand uses the expression 'male and female' in 1: 27 and 6: 19; the other uses in Gen. 2: 25 'the man and his wife', in Gen. 7: 2 'the male and his female'. One strand

speaks in Gen. 15: 18 of 'making a covenant', the other in Gen.
17: 7 of 'establishing a covenant'. In Gen. 12: 6; 50: 11 the inhabitants of the land are called Canaanites, in 15: 16 and 48: 22 Amorites; similarly the name of the mountain of God alternates between
Sinai in Exod. 19: 11, 18 and Horeb in Exod. 3: 1; 17: 6, and that
of the patriarch in the story of Joseph between 'Jacob' (Gen. 37:
1, 34 and *passim*) and 'Israel' (Gen. 37: 3, 13 and *passim*). The
best known variation, occurring continuously up to Exod. 3 and
6 respectively, is in the use of Jahweh and Elohim for the name
of God; this gave rise to the scientific criticism of the Pentateuch
and from it are derived the designations of the separate sources as
Jahwist or Yahwist (J) and Elohist (E). Dahse has attempted to
use the variations in the LXX to explain the different names for
God in Genesis as due to its division into selected portions for
reading; but, even so, this theory of Pentateuchal criticism has
not up to the present time been generally shaken. Thus the two
names of God, e.g. in the story of the flood, have been clearly
preserved side by side. Exod. 3 and 6 enables us to see that the
use of different names for God is based on quite definite theories
which point to different trends in the separate sources. We can,
therefore, consider it to be both the result of Pentateuchal criticism and a firm foundation for it, that the Pentateuch first came
into being after the time of Moses in Canaan and represents a
literary composition made up of strands of different kinds and
periods, each with a character of its own.

12. The history of Pentateuchal criticism

Pedersen, 'Die Auffassung vom AT', ZAW 49 (1931) 161–181; Literature: Simpson, *The Early Traditions of Israel*, 1948, 19–49; North, 'Pentateuchal Criticism',
OTMSt. 1951, 48–83; Eissfeldt, ThR 18 (1950), 91–112, 179–215, 257–287.

Even in the times of the Early Church doubts, never wholly
silenced, were thrown on the tradition of the Mosaic authorship
of the Pentateuch; they arose in part out of dogmatic and ethical
considerations (see section 1, paras. 1, 2, 3). Nor was there lacking
incipient criticism based on the observation of individual points,
such as those mentioned in section 11.

1. Nevertheless, the beginnings of really scientific criticism of
the Pentateuch, dealing systematically with the literary problem,

do not appear till the eighteenth century. In the year 1711 Pastor Witter of Hildesheim published his work 'Jura Israelitarum in Palaestinam', in which he brings forward the fundamental criterion of the alternating names of God, Yahweh and Elohim, in Genesis, as well as doublets and considerations of style, as the first scientific method of establishing the truth of what had been assumed already earlier, namely that Moses had compiled the Pentateuch out of older written and oral traditions. The credit due to him for Pentateuchal criticism became forgotten. The same fate befell at first also a French Catholic physician, Jean Astruc, who was still, until ten or twenty years ago, regarded as the founder of the modern criticism of the Pentateuch, and who in 1753, likewise on the basis of the names of God in Genesis, distinguished two main and ten fragmentary, secondary sources used by Moses in the composition of Genesis. Both attempts were intended to be apologetic; by means of analysing the sources they wished to retain the tradition of the Mosaic authorship for the whole of the Pentateuch in the face of the considerations adduced against a single writer.

2. It was Eichhorn, however, who first brought out the fact in his *Einleitung in das Alte Testament*', 1780 ff. that the difference in literary style was found throughout both main sources and who thereby furnished the scientific proof of their existence. The work of the redactor of these sources, whom he finally distinguished from Moses, was also recognized by him as a well-planned composition. These studies were carried further by the work of Ilgen *Die Urkunden des Jerusalemer Tempelarchivs*, I, 1798, who was the first to point out two Elohist sources, though their existence was not recognized until later. The thesis, propounded by Witter, Astruc, Eichhorn and Ilgen, is called the *Early Documentary Hypothesis*. It considers the sources of Genesis to be a connected series of stories which were used by the latest author of Genesis as 'documents' and were put together by him. But this explanation could satisfy only so long as it was confined to Genesis; it was bound to break down as soon as the parts dealing with the law were subjected to examination.

3. A closer scrutiny of the legislative components of the Pentateuch gave the impression on the contrary that they were separate fragments independent of each other, some greater, others smaller,

which appeared to be placed side by side without any internal connexion. This led to the so-called *Fragmentary Hypothesis* which was represented in England by Geddes, in Germany by Vater (*Kommentar über den Pentateuch*, 1802 ff.). Vater assumes Deuteronomy to be the matrix to which gradually other legal and narrative portions attached themselves, and that these are now before us in a 'Yahwist' and an 'Elohist' group. The flaw in this hypothesis lies in the fact that it fails to notice the systematic connexion visible in the construction and arrangement of the whole and above all in the consistent chronology.

4. These considerations induced Ewald (ThStKr 4, 1831, 595 ff.) to suggest the so-called *Supplementary Hypothesis*, supported later by von Bleek and in the commentaries on Genesis of Tuch and Franz Delitzsch. This regards a homogeneous Elohist basic document as the core which was then completed later with Yahwist passages. Ewald himself was convinced that the Yahwist passages were independent and was inclined to combine the Early Documentary and the Supplementary hypotheses, emphasizing more and more strongly the independence of the separate sources. Thereby he led the way to the New Documentary hypothesis which has formed the basis of Pentateuchal criticism right up to the present.

5. The real founder of the *New Documentary hypothesis* is considered to be Hupfeld, who in his book, *Die Quellen der Genesis*, 1853, by means of fresh evidence, procured the victory for the assumption previously made by Ilgen that there are two Elohist sources running through. A Yahwist source is introduced as a third. These three originally independent documents have been amalgamated by a redactor. Almost at the same time Riehm's *Die Gesetzgebung Mosis im Lande Moab*, 1854, won recognition for the view that Deuteronomy was an independent writing. After Nöldeke and Dillmann in his commentary had done more work on the separation of the Priestly source (P), a foundation of literary criticism had been laid on which research could continue to build.

6. The next generation of scholars was more occupied with the combined *literary and historical question* of fixing the dates of the sources. Up till then, with the 'Supplementary hypothesis' in view, there had been a tendency to start from the chronological arrange-

ment and the clear construction of the Priestly writing which gives its character to the present form of the Pentateuch and to consider P to be the foundation and oldest source which would be followed in its development in time by the second Elohist document, E, then by the Yahwist, J, and finally by Deuteronomy, D. The revolution in this field was brought about by the researches of von Graf, Kuenen and Wellhausen. It is true that several decades earlier Reuss and Vatke had already urged that P was included at a relatively later date, but this theory had to wait for its acceptance until the scientific foundation for it had been laid by the works of von Graf, *Die geschichtlichen Bücher des Alten Testaments*, 1866, of Kuenen, *Godsdienst van Israel*, 1869 ff., and Wellhausen's brilliantly written *Geschichte Israels*, I, 1878 (later *Prolegomena zur Geschichte Israels*, ²1883, ⁶1905). It is Wellhausen's enduring service to have proved by means of a comparison with the information in the rest of the Old Testament that the historical place of the 'Mosaic law' (P) is not at the beginning, but at the end of the development of Old Testament religion, and that the Yahwist source must be considered to be the oldest document in the Pentateuch.

7. The importance of Wellhausen is also made evident by the fact that in the subsequent period the whole of Pentateuchal criticism was determined by the discussion of his labours. It has become generally recognized that P is not the oldest source. Nevertheless, no agreement has been reached with regard to the absolute dating. Whilst, e.g. Dillmann, Kittel (earlier), Baudissin place E at 900–850, J at 800–750, P at 800–700, D at 650–623, and other scholars (König, Orelli, Strack and others) assume them in general to be older (e.g. E 1200, J 1000, D 700–650, P. 500), the majority of scholars such as Reuss, Duhm, Stade, Smend, Marti, Cornill, Baentsch, Benzinger, Holzinger, Kautzsch, Steuernagel, Bertholet and others take their stand with Wellhausen's school in approving the sequence: J ninth century, E eighth century, D seventh century, P fifth century; it can thus certainly be said that the foundation of Wellhausen's theory has won recognition.

8. Yet opponents of Wellhausen's school have not been lacking. Klostermann supposes that the Pentateuch originated in amplifications which crystallized at different periods round the basic Mosaic law proclaimed at religious and public recitals.

Eerdmans is led by a critical consideration of the material and of the content to reject the four sources theory. He says that the primary constituents of the Pentateuch are not sources running through it, but various fragments differentiated from each other by their subject-matter, which belonged originally to the polytheistic stage of religion and were revised to fit a monotheistic outlook in the post-Deuteronomic and post-exilic times. Dahse, basing his argument on textual criticism and referring to the LXX, rejects the variation in the names of God as a criterion for distinguishing the sources and speaks of a prophetic and a priestly liturgical revision of the early narrative material. Löhr assumes that the Hexateuch was composed by Ezra who put together the early material some of which went back to Moses. The works of Wiener, *Essays in Pentateuchal Criticism*, 1913; Möller, *Die Einheit und Echtheit der fünf Bücher Mosis*, 1931; D. B. MacDonald, *The Hebrew Literary Genius*, 1933; Cassuto, *La questione della genesi*, 1934; Jacob, *Das erste Buch der Thora*, 1934 and Rabast, *Die Genesis*, 1951, return to the tradition and endeavour to retain the literary homogeneity of the Pentateuch and the authorship of Moses in the face of the critics; also Helling too, *Die Frühgeschichte des israelitischen Volkes*, 1947, and Levy, *The Growth of the Pentateuch*, 1955, make an attempt to support the tradition with fresh arguments. Volz and Rudolph have rejected the literary independence of the Elohist as a narrator. Volz (similarly Jepsen) will admit only *one* narrator, the Yahwist, to whom he ascribes a series of E passages (nor does he recognize P as a narrator); E is not a source running through the Pentateuch, but at most a reviser of J who might possibly be the same as the Deuteronomic redactor. Rudolph also wishes to explain the Elohist passages as interpolations on the lines of the Supplementary hypothesis, yet he does not go as far as Volz in his negative criticism of E.

9. In the last generation the work of literary cricitism and the historical study of the literature was enriched by the *critical examination of the subject matter and the form* in association with archaeology and the general history of religion carried out by Gunkel and Gressmann (*Mose und seine Zeit*, 1913). The main interest was directed to the individual narratives and separate topics, whilst examining also the pre-literary stage of their history. It is easy to see that when attention is concentrated on the origin

and growth of the oral tradition, on its place in the practical life of the people and of their religion, the purely critical and historical work on the literature falls into the background. Gunkel's line of research approached a kind of fragmentary hypothesis, so that the sources of the Pentateuch appear to be collections of older traditions rather than free literary productions. The strong interest taken in the broad types of literature favoured by the people caused the importance of the author's personality for the origin of the Pentateuch to be reduced. For this reason Gunkel does not see in J, E and P individual personalities, but schools with a definite stamp.

10. Meanwhile, however, the work of literary criticism on the Pentateuch had not stood still. It was marked by the attempt to divide up the sources, J, E, P themselves into separate strands of tradition. Budde (*Die Urgeschichte*, 1883) had already worked out the separation of two threads of narrative J^1 and J^2. Bruston, 'Les Deux Jéhovistes' (*Revue de théologie et de philosophie*, 1885) had endeavoured to divide up the whole work of J. When sorting out the older material from the rest of J, Morgenstern assumes a Kenite source, Pfeiffer a source of Edomite origin. Smend and Eissfeldt, keeping strictly to the theory of the Documentary hypothesis, which considers J^2 not only as a supplement and addition but as a document parallel with J^1 running independently through the whole Hexateuch, have followed this path further. Leaving aside Deuteronomy, they have arrived at a four-sources theory which Eissfeldt expresses explicitly by naming the oldest source no longer J^1 but L (the lay source) in order to emphasize how comparatively far this source is removed from the cultic and priestly interests of the priesthood. The fact that the same narrative theme occurs four times, which indeed cannot always be established without postulates, is Eissfeldt's chief argument in his analysis of the sources. Simpson breaks up the Yahwist strand and thus combines the Documentary with the Supplementary hypothesis by claiming that J^1 is the tradition of the Southern tribes, and that J^2 on the other hand is a supplement to J^1 in which the traditions of Northern Israel from the 'House of Joseph' find expression. For the Elohist, Procksch, *Das nordhebräische Sagenbuch*, 1906, undertook to prove the existence of a source E^1 written in the Northern kingdom and of an expansion made in

the Southern kingdom after the fall of Israel. Meanwhile Kuenen, *Einleitung in das Alte Testament*, in German, 1887, had already pointed out that the Elohist strand was not homogeneous. In the case of the priestly writings their composite character had been recognized for some time, especially as regards individual strands of the legal material. Recently von Rad, 'Die Priesterschrift, BWAT 65, 1934, has attempted to prove the existence of a double strand in the narrative of P also and to divide it into two continuous narrative threads by means of a literary critical analysis. Yet in view of the widely differing attempts to dissect the sources of the Pentateuch further, it is hard to resist the impression that the method of literary criticism for identifying the sources down to the individual wording has reached its limit and has sometimes exceeded it.

The results achieved by the Pentateuchal researches of the last 150 years command our respect. Nevertheless, the aim of literary criticism to carry out the analysis of the sources as far as the individual wording can hardly be reached in view of the state of the form of their transmission. The fact must be faced that much of the material had behind it a very long history full of vicissitudes before it was fixed in writing, and that the sources, too, after their amalgamation themselves experienced as traditions a further active history which we are not yet in a position to survey; for we do not know for how long the oral tradition continued beside the written one and what influence it had on the latter; we should, therefore, do well to be cautious with regard to an analysis which is too mechanical, formally logical and based merely on literary criticism. We can no longer grasp the strands of the Pentateuch as though they were entities fixed in detail, and the understanding of their nature must therefore be determined by the whole, by their religious ideology, rather than by the separate traditions which were subjected to more violent, no longer clearly discernible historical changes. Nevertheless, it would be a mistake to give up altogether with Pedersen and Engnell the methods and results of literary criticism; for the criteria it has worked out retain their appropriate validity for the oral tradition also. Old Testament studies are standing today at a stage when literary criticism is being scrutinized afresh with the help of researches into the history of the tradition, and of the form and the cult. Here the discussion of the questions to be asked and of the possibilities of answering them still remains completely open.

13. How the sources of the Pentateuch were formed

Jirku, *Die älteste Geschichte Israels im Rahmen lehrhafter Darstellungen*, 1917; Alt, 'Der Gott der Väter', BWAT 1929=Alt I, 1 ff.; idem, 'Die Wallfahrt von Sichem nach Betel, In piam memoriam Alexander von Bulmerincq'. *Abhandlungen der Herdergesellschaft und des Herderinstituts zu Riga.* 6th vol., No. 3, 1938, 218 ff.=Alt I 79 ff.; von Rad, 'Das formgeschichtliche Problem des Hexateuch', BWAT 1938, Noth, 'Die Gesetze im Pentateuch', *Schriften der Königsberger Gelehrten-Gesellschaft Geisteswissenschaftliche Klasse*, vol. 17, No. 2. 1940; idem, Überlieferungsgeschichtliche Studien, loc. cit., 18, No. 2. 1943, ²1957; von Rad, 'Deuteronomium-Studien', FRLANT NF40, 1947, ²1948; Eissfeldt, 'Die Geschichtswerke des Alten Testaments', ThLZ 1947, col. 71 ff.; Weiser, 'Psalm 77. Ein Beitrag zur Frage nach dem Verhältnis von Kult und Heilsgeschichte', ThLZ 1947, col. 133 ff.; Noth, *Überlieferungsgeschichte des Pentateuchs*, 1948.

A survey of the history of Pentateuchal criticism reveals no single line of development and no single road to the solution of the problems. It is just the latest researches which lead Gunkel to favour the Fragmentary hypothesis, Eissfeldt and von Rad (*Die Priesterschrift*, 70) the Documentary hypothesis, Volz and Rudolph the Supplementary hypothesis and in the case of J the Fragmentary hypothesis also in a certain sense; at the same time they show clearly that each of these methods has its measure of truth, but also its limitations. The Documentary hypothesis provides the basis for the analysis of the narratives and of their contexts; the use of the Supplementary hypothesis is justified where fresh material is admitted both into the original strands of the sources and also during the continuous growth of the tradition; in view of the development and employment of the oral traditions and for the legal matter and the older material embedded in the sources the method of the Fragmentary hypothesis cannot be discarded. The limitation of these methods lies in the fact that no one of them by itself is able to do justice to the contents of the tradition as a whole. The history of the formation of the Pentateuch is richer and more manifold, the strands of the sources themselves are by no means literary documents defined in all their details, but entities growing and developing through the vicissitudes of religious and national happenings, handed down, and combining with each other, as a living tradition. Therefore, they cannot be accounted for simply on the assump-

D

tion of literary criticism that they are the more or less mechanical addition of purely literary works with an unalterable shape. The history of the literature of the Old Testament, and even if it is only of the collection of the sources by the redactor, is more than a sum in arithmetic; and the problem, too, of the formation of the Pentateuchal sources reaches out beyond not only the sphere of literary criticism, but also beyond that of the pure history of literature.

In order to understand the formation of the Pentateuch as a whole and of its individual literary sources, it will be necessary to penetrate with the help of the history of the material, the form and the tradition to those points in Old Testament history where the rise and preservation of such remarkable productions as are presented by the strands of the Pentateuch can be explained by the actual circumstances. The fact that the most varied literary forms, such as popular tales, folk-tales, myths, sagas, cultic legends, songs and legal corpora have been amalgamated and preserved in their different shapes side by side and intertwined, requires to be explained by the peculiarity of Israel's history, by its spiritual and religious *life*. For the sources of the Pentateuch are not historical works in the modern sense, written perhaps from a learned interest in recording and keeping the tradition of past events for a cultured class; this fact emerges clearly enough from their pronounced ideology with its particular concern for religion as well as from the reshaping of the early material by the authors of the Pentateuch, observable in almost every part. But in that case the question cannot be evaded: from what motives, in what spiritual and intellectual atmosphere, for what needs in the life of Israel, did the compilation of the Pentateuchal traditions and their sources arise, become written down and preserved with continuing care? In this process the literary fixation is merely *one* link—and not even the most important one—in a long chain of development which led to the formation and preservation of the Pentateuchal sources, and the problem of their formation cannot be considered to be primarily a process of literary creation, but a process in a more wide-spread and deep-seated sphere of their life. After the analysis of literary criticism has reached a certain finality, or one might say its limits, it has become the next task of Pentateuchal research to determine the 'setting in life' (*Sitz* *im Leben*) which will explain not only individual traditions, but also the Pentateuchal sources as a whole, and this is where research must go beyond Gunkel and von Rad too. Von Rad has pursued this so-called 'form-historical' problem of the Hexateuch in a special investigation, on the theses of which Noth also has built up his traditio-historical studies of the various 'themes' in Pentateuchal narrative. Referring back to the work of Klostermann, Pedersen and Mowinckel, von Rad is right in seeking for the roots of the Pentateuchal tradition in the *festival cult* of the early Israelites. He takes over from Mowinckel the well-founded thesis that the *Sinai tradition* grew out of the *'festival legend' of the renewal of the covenant at the autumn festival.* Von Rad takes the sanctuary at Shechem to be the home of the festival and its tradition and believes that he can reconstruct its course in all particulars from Exod. 19, Jos. 24, Deut. 27 and Jos. 8: 34. But it must be doubted whether it is admissible and possible to reconstruct the festival in detail on the basis of these elements of the tradition which are disparate as regards both their date and their literary quality.*

Von Rad detaches from this Sinai tradition belonging to the autumn festival the *Conquest tradition* and wishes to recover its earliest attainable form in Deut. 26: 5 ff.; the so-called 'little historical credo', which he considers to be the 'festival legend' of the *festival of Weeks* celebrated at the *sanctuary of Gilgal*; however, it remains obscure for what period and for which circles (tribe of Benjamin?) the assumption of such a festival at Gilgal with a separate Conquest tradition claims to be historically valid.†

Both in its presuppositions and in its deductions, this hypothesis arouses serious misgivings and is more likely in its turn to add fresh unsolved problems to the real question of the formation of the Hexateuch in its transmitted state. In the opinion of von Rad the Pentateuch, which had grown out of such a 'historical credo', and also out of its sources, must be judged as a 'baroque elaboration of simple dogmas' and as an inflated literary composition pressed 'to the limits of the possible and the readable'. For the present it may remain an open question whether this is really the

---

* cf. also Noth, *Geschichte Israels*, ²1954, ⁴1959, p. 97.
† cf. also Noth, *Überlieferungsgeschichte des Pentateuchs*, p. 55, note 170, against localizing the Conquest tradition at the sanctuary of Gilgal.

general impression forced upon the unprejudiced critical observer. In any case, even the foundation on which von Rad constructed his thesis shows itself on close examination to be unable to bear the load. It is by no means proved, nor can it be proved from the existing material, that the delivery of 'The first of all the fruit of the ground' at the sanctuary by a pious individual with a prayer relating this cultic custom to Yahweh's saving acts, took place on the occasion of the feast of Weeks at Gilgal. In Deut. 26: 1 ff. there is no mention at all of a feast, nor does the corresponding legal precept concerning the offering of the first fruits in Exod. 23: 19 (Exod. 34: 26) name any feast as the appointed time (cf. Dillmann on Exod. 23: 19); moreover, the context runs counter to the view that the feast of Weeks may perhaps be tacitly implied. It is just as possible and, judging by the context and the subject matter (the first of *all* the fruit of the ground), more likely that different offerings at different times, unrelated to any particular feast, are meant here (cf. Eissfeldt, 'Erstlinge und Zehnten im Alten Testament', BWAT, Vol. 22, 1917, 27 f., 42; also Noth, *Überlieferungsgeschichte des Pentateuchs*, 55). The liturgical prayer prescribed for the man when he makes his offering and with which he is to confess his belief in Yahweh's historical acts of salvation merely reveals the intention to draw the rite originating in an agricultural religion into the sphere of the tradition of salvation-history associated with the Yahweh religion by providing a 'historicizing' reason for it, thus detaching it from its native soil in an originally alien religion. This is a secondary and later process in the history of religion and of form and transmission which can be observed in the Old Testament in the case of other cultic customs of similar origin and which is justified by the theology of the prophets, e.g. in Hos. 2: 7, 10. Here the tradition of the Yahweh religion concerned with salvation history is already presupposed; it cannot, therefore, have had its original home in the custom mentioned in Deut. 26: 1 ff. Consequently, the form-historical examination of the Pentateuchal problem must start at a different point in this tradition than at that of the credo in Deut. 26: 5 ff.

Owing to the absence of any connecting links, von Rad's thesis and Noth's deductions concerning the history and the tradition provide no explanation how out of such a credo there should have developed the Pentateuchal presentation of salvation history, which, in spite of all von Rad's efforts to make the subject matter of the credo appear similar to that of the Pentateuch, is after all generically something essentially different from an expanded hymn-like prayer or creed. The real problem concerning the motives and the practical purpose of the individual Pentateuchal sources themselves and their combination into a whole, is brought no nearer to a solution than before by von Rad's thesis, which traces them back by the methods of 'Formgeschichte' to the two festival legends of the Conquest and the Sinai traditions attached to separate places and festivals. For such assumptions make the Yahwist appear again as a collector of different traditions with a more or less recognizable power of composition and theological individuality. It is obvious that in this case there is no reason to look for the actual setting, the *Sitz im Leben*, of the Pentateuchal sources themselves or of their compilation, when they are regarded merely as literary compilations concerning which we are not told for whom or for what purpose they were collected. And yet this question cannot be suppressed in view of the juxtaposition and interweaving of differing parallel source-strands. These facts cannot just be explained as a process of literary ossification, but must be understood to be the outcome of the living importance which tradition had and maintained up to a late period. Thus the question as to the actual setting, the *Sitz im Leben*, of the Pentateuchal sources still remains the decisive one—not answered by von Rad either—for the problem of the origin of the Pentateuchal tradition. It continues to exist also in spite of Noth's assumption (*Üb. Pent.*, 43 f., 216 ff.)—which is able, in some cases, to offer a better explanation—that the growing together of different traditions took place in the anonymous period of pre-literary development.

Von Rad has barred his way to making this inquiry by choosing the so-called 'credo' (Deut. 26: 5 ff.) as the starting point of his investigation, instead of proceeding from the Pentateuch or its sources as a whole and feeling his way back from there. Relying on this insecure foundation he separates, not without a certain forcible simplification, the tradition of the history of the Conquest from the Sinai tradition of the renewal of the Covenant, and assigns each to a particular festival and sanctuary. It is indeed correct, as von Rad maintains, that a distinction exists between the Sinai tradition with its theophany and its covenant-making on the one hand and the tradition of Yahweh's savings acts as historical events on the other, but the deduction drawn by von Rad from this, that there would not have been room for both these traditions side by side in the same festival cult, is too subtle and not conclusive. For the absence of any mention of the Sinai tradition in the enumeration of the historical saving acts of Yahweh, as in Deut. 26: 5 ff.; 1 Sam. 12: 8 ff.; Exod. 15; Ps. 136, etc. which von Rad (and Noth similarly) uses to support his thesis, is by no means so striking as he supposes. We must bear in mind the fact which von Rad himself recognizes in another place, but has left out of account at this point in his argument, that the subject matter of the Sinai tradition is not a historical event in the same sense as the historical events of the exodus and the entry; it is on the contrary an encounter with God which leads up to the acceptance by the people of the will of God proclaimed in the commandments; and in its cultic setting it represents a particular action in the course of the festival. Consequently it is not mentioned in the same breath with God's acts of salvation in those texts which are concerned only with the latter. The reason why certain texts do not mention the Sinai tradition beside the saving acts of Yahweh (exodus, conquest, etc.) does not spring from their ignorance of this tradition which would in that case have to be assigned to another cultic sphere; it is due to the fact that they *restrict* themselves to the recital of the saving acts in history on grounds which make it clear that their silence concerning the Sinai tradition cannot be used as an *argumentum e silentio* for the reconstruction of the whole contents of the festival cult, as is done by von Rad. For Deut. 26: 5 ff. cannot be considered to be the 'festival legend' of the feast of Weeks. It is a prescribed confession giving the reasons for Yahweh's claim to the first fruits of the ground and for the duty of offering them. This purpose is completely fulfilled by the mention of the historical acts of salvation which led to the grant of the land (Deut. 26: 5 ff.); to bring in the people's pledge at Sinai would only be disturbing in this circumscribed train of thought. The range of ideas in this confession is determined by the concrete situation of this particular agricultural custom and therefore proves nothing about the whole subject matter of the festival cult; it is only using a part of its tradition.

The situation is similar with regard to the hymns which celebrate Yahweh's deeds of salvation in history, as in Exod. 15, Ps. 105, 136, etc., although with this difference, that these hymns are directly connected with the festival-cult and must be judged as parts of the festival-liturgy at a definite point in which they were performed. By their use the congregation is echoing Yahweh's saving deeds in hymns which look back on them and presuppose the detailed cultic presentation of this salvation history which is summarized and recapitulated in them (cf. Ps. 44: 2 ff.; 77: 12 ff.; 78: 2 ff.; 111: 4, 6, etc.). It cannot be expected of such separate parts of the festal liturgy that they should present the entire substance of the festal performance, especially as the subject of the hymn is usually concerned with Yahweh's acts of salvation as proofs of the divine greatness and power. The Sinai tradition on the other hand with its pledge of the cult-congregation to the proclamation of the divine will is outside the range of vision of these hymns; yet this does not allow the conclusion to be drawn that this tradition could not have had a place at another point in the festal liturgy. The situation is different in 1 Sam. 12. Without going into the question of the relationship between Samuel's speech and the festival tradition, this severe lecture clearly presupposes just those things which form the substance of the Sinai tradition (cf. Pss. 78, 106). Apart from this implied presupposition which was the motive for (vv. 6 f., 10) and the purpose (v. 14) of the speech, Samuel's undertaking would be meaningless. But if the fundamental idea of the Sinai tradition runs like a red thread through the whole speech, then naturally a special mention of the 'Sinai events' would be superfluous.

Therefore, the omission to mention the Sinai tradition in the passages quoted does not prove that it was impossible for the traditions of the Conquest and of Sinai to exist side by side in the same festival cult and that they must consequently be allotted to two different festivals and sanctuaries.

But von Rad has overlooked the fact that in the account of Jos. 24 which goes back to an early cultic tradition, the two sets of tradition are already combined and are clearly regarded as belonging essentially together because they supplement each other: the recapitulation of the events of salvation history in Jos. 24: 2–13 *and* the people's commitment to the covenant in Jos. 24: 14–26.

It can be seen from the style in which these historical events are presented, namely as God's word using the first person singular, that in the background there stands the conception of the encounter between the people and God who appeared to his worshipping congregation (theophany) and is now speaking to it. Thus this manner of speech which is original as compared with Deut. 26 and is still preserved in Jos. 24 (cf. Ps. 81: 9 ff.) shows the original connexion between *God's revelation of his nature in his saving acts* in history *and his revelation of his will leading up to the pledge of the congregation.* At the same time this explains the 'canonical weight' which this tradition of God's double manifestation in 'history and law' had in shaping the literary tradition of the Pentateuch. It is generally recognized today that behind the form of the presentation in Jos. 24 a sacral act of the tribal union, repeated in the festal cult, is to be assumed; therefore, this juxtaposition of God's activity in salvation history and of the commitment to the covenant resulting from the theophany can be understood only if 'history and law' were from the earliest days the two fundamental pillars of the tradition in one and the same cult festival for the sacral union of the tribes of All-Israel.*
Therefore the differentiation of the Sinai tradition from that of the Conquest does not justify separating the two traditions and assigning them to the cult of two different festivals parted by time and place.

The extremely peculiar linking of theophany (manifestation at Sinai) and historical tradition (Exodus and Conquest), of God's proclamation of his nature and of his will in the Pentateuch, remains fundamentally unexplained by von Rad's assumption that it was the Yahwist who first effected the combination of the two cult traditions which were originally quite separate. What could have induced him to effect such a decisive operation on the tradition if he was not tied to what was already handed down in the cult regarding the intimate connexion between the traditions of Sinai and the Conquest? Could the 'canonical' weight of just this combination of the traditions of Exodus, Sinai and the Conquest

---

* The question must be left in abeyance here whether the history of these traditions may be pursued further back to their formation, and as to who in that case first held them. The reflexions of Noth tending in this direction only confirm the fact that we do not get beyond conjectures and do not by these means reach any reliable foundation for the Pentateuchal problem.

which has been recognized in the general plan of all the Pentateuchal sources, and even beyond them, be understood as the consequence merely of the literary undertaking of a single individual whose work, moreover, von Rad wants to render intelligible as a late appearance in the whole development? The linking together of the two sets of tradition was not carried out first by the Yahwist, but was handed down to him as an established datum.* This follows also from the fact that, apart from Jos. 24, it is presupposed in passages, all of which it would be scarcely possible or desirable to explain by literary dependence on the Yahwist, as for example in the introduction to the Decalogue; in Exod. 3: 18; 19: 3 ff.; Deut. 6: 20–25; 1 Sam. 12: 7, 14 ff.; Ps. 44: 2 ff.; 81: 6 ff.; 97: 10 ff.; 111: 4, 6 f.; Jer. 7: 22 ff.; 31: 31 ff. In this matter it will not indeed be possible to get by without assuming the bond of a common tradition fostered in the cult and made known by it. Moreover, in the case of a number of the psalms concerned, the assumption of their pre-exilic origin cannot be refuted. So this aspect of the matter, too, raises the fundamental question whether the starting point for solving the problem of the formation of the Pentateuchal tradition may not be found just in this remarkable linking together of its two basic elements. This solution would also be able to do justice to the juxtaposition of the story-telling historical accounts and the legal components of the Pentateuch. In other words, von Rad's question should be posed from the opposite end with the idea that the *theophany* (Sinai) tradition with *the manifestation of God's will* and *the making of the covenant* on the one hand and *the account of God's historical acts of salvation* as *the manifestation of his nature* on the other hand were the original basic component parts of one and the same festival celebrated at the central sanctuary of the tribes (the holy Ark). These components appear already at the foundation of this union at the 'Assembly' at Shechem (Jos. 24) and from then onwards had a certain normative significance in the festival of the covenant for the whole of 'Israel', i.e. the sacral union of the tribes, and for the shaping of its tradition. Here is to be sought the original cultic environment into which all the Pentateuchal sources were compelled by the weight of a living tradition to fit their presentation of the history of salvation. Hence also the Pentateuch as such is

* Thus now also Noth, *Uberlieferungsgeschichte des Pentateuchs*, p. 43.

not to be judged merely as a literary precipitate of tradition long since detached from the cult (von Rad), but as a fixation of traditions intended for liturgical recitation which sprang directly out of the cult and still stood in active relationship with it. Account must be taken of the fact that the institution of the sacral union of the tribes, which in my view has no rival as the original bearer of the Pentateuchal tradition, continued to exist still in the time of the kings. The basic characteristic common to all the Pentateuchal sources lies in their collecting and developing older traditions of different kinds and origins into a complete presentation of history as directed by God, the purpose of which is to realize divine salvation in and for 'Israel', the people of the twelve tribes. It is not 'history' in the usual sense, but *salvation-history* which is the real subject matter of the descriptive parts of the Pentateuch, and this belongs to the sacral sphere of the cultic celebration, as the place where salvation is mediated and realized. Therefore, we do not do justice to the nature of the Pentateuchal strands if we place the 'story-telling' character of the presentation of piously interpreted historical events in the foreground and at the same time pay no attention to the decisive dynamic way, characteristic of ancient cultic thought, of understanding the presentation of salvation-history as an actualized happening continuing into, i.e. still influencing, the present (against Noth, *Üb. Pent.*, p. 53). In all the strands of the sources there are combined with the presentation of salvation-history legal passages as the ordinances of the covenant. Thus the Pentateuch also by combining 'history and law' expresses the fundamentals of salvation as the manifestation of the nature and the will of God in the form which is typical of and valid for the Old Testament.

The need to present it in this way assumes three things: (1) that different kinds of tradition came together in the 'Israelite' cultural sphere as a result of the different tribes and sections of the population in Palestine joining to form the sacral union of 'Israel', the people of God; (2) a cultic tradition of this sacral Yahweh union, fostered at the common shrine, which had as its object the revelation and realization of salvation by presenting and reproducing the history of salvation and the renewal of the covenant; (3) in connexion with this a faith in Yahweh as the God whose nature and power manifests itself in the history of the past and the present, a faith which tends to absorb the traditions of foreign religions and to bring them into its service. These assumptions were satisfied when Israel had won the control of Palestine, had admitted a part of the inhabitants into its union, which was both religious and national, and had come to terms with its material and intellectual civilization. The circle which was interested in that presentation of salvation-history is the tribal union which was both sacral and national and was originally the bearer of the name 'Israel'; it was made one by the common worship of Yahweh as 'the God of Israel'. The occasions, at which that salvation-history was brought to life, must be sought in the regularly recurring cultic festivals, when the tribes came together for their common worship of Yahweh at the central sanctuary (the ark) for the feast of the covenant, which probably took place in the autumn. Their purpose was to hear from a qualified person how their God had revealed his nature and his will in history, to experience this history as it was made present and real to them in the action of the cult, and to seal afresh their communion with God in the act of concluding the covenant.

The Old Testament contains in several passages from different periods pointers to such solemn occasions when the traditions of the past effective for salvation in the present were publicly recited. In connexion with the national worship of Yahweh the Song of Deborah with its hymn-like introduction and its conclusion is evidence of the comparatively early existence of the religious presentations of history in the framework of the festival cult of the national tribal union; it draws particular attention itself to the rehearsing of 'the righteous acts' of Yahweh to his people (Jgs. 5: 11). (Owing to the corrupt text it is no longer possible to know the concrete situation for this allusion.) With regard to the hymn-like setting and also to the sayings about the individual tribes Deut. 33 is on the same level. Genesis 49 belongs here too, although here the setting is lacking for intelligible reasons (pre-Mosaic period!). In these chapters, where in the presence of the heads of the people at the assembly of the twelve tribes (Deut. 33: 5) the rule of Yahweh as king is celebrated, the tradition of the history of the tribes is set forth in the shape of blessings and cursings, thus standing in close relation to the performance of salvation in the cult (cf. Mowinckel, *Psalmenstudien*, V, 1924). It is not without reason that these concluding oracles of blessings and cursings concerning the individual tribes are fitted into salient positions in the Pentateuchal sources (the end of the story of the patriarchs, and of the Mosaic tradition). Similarly at a significant place in the Hexateuch (the end of the narrative of the conquest) there appears the early, perhaps the earliest, information about the combined national and cultic gathering of the tribes at the sanctuary at Shechem in Jos. 24, behind which probably stand the historical events which led to the foundation of the sacral union of the twelve tribes in Palestine. Here the retrospective historical tradition, which must be older than the Genesis narrative since it does not conform to its scheme, is closely connected with the pledge of the people at the cultic covenant-making before Yahweh, and this proves its early association with the cultic celebration of the covenant; therefore, the fact previously mentioned that in this account of the sacral covenant-making of the twelve tribes the presentation of *salvation-history* is formulated in the style of a revelation. i.e. as a word of God mediated by Joshua to the cultic community, must be considered from the point of view of form-history also as being that style of cultic presentation which comes nearest to its original form. With this in mind the assumption which is necessary to explain the *narrative form* of the Pentateuch, namely the transition in the Pentateuch from the style of revelation to that of narrative (cf. 1 Sam. 12: 8 ff.) observable elsewhere (e.g. in the prophets) presents no further difficulties.

Moreover Mowinckel (Le Décalogue, 1927, 114 ff.) has already pointed out that the Sinai narrative of JE still contains clear indications which make it probable that in its present form it grew out of the liturgy of the covenant festival. Besides we know from Exod. 12: 2 ff. that together with the rites of the passover, the transmission of its 'historical' basis resting on the story of the exodus from Egypt was laid on the people as a sacred duty. This frequently observed 'historicizing' of the feasts of cattle-breeders and Bedouins, which arose originally within other ways of life, namely their subsequent admission into the genuinely Israelite tradition of Yahweh's salvation history, proves not only that the superior vitality of the worship of Yahweh absorbed and incorporated other cultic domains, but also that the tradition of salvation-history and the Yahweh cult cannot be separated from

each other. Further the idea of a 'Great Israel', i.e. the later extension to 'All Israel' of the traditions which originally sprang from
smaller groups and at first concerned them alone, an extension
obliterating the facts, can be traced throughout the exodus-
Moses-conquest traditions in the Pentateuch, the book of Joshua
and the Deuteronomistic framework of the book of Judges,
and must be understood against the background of the cultic
tradition; in this tradition salvation-history was experienced
as a contemporary re-enactment of Yahweh's dealings with the
sacral tribal-union even by those tribes and members of the
covenant, who—from the historical point of view—had originally
no share in the events presented (cf. Jos. 24). These examples of
the association between the Pentateuchal traditions and the cultic
festival celebration make it evident that the place where the presentation of salvation-history was cradled and nurtured must be
sought in the cult of Yahweh's festival of the tribal union 'Israel'.
In view of the existence of a religious tradition and interpretation
of history related to Yahweh—not so much as regards particular
characteristics—it seems to me that the oldest cultic traditions of
salvation-history, the Pentateuchal sources, the prophets' outlook
on history, the presentation of history in Deuteronomy and by
the Deuteronomists, the picture of history in the Priestly writing,
and also the historical reflexions given in the psalms, e.g. in Pss.
78, 105, 106, 135, 136, all stand in *one* unbroken series transmitted and continuously kept alive in the cult. The significance
of such a cultic tradition, as the common centre of the manifold
ways in which salvation history was shaped in the OT, needs
to be appreciated more thoroughly than hitherto, and it must
receive consideration also when examining the problem of the
formation of the Pentateuchal sources.

The connexion between God's revelation of his nature and of
his will in law and history to be noticed in the Decalogue, in
Jos. 24; in Pss. 44, 78, 81, 95, 105 f., 135 f., etc. and in the Sinai
tradition suggests from the outset that the cultic celebration of
salvation-history issued in the renewal of the covenant with Yahweh, as the guarantee of the divine salvation which linked God's
salvation and blessing to the cultic community's pledge of obedience. It can, therefore, be assumed that in the case of the *legal
elements* of the Pentateuch, they, too, were transmitted in the

festival cult and that the sacral union of tribes carried on this tradition. Deut. 27 gives an account of a sacral act of this kind at the national sanctuary of Shechem which was probably based on a well-established regularly performed rite; there in the presence of the congregation of the people gathered from all the tribes the circumstance that Israel has become the people of Yahweh (v. 9), is connected with the sacral act of blessing and cursing (v. 12 f.) and at the same time a liturgy of curses is recorded which refers to Yahweh's legal requirements from the people. The writing of the commandments on lime-washed stones set up in the sanctuary (Deut. 27: 2 ff.; Jos. 8: 30 ff.; cf. Jos. 24: 27) again reflects clearly the original association of the law and the covenant cult. Deut. 31: 9 ff. also tells how the Deuteronomic law was written down and preserved and, at the same time, how it was recited regularly every seventh year in the presence of the whole congregation of the people, consisting of men, women, children and strangers. It is probable that, as Alt (*Die Ursprünge des israelitschen Rechts*, 63 ff.) has shown, behind this there stands the much earlier custom of the sacral legal recitation of series of commandments of the old Israelite code, to which the people pledged themselves afresh regularly at the beginning of the Sabbatical year. Beside the renewal of the material foundations of its existence (cancellation of the ownership of landed property and a fresh distribution by lot of the fields to the individual family houses in Exod. 23: 10 ff.; Deut. 15: 1 ff.; Lev. 25: 1 ff.) they celebrated regularly in the cultic act the renewal also of the covenant between Yahweh and his people. Presumably this custom, too, goes back to the festival of the covenant, celebrated annually in the autumn (cf. Deut. 31: 11 and 1 Kgs. 8: 2; 12: 32) at the sanctuary of the ark (Deut. 31: 9 f.). Thus here is to be found in the Hexateuch the focal point in the cultic setting of the conquest traditions of the individual tribes and their connexion with the law of the covenant; their cultic function is to confirm the ownership of the land as the foundation for the sacral legal act of distributing it (cf. Ps. 16: 5 f.; 60: 8 ff.). Now, beside the remnants of old separate traditions handed down about the conquest, which are preserved in the story of the spies in Num. 13 f. and Jos. 14: 6 ff. (cf. Deut. 1: 22 ff.) and Jgs.1: 27 ff., the book of Joshua has accepted in the main, in a form extended to 'all Israel', the conquest-tradition of the tribe of Benjamin which presumably was attached to the sanctuary of Gilgal. The explanation of this is probably to be traced to the time of Saul when the tribe of Benjamin and its sanctuary had risen to be especially important and could be considered as representing Israel. Accordingly, the national Yahweh festival cult of the tribal union was the place where the genuine Israelite law was handed down in living form, as it was also the place for the authentic Israelite tradition of salvation-history. Thus the religious and moral prohibitions of the Book of the Covenant, as Noth has shown, are probably compilations from the Amphictyonic law in force among the union of the twelve tribes. The laws of Deuteronomy and of the Law of Holiness had their home (*Sitz im Leben*) in the care devoted to the tradition and to the Torah provided by this sacral union (cf. now, too, von Rad: in *Deuteronomiumstudien*). It is only when we keep this in view that we can understand that remarkable combination of laws and history which we have in the Pentateuchal sources, especially for the Mosaic period: they both grew in the same soil and they were kept alive and developed in the regular maintenance of the cultic tradition.

In proportion as the Israelite people assimilated the Canaanite civilization and had to come to terms with it, the Yahweh tradition admitted new elements and permeated them. These originated partly in the indigenous civilization of Canaan, partly in the tribal traditions of the pre-Mosaic Hebrews, such as e.g. Palestinian local sagas and legends and customs of the sanctuaries (cf. also Alt, 'Die Wallfahrt von Sichem nach Betel', *Festschr. für Bulmerincq*, 1938, 218 ff.), traditions of the Canaanite peasant-law, primeval myths, and historical traditions of families and tribes concerning the history of the patriarchs. The exclusive vitality of the faith in Yahweh did not tolerate as a permanency the existence side by side of different forms of culture and religion. It absorbed these foreign elements and made them serviceable to itself by building them into its own tradition, partly after a vigorous transformation of the old material. When and where this process set in, and what course it took in detail, cannot be clearly perceived. Traditions of tribal history and religious traditions, which were originally indigenous in different circles, had been merged here and there into larger groupings already before the rise of the worship of Yahweh in Palestine in the patriarchal era. This pro-

cess was promoted by contractual agreements with invocations
to the gods by whose names the individual partners swore their
oaths, especially in the border-sanctuaries, such as Beersheba,
Bethel, Mizpah, which were visited by different tribes (cf. Gen. 31:
44 ff. and Alt, *Der Gott der Väter*). Nevertheless, the decisive impetus was given to this process by the expansive power of the
Yahweh-religion of Mosaic origin. The Song of Deborah (cf.
especially Jgs. 5: 8) as well as Jos. 24 teaches us that it played a
significant role even in the time before the kingdom. Yet it seems
to have been stimulated anew by the national unification of the
tribes under David. Probably the combination of the diverse
traditional elements, as we find it in the work of the Yahwist, is
to be traced back to the incentive to cultic and theological unification springing from David's political measures for the cult, for
which the building of Solomon's temple provided the outward
cultic and artistic manifestation in architecture.

The manner in which the different traditions were worked up
within the framework of the cult of the covenant festival cannot
yet be shown in detail. Yet on the one hand the conception of the
covenant has long since been recognized as significant for the
sociological structure of Israel's religion in the tribal union and
the kingdom (cf. for this Weiser, 'Glaube und Geschichte im AT',
BWAT 1931, 12 f., 57 ff. and Eichrodt, *Theologie des AT*, 6 ff.).
On the other hand this conception plays a role in all the sources of
the Pentateuch (in J and P it is brought into the story of the
patriarchs also in Gen. 15, 17 and in P even into primeval history
in the covenant with Noah). These facts prove a close connexion
between the shaping of the political and cultic life in Israel and the
development of the Pentateuchal tradition. In other words, the
individual strands of the Pentateuch which we call JEDP are
stages and types in the shaping of the tradition of salvation-
history, which had its home in the cult of the union of the twelve
tribes and maintained itself by its sacral recital at the feast of the
covenant all through the period of the political division of the
tribes as the living possession of the religious congregation of the
people right up to the reading of the Torah in the synagogues.
Thus its coming into existence and its growth, the incorporation
of legal components, such as e.g. the Decalogue in E and D, the
Book of the Covenant in E and the Law of Holiness in P, and also

the combination of the sources into the complete Pentateuch, can only be understood in connexion with the history of 'Israel', i.e. of the sacral union of the tribes and of its changing mingled religious and political concerns. Therefore we must not regard as the prototype of the Pentateuchal sources the credo spoken by a layman, but the recitation and representation of salvation-history proclaiming the nature of God and leading up to the proclamation of his will and the act of renewal of the covenant, which is mediated at the regular covenant-festival of the sacral union of the twelve tribes by a cultic person (priest or prophet; cf. Jos. 24; 1 Sam. 12; Pss. 78: 5; 81: 6 ff.; 105: 5 ff.) divinely commissioned to speak. Accordingly, these recitations are to be understood as a kind of lectionary, i.e. as the written records of the tradition of salvation-history belonging to the union of the twelve tribes, and fostered by oral recital and transmission. The agreements between J and E as regards the elements transmitted and their arrangement is attributed by Noth (*Üb. Pent.*, 40 ff.) to a common written or oral basis (G), on which both Pentateuchal sources drew independently of each other. This reliance on a common basis is remarkable in view of the frequently wide divergence of the material peculiar to each of the two sources. It is explained by the fact that a certain hard core of the salvation-history tradition had developed by its repeated proclamation in the cult and had become so well established that a sort of normative authority was accorded to it already in the pre-literary stage. The function of the authors of the sources consisted less in the collection and literary preservation of old popular traditions (Gunkel) and much more in the written development, transformation and combination of the material and the traditions handed down in the festival cult. For this at any given moment the determining factors were the particular cultic needs and intellectual trends of the historical situations in which the Pentateuchal sources came into being. Without this cultic-sacral background the fact that the different strands of the sources were placed side by side and worked up together as literature would remain unexplained, since in view of the intention evident in the later strands to replace the earlier ones it would be incomprehensible why these continued to exist as literary entities. Their neutralization seems to have taken place not in the literary sphere, but in the framework of the cultic recitation, by the choice of those pieces for recital at any given time which met the needs of the day and were intended to be substituted for the earlier forms of the tradition. Thus what was early was left in its literary form, as it was, beside the late, but was replaced at the cultic recital by the new tradition, a procedure of continuously active fashioning of the tradition which only reached some finality with the last redaction of the Priestly Code and the uniform liturgical use of the Torah since Ezra. We must also reckon with the fact that once the tradition had been written down, it had had a history within the framework of its actual proclamation in the cult and was thus subjected to changes and extensions which were not unimportant; probably the oral tradition continued to exist for some time beside the written one and influenced it. Thus it becomes intelligible why one often cannot manage to sort the sources out neatly from each other, including the details of the wording. Yet it would be going too far, if on the basis of these considerations the significance of the personality of the authors of the sources was allowed to become altogether unimportant, and if the Pentateuchal sources were seen, as Gunkel does, to be only the fruit of the activity of Schools (J.E.); the sources have not lost the personal stamp of their origin even in their further historical development. Finally we must remember that, according to the way of thinking peculiar to the ancient cult, the cultic recapitulation of salvation-history means something different from just the retention of the memory of events in past history. The Pentateuch which issued from the festival-cult means something different from the 'narrative' literature of history in the more or less modern sense. The cultic presentation of salvation-history, like the theophany itself (Jgs. 5: 4 ff.; Ps. 18: 8 ff.; Is. 6; Deut. 33; Hab. 3. Pss. 68: 25; 77: 17 ff. etc.), with which it has an outward and an inward connexion, is the actual reproduction and application of salvation to the present; and in this the festival congregation takes a direct part, itself renewing the experience each time afresh, as a witness by eye and ear and as the object of the divine saving activity, of its meeting with the God of this salvation-history, thus confirming and realizing its own salvation (cf. Pss. 95: 7 ff.; 96: 6). The sacral importance of the recapitulation of salvation-history rests on this, that it was made actual within the framework of a sacramental happening as the revelation of the nature of God believed to be present in the cultic act. In this lies the final ground for the canonical authority of the tradition of salvation-history and for the tenacity with which its design has maintained itself, setting the course across the centuries and throughout all the strands of the Pentateuch in spite of all variations of detail, and has been reflected in a diversity of forms, in many parts of the OT literature, including Deut. 26: 5 ff. This, too, is the basis for the special position of the Pentateuch and its tradition within the rest of the historical tradition and literature handed down in the OT. 'Salvation-history', in the sense of the Pentateuchal tradition grown out of the festival-cult, is something different from history. It is the act itself of salvation, taking place sacramentally, brought into the present by the cultic act and experienced directly. In consequence, the question of the formation of the Pentateuch is something more than a problem of history and of the history of literature. This is what we must keep in mind, as after these general considerations on the history of the form and the cult we turn to the individual strands in the Pentateuch.

14. The Yahwist strand

For the literature see beginning of section 10, pp. 69–70. Also Budde, *Die bibl. Urgeschichte*, 1883; Luther, *Die Persönlichkeit des Jahwisten*; bei ed. Meyer, *Die Israeliten und ihre Nachbarstämme*, 1906, 105 ff.; Gunkel, *Genesis*³, 1922, pp. LXXX ff.; Procksch, *Genesis*,² 1924, 16 ff.; Hellbardt, *Der Jahwist und die biblische Urgeschichte*, Diss. 1935; H. Schmidt, 'Das Meerlied, Exod 15', ZAW 1931, 59 ff.; Frank M. Cross, jr. and David Noel Freedman, 'The Song of Miriam', JENSt XIV (1955) 237 ff.; Mowinckel, 'Der Ursprung der Bileamsage', ZAW 1930, 233 ff.; Eissfeldt, 'Die Komposition der Bileamerzählung', ZAW 1939, 212 ff.; Hölscher, 'Die Anfänge der hebräischen Geschichtsschreibung, *Sitzungsberichte der Heidelberger Akademie der Wissenschaften*, Phil.=hist. Klasse, 1942; Eissfeldt, *Geschichtsschreibung im Alten Testament*, 1948; Noth, *Überlieferungsgeschichte d. Pentateuchs*, 20–44; Hölscher, *Geschichtsschreibung in Israel* (see beginning of section 9); Rowley, 'Moses and the Decalogue', BJRL 34 (1951); Jepsen, *Zur Überlieferungsgeschichte der Vätergestalten* (see lit. section 10).

The Yahwist source-strand derives its name from the fact that throughout this strand, unlike the others, the name used for God is Yahweh (Jehovah) even for the pre-Mosaic period. Beside this it is thought that other criteria characteristic of J can be noted: as for example the name of the mountain of God, Sinai (in E Horeb), the designation of the inhabitants of Palestine as Canaanites (in E Amorites), etc. (Further details in Steuernagel, *Einleitung*, pp.

214 f.) Yet we must remark here that in view of the history of the traditions and their. oral development the use of linguistic arguments by means of which to separate the sources cannot be considered reliable in every case. It is characteristic of the Yahwist strand that in it the racy, vivid, often even coarse style of the popular manner of presentation has been most clearly preserved and that even there, where the subject matter of the old national tradition has been vigorously redirected towards a spiritual outlook, the old ways of visualizing and of expressing things have been retained. This endows the whole with lively animation and realistic power. But however noticeable this aesthetic aspect of J's method of presentation may be as compared with that of E or P, yet the essential significance of the Yahwist strand does not lie in the individual features of the narrative, but in the spirit which controls the whole presentation and out of stories fashions 'history' possessing the widest horizon and the deepest range. This is achieved by looking at each event as one item in a larger sequence, shot through with meaning, and as a purposive saving action of God with human actors playing their part in it. In this theocentric conception of history, God is considered to be the one who really shapes all history without this fact causing the human side in the happenings to be curtailed or neglected. It is just by the manner in which the divine and human factors in history lie undiminished side by side and intertwined that the peculiar greatness of the Yahwist work consists. It is on this that there depends in the last resort the tremendous realism, truthfulness and depth of his presentation which is woven together out of a variety of materials, derived partly from mythology (creation, paradise, marriages of angels, story of the flood), partly from tribal tales (the Cain and Lamech traditions). It begins at the farthest limit of history with the creation and in the story of Paradise it immediately presents the foundations of human existence from the viewpoint of creation, sin and judgment. This outlook on history as judgment on sin is the inner link holding together the different narratives concerning primeval history in Gen. 1–11 with increasing dramatic effect.

Along parallel lines, this piece of the universal history of mankind is linked together externally by genealogies which are brought down to Abraham by the process of elimination. Thus primeval history prepares both inwardly and outwardly for the story of the patriarchs in Gen. 12–50. Here, after the attempts of mankind to construct history according to their own will have suffered shipwreck on God's judgment, the initiative for what happens passes to the hand of God and with the choice of Abraham the real salvation-history for Israel and through Israel for the world (Gen. 12: 3) begins. The external scheme for the story of the patriarchs leads through the genealogical line of the three generations of the patriarchs and the twelve sons of Jacob up to the beginnings of the history of the people in the Mosaic period. Its fundamental note, the accomplishment of the divine plan of salvation in defiance of all human obstacles, fears and hopes, forms an internal link between the most varied material and is sounded as a reminder again and again in the promises of descendants and possession of the land handed on through the cult-tradition of the tribal union. The story of the youth and call of Moses, of the oppression of the people, and their deliverance out of Egypt, of their journey to Sinai and the revelation and the pledge which took place there, of their departure and wandering past Kadesh up to the frontiers of the promised land, all this is held together by the basic conception that the people are preserved in face of the might of their enemies and in spite of the repeated rebellion of Israel against their leaders. Here, too, the story serves to demonstrate the ascendancy of God in his power, his claim and his mercy by means of which he achieves his plan for salvation-history. Nothing more is needed to show that the Yahwist strand must also have told of the realization of the promise, and so of the conquest of Canaan by Israel, that is to say that the story of J must have reached its conclusion only beyond the present Pentateuch.

The following passages are generally ascribed to the Yahwist strand (for the detailed analysis see the commentaries. x signifies intermixture with the strands added in brackets): Gen. 2: 4 b–4: 26; 5: 29; 6: 1–8; 7–8^x (P); 9: 18–27; 10: 8–19, 25–30; 11: 1–9, 28–30; 12; 13^x (P); 15^x (E); 16^x (P); 18: 1–19; 28, 30–38; 21: 1–7^x (P), 32–33^x (E); 22: 14–24^x (E); 24^x (E); 25^x (P); 26^x (P); 27^x (EP); 28: 13–16; 29: 2–14; 31–35; 30: 9–16, 24–43^x (E); 31^x (EP); 32^x (E); 33^x (E); 34^x (E); 36^x (EP); 37^x (EP); 38; 39^x (E); 40–42^x (E); 43; 44; 45^x (E); 46^x (EP); 47^x (P); 48^x (EP); 49: 1–27; 50: 1–11;

Exod. 1^x (EP); $2-5^x$ (EP); $7-10^x$ (EP); 11: 4–8; 12: 21–27; $13-14^x$ (E); 15: $22-27^x$ (E); 16^x (EP); 19: 20–25; $23-24^x$ (EP); 32^x (E); 33^x (E); 34: 1–28;

Num. 10: 29–33; 11^x (E); $13-14^x$ (EP); 16^x (EP); $20-21^x$ (EP); $22-24^x$ (E); 25: $1-5^x$ (E); 32^x (EP);

Deut. 34^x (EDP).

In view of the origin and use of the Pentateuch in connexion with the festival-cult of the union of the twelve tribes, which has been discussed in section 13, this allocation to the sources can only claim validity subject to the proviso that the continued existence of the oral tradition alongside its fixed written form and the liturgical use of the transmitted salvation-history were not without influence on the later development in matters of detail. Therefore it is no longer possible to sort out the individual words and phrases in many of the passages.

We can only guess at the particular *circumstances in which the J strand arose*. It is no doubt the earliest complete description of the early tradition of salvation-history; its roots seem to be in the Davidic-Solomonic period, its author may have been closely associated with the royal house of Judah. It follows from the continuity of the arrangement and the homogeneous ideology with which the individual traditions are fitted into one general pattern of thought, that in J we have to do with a complete presentation, that is to say with an approximately *independent and homogeneous* work within the limits of what was said in section 13. Many scholars divide up the Yahwist strand into two narrative threads, J[1] (Eissfeldt: L) and J[2], particularly in the primeval history (especially Budde) but also elsewhere. But the evidence for two such threads of narrative within the Yahwist composition, each worked up according to its thought and style into a homogeneous sequence, cannot be considered convincing. Simpson's attempt to detach from the Yahwist strand a thin thread of narrative with traditions of the Southern tribes from the Davidic period (J[1]) which were then said to have been completed by traditions of the Northern tribes (J[2]) also lacks effective cogency.* Pfeiffer (see also *Introduction to the OT*, 159 ff.) from similar considerations wishes to postulate as a source of Genesis a south

* For the criticism of this analysis cf. Eissfeldt, 'Die ältesten Traditionen Israels', BZAW 71 (1950).

Palestinian strand, enlarged by later additions which originated in Edom, and would like to assign to it the mythological stories of primeval history (e.g. Gen. 3, 6: 1 ff.; 9: 20 ff.; 11: 1–9) and sagas from Southern Palestine and Transjordania (e.g. passages from Gen. 14, 19, 34–36, 38). But against this attempt too the same arguments must be urged as against the four sources theory, quite apart from the fact that its acceptance destroys obviously continuous literary passages and that the question of how such a non-Israelite strand of tradition came to be incorporated into the Pentateuch is faced with almost insoluble difficulties. Another line of thought is opened up by the thesis advanced again by Mowinckel and Hölscher and substantiated anew by the use of both the divine names 'Yahweh' and 'Elohim' in Gen. 2: 4–3: 24, as well as by remnants of older linguistic usages in the Septuagint. This thesis is to the effect that the Elohist strand also had an account of primeval history of which those passages are still preserved which had up till now been designated as J¹. The remaining inconsistencies, breaks and unevennesses of the J strand are explained for the most part by the heterogeneous material used by the Yahwist. The reshaping hand intervened vigorously in some passages (e.g. in the case of the subject matter underlying the story of Paradise, where individual passages still enable its original background of polytheistic mythology to be recognized). Yet in general it transmitted the old pieces very faithfully and with little change, so that they often still stand out clearly and frequently receive their special 'Yahwistic' impress only by the context into which they are inserted. The following are examples of mainly *earlier material* which has been taken over:

(a) The *Song of Lamech* (Gen. 4: 23 f.) a profane, blood-thirsty song of a braggart, which extols the cruel ferocity of revenge. The comparison with Cain's bloody revenge suggests perhaps an original connexion with Kenite tradition. It is characteristic of J that, by means of the context in which he has placed the song, he makes it appear as an example of unrestrained excess in a blood-feud and of the growing depravity of mankind, and this serves him as an ethical and religious reason for introducing the story of the flood.

(b) The *oracles of Noah* concerning Shem, Japheth and Canaan (Gen. 9: 25–27). It seems that the tradition of the three sons of

Noah is firmly rooted historically in an earlier period; Gunkel thinks of the circumstances of the nations in the middle of the second millennium B.C. In their present form the oracles probably envisage the time of David who first succeeded in subduing the Canaanites. In that case Japhet probably means the Hittites who came from Asia Minor (cf. Japetos in Cilicia) and were strangers in Palestine; Shem would be understood to be the Israelite tribes united in the worship of Yahweh. It is in the sacral tradition of these tribes that the *Sitz im Leben* of blessings and curses such as these is to be sought (see above and sections c, d.).

(c) The *blessing of Jacob* (Gen. 49) is a collection of oracles concerning the individual tribes which is now placed as *vaticina ex eventu* in the mouth of the dying patriarch. Parallels to it are found in Deut. 33 (E) and in the tribal sayings in the Song of Deborah (Jgs. 5: 15 ff.). The introduction to Deut. 33 and Jgs. 5 enables us still to perceive the original connexion of such blessings with the Yahweh festival of the union of the twelve tribes; the same connexion can be assumed also for Gen. 49; the blessing of the tribes in the patriarchal tradition offered no possibility of including in it the introduction with the manifestation of Yahweh on Sinai, so this is lacking in Gen. 49. The individual oracles are older than the whole. They assume that the tribes are settled in Palestine and originated perhaps in the period when the tribes led separate lives. The intentionally mysterious allusive nature of the oracles does not allow a precise date to be fixed. It cannot have been put together as a whole before the time of the judges; in its present form it is probably intended to support the claim of Judah to the leading position among the tribes. But it is in itself no finished unit, since sometimes the tribes as such, sometimes their personified eponyms, and in the case of the individual oracles conditions of different ages, are visualized. The difference in their length (that of Judah consists of three contrasting parts, Dan has two different ones) is an indication of the composite nature of the whole. Since the oracle concerning Judah points to the kingship of David, the present form of Jacob's blessing cannot be any older than that event.

(d) *The Oracles of Balaam* (Num. 24: 3–9, 16–19). These two oracles, now incorporated into the saga of Balaam, do not presuppose the saga itself, as Mowinckel has shown, and were, therefore, originally independent sayings, comparable with the tribal sayings just mentioned (Eissfeldt differs). They concern the whole people of Israel, thought of as settled in the land; therefore they did not originate in the time before the conquest. They are pure Israelite productions which, with their prediction about David (star out of Jacob, verse 17 and his victory over Moab and Edom, verse 7) and the allusion to king Agag (cf. 1 Sam. 15) probably come from the time of Saul or else of David (Rudolph). The note of unshaken national self-consciousness leads to the same conclusion. The original setting (*Sitz*) of the songs seems to have been the tradition of salvation-history in the national cúlt of Yahweh. The oracles concerning the other nations (verses 20–24) are of later growth. The Balaam saga was subsequently woven round the oracles by attaching itself to an early tradition about the seer Balaam from outside Israel and developing it further, and this gave the cultic sayings their historicizing framework. One can imagine this process, too, to have taken place in the era of David and Solomon (Mowinckel suggests the time of King Mesha of Moab, ninth century). The situation regarding the Elohist sayings of Balaam is different (see below).

(e) The so-called *Yahwistic decalogue* (Exod. 34: 10–26) was considered first by Goethe, *Was stand auf den Tafeln des Bundes*, 1773, then by Wellhausen and many others, in view of Exod. 34: 1, 28, to be the original earlier decalogue, on the basis of which the covenant of Sinai was supposed to have been made, and out of which the 'ethical' decalogue of Exod. 20 is thought to have sprung after a process of recasting. At any rate, the passage in its present form is no decalogue and can no longer be reconstructed as such, in spite of many efforts to do so. Different points suggest revision and enlargement (verses 15, 16, 24). Some of it is paralleled in the Decalogue of Exod. 20; other parts correspond to the language of the Book of the Covenant. The passage as a whole gives the impression of a conglomerate of heterogeneous regulations, in which the cultic rules of the priests for the laity predominate. It is a proof of the admission of Canaanite cultic (the feasts of unleavened bread, of weeks and of ingathering) and legal customs into the religion of Yahweh and of the historicizing and assimilation of these foreign elements into the framework of the cult of Yahweh.

(f) *The Red Sea Song* (Exod. 15: 1–18) is a festival hymn to Yahweh, the 'man of war' and eternal king, which sets forth the two dramatic crowning points at the beginning and end of the first epoch of Israel's history; the deliverance at the Red Sea and the conquest of Canaan, and ends in the glorification of Yahweh and his sanctuary (of Zion?). The song seems to have sprung from the earlier shorter song transmitted in E (Exod. 15: 21) and to have been composed for the enthronement of Yahweh, which was celebrated at the national feast of the covenant. It is no longer possible to determine exactly the date of its origin; it could hardly have come into existence before the period of David and Solomon; others suggest Deuteronomic influence and give it a correspondingly later date. It is remarkable with what freedom it deals with what was handed down, a sign of the way in which the tradition no doubt continued to be moulded actively even after the composition of the Pentateuchal sources and which was not without influence on its further development, although the inconsistencies this involved were not adjusted in every case. Cross and Freedman give an explanation of the Song of Miriam which differs in many respects from the usual understanding of it. It is based on a comparison of its poetic style with the Canaanite (Ugaritic) phraseology and they come to the conclusion that it was the earliest hymn which had been preserved, that it was in the hands of J and E and dates from the twelfth to the eleventh centuries. However, they do not throw enough light on the difficulty of imagining Ugaritic models being taken over into the Yahweh tradition in those days.

The questions how far J was tied in detail to pre-existent traditions, what he took over from them or added on his own account and how far he reshaped what he found, must be reserved for the examination of individual passages. Only a few examples may be mentioned here. It has been shown in section 13 in opposition to von Rad's interpretation that the association of law and history, that is in concrete terms, of the Sinai and the exodus-conquest traditions, was not the 'independent bold venture' of J, but a well-established cultic tradition. In the same way the association of the patriarchal history (at least of the figure of Jacob) with the salvation-history traditions of the union of the twelve tribes seems to have been already in the hands of J (cf. the story of Jacob's change of name to 'Israel' who thus becomes the ancestor of the Covenant, see Gen. 32: 29; 35: 10). On the other hand, the following points give the impression of being J's own contribution: firstly, that the tradition of Abraham receives precedence over that of Isaac, which is impoverished in its favour, and that its theological aspect as the history of salvation is stressed by the conception of election (Gen. 12: 2 ff.) which is carried on in the promises concerning the land and his descendants and in their accomplishment in the face of all risks; secondly, that the figure of Abraham has a cultic significance which can be seen in the brief remarks concerning Abraham's founding altars at Shechem and Bethel (Gen. 12: 6, 8) with its veiled pointed allusion to the local cultic sagas of the history of Jacob (Gen. 28, 33, 35). The internal association of the stories of primeval history as the manifestation of God's judgment on the sins of mankind with the history of salvation which begins with the history of the patriarchs was probably modelled on the tradition of the theophany in the cult of the Covenant festival (cf. section 13 and Amos 1: 3 ff.; Mic. 1: 2 ff.; Hab. 3: 2 ff.; Pss. 9: 8 f., 17 ff.; 47: 4; 94: 2; 97: 2 ff.; 98: 9; 135 f. and the designation of Yahweh as the 'Judge of all the earth' (Gen. 18: 25), which makes the impression of an accepted stereotyped formula). This basic conception of primeval history cannot, therefore, be claimed simply as the independent invention of the Yahwist, even though its execution in detail may be taken as evidence of the power of the author of this strand to mould it.

(2) The question of the *time when the Yahwist strand came into being* is not easy to answer in view of the peculiar circumstances in which the tradition was formed and it can be answered only approximately. As contrasted with the other strands the Yahwist one is marked by its being closer to the popular forms in which stories were conceived and transmitted, and by its realistic way of presenting them, observing them unselfconsciously and therefore reflecting less about them. In general, there is less interference with the state of the early traditions than in E and P. Thus the J version in Gen. 12 reports without misgivings that the patriarch lied, whilst E endeavours to remove this blemish at least in part. In Gen. 30: 37 ff. J makes Jacob obtain his wealth in flocks by cunning, in the parallel passage in E in 31: 5 ff. it is by divine

dispensation which appears as a retaliation for Laban's conduct. The natural account of the motives for what happened in J as contrasted with the strongly theologizing tendency in E, the unaffected, anthropomorphic and vivid way of speaking of God shows, by comparison with the Elohistic endeavour to make the religious conception of the world more spiritual, that the J strand is relatively the older one. As regards the absolute chronology, judging by the oracles of Noah and Balaam (Num. 24: 16 ff., see above), by the oracle concerning Judah in Jacob's blessing (see above) and by the allusion to Edom's attempt to free itself (Gen. 27:·40) which probably refers to 1 Kgs. 11: 14–22 (others think of 2 Kgs. 8: 20 in the ninth century), the era of David and Solomon may be assumed for the origin of the Yahwist. This period would supply the explanation for the concept of a Greater Israel which pervades the whole strand and which forms the historical and political bond, gathering together into a complete work the different tribal and local traditions. It would also account for the optimism of national and religious exultation which meets us, e.g. in the Balaam oracles, in Jacob's blessings and in Exod. 14: 13 f.* David's brilliant cultic policy showed itself in his transferring the holy ark, the old central sanctuary of the tribes, to his new residence in Jerusalem (2 Sam. 6) and in linking by this means the sacral union of tribes to his kingship and to the political concept of the kingdom; this was carried to its final conclusion in the history of the cult by the plan to build the temple, the execution of which was to be reserved for his son Solomon (cf. 2 Sam. 7 and 1 Kgs. 6 ff.). This policy is likely, also, to be the background against which the different sacral traditions and those of the tribal history were powerfully drawn together into one homogeneous presentation of salvation history, such as lies before us in the work of the Yahwist. Yet at the same time we must not lose sight of the fact that the Yahwist tradition, together with the national cult, was subject to developments later on also, and that the history of the Yahwist strand was by no means ended when it came into being in the tenth century. Hölscher, who considers the work of the Yahwist to be 'historical writing' in the strict sense, assumes that J's account extended beyond the Pentateuch as far as 1 Kgs. 12: 19 and, with many others, places its origin at the end of the

* cf. Schmöckel, ZAW 62 (1950), pp. 319 ff.

ninth century. Jepsen includes the passages ascribed to the Elohist also in the Yahwist work and brings its date down to the eighth century.

There is wide agreement amongst scholars that the *place of origin* is the land of the tribe of Judah in the South of Palestine. In Gen. 49: 8 ff. Judah is the royal tribe; in this passage and the Balaam oracles the Davidic kingship is judged so favourably that J can be most readily imagined in the immediate surroundings of the king's court at Jerusalem. In other places too the traditions of Judah are to the fore, e.g. in Gen. 38. In the story of Joseph Judah is the spokesman for the brothers. Moreover, the closer relations of J to the traditions of the Southern tribes as compared with E, point in the same direction, e.g. in Gen. 34 Simeon and Levi undertake the attack on Shechem, whilst E, with his secondary generalizing tendency, gives all the sons of Jacob a share in it. The traditions of Sodom and Lot attached to the district of the Dead Sea, and of Abraham concerning Hebron and its sanctuary are peculiar to the Yahwist. In the story of Hagar too (Gen. 16) the greater interest of J in the local cultic tradition of Beer-lahai-roi, which lies far to the south is obvious, whilst E in Gen. 21 has obliterated the individual local features. A special concern is felt for the figure of Abraham who belongs to the south and the tradition about him is decked out with greater detail. This is brought out, for instance, in the transference of themes from the Isaac narrative (Gen. 26) and the Jacob tradition (Gen. 28: 10 ff.; 35: 1 ff.; 33: 20) to Abraham (Gen. 12: 10 ff.; and also 12: 6–8) and in the emphasis on the covenant made between Yahweh and Abraham (Gen. 15). All these points lead to the same conclusion. It may be conjectured that the covenant with Abraham was intended to depreciate the Sinai covenant of Moses which was handed down as part of the tradition of the Joseph tribes. Similarly perhaps the use by J of the divine name Yahweh in the pre-Mosaic period, which might go back historically to earlier relations of the Southern tribes with the God of Sinai (a union of six tribes under the leadership of Judah? cf. Noth, 'Das System der zwölf Stämme Israels' BWAT 1930, pp. 107 f.), was intentionally designed to weaken in favour of the tradition which was alive in the South the significance of the revelation of this name in the time of Moses, which fitted in with the tradition of the northern tribes who entered the country only in the post-Mosaic time. The fact that North-Israelite traditions about Joseph and the sanctuaries of Shechem and Bethel have been admitted into the J strand as well, is no proof of the northern home of J (thus amongst others De Wette, Reuss, partly Kuenen and Simpson). For after all J consciously transferred to Abraham (Gen. 12: 6, 8) the sagas about the founding of the sanctuaries which according to Gen. 33: 20; 28: 10 ff.; 35: 1 ff. had, in the first instance, been connected only with the figure of Jacob, and had thereby reduced the northern Israelite bias of these traditions for the benefit of the figure of Abraham whose home was in the south. The union of the tribes in the Davidic kingdom had also led to their traditions being linked up more closely; but the stress laid on these traditions by J in comparison with E certainly points to Judah rather than to Israel. It is a remarkable fact that the story in Gen. 22, which seems to be based on an early pre-Israelite sanctuary-legend about Jerusalem, is preserved only in E and not in J; the reason for this may be that the temple tradition associated with David (2 Sam. 7, 24) and Solomon had ousted the earlier Canaanite local saga. The Yahwist combined the concept of the kingship and the people, including all its tribes and its traditions, with the overlapping concept of the tribal Yahweh-cult concerned with salvation-history. Thus he took up and carried forward that line of development which is most clearly visible in Samuel, and this suggests the conjecture that the formation and preservation of the Yahwistic book of traditions is to be sought amongst priests and prophets in Judah who stood in close relationship with the royal court and with the Yahweh-cult of the sacred ark which it adopted and elaborated.

Notwithstanding its nearness to popular traditions, the work of the Yahwist as seen from the viewpoint of the history of ideas belongs after all to the prophetic line in the development of the OT. For this work with its serious, theocentric conception and presentation of history is basically a witness to the living power of God, and this witness, so far as we can see, is the first to open up in OT literature those wide and deep perspectives in which the spirit of the prophets continued to meditate. The faith of Yahweh, with its theocentric attitude of mind and its belief in salvation-history, supplied the Yahwistic outlook on history with its far-flung and all-embracing framework into which it placed all that happened between creation and eschatology. In the light of this faith it arrives at a religious interpretation of the meaning of the rich and manifold cultural inheritance of the Early East which it brings into association with the most characteristic religious experiences of the Israelite people. This work is a witness to the transcending power of God who rules in nature (creation) and in history, and whose reality is recognized and experienced just as deeply in judgment as in mercy; it also presents the true state of man, and with a clear insight into the realities of life and with uncorruptible truthfulness it draws a picture of mankind with all its contradiction of sin and faithful obedience; and because of this, it has throughout the centuries again and again won recognition for the basic concepts of biblical revelation and salvation-history.

15. The Elohist strand

For the literature see at the head of section 10 and section 14; Procksch, *Das nordhebräische Sagenbuch*. *Die Elohimquelle*, 1906; Hölscher, 'Das Buch der Könige, seine Quellen und seine Redaktion', *Gunkelfestschrift* 1923, 158 ff.; Hellbardt, 'Der Elohist als selbständige Geschichtsquelle', ThBl 1933, col. 342 ff.;–Budde, *Deuteronomium* 33, 1922; Löhr, 'Deuteronomium 32', *Prot. Monatshefte* 1903, 1 ff.; Hauri, *Das Moselied*, Diss. 1917; Budde, *Das Lied des Moses*, 1920; Sellin, ZAW 1925, 161 ff. –Matthes, 'Der Dekalog', ZAW 1904, 17 ff.; H. Schmidt, 'Mose und der Dekalog', *Gunkelfestschrift*, 1923, 78 ff.; Mowinckel, *Le Décalogue*, 1927; Meinhold, *Der Dekalog*, 1927; L. Köhler, 'Der Dekalog', ThR 1929, 161 ff. (further literature there); Rowley, 'Moses and the Decalogue', BJRL 34 (1951); Eberharter, *Der Dekalog*, 1929; Volz, *Mose*,[2] 1932, 58 ff.; Alt, *Die Ursprünge des Israelitischen Rechts*, 1934=Alt I, 278 ff.; Stamm, *Der Dekalog im Lichte der neueren Forschung*, 1958; –Rothstein, *Das Bundesbuch und die religionsgeschichtliche Entwicklung Israels*, 1888; Baentsch, *Das Bundesbuch*, 1892; Nowack, 'Das Bundesbuch', BWAT 1927; Menes, 'Die vorexilischen Gesetze Israels', BZAW 1928; Pfeiffer, 'The Transmission of the Book of the Covenant', HThR, 1931, 99 ff.; Morgenstern, 'The Book of the Covenant', *Hebr. Union College Annual*, 1928, 1 ff.; 1930, 19 ff.; 1932, 1 ff.; Cazelles, *Études sur le Code de l'Alliance*, Paris, 1946; Mowinckel, 'The two sources of the Predeuteronomic Primeval History (JE) in Gen. 1–11', *Norske Videnskaps*. Academi i Oslo (II Histor. Filos. Kl., 1937, No. 2); Hölscher, *Die Anfänge der hebräischen Geschichtsschreibung*, 1942; Hölscher, *Geschichtsschreibung in Israel* (see Lit. section 9); Jepsen, *Zur Überlieferungsgeschichte der Vätergestalten* (see Lit. section 10); Eissfeldt, 'Die Umrahmung des Moseliedes Deut, 32 : 1–42 und des Mosegesetzes Deut. 1–30 in Deut. 31 : 9–32 : 42', *Wiss. Ztschr. d. Martin-Luther-Univ. Halle-Wittenberg*, Ges. Sprachwiss. Jg. 4, vol. 3 (1955); 411–418; idem, Berichte über die Verhandlungen der sächs. Akad. d. Wissensch. zu Leipzig. Phil.-hist. Kl. B. vol. 104 Part No. 5, (1958) pp. 5–25.

The problem of the 'Elohist' presents to start with greater difficulties than that of the Yahwist, because the Elohist strand is not preserved to the same extent and also not in the same degree of completeness as that of the Yahwist (see below). This, so it seems to me, has eased the recent doubts thrown by Volz and Rudolph on the independence of E. Yet in spite of some legitimate objections raised by them to the method used by literary criticism in segregating E, the fact of the former existence of an independent Elohist strand can hardly be contested. The passages generally assigned to the Elohist strand on the basis of doublets, contradictions, etc., are marked out as belonging together, not only by a definite coherence with each other, but also by language, style, by a world of ideas and conceptions possessing the same aims, as well as by the homogeneity of a characteristic inner design. Consequently, although they are closely linked with J passages in the present composition of the Pentateuch, they are not to be esteemed as redactional expansions of J, but as traces of a special strand, and these justify us in speaking on the analogy of J of an independent Elohist strand which gives an individual intellectual aspect and stamp to the tradition held by them in many respects in common, but which makes use as well of matters separately transmitted.

The following passages are usually assigned to the stock of the E strand which is still preserved: Gen. 15^x (J); $20–21^x$ (J); 22^x (J); 24^x (J); 27^x (JP); 28: 10–12, 17–22; $29–34^x$ (J); 35^x (P); 36^x (JP); 37^x (JP); 39^x (J); $40–42^x$ (J); 45^x (J); 46^x (JP); 48^x (JP); 50^x (JP);

Exod. 1^x (JP); $2–5^x$ (JP); $7–10^x$ (JP); 11: 1–3; 12^x (JP); $13–14^x$ (J); 15: 20 f.; 16^x (JP); 17–18; 19^x (J); (20: 22–23: 19=Book of the Covenant); $23–24^x$ (JP); 32^x (J); 33^x (J);

Num. 10^x (JP); 11^x (J); 12; $13–14^x$ (JP); 16^x (JP); $20–21^x$ (JP); $22–24^x$ (J); 25: 1–5^x (J); 32^x (JP);

Deut. 31: 14 ff.; 32; 33; 34^x (JDP).

As regards E's linguistic usages, although in some passages we must allow for later revision, we find *inter alia* in E that '*elōhîm* or *hā* '*elōhîm* is used to designate God in the pre-Mosaic period, i.e. up to Exod 3; also that the inhabitants of Palestine are called Amorites, the mountain of God Horeb (disputed by Noth, *Überlieferungsgeschichtliche Studien I*, 29, note 4; for further information see Steuernagel, *Einl. in das AT*, 214 f.). A survey of the passages belonging to E shows that the E strand, as it is in our hands today, runs parallel to the Yahwist strand as regards its plan, and was, therefore, probably tied to a traditional form, such as we have in the Yahwist work. We can understand this at once when we consider the care given to the tradition of salvation-history in the cult, from which it was neither possible nor was it intended to break away. Yet, on the other hand, within these limits we can note in E a very high degree of independence which had been developed regarding the manner of presenting the tradition. The question must be considered whether there was in E any primeval history, and if so, how far it is still preserved (Dillmann, Mowinckel, Hölscher, see above, p. 103). There is the further question whether the fact that E, unlike J, knew that the patriarchs worshipped strange gods (Jos. 24: 2 ff.) entitles us to draw conclusions about his manner of presentation; which in other respects also is opposed to paganism more definitely than that of J (cf. Gen. 35: 2 ff. E with 31: 19 J) and thus reveals a relationship with the stock of ideas of the sacral tribal union. E lacks the specifically Judean traditions; there is no mention of the Lot–Sodom circle, of Abraham in Hebron, of the story in Gen. 38 about Judah. The figure of Abraham withdraws and so Jacob advances more into the foreground. Greater interest is shown by E in the cultic traditions of the local sanctuaries, especially of Bethel and Shechem, where he uses earlier and more precise traditions than J (cf. also Exod. 17: 15; 18: 12) as he does also in the story of Joseph (König and Jepsen). The person of Moses, too, in addition to the fact that to him for the first time the name of Yahweh was revealed (Exod. 3), is brought out more prominently and the tradition about him is supplied with fuller detail than J (e.g. Exod. 2); Moses as the intermediary of God at the deliverance from Egypt and at the Red Sea is characterized more clearly than in J (Exod. 3; cf. Exod. 14: 21a, 26 f. E with 14: 21 b, 27 b J). His pre-eminent position is underlined particularly in E in Exod. 11: 3; 14: 21a, 31; 33: 11; Num. 12: 6; and the fact that the oracles concerning the tribes are placed in the mouth of the dying Moses (Deut. 33) (in J in Gen. 49 in that of Jacob) points in the same direction. Further it is to be remarked that E seems to stand in a closer relationship to the prophetic movement. In Gen. 20: 7 Abraham is already described as a prophet and entrusted with the prophetic function of intercession (Gen. 20: 7 ff.). It is Moses especially who is considered by E to be a prophet, inspired

E

by Yahweh and endowed with power (Exod. 4: 21; Deut. 34: 10 ff.); in Exod. 32 and Num. 21: 4 ff. he is the great intercessor; in Num. 12: 6 ff. (Exod. 33: 11; Deut. 34: 10) he is even raised above all prophets. The thoughts on the prophets in Num. 12 and the wish expressed in Num. 11: 25 ff. in connexion with the endowment of the spirit and the ecstatic state of the seventy elders that all the people might be prophets, shows clearly this positive interest in and the close relationship of E to the prophetic movement.

It is in this context that his own *characteristic theological* views must be understood. A certain tendency towards making his conception of God less material and more spiritual is to be observed. God is imagined as mainly in heaven and having intercourse with man through intermediaries (angels) (Gen. 28: 12; 31: 11), as revealing himself at night in dreams and visions (Gen. 20: 3, 6; 21: 12; 28: 12; 46: 2 and *passim*); thus he is withdrawn from the material sphere. By these means and by reducing the anthropomorphisms the distance between God and man is emphasized more strongly. Parallel with this, the wonders of God are raised to the miraculous in order to give expression to the supernatural power of God. Whilst in J, direct religious intuition receives a literary form, in E theological reflexion predominates. As regards the narrative, this means a falling away from the realistic closeness to life and the fresh vividness which distinguishes the Yahwist strand into an occasionally ponderous theological rationality. The same difference is to be observed in the matter of anthropology in which E is more interested than J. A more delicate ethical feeling reveals itself in the effort to present the patriarchs as models. This often gives E's description a certain air of exhortation (cf. Gen. 20: 12 E with 12: 10 ff.; 26: 7 f. J; 30: 37 ff. J with 31: 5 ff. E). The faith of Abraham (Gen. 15: 6), his sympathy for the banished maid (Gen. 21: 11–14; cf. the contrast in 16: 6 J) and the deeply moving, masterly account of the patriarch, prepared with unexpressed sorrow for the ultimate sacrifice (Gen. 22), may serve to illustrate E's special feeling for the human side of his characters. Another consequence of his theological reflexions in this sphere is the exclusiveness with which Israel and the heathen are separated from each other. In the Elohist strand the coming to terms with the traditions of the foreign religions often took a

different form than it did in J, although the sources of both of
them sprang from the same cultic soil. In this matter the altered
historical situation and the political aspect of the cult in the
Northern Kingdom, as contrasted with that of the South, makes
itself felt. Foreign gods are rejected and thrust aside (Gen. 35: 2,
cf. 31: 19; Jos. 24: 14 ff., see above); their worship is condemned
as apostasy (Exod. 32; Num. 25: 1 ff.); the tendency to avoid
human sacrifice in Gen. 22 is in the same line of thought. This
absolute declaration of war is not, indeed, extended to the sacred
pillars (Gen. 28: 18; Exod. 24: 4). Yet E has a tendency to divest
them of their cultic character: in Gen. 28 the pillar is a memorial
stone; in Gen. 35: 1 only the altar at Bethel is mentioned; in
Gen. 35: 20 it is a question of Rachel's grave; in Exod. 24: 4 the
pillars are transformed into symbols for the twelve tribes. This
process shows clearly the absorptive power of the Yahweh
religion of the union of the twelve tribes, a power which it derives
from the concerns of the cult. The theological ideology combined
with the exclusiveness of the united religious and ethical demand
of God can be grasped most clearly in the sentence in Exod. 19: 6
announcing a programme: 'Ye shall be unto me a kingdom of
priests, and an holy nation'. The sacral and anthropological side
of the idea of election is outlined and the national interests are
merged completely in the religious demand. Thus the way is
prepared for the conception of the 'people of Israel' which plays
an important part in Deuteronomic thought. For the roots of this,
too, are in the sacral union and the covenant cult of 'Israel', the
union of the tribes, which can still be recognized by its terminology. In general we can observe in E an inclination to systematize
what has happened outwardly and inwardly. We are conscious of
an attempt to divide up the history of salvation into separate
epochs by means of the use of different names for God in the
periods before and after Moses, as well as in the retrospect on
salvation-history (Jos. 24). In some passages there is a marked
effort to look at history from the viewpoint of God's judgment
on human guilt (Gen. 15: 16; Exod. 32: 34), as in Gen. 20 which
differs from its counterparts in J (12, 26) in that E pursues the
problem of 'Guilt and Fate' and reflects on the question of
theodicy.

In this connexion pessimism has been attributed to E, but perhaps not quite rightly; for it is nothing other than the thought of judgment, which is also rooted in the Israelite festival cult of the covenant and which, taken up, developed and deepened by the prophets, is used here as the basis from which to interpret history. Yet the seriousness with which the prophets regard history has fundamentally nothing to do with pessimism. The fact that von Rad, without going into details, considers it the peculiarity of the Elohist, as compared with J, to be 'more popular' and less concerned with theological problems, is connected in part with his over-estimate of the Yahwist's own theological achievement.

On the other hand, it is noticeable that especially in the case of Ephraimite traditions E often enters more into details, brings in, so to speak, learned notes (Gen. 35: 8, 19; 31: 20, 24; Exod. 1: 11; 13: 18) and to a much greater extent than J refers to earlier literary sources, so that we sometimes receive the impression of greater historical accuracy (cf. e.g. Exod. 17: 14). We may mention in this connexion the most important separate literary passages taken up into the E strand:

(a) *Miriam's Song of the Sea* in Exod. 15: 21, a short hymn to Yahweh, the deliverer at the Red Sea, probably sung antiphonally; it is likely that it was near in time to the event it celebrated and was transmitted in association with the festival liturgy (see above, p. 106).

(b) *The oath at the throne* (?) *of Yahweh* in Exod. 17: 16: 'there is a hand against the throne (?) of Yahweh, Yahweh will have war with Amalek from generation to generation!'

(c) The *ark oracles* in Num. 10: 35 f., spoken according to the present context when the sacred ark set out and when it rested. But probably they were originally parts of the liturgy from the earliest cult of the ark, associated with the tradition of theophany (cf. Torczyner, *Die Bundeslade*, 1930, 7 ff.) and used in the holy wars of the tribal union. They appear to have been handed down amongst the priests of the ark.

(d) *The quotation from the book of the Wars of Yahweh* in Num. 21: 14 f. a fragment of an early description of the country, which is meant to prove that the Arnon was once the boundary between the Moabites and the Ammonites.

(e) The *Song of the Well*, Num. 21: 17 f., a secular working song, see above p. 27.

(f) The *taunt-song* against Sihon, king of the Amorites, in Num. 21: 27–30, which perhaps grew out of an Amorite song of victory; Noth, in ZAW 1940–41, 107 ff. considers it to be originally an Israelite song of victory against the domination of the city of Heshbon.

(g) In the above passages E has made use of early poetic material peculiar to itself, some of which only fits with difficulty into the context of his account (Mowinckel conjectures that these and other poetic passages are fragments of a Judean national epic of which the Elohist has made use). In the *saga of Balaam* he has replaced the old oracles handed down to us by J, with other poems adapted to the tale itself (Num. 23: 7–10, 18–24), which celebrate the exclusiveness and individuality of Israel as contrasted with the heathen (Num. 23: 9, 23) and the rule of Yahweh as king (Num. 23: 21 f.) instead of the kingship of David (thus J Num. 24: 7, 18 f.) a clear proof that these are based on other times and circumstances, but yet that the connexion with the tradition of the festival cult of Yahweh is still being maintained (thus also Bentzen).

(h) In the *Blessing of Moses* in Deut. 33, unlike the parallel passage in Gen. 49, the old liturgical framework is still preserved which enables the *Sitz im Leben* of the song to be recognized, namely the assembly of the tribes of Israel for the celebration of Yahweh's theophany when he enters upon his dominion as king over his people (verse 4 f.). We must think of this recurring regularly as a remembrance and cultic repetition of the events in the Mosaic period which culminated in the sacral covenant-making. Of course the poem was not composed by Moses; the tribes are settled in Palestine, verses 7, 12, 22 f.; and what is true for Gen. 49 is true also for Deut. 33, namely that the individual oracles are earlier than the whole. In general the conditions assumed in Deut. 33 seem to be later than those in Gen. 49. Simeon (cf. Gen. 49: 5 ff.) has lost its independence, so that there is no longer any question of it as a separate tribe. Levi exists no more as a secular tribe; it has only spiritual functions in the Blessing of Moses. In the saying concerning Judah it is not made clear whether Judah's wish 'to return to his people' is to be understood as thinking of the time before the kingdom or after its disruption. The formulation as well as the lack of any mention of the Davidic kingship and the exuberant praise of Joseph probably point to a Northern-Israelite origin. Contrasted with the underlying coarse, heroic-warlike temper of Gen. 49, Deut. 33 is more strongly imbued in general with a religious strain and with the more peaceful ideal of ownership in rest and security, also no doubt a sign of a relatively later age. No certainty can be reached with regard to determining an absolute date for the song. Some suggest the time of the judges, others the age of Jeroboam II (eighth century); at any rate the collection was made before the fall of Israel in 721.

(i) Here we must mention also the *Song of Moses*, Deut. 32: 1–43, which, owing to the poetic force of its language, was thought worthy of a Moses, but owing to its looking back on the period of Moses as long past (verse 7) and on the attitude of the people after they were settled in Canaan, cannot have originated with him. Budde considers the song to be a sort of double of Moses' Blessing interpolated later to replace it. It is almost universally regarded as a secondary interpolation which betrays its post-exilic origin by certain reminiscences of prophetic trains of thought (e.g. Is. 63: 7–65: 25). The allusion in it to 'those which are not a people' in verse 21 whom Yahweh appointed to be a punishment for Israel's apostasy to 'those who are no gods', but whom he himself will punish later, is thought to refer to the mixed population of the Samaritans (Sellin) and the vine of Sodom and Gomorrah (verse 32) to the Moabites and Ammonites. Nevertheless, since the exile is not mentioned as the obvious punishment of Yahweh and, as Eissfeldt has shown, since the passages placed as an introduction and a conclusion to the song (31: 9 ff.; 32: 45 ff.) indicate that it will be replaced by the 'law', it is natural to suppose that it was originally transmitted within the framework of the E strand and is to be explained as a product of pre-exilic times. It presupposes the circumstances of a divine service (verses 3, 7, 15, 43) and moves in cultic forms and prophetic ideas which contemplate salvation-history in hortatory fashion in the stereotyped sequence of Yahweh's deeds of salvation, namely, Israel's apostasy, God's judgment and the promise of his mercy by which he procures absolution and justice for his people and takes vengeance on his enemies. Presumably the song which might be imagined as spoken by a cultic prophet is based on a scheme of preaching followed at divine service, the elements of which have been preserved right up to the rules of the sect of Qumran. The basic key-note, echoed in the hymn-like context of the song, emphasizes in a concentrated form the strength of the theological interpretation of history. It is for the sake of himself that God acts in history which in its many forms of judgment and salvation makes manifest the power and divinity of himself alone (verses 27, 39).

(k) The *Decalogue* in Exod. 20: 1–17 (cf. Deut. 5: 6–18). In the context of the E strand the Decalogue seems originally to have played the part of the record on the basis of which the covenant between Yahweh and Israel was concluded at Horeb in Exod. 24: 3 f. According to the present state of the text, which is due to the insertion of the 'Book of the Covenant', the latter took over this function. This was probably effected by 20: 18–21 being moved from its earlier position in front of the Decalogue to become the introduction to the Book of the Covenant. The association of legal ordinances with the historical tradition of the manifestations at Sinai has been preserved through all the strands of the Pentateuch; it evidently goes back to a sacral tradition cherished no doubt since early days in the cult of Yahweh (see section 13). The introduction to the Decalogue also presupposes this connexion between historical manifestation and God's demand. By comparing the apodictic form of the commandments with similar structures of law handed down in the OT, Alt has made it probable that the Decalogue and similar legal corpora are the embodiment of a genuinely Israelite shaping of its laws which had its place in Israel's life (*Sitz im Leben*) as the unconditional demand of God in the regular sacral recital of the law in the presence of the religious community of the people. Moreover, Alt, by inferring that Deut. 31: 9 ff., applied to earlier times, sees the sacral recital of the law as the point at which the tradition of the summary of the divine demand was regularly kept alive. This happened every seven years when the renewal of the covenant at the national shrine of Yahweh (in the time before the kingdom this may have been held at Shechem, Shiloh or Gilgal) was celebrated at the feast of tabernacles in the presence of the whole congregation of the people. In this context, in view of the revelation of God's name and nature declared in the introduction to the Decalogue, the fact that the commandments are formulated in the indicative probably points to the corresponding description out of God's mouth of the nature of the people of God, who are marked off by the negative forms of the commandment from their heathen neighbours.

As regards its shape, the Decalogue represents a collection of fundamental demands, both religious and ethical, designed for learning by heart (ten in number!) and formulated as comprehensively as possible. The present form of the ten commandments still shows clearly the traces of changes to which its wording has been subjected in the course of history. The reason given for the commandment about the sabbath presumes knowledge of P's story of the creation in Gen. 1 and is, therefore, hardly conceivable before the exile. The traces of sermon-like amplifications in Exod. 20 as in Deut. 5, as well as the existence of a two-fold form of transmission diverging from each other at several points, indicate that the tradition changed its shape actively right up to later times. Moreover, the fact that the commandments concerning the sabbath and parents are stated as a positive command in contrast to the other negative prohibitions, shows that the wording of the Decalogue has had its history, and indeed nothing else can be expected from its use in the framework of the sacral recital of the laws. It seems, too, that we must think of the striving after the most comprehensive and general statement of the demands discernible in the Decalogue as compared with similar legal material (Exod. 21: 12 ff.; Deut. 27: 15 ff.) as a later stage in the development of this type rather than as its beginning.

It is with these considerations in mind that the question of the *Mosaic origin* of the Decalogue must be discussed. As its present form represents merely the result of a long history of the tradition, the question concerning the Mosaic derivation can have a meaning only in the sense of asking whether the individual demands of the ten commandments are possible in the conditions of Moses' time. For a scientific proof, that the decalogue *must* have originated with Moses, cannot be produced with our present methods of ascertaining the truth. We must not reject out of hand the possibility that these demands may reach back into the period in the desert. The fact that the apodictic form of the law sprang from the genuinely Israelite cult of Yahweh seems to me to have been firmly established by Alt. From there the lines of legal development may go back to the historic roots of the Yahweh religion of Israel and its first organizational form. That there were images of gods or of Yahweh in Israel later on is no argument against the existence of a prohibition of images. If we fail to observe the effects of the ten commandments in the life of the post-Mosaic period, we must not generalize this objection in one direction only and lose sight of the development of the Israelite religion under the influence of the neighbouring religions. As a matter of fact in the daily life of the Israelite peasant other forms of religion persisted beside the Yahweh-cult of the sacral union of the tribes. In the long run the saying holds good here too: *abusus non tollit usum*. That the sabbath could not be kept in the desert is a postulate which cannot be verified. The opinion that in the ten commandments a settled life in Palestine is presupposed, applies in part only to later additions (strangers, gates); the designation *bêt* does not necessarily mean a fixed dwelling-house, but can be the name for a 'tent' or 'the property of the family'.

Nevertheless the main question is not the Mosaic origin of the Decalogue. More important is it to recognize that the tendency visible in the Decalogue as compared with other series of laws to thrust aside the purely legal tenets in favour of a more comprehensive religious and moral content has given just to this collection of commandments its universal historical significance.*

(1) The *Book of the Covenant* in Exod. 20: 22–23: 33. It derives its name from its present literary connexion with Exod. 24: 7, but this is secondary. Originally the 'record of the covenant' probably meant the Decalogue. It is not certain what position in the Elohist strand was formerly occupied by the Book of the Covenant. The most likely conjecture is that it was fitted in after Jos. 24. In Jos. 24: 25 it is recorded that Joshua gave the people in Shechem 'a statute and an ordinance' and wrote 'these words in the book of the law of God'. In that case the Book of the Covenant would have been in E's scheme that record of the law which was connected with the making of the covenant in Shechem. When the Pentateuch was later worked into a unity (perhaps when Deuteronomy was inserted) it was dislodged from its original position and attached to the Sinai-narrative. Rost, who also underlines the relation of the Book of the Covenant to the

* For the literature and discussion about the Decalogue see the recent book by Rowley, *Moses and the Decalogue*.

Shechem tradition, suggests its former position to have been in front of the section of Deut. 27: 2–8, which he assigns to E; he thinks it was displaced from there later by Deut. 12–26.

As regards its contents the Book of the Covenant is a collection of heterogeneous ordinances which did not all stem from the same root. A short introduction in Exod. 20: 22 is followed by cultic rules about images of God and altar building in Exod. 20: 23–26; the passage of 21: 1–22: 16 is supplied with a special title and is a collection, no longer completely preserved, of legal statutes, mainly (except for 21: 12–16) in the 'if' style of case-law, which deal with the law about persons and things, about slaves and homicide, personal injuries, damage to cattle, and about fields and marriage law. In 22: 17–23: 19 several cultic and moral requirements are put together, amongst which we may emphasize especially in Exod. 22: 20–27 humanitarian rules for the protection of those in need of help, in Exod. 23: 4 f. commands to love your enemy, in 23: 1–3, 6–9 right behaviour in legal matters, as well as cultic ordinances about rest from work, agricultural feasts and sacrifices in 23: 10–19. In conclusion in 23: 20–33 warnings are given with divine promises in the case of obedience.

The ordinances gathered together here are multifarious and their apparently variegated arrangement, like a patchwork, does not reveal any orderly principle based on their subject matter. This has led to the literary homogeneity of the whole being disputed and its being regarded, apart from secondary amplification, as the more or less accidental construction of the redactor. Merx has vigorously upheld the literary unity of the Book of the Covenant as being carefully and systematically thought out. He is probably correct, if we consider the analogy of other legal corpora, such as Deuteronomy and the law of Holiness, which are composed in similar fashion. Beer, *Exoduskommentar*, p. 125 wishes to see in the Book of the Covenant an instruction to reform the law. In any case, we must bear in mind that the impression given by its manifold variety is due, in part, to the different roots out of which the Israelite law was formed and the ordinances of the Book of the Covenant have grown. The case-law has been taken over from Canaanite law. This is what explains the striking relationship of certain parts of the Book of the Covenant, as regards the legal material and its arrangement, to the Code of

Hammurabi and Assyrian, Sumerian and Hittite laws. This does not mean literary dependence, but that Israel took over Canaanite legal forms and customs in Palestine, and that these for their part were probably introduced from the cultural stock of Mesopotamia through the alien ruler-class in the Canaanite city states into Western Asia where they experienced a partial further development of their own. The apodictically formulated legal precepts of the Book of the Covenant go back as regards their form to the genuinely Israelite sacral embodiment of the law which has therefore a more definitely religious and ethical impress, and its roots may reach back into the beginnings of the history of the Israelite people. We can observe already in the Book of the Covenant that the independent Israelite law reaches out beyond the sacral sphere and appropriates the secular legal sphere of Canaanite law. The history of the types confirms this by the mixed forms. Consequently a certain development since the conquest must be presumed for this process of absorption of alien law by Israel. The period when the Book of the Covenant came into being can, therefore, hardly be fixed before the time of the judges. The attempts to regard it as the legal precipitate of the reaction from Jehu's revolution (Menes), or to bring it into connexion because of the commandment about the altar with the Rechabite reaction or with the circles round Elisha (Morgenstern) imputes to it trends which on the whole are not to be found in it. Nor can any convincing conclusions as to its origin in the seventh century be drawn from its secondary literary position (Eissfeldt). The majority of the ordinances point to an earlier age and it contains no precept which would need to be dated so late. Noth in *Die Gesetze im Pentateuch*, p. 75, sees in the combined religious and moral prohibitions in the Book of the Covenant the original basic material, namely a compilation of the Amphictyonic law. Later further different collections of legal maxims in force in the region of the union of the twelve tribes were associated with them and those which were formulated as case-law were derived from the world of culture of the Canaanite city states. The Book of the Covenant is a proof that Israel had come to terms with Canaanite civilization and had permeated it in early days with its own religious and ethical forces. The most likely seat of the tradition is to be sought in one of the national sanctuaries. This association would also provide the reason for its admission into the Elohist strand.

By general agreement the Northern Kingdom is to be regarded as the *home* of the Elohist tradition. Only Smend and Hölscher who thinks that E came to birth in the exile, support a Judean origin, which has recently been advocated also by Noth. But apart from the observations already made above in the description of the characteristics of E, the preference for Joseph in the Mosaic blessing and the naming of the ancestral graves in the Northern Kingdom (Deborah in Gen. 35: 8; Rachel in 35: 16 ff.; Joseph in Jos. 24: 32; Joshua in Jos. 24: 30, 33) as well as the omission of certain Judean traditions point to an origin in the Israelite Northern Kingdom. The silence concerning Hebron and the transference of Abraham to Beer-sheba (Gen. 21: 22 ff.) must be interpreted as an attack on the Judean sanctuary at Hebron. In those passages in which traditions from the Southern Kingdom have been used (Gen. 22, oracles of Balaam) the features indicating its place of origin have probably been intentionally effaced. The traditions about Beer-sheba in E most likely go back to the connexions of the Northern Kingdom with this place (see Am. 5: 5; 8: 14).

In order to ascertain the *period* when the Elohist strand came into being, we must take into account its relation to the prophetic circles and their way of thinking as well as the allusions to the situation as regards the government of the Northern Israelite Kingdom (Gen. 37: 8; Deut. 33: 7; Num. 23: 21). The defeat of the Aramaeans seems to lie in the past, the nation is enjoying a certain amount of peace and security, and the Assyrian danger does not yet appear threatening. That would suggest the age of Jeroboam II in the middle of the eighth century; but perhaps we must allow for an even earlier origin. Consequently the Elohist strand was the book of the Northern Israelite tradition, which came into existence at the time of the independent development of the cult at the national shrines of the Northern Kingdom (cf. 1 Kgs. 12: 26 ff.); for this had become necessary on the disruption of the kingdom so as to counteract the cult at Jerusalem and its tradition. The same explanation accounts for its running parallel with J, which arose from its adoption of the common tradition, shared up till then, and also for the differences due to the contrast between north and south and to its somewhat lengthy history in the Northern Kingdom. In that kingdom, as we can see from the stories of Elijah and Elisha, the prophetic movement was the influential bearer of the Yahweh tradition of the national religion and so it is just in this soil that the relationship of the E-tradition to prophecy can be most readily understood. Accordingly in the history of ideas the Elohist source stands on the line separating Elijah on the one side from Amos and Hosea on the other. We cannot yet identify any direct influence of the latter.

The fact that, after the catastrophe of 721, the Northern Israelite production continued to be handed down by Judean hands (perhaps amongst the prophets) and was incorporated into the Yahwist tradition, no doubt resulted in manifold alterations and probably also in abridgements of the E material; so the present condition of its tradition is no longer able to provide us with a faithful picture of its original form. It is not possible to ascertain exactly whether, and for how long, the E tradition still had a separate existence beside J in the Southern Kingdom also. At any rate we must guard against too mechanical a conception of the redactor's work; it probably stands in close connexion with the practical use of the tradition in the cult and appears to have been a process of absorption continuing for a longer period. The customary sign for this, RJ[e], designates not so much a literary personality, as the summing up of different processes which have led finally to the form now before us in the combination we have today. The Elohist tradition is significant also because in the course of its use in divine service it was developed further in the direction of a hortatory sermon-like shape which represents the bridge between E and the Deuteronomic tradition of history.

16. Deuteronomy

Commentaries: (see literature, head of section 9).–Steuernagel, *Der Rahmen des Deuteronomiums*, 1894; idem, *Die Entstehung des deuteronomischen Gesetzes*, 1895, [2]1901; Stärk, *Das Deuteronomium*, 1894; Puukko, 'Das Deuteronomium', BWAT 1910; Hempel, *Die Schichten des Deuteronomiums*, 1914; König, *Das Deuteronomium*, 1917; Kegel, *Die Kultusreform des Josia*, 1919; Hölscher, 'Das Buch der Könige, seine Quellen und seine Redaktion', *Gunkelfestschrift* 1923, 158 ff.; idem, 'Komposition und Ursprung des Deuteronomiums', ZAW 1922, 161 ff.; Oestreicher, 'Das deuteronomische Grundgesetz', *Beitr. z. Förderung christl. Theologie*, 1923; Horst, 'Die Kultusreform des Königs Josia', ZDMG 1923, 220 ff.; Stärk, Das Problem des Deuteronomiums, *Beitr. z. Förderung christl. Theologie*, 1924; Gressman, 'Josia und das Deuteronomium', ZAW 1924, 313 ff.; König, 'Stimmen Ex. 20 : 24 und Dt. 12 : 12 f. zusammen?' op. cit., 337 ff.; Budde, 'Das Deuteronomium und die Reform

König Josias', ZAW 1926, 177 ff.; Bentzen, *Die josianische Reform und ihre Voraussetzungen*, 1926; Procksch, 'König Josia', *Zahnfestgabe* 1928, 19 ff.; Baumgartner, 'Der Kampf um das Deuteronomium', ThR 1929, 7 ff. (more literature there); v. Rad, 'Das Gottesvolk im Deuteronomium', BWAT 1929; Horst, *Das Privilegrecht Jahwes*, 1930; Östreicher, 'Reichstempel und Ortsheiligtümer in Israel', *Beitr. z. Förderung christl. Theologie*, 1930; Welch, *Deuteronomy*, 1932; Breit, *Die Predigt des Deuteronomisten*, 1933; Dornseiff, ZAW 1938, 64 ff.; v. Rad, *Das formgeschichtliche Problem des Hexateuchs*, 1938, 23 ff.; Noth, *Die Gesetz im Pentateuch*, 1940, 28 ff., 34 ff.; Hospers, 'De numeruswisseling in het boeck Deuteronomium', *Diss. Utrecht*, 1942; v. Rad, *Deuteronomium-Studien*, ²1948; Alt, *Die Heimat des Deuteronomiums*, Alt II, 250 ff.

The name 'Deuteronomy' for the 5th Book of Moses goes back to a misunderstanding of Deut. 17: 18, where the LXX reproduces the words *mishnēh hattôrāh* (beside the customary title [*'ēlleh*] *dᶜbārîm* current for Deuteronomy in Jewry also) designating a 'copy' of the law as δευτερονόμιον (a reiteration of the law). Compared with the other sources of the Pentateuch, Deuteronomy shows itself to be a great independent literary work. Its style and use of language, its ideology and the fact that its design is relatively complete in itself distinguish the work clearly from the rest of the strands in the Pentateuch. The peculiarity of the language in Deuteronomy shows itself not so much in the special use of individual words as in the combination of words into formal phrases, and in a pleonastic, impressive breadth of style, to suit the hortatory intention of the author, e.g. 'the place which Yahweh shall choose to put his name there' (12: 5, 11, 21; 14: 23, 24 and *passim*); or 'with all thy heart and with all thy soul' (4: 29; 6: 5; 10: 12; 11: 13; 13: 4 and *passim*). (For further details see the statistics of the language in Steuernagel's Commentary, pp. 41 ff.). All thought is concentrated on the one and only worship of Yahweh, on the forcefulness of the demand for faithfulness and obedience to God, for which the motive is gratitude and love in return for the faithfulness and love of Yahweh for his people manifest in their history. This draws the whole together from within in the same way as does the external design, namely the homogeneity of the situation before Moses' death which encircles all Deuteronomy· and stamps it as the legacy of the dying Moses. The *substance*, chapters 12–26, which contains the 'statutes and the judgments' of the Moab covenant, is surrounded by the *frame*: chapters 1–11, the introductory speeches as a preparation for the legislation with exhortations to observe the commandments and singling out individual demands; chapters 27–30 looking back on the law, with indications of the consequences that obedience will bring with them. Apart from the historical appendix, chapters 31–34, in which traces of the other Pentateuchal sources recur again, Deuteronomy is a unity which taken as a whole is complete in itself and requires separate consideration.

This character of its own is evident when compared with the rest of the Pentateuchal sources, and is connected with *its origin*. The tradition of Mosaic authorship must be rejected for Deuteronomy, for the reasons already discussed concerning the authorship of the Pentateuch as a whole. To this must be added the fact that Deuteronomy assumes the E tradition to be known and also shows itself to be later than individual legal ordinances of the Book of the Covenant (cf. e.g. Deut. 15: 12 ff. with Exod. 21: 2–11; for further details see Bertholet's *Commentary*, pp. XIV f.). For the question of the origin of Deuteronomy the connexion between it and the reform of Josiah is of particular importance. Already Chrysostom, Jerome and Athanasius recognized that it was connected with the law-book on which Josiah's reform was based. After Lessing had pointed incidentally to the identity between Josiah's legal reformation and the chief subjects in Deuteronomy 'which contain the second law', De Wette (*Dissertatio critica*, 1805) advanced the scientific thesis that Deuteronomy was a later work differing from the earlier books of the Pentateuch and originating during the period of its discovery in 621 B.C. In spite of its being frequently disputed, and especially vigorously in recent times, this thesis has won almost universal recognition. The reasons for the connexion between Deuteronomy and the legal reformation of Josiah are convincing: according to the account of the reforms (2 Kgs. 22 f.) which is on the whole reliable. Josiah, acting on the basis of the law-book found in the temple by Hilkiah, the high priest, abolished all sanctuaries outside the temple in Jerusalem, cleansed the temple itself of all foreign cults and transferred to the temple the celebration of the passover, which up till then had been kept in the family circle. Amongst all the collections of laws which we have in the OT, Deuteronomy is the only one which sets up as requirements those things which were carried out in Josiah's reforms (for the centralization of the worship in 2 Kgs. 23: 8 f., 19 cf. Deut. 12: 13 ff.; for the abolition of sun-worship in 2 Kgs. 23: 11 f. cf. Deut. 17: 3; for the removal of the houses of the Sodomites in 2 Kgs. 23: 7 cf.

Deut. 23: 18; for the extirpation of those who exorcized the dead in 2 Kgs. 23: 24 cf. Deut. 18: 11 ff.; for the prohibition to sacrifice children in 2 Kgs. 23: 10 cf. Deut. 18:10; for the celebration of the Passover in 2 Kgs. 23: 21 ff. see Deut. 16: 1–8). In face of these fundamental agreements between Josiah's law-reforms and Deuteronomy, the difference between 2 Kgs. 23: 8 f. according to which the priests of the high places were assigned a subordinate place under the priests of Jerusalem and the requirement in Deut. 18: 6 ff. to give the priests of the high places the same privileges as their colleagues had in Jerusalem, cannot be used as counter-evidence, since probably the execution of this ordinance was frustrated by the—understandable—resistance of the temple priesthood. König and Budde have proved the impossibility of Oestreicher's attempt to deny that Josiah's reform and Deuteronomy were concerned with centralizing the worship and to place the date of Deuteronomy much earlier (similarly Sanda, *Komm. z.d. Königsbüchern*). The view, supported by Löhr, Welch and Dornseiff, that Deuteronomy is an older book going back in part to the time of the Judges and Moses or into the ninth century, is just as untenable in face of the agreements mentioned above as the opposite opinion set forth by Hölscher that Deuteronomy must be pronounced post-exilic owing to its utopian character (cf. for this last especially Gressmann, Budde and Noth). The connexions between Josiah's reform-law and Deuteronomy are of such a nature that the two do not only stand in a close relationship but are, to a certain extent, identical, or, as it is customary to formulate it, that Josiah's book of reforms was the 'original Deuteronomy'. Thus the Deuteronomy we have today has grown out of Josiah's law-book of reforms. This does not affect the fact that, as Oestreicher has rightly recognized, Josiah carried out certain reforms (2 Kgs. 23: 4, 6 ff., 11 f.) already before the Deuteronomic law-book was discovered.

It is generally admitted that Deuteronomy in its present state represents by comparison with the 'original Deuteronomy' a form expanded by revision and additions. The two introductory speeches, chapters 1–4 and 5–11, the differing final exhortations 30: 15–20; 32: 45–47, after 28: 69 had already preceded them with a closing colophon, the incorporation of the ceremony of blessing and curses on Gerizim and Ebal in 27: 11–13, 14–26, which is, perhaps, taken from the E tradition, beside passages which betray their secondary, i.e. exilic, origin, such as 4: 25–30, 14: 1–21, 28: 25–69; 30: 1–10, all these make it clear that the original Deuteronomy is separated from its present state by a long process of growth in its literary history which probably goes back to the historical development of the cult. Opinions diverge as to how this process is to be imagined. There are in the main two groups of questions involved. (1) What was the original Deuteronomy like? (2) How is the present condition of Deuteronomy in its relation to the original Deuteronomy to be explained?

(1) The attempts to peel the original Deuteronomy out of the present one fluctuate between two extremes. Either the original Deuteronomy has ascribed to it only that which is mentioned in the account of the reforms in 2 Kgs: 22 f.(Puukko), or only that is cut out which cannot be explained from the time of Josiah (Bertholet). Yet in this matter we must reflect that the short account of the reform, no longer transparently clear in everything, offers no sort of warrant that all the measures of reform were taken because of the original Deuteronomy and that all those required by it were mentioned in the account; besides, even if they were, it is not certain whether all its requirements were carried out at once. This at least seems to follow from the account of the reforms, that the original Deuteronomy must have included not only the legal kernel of chapters 12–26, but probably also introductory and concluding exhortations with blessings and curses, otherwise the terrifying effect of its reading on the king (2 Kgs. 22: 11, 19) would not be explained. The wording of the original Deuteronomy can no longer be reconstructed and all attempts in this direction are hypotheses. Out of the abundance of various proposals, we may mention that of Sellin who wants to recover the fundamental law of Josiah in the following passages: 4: 44, 46–49; 6: 4–15; 12: 13–27; 13: 2–19; 14: 22–29; 15: 1–26, 15; 28: 1–25; 30: 15–20. But Sellin allows for the possibility that some of this might only be the precipitate of Josiah's reform itself.

(2) The other question to be asked lays more weight on the critical analysis of the Deuteronomy of today from the literary point of view and seeks by this means to approach the relationship of the original Deuteronomy to the present one. Here two

groups of attempted solutions face each other. The one proceeds on a documentary hypothesis and wishes to think of Deuteronomy as the addition of two (or three: Steuernagel) different 'editions' (Kuenen, Wellhausen, Steuernagel, Stärk, Marti, Smend, Eissfeldt and others); the other explains the development of Deuteronomy by the way of a supplementary hypothesis, so that by additions and expansions which attached themselves to the original book in the course of history the final shape of Deuteronomy came into being (König, Hölscher, Sellin, Noth and others). The separation into continuous parallel lines according to the use of the singular and the plural in addressing Israel, such as Steuernagel and Stärk have attempted, runs into difficulties and in chapters 12–26 cannot be carried out at all. Since no cogent proof for the existence of parallel editions of Deuteronomy is produced, the formation of Deuteronomy out of the original one must be thought of more probably as the accretion of supplements within the framework of the oral, partly sermon-like recital at the festival cult of the covenant, in which above all the hortatory passages such as chapters 5–11 and probably also the historical retrospects in chapters 1–4 had their *Sitz*. In that case the passages with the singular form of address would be ascribed to the original Deuteronomy, whilst those formulated in the plural would be considered to be expansions. This growth of the Deuteronomic tradition goes on right up to the post-exilic period.

But when the relation between the original Deuteronomy and the present one has been elucidated, we have still not yet given an exhaustive answer to the Deuteronomic problem. Even the original Deuteronomy itself is by no means a creation at first hand, but goes back to older sources and stands in a broader traditional context. This question has been investigated above all by Hempel (and by Horst also for a part of the ordinances). Hempel believes that Deuteronomy arose out of a Rule of the Jerusalem temple revised with a view to the centralization of the worship, a Rule which had received various expansions partly from other sources. There is no doubt that Deuteronomy stands in a line of historical development, both ideological and literary, which reaches back even beyond the original one and is not without significance for understanding its formation and origin. We must mention first its relationship to the Elohist tradition and especially to the Book of the Covenant. That Deuteronomy depended on the Book of the Covenant can be observed in several passages: in Deut. 15: 12 ff. the regulation for setting free Hebrew slaves is taken partly verbatim from Exod. 21: 2 ff. The regulations about the cities of refuge in Deut. 19: 1–13 are probably to be considered as an expansion and modernization of the older and shorter regulations of Exod. 21: 22 ff. (cf. further Bertholet's *Commentary*, p. XIV f.); the agreements as regards subject-matter go so far that there was an inclination to regard Deuteronomy actually as an expanded edition of the Book of the Covenant (Kuenen, Wellhausen). Moreover, Eissfeldt (*Einl.* 264 ff.) has shown that Deuteronomy was conceived from the literary standpoint as a substitute for the Book of the Covenant with the intention of neutralizing it by including the old ordinances, and by shedding on them the light of a fresh insight from having only one place of worship. We may enlarge upon this comment by saying that Deuteronomy was intended to replace the Book of the Covenant, not only from the literary, but also from the cultic standpoint, when the law was read out at the feast of the renewal of the Covenant, and did in fact replace it. Von Rad, too, starting from form-historical considerations, has now rightly pointed to the cultic quality of the structure of Deuteronomy. The fact that Deuteronomy is traced back to Moses allows us also to conjecture that it was originally associated with the covenant-making at Sinai and was admitted for recital before the congregation of Yahweh at the feast of the renewal of this convent (cf. Deut. 31: 10 ff.). It is probably a consequence of its cultic and literary incorporation into the tradition of the Pentateuch that it is transferred to the end of the wanderings in the desert, as is presumed already in the earliest introductory speech (8: 2 ff.). The fact, too, that the whole of Deuteronomy is considered by the later commentators of Deut. 5 to be the exposition of the Decalogue, shows how tenaciously the connexion between Deuteronomy and the cultic tradition of the Sinai-covenant was preserved.

The relations of Deuteronomy to the *E tradition* probably have a similar explanation. The admission of the Decalogue, the remarkable dependence on the Elohist shaping of the tradition, with the special emphasis in the historical retrospect on what had been handed down from Moses, is probably due to the intention to give fresh weight and at the same time a fresh interpretation to and to throw a fresh light on the tradition of the sacral union of the twelve tribes, in whose cultic sphere Deuteronomy came into being and for which it was intended. The Elohist tradition with its fight against strange gods and heathen customs and with its hortatory view of history is carried on, but its interpretation is adapted to the new age and its spirit. The relationship, too, between Deuteronomy and *prophecy* observed at different times is accounted for in the same way. Serious consideration must therefore be given to the view that Deuteronomy is a 'restoration programme', originating after the overthrow of the Northern Kingdom in the circles there faithful to Yahweh. Alt supports this by the relationship of Deuteronomy to Hosea and by its attitude to the kingship. By what routes Deuteronomy then came to Jerusalem and was considered there significant enough to be deposited in the temple, can only be surmised for lack of the necessary information. Perhaps it was some of the Judean (cultic) prophets who, after the fall of the Northern Kingdom, were concerned to preserve and cherish the Elohist prophetic tradition received from there; they may have been interested in Deuteronomy because of its relations with the E tradition, and especially for its social and humane ethos and for the prophetic strain expressed in the promises and warnings. The *priestly* element and the concern of Deuteronomy for the cult is explained in this way without the necessity of declaring with Wellhausen, Bertholet, Budde and others that Deuteronomy is the result of a compromise between the priesthood and the prophetic movement. The cultic prophets and the country priests who were to a large extent like-minded with them (but not the temple-priesthood of Jerusalem, cf. Deut., 18: 6 ff.) appear to have been the supporters of that movement, which in the end, when the particular political situation in Josiah's time offered the occasion, led to the Deuteronomic reform.

But we must not overlook the combined *political and national* motives for the production of Deuteronomy which suggest that we must not relegate the production of the reforming book too far away from the reform itself, even if, as Noth has shown, Deuteronomy was not drawn up as a political law of the land and was not given recognition as such by Josiah. Many factors must be taken into consideration. They include Josiah's attempt to free himself from the rule of the declining Assyrian world-empire, to which cultic expression was given by abolishing the Assyrian worship of the stars, the endeavour to win over the Northern Kingdom by a Davidic Renaissance policy (cf. 2 Kgs. 23: 15 ff.) which can be detected in Deuteronomy also (Hempel, Welch), the self-consciousness and concentration on their own religious and national forces which bore fruit in the ideology of the tribal union, 'one God, one people, one cult', and in the centralization of its religious life, both as regards the Mosaic tradition and also with the cultic reorganization in view. All these factors enable us to recognize that Deuteronomy, together with the reform it strove to bring about, owes its origin and its effectiveness to the concurrence of long cherished forces in the sacral tradition of the union of the twelve tribes with the historical conjunction of circumstances in Josiah's policy. This provides an adequate explanation for the use of older and heterogeneous material in Deuteronomy as well as for the relatively harmonious manner by which they are combined with novel tendencies and perspectives. Von Rad has recently (*Deuteronomium-Studien*) on the basis of form-historical investigations thrown fresh light on Deuteronomy's double nature, the priestly and cultic and the national and warlike; he attributes to the prophetic spirit—in my opinion wrongly*—only the significance due to the general influences of the currents of the times; in this way he comes to the conclusion that Deuteronomy was produced by the 'country Levites' amongst the levies recruited from the land-owing rural population. Since the political and military catastrophe of the year 701 the conservatively inclined landed gentry had risen to fresh importance and fresh influence. Thus we may agree with von Rad so far as to place into this political and cultural context the restoration policy of Josiah who owed his accession to the throne to these very circles (2 Kgs. 21: 24) and also the tendency of Deuteronomy to secure recognition once again for the old covenant-religion of the tribal union.

The account of the discovery of Josiah's law-book (2 Kgs. 22 f.) does not conflict with these conclusions. In itself the brevity of the

* cf. also Fohrer, 'Die Hauptprobleme des Buches Ezechiel', BZAW 72 (1952), p. 165.

report of the discovery admits of different possibilities. The information that the law-book was 'found' in the temple may be interpreted by an Egyptian analogy, according to which a newly produced sacred book was said to have been 'found' in the temple at the feet of Thot, the revealer of books, thus providing divine authorization for the law-book produced immediately before it was brought in. If we do not wish to do this, we can accept the obvious explanation of the 'find' in the temple, without being obliged with Cornill, H. Schmidt and others, to suppose a priestly fraud for which the account gives no support. In that case the law-book seems to have been deposited in the temple according to a custom for which there is also evidence elsewhere in the OT (cf. 1 Sam. 10: 25; Deut. 31: 26; Is. 37: 14), to have been found there later in fact by Hilkiah and then to have been used as the basis of Josiah's policy of reform which was already probably in progress. We cannot learn anything more from 2 Kgs. 22 about the fate of the book in the period between its composition and its discovery; but if we assume a Northern Israelite home for certain passages of Deuteronomy, we may conjecture that many accretions to its original state took place in the Jewish circles mentioned above which were interested in its preservation.

The rest of Deuteronomy's fate after the reform is probably associated with its being read during the act of worship at the regularly recurring celebration of the renewal of the covenant (Deut. 31: 9 ff.). It seems that we must find here the reason for the production of the hortatory expansions, the sermon-like framework of the introductory and concluding admonitions, and the place where they came into being. The historical retrospect of the introductory speech in chapters 1–4 also probably originated in this soil. Noth in *Überlieferungsgeschichtl. Studien* I, 14 ff. sees in Deut. 1–3 not the original introduction to the Deuteronomic law, but the beginning of a 'Historical book of the Deuteronimist', which he assumes to have existed and to have included Deuteronomy, Joshua, Judges, Samuel and Kings and to have been composed with the use of older traditions in the middle of the sixth century B.C. according to a homogeneous plan and arrangement; but for this see pp. 146, 157, 168, 181. There is, therefore, no need to assume different editions of Deuteronomy in order to give a historical explanation of its present shape. Its further growth can also be understood in the course of its being read in the cult. The deposit of the experiences of later days is to be found mainly in the final sections, 28: 69–29: 28; 30: 1–10. Allusions to the exile (cf. 4: 25–30) show that in the sixth century, too, Deuteronomy was a living tradition. It is no longer possible to ascertain at what moment Deuteronomy had passages of the earlier tradition from J and E incorporated into it and was fitted with these into the whole Yahwist–Elohist tradition. Since passages from P have been taken over, the final shaping of the conclusion, Deut. 31–34 must be deferred to the post-exilic period.

Deuteronomy stands on the threshold between two eras. Hence it shows two faces. Its roots reach back to the most vigorous sources of the old national and religious tradition of the OT, and with its intense concentration on God's love and the love of God and of one's neighbour it is the mature fruit of the prophetic preaching, which by Jesus' references to it (Mt. 22: 37, cf. Deut. 6: 5; 7: 7 ff., 13; 10: 12) receives its sanction from the NT. On the other hand, if we consider its effects with its partly rational, theological ideology of retribution and its propensity for a certain 'legality', it stands at the beginning of a development, the outcome of which became a religion which can be taught and learned (cf. Deut. 7: 6 ff.; 30: 11 ff.), the religion of Judaism.

17. The Priestly Writing

Ed. Meyer, *Die Entstehung des Judentums*, 1896; Budde, 'Ellā toledoth', ZAW 1914, 241 ff.; ZAW 1916, 1 ff.; Löhr, 'Untersuchungen zum Hexateuchproblem, I. Der Priesterkodex', BZAW 1924; Meinhold, 'Esra der Schriftgelehrte', *Martifestschrift*, 1925, 197 ff.; R. Kittel, *Geschichte des Volkes Israel* III. 2, 1929, 584 ff.; Jepsen, 'Zur Chronologie des Priesterkodex', ZAW 129, 251 ff.; Kauffmann, 'Probleme der israelitsch-jüdischen Religionsgeschichte', ZAW 1930, 23 ff.; op. cit., 1933, 35 ff.; H. H. Schäder, *Esra der Schreiber*, 1930; v. Rad, 'Die Priesterschrift', BWAT 1934; Luther, ZAW 1938, 44 ff.; Humbert, 'Die literarische Zweiheit des Priesterkodex', ZAW 1940–1, 30 ff.; Noth, *Überlieferungsgeschichtliche Studien* I, 180 ff.; idem, *Überlieferungsgeschichte des Pentateuchs*, 1948, 7 ff.; Elliger, 'Sinn und Ursprung der priesterlichen Geschichtserzählung', ZThK 1952, 121 ff.; Kornfeld, *Studien zum Heiligkeitsgesetz*, 1952; Rendtorff, 'Die Gesetze in der Priesterschrift, FRLANT 62, 1954; Elliott-Binns, 'Some problems of the Holiness-Code', ZAW 1955, 26 ff.; Hempel, Art. 'Priesterkodex' in Pauly-Wissowa, *Realenzyklopädie des klass. Altertums* 22, 1954, col. 1943–1967.

The Priestly Code is the strand which is most sharply differentiated from the other sources by its language, style and theological outlook and was, therefore, the earliest to be recognized by scholars and to be disentangled. The lively narrative gives way here to a more formal presentation, in which a certain erudite interest in cultic and ritual institutions and regulations for priests prevails; that is the reason for its scientific name, the Priestly Book. Its learned character is shown above all in the precise (artificial) chronology on which even now the Jewish calendar is based. It is seen also in the way events are arranged into periods (cf. e.g. Exod. 6: 3). The schematic arrangement visible in P can be traced right through down to the stylistic shaping of the individual literary paragraphs. The Priestly Book is distinguished from the other sources by its linguistic usage as well. To describe the creative activity of God it uses the *terminus technicus, bārā'*; it says 'to establish a covenant' (J: 'to make a covenant.); the months are indicated by figures, etc. (Further details in Steuernagel, *Einleitung*, pp. 233 ff.).

There is far-reaching agreement in attributing the following passages to P: Gen. 1: 1–2: 4a; 5: 1–28, 30–32; 6: 5–9: 19^x (J); 9: 28 f.; 10^x (J); 11: 10–26, 27, 31–32; 13: 6, 11 f.; 16: 1, 3, 15 f.; 17; 19: 29; 21: 3–5; 23; 25: 7–20; 26: 24 f.; 27: 46–28: 9; 31: 18; 35: 9–13, 15, 22–29; 36^x (JE); 37: 1–2; 46: 6–27; 48: 3–6; 49: 28–33; 50: 12 f.

Exod. 1: 1–5, 7, 13 f.; 2: 23–25; 6: 2–30; 7: 1–13, 19 f., 23; 8: 1–3, 12–15; 9: 8–12; 11: 9, 12: 20, 28; 12: 40–51; 16^x (JE); 24: 16–18; 25–31; 34: 29–35; 35–40.

Lev. the whole.

Num. 1–10, 13–14^x (JE); 15, 16^x (JE); 17–19; 20^x (JE); 25: 6–31: 54; 32^x (JE); 33–36 (secondary appendices).

Deut. 32: 48–52; 34: 1a, 7–9.

The Priestly writing starts off like the Yahwist with the story of the creation, but deals with primeval history and with that of the patriarchs merely as an introduction to the revelation to Moses, on which the chief emphasis is laid. Only in isolated passages does P give greater detail in Genesis: namely, in the story of creation, which goes back to a separate tradition, in the story of the flood and in the case of the covenant with Noah 6–9, when circumcision was introduced in the covenant with Abraham in 17, when the hereditary burial-place for the patriarchs was bought in 23. In other places this strand restricts itself to shorter statements, which make it clear that the older fuller tradition is known and that its plan is being followed. The separate passages of P are linked by the equally characteristic genealogies. The chief material of the Priestly source has a place found for it in the story of Moses; here the legal passages predominate, and even where historical narratives are given, the story serves to give a theological basis to the religious institutions binding on later times (e.g. Gen. 2: 3; 9: 3 ff; 17: 9 ff.; Exod. 12: 1 ff., 14). The subjects which in this way receive in P their historical sanction include the sabbath, the food rules, circumcision, passover, the sanctuary, priests, sacrifices, levites and the Aaronic priesthood. Beside the fact that both the Priestly writing and Deuteronomy refer their most important laws back to Moses' time, they also have this in common that they are planned as a programme. But as regards its contents P shows itself to be in spirit an independent unit.

Yet in spite of being homogeneous in spirit, the Priestly Book is no literary unity. The same criteria that we meet with elsewhere in Pentateuchal criticism, such as doublets, discrepancies, interruptions in the continuity, indicate that the Priestly writing, too, is a literary compilation. Thus e.g. in Exod. 29: 7, 29, Lev. 4: 3, 5, 16 and *passim*, it is only Aaron and the high priest for the time being who are anointed, yet according to Exod. 28: 41; 30: 30 and *passim*, it is all the priests; according to Num. 4: 23 ff. the duty of the Levites to serve the temple begins at 30 years of age, according to Num. 8: 24 at 25 years; according to Lev. 4: 14 a bullock, according to Lev. 9: 3; Num. 15: 24 a he-goat is brought as a sin-offering for the congregation; Exod. 27–29, Lev. 8 f. speak only of an altar for burnt offerings, Exod. 30: 1–10, Exod. 35–40 add to this an altar to burn incense. Besides, Lev. 1–7 and 11–15 interrupt the continuity and show themselves to be interpolations; Lev. 17–26 also stands out as an isolated section; in addition Exod. 25: 1–10; 30: 11–38; 31: 1–11, also parts of Exod. 35–40; Num. 4–7; 15; 18: 8–32; 19, 28–30 are generally regarded as peculiar to the Priestly writing. Von Rad has gone beyond this in an attempt to dissect it into sources running right through it. Whilst he thought he was able to detect far more material crammed in than had been noted hitherto; he wishes this to be regarded not as secondary expansions of a basic document (Pg) but as the addition of two independent source-threads, beside the 'book of the generations' which he deduces from Gen. 5: 1.* There are prob-

* Yet cf. *Eissfeldt, Biblos geneseos, Festschrift Fascher* (1958), pp. 31–40.

ably two sets of tradition for some passages, e.g. concerning the
Levites in Num. 1: 50 ff.; 3: 5 ff.; 8: 5 ff.; 18: 1 ff.; but taken as a
whole, the reasons for a division into continuous sources are
insufficient. Some verses may be considered as glosses (Gen. 27:
46 ff.; Exod. 6: 10 ff. and *passim*), others as expansions to supplement a basic statement (Exod. 35: 40; Lev. 16). Considerations
of literary criticism have induced Humbert especially to express
misgivings about von Rad's two sources theory. Besides this there
are chronological difficulties which von Rad (pp. 164 ff.) himself
has to admit. Above all the ideological differences in the strands
worked out by von Rad are not such as to justify, when seen as a
whole, an analysis in the sense of a documentary hypothesis for P
based on literary criticism alone. A solution tending towards a
supplementary hypothesis seems more likely to do justice to the
literary and historical process of growth of the P tradition, which,
like the other Pentateuchal sources, can in the last resort only be
understood in connexion with its practical use in the cult.

As regards the *history of the origin and growth* of P, its relative
dating as the youngest of the Pentateuchal sources is proved by
the fact that the centralization concerning the place of worship is
no longer at all under discussion, but is simply assumed. For fixing
the absolute date we must note that prophets like Deutero-Isaiah,
Haggai, Zechariah and Malachi do not presuppose P, that Ezekiel
knows no high priest and has references only to Lev. 17–26 and
not to the rest of the stock of P. As valid law, therefore, P cannot
have gained significance before the beginning of the fifth century.
It is almost universally agreed that the Priestly Book was the law
on which the reform under Ezra and Nehemiah was based. According to Ezr. 7: 1 ff. Ezra, 'the scribe of the law of the God of
heaven'* came to Jerusalem in the year 458 with the authorization
of the Persian king, so as to put things there in order on the basis
of the law 'which is in thine hand'. This law was the foundation
of his attempts at reform and after his fall it was brought forward
again by Nehemiah in the year 444 and carried into effect (Neh.
9: 1 ff.; 13: 1 ff.; 10). The relations between this reform and the
ordinances in P (cf. Neh. 8: 13 ff. with Lev. 23: 40; Neh. 8: 18

---

* *Sapar*, a technical expression in Aramaic, the official language of the empire,
originally meant something like 'secretary'; through its transference into Hebrew
as *sōpēr* the tradition of Ezra 'the scribe' arose.

with Lev. 23: 36, ordinances about the feast of tabernacles; and Neh. 10: 36 ff. with Num. 18: 12 ff., about first fruits) hardly leave any doubt that the Priestly Book formed the foundation of the reform of Ezra and Nehemiah. The only question is whether P by itself, or the whole Pentateuch enlarged by P, was the law-book which Ezra brought with him from Babylon. Since Neh. 13: 1 ff. and 10: 31 (no intermarriage with the people of the land) refers back to Deut. 23: 4 ff.; Exod. 34: 16 and Deut. 7: 2 ff. and the renunciation of claims in the sabbatical year in Neh. 10: 31 is based on the remission of debts in Deut. 15: 2, it is probable that the whole of the Pentateuch formed the basis of the reform. Moreover the fact that the Samaritans took over all the Pentateuch in the fourth century is more easily understood if it had been sanctioned as a whole to be the law by the King of Persia and the Samaritans were striving to obtain official recognition as a Jewish religious community. Consequently the Priestly writing came into being before 458 amongst the Jews in Babylon in the circles of the priests as a programme of reform built into the tradition of salvation-history, perhaps in connexion with the movements and aspirations which at the time of Artaxerxes I led to the return under Ezra; the language of P also points to about that period. These things explain the strong emphasis placed on the sabbath (Gen. 2: 2f.) and circumcision (Gen. 17: 9 ff.) as distinctive marks amongst the heathen surroundings of the *Gôlāh*. Noth doubts whether the Priestly Book is identical with Ezra's law of reform. He considers it to be originally a purely narrative book which turned on the establishment of the national and cultic community at Sinai, but without the laws which were inserted later. With regard to these he leaves open the question whether, and to what extent, they were taken into the Priestly writing when the latter was already incorporated into the Pentateuch. But the close association of historical narrative and legal ordinances and arrangements (see above) argues against sorting out on grounds of literary criticism an independent historical narrative, which Elliger, following Noth, would like to consider a work of consolation composed during the exile. Nevertheless the Priestly Book is no completely new creation. It has admitted and assimilated earlier material into its legal as well as its narrative components. The most comprehensive and important legal corpus included in

P is the *Law of Holiness*, Lev. 17–26 (P^h), named thus by Klostermann on account of the repeated fundamental demand 'Ye shall be holy, for I, Yahweh your God, am holy' (19: 2; 20: 7 f., 26 and *passim*). In spite of later revision by the circles round P it can still be clearly recognized as an independent corpus by its original individuality and its self-contained character. A systematic arrangement strictly carried through cannot be discovered in the Holiness Law any more than it can in the Book of the Covenant or in Deuteronomy. We may draw attention to chapter 19, a collection of individual commandments mostly apodictic in form as a supplement to the Decalogue; to chapters 21 f., ordinances concerning priests and holy offerings; to chapter 23 a calendar of festivals. Several doublets (e.g. 17: 12=19: 26; 19: 27 f.=21: 5; 18: 6–30 parallel to 20: 10–26) suggest the conclusion that this law was assimilated to P later. But even apart from this, the whole is no literary unity, but a compilation of different, smaller collections which lead us to assume for its origin a longer process of growth. Since in chapter 17 the concentration of the cult is presupposed and a relationship with Ezekiel can be observed (some people think Ezekiel is the author of the Law of Holiness), this corpus may come from about the time of Ezekiel at the beginning of the sixth century. Merx has shown that older rituals from the worship on the high places are incorporated, which suggests a more prolonged history for the traditions used in the Holiness Law, in the course of which the Yahweh worship of the tribal union has absorbed and assimilated foreign traditions. The incorporation of this corpus into the Priestly writing proves amongst other things that P is built up on earlier priestly traditions.

These include also the collection of *tôrôṯ or directions concerning sacrifices* in Lev. 1–7 (P^o), brought together into a unity by the ending in Lev. 7: 37. As the different introductions to the separate *tôrôṯ* show, there are gathered here smaller, originally independent collections put together by a priestly hand and probably expanded in chapters 6 and 7 by later supplements.

The groups of laws concerning *purification* in Lev. 11–15 represent a special unit within the framework of P, which separate endings (11: 46 f.; 13: 59; 14: 32, 54 ff.; 15: 32 ff.) prove to be a collection of priestly learning made up of smaller units. Since in

12 f. the ordinance of 15: 19 is already assumed, these chapters seem to be inserted later. The laws concerning both sacrifices and purification probably date from the pre-exilic worship at the temple of Jerusalem and at the sanctuaries in the country.

But in addition to what has been mentioned and to further legal material P has used earlier sources. For apart from the general plan of the narrative in which P proves its independence from JE, the mythological background of the creation story, especially the representation of chaos, and similarly some features of the flood story (e.g. the rainbow) show that the Priestly writing has used sources of its own as well. In the Mosaic tradition, too, P has based his narrative on older transmitted material unknown to the other strands (e.g. Exod. 34: 29 ff.). This raises the question whether, and how far, the genealogical and chronological structures of P do not also go back to early priestly learning. Observations such as these are not sufficient to prove the conjecture that the historical narrative of the Priestly writing is a revision of a history book by the priests which came into being already in pre-exilic times (Rost). This older material in P is better understood as coming from the oral tradition of the priests handed down in the course of the divine service (cf. now also Hempel, who seeks the origin of the old isolated traditions in the scenes of the cultic drama).

Compared with the other Pentateuchal sources, the Priestly writing represents an independent unit on account of its form and the intellectual and religious lineage into which the whole is placed to serve its times. Yet it is also to be valued for itself as the outcome of a long history of tradition stretching right back into the past, which in part and in its own way, enabled the inheritance of Moses and the prophets to bear fruit for the new era. Its significance lies in the fact that it became the foundation for the post-exilic religious community and for its structure organized as a cultic fellowship led by the hierarchy. It is important, too, from the point of view of the history of literature, for it was made by the redactors the point of departure and the guide-post for the final shaping of the Pentateuch which fixed the tradition. In consequence it was long considered to be the controlling and earliest strand in its composition. P brought to completion the rationalization of the religious life and thought, which set in with

Deuteronomy, by causing the ritual law with its individual regulations to embrace the entirety of life and by its ordinances to guarantee the security of existence. The political and national aspect is eliminated; the ethical aspect is indeed included (cf. Lev. 19) but it is pushed into the background by the preponderance of ritual observances. The conception of God's sublimity is heightened to a remote transcendence; the mediation between God and man is now the task of the priest with his office directed to expiation. Thereby the direct, living relationship of faith is made difficult, if not quite impossible, for the individual. The Priestly Book paved the way for the deadening forms of the legalistic piety of Judaism. But in its own day it took its share in preventing the Jewish religious congregation from breaking up, and in enabling it to become the bearer of the OT tradition until this tradition found its fulfilment in Jesus.

The historical books from Joshua to 2 Kings, forming in the Hebrew Canon the first half of its second part, are called there former (earlier) prophets because they were thought to have been written by prophets. A later revision gave the separate books the stamp of a homogeneous historical book which includes the narratives from the conquest of Canaan up to the Babylonian exile.

18. The Book of Joshua

Commentaries: KeH: Dillman, 1886.–SZ: Öttli, 1893.–HK: Steuernagel, [2]1923.– KHE: Holzinger, 1901.–HSAT: Holzinger, 1922.–SAT: Gressman,[2] 1922.–HS: Schulz, 1924.–TU: De Groot, 1931.–HAT: Noth,[2] 1953.–Garstang, Joshua, Judges, 1931.–ATD: Hertzberg, 1953.–LStB (Clamer): Gelin, 1949.–LStB: Abel, 1950.– EB: Nötscher,[2] 1955.–BOT: Alfrink, 1952.–LSB: Baldi, 1952.–IB: Bright and Sizov, 1953.–SBB: Freedman, 1950.–Alt, 'Judas Gaue unter Josia', PJB 1925, 110 ff.= Alt II, 276 ff.; idem, 'Das System der Stammesgrenzen im Buch Josua', Sellinfest- schrift, 1927, 13 ff.;=Alt I, p. 193 ff.; idem, 'Eine galiläische Ortsliste in Jos. 19', ZAW 1927, 59 ff.; Noth, 'Studien zu den historisch-geographischen Dokumenten des Josuabuches', ZDPB 1935, 185 ff.; Alt, 'Josua', BZAW 66, 1936, 13 ff.=Alt I, 176 ff.; Möhlenbrink, 'Die Landnahmesagen des Buches Josua', ZAW 1938, 238 ff.; Noth, Überlieferungsgeschichtliche Studien I, 1943, 40 ff.; Mowinckel, Zur Frage nach dokumentarischen Quellen in Jos. 13–19, 1946; Snaith, 'The Historical Books', OTMSt (1951), 84 ff.; Roussel, Le Livre de Josué, chap. 1–12, 1955; Kaufmann, The Biblical Account of the Conquest of Palestine, 1953; Eissfeldt, Die Eroberung Palästinas durch Altisrael, Die Welt des Orients II, 2 (1955), 158 ff. See bibliography, section 14.

The book of Joshua bears the *name* of its chief hero and is said according to the tradition of the Talmud (*baba bathra* 14*b*) to be composed by Joshua. Its *contents* form the continuation of the narrative in the Pentateuch and describe how Israel took posses- sion of the land west of the Jordan in the period from the death of Moses to that of Joshua. Chapters 1–11 deal with the conquest of Canaan by the whole of Israel under the leadership of Joshua; chapters 13–22 with the apportionment of the land; the two last chapters make up the conclusion; chapter 23 with a farewell address by Joshua, chapter 24 with the story of the assembly at Shechem and a short account of Joshua's death.

The book is an anonymous work which nowhere professes to have been composed by Joshua. The information about Joshua's death and passages which were written after Joshua, such as 4: 9; 7: 26; 8: 28, etc. ('unto this day') point as in the similar case of the Pentateuch to a later time for the origin of the work as a whole.

From the point of view of literary history and of its contents the book of Joshua belongs to the Pentateuch: it contains the necessary continuation of its story. Exod. 13: 19 in E when it mentioned the burial of Joseph's bones in Canaan is referring to Jos. 24: 32 ff.; Num. 27: 1 ff. in P has the entry under Joshua in view and points to Jos 17: 3 ff.; Deut. 11: 29 f. and 27: 11 ff. allude to the ceremony of blessing and cursing on Mounts Gerizim and Ebal respectively, which was carried out in Jos. 8: 30 ff. These facts prove not only that the book of Joshua and the Pentateuch belong together, but at the same time that the separate Pentateuchal strands are also continued in the book of Joshua. The criteria too which distinguish the sources are to be found there as in the Pentateuch (doublets, discrepancies, etc., cf. Jos. 8: 9 with 8: 12; 11: 21 f. with 15: 13 ff.; 15: 63 with 18: 28; 23: 8 with 24: 14). But the interweaving of the strands and the way in which they are combined differs from the method used in the Pentateuch. The basis of chapters 1–12 is in the main the E strand, though it was subject to a Deuteronomic revision. Deuteronomic passages can be identified particularly in chapters 1, 10 ff., 23. In the first part of the book of Joshua the characteristics of the Priestly writing can be recognized in a few passages only: 4: 19; 5: 10–12; 9: 17–21 (perhaps in these cases it is even only a question of supplementary material in the style of P); on the other hand in the second part P has his say at greater length. An analysis of the individual strands in Joshua after the manner of the Pentateuch has led to no satisfactory result in spite of various attempts (Gressmann, Smend, Eissfeldt who wishes to trace LJE side by side). The difference between J and E can be recognized chiefly in their differing conception of the conquest of Canaan. Whilst E describes the conquest as a united undertaking by the whole of Israel under the leadership of the Ephraimite Joshua, followed by the distribution of the land, J seems to know, according to 17: 14 ff. and Jgs. 1: 3, of its apportionment before the conquest; he describes the conquests as having been achieved by individual separate tribal groups at different times and in different places, without Joshua playing the predominant part as related in E. Moreover it was not possible at first to conquer the plains and their cities (15: 13–19; 16: 10; 17: 11–13. Cf. Jgs. 1: 10–15, 20 f., 27–29). Thus the material of the Yahvist is found only in short passages which do not determine the character of the whole work. The E strand plays the main role dominating the picture of the conquest of the land. Yahweh's miracles at the crossing of the Jordan in 3: 5 ff. and at the capture of Jericho in 6, the claim in 24: 23 for Yahweh alone to be worshipped, which is the practical deduction from the story of the conquest which God has directed, all reveal the Elohist's tendency to lead up to exhortation, which can be observed elsewhere in E. In chapters 1–11 E has transformed old Benjaminite traditions, some of them local and explanatory (cf. 4: 7, 20 ff.), in such way that they serve his conception of a conquest of Canaan at one stretch by the whole of Israel under Joshua. The question how far these traditions of the conquest and these stories of the heroes had already been formed previously into one or more general collections has received different answers from Möhlenbrink and Noth and cannot be decided with confidence. I think it worth while noting Möhlenbrink's observation that the tradition came to birth in the sacral tribal union, although I cannot accept his thesis as regards the division of the material into two different sets of tradition and cultic unions. The various tribal traditions, presumably nurtured at local sanctuaries (e.g. the Benjamite Gilgal), seem to have had a long history, of which the details are no longer clear, before they were taken up into the tradition of the whole of Israel. Both their association with the person of Joshua, the tribal hero of Ephraim, and their extension to the nation do not belong to the old stock of sagas, as Alt has shown; it is only in chapter 10 that the Elohist uses a piece of an Ephraimite heroic saga in which the figure of Joshua is original and in this instance (10: 12 f.) the Elohist mentions an old heroic song out of the 'Book of the Upright'. Although he stamps Joshua as the successor of Moses (cf. Exod. 17: 8 ff.; 24: 13; 32: 17 f.), probably owing to his importance in consolidating the tribal union at the national sanctuary of Yahweh at Shechem (chapter 24), yet in his presentation of the history he gives to the Ephraimite tradition a bias, which allows the characteristics of Northern Israel to stand out clearly here too in his transmission of it as compared with those of the Yahwist.

F

The Deuteronomic revision, the form in which we now have the Elohist tradition of Joshua, agrees with the picture given by E of the conquest of the land as a whole. Beside the Deuteronomic sections in 1: 3–9, 12–18; 10: 16–43; 11: 10–12: 24; 22: 1–8; 23, we can identify by a number of shorter passages also (e.g. especially 8: 30 ff.) a Deuteronomic revision, carried through continuously up to chapter 12, which has made use beside E of other earlier material (lists of captured towns and subjugated kings in 10: 16 ff.; 11: 10 ff.). In the second part of the book of Joshua on the other hand Deuteronomic traces can only be discovered here and there. The tradition derived from E of the conquest of the land as a whole and the extermination of its inhabitants means for the theological outlook on history of the Deuteronomist the abolition of the danger of syncretism. Later the Deuteronomic form of the Joshua tradition seems to have been expanded. There are no sufficiently convincing and valid arguments for assuming two Deuteronomic editions of the book of Joshua, as some scholars have proposed.

Whilst the share of the *Priestly writing* in the first part of the book of Joshua can be observed in some few passages at the most and the Deuteronomic revision prevails, it is P which underlies the description in chapters 13–21. P also agrees with the E tradition, but has developed it independently and incorporated older material (in 22: 9 ff. and in lists in chapters 15 and 19). The priestly characteristics can be seen e.g. in the prominence given to the priest Eleazar beside Joshua and the heads of the tribes (14: 1; 17: 4; 19: 51) and in the mention of the 'congregation of the children of Israel' and the 'tent of meeting' (18: 1). Noth (*Über-lieferungsgeschichtliche Studien* I, section 22), who ascribes the first part of the book of Joshua to the historical book, which he assumes to have extended from Deut. 1 to 2 Kgs. 25, sees in the second part, chapter 13–19, an appendix to this book, in which older material of tribal geography has been incorporated and expanded by later additions (against this Mowinckel and Kaufmann). He thinks that he must deny the existence of traces in the book of Joshua of the P strand of the Pentateuch. The passages of importance for distinguishing the strands Noth explains mostly as additions largely of unknown origin. Thus his attempted solution, which confines itself too much to considerations of pure literary and form-criticism, is confronted with fresh unsolved problems. Both the Deuteronomic revision, as well as the incorporation of P's apportionment of the land, presupposes that the book of Joshua is still connected with the Pentateuch. Its *separation from the Pentateuch* must therefore have taken place only after the Priestly writing came into existence. As the Samaritans took over the Pentateuch without the book of Joshua, this fixes its lower limit. Probably the attempt under Artaxerxes to organize Jewry afresh, which was begun by Ezra in the year 458 (Ezr. 7: 1 ff.) and which implied that both political independence, and therewith also the programme for the apportionment of the land as set out in the book of Joshua, had been relinquished by the Jews, provided the occasion for this book to be cut off from the Pentateuch and for this latter without the former to be sanctioned as the basis of the reform. From then onwards the book of Joshua had an independent literary fate. The state of the text too, as a comparison of the versions teaches us, was not transmitted with the same care as that of the Pentateuch which was earlier in achieving canonical authority. This also justifies us in making a separate examination of the book of Joshua.

19. The Book of Judges

Commentaries: KeH: Bertheau,[2] 1883.–SZ: Öttli, 1893.–HK: Nowack, 1902.–KHE: Budde, 1897.–ICC: Moore,[3] 1949.–EH: Zapletal, 1923.–CEB: Lagrange, 1903.–HSAT: Kittel, 1922.–SAT: Gressmann,[2] 1922.–HS: Schulz, 1926.–Burney, [2]1920.–Garstang, Joshua Judges, 1931.–LStB (Clamer) Tamisier, 1949.–SBB: Slotki, 1950.–EB: Nötscher, [2]1955.–COT: Goslinga, 1951–52.–LStB: Vincent, 1952.–ATD: Hertzberg, 1953.–IB: Myers, Elliott, 1953.–BOT: de Fraine, 1956.–Budde, *Die Bücher Richter und Samuel. Ihre Quellen und ihr Aufbau*, 1890; Kittel, 'Die pentateuchischen Urkunden in den Büchern Richter und Samuel,' ThStKr, 1892, 44ff., Frankenberg, *Die Komposition des deuteronomischen Richterbuches*, 1895; Wellhausen, *Die Komposition des Hexateuchs und der historischen Bücher des AT*[3], 1899; Gunkel, 'Simson' (*Reden und Aufsätze*, 1913, 38 ff.); Smend, 'JE in den geschichtlichen Büchern des AT', ZAW 1921, 181 ff.; Eissfeldt, *Die Quellen des Richterbuchs*, 1935; Wiese, 'Studien zu dem Buch der Richter', BWAT 1926; Auerbach, 'Untersuchungen zum Richterbuch', ZAW 1930, 286 ff.; ZAW 1933, 47 ff.; Noth, 'Das System der zwölf Stämme Israels', BWAT 1930, 162 ff.; Eissfeldt, Der geschichtliche Hintergrund der Erzählung von Gibeas Schandtat (Ri, 19–21), *Beer-Festschrift*, 1935, 19 ff.; Alt, *Die Ursprünge des israelitischen Rechts*, 1934, 31 ff.=Alt I, 278 ff.; Buber, *Königtum Gottes*,[3] 1956, 15 ff.; Noth, *Überlieferungsgeschichtliche Studien* I, 1943, 47 ff.; Noth, Das Amt des 'Richters Israel', *Bertholet-Festschrift*, 1950, 404 ff.; Snaith, 'The Historical Books', OTMSt (1950), 90 ff.; (see literature for section 14).

The book of Judges takes its *name* from the heroes whose deeds are told in the main part of the book; these men, inspired by

Yahweh to save the people, are called according to 2: 16 and *passim* 'judges'—those who procure justice, helpers, rulers. But this designation can be considered appropriate only for the middle portion of the book of Judges. Its contents as a whole are supposed to fill up the period between Joshua and Samuel, and at the beginning and end of it there are narratives which do not deal with individual 'judges'. According to the tradition of the Talmud Samuel was considered to be the *author* of the book. Yet this is refuted by the evidence of literary criticism which enables stages in the redaction reaching down into late times to be clearly identified.

The *contents* of the book of Judges are divided into three dissimilar parts. The *introduction* 1: 1–2: 5 gives a short account of two different invasions by the southern and the Joseph tribes and notes the regions which the other tribes were unable to conquer. To this extent this part overlaps as regards its subject matter the contents of the book of Joshua in spite of its being inserted chronologically after the death of Joshua (1: 1). The *second part* 2: 6–16: 31 contains the actual stories of the judges introduced by a preface (2: 6–3: 6) which links them with Jos. 24 and emphasizes as its programme that point of view which is to provide a uniform explanation for the individual narratives which follow. Stories are told in detail about Othniel in 3: 7–11; Ehud in 3: 12–30; Deborah and Barak, in 4 (for the Song of Deborah in 5, see above, pp. 30–31, 106); Gideon in 6–8 (with which is connected the story of Abimelech's city monarchy of Shechem in 9); Jephthah in 10: 6–12: 7 and Samson in 13–16. Short notes are considered sufficient for Shamgar in 3: 31, Tola and Jair in 10: 1–5 and Ibzan, Elon and Abdon in 12: 8–15; so we speak of the six greater and the six lesser judges. The *third part* contains two narratives which in their present form and their loosely attached position are intended to prove the need for a monarchy from the unstable conditions in the time before the kings (17: 6; 18: 1; 19: 1) when 'every man did that which was right in his own eyes' (17: 6; 21: 25). Chapters 17–18 describe the founding of the tribal sanctuary of Dan by means of the theft of an idol from the private sanctuary of the Ephraimite Micah. The second narrative in 19–21 relates a shameful crime of the Benjamites in Gibeah, of their punishment and of the preservation of the remnant by providing them with foreign wives.

From the point of view of literary history too the three parts of the book of Judges differ from each other and suggest the need for separate examination. The *introduction* 1: 1–2: 5, is put together out of tales of tribal history concerning the conquest of Canaan in a terse style with short passages interspersed containing anecdotes and assigning causes. It includes a survey, almost like a list, of the conquered and unconquered districts respectively (see especially 1: 27–35). It makes the impression of being a selection out of a more extensive tradition. Unlike the Elohist-Deuteronomic tradition in the book of Joshua this section does not presuppose the idea that the land was conquered by all Israel under one leader, but knows of several separate thrusts by individual tribal groups which were not always successful, as appeared from some passages of the Yahwist tradition in the book of Joshua (Jos. 15: 63; 16: 10; 17: 12 ff.). There are partly verbatim parallels to the J strand in Joshua (cf. e.g. Jgs. 1: 11 ff. with Jos. 15: 15 ff.). In the lists older traditional material seems to be utilized and reshaped, for 1: 34 supposes Dan still to be living in his former home (cf. chapter 17 f.). Moreover since in Jgs. 1 the active interest of the narrator is fixed on the enterprise of the southern tribes, the introduction to this book must be judged to be an extract from the Yahwist tradition, which has been inserted by a later hand into the book of Judges, following on after the death of Joshua (Jgs. 1: 1); for within the structure of the book of Joshua it stood in the way of the Elohist presentation favoured in that book. In the context of the present book of Judges the Yahwist introduction appears as a foreign element which stands closer to the book of Joshua than to the succeeding narratives in the book of Judges. Thus 2: 6 ff. follows directly on Jos. 24 and tells of Joshua's death without paying any attention to 1: 1–2: 5.

The main part of the book of Judges (2: 6–16: 31) is characterized by a common homogeneous literary arrangement of the narratives put together in it. The individual stories are in contrast, both as regards their language and their theological interpretation of the events, with the *frame-work*, by which these originally independent stories of the judges are gathered together into a 'history' regarded and arranged from the same point of view. In this frame-work the individual tribal heroes appear as 'judges' over the whole people, whilst in the narratives themselves they are known only as leaders of separate tribes or groups of tribes. Each time at the beginning of the story we are told that Israel deserted Yahweh, that he gave them to be punished into an enemy's hand and that when the people repented, he raised up a saviour for them. The conclusion usually consists of a short note on the length of time the respective leader 'judged' and on his death. This stereotyped scheme of theological pragmatism with its regular rhythm of apostasy, punishment, repentance and deliverance has clearly been impressed on the stories at a later date and placed at the beginning in the preface which sets out the programme (2: 6 ff.) as if it were the common theme of the collected stories of the judges. The form and content of these passages convey the spirit of the Deuteronomic writings which set out to present history from the point of view of edification. The chronological scheme, too, into which the stories were subsequently fixed is Deuteronomic in origin and perhaps constructed out of earlier statements about dates; it is now connected with the calculation that the time between the exodus and the building of Solomon's temple was 480 years (1 Kgs. 6: 1 [Deuteronomist]). This Deuteronomic revision of the book of Judges probably took place about the time of the exile and its style and outlook reveals the fact that it arose out of the instruction given in the divine service. Yet the pragmatic theology by which history is reviewed in the book of Judges is not a completely new conception. Even the Song of Deborah shows traces of that linking of their defencelessness and the menace of their enemies with the slackening in their religious obligations towards Yahweh, the god of war, and with the influence of Canaanite civilization and its gods (Jgs. 5: 6–8, 16 f., 23) (against Bentzen). Neither the introduction in 1: 1–2: 5 nor the conclusion in 17–21 bear the marks of Deuteronomic revision we have mentioned, and nor does the Song of Deborah in 5, the story of Abimelech in 9 and the notes about the lesser judges. Moreover the Deuteronomic chronology was believed to take no account of Abimelech and the lesser judges. All these considerations led to the conclusion that these passages could not have been in the Deuteronomic book of Judges. In the story of Samson the final Deuteronomic comment occurs already in Jgs. 15: 20, so the tale of Samson and Delilah and that concerning Samson's death (Jgs. 16) are assumed to have been added later and brought to a close in 16: 31 by a redactor who appended a further concluding remark. According to this hypothesis the Deuteronomic book of Judges would have included only Jgs. 2: 6–15: 20 omitting Jgs. 5 and 9 and the lesser judges. Those who support this view are forced to suppose that those passages not stamped as Deuteronomic were cut out by the Deuteronomic redactor of the book of Judges and were then reinserted at a later redaction (Budde, Pfeiffer, Rost and others). Another possible way of explaining these facts is that the passages named were not subjected to the edifying Deuteronomic revision because like the lists of the lesser judges and the introduction in 1: 1–2: 5 (but see 2: 1–3) they were not suited for it, or themselves already tended to edification (Jgs. 5: 8, 31; 9: 56 f.) or, as is likely in the case of chapters 17–21, because they were to be made fit for use in the divine service by omitting the Deuteronomic framework (similarly Eissfeldt).

The old *stories of heroes* stand out in clear contrast from the Deuteronomic framework of the book of Judges. Probably they had already been collected and were at hand for the Deuteronomic reviser. Yet this collection itself already bears the marks of a compilation, the traces of which can be observed both in the preface in 2: 6 ff. and in the separate tales of the judges. Thus at least in the narratives of Gideon and Jephthah two parallel traditions can be identified: according to the one which is no longer completely preserved Gideon undertakes an expedition against Zebah and Zalmunna (cf. 8: 4–21) from personal motives of blood revenge, according to the other he is chosen by Yahweh to be the deliverer of the people from the predatory incursions of the Midianites and their kings Oreb and Zeeb. In the story of Jephthah two traditions are interwoven (Noth supposes a basic narrative enlarged by later supplements); according to these on the one occasion Jephthah is a chieftain who is recalled from banishment and fights against the Ammonites and later against Ephraim (10: 17–11: 1; 11: 29, 33b; 12: 1–6); on the other he lives in Mizpah, leads the struggle against Moab and makes the well-known vow (11: 2–28, 30–33a, 34–40). In Jgs. 4 a tradition concerning Jabin (cf. Jos. 11: 1 ff.) is united rather superficially with one concerning Sisera, whilst the Song of Deborah is acquainted only with the latter; yet there can be no question of parallel threads here any more than in the Abimelech narrative, into which is admitted in addition to the main thread the story of Gaal in 9: 26 ff. and the fable of Jotham in 9: 8–15 which has clearly been taken out of other contexts. In the preface in 2: 6 ff. beside the Deuteronomic ideology represented by 2: 11–19, the failure to conquer Canaanite cities is accounted for once by the divine intention 'to teach the children of Israel war' (2: 23a; 3: 1b, 2, 5 f.), at another time 'to prove' them (2: 22; 3: 1a, 4). It is easy to understand that such duplications encouraged the attempt to find again in the pre-Deuteronomic book of Judges the Pentateuchal strata J and E (Eissfeldt LJE) and to wish to divide up the book into two parallel collections, particularly since especially in the Gideon story (e.g. in 6: 25–32, 36–40) a certain affinity with the spirit of the E passages in the Pentateuch cannot be denied. Yet this hypothesis, supported by Budde, Cornhill, Smend, Eissfeldt, and in a certain sense also by Pfeiffer, Kittel and Sellin, is contradicted by two facts: neither of the two theories announced as a programme in the preface are really followed out in the separate stories (this must also be held against Noth's hypothesis, when he considers the book of Judges to be a part of a great historical work composed by the Deuteronomist); and the ideology of the Penta-teuchal strands cannot be perceived right through the narratives of the book of Judges. Here the activity of J and E would have restricted itself chiefly in fundamental contrast to the Pentateuch to the collection of old narratives; a more thorough transforma-tion of the old material cannot be established for the book of Judges as it can for the Pentateuch. The affinity of individual passages with E can be explained without assuming the Penta-teuchal sources to have been carried over into Joshua and Judges 1 by supposing that these passages were handed down in circles associated with the E tradition. On the other hand it seems as if 6: 7–10 and 10: 6–16 belong rather to the Deuteronomic tradition than to those passages akin to E (against Eissfeldt); yet neither of them are by any means to be considered in all respects the free invention of their author, for they were shaped in dependence on strongly marked traditional material. Both their backward glance on the history of salvation and the formula of the theophany in Jgs. 6: 7 ff.; as well as the renunciation of strange gods in 10: 16, go back to cultic tradition. Yet we must add that in view of the affinity of the Deuteronomic view of history with the ideas of the

Elohist tradition (e.g. in 9: 56 f.) it is not always possible to draw with certainty the line dividing the pre-Deuteronomic from the Deuteronomic revision.

The pre-Deuteronomic tradition of the judges had probably had an active existence for a long time. Individual tales, like the story of Ehud and Jephthah in particular, which were originally handed down in their tribes by word of mouth as tribal tales, maintained themselves in their isolated state longer than those in the Pentateuch. Others, such as e.g. the stories of Gideon and Samson, were combined with different kinds of narrative themes and types and were expanded to form a cycle of sagas. In the Gideon narrative explanatory cultic sagas (6: 25 ff.; 8: 24 ff.) are interwoven with heroic and tribal sagas and historical accounts. The Abimelech story is one of the most notable examples of very early Israelite historical narrative. The saga of Samson includes in the story of his call, which is probably later, themes of an old cultic saga, and besides there are heroic tales, comparable to the labours of Hercules, perhaps coloured by myth, folk-tales (pranks in the style of the popular books about Till Eulenspiegel or Peer Gynt, wedding riddles), in the later expansion of the Delilah-story themes from folk-tales, and all these are combined with historical memories of the times of the Philistine danger. Already in the pre-Deuteronomic period different traditions concerning individual figures and events had coalesced within the different stories of the judges. Yet the separate tales of the heroes do not seem to have been united by any internal connexion with each other. The traditions concerning the judges were collected, so far as we can see, in a much more external and desultory manner than was done in the case of the Pentateuchal strands. The collection gives the impression of being a selection from historical material of the tribes which was originally more extensive. The occurrence of the name 'Israel' in the old stories of heroes suggests the conclusion that the pre-Deuteronomic collection of these tales had already been a tradition held in common in the Israelite tribal union and had provided the foundation for the expansion to the Greater Israel presented by the Deuteronomist. Perhaps the anti-monarchical tendency also which Buber thinks he can discover in the stories of Judges 1–16 is to be explained by the range of ideas of the sacral union of the Israelite tribes in which religion and politics were combined, and which by reason of its nature had a democratic bias in politics. At first the collection of the stories of the judges probably served to close the gap in the tradition between the conquest of the land and the rise of the kingdom by a literary production. It was the Deuteronomic revision which first effected a closer union of these stories by stringing them on to a chronological and theological thread.

The information about *the lesser judges* consists merely of notes concerning the length of their activity as judges, their origin, kindred, death and burial. As these with their more exact dates do not seem to fit into the chronological scheme of the Deuteronomic book of Judges nor in other respects to show any of the marks which distinguish the Deuteronomic revision, they are usually considered to be a later addition. But the possibility must not be excluded that these notes go back to an older tradition with a historical background (old official lists of those who administered justice in the tribal union). They were inserted into their present position before and after the narrative about Jephthah probably because his name was handed down both in the old stories of the heroes as well as in the list of the lesser judges (12: 7), thus providing the occasion to combine both sets of traditions (Noth).

The two narratives at the end of the book of Judges, 17–18 *and* 19–21, also require separate consideration. Their position as well as the explicit allusion to the disordered conditions of the time 'when there was no king in Israel' reveal the intention of him who placed them there. For they now serve as a bridge to the narratives dealing with the origin of the kingship in the book of Samuel and are probably to be considered in their present position as a later appendix to compensate for the anti-monarchical line in the book of Judges. Yet this was not their original meaning and purpose. For we are concerned here with two quite different stories, independent of each other. The first one in 17–18 gives us a primitive story of extreme value for the history of religion about the founding of the sanctuary of Dan with the obvious intention of throwing a scornful light on the far from laudable circumstances of its origin. Thus the passage cannot be considered to be a genuine ἱερὸς λόγος of that sanctuary and can hardly have come into being in Danite circles themselves. In its present form we can still recog-

nize clearly two intertwined parallel traditions, although it is no
longer possible to separate them in detail. The one account tells in
17: 3 f. and elsewhere of a graven image, and a molten image, the
other in 17: 5 of an ephod and teraphim. According to one variant
in 17: 7a, 8 and elsewhere the priest is a man from Judah who in
18: 20 is persuaded by the Danites to accompany them and to take
the image of the god with him; according to the other in 17: 9,
12 f. a young Levite is concerned and here the image of the god is
stolen by the Danite. There is insufficient evidence for the obvious
attempt which has often been made to find again in the two variants the sources J and E. At any rate we have to do with an old
tradition, the origin of which may reach back into the earliest
times of the kings.

The second story in 19–21 is of quite a different kind. It tells of
a shameful crime committed by the Benjamites of Gibeah on the
wife of a Levite and of its punishment by the national Israelite
community. The tale might go back, as Noth has shown, to a
tradition of the tribal union before the kingdom existed; on the
other hand Eissfeldt supposes it to be originally a tribal tale which
has now been transferred to Israel as a whole and formerly dealt
with the origin of the tribe of Benjamin when it split off from
Ephraim. In the case of this passage too the attempt has been made
in different ways to divide it up into two sources (JE). Only in
chapter 21 can two parallel traditions be demonstrated with confidence, namely where the accounts in verses 1–14 of women being
procured from Jabesh and in verses 15–23 of their being carried
off at a feast in Shiloh stand as doublets side by side. Perhaps the
later version in verses 1–14 with its allusion to Jabesh (cf. 1 Sam.
31: 11 ff.; 2 Sam. 2: 5 ff.) contains a subsequent reinforcement of
the prejudice directed against the tribe of Benjamin and the kingship of Saul who belonged to it, a prejudice which lies hidden in
the whole story and could be explained by the period of antagon-
ism between David and the house of Saul. However, this duplica-
tion in chapter 21 is not sufficient to enable the whole story to be
divided up into two sources. On the other hand in several passages
(e.g. 20: 15–17, 18) the work of redaction can be observed which
has incorporated features of other OT narratives into the original
context and has probably in 20: 2, 17, 21 and elsewhere exaggerated
to an improbable extent the figures it gives. Presumably this is a

midrash-like revision of the tradition, which most likely did not take place till the post-exilic period.

The fact that neither of these two stories bears the marks of Deuteronomic revision has been interpreted to mean that they were removed from the book of Judges by the Deuteronomic redactor and admitted into it again later by a post-exilic one. In itself, there is of course also the possibility that right down to a late age old traditions had been preserved and had found their way only in post-exilic times into the literary context of the book of Judges. Yet the Deuteronomic revision may also have been omitted because these stories, whose nature is distinct from those of the rest concerning the judges, were unsuited for the Deuteronomic ideology of this book and consequently were passed over in this revision, with the result that they were excluded from practical use in the cult without being eliminated from their older traditional place.

Accordingly we can picture the way in which the book of Judges came into being somewhat as follows: at the beginning there was the period of the oral transmission of separate stories of heroes told against the background of individual tribal unions or of groups of unions drawn together by common undertakings (in an Amphictyonic league as e.g. in Jgs. 19 ff., probably also in the Song of Deborah). To this stage of development belongs also the growing together of different types of narratives (explanatory, local, cultic, heroic and tribal sagas with historical traditions) which can be observed particularly clearly in the stories about Gideon, Abimelech and Samson. The pre-literary development is followed by a period of literary activity when the tradition was elaborated and strung together to form a loosely connected whole. Perhaps already at this point it was intended to fill the gap in the tradition between Joshua and Samuel with help from the Yahwist introduction and the re-interpreted final chapters 17–21. We must probably also ascribe to this period the merging of parallel traditions in the stories of Gideon and Jephthah and in Jgs. 17 f.; 21 and the accretion of expansions (e.g. in Jgs. 4 and 9). It cannot be established with certainty how far this pre-Deuteronomic book of Judges was already internally braced together in detail by a chronological or a more deep-seated ideological framework which in that case would have served to a certain extent as a preparation for the Deuteronomic revision which succeeded it. In this stage the whole is gathered together more closely into the framework of a chronological scheme of theological pragmatism, whilst the traditions unsuited to it are neutralized (introduction, chapter 9: 17–21). To the post-Deuteronomic or post-exilic period there seems to belong the midrash-like revision of Jgs. 19–21, according to others the insertion of Jgs. 17–21 as a whole. Noth denies the existence of a 'Deuteronomic book of Judges' and considers Jgs. 2: 6–12, 15 to be part of the historical work of the Deuteronomist which he has conjectured (see above) and which possibly originally passed directly from Jgs. 13: 1 to the Samuel tradition and was only enlarged subsequently by the story of Samson and Jgs. 17–21.

The book of Judges is significant not only as a valuable source in many respects for the conditions and growth of the people and the religion in the first period of Israel's settled life. At the same time the various stages of its development afford a proof of the constantly renewed internal discussion of the history and tradition which belongs to the nature of OT religion.

The book of Judges has become of special importance in the study of the Septuagint—inasmuch as it was the means by which first Grabe (*Epistola ad Millium*, 1705) then Lagarde established the existence of several versions of it. Pretzl (*Biblica* 7, 1926) has shown that these were a matter of recensions of which the text-recension of Lucian is the one to be preferred for the book of Judges.

20. The Books of Samuel

Commentaries: KeH: Thenius-Löhr,³ 1898.–SZ: Klostermann, 1887.–HK: Nowack, 1902.–KHE: Budde, 1902.–Schlögl, 1904.–KAT: Caspari, 1926.–EH: Schulz, 1919–20.–ICC: Smith, 1953.–CEB: Dhorme, 1910.–HSAT: Kittel, 1922.–SAT: Gressman,² 1921.–TU: De Groot, 1934–1935.–HS: Leimbach, 1936.–HBK: Ketter, 1940.–COT: Goslinga I, 1948.–EB.: Rehm, 1949.–LStB (Clamer): Médebielle, 1949. –SBB: Goldman, 1951.–LSB: Bressan, 1954.–LStB: de Vaux, 1953.–IB: Caird, Schroeder, Little, 1953.–ATD: Hertzberg, 1956.–BOT: van den Born, 1956.–See the bibliography for section 19–Wellhausen. *Der Text der Bücher Samuelis*, 1872; Cornill, 'Ein elohistischer Bericht über die Entstehung des israelitischen Königtums in 1 Sam. 1–15 aufgezeigt', ZKWL 1885, 113 ff.; idem, 'Zur Quellenkritik der Bücher Samuelis'. *Königsberger Studien* I, 1887, 25 ff. idem, ZAW 1890, 96 ff.; Caspari, 'Literarische Art und historischer Wert von II Sam. 15–20', ThStKr 1909, 317 ff.; Procksch, Die letzten Worte Davids, *Kittelfestschrift* 1913, 113 ff.; Tiktin, 'Kritische Untersuchungen zu den Büchern Samuelis', FRLANT 1926; Rost, 'Die Überlieferung von der Thronnachfolge Davids', BWAT 1926; Mowinckel, 'Die letzten Worte

Davids, II Sam. 23: 1–7', ZAW 1927, 30 ff.; Lods *Israël des origines au milieu du VIIIe siècle*, 1930, 408ff.; Eissfeldt, *Die Komposition der Samuelisbücher*, 1931; Hylander, *Der literarische Samuel–Saul—Komplex* (1 Sam. 1–15), 1932; Weiser, '1 Sam. 15', ZAW 1936, 1ff.; Alt, 'Zu II Sam. 8 : 1', loc. cit., 149 ff.; Press, 'Der Prophet Samuel', ZAW 1938, 177 ff.; Noth, *Überlieferungsgeschichsliche Studien* I, 1943, 54 ff.; Eissfeldt, *Geschichtsschreibung im Alten Testament*, 1948; Bentzen, 'The Cultic Use of the Story of the Ark in Samuel', JBL 57 (1948), 37 ff.; Snaith, 'The Historical Books', OTMSt (1951), 97 ff.; Alt, 'Das Grossreich Davids', ThLZ (1950), col. 213–220=Alt II, 66 ff.

As we learn from Eusebius and Jerome the books of Samuel were handed down in Hebrew as only *one* book. It was the LXX which probably on account of its size brought together into one the books of Samuel and Kings under the title 'Book of the Kingdoms' (βασιλειῶν) (Jerome, Regum=Book of the Kings) and divided it into four parts (βασιλειῶν α=1 Sam.; βασιλειῶν β= 2 Sam.; βασιλειῶν γ=1 Kgs.; βασιλειῶν δ=2 Kgs.). The Vulgate accepted this division which was introduced into a Hebrew manuscript of 1448 and into the Bible of Bomberg in 1517 (see section 57). Nevertheless the concluding massoretic statements which stood originally at the end of the books of Samuel were still left in that position. The separation between the books of Samuel and of the Kings was not carried out skilfully; for the narratives about the last events in the Davidic period which should be in the books of Samuel both because of their contents and from the literary point of view, are now found at the beginning of the books of the Kings. (See below.)

According to the Jewish tradition in the Talmud (baba bathra, 14b), Samuel was considered the author of these books. But that is not possible if only because the main part is concerned with events which stretch out far beyond Samuel's death, recorded already in 1 Sam. 25. Probably the high esteem in which Samuel was held later as a prophet and as the chief character in what is described led to the book being called after him and finally also to the assumption that he was its author (cf. 1 Chron. 29: 29 f.).

As regards its *contents* the book of Samuel forms the continuation of the course of events indicated at the end of the book of Judges: it continues the story of the rise of the Israelite monarchy and of its first kings Saul and David. Thus far the designation of the LXX is justified by its subject-matter. In detail the sections are as follows: I. 1–7 *Samuel* (1–3 Samuel's childhood, 4–6 the story of the sacred ark, its loss in the war against the Philistines, the marvels it performs in the enemy's country and its voluntary restitution by the Philistines, 7 Samuel's decisive victory over the Philistines, Eben-ezer, Samuel as 'judge'). I. 8–15 *Samuel and Saul* (8–11 different accounts concerning the origin of the monarchy, 12 Samuel lays down his office of judge, 13–14 Saul's wars, 15 Saul's rejection and the parting of Samuel and Saul). I. 16–31 *Saul and David* (16 David is anointed and comes to Saul's court, 17 David's victory over Goliath, 18–20 David's relations to Saul, Jonathan, Michal, his flight, 21–27 David flees from the pursuit of Saul, 28 Saul with the witch of Endor, 29–30 David's raids into the southern territory, 31 battle at Gilboa, Saul's death). II. 1–8 *David becomes king of Judah and Israel* (1 David hears of Saul's death, his lament for Saul and Jonathan, 2–4 David king in Hebron, war with the house of Saul, 5 David king over Israel, conquest of Jerusalem, victory over the Philistines, 6 transfer of the ark to Jerusalem, 7 David's intention to build a temple, Nathan's prophecy concerning David's dynasty, 8 Survey of David's successes in war and his officials). II. 9–20 *the story of David's succession* (9 David's magnanimity towards Jonathan's son, 10–12 war with the Ammonites, David's adultery with Bathsheba, the murder of her husband Uriah, Nathan's intervention (Parable), 13–18 Absalom's rebellion, 19 David's return to Jerusalem, dispute between Judah and Israel, 20 rebellion of the Benjamite Sheba). II. 21–24 *Appendices* (21: 1–14 famine and blood revenge of the Gibeonites, 21: 15–22 David's heroes in the battles with the Philistines, 22=Ps. 18, 23: 1–7 David's 'last words', 23: 8–39 lists of David's heroes, 24 census and pestilence, purchase of the site of the future temple).

Although when we look at the whole we cannot fail to recognize the attempt to give a continuous account of the events, yet even a superficial inspection shows that the narratives in the books of Samuel are not all of a piece. Repetitions, doublets, inconsistencies between mutually exclusive parallel passages, narratives telescoped into each other and trends straining away from each other, all these lead to the inescapable conclusion that the books of Samuel must be regarded as a compilation of heterogeneous literary compositions. We may name as a specially clear example the accounts of the origin of the monarchy. In I. 9: 1–10: 16 we are told in a popular style permeated with themes of folk tales that Samuel at the instigation of Yahweh anointed the lad Saul, commissioning him to deliver the people from the oppression of the Philistines. In I. 8+10: 17–27 on the other hand Samuel gives way only against his will to the demand of the people to have a king 'like all the nations', and the wish of the people for a king is especially stigmatized by God as a rebellion against the one and only kingship of Yahweh. According to I. 11: 15 Saul is made king in Gilgal, according to 10: 17 ff. he is chosen by lot in Mizpah. The proverb 'Is Saul among the prophets?' is given a different derivation in each of the contexts of I. 10: 11 and 19: 24. Again the circumstances under which David was introduced to Saul and came to his court are handed down differently. According to I. 16 he is fetched to the royal court as a harpist to drive away Saul's evil spirit and becomes the king's armour-bearer; in I. 17 on the other hand David is still a boy who becomes known to the king first through the fight with Goliath. Again David's magnanimity towards Saul is related in I. 24 and 26 in two forms, and his going over to the Philistines is told in I. 21: 11–16 in one way and in I. 27 in another. Observations like these which can easily be increased have led already from Eichhorn onwards to attempts, as in the case of the book of Judges, to divide the tradition of the book of Samuel between two sources (Ewald, Thenius, Löhr, Wellhausen, Kittel, Sellin). The identification of these two strands with the J and E of the Pentateuch has been championed especially by Budde, Cornill, and Hölscher and has found many followers. Then Smend and Eissfeldt urged the inclusion of the book of Samuel also in their theory of three sources to correspond with their hypothesis of the Hexateuch sources. But the division into two or three continuous literary threads arouses serious doubts. The activity of the authors of these sources would be confined to an even greater degree than in the book of Judges in the main to a mechanical collection and mostly to a mere superficial stringing together of older traditions without any generally recognizable principle of arrangement, and this would be remarkably out of keeping with the creative power of J and E to be observed in the Hexateuch. The peculiarities as regards style, structure and interests of the individual groups of narratives in the book of Samuel, and hence also of the circles to be considered as authors and bearers of the tradition, show such diversities, which have also been preserved, that it is fruitless to search for a comprehensive and continuous ideological plan. Thus even the less practised eye notices at once the difference in more than one respect between the narratives concerning the ark in I. 4–6 and II. 6 and the stories of the wars in I. 13 f., or between the popular account of the anointing of Saul in I. 9 f and the story of David's reign in II. 9–20. There can hardly be any other explanation than that here quite dissimilar literary traditions originating in different circles have been placed side by side without adjusting the differences between them. The discrepancies between I. 17 and 18 are substantially ironed out by the Septuagint giving a text in 17 which is probably older and presents less difficulties. But even in the case of those passages which have been ascribed to the E sources (especially I. 7, 8, 10: 17 ff., 12, 15, 28) owing to their critical attitude towards the monarchy and their theological position, it can be pointed out that the trends of these passages when examined closely differ from each other. Thus here too we are not concerned with a literary work of homogeneous character (in such a work chapter 12 would be impossible e.g. when followed by chapter 15). Nor is this fact favourable to the thesis of Noth who assigns most of the passages named to the large Deuteronomic history which he has conjectured (see above). It is not without some violence that he attempts to adjust or to explain the contradictions and discrepancies; but his efforts reveal the weaknesses and limitations of the simplifying method of literary criticism which he applies rather one-sidedly and they are unable to remove the difficulties conclusively. In view of the diversity of motives and points of view in the passages under discussion we must on the contrary take into account a many-stranded process of utilizing and shaping the traditions which developed over a long period and set in at different points and different times. Their common characteristic is a theological outlook on history such as was fostered in prophetic circles and is found in the Elohist work, but which came into existence considerably earlier than E. It goes back, as can be shown from I. 15, and also from I. 7–12, to the political and religious difficulties which hampered the rise of the monarchy from the beginning. Yet this appears only in isolated passages in the book of Samuel partly when older traditions are being used, but it gives no con-

tinuous and complete presentation of history like E in the Pentateuch. Therefore we must start to explain the formation of the
books of Samuel by beginning, not as in the case of the Pentateuch, with vertical sections out of the traditional material, but
rather with horizontal literary sections, i.e. with greater or smaller
groups of narratives which are not so much intermingled with
each other as strung after each other, partly on a very loose thread.
Rost has demonstrated this for part of the material by means of
comprehensive comparisons of style and subject matter.

We can name as the main original *independent fundamental literary
units*: (1) The narrative concerning the ark I. 4–6, II. 6; (2) The
story of Saul's rise I. 9–10: 16; 11, 13–14; (3) The story of David's
rise I. 16: 14–II. 5 (8); the story of David's reign II. 9–20 and
1 Kgs. 1–2.

(1) *The narrative concerning the ark* 1. 4–6, 2. 6. This narrative
concerning the destinies of the ark stands out from its surroundings as an independent literary entity. Of Samuel there is no mention at all; this marks off the story clearly from 1. 1–3 and 7. The
whole, now torn apart and divided between chronologically
appropriate positions, shows itself by its style, vocabulary and
mode of expression and by its plainly evident cultic interests to be
a self-contained traditional production which tells the story of the
ark from the time when it was lost to the Philistines till it was
fetched back by David. The religious outlook and the tendency of
the narrative to emphasize the power and importance of the ark in
face of its not particularly glorious fate directs our thoughts towards the circle of the priests of the ark in Jerusalem as the
authors and preservers of this cultic legend which was perhaps
intended to provide from history legitimate authority for the cult
of the ark in view of intelligible doubts. It is most easily understood as belonging to the era of David and Solomon, and to judge
from Psalm 132 it may have been the festal legend on which a
dramatic performance in the temple of Jerusalem was based in
later times (Bentzen).

(2) *The story of the rise of Saul.* I. 9–10: 16, 11, 13, 14. Here are
placed loosely connected together several early isolated narratives
which deal with the rise of Saul to be king and his first acts of war.
This collection is brought to a definite close in a survey in
14: 47–52 which sums it up. The original separate narratives are of

varied origin: 9: 1–10: 16 is a popular saga, interwoven with themes from folk-tales and miracles and presenting the main persons lovingly with colourful vivacity. Chapter 11 is a historical narrative strongly stamped with realism in the style of the stories of the heroes in the book of Judges; it is now planned as the close of the history concerning the origin of the monarchy and refers back to 10: 16 (cf. 11: 1), but at no point does it assume the contents of chapter 9 f.; it was therefore originally independent. Chapter 13 f. is a historical narrative intermingled with themes from sagas about Saul's wars with the Philistines, and is derived from military circles; 13: 1–15 was incorporated later; the piece anticipates Saul's rejection (chapter 15) and is firmly anchored by 10: 8 to the preceding narrative. The narrative of the wars against the Philistines is likewise an independent complete whole, but is now probably understood by its loose association with the story of Saul's rise (cf. 13: 3 with 10: 5) as the fulfilment of the commission which was given to Saul at his anointing. A comparison of 10: 1 with 14: 47 f. brings out the rounding off of the themes of this collection. Possibly the narrative of Saul's tragic end, now placed in its chronological place in 1. 31, is to be considered as a kind of completion of this traditional series, since 14: 52 seems to point to a story of this kind. Although the difficulty of Saul's position is clearly seen (14: 39, 45 f.) yet the story is inspired by veneration for the king and respect for his rule. The origin of the narrative is probably not too far removed from the events it describes; its home may perhaps be found in Benjaminite circles.

(3) *The story of David's rise* in I. 16: 14–2. 5 (8) is built up on another foundation; it starts off at once by emphasizing that the spirit of Yahweh had departed from Saul (16: 14) and uses the sombre picture which it sketches of Saul as a foil to set off effectively the fateful rise of David to become king of Judah and Israel. An almost uninterrupted and consistent account tells with realistic candour without a tendency to exaggeration the events and deeds which led David by many tortuous and devious paths. through persecution by Saul, the life of a freebooter and the condition of a vassal to the Philistines, until after the death of Saul and his son Ishbosheth, the ripe fruit of shrewd waiting, yet of a purposive, energetic policy, aided by fortune, fell into his lap. The narrative clearly ends at II. 5: 10, 12 when, after the capture of

Jerusalem and the defeat of the Philistines he has reached his goal, to be the king over the whole of Israel, and this is recognized in retrospect as the divine endorsement of his power. II. 5: 17–25 fits on to 5: 3, and 8. 1 ff. is by the hand which had inserted here chapter 6 and 7 out of other literary works. It is separated from the story of David's rise, to which it was probably attached previously, as a kind of final rounding off (see 8: 14 f.); Noth conjectures here the revising hand of the 'Deuteronomist'. The author, a man qualified by his gift of observing facts at close quarters and of skill in literary presentation as well as by a feeling for deeper historical, psychological and religious relationships, is familiar with the circumstances he is describing. David's lament on the death of Saul and Jonathan also (II. 1: 17–27) out of the 'Book of the Upright'—owing to a textual error often wrongly called the Song of the Bow—and David's dirge on Abner (II. 3: 33 f.) go back to reliable traditions. The author of the whole must be sought at the court amongst David's intimates.

The group of narratives concerning David's rise had a history of its own. Many stories are preserved in duplicate; thus e.g. in I. 20 two different versions of David's flight are incorporated (a: 20: 1–10ˣ, 12–17, 24–34; b: 20: 1–3, 11, 18–23, 35–42); David's going over to the Philistines in I. 21: 11–16 and 27: 1–6; David's magnanimity towards Saul in I. 24 at Engedi and in I. 26 in the desert of Ziph are also reported in different versions. Doublets such as these, which cannot be gathered together by themselves into a homogenous literary sequence and disturb the course of the story, must be understood as accretions from oral tradition, all the more confidently since in the case of I. 17 comparison with the substantially shorter text of the LXX enables it to be seen that tradition was developed and admitted right up to a late period.

(4) The most significant historical source for the Davidic era is, however, the *court history of David* in II. 9–20 and 1 Kgs. 1–2. After using older sources (e.g. the narrative of the ark, to which the beginning of the story is geared, also in II. 7 an oracle of Nathan about David's reign later expanded several times and an account of an Ammonite war in II. 10 ff.), the story proceeds to a comprehensive objective presentation of a Court History of David which according to the verdict of the ancient historian Ed. Meyer 'stands far above all that we know of other early

oriental historical writings'. Its author has equal command of the art of the dramatic construction of a tale and of the realistic characterization of the persons whom he presents true to life and unadorned. He keeps himself in the background, and yet quite a small number of indications (II. 11: 27; 12: 24; 17: 14) reveal the fact that he regards even the ultimate relationships in history to be between earthly events and divine dispensation. The history of the reign is written by a well-informed eye-witness; Ahimaaz, the son-in-law of Solomon (Klostermann, Budde) or Abiathar, David's priest (Duhm, Rost) have been thought to be the author. At any rate the employment of expressions in use at a court and the exact knowledge of the events at the royal court point to a member of it who probably wrote the work during the era of Solomon in order to justify the succession of the latter from the course of the history.

What we have observed in the case of the Court History, is valid also for the question of the *formation of the whole book of Samuel* out of its basic components. Individual groups of narratives are associated with each other as a result of a historical consciousness nourished by the national successes of the Davidic period. Perhaps they were linked together by oral recital in the framework of the royal cult which was coming into use and of its tradition which was in process of formation (cf. also Bentzen). Thus there comes into being a general presentation of the rise and development of the monarchy in chronological order. (Noth considers I. 13: 1 to be the Deuteronomic introductory formula for Saul's kingship and II. 2: 10a, 11 for that of Ishbosheth as well as a provisional one for David; he considers II. 5: 4 f. to be the full introductory formula for David). In its course many a narrative was taken out of its original literary context and inserted into the place required by the chronological scheme. Thus for example II. 6 from the story of the ark was brought in with II. 7 at the end of the story of David's rise. In the same way I. 31 from the story of Saul was put before II. 1 in its correct place as regards time and subject matter. In addition to the doublets mentioned above it seems as if passages from other traditions had also been fitted in, which do not correspond to anything in the existing series of narratives; these include lists and passages from annals such as we find in I. 14: 49–51; II. 8: 16–18; II. 21: 15–22 and 23: 8–23, 24–39.

It is intelligible that such comprehensive lists and surveys should be given a place where the end of early series of narratives and so the end of the period described in them offered the natural opportunity. In the case of I. 14 and II. 8 no further explanation is required. The position of the appendices in II. 21 ff. before the actual ending of the story of the reign in 1 Kgs. 1–2 is probably due to the fact that these last chapters already extend into Solomon's era and consequently the traditions relating to David's reign could only be fitted in earlier. This may also be the reason for the interpolation as appendices at this point in the Court History of II. 21, of the narrative of the famine and of the blood revenge of the Gibeonites, which from the literary point of view belongs to II. 24 (cf. 24: 1), the story of the pestilence, and the purchase of the future site of the temple—both old traditions for which no suitable place was found in the history of David's reign. The connexion between them is then interrupted by the later insertion of the poetic passages in chapters 22 and 23.

However, another series of developments in the history of the tradition has determined the literary aspect of the books of Samuel even more definitely than the alteration and shaping of the basic literary elements; this was *the prophetic interpretation of the history and its traditions* which proceeds side by side with the traditions of the people and the court, though it also stands in antithesis to them. We meet it above all in the stories of Samuel and Saul. Here belong narratives such as the rejection of Saul in I. 15, Saul with the witch in I. 28, as well as the account considered hostile to the king concerning the origin of the monarchy in I. 8 and 10: 17–27, Samuel's victory over the Philistines in I. 7 and his retirement in I. 12; and also the story of Samuel's boyhood I. 1–3 and probably also the later parallel to Saul's rejection in I. 13: 7–15 and the passages belonging to it in 10: 8 and finally the story of David's anointing in I. 16: 1–13 which now together with I. 15 forms the bridge between the story of Saul's rise and that of David. The late narrative of David's victory over Goliath, which is inconsistent with II. 21: 19, might be included in this category owing to its theological slant (I. 17: 45 ff.). All these narratives are probably associated together in the same intellectual and religious context of a theological presentation of history; but they do not represent a literary unity, as is often maintained. After all they differ too

much in their outlook and conceptions for their composition at
the same time by one hand to be possible (cf. in particular the
varying conception of Samuel as priest, prophet and judge). From
the point of view of the history of tradition and of literature a new
manner of presenting and interpreting history is being worked out
here which undertakes to explain what has happened and to render
it intelligible from the religious point of view. In the background
there stands the conflict between worldly and divine power, the
clash between king and prophet or judge which brought strong
feelings into this manner of regarding history. The roots of the
earliest passage in this series, I. 15 reach back to the circles round
Samuel (Weiser, ZAW 1936, 1 ff.) and form the starting point of a
development of the tradition in the book of Samuel which unlike
the popular tradition (I. 9: 1–10: 16) rejects on principle from
religious considerations the desire of the people for a king 'like
all the nations'. The specially high esteem in which Samuel is held
as a prophet in these passages shows that this form of the tradition
was developed in the circles of the prophets who regarded Samuel
as their ancestor. This is the reason too for its spiritual relationship with the E strand of the Hexateuch, which likewise, though
only later on, arose out of the interpretation of history in these
circles. This presentation of history which was both prophetic and
edifying had at its disposal to some extent earlier traditions of its
own, which supplement the popular tradition at material points.
Other parts of it must be judged to be later reshaping of existing
traditions or new legendary creations (e.g. passages from the story
of Samuel's boyhood, David's anointing and the victory over
Goliath); these were probably intended to neutralize or reinterpret earlier narratives within the framework of the edifying
recital of history during the cult (cf. I. 12: 7 ff.); to assign the
greater part of the Samuel-stories to priestly circles (Press) is
too one-sided and not sufficiently well-grounded. This prophetic
shaping of tradition tended to deprecate the monarchy rendering
itself independent in its own strength, it made war on the Canaanite local and popular religion (cf. I. 15: 23; 28: 3, 9 ff.), it endeavoured to survey longer periods of time in a comprehensive
way (cf. the association of the tradition of Eli and Samuel in the
stories of the judges) and to link their tradition through their
ideology; all these trends paved the way in the course of the

history of this tradition for the Deuteronomic outlook on history and for the revision of the historical books; indeed they approximate to it in the book of Samuel, as they do in that of Judges.

But the books of Samuel differ from the book of Judges in that the *Deuteronomic revision* of the subject-matter is not very prominent, probably because owing to the prophetic revision of the tradition the substantial preparatory work for the object which the Deuteronomic revisers strove to reach had been already accomplished. Noth substantiates this by the thesis that the Deuteronomist had already in I. 8–12 expressed his rejection on principle of the institution of the kingship and therefore had no occasion to interfere with the received tradition by interpreting or criticizing it; this is nevertheless a striking difference when compared with the Deuteronomic method in the book of Judges, and one not exactly favourable to his hypothesis of the Deuteronomist's homogeneous historical composition extending from Deut. 1 to II Kgs. 25. Traces of the Deuteronomic reviser's activity are found e.g. in I. 2: 35 f., a *vaticinium ex eventu* which has an eye to the circumstances of the Deuteronomic reform; in the chronology of I. 4: 18b; 7: 2b; II. 5: 4 f.; in the statement about the building of Solomon's temple in II. 7: 13. On the other hand there is no proof for the thesis, accepted by many from Budde, that I. 15, the court history in II. 9–20 and the appendices in II. 21–24 were removed by a Deuteronomic hand and inserted again in the post-exilic period. These few signs of a Deuteronomic revision allow us to recognize here also the attempt to gather together the traditions more tightly and to interpret them homogeneously in both a theological and rational manner.

The Deuteronomic revision does not even yet bring to an end the history of the formation of the books of Samuel. It was presumably in connexion with its transmission in the cult at an indeterminate time, that some poetic pieces were inserted, namely the psalm of Hannah I. 2: 1–10, a hymn out of the festival-cult in the period of the kings which is admitted into this context on account of verse 5, but is shown by verse 10 to be an anachronism. The psalm of David in II. 22, a duplicate of Ps. 18, the title of which alludes to David's deliverance from Saul's persecution, is the royal Song of Thanksgiving, usually assigned to a festival of thanksgiving for victory from the later period of the kings, but is

THE BOOKS OF SAMUEL

better understood as coming from the festival cult of Yahweh in the Davidic period. Finally the so-called 'last words of David', in II. 23: 1–7, a mirror for rulers, with an introduction akin to the style of the oracles of Balaam, by its type a combination of prophetic oracle and wisdom-saying, which in its present form could hardly go back to David himself, but presumably had its place in the cult of the king in Jerūsalem already in early days (cf. Ps.101). This interpolation probably caused the original connexion between II. 21 and II. 24 to be broken and the arrangement in the 'appendices' to be disturbed; it probably provided the occasion for the book of Samuel to be cut off later at the end of II. 24 as a separate entity. Yet even after this the shaping of the tradition did not reach finality, as we see from a comparison of the Massoretic text with the Septuagint in which e.g. I. 17: 12–31, 41, 50, 55–58; I. 18: 1–5, 9–11, 17–19, 21b are lacking. A new light has been thrown on the significance of the LXX text, pointed out already by Wellhausen, by the discovery of numerous fragments of Samuel in cave 4 of Qumran, which clearly stand close to the Hebrew prototype of the LXX.*

From all this we can make something like the following picture of those stages in the literary development which are significant for the formation of the book of Samuel. At the same time we must not overlook the fact that these stages occasionally overlap in time and may not be regarded simply as coinciding with definite epochs: (I) *Individual traditions* formed by the people and the court; to these belong no doubt the stories of the wars in the time of Saul in 1. 11, 13 f. and David's war against the Ammonites in 2. 10 ff.; the popular narrative of the beginning of the monarchy in 1. 9 f., the narrative about the ark in 1. 4–6; 2. 6, Nathan's earlier prophecy in 2. 7 and also the lists and annals in 2. 8, 21, 23 and David's dirges in 2. 1: 17–27; 3: 33 f. (II) *Comprehensive accounts* based on existing traditions (the classical period of historical writing): the stories of the rise of Saul in 1. 9 f., 11, 13 f., that of David in 1. 16: 14–2. 5 (8), the court history in 2. 9–20, 1 Kgs. 1–2. (III) *The collection and combination of accounts* named in (II) and their welding into one comprehensive tradition arranged chronologically, and the accretion of parallel and later

* cf. F. M. Cross, jr., A report on the Biblical fragments of cave four in Wadi Qumran, BASOR 141 (1956), 9–13.

traditions probably in connexion with the practical cultic use of the tradition. (IV) *The prophetic formation and re-shaping of the tradition into a complete history interpreted theologically* in 1. 1–3, 7, 8, 10: 17 ff., 12, 15, 16: 1–13, 28. (V) *The Deuteronomistic revision* of the book of Samuel. (VI) *Later expansions* by the insertion of poetic pieces of cultic origin in 1. 2: 1–10, 2. 22, 23: 1–7, expansions in 1. 17 and 18.

The growth of the book of Samuel reflects at the same time the awakening of the combined historical and national consciousness in Israel which above all with the rise and the success of the Davidic monarchy makes an immediate and effective appearance and reveals too the wealth of the historical traditions, noteworthy also from the artistic point of view. This book bears witness at the same time to that spiritual understanding of history as a religious problem which is rooted in the genuinely OT conception of Yahweh as the God of history and which, enshrined in the cult of the covenant, sustained and deepened by the spirit of the prophets, itself influenced in its turn the shaping of history.

21. The Books of the Kings

Commentaries: KeH: Thenius-Löhr,[3] 1898.–SZ: Klostermann, 1887.–HK: Kittel, 1900.–KHE: Benzinger, 1899.–EH: Sanda, 1911–12.–HSAT: Eissfeldt, 1922.–SAT: Gressmann, [2]1921.–HS: Landersdorfer, 1927.–EB: Rehm, 1949.–LStB.: de Vaux, 1949.–LStB (Clamer): Médebielle, 1949.–SBB: Slotki, 1950.–ICC: Montgomery, ed. by Gehman, 1951.–LSB: Garofalo, 1951.–HBK: Ketter,1953.–IB.: Snaith, Sockman, Calkins, 1954.–See bibliography for section 19. Gunkel, 'Elias, Jahwe und Baal', RVB 1906; Benzinger, 'Jahwist und Elohist in den Königsbüchern', BWAT 1921; Gunkel, *Meisterwerke hebräischer Erzählungskunst, I Geschichten von Elisa*; Hölscher, 'Das Buch der Könige, seine Quellen und seine Redaktion', *Gunkelfestschrift*, 1923, 158 ff.; Begrich, *Die Chronologie der Könige von Israel und Juda und die Quelle des Rahmens der Königsbücher*, 1929; Mowinckel, 'Die Chronologie der israelitischen und jüdischen Könige', *Acta Orientalia*, 1932, 161 ff.; Alt, 'Das Gottesurteil auf dem Karmel', *Beer-Festschrift*, 1935, 1 ff.=Alt II, 135 ff.; Jepson, 'Israel und Damaskus', AfO, vol. 14, No. 3–4, 1942; Noth, *Überlieferungsgeschichtliche Studien* I, 1943, 66 ff.; v. Rad, *Deuteronomium-Studien*,[2] 1948; Snaith, 'The Historical Books', OTMSt (1951), 102 ff.; Jepsen, *Die Quellen des Königsbuchs*, 1953,[2] 1956; Eissfeldt, 'Der Gott Karmel', Sitzgsber.d. deutsch. Akad.d.Wiss. zu Berlin, Kl. für Sprache, Lit.u.Kunst, 1953. No. 1; Galling, 'Der Gott Karmel und die Ächtung der fremden Götter', *Festschrift für Alt* (1953), 105 ff.; Calier *La chronologie des rois de Juda et d'Israël*, 1953.

The book of the Kings was once linked to the books of Samuel and like these formed originally only *one* book. This is evident from this fact amongst others that the Court History of David extends into 1 Kgs. 2 and that the LXX has included the books of

Samuel and the Kings under the same title (βασιλειῶν). In the Jewish canon the book bore the name *mᵉlākîm* which has become the general usage since Jerome (*Regum*). As in the case of the book of Samuel the division of the book of Kings into two has also been taken up into the Hebrew Bible from the LXX and the Vulgate; this division makes an awkward rent in the narrative about Ahaziah. The late-Jewish dogmatic tendency to ascribe the authorship of the books of the OT to prophets led to the opinion (baba bathra 14b) that Jeremiah wrote the book of the Kings, but this cannot stand up to a scientific examination.

The *contents* of the books of the Kings are divided into three parts: 1. 1–11 the story of Solomon; 1. 12–2. 17 the story of both kingdoms till the fall of Israel; 2. 18–25 the story of the kingdom of Judah until the exile, or rather until King Jehoiachin was pardoned by Evil-Merodach in the year 561. The information about Solomon has been put together in such a way that there is a description in chapters 1–2 of his establishment on the throne, in 3–10 of the splendour of his reign and in 11 of his inglorious end. The rest of the history is arranged chronologically so that the information about the individual kings follows in the order in which each one began to reign.

But the intention which this reveals, to make the whole a homogeneous *composition*, becomes still more evident from the *framework* into which the accounts of the individual kings are placed and which gives a uniform stamp to the whole book much more definitely than in the case of the book of Judges. This framework consists of stereotyped opening and closing formulas and contains at the beginning a synchronization of the dates of accession, fixed in the case of the Israelite kings according to the corresponding year in the reign of the contemporary king of Judah, and *vice-versa*. In addition a statement about the king's capital, the length of his reign (in the case of the kings of Judah his age at his accession, the name [and place of origin] of his mother is added) and lastly a judgment on his piety. The closing formula refers to more detailed sources for the history (occasionally with an indication of their contents), a note of the king's death, place of burial and successor. Where this schematic framework is missing or appears in a divergent form, various material reasons connected with the subject matter have been brought forward. (Details in Steuernagel, *Einl.* 345). This framework stands so prominently in the foreground dominating the whole of the picture that its author has been almost universally supposed to be also author of the present book of Kings. Jepsen gives another explanation: in 1. 2: 10–2. 18: 8 he attempts to lay bare a synchronistic chronicle of the Kings, without any kind of religious reflexions, which he thinks was composed in the form of Babylonian chronicles on the basis of written records from the palace archives at the end of the eighth century in order to contrast the changes in the Israelite dynasties with the permanence of the house of David. Jepsen ascribes to later editorial revision the fact that the framework was expanded and supplemented in the case of the kings after Hezekiah (see below). At any rate from a comparison with the Deuteronomic framework of the book of Judges, and still more from the religious judgments on the kings, it is clear that the book of Kings as a whole owes its origin to Deuteronomic hands. In the case of the kings of Israel the worship of idols ('the sin of Jeroboam' cf. 1. 12: 26 ff.) is named as the reason for their condemnation by the Deuteronomist; in the case of the kings of Judah the retention of the worship in the high places is what usually causes the praise to be qualified; it is deserved fully only by Hezekiah and Josiah for their removal of these places. Without doubt it is the reform of Josiah (621) of which the intention (uniformity and purity in worship) is applied as a standard for the conduct of the kings. Consequently the Deuteronomic book of Kings cannot have originated before 621. Since 2. 22: 20 is not yet aware of the unfortunate death of Josiah and other passages, such as 1. 8: 8; 9: 21; 11: 36; 2. 8: 19, etc., know nothing as yet about the exile, it has been assumed—on the supposition that these passages are to be ascribed to the Deuteronomic author—that the Deuteronomic book of Kings came into being whilst Josiah was still alive (between 621 and 609) and to begin with extended as far as 2. 23: 25a. In that case this book would have been continued in the same spirit and style up to its present conclusion during the exile—the return is nowhere mentioned. The allusions to the exile in 1. 8: 46 ff.; 9: 6 ff.; 2. 21: 11 ff.; 22: 16 ff., etc., would also have to be ascribed to this second Deuteronomic revision. But we must still consider whether 2. 22: 20 and the passages named which do not seem aware of the exile should not be assigned to earlier sources used by the Deuteronomic author whose work would be placed with Noth and Jepsen during the exile; in that case the assumption of a second Deuteronomic redaction would be superfluous. However, the discrepancy between those sources (e.g. 1. 8: 8) and the days in which the Deuteronomic author lived would even on this view remain unexplained.

The Deuteronomic book of Kings contains no complete history of the individual kings, nor was it in any way intended to do justice in it to the historical and political significance of the different representatives of the monarchy. This has always attracted attention, e.g. in the case of personalities like Omri and Ahab, and is very regrettable from the point of view of the historian. Within the framework of a chronological scaffold the Deuteronomic book of Kings provides us with excerpts which it relates with theological pragmatism to the fundamental trend of the Deuteronomic reform. More details are given only in those passages where such a relationship suggested itself, as in the story of the building of the temple and of its fate, also in narratives of the prophets who are regarded to a certain extent as precursors of the reform. Sometimes the relationship is produced artificially, as for example where the shrines and the worship of idols under Solomon are regarded as a reason for the disruption of the kingdom contrary to the historical circumstances.

The Deuteronomic author did indeed work up his material and fit it into his framework (thus e.g. 1. 17 presupposes the Deuteronomic passage in 16: 30 ff. and 2. 9 refers back to 8: 28) but he did not create his material himself. Not even the chronology of the framework, as had long been thought, is derived from the Deuteronomist. This holds good whether the explanation of Begrich is accepted that the chronological statements are based on differing systems of reckoning in the sources and that the discrepancies which had long been observed are due to the attempt to harmonize these different calculations with each other, or the assumption of Jepsen that there was originally a basis of a uniform chronological system of reckoning and that this became confused owing to wrong interpretation of individual passages.

As regards the *sources* used in the Deuteronomic book of Kings, the author himself names three of them: in 1. 11: 41 *the book of the acts of Solomon* (*sēper diḇʿrê shʿlōmōh*), in 1. 14: 29; 15: 7 and *passim*;

the book of the chronicles of the kings of Judah, and in 1. 14: 19; 15: 31
and *passim, the book of the chronicles of the kings of Israel*. The two last-
named (*sēper dibᵉrê hayyāmîm* ...) are no doubt two different works.
Hölscher conjectures that only one work cited by the different
names is concerned, namely the historical work of the Elohist (for
this see below). Jepsen too thinks of the sources cited by different
names as a uniform book of annals which originally gave a survey
of the history from Solomon to Manasseh and was produced in
the priestly circles in Jerusalem in the first half of the seventh
century. Yet against this we have the different names given to the
sources used and the fact that one of these sources is still referred
to for the later kings, Amon, Josiah and Jehoiakim; no satisfactory
explanation is given by Jepsen for these points. Although the
Deuteronomist when referring to the sources quoted indicates
only what he has not taken from them, yet we may surely assume
that what he has told us also comes from them. It is not possible
to gain a reliable and adequate picture of these sources. The book
of the acts of Solomon which is utilized in 1. 3–11 seems to have
been of a biographical nature, courtly historical writing composed
ad majorem regis gloriam. We are led to this conclusion by the
accounts of the buildings, the display of the splendours, the com-
mercial relationships, the wisdom and fame of Solomon which
we find recorded separately, without any order, beside official
annals and lists concerning officials and furnishings. The dedication of the temple in 8: 12 f. is inserted according to the LXX at
another place (after 8: 53) and derived in another (earlier?) form
from the '*Book of the Songs*' (see above p. 31). In the case of some
passages the narrative has been worked up independently by the
Deuteronomist himself (e.g. 5: 17 ff.; 8: 15 ff.), but it has usually
been taken over from the source as it stood. The arrangement of
the history of Solomon probably goes back to the Deuteronomist
himself. It is still less possible to gain a clear idea of the two other
sources cited, the books of the chronicles of the kings of Judah
and of Israel. The manner in which these books are cited, as being
generally accessible, and the style which is not official but rather
both personal and private (cf. e.g. 1. 12: 2–20) permits us to conjecture that here we are not concerned with an official piece of
writing. Moreover particularly in the case of the kingdom of
Israel it cannot well be assumed that with the frequent revolutions

a continuous book of annals had existed permanently and been preserved there. The various pieces of information about the individual kings, their families, buildings and wars are probably gathered together out of different sources, including also official ones. Although the book of the chronicles of the kings of Israel is mentioned last in 2. 15: 31 in the case of Pekah, yet it may be assumed that it also gave an account of the last kings Hoshea and of the downfall of Israel. The chronicles of the kings of Judah are mentioned for the last time in the case of Jehoiakim in 2. 24: 5; from this we can conclude that this tradition of a chronicle was carried on to the beginning of the sixth century.

The Deuteronomic book of Kings is based on still further sources beside those expressly cited. 1. 1–2, with the exception of 2: 1–4 where the Deuteronomic author has supplied his own material belongs to the Court History of David (cf. pp. 164 f.). Considerable space is occupied by the *stories of prophets*, inserted into the chronological scheme. Within the frame of the Deuteronomic historical picture these serve to display the prophets as rivals of the kings. The traditions of Elijah and Elisha in particular belong here; from their style, content and religious outlook they must be judged to be from separate sources.

The *story of Elijah*, of which the beginning was broken off when being fitted into the Deuteronomic book, is contained in chapters 17–19; 21; 2. 1; in chapters 1. 20 and 22 the story of Ahab has now been interpolated. In the LXX 1. 21 follows on 19; the arrangement in the MT can probably be explained by the intention to place the threat of Ahab's death in 21 immediately before the narrative of its fulfilment. The tales about Elijah are originally independent, isolated accounts arising out of the oral tradition amongst the prophets' disciples. 1. 17 and 18 are now held together by the report of a famine which frames them, but is not presupposed in the narrative of the raising of the dead boy nor in the core of the story of God's judgment on Carmel (cf. 18, 34 f.); the famine must therefore belong to a later strand than the separate traditions. In 1. 18 a local cultic narrative of the shrine on Carmel (Alt) is both introduced and followed by legendary material in which the powerful position and importance of the prophet in relation to the king, is strongly emphasized. The story too of God's appearance on Horeb in 1.19 is set merely artificially into the whole context; like the tale of Naboth in 1. 21 it is an original isolated narrative. All these narratives express the high esteem and veneration for the prophet and master which is really only conceivable in the circles of the prophet's disciples. Out of historical reminiscences, embellished in legendary style, these circles created probably as early as the ninth century masterpieces of Hebrew narrative skill. In comparison with the stories of Elisha the high intellectual and religious level of the Elijah traditions is remarkable. The fundamental questions of monotheism in 18: 21, 39; 17: 24, the problem of 'king and prophet' in 18: 1 ff.; 21, the enquiry into the nature of God in 19: 9 ff. are set against concrete historical situations, recognized as significant and grasped at their deepest level. Some of the themes, such as the story of the never failing cruse of oil and the raising from the dead in 1. 17 are told in another form about Elisha too in 2. 4 (cf. also 2. 2: 12 with 2. 13: 14). Such transference of themes is understood most easily at the stage of oral tradition. In 1. 19: 15 f. Elijah is commissioned to anoint Hazael and Jehu, but it is Elisha not Elijah who is reported to have carried out the commission in 2. 8: 7 ff.; 9: 1 ff. This shows us that there was originally a fuller tradition concerning Elijah and that we have only a selection of it in the Deuteronomic book of Kings. It is no longer possible to decide whether and to what extent the stories of Elijah and Elisha had already been collected into a literary unit in the pre-Deuteronomic tradition.

At any rate the stories of Elisha which fill the main part of the section 2. 1–13: 21 must also be considered to have been shaped as independent traditions of the prophet in earlier times. The contrast with the stories of Elijah in respect both to form and subject-matter and particularly as regards their intellectual and religious quality is so obvious that there can hardly be a question of a common author. On the one hand the Elisha tradition proceeds on the lines such as produced popular anecdotes, in which tales of miracles decked out with themes of magic predominate; on the other hand it lives in the sphere of legends standing between historical narrative and saga in which the prophet is more or less in the foreground. To the first kind belong narratives like the story of the miracle of the oil in 2. 4: 1–7, of decontaminating the food with flour in 4: 38–41; of feeding a hundred men in 4: 42–44, of the floating axe in 6: 1–7 and of the life-giving energy in his bones in 13: 20 f.; the narrative of Elijah's ascension and the transference of the prophet's power to Elisha in 2. 2: 1–18 is akin to these. There is more of the nature of a saga in the story of the Shunammite woman in 4: 8–37, and in 8: 1–6 (now torn apart for chronological reasons and thereby rendered inconsistent) and in the narrative of Naaman in 2. 5, an originally isolated narrative composed for the glorification of Elisha and Yahweh; in its religious attitude this story stands closest to the narratives of Elijah. Whilst these legends and sagas of the prophet came into existence owing to the veneration for the man of God amongst the prophets' disciples, the roots of the traditions lying on the borderland between saga and history (2. 3: 4–27 Jehoram's war against Mesha of Moab; 16: 8–23 the blinding of the Aramaeans; 6: 24–7: 20 the famine in Samaria; 8: 7–15 the anointing of Hazael; 9: 1 ff. the revolution of Jehu; 13: 14–19 Elisha's death) go back to historical traditions and seem to have arisen only when older historical narratives were combined with traditions of the prophets; this is shown also by the fact that the historical traditions are linked together more successfully than the legends of the prophets. For this reason the group of the Elisha-stories might be rather later than the Elijah narratives.

The combination of good historical narrative with prophetic traditions can be observed also in *another source* which has been taken up into the Deuteronomic book of Kings. In 1. 20 and 22 an account of Ahab's war against Syria and of his death, together with the story of a prophet, Micaiah, son of Imlah, has been preserved; this must probably be considered as a fragment of a more detailed historical tradition such as we should expect particularly in the case of this important king. As contrasted with the disapproving verdict of the Deuteronomist on Ahab (cf. 1. 16: 30 ff.) we are struck by the objective account of this Ahab source with its frank appreciation of Ahab's political and human greatness, a proof that this is an independent one. At the same time we can understand that the Deuteronomist with his estimation of Ahab did not let it have its full say. This Ahab source stands comparatively close to the events of which it gives a reliable account and may have originated as far back as the ninth century.

A larger *collection of legends about Isaiah* has been included by the Deuteronomist in 2. 18: 13–20: 19 and fitted into the history of

G

Hezekiah. It has also been taken into the book of Isaiah (Is. 36–39). The information about Hezekiah's tribute to Sennacherib in 18: 14–16. which is not found in the book of Isaiah, seems to have been added by the Deuteronomist from the 'chronicles of the kings of Judah'. In the three legends about Isaiah different kinds of material have been worked up: the narrative of Sennacherib's threat to Jerusalem in 18: 13–19: 37 makes use of two sources; just like that of the embassy of Merodach-Baladan in 20: 12–19 it is a mixture of historical narrative and prophetic legend whilst the account of Hezekiah's illness and cure in 20: 1–11 displays the features of a legendary miracle story. This tradition may have arisen amongst Isaiah's disciples or later prophets of the seventh century.

The *other narratives concerning prophets* which have been included in the book of Kings show that up to a late period the prophetic tradition received keen attention. In 1. 11: 29–39, 12: 15; 14: 1–18; 15: 29 the Deuteronomist used the traditions concerning Ahijah the Shilonite for his own ideas. In 1. 12: 21–24 the later reflexions of the prophets on history were woven into the narrative concerning the prophet Shemaiah. Similarly we must consider as appendices which were probably put into the book of Kings only in the post-Deuteronomic period, the appearance of an anonymous prophet to denounce the altar at Bethel and the story of the prophet attached to it in 1. 12: 32–13: 32 (in 13: 2 Josiah is named! Noth conjectures a local tradition of Bethel dating from the period after Josiah's reform of the cult) and also the equally nameless prophecy against Manasseh in 2. 21: 7–15.

The material out of which the Deuteronomic author of the book of Kings constructed his composition is of different kinds. There has indeed been no lack of attempts to regard the pre-Deuteronomic sources of this book as condensed continuous literary units, which were then allotted to two sources in order to find the continuation of the Yahwist's and Elohist's work in the books of the Kings as well. But the parallel traditions brought forward as proofs are not sufficient to carry through the apportionment either of the stories of Elijah and Elisha or of the other pieces, let alone to solve the question whether the indications of a consistent ideology as in the Pentateuchal sources could be recognized running through them. In view of the diversity of the sources utilized in the book of Kings it is not surprising that no one has yet succeeded in sorting them out into two strands and the attempts produced so far diverge widely from each other. The hypothesis that J and E were continued right into the book of Kings raises particular difficulties too in the matter of their dating. Thus Benzinger wishes to connect J whom he traces as far as 2. 17: 3 f. with Hezekiah, and E the last signs of whom he finds in 2. 23 f. with the Deuteronomic reform, whilst Hölscher takes the work of the Yahvist up to the disruption of the kingdom in 1. 12 and thinks the Elohist did not write until the exile. Smend and Eissfeldt propose a division into three sources here also, but have given up the task of carrying the work through in detail. But even if it is not possible to obtain a more accurate insight into the individuality and history of the sources underlying the Deuteronomic book of Kings, yet the condition in which it has been handed down to us today in no way suggests the hypothesis of continuous historical traditions in the manner of the Pentateuchal sources. Jepsen assumes a revision in about 580 when the temple priests in Jerusalem united the above mentioned synchronizing chronicle with extracts from the royal annals and added a few supplements (e.g. 2. 23: 4–15); but he does not think that this revision already shows any connexions with Deuteronomy by its concern for the history of cult. He believes that he has found these first in a revision by the nabi to which the book of Kings owes its present size and contents particularly by fitting the narratives of the prophets into the framework supplied by the priests' revision, and that the 'Deuteronomic' judgment of history in its present form is due to the same revision. He conjectures that the author of this revision, placed by him after 561 (2. 25: 27 ff.) in Mizpah, was a disciple of Jeremiah. Yet it remains open to question whether an attempted solution concentrating so definitely on a person and a place is able to do justice to the diversity of the traditions and their history, above all in the case of narratives concerning the prophets.

Thus the book of Kings obtained its present form substantially through its Deuteronomic author and perhaps after a second Deuteronomist had revised and expanded it in the Deuteronomic sense and style during the exile. In later times only a few smaller pieces were added. Amongst these we may mention the revision of the accounts in 1. 8: 1 ff. of the removal of the ark into the temple, into which interpolations in the manner of P were inserted beside a number of smaller expansions. The fact that the LXX frequently diverges from P and often shows a shorter text proves that additions were made up to very late times.

The Deuteronomic book of Kings can be understood only in connexion with the Deuteronomic movement, its motives and its results in the so-called Deuteronomic *writing of history*. The historian may indeed regret that owing to the manner in which the Deuteronomist dealt with the historical tradition, merely a bare skeleton and condensed excerpts, lit from one side only, have survived from a much more plentiful tradition; but we do not do justice to the Deuteronomic historical work if we regard it as a source of political history. The pen of the Deuteronomist was not guided by his concern for either secular or church history. The utilization and revision of the old traditions is of both a devotional and a didactic nature and is intended to serve practical religion. The sermonizing use of history as an example in order to exhort and to educate is on the same lines as the introductory and concluding speeches of Deuteronomy which had grown out of the religious discourse in the cult. The peculiar character of the Deuteronomic historical work is intelligible only if it is connected with the Deuteronomic movement itself. In the age of Josiah and still more during the Babylonian exile the nation was confronted with the problem of its existence. Under Josiah there appeared the last possibility of a deliverance from the threat of external destruction and internal decay. As a result of the preaching of the prophets at that time the people were recalled to their senses and their religious life was rekindled and concentrated by the Deuteronomic reform. This took the form of a radical break with their half-heathen past, as seen especially in the worship at the high places and of idols, and of an equally radical turning towards the fundamentals of the religion of Yahweh which imposes an ethical responsibility for society. This meditation on their real nature combined with their cultic and prophetic tradition extended also to their consideration of the nation's past. Here the concentration of their energies on *one* goal produced that one-sidedness in their pragmatic view of history which is the most conspicuous characteristic of the Deuteronomic work. When a king waged war on religious fragmentation, as was done by

Hezekiah and Josiah, then the Deuteronomist praised him and held him up as an example; the rebuke which he administers to a greater or lesser extent to the other kings is intended to be a warning lesson. In the same way the one-sided concentration on the urgent Deuteronomic demands of the times explains why the Deuteronomic revisers of the history cut out or neutralized ruthlessly everything which could not be related to these demands.

But the Deuteronomic movement did not gain real significance until the exile. The destruction of the nation, foretold long ago by the prophets, had now brought wider classes of the people to an awareness of their real selves. They recognized now the guilt of the responsible class, above all of the monarchy, they acknowledged that the collapse of the nation was the punishment of the just God and they were ready for solemn penance. Now the existence of the whole of their faith in Yahweh was at stake. In this matter the Deuteronomic view of history rendered the service of showing by the events of the past the justice of God and the sternness of his demands, revealed in prophecy and in the fulfilment of his words which had power over history; it also helped to win respect for these ideas with renewed and intensified force under the impact of the catastrophe. The whole historical tradition was included in the range of their thought. The old traditions of J and E, of the period of the judges and the early period of the kings were combined with the Deuteronomic history of the kings to form a great symposium of the tradition. Thus they served as a textbook for the generation which wanted to find its way back while in exile to the sources of its religion and by this means it has preserved for us its religious literature. It is from this point of view that the Deuteronomic historical work must be judged.

Probably several hands had a share in it, as can be deduced from the different ways in which Joshua, Judges, Samuel and Kings have been revised, whilst in the case of J and E in the Pentateuch only quite insignificant traces of Deuteronomic work can be detected e.g. Exod. 23: 20 ff.; 34: 10 ff. Noth (*Überlieferungsgeschichtl. Studien I* section 12 f.) has attempted to harmonize these different ways of treating the existing traditions with his basic thesis, namely that the essential substance of the traditions in Deut. 1 up to 2 Kgs. 25 is to be regarded as the historical work of a single author, the Deuteronomist, who in the middle of the sixth century probably in Palestine collected old material, then sifted and arranged it according to a definite personal point of view which combined history with theology. But Noth's efforts to achieve this lay bare, partly unwittingly, the difficulties which obstruct his noteworthy and comprehensive attempt at exegesis, to which full justice can be done only by a discussion of the details. Something similar applies to Jepsen's endeavour, which resembles Noth's thesis and modifies it to the extent that some of its difficulties are removed. However, he overestimates what can be achieved by the discussion of language and style according to the methods of literary criticism, on which he relies in the main for analysing the different sources. In view of the trend towards edification of the Deuteronomistic historical writing and of the different manner of utilizing the existing traditions, we shall have to take account, to a greater extent than Noth and Jepsen have done, of a more sharply differentiated and varied history of the transmission and its connexion with cultic traditions. We owe it to the Deuteronomistic revision of history that faith was kindled afresh by a re-examination of the historical tradition resulting from new stimuli; and this meant at the same time the preservation of a great part, probably the most valuable part, of this tradition. Yet at the same time we must not overlook the fact that as a result the rich vitality of historical reality was curtailed and restricted and the relations between God and man were rationalized in accordance with a theological scheme, which led in the end to the deadening forms of the religion of the Judaic law.

C. THE LATTER PROPHETS

W. Robertson Smith, *The Prophets of Israel*, 1882; [3]1908; Cornill, *Der israelitische Prophetismus*, 1894; [13]1920; Giesebrecht, *Die Berufsbegabung der alttestamentlichen Propheten*, 1897; Gressmann, 'Der Ursprung der israelitsch-jüdischen Eschatologie', FRLANT 1905; Sellin, *Der alttestamentliche Prophetismus*, 1912; Duhm, *Israels Propheten*, 1913; [2]1922; Hölscher, *Die Propheten*, 1914; Gunkel, *Die Propheten*, 1917; Hänel, 'Das Erkennen Gottes bei den Schriftpropheten', BWAT 1923; Lindblom, *Die literarische Gattung der prophetischen Literatur*, 1924; Th. H. Robinson, 'Neuere Prophetenforschung', ThR 1931, 75 ff.; Häussermann, 'Wortempfang und Symbol in der alttestamentlichen Prophetie', BZAW 1932; Jepsen, *Nabi*, 1934; Lindblom, 'Die Gesichte der Propheten', *Studia Theologica* I, 1935; 7 ff.; Prugh, *Der Patriotismus der Propheten Israels* (Diss. Heidelberg) 1935; Graham, *The Prophets and Israel's Culture*, 1935; Heschel, 'Die Prophetie, *Poln. Akademie der Wiss. Memoires de la commission orientaliste* No. 22, 1936; Volz, *Prophetengestalten des Alten Testaments*, 1938; Guillaume, *Prophecy and Divination among the Hebrews and other Semites*, 1938; J. M. P. Smith, *The Prophets and their Times*,[2] ed. by W. A. Irwin, 1941; Rowley, 'The Nature of O.T. Prophecy in the Light of recent Study', HThR 38 (1945) 1–36=*The Servant of the Lord*, 1952, 89–128; idem ed., Studies in Old Testament Prophecy, 1950; Mowinckel, *Prophecy and Tradition; The prophetic books in the light of the study of the growth and history of the tradition*, Oslo, 1946; Allen, *Prophet and Nation*, London, 1947; Knight, *The Hebrew Prophetic Consciousness*, London, 1947; Seierstad, *Die Offenbarungserlebnisse der Propheten Amos, Jesaja und Jeremia*, Oslo, 1948; Eissfeldt, 'The prophetic Literature', OTMSt (1951) 115 ff.; Fohrer, 'Neuere Literatur zur atl. Prophetie', ThR 20 (1952), 193–271, 295–361; Church, Brook, *The Private Lives of the Prophets and the Times in which they lived*, 1953; Fohrer, *Die symbolischen Handlungen der Propheten*, 1953; T. H. Robinson, *Prophecy and the Prophets in Ancient Israel, Studies in Theology* 28 (1953); Neher, *L'essence du Prophétisme*, 1955; Rowley, 'Ritual and the Hebrew Prophets', JSS, Vol. I (1956), 338 ff.; Kuhl, *Israels Propheten*, 1956.

In the second part of the Hebrew canon the 'Former Prophets' are followed by a second section containing the prophetic writings proper, called by the Jews 'the Latter Prophets'. This collection contains (a) the three Great Prophets, Isaiah, Jeremiah, Ezekiel; (b) the Book of the Twelve Minor Prophets, Hosea, Joel, Amos, Obadiah, Jonah, Micah, Nahum, Habakkuk, Zephaniah, Haggai, Zechariah and Malachi. In the form in which we now have them, this collection of prophetic writings is the result of the work of Jewish scribes, which was brought to a close in a general way about the year 200 B.C.

22. Isaiah

Commentaries: KD: Delitzsch[4], 1889.–KeH: Dillmann-Kittel,[6] 1898.–SZ: Orelli,[3] 1904.–KHC: Marti, 1900.–WC: Wade, [2]1929.–HK: Duhm,[4] 1922.–KAT: Procksch, Jes. 1–39, 1930.–ICC: Gray-Peake, Isa. 1–27, 1949.–EH: Feldmann, 1925–26.–CEB: Condamin, 1905.–HSAT: Guthe, Eissfeldt, 1922.–SAT: König, 1926.–Kissane

I, 1941. II, 1943.–Bentzen, 1943–1944.–LStB (Clamer): Dennefeld, 1947.–EB: Ziegler, 1948.–SBB: Slotki, 1949.–ATD: Herntrich (chapters 1–12)²1954.–Steinmann, 1950.–Bewer, 2 vols., 1950.–LStB: Auvray, Steinmann, 1951.–Hertzberg, ²1952.– LSBR: Vaccari, 1953.–IB: Scott, Kilpatrick, 1956.–Cornill, 'Die Composition des Buches Jesaja', ZAW 1884, 83 ff.; Giesebrecht, *Beiträge zur Jesaja Kritik*, 1890; Cheyne, *Introduction to the Book of Isaiah*, 1895; in German, 1897; Meinhold, *Die Jesajaerzählungen Jes*, 36–39, 1898; Guthe, 'Jesaia', RV, 1907; Fullerton, 'Viewpoints in the discussion of Isaiah's hopes for the future, JBL 1922, 1 ff.; Budde, 'Über die Schranken, die Jesajas prophetischer Botschaft zu setzen sind', ZAW 1923, 154 ff.; idem, *Jesajas Erleben*, 1928; idem, 'Zu Jes 1–5, ZAW 1931, 16 ff.; 182 ff.; 1932, 38 ff.; Mowinckel, *Profeten Jesaja*, 1925; Boutflower, *The Book of Isaiah in the Light of Assyrian Monuments*, 1930; Mowinckel, 'Die Komposition des Jesajabuches Kap. 1–39', *Acta Orientalia*, 1933, 267 ff.; Fichtner, 'Jesaja unter den Weisen', ThLZ 1949, col. 75; Scott, 'The Literary Structure of Isaiah's Oracles', *Studies in OT Prophecy* (ed. by Rowley) 1950; von Rad, *Der heilige Krieg im alten Israel*, 1952, 175 ff.; Young, *Studies in Isaiah*, 1954, 56–61; Würthwein, 'Jes. 7 : 7–9, ein Beitrag zum Thema Prophetie u. Politik', *Festschrift für Heim*, 1954, 47–63; Weiser, ThWB, VI, 189 f., 195; Fullerton, 'Immanuel', AJSL 34, 1918, 256 ff.; Kraeling, 'The Immanuel Prophecy', JBL 1931, 277 ff.; Budde, 'Das Immanuelzeichen und die Ahaz-Begegnung Jes. 7', JBL 1933, 22 ff.; v. Bulmerincq, 'Die Immanuelweissagung (Jes 7) im Lichte der neueren Forschung', *Acta et Commentationes Universitatis Tartuensis* 37, I, 1935, 1 ff.; Graham, 'Isaiah's Part in the Syro-Ephraimitic Crisis', AJSL 50, 1934, 210 ff.; Mowinckel, 'Immanuelprofetien', *Norsk Teologisk Tidskrift*, 1941, 129 ff. W. Vischer, 'Die Immanuelbotschaft im Rahmen des königlichen Zionsfestes', *Theol. Stud.*, vol. 45, 1955; Stamm, 'Neuere Arbeiten zum Immanuel-Problem', ZAW 68 (1956), 46 ff.; Alt, 'Jes. 8 : 23–9 : 6, Befreiungsnacht und Krönungstag'. *Bertholet-Festschrift*, 1950, 29 ff.;=Alt II, 206 ff.; Smend, 'Anmerkungen zu Jes. 24–27', ZAW 1884, 161 ff.; Lohmann, 'Die selbständigen lyrischen Abschnitte in Jes 24–27', ZAW 1917–18, 1 ff.; Rudolph, 'Jesaja 24–27', BWAT 1933; Lindblom, *Die Jesajaapokalypse* Jes 24–27, 1938; Gunkel, 'Jesaja 33, eine prophetische Liturgie', ZAW 1924, 177 ff.; Caspari, 'Jesaja 34 und 35', ZAW 1931, 67 ff.; Begrich, 'Der Psalm des Hiskia, FRLANT 1926.

In the customary order of the Great Prophets Isaiah comes first; yet the rabbinic tradition in *baba bathra* 14 places his book after Jeremiah and Ezekiel, perhaps remembering its late ending, perhaps too in order to underline in this way the connexion between Jeremiah and the books of the Kings (see p. 171). Its author is considered to be the prophet Isaiah, son of Amoz (not to be confused with the prophet Amos). Of *his life* we know only what has been handed down in connexion with his prophecy. Probably he was born in Jerusalem and lived there; he carried out his function as a prophet from 746 until at least 701. He was married; his wife is called a 'prophetess' in 8: 3, because Isaiah realized that his whole family, including his two sons whose prophetically symbolic names we are told (Shearjashub='a remnant shall return' in 7: 3 and Maher-shalal-hash-baz='the spoil speedeth, the prey hasteth' in 8: 3), had been enrolled in the service laid on him by Yahweh. We can gather from the circle of his friends in 8: 2 and above all from the whole style of his message that Isaiah belonged to the aristocratic and educated class. Hardly any convincing evidence can be derived from the words of the prophet for the conjecture that Isaiah was by profession a teacher of wisdom or of the law. In 746, the year that king Uzziah died, he was called as a young man to be a prophet (6: 1 ff.) and he exercised his prophetic function in his native city in a period of political troubles under Jotham, Ahaz and Hezekiah. The incursion of the Assyrians into the history of Palestine under Tiglath-Pileser III, as well as the various attempts of the Syrian and Palestinian states to preserve their freedom from Assyria are reflected in Isaiah's prophecies. Therefore politics and religion are together the theme which stands in the foreground of his message since his clash with king Ahaz (chapter 7). In the Syro-Ephraimite war (733–32) in which the allied Syrians and Israelites wished to force Ahaz of Judah to join a defensive alliance against the Assyrians, the prophet opposed the policy of fear with undaunted confidence in his faith. After he had attempted in vain to deter Ahaz from his plan to invoke Assyrian aid against his Palestinian foes, he seems to have withdrawn for a time from public activity (8: 16 ff.). He witnessed the fall of Damascus in 732, the rebellion of Hoshea, king of Israel on the death of Tiglath-Pileser in 727 and the end of the Northern Kingdom which followed in 721. He lived to see the further revolts in which Hezekiah of Judah took part thus breaking with the policy of his father Ahaz, namely the rising in 713–11 of Philistia, Moab and Judea, probably instigated by Egypt, and ending with the capture of Ashdod by the Assyrians (Is. 20: 1 ff.), and the insurrection which after Sargon's death in 705 spread through nearly the whole of Palestine and led to the devastation of Judea and to the serious threat to Jerusalem by Sennacherib in the year 701 (Is. 1: 7 f.; 36 f. and *passim*). The last words of the prophet to which we can affix a date were spoken in the year 701. That Isaiah suffered a martyr's death under Manasseh seems to be a later legend (cf. Ascensio Isaiae 5: 11–14 and Heb. 11: 37).

The chief burden of his activity as a prophet lies in the oral proclamation of separate oracles of thrilling poetic power and inimitable certainty of aim, spoken in concrete historical situations. Once only in 20: 1 ff. do we hear of a symbolic action when Isaiah walked for three years without his outer garment and barefoot in order to announce the coming defeat of the Egyptians. The words of the prophet were set down in writing and consequently the book of Isaiah came into being merely as a secondary occurrence which seems in his case to be connected with the failure of his oral message. In 30: 8 he is commissioned to write his oracles down so that they may serve as a witness to later times; and in 8: 16 he seems to hand over his counsels to the safe keeping of his disciples at the moment when he retires from public work. The small amount which he recorded himself has been preserved by his pupils; the largest part of the Isaianic oracles in our possession were probably written down and collected by his disciples.

Yet the contents of the *book of Isaiah* consists to a small extent only of authentic prophecies of Isaiah. It is not without good reason that this book has been called 'a whole library of prophetic writings'. A survey of the entire book reveals at once *three parts* clearly marked off from each other: chapters 1–35, 36–39, 40–66. The chapters 36–39 form, as a comparison with Jer. 52 teaches, the historical, biographical conclusion of the book of Isaiah proper and have been taken over from the book of Kings (see above pp. 177 f.). Nowhere in chapters 40–66 are there any more references to Isaiah, whilst these occur frequently in 1–39. Moreover 2 Chron. 36: 22 ff.=Ezr. 1: 1 ff. allude to Is. 44: 28, but attribute the passage not to Isaiah, but to Jeremiah. All this shows that quite apart from the arguments concerning style and subject-matter Is. 40–66 has nothing to do with the prophet Isaiah. But even the remaining chapters 1–35 do not represent a homogeneous collection from the literary point of view. This is shown already by the various headings in 1: 1; 2: 1; 13: 1, etc. These identically recurring headings (*maśśā'* = the oracle concerning . . . in 13: 1; 15: 1; 19: 1; 21: 1, 11, 13; 22: 1; 23: 1) throw chapters 13–23 into clear relief as a sub-section. Thus *chapters 1–35 can again be divided into three parts:* 1–12, 13–23, 24–35. There seems to be a particular principle underlying the arrangement of these groupings which is found also in Ezekiel and in the LXX version of the book of Jeremiah: The first part, 1–12, contains in the main *denunciations against his own people,* the second part 13–23 *oracles against foreign nations*; in the third part *prophecies of salvation* predominate. Not all the individual oracles fit into this scheme because whoever arranged them was tied by existing collections of a different kind. In fact each of these three parts is made up of smaller collections.

(I) Is. 1–12. The heading in 1: 1 gives the keynote to this section which contains in the main genuine oracles of Isaiah 'concerning Judah and Jerusalem'; it ends with a psalm-like doxology with an eschatological outlook suggesting that this collection in its final form was used for liturgical recitation. The heading in 2: 1, which must be regarded as the beginning of a separate collection, shows that this piece has not come to us at first hand, but was put together by the collector out of smaller groups of sayings which already existed. It is also likely that chapter 6, the account of the call, stood not in the middle but at the beginning of a literary unit, as in the case of Jeremiah and Ezekiel, so that chapter 6 seems to begin another collection. This is all the more probable because chapter 6: 1–9: 6 now tears apart the passage in 5: 25–30 and 9: 7–20 sharing a common refrain, as well as the continuity of a sevenfold cry of woe in 5: 8–24 and 10: 1–4; thus chapters 6: 1–9: 6 appear to be a self-contained unit no doubt existing originally by itself, then inserted later between chapters 5 and 9 ff. which belonged together. Thus in the section 1–12 there are the following five sub-sections: (a) chapter 1; (b) 2–4; (c) 5+9–11; (d) 6: 1–9: 6; (e) 12.

(a) Chapter 1 is a compilation of diverse oracles of Isaiah which were once probably independent. The one about the devastation of Judea in 1: 4–9 dates from the year 701, whilst no exact date can be assigned to the other oracles, because of the lack of concrete historical allusions. Owing to the general nature of their subject-matter the collector seems to have placed them at the beginning of the collection in chapters 1–12 as a sort of introduction out-lining its content, thus anticipating some of the main and funda-mental ideas in Isaiah's prophecy; he then gave it a heading (1: 1). Thus for example the very first oracle about Israel's ingratitude and failure to respond to God provides a good opening for the oracles against Judah and Jerusalem put together here. The oracle denouncing the ritual in 1: 10–17 couched in the form of the Torah is connected externally by a catchword with what pre-cedes it. A saying about God's wonderful mercy in 1: 18–20 is followed in 1: 21–26 by a denunciation of the sins of Jerusalem in the form of a dirge and in 1: 27–31 by fragmentary oracles

dealing with deliverance and judgment. In this chapter no principle of arrangement can be detected.

(b) Chapters 2–4 is an older collection with its own title in
2: 1; it contains oracles from Isaiah's early days which is probably
the reason why it was placed before 6: 1–9: 6. At the start in 2: 2–5
and at the end in 4: 2–6 there are now placed oracles of promise
which do not belong to Isaiah, whilst in between are denunciations
and their justification. This enables some kind of an arrangement
by the collector to be observed. The eschatological prophecy of
salvation, describing the pilgrimage of the Gentiles to the temple
mount at Jerusalem and the destruction of weapons and the end
of wars in 2: 2–5, which is found in the same words but with a
different liturgical conclusion in Micah 4: 1–4, is an anonymous
oracle inserted both into the book of Isaiah and into that of
Micah; it is not possible to show that either form is in any way
dependent on the other, so that we cannot prove either the oracle
in Isaiah or that in Micah to be prior to the other. In 2: 6–21 there
follows a poem full of threats about the day of Yahweh divided
into strophes by a refrain, an outstanding revelation both of
Isaiah's powerful conception of God and of his language. It is
succeeded in 3: 1–15 by a denunciation probably composed also
before 735 against Jerusalem's leaders, which arrests attention by
its trenchant pictures of revolutionary anarchy. The derision cast
on the arrogance of the women of Jerusalem in 3: 16–4: 1 con-
cludes this collection of genuine Isaianic oracles. The prophecy
of the salvation which God will give to Zion, contained in 4: 2–6,
is very inferior in its diction to the authentic words of Isaiah; it is
probably alien matter placed here by the collector to bring this
small collection to a close.

(c) Chapter 5 starts a fresh collection consisting likewise of
older oracles of Isaiah. This included also his work contained in
chapters 9–11 and has probably become disarranged by the interpolation of 6: 1–9: 6 (see above). The parable of the unfruitful
vineyard which begins with the seductive sounds of a playful
love-song and ends by breaking out in strongest contrast into that
powerfully suggestive (untranslatable) play upon words 'judg-
ment-oppression', reveals all the highly-charged tension in
Isaiah's skilled use of words and the daring breadth and freedom
of his religious thought. In 5: 8–24 and 10: 1–4 we have a seven-

fold woe; its individual oracles were probably proclaimed by Isaiah at different times and were brought together here subsequently partly in a mutilated form. 5: 25–30 is connected with 9: 7–20 by the refrain: 'For all this his anger is not turned away, but his hand is stretched out still'; in his use of a pattern of calamities, Isaiah seems here to fall back on Am. 4: 6–12 and on an even older tradition. It is not possible to give the poem an exact date. On the other hand the woe on Assyria in 10: 5–34 which starts a compilation of Isaiah's oracles dealing with parallel subjects, belongs to a later period when the prophet realized that Assyria had gone beyond its mandate to be God's rod of discipline. This collection too was no doubt brought to an end in 11: 1–9 with a promise of salvation, namely the well-known Messianic oracle concerning the 'shoot out of the stock of Jesse' on whom the spirit of Yahweh shall rest. The authenticity of the prophecy is much in dispute. Yet the more spiritual treatment of the messianic ideal in 11: 1–5 belongs to a range of ideas which cannot be declared absolutely beyond Isaiah's vision. It is more open to question whether the description of the ultimate peace in nature (11: 6–9) originated with Isaiah. In any case 11: 10–16 is a post-exilic prophecy of salvation which presupposes that Israel and Judah are in banishment and was composed and inserted after 11: 1 ff. at a later date.

(d) The continuity of the collection discussed above is broken by 6: 1–9: 6, a group of Isaianic oracles which to judge by their style in the first person (chapter 7 also seems originally to have been autobiographical in form) were probably put together already by Isaiah. The account in chapter 6 of his call in the temple at Jerusalem, matchless in its terse dramatic force, opens this group of his writings. Chapter 7 from the time of the Syro-Ephraimite war follows with oracles in 7: 1–9 about faith and in 7: 10–17 about the sign of Immanuel, then with several threats of judgment carried out by the Assyrians. It may perhaps be concluded from 8: 16 ff. that Isaiah, after his fruitless efforts to bring the king to his side by making the decision demanded by faith, withdrew for a certain time from public activity and entrusted his disciple with his prophetic legacy concerning the Syro-Ephraimite war. This may have been the booklet 6: 1–9: 6. The prophecy of salvation concerning the Davidic messianic child in 9: 1–6 contains nothing which would prevent its being traced back to Isaiah; its position here would be best explained as a word of consolation, pronounced for the first time not in public but in the intimate circle of disciples. Then perhaps the fact that this booklet of Isaiah ended with an oracle of salvation had an influence on the shaping of the other collections in 2–4 and 5 and in 9: 7–11: 9.

(e) Chapter 12 is composed of two songs each with a special introduction; 12: 1–3 is a song of thanksgiving, 12: 4–6 is an eschatological hymn in the style of a liturgical psalm. It seems to have been first admitted as a concluding doxology by the collector of the whole group of chapters 1–12.

(II) Is. 13–23. These chapters are shown to be a separate literary unit both by the formal distinctive mark of the ten times repeated heading of *maśśā'*=burden, as well as by their subject-matter, inasmuch as they are mainly composed of oracles against foreign nations. The oracle against the official, Shebna, in Jerusalem in 22: 15–25 has been included because in verse 16 he is described contemptuously as a foreigner. The oracle of the valley of vision in 22: 1–14 directed against Jerusalem includes in verse 5 f. foreign lands and peoples in its survey and is on that account fitted into the oracles of foreign nations. Therefore both the compilation of the individual 'burdens' which answer to this description and their headings are due to the collector of the whole piece. It is no longer possible to discover why some sayings lack a heading; perhaps these are later appendices. The following pieces in the collection go back to Isaiah: an oracle against Assyria in 14: 24–27; the warning to Philistia in 14: 28–32 dated by the year in which Ahaz died (726); in 17: 1–11 a threat against Damascus and Israel from the time of the Syro-Ephraimite alliance and in 17: 12–14 a woe to the tumult of the nations which will be destroyed in a night, probably referring to the Assyrian army (perhaps from the year 701). Chapter 18 is an oracle of Isaiah to the Ethiopian embassy which might be brought into connexion with the revolt of the year 713 or 705. Chapter 20 contains a reliable report in the third person of Isaiah's symbolic and prophetic action during the years 713–11 as a warning against the Egyptian alliance. Finally in chapter 22 two genuine pieces by Isaiah are placed together, a sharp denunciation in 22: 1–13 of the unforgivable sin of Jerusalem frivolously revelling in the joy of imaginary victory: 'Let us eat and drink, for tomorrow we die!', probably from the time of the fortunate deliverance from Sennacherib's army in 701, and in 22: 15–25 the oracle against the domestic official, Shebna and his successor, Eliakim, to which no exact date can be given.

The rest comes from other hands: 13: 1–14: 23 is an oracle on the destruction of Babylon with a magnificent taunt-song on the king of Babylon in 14: 4–21, composed before 538, because Babylon's extinction by the Medes is in mind and its conquest by Cyrus is not known. Chapters 15–16 contains an extensive older oracle on Moab in 15: 1–16: 12, provided with an appendix by a later hand in 16: 13 f. which is partially used in Jer. 48: 29 ff. and is there ascribed to Jeremiah; consequently it is an anonymous oracle the date of which remains uncertain (oppression by Moab in the eighth or fifth century or even later?). Chapter 19 is an oracle against Egypt expanded subsequently; the universal belief, that after the judgment Egypt will be converted and together with Assyria will be called the people of Yahweh beside Israel, recalls the soaring hopes of Deutero-Isaiah; this oracle too can hardly be dated with confidence (some think the 'fierce king' who shall rule over them in verse 4 is a king of Assyria of the seventh century, others that he is Psammetichus or one of the Persian kings of the fifth or fourth centuries). In 21: 1–10 the heading 'of the wilderness', like that in 21: 11, 13; 22: 1, is taken by the collector himself from the oracle; it has the fall of Babylon in mind and its characteristic visionary outlook of a prophet is akin to the oracle of Edom in 21: 11–12; probably both come from the same hand. 21: 13–15 is an oracle 'upon the steppe' for which no date can be given; in verse 16 f. it is transferred to Kedar. The oracle of Tyre in chapter 23 seems to have been welded together out of one of Tyre and another of Sidon (see verses 2, 12); an appendix in verses 15–18 refers perhaps to the destruction of Tyre by Alexander the Great (332) and to the renewed prosperity of the city after seventy years when it received a republican constitution through Ptolemy II in the year 274. As regards the time when the whole collection in 13–23 was formed only the post-exilic period can be considered; the fact that appendices are added as late as the third century proves its continuing active literary life.

(III) Chapters 24–35. This part of the book of Isaiah shows no indications anywhere which would mark the whole of it as a separate book. It must therefore be assumed that this section was completed only at a late date, its contents having been gathered together probably because their subject-matter was in the main full of promise. It is composed of three independent collections clearly distinguished from each other: (a) 24–27; (b) 28–33; (c) 34–35.

(a) Chapters 24–27 is an apocalypse; in powerful language and splendid pictures it speaks of the end of all things. At the beginning is placed the end of the world, at the conclusion the return of the Dispersion, these form the cardinal points of its eschatology. The book itself is made up of *eschatological prophesies* in 24: 1–3, 17–23; 25: 6–8; 27: 1, 12–13 and of *songs*, especially eschatological hymns as in 25: 1–5, 9–12; 26: 1–6, etc. Up till now the problem remains unsolved whether the prophecies or the songs are the later. The general nature of the eschatological statements makes it difficult to assign an absolute date; the religious ideas about the angels and the resurrection point to a comparatively late date.

Different results are reached according to the name given to the city in question: Lindblom thinks of the occupation of Babylon by Xerxes in 485 (Olmsted, AJSL 35, 1938. 3, pp. 392 ff. places it in the year 478–7), Rudolph of that by Alexander the Great in 331, Procksch of the conquest of Carthage by the Romans in 146, Duhm of the destruction of Samaria under John Hyrcanus in 110, Smend and Eissfeldt of Moab. No definite decision is possible; at any rate the booklet which is important for the development of the mingled eschatological and apocalyptic conceptions can hardly have come into being before the fifth century.

(b) The chapters 28–33 contain for the most part genuine sayings by Isaiah, especially 28–31, usually called the *Assyrian cycle* because the oracles with *one* exception all come from the time of the revolts against Assyria of the years 713–701. Only 28: 1–4 a woe against Samaria, 'the crown of pride of the drunkards of Ephraim', was composed before the fall of Israel. In its original form this booklet goes back to Isaiah himself, if we may apply to the oracle brought together here the order in 30: 8 to write down the words as a witness for later times; for this is the most likely assumption, in spite of all the doubts expressed about it, because we have preserved here the most important oracles from the later period of the prophet's activity. The individual sayings were spoken at different dates. Amongst them we may note especially the saying in 28: 4–22 about the foundation corner-stone which Yahweh will lay in Zion: 'he that believeth shall not make haste'; 28: 23–29 is a didactic parable about the different kinds of work performed by the farmer as an illustration that God does not always act in the same way and yet acts with a purpose; 29: 9–12 deals with hardness of heart; 29: 13–14 with the cult as lip-service and commandments of men learned by rote; in 30: 15–17 we read 'in quietness and confidence shall be your strength' and finally in 31: 1–9 the warning against trust in the strength of men: 'the Egyptians are men, and not God'; thus expressing the contrast in history between 'flesh' and 'spirit'.

The oracles in 29: 17–24 and 30: 18–26 are later interpolations. The first clearly presupposes the exile; the saying too about the princes and people of the future in 32: 1–8 which recalls Is. 11, but falls far short of it, must be considered an appendix. As Gunkel has shown, chapter 33 is not a real piece of prophecy, but a liturgy shaped like a prophetic prediction of the future which in imitative fashion combines different literary types (woes, popular laments, a liturgy of the Torah, oracles and prophetic sayings). This prophetic liturgy is certainly post-exilic, and to be assigned to the Persian or Greek ascendancy according to the interpretation given to the destruction of the hostile world-power mentioned in it.

(c) Chapters 34–35 are an apocalypse dealing with the annihilation of Edom and the deliverance of Zion. It presupposes the Jewish dispersion and shows definite points of contact with Deutero-Isaiah so that it can have come into existence at the earliest towards the end of the sixth century. Its final note of salvation at the end of time will have been the reason for its place at the end of Isaiah's prophecy.

Chapters 36–39 were taken over from the book of Kings by the collector of the whole work as a kind of biographical conclusion and placed at the end. When compared with the parallel text in the book of Kings, we find that the account of Hezekiah's tribute (2 Kgs. 18: 14–16) is omitted and that on the other hand the 'psalm of Hezekiah' in 38: 9–20, a personal song of thanksgiving, is added and placed in the mouth of the convalescent Hezekiah though originally it had nothing to do with him. The oracles of the prophet handed down in the legends of Isaiah may go back to a relatively reliable tradition of his disciples. The biographical ending was admitted into the book of Isaiah only in post-exilic times; perhaps we can gather from 2 Chron. 32: 32 that the chronicler had not yet read these chapters in the book of Isaiah (the remark relating to the book of Isaiah is probably an addition). In that case 36–39 would not have been appended before the third century.

The separate diverse happenings which went to *the formation of the book of Proto-Isaiah* (occasionally Isaiah 1–39 is so called to distinguish it from Deutero-Isaiah) and which have led to its present form can no longer be clearly seen. In the course of a lengthy history it has grown out of different basic units. In addition to the period of the prophet's oral pronouncements which was the most important, we can distinguish in this history roughly three different stages: I. Two basic collections from Isaiah himself, namely 6: 1–9: 6, the legacy resulting from the Syro-Ephraimite war, and 28–31, the testimony from the second period of his activity. Stage II may be called that of the work of *Isaiah's disciples* who had a material share in preserving the two pieces just named and in collecting the oracles of Isaiah. To them are due the collection of genuine sayings in 2–4 from Isaiah's early days, the groups of 5 + 9: 7–11: 9, now interrupted by 6: 1–9: 6 and also chapter 1 and the genuine items of the section 13–23 (see above). Presumably following the pattern of 6: 1–9: 6 the two first-named collections are each concluded with a message of salvation. Stage III in the history of the development of the book of Isaiah is marked by expansions and by the gathering together of existing basic units into larger collections: 2: 2–4; 4: 2–6; 11: 10–16 are taken in and combined by the collector into the larger unit, 1–12 by adding chapter 12 to the older collections. We must imagine a similar process in the formation of the group of oracles about foreign nations in 13–23: the items were accepted, completed with others of foreign origin and amalgamated in accordance with a common outlook with other oracles which had already been collected. In the third part of the book of Isaiah at first small amplifications are probably inserted into the context

of the old collection of 28–31, especially at its end (29: 17–24;
30: 18–26; 32: 2–8; 33; 34 f.) and finally the apocalypse in 24–27
is added to the whole. The biographical conclusion from the
books of Kings rounds off the Isaianic tradition in a literary style
from the point of view both of its subject-matter and of its
literary history.

We must imagine the history of this development of the book
of Isaiah to have been much more complicated in its details than
it is possible to describe in a rough survey. Its motives can be
understood only if we take account of the fact that the various
changes and the growth of the book are due to this literature
being employed liturgically, and especially to its being read
aloud at the service in the synagogue. The impression gained by
the methods of literary criticism, that the condition of the book
of Isaiah was neglected from the literary point of view, is not
derived from the neglect of Isaianic prophecy; on the contrary it
is the consequence of the increased use of this book and of its
significance for the religious life of later generations who brought
out of it and put into it the answers to their own vital problems.
It is only by this route that the prophetic writings—like the
historical literature—of the OT have been preserved as a living
book. The fact, that it is just the book of Isaiah which is so rich
in additions from the most diverse epochs, is a proof that this book
has been taken up afresh again and again and that in the end the
true significance of this regal figure among the prophets was after
all recognized and appreciated.

The *significance* of Isaiah can be realized best from his encounter
with God at the hour of his call, for it became crucial for his
whole prophetic work. The nature of God is described in this
story by means of two concepts: *kādôsh* and *kābod*; God is the holy
one, i.e. who is the personal power of awful reality, exalted above
all things human and indeed who stands in complete contrast to
man, before whom man becomes conscious for the first time of
his complete impotence and insufficiency, indeed of his forlorn
state; God is at the same time the majesty (*kābôd*) who pervades,
encompasses and controls the whole world, who moulds history
by his own power according to his own plan, who makes known
his exalted state in judgment and salvation and brings his purpose
to its fulfilment. In the face of this divine reality only *one* posture

is possible for man, that which Isaiah describes with the word 'believe' (7: 9; 28: 16; 30: 15. For Isaiah this word embraces the whole attitude of the man who perceives God in his holiness and majesty, acknowledges him and trusts and obeys him to the exclusion of all others. Therefore the prophet rejects all trust in human power and human wisdom; there is only *one* fear and only *one* trust, namely God. (8: 13.) This belief is not the feeble fatalism of the quietist, but the highest deployment of strength with unsuspected energies even there where man has no longer a rational support for his confidence and is face to face with the God who hides himself (8: 16). In the matter of politics and religion Isaiah does not advocate a Utopia, but stands for a realism based on religion; for him there is only one policy derived from responsibility to God. Therefore Isaiah understands the nature of sin to be fundamentally the refusal to see and to recognize in life the exalted reality of God. What he denounces with scathing words is self-assurance, injustice, avarice, luxury, the power-politics of men, a man-made cult, all these grow out of this ultimate root. Nor is the responsibility to God cancelled for Isaiah by the fact that in his theocentric thought he recognizes sin to be the consequence of hardening by God, of the judgment of God (6: 10 ff.; 29: 9 ff.). For him judgment too means that the exalted majesty of God prevails against everthing that resists it (2: 7 ff.). To this fundamental thought of his Isaiah remained faithful all his life long, even though there are changes in his conception of the way in which judgment is carried out. For the purposive rule of the living God will not allow itself to be yoked with rational human ideas (28: 23 ff.). Therefore his conceptions too of salvation are not always the same. Beside oracles of complete annihilation he proclaimed already in his early days that a remnant would be saved (Shear-jashub was born before 734); in the Syrian-Ephraimite war he seems to have applied the idea of the remnant to the whole of Judah or to the kingdom of David which is to be restored (Alt); later he made a clear distinction between nation and religion and in 28: 16 saw the remnant as a community of believers without giving up the hope that Jerusalem would be saved. The emphasis is now transferred to the individual's decision to believe and thereby the position is reached where faith could survive the collapse of the nation. This change is fundamental for the history of religion. Side by side with it the national messianic idea, which in 9: 1 ff.; 11: 1 ff. is rooted in the coronation ritual is now treated as a matter of the spirit; this presupposes a break with the line of the Davidic house which had reigned up to that time. And when the NT refers back to Isaiah's messianic prophecies, this is an indication that Isaiah had set foot on the road of which the goal is Jesus Christ.

23. Deutero–Isaiah (Is. 40–55)

Commentaries: see section 22.–KAT: Volz, 1932.–HSAT: Budde, 1922.–SAT: Haller,[2] 1925.–Frey,[3] 1938.–Bentzen, 1943.–TBC, North, 1952.–IB: Muilenburg, Coffin, 1956.–Kittel, *Jes.* 53 *und der leidende Messias im AT*, 1899; Füllkrug, *Der Gottesknecht des Deuterojesaja*, 1899; Budde, *Die sog. Ebed-Jahwe-Lieder*, 1900; Cornill, ThR 1900, 409 ff.; Sellin, *Studien zur Entstehungsgeschichte der jüdischen Gemeinde*, 1. *Der Knecht Gottes bei Deuterojesaja*, 1901; Stärk, 'Die Ebed-Jahwe-Lieder in Jes. 40 ff.', BWAT 1913; Gressman, 'Die literarische Analyse Deuterojesajas', ZAW 1914, 254 ff.; Fischer, 'Isaia 40–55 und die Perikopen vom Gottesknecht', *Atl. Abh.* VI, 4–5, 1916; idem, 'Wer ist der Ebed?', *Atl. Abh.* VIII, 5, 1922; Mowinckel, *Der Knecht Jahwäs*, 1921; Gunkel, *Ein Vorläufer Jesu*, 1921; Sellin, *Mose*, 1922; Köhler, 'Deuterojesaja, stilkritisch untersucht', BZAW 1923; Haller, 'Die Kyroslieder Deuterojesajas', *Gunkel-Festschrift*, 1923, 261 ff.; Rudolph, 'Der exilische Messias', ZAW 1925, 90 ff.; idem, 'Die Ebed-Jahwe-Lieder als geschichtliche Wirklichkeit', ZAW 1928, 156 ff.; Torrey, *The second Isaiah*, 1928; Gressman, 'Der Messias', FRLANT 1929, 285 ff.; Hempel, 'Vom irrenden Glauben', ZSTh 1929–30, 631 ff.; Sellin, 'Tritojesaja, Deuterojeseja und das Gottesknechtsproblem', StKZ 1930, 73 ff.; 145 ff.; Mowinckel, 'Die Komposition des deuterojesajanischen Buches', ZAW 1931, 87 ff., 242 ff.; Eissfeldt, *Der Gottesknecht bei Deuterojesaja im Lichte der israelitischen Anschauung von Gemeinschaft und Individuum*, 1933; Elliger, 'Deuterojesaja in seinem Verhältnis zu Tritojesaja', BWAT 1933; Caspari, 'Lieder und Gottessprüche der Rückwanderer (Jes 40–55)', BZAW 1934; Glahn und Köhler, *Der Prophet der Heimkehr*, 1934; Stevenson, 'Successive phases in the career of the Babylonian Isaiah', BZAW 66, 1936, 89 ff.; Mowinckel, 'Neuere Forschungen zu Deuterojesaja, Tritojesaja und dem 'Äbäd-Jahwe-Problem', *Acta Orientalia*, Vol. XVI, 1938, 1 ff.; Sellin, 'Die Lösung des deuterojesajanischen Gottesknechtsrätsels', ZAW 1937, 177 ff.; Begrich, 'Studien zu Deuterojesaja', BWAT 1938; Bentzen, *Messias, Moses redevivus, Menschensohn*, 1948; Engnell, 'The Ebed Yahweh Songs and the Suffering Messiah in Deutero-Isaiah', BJRL 31, 1, 1948, 54–93; North, *The Suffering Servant in Deutero-Isaiah*, 1948; Snaith, 'The Servant of the Lord in Deutero-Isaiah', *Studies in OT Prophecy* (ed. by Rowley) 1950, 187 ff.; Lindblom, 'The Servant Songs in Deutero-Isaiah', *Lund. Univ. Årskrift*, N.F. Avd. Vol. 47, No. 5 (1951); Rowley, *The Servant of the Lord*, 1952, 1 ff.; von Waldow, 'Anlass und Hintergrund der Verkündigung des Deuterojesaja', *Diss. Ev. theol. Fak. Bonn*, 1953; Rendtorff, 'Die theol. Stellung des Schöpfungsglaubens bei Deuterojesaja', ZThK 51 (1954), 3–13; Jenni, 'Die Rolle des Kyros bei Deuterojesaja', ThZ 10 (1954), 241–256; de Boer, 'Second-Isaiah's Message', OSt Vol. XI, 1956; Rignell, *A Study of Isaiah*, ch. 40–55, 1956, Lund, Univ. Årskrift N.F., I, Vol. 52, No. 5; O. Kaiser, 'Der Königliche Knecht. Eine traditionsgeschichtlich—exegetische Studie über die Ebed–Jahwe-Lieder bei Deuterojesaja, 1959, FRLANT 70.

Chapters 40–55 of the book of Isaiah did not originate with Isaiah, but with an unknown prophet to whom the name of

Deutero-Isaiah has been given in scientific studies because of the position in which his writings are placed. Already in the early Middle Ages some rabbis doubted the traditional attribution to Isaiah; since Döderlein in 1775 and Eichhorn in 1782 a growing number of scholars have recognized that we have to do with a writing produced about two centuries later. Its form and subject-matter as well as the historical and intellectual background of its times show that these chapters belong to a different period from the sayings of Isaiah. Scholars were not wrong in speaking of a style peculiar to Deutero-Isaiah; it is characterized by a certain uniformity, by repetitions, by the prominence of particular types of speech, namely oracles of salvation, songs of lament and thanksgiving, hymns and controversies, whilst the genuine prophetic forms of speech are remarkably scarce. We may agree with Volz in explaining this as being due to preaching by word of mouth in the synagogue which was coming into existence and of which Deutero-Isaiah may be considered the spiritual leader. This might also account for the inner relationship of his oracles to the cultic traditions concerned both with the history of salvation and with eschatology (cf. now v. Waldow; a different view is taken by Begrich, who—in spite of the form of the prophet's oracles—is thinking exclusively of written prophecy). Already the first words of the book lead us into another world: the people are in need of consolation; Israel is in exile in Babylon, dejected, near to despair in 42: 22; 43: 14; 46: 1 ff.; 47: 6 and *passim*, Jerusalem and Judah are destroyed in 44: 26 ff.; 49: 8, 16 ff.; 51: 3; the prophet is attempting to rouse the people to fresh hope for their imminent deliverance through the omnipotence of Yahweh in 40: 2; 41: 10 ff.; 42: 15 ff.; 43: 1 ff. The Persian king Cyrus who is named in 44: 28 and 45: 1 and who according to 41: 2 f. has already made his appearance in history as a victorious conqueror, is seen by the prophet to be 'Yahweh's Anointed', charged by God to deliver Israel. Since the expectations expressed in 46: 1 f. and in 47: 1 ff. regarding the fall of Babylon were not fulfilled, the oracles of the prophet—at least chapters 40–48—must be placed in the time between the war with Croesus of Lydia in 546 and the capture of Babylon by Cyrus in 538. In chapters 49–55 there is no more mention of Cyrus and of the approaching fall of Babylon. Baudissin and Volz explain this by saying that these oracles belong to the time immediately after the conquest of Babylon, but before Cyprus published his edict of liberation; in their view, as the hopes placed by the prophet on Cyrus, that he would worship Yahweh and prepare the way for his worship in the world, had not been fulfilled, Deutero-Isaiah mentions him no more in chapters 49 ff. But there may be another reason for this which we cannot now discover. Begrich overrates the influence of historical events on the message of Deutero-Isaiah. He makes a sharp distinction between an 'eschatological' form of his hope which he connects with Cyrus's revolt against Astyages of Media in the year 553–2 and the transference of this hope to Cyrus as the deliverer sent by God, which was due to the Lydian war in 547–6; in this case a fundamental 'transformation' of the prophet's hope for the future must be assumed. Begrich thinks that the actual activity of Deutero-Isaiah is limited by these two events. But in spite of the ingenuity employed by Begrich in this matter he has not produced decisive proof that the 'hope set on Cyrus' excludes the eschatology taken over from the cultic tradition by Deutero-Isaiah and that his silence concerning Cyrus in the other passages could only be explained by a period in which the prophet knew nothing of Cyrus 'as yet'.

The author is well acquainted with conditions in Babylon; moreover most of his oracles which bear the marks of oral utterance are addressed to the exiles. Thus it is likely that Deutero-Isaiah himself exercised his ministry in exile and had grown up in the Babylonian captivity. This would explain the fact that owing to his trenchant criticism of Babylon the prophet let the written version of his pronouncements go out without his name. Others conjecture on less convincing grounds that Deutero-Isaiah lived in Egypt (Ewald, Marti, Hölscher) or Palestine (Seinecke, Mowinckel), or in the Lebanon (Duhm). Others again think he joined in the return from exile and did not write chapters 49–55 until then (Kittel, Procksch and others); yet the passage in 52: 11 supporting this conjecture ('go ye out from thence' = Babylon; but cf. 52: 5 'here') does not necessarily lead to this conclusion. The view of Volz seems to me more probable that Deutero-Isaiah remained in Babylon and devoted himself there to the missionary task, especially if the missionary ideas of the Servant Songs (see below) may be applied to the prophet himself.

The prophetic writings preserved in chapters 40 to 55, considered as a whole, must be pronounced a unity; that which distinguishes chapters 40–48 from 49–55 is not so marked that they must be assigned with Staerk to two different authors. The writing is composed of about fifty loosely connected short sayings and songs which were probably originally declaimed during the gatherings on the Sabbath or for lamentations (v. Waldow). This is suggested by the rhetorical strain which we cannot fail to notice (rhetorical questions, harangues, appeals, repetitions and a preaching style). As a result of this an internal progressive movement of connected thought throughout the whole work cannot be detected (against Budde); but the opposite explanation, namely that the sayings are strung together according to a purely external concord of catchwords without any kind of arrangement (Mowinckel) also goes beyond the mark. For we can after all observe a certain arrangement as regards chronology and subject matter, in so far as the sayings contained in 40–48 are probably to be placed earlier in time than those in 49–55, and the conclusion in 55: 11 clearly refers back to the beginning of the writing in 40: 8. Thus nothing stands in the way of the hypothesis that Deutero-Isaiah himself wrote down his utterances and put them together on the whole in the shape in which they have been handed down. Elliger is hardly right in wishing to assign a number of oracles to the pupil of Deutero-Isaiah, called 'Trito-Isaiah', whom he regards as the actual collector and reviser of his master's prophecies. But apart from perhaps 44: 12–20 and 52: 3–6 we can scarcely identify in 40–55 any additions or revisions and the difference between 40–55 and the chapters 56–66 attributed by Elliger to Trito-Isaiah is so great that it justifies us in regarding 40–55 as a homogeneous work with a character of its own.

In these chapters the much-discussed 'Servant Songs' in 42: 1–4; 42: 5–9; 49: 1–6; 50: 4–9; 52: 13–53: 12 occupy a special place. They are scattered amongst the other songs and oracles of the prophet without any recognizable connexion of subject-matter, and they can be detached from their literary environment without disturbing the continuity. This leads to the conclusion that these songs were inserted at a later date and must be considered as separate passages in relation to the rest of Deutero-Isaiah's prophecy. The songs are connected with each other so closely by their language, their style and the content of their thought (42: 4 points to 53: 1 f. as its goal) that in spite of their being dispersed they may be regarded as a unity. The problem of the Servant Songs lies in the remarkable existence side by side of similarities and differences as compared with the rest of Deutero-Isaiah's prophecy. This is seen already in the language in which he expresses himself; words characteristic of Deutero-Isaiah which in his prophecy refer to Israel or Cyrus are here applied to the servant ('call by name', 'hold by the hand'); the style of Deutero-Isaiah is particularly apparent in 42: 8 f. The monotheistic, universal conception of God as the theocentric cause and goal of the work of salvation, the idea of mission, the waiting of the Gentiles for this salvation, these are fundamental thoughts which play the same decisive role in the Servants Songs as they do in the prophecy. On the other hand the songs differ from the rest of the sayings of Deutero-Isaiah, in which the prophet keeps everything personal in the background, by their avowedly individual, indeed autobiographical quality, as well as by the use of the designation 'servant' for a single person, whilst elsewhere in Deutero-Isaiah the expression indicates the people of Israel collectively (41: 8 f.; 42: 19; 43: 10 and *passim*). Moreover the missionary purpose which is expressed in the prophecies by the passive witness of Israel to God's power and dominion, is envisaged in the Servant Songs as the active missionary work of the Servant; and in connexion with this the eschatological character of salvation recedes and the method by which the Gentiles receive salvation is modified.

Two problems above all demand a solution, that of the authorship of the Servants Songs and the problem raised already in Acts 8: 34 as to who is meant by the Servant. With regard to the problem of authorship the affinity of the Servant Songs with the prophecy of Deutero-Isaiah is after all so close that it is most natural to assume that the Songs originated with Deutero-Isaiah himself; on the other hand the differences are not such as to exclude him as their author.

Now if Deutero-Isaiah is the author of the Songs, then, judging by the use of the first person singular in 49: 1 ff. and 50: 4 ff., the simplest answer to the second question as to the person of the Servant must be that it is the prophet himself. In that case the

differences which have been mentioned between the Servant
Songs and the prophecies are explained, especially as regards their
autobiographical scheme, by the assumption that they are not intended to be proclaimed in public, but were addressed to a
smaller circle, perhaps to the prophet's disciples; to these the prophet grants a glimpse into his inner self whilst he calls himself to
account and he probably does so at a time which suggests such a
retrospect on the meaning of his past ministry. According to
50: 5 ff. the prophet seems to be persecuted and involved in legal
proceedings, probably the all too intelligible result of his by no
means unobjectionable political activities. His life's work, the
message of deliverance to Israel and the mission to the Gentiles,
is at stake in view of this situation; at that moment, confronted
with certain death by execution, which the prophet in 52: 13 ff.
looks boldly in the face as though it had already happened, his
faith soars to the audacious hope that his suffering and death do
not signifiy the failure of his God-ordained life's work, but that as
vicarious suffering 'for many' it is part of this work of converting
Israel and the Gentiles to Yahweh. In a passage fitted in between
two divine oracles in 52: 13–15 and 53: 11b–12 expressing this
certainty, the prophet makes those who remain behind confess in
53: 1–11a how by the suffering and death of the innocent one they
come to acknowledge their sin, to repent and to become converted and how in this way God's plan of salvation is accomplished in them. According to this interpretation the Servant
Songs seem to be the legacy of the prophet as he struggles in face
of death to find the meaning of his life's task, a divine revelation
granted him in his last hour as a faith victorious over death, and
passed on by him to his disciples shortly before he dies. It is they
who probably handed down these songs and fitted them in
amongst the other prophecies, though it is no longer possible to
understand why they are assigned to different places (perhaps
according to a certain biographical and chronological outlook).

The solution presented here, which is put forward in a similar
form by Mowinckel (earlier), Gunkel, Haller, Sellin, Begrich and
Volz (for the first four songs) has the advantage that the new
knowledge of faith breaking through to evangelistic comprehen-
siveness is consistent and vital; it is a knowledge such as cannot
be gained by meditating on others, but bursts forth only as a per-

sonal experience of reality (i.e. 'existentially'). The fact that the last Servant Song differs from the others in its silence about the active missionary work of God's slave is intelligible in view of the prophet's situation which of course leaves no room at all for any kind of activity; it cannot therefore be adduced as a reason for applying this song to another servant figure (against Volz). The road to salvation is now a different one (the effect of the vicarious death and suffering of the innocent servant of God); the goal of salvation in 52: 13; 53: 10 remains the same.

Beside this interpretation of the servant figure as an individual, it has since the LXX and the Targum right up to the present day been given a collective interpretation by well-known scholars. It takes into account especially the fact that in the OT nations frequently appear personified as individuals and that there is thus no need to distinguish between the servant of the songs and the one of the prophecies if they both indicate the people of Israel (Hitzig, Reuss, Stade, Wellhausen, Smend, Marti, Giesebrecht, König, Budde, Cornill, Meinhold, Steuernagel, Eissfeldt). But a whole series of personal traits which are repugnant to an allegorical interpretation as a collective entity (42: 2-4; 49: 4; 50: 4 ff.) after all advise against it. The conception too of the servant as an individual has been put forward in the most varied forms: amongst historical figures, besides Deutero-Isaiah, the following have been suggested, Moses (Sellin earlier), Jeremiah (Duhm earlier), Jehoiachin (Sellin earlier, and others), Zerubbabel (Sellin earlier), or a teacher of the Torah in the early post-exilic period (Duhm). Kittel and Rudolph have advocated the view that an unknown contemporary martyr is indicated by a combination of history and eschatology; Delitzsch, Orelli, Staerk, Gressmann, Fischer and others support a Messianic interpretation. Bentzen is impressed by the fact that various themes of Israelite and non-Israelite tradition meet in the figure of the servant and puts forward the idea that it can be interpreted as applying to the prophet as an individual and to Israel collectively combined with a messianic interpretation; this places him in the ranks of those who like Delitzsch, Torrey and Rowley emphasize the fluid nature of the conception of the servant. Gressmann, Staerk, Haller, A. Jeremias, Mowinckel and Bentzen have conjectured that there are in the songs and figure of the servant cultic mythological influences of the conception of the vegetation-god (Tammuz-Adonis) who dies and rises again. Engnell has applied to the Servant Songs Gyllenberg's suggestion (*Svensk Exegetisk Årsbok*, 1940, p. 87) to regard the book of Deutero-Isaiah as a prophetic imitation of the liturgy for the festival of Yahweh's accession; in the songs Engnell thinks he sees, on the strength of comparisons with the texts from Ras Shamra, beside the Tammuz themes others from ideologies of kings and primeval man of the Near-East. The figure of the servant he interprets as a future Messiah in whom the features of the Davidic conception of the Messiah are thought to be combined with the suffering and victorious slave of God as he is understood in the light of the cultic ideology concerning the king. But doubts have rightly been raised both as to such a far-reaching use of 'parallels' from the history of religion and of cults, as well as to the merging of the varied features of the messianic figure. Whatever the extent of the influence on the Servant Songs which one is prepared to concede to existing traditions within and outside the OT, yet the fact remains that they are entwined with the fate of the prophet and of his task. This is what explains also the anonymity of his writing which was placed after Isaiah 1–39 on account of some similarities of language.

In its historical aspect the *significance of Deutero-Isaiah* lies in the fact that as a spiritual leader in exile he not only preserved the legacy of the great prophets right through the internal crisis of the nation, but that in the changed external and internal situation of Israel he aroused it and led it forward to a new life. *His way of conceiving God* unites the ideas of the cultic tradition with those expressed by his prophetic predecessors to form a concept of comprehensive completeness and power. God is 'the first and the last', the unrivalled, sublime and eternal creator and lord of *nature and history*. By combining on a grand scale universal creation, universal history, and universal redemption (salvation) Deutero-Isaiah advanced beyond his predecessors to that homogeneous theocentric view derived from the world-wide monotheistic conception of God which belongs to the essence of the biblical *Weltanschauung*. This God, to whom the forces of nature and the powers of history do service, makes use both of the orderliness of nature and history and of the incomprehensible miracle in order to glorify himself before the world. Yet the God who does all

things for his honour is at the same time the God of incomprehensible love, the shepherd and redeemer of his people. His coming which the prophet announces again and again in rapturous
tones and hymns derived from the old tradition of the cult is the
dawn of the ultimate (eschatological) reign of God on earth. In the
face of this God 'all flesh is as grass'; but the prophet knows too
that the everlasting God gives 'power to the faint, and to him that
hath no might he increaseth strength'. Deutero-Isaiah is the prophet of the hope like the flight of an eagle, of the waiting on God
which never grows weary. And yet behind the soaring optimism
of his faith there is a severe struggle to win the certainty of this
faith in God. Although we learn little from the writings themselves about the personality of Deutero-Isaiah, yet the characteristic form in which he argues both about God and in his predictions, the style of his rhetorical questions and controversial discourses cannot hide the fact that the prophet is addressing himself not only to the paralysing doubts amongst the nation, but also
to the temptations in his own breast. His hope in Cyrus failed him;
visible success was denied to the great missionary task which the
prophet himself took in hand, he is seized by misgivings that 'he
has laboured in vain' (49: 4). The Servant Songs are a moving
witness to the manner in which the prophet had to fight his way
through again and again even in the face of persecution to the
certainty of God, and finally he was led through the 'martyrdom'
of his own suffering and death to the knowledge of the un-
searchable greatness of God, who builds up even as he destroys
and who creates new life out of ruin. The things he had thus
come to know have helped Christendom to comprehend the
passion of Christ; in this there lies the deep meaning of the
messianic interpretation of the songs of the suffering slave of
God, an interpretation which is recently being stressed more
strongly. Thus Deutero-Isaiah has been called not without good
reason a 'forerunner of Jesus' (Gunkel) and 'the evangelist of the
OT' (Seinecke).

24. Isaiah 56–66

See Commentaries and literature for section 22 and section 23.–Kosters, 'Deutero-
en Trito-Jezaja'. *Theol. Tijdschrift* 1896, 604 ff.; Gressman, *Über die Jes 56–66
vorausgesetzten zeitgeschichtlichen Verhältnisse*, 1898; Littmann, *Über die Abfassungszeit*

des Tritojesaja, 1899; Cramer, *Der geschichtliche Hintergrund der Kap.* 56–66 *im Buch Jesaja*, 1905; Zillessen, ' "Tritojesaja" und Deuterojesaja', ZAW 1906, 231 ff.; Abramowski, 'Zum literarischen Problem von Jes 56–66', ThStKr 1925, 90 ff.; Elliger, 'Die Einheit des Tritojesaja', BWAT 1928; idem, 'Der Prophet Tritojesaja', ZAW 1931, 112 ff.; Odeberg, *Trito-Isaiah*, 1931; Glahn and Köhler, *Der Prophet der Heimkehr*, 1934.

Since Duhm in 1892 detached chapters 56–66 from Deutero-Isaiah and assigned them to another prophet of the Ezra-Nehemiah period, the spread of this hypothesis has brought the name *Trito-Isaiah* (third Isaiah) into use for the alleged author of these chapters. Yet this name is really legitimate only under two conditions, namely that chapters 56–66 do not belong to chapters 40–55 and at the same time that they represent a literary unit which is ascribed to a *single* author.

(1) The view that chapters 56–66 must be separated from chapters 40–55 has with few exceptions (König, Torrey and others) generally prevailed. Most of the oracles have other historical circumstances in view. The nation is living in Palestine; Jerusalem is built up again. The subject-matter of these prophecies is no longer the great longing for deliverance and for the return home, but miserable conditions, details and quarrels in the life of the community. We hear of the shortcomings of bad leaders of the people in 56: 9 ff., of syncretistic tendencies and the worship of idols in 57: 3 ff.; 65: 1 ff.; 66: 3 ff.; of arguments against building the temple, 66: 1 ff. As contrasted with Deutero-Isaiah the expectations of salvation bear a marked worldly and materialistic colouring; the nations have a different relationship to salvation. The conception of God is not as lofty as that of Deutero-Isaiah and his strong trustful optimism will be sought in vain. The fact that especially in 60–62 sayings of Deutero-Isaiah are frequently employed and quoted, their original meaning being distorted, supplies a complete proof that there is a deep gulf between Deutero-Isaiah and the passages in Is. 56–66.

(2) There are substantially greater differences in the views of scholars as regards the second question about the homogeneity of the prophecies in Is. 56–66 and their dating which is bound up with it. The opinion of Duhm that Is. 56–66 is derived from a single author, namely a forerunner of the reform of Ezra and Nehemiah in the fifth century has been followed by Marti, Cornill, Hölscher, Littmann and Pfeiffer. By means of critical investiga-

tions into the language and the style Elliger in particular has attempted to prove that Trito-Isaiah was a disciple of Deutero-Isaiah, to whom chapters 56–66 as well as the revision and publication of his master's prophecies are supposed to be due. This view which would make of Trito-Isaiah a contemporary of Haggai and Zechariah is supported also by Sellin, Meinhold and others. But Elliger relies too much on linguistic evidence; after a critical scrutiny not many phrases are left over which are actually used in common and after all the differences carry too much weight to be overlooked. Thus for example the word *sedek* includes in Deutero-Isaiah the whole of divine salvation, whilst in 56 ff. it is used mainly for human uprightness. It is still less possible to prove in 56 ff. a spiritual homogeneity of subject matter which would reach the height of 40–55 and could be understood as arising in the same historical period and in one and the same spiritual epoch of post-exilic Judaism. The individual passages reflect quite different circumstances. Thus, for example, the passage 56: 1–8 dating perhaps from the beginning of the fifth century deals with problems concerning the ordering of the community and contains the far-sighted phrase about the temple as a 'house of prayer for all peoples'; 56: 9 ff. is a sharp indictment of the bad shepherds who pursue only their own gratification and gain, but amongst their people are like dumb dogs who cannot bark. In 60–62 a series of quotations attracts attention and has suggested the idea of a small collection by an imitator and follower; these passages might have come from early in the post-exilic time. On the other hand in 63: 7–64: 11 which shows a certain affinity with Lamentations no relationship with Deutero-Isaiah can be established, probably because we are concerned here with a product of the first exilic days which are earlier than Deutero-Isaiah. 65 and 66: 3 ff. are thought to have originated in Hellenic times because it was then that the attack on the deities Gad (fortune) and Meni (Destiny) seems to have gained greater influence and customs are contemplated probably belonging to the practices of the mysteries which were beginning to spread at that time. Scrupulous exegesis must fill in the details; at any rate these examples suffice to show that in Is. 55–66 we are not concerned with the work of a single prophet 'Trito-Isaiah' but with a collection of appendices to the book of Isaiah by different hands and from different times. Moreover this view is upheld by a number of scholars amongst whom we may name Kuenen, Cheyne, Kosters, Baudissin, Kittel, Budde, Volz and Eissfeldt.

It can no longer be determined whether these appendices existed in the first instance as smaller collections of anonymous prophecies and songs or were added individually to the book of Isaiah, and whether perhaps the vigorous use of the book of Isaiah in the liturgy or a certain affinity with Deutero-Isaiah prompted their being attached to Is. 55. Is. 56–66 is a valuable source of information for our otherwise very scanty knowledge of post-exilic Judaism; we derive an insight into the significance of the Sabbath from 58: 16 f., of the temple from 56: 7, into the progress of eschatology from 65: 17, into the difficulties of building up the community from 56: 1 ff.; 59: 1 ff., 65: 1 ff., and we see how in spite of everything the sternness of the prophet's conception of God and of the recognition of sin in 57: 14 ff.; 59: 1 ff.; 64: 5 ff. remained alive.

25. Jeremiah

Commentaries: KeH: Hitzig,[2] 1866.–KHE: Duhm, 1901.–SZ: Orelli[3], 1905.–HK: Giesebrecht,[2] 1907.–WC: Binns, 1919.–HSAT: Rothstein, 1922.–SAT: H. Schmidt,[2] 1923.–KAT: Volz,[2] 1928.–TU: van Ravenstejn, 1925–27.–HS: Nötscher, 1934.– CEB: Condamin,[3] 1936.–HAT: Rudolph, 1947, [2]1958.–Cornill, 1905.–Riciotti, 1923. –EB: Nötscher, 1947.–LStB (Clamer): Dennefeldt, 1947.–SBB: Freedman, 1949.– LStB.: Gelin, 1951.–Bewer, Vol. I, 1951; Vol. II, 1952.–LSB: Penna, 1952.–ATD: Weiser I[2], 1956; II, 1955, [4]1960.–LSBR: Vaccari, 1953.–IB: Hyatt, Hopper, 1956. Schwally, 'Die Reden des Buches Jeremia gegen die Heiden, XXV, XLVI–LI', ZAW 1888, 177 ff.; Cheyne, *Jeremiah, his life and times*, 1888; Marti, *Der Prophet Jeremia von Anatot*, 1889; Stade, 'Bemerkungen zum Buche Jeremia', ZAW 1892, 276 ff.; Erbt, *Jeremia und seine Zeit*, 1902; Kieser, 'Das Jeremiabuch im Licht der neuesten Kritik', ThStKr 1905, 479 ff.; Jakoby, 'Zur Komposition des Buches Jeremia', ThStKr 1906, 1 ff.; Mowinckel, *Zur Komposition des Buches Jeremia*, 1914; Baumgartner, 'Die Klagegedichte des Jeremia', BZAW 1917; Volz, *Der Prophet Jeremia*, 1918; [3]1931; idem, 'Studien zum Text des Jeremia', BWAT 1920; Skinner, *Prophecy and Religion*, 1928, [2]1951; Horst, 'Die Anfänge des Propheten Jeremia', ZAW 1923, 94 ff.; Hertzberg, 'Prophet und Gott', *Beitr. z. Förderung christl. Theologie*, 1923; Th. H. Robinson, 'Baruch's Roll', ZAW 1924, 209 ff.; Lofthouse, *Jeremiah and the New Covenant*, 1925; Welch, *Jeremiah, his Time and his Work*, 1928, [2]1951; G. A. Smith, *Jeremiah*, [4]1929; Kost, 'Jeremias Stellungnahme zur Aussenpolitik der Könige Josia und Jojakim', *Christentum und Wissenschaft*, 1929, vol. 2, 3 ff., Rudolph, 'Zum Text des Jeremia', ZAW 1930, 272 ff.; Gross, *Die literarische Verwandtschaft Jeremias mit Hosea*, 1930; Calkins, *Jeremiah the Prophet*, 1930; Gross, 'Hoseas Einfluss auf Jeremias Anschaungen', NKZ 1931, 241 ff.; 327 ff.; Morgan, *Studies in the Prophecy of Jeremiah*, 1931; Gordon, *The Rebel Prophet*, 1932; Bardtke, 'Jeremia, der Fremdvölkerprophet', ZAW 1935, 209 ff.; ZAW 1936, 240 ff.; Birkeland, *Zum hebräischen Traditionswesen, Die Komposition der prophetischen Bücher des AT*, 1938; Herntrich, *Jeremia, der Prophet und sein Volk*, 1938;

Rudolph, 'Zum Jeremiabuch', ZAW 1944, 85 ff.; Birkeland, *Jeremia, Profet og Dikter*, 1950; Rowley, *The Prophet Jeremiah and the Book of Deuteronomy, Studies in OT Prophecy*, 1950, 157 ff.; Steinmann, *Le prophète Jérémie: sa vie, son œuvre et son temps*, 1952;–Leslie, *The intimate Papers of Jeremiah*, 1953; idem, *Jeremiah, Chronologically arranged, translated and interpreted*, 1954; Miller, *Das Verhältnis Jeremias und Hesekiels sprachlich u. theologisch untersucht mit besonderer Berücksichtigung der Prosareden Jeremias* (Van Gorcums Theol. Bibliothek) 1955; Birmingham, *Jeremiah the Prophet*, 1956.

I. *Life and Ministry*. We have far more information about Jeremiah's life and ministry, and also about his inner struggles, than we have in the case of the other prophets. The reason for this is not only that we possess records of it from the hand of Baruch, his friend and fellow-worker, but also that in Jeremiah's prophecy his personal life as an individual is more prominent, and we are given especially in the 'confessions' an insight into the life of the prophet's soul. Four periods can be distinguished in his ministry: (1) his activity under King Josiah from his call in 627 to the Deuteronomic reform in 621; (2) under Jehoiakim from 608–604 (597); (3) under Zedekiah to the fall of Jerusalem from 597–587; (4) after the destruction of Jerusalem until Jeremiah's death in Egypt.

(1) Jeremiah was born the son of a priest in Anathoth about 4½ miles north-east of Jerusalem in the middle of the seventh century, but he was not himself a priest. He was called by God in his youth to be a prophet and he gives an account of this in chapter 1. It is open to question whether after his call he began by appearing as a prophet in his native town and was only induced by disappointments to turn to Jerusalem, as Duhm infers from 5: 1 ff. and 11: 18 ff. For already in his early oracles he addresses the 'men of Judah and Jerusalem' and it is most likely that this probably may have taken place on the occasion of the gatherings for the feasts in Jerusalem. Starting from the original tradition of the covenant with Yahweh, he scourges the adulteration of religion and its admixture with heathen elements, which marked the period of King Manasseh and the first years of the reign of the young Josiah, as faithless back-sliding into the nature-religion of Baal which was both materialistic and sensual; and he is forced to pronounce upon it the judgment which threatens it 'from the north' if the people do not 'return' to Yahweh. Side by side with the oracles of judgment there stands the call to return; starting again from the fundamental tradition of the covenant the prophet

H

promises the contrite people the return home of the prisoners of the Northern Kingdom and the reunion of the separated sister-kingdoms for the common worship of Yahweh in a freshly organized covenanted relationship (3: 1–4; 4; chapter 30 f.). Thus perhaps he prepared the way for the aspirations which led to the political and religious reforms under Josiah. This would explain the fact that from the period after the Deuteronomic reform until the death of Josiah we can identify no oracle of Jeremiah to which a reliable date can be assigned. We may conclude from this that, though Jeremiah expressed no opinion on the subject of Deuteronomy, he recognized a certain measure of success for his prophetic preaching when the Josianic reform recalled the people to their senses and abolished the foreign cults. This led him to expect a change for the better without the need of any intervention on his part in the process of reclamation which had begun. The same point of view appears in the favourable general verdict which Jeremiah pronounced on the reign of Josiah in 22: 15 f.: 'he did judgment and justice . . . then it was well'. Kost wishes to find in chapter 31 Jeremiah's assent also to Josiah's policy of national expansion.

(2) A different situation arose when with the death of Josiah the national and religious hopes were shattered and Jehoiakim, installed as king in 608 by the Pharaoh Necho against the people's will, began to subject them to a cruel and unscrupulous rule under which the Deuteronomic reform became practically ineffective. The severe strictures with which Jeremiah denounces the arbitrary despotism of the king (22: 13 ff.) has the result that from then onwards king and prophet are bitter enemies. To this must be added the opposition of the priests who cannot bear Jeremiah's attack in 7: 26 on the frivolity of their outward confidence in the temple and his prophecy that it would share the fate of the sanctuary at Shiloh. The prophet is accused of blasphemy, but for the time being escapes punishment, because a similar prediction by the prophet Micah was recalled as a precedent (Mic. 3: 12). But the enmity of the priests continues; Jeremiah is threatened by informers and attempts on his life (18: 18; 20: 10). When with prophetic symbolism he breaks a pitcher as a sign of the complete destruction of Jerusalem (19: 1, 10 f.) his first martyrdom begins; he is scourged, put in the stocks (20: 1 ff.) and prevented from

entering the temple in future. One day he learns with horror that even in his own family a secret plot to murder him is being hatched (11: 18 ff.). Shunned by the people, excluded from the joys and successes of life, the lonely man struggles in bitter despair with his God; presumably it was at this time that he produced and wrote down those personal confessions of his inner sufferings and distresses which stir us deeply by their candour in 12: 1 ff.; 15: 10 ff.; 16: 1 ff.; 20: 7 ff., and probably also the vindictive prayers in 11: 18 ff.; 17: 12 ff.; 18: 19 ff. which show to what depth the prophet was brought and yet how he raised himself again through the help of God. When in the decisive battle between Babylon and Egypt in 605 the world dominion passed to the victorious Babylonians and the 'foe from the North' announced by Jeremiah assumed a concrete historical shape in the person of Nebuchadnezzar, the hour had come for the prophet's threats to be fulfilled; a fresh sense of reality and urgency enters into his preaching of repentance. He receives the divine commission to write down the oracles he had delivered up till then and dictates them to his friend Baruch. On a fast-day in December 604 Baruch reads this manuscript aloud at a public meeting in the temple. The people and their leaders are deeply impressed by the oracles; the king to whom in his turn the manuscript is read, remains unmoved by it; coolly and scornfully he cuts the roll up into pieces column by column and throws it into the fire (36: 1 ff.). Jeremiah and Baruch can escape the king's order of arrest only by remaining hidden on the advice of the officials.

(3) Jeremiah's threats of disaster proved correct. In the year 597 Jerusalem is besieged and leading men amongst the people are taken into captivity in Babylon. This raised the prophet's reputation. The last king Zedekiah had the wish to listen to Jeremiah, but not the strength to assert himself against the leaders of the party in favour of war. Jeremiah advises submission to Babylon; for he regards its world domination as the instrument of Yahweh and Nebuchadnezzar as God's servant (27: 6). Now it is above all the fanatical nationalistic prophets of salvation who oppose Jeremiah. During the Syrian insurrection in 594 he has an embittered clash with Hananiah, a representative of this prophetic movement (27 f.). Jeremiah turns also to the exiles in Babylon by letter (29) and urges them to work and to hold out in patience, and even to

care and pray for the welfare of Babylon. When Jerusalem is besieged a second time in 588, Jeremiah's martyrdom begins afresh, for he is inflexible in maintaining his conviction. He is accused of treachery and desertion to the enemy, is thrown into prison and into a cistern and narrowly escapes death (37 f.). The king indeed seeks to communicate with him privately, but yet has not the courage to free him from custody. Only with the fall of the capital is there a change in his situation. He is treated with respect by the Babylonians, remains with his people and wishes to take part in the last attempt at reconstruction under the governor Gedaliah in Mizpah. After Gedaliah's murder he is forced to flee to Egypt (42 f.) and there carries on the fight against idolatry into his old age (44). Legend reports that he suffered a martyr's death in Egypt but its truth cannot be established.

II. In its present form *the book of Jeremiah* is the production neither of Jeremiah nor of Baruch, but like the other prophetic books it is the result of a long history of transmission, which can no longer be clearly surveyed in detail and in which several hands had a share. As in the case of his predecessors Jeremiah's prophetic activity consisted to begin with and principally in oral proclamation, for which he uses the customary forms of speech of the prophets (see section 7) and the liturgical types and the exhortation at the divine service as well; to all these he gave fresh life and colour, for he is one of the greatest poets of the OT. After this it is only a secondary stage in the history of the transmission, when the separate oracles of the prophet are set down in writing and collected. Chapter 36 (see above) gives us a valuable insight into how the book of Jeremiah began to come into existence. We are told there of the written record of the prophet's sayings from the period 626–605, which Jeremiah dictated to Baruch in 605 in order that it might be read aloud in public. This original roll was not the whole of the book of Jeremiah, but presumably only a smaller collection, since it was read aloud three times in one day. King Jehoiakim destroyed it; then according to 36: 27 ff. the oracles in it were dictated a second time to Baruch and 'there were added besides unto them many like words' (36: 32). This second enlarged edition of the original Jeremiah forms no doubt the nucleus of his book; it consists presumably of oracles in the first person singular from the years 626–605. As we do not know

exactly either when the amplifications of the collection were
written down, nor how extensive the additions were, the natural
attempt which has often been undertaken to extract this second
record from the book as we now have it can hardly be realized.

The contents of the present book of Jeremiah are divided into five
parts: (a) 1–25; (b) 26–36; (c) 37–45; (d) 46–51; (e) 52.

(a) The first part 1–25: 14 is marked out as a distinct section by
the fact that 25: 1–14 in its original form was intended to be a
final summary and that in the LXX, which has probably preserved
an older arrangement, 25: 14 is followed by the group of poems
about the nations (MT chapters 46–51 and 25: 15–38). The clearly
recognizable division of the LXX into I. oracles of doom against
Judah and Jerusalem in 1–25; II. threats against foreign nations in
25: 15 ff.; 46–51; III. prophecies of salvation in 26–36 corresponds
to the tripartition to be observed in Is. 1–35 and in Ezekiel, and
may go back to a later redactional arrangement. The first part of
the book of Jeremiah contains the prophet's oracles apparently
set out according to the three historical periods of Jeremiah's
ministry: 1–6 out of the time of Josiah; 7–20 mainly out of the
time of Jehoiakim and 21–25 for the most part out of the time of
Zedekiah. 25: 1–14 from the year 604 was placed at the end out of
regard for chapter 36. It is not possible to say for certain whether
this arrangement indicated a certain concern for biography; we
might most readily ascribe this to Baruch to whom we owe the
narratives concerning Jeremiah's trials (37–45) and whose hand
may be presumed also in 19: 14 ff.; 21: 1 ff.; 25: 1 ff. What Baruch
contributed to the production of the book of Jeremiah cannot in
any case be called a biography. The biographical sequence is interrupted at various points by oracles grouped according to their
subject-matter, such as those about the cult in 7: 1 ff.; laments in
9: 9 ff.; droughts in 14: 1–15: 9; wisdom-sayings in 17: 5 ff.; sayings concerning the king's house in 22: 1 ff. and against the prophets in 23: 9 ff. Here perhaps earlier combinations of Jeremiah's
oracles may have been used. Thus Baruch or a later collector seem
probably to have inserted Jeremiah's own notes according to
their subject-matter. It is no longer possible to discover why the
'Confessions' (see above) which like other passages not intended
for public recital (e.g. 3: 6–11; 7: 16–20; 11: 18 ff.) go back to notes
made by Jeremiah for his own use, are now scattered in several

places. The oracles in the first person singular against Israel and Judah in 36: 2 dating from the time before 605 no doubt belonged to the original roll of which 25: 1–14 perhaps once formed the conclusion.

(b) In chapters 26–36, unlike the account in 1–25 in the first person singular, the third person singular predominates, since the words and actions of Jeremiah are fitted into a framework of historical narrative. It is very instructive for this method of presentation to compare the speech about the temple reproduced in chapter 7 as dictated by Jeremiah with the account in chapter 26 dealing with the same material in which the description of the events connected with it forms the main interest. These may have been independent notes of Baruch, especially where a record in the third person singular was at hand; where the first and third persons alternate (chapters 27, 28, 30 f., 32, 35) Baruch seems to draw on direct information from the prophet or Jeremiah's personal notes; 30: 2 offers positive evidence for this in the case of the oracles of salvation collected in chapters 30–31. In chapters 27–29 we can see indications of a special mode of transmission, yet we can determine nothing more precise about its origin and history. The arrangement of the separate pieces is partly chronological in 26–29, partly by subject-matter in 30 ff.; it is no longer discernible in 34 f. Chapter 36 which belongs chronologically before chapter 34 f. is placed intentionally at the end as the retrospect of the editor on the way the book of Jeremiah's oracles came into being.

(c) Chapters 37–45. Chapters 37–44 contain continuous narratives in the third person singular concerning the ministry and sufferings of Jeremiah during the siege of Jerusalem and after the fall of the city until his last activities amongst his fellow-emigrants in Egypt. The intimate knowledge of the individual personalities and events suggest that Baruch was the author although he is not named anywhere. It cannot be proved that all the passages composed by Baruch were once collected into a homogeneous chronologically arranged 'biography by Baruch' and were torn apart by a later redactor (thus Rudolph, Rost and others). In chapters 37–44 the concern for the prophet's unhappy fate is connected in such a way with the concern that the divine oracles should be upheld that the question of the truth of these oracles, raised once again at the end (44: 22 ff.), stands out in view of the external and in-

ternal tragedy of Jeremiah's ministry as the unsolved problem of
the prophet's fate. By adding as a conclusion in chapter 45 a
divine oracle which had been addressed to him personally by
Jeremiah in 605, Baruch supplies the answer that the passion of
God's messenger and his prophetic mission belong together in
accordance with God's will, and that it is just this which confirms
the truth of God's word which Baruch had been obliged to experience for himself too at Jeremiah's side. If this is so, chapters
37–45 must be regarded as a legacy composed perhaps only after
the death of his master, the truth of which Baruch himself also
acknowledges as he hands it on to faithful hands amongst the
future generations. In 39: 1 f., 4–10, 13 a summary of the account
in chapter 52 about the fall of Jerusalem is merged by a redactor
with Baruch's narrative, so that the historical sequence of the
events is obscured.

(d) Chapters 46–51 occupy a position apart. They contain
prophecies against foreign nations: in 46: 2–28 against Egypt, in
47: 1–7 against the Philistines, in 48 against Moab, in 49:1–6
against Ammon, in 49: 7–22 against Edom, in 49: 23–27 against
Damascus, in 49: 28–33 against Kedar and Hazor, in 49: 34–39
against Elam and in 50 f. a lengthy oracle against Babylon. This
collection reveals a larger number of interpolations as compared
with other parts of the text of Jeremiah and its independent
character can be recognized chiefly by the fact that the LXX has
put these oracles in a different position in the book of Jeremiah
and in a different order, namely after 25: 13, so as to connect them
with 25: 15–38, which is placed at the end. The LXX has therefore
treated them as a unity. This arrangement represents an earlier
stage in the redaction as compared with that of the MT and probably grew out of the needs of public worship. The reason for
placing the poems about the nations subsequently at the end of the
book of Jeremiah was presumably the fact that after the end of the
exile the great minatory poem against Babylon became for the
general public of greater immediate importance and seemed a
more suitable conclusion than the oracles about the downfall of
Jewry in Egypt (chapter 44). When considering the oracles about
the Gentiles opinions diverge widely both as regards their authorship and also their unity. Bardtke conjectures that Jeremiah wrote
the nucleus of these oracles which were revised and expanded and

he assumes the existence of an originally independent booklet of oracles against the foreign nations with which he includes besides the kernel extracted from 46–49 also 25: 15–17 and 25: 27–29 and the account of Jeremiah's call in 1: 2, 4–10. He attributes this booklet to the period of Jeremiah's first ministry in which he says that Jeremiah appeared as a member of the order of Nebiim to be a prophet against foreign nations. His very ingenious argument, for which 1: 10 hardly supplies a sufficiently strong foundation, leads nevertheless to consequences (a radical change in Jeremiah's prophecies, a different sequence of events, the absence of an oracle against Assyria which still existed at that time) of which there is no trace in the rest of the book. Volz also maintains the original unity of these oracles. But he denies that this booklet originated with Jeremiah and traces it back to a follower of the prophet who composed it as a homogeneous work in the time after the death of Nebuchadnezzar (562), making use of the writings of earlier prophets (Amos, Isaiah and particularly Jeremiah). This work is then said to have been added later as an appendix at the end of Jeremiah, as was done in the case of Deutero-Isaiah, with the knowledge that it did not originate with Jeremiah (similarly Mowinckel, Pfeiffer and Rost). Yet this seems to be controverted by the fact that unlike the book of Isaiah Jer. 52, the historical appendix from the book of Kings, stands not before, but after 'Deutero-Jeremiah'; moreover the difference from the undisputed oracles of Jeremiah is emphasized too strongly, and on the other hand too little attention is paid to the secondary revision of individual poems, whilst it is dated by chapters 50–51 which do not come from Jeremiah. The majority of the scholars consider 46–51 to be a compilation of various oracles concerning foreign nations which came into being as a whole in the period after Jeremiah, but of which some pieces (especially the oracle against Egypt, but perhaps also the sayings against Edom, Moab, Ammon and Elam) might go back to a Jeremianic matrix of the year 605 (cf. 46: 1 f.) or else 597 (cf. 49: 34). The comprehensive oracle against Babylon (chapters 50–51), which was produced between 587 and 538, was inserted by a redactor in connection with Baruch's narrative of Jeremiah's letter prophesying doom sent to Babylon (51: 59 ff.) and was interpreted by him as the contents of that prophecy. Only an exegesis of the details can procure a more precise verdict on this question which is still in debate and depends on the method yet to be definitely established which was used in the subsequent revision of this section.

(e) Jer. 52 is a historical appendix taken from the book of Kings and is parallel with 2 Kgs. 24: 18–25: 30. Yet unlike Is. 36–39 there is here no mention of oracles of Jeremiah nor of him himself. Perhaps the narrative of Jerusalem's ruin is to be understood as a pointer to the fulfilment of Jeremiah's pronouncement of doom, and the information about the liberation and the honour done to the captive king Jehoiachin as the first indication of a return of salvation, both of which Jeremiah had announced in different oracles.

The origin and growth of the book of Jeremiah can indeed no longer be discerned or described as a coherent process in the history of the transmission to be pursued backwards into its details without any gaps. Nevertheless different stages in the form of the tradition stand out as distinct from each other, and these afford a general survey of the development of the book of Jeremiah.

The book was based to begin with on Jeremiah's notes of various kinds, such as the oracles of the original roll dictated to Baruch in the year 605 or else its second enlarged edition, and also on his writings, such as e.g. his confessions, the prophecies of restoration in 30 f., the prayers for vengeance, etc.; the second stage of development consists of the sayings composed and rearranged by Baruch partly by utilizing the above-mentioned material, partly by elaborating it on his own account; to these we may add the story of the prophet's sufferings in 37–45. The third stage is characterized by the interpolation of foreign matter and revisions; usually these are considered to include those oracles of Jeremiah which have been given a more instructive and edifying form and set in a framework which recalls the Deuteronomic style and was the regular usage for the cultic recital of the prophetic writings (in the synagogue) (cf. 7: 1 ff.; 11: 1 ff.; 16: 1 ff.; 18: 1 ff., 21: 1 ff.; 22: 1 ff; 25: 1 ff.; 34: 8 ff.; 35). Mowinckel and Rudolph assign these pieces to a special Deuteronomic source which came into existence during the exile. But the fact that pieces such as 7: 1 ff. and 11: 1 ff. run counter to the fundamental trend of Deuteronomy (cf. on this now Miller) suggest that here it is a matter of the phraseology in public worship, employed already before the 'Deuteronomic' view of history and revision, and used by Jeremiah himself or by Baruch, as seems to be the case in 21: 1 ff.; 22: 1 ff.; 25: 1 ff.; 34: 8 ff. and 35. But since such instructions and exhortations were suitable for repeated use in worship it is not possible in every case to keep apart the original wording of Jeremiah's sermons and any later liturgical elaboration.

The following are almost universally regarded as subsequent insertions of considerable extent: 10: 1–16, a saying about the unreality of idols reminiscent of Deutero-Isaiah; 17: 5–13 some Wisdom sayings; 17: 19–27 a saying about the commandment for the Sabbath; a catalogue of sins in 32: 29–35 and a promise of deliverance in 32: 37–41; also oracles of salvation in chapter 33. Yet there is no compelling reason to deny the Wisdom sayings to Jeremiah, and in the case of 10: 1–16 and 17: 19–27 we must consider whether the secondary elaboration does not go back to original sayings of Jeremiah. Smaller additions may in part be deduced from the shorter text of the Septuagint. The oracles concerning foreign nations in 46–51 also were subjected to revisions, expansions and reinterpretations; the great oracle against Babylon especially which seems to depend on Is. 13 f. is an exilic addition, which was later given an eschatological significance (see 51: 46).

A proof of the growth of the text is supplied by a *comparison of the MT with the LXX*. The text of the LXX is shorter by about one-eighth than the MT. Something may certainly be explained by the Septuagint's efforts to abbreviate; yet there are also lacking some longer pieces which could not have been in the text underlying the LXX and this provides proof of a later growth since the LXX text is on the whole an earlier one. The fact that work was still done on the MT at a relatively late date, as well as the not inconsiderable number of additions and revisions are signs of the living significance which the book of Jeremiah had in public worship and in the religious life of the later congregation.

When considering *Jeremiah's religious significance* we must start with his relationship to the tradition of the cult of Yahweh. That this tradition meant to Jeremiah, the priest's son, the world in which his personal religious life was at home, is evident from the liturgical forms and traditional images in which his private prayers and confessions are expressed (15: 10 ff.; 17: 12 ff.; 18: 18 ff.; 20: 10

ff.; 32: 16 ff.). His prophetic message too was not infrequently proclaimed as part of the festival cult at the temple of Jerusalem (cf. e.g. 2: 4; 5: 7; 7: 2 ff.; [26: 11]; 8: 17; 10: 1 ff. and *passim*) where he occasionally assumes cultic functions as a prayer leader or intercessor (9: 1 ff.; 10: 17 ff. 1; 14: 1 ff., 17 ff.; 16: 19 ff.). The fundamental data of the covenant with Yahweh, which he assumes to be known to his hearers, are used by him as points of contact from which to start his preaching, when with diverse variations he refers back to the saving deeds and the demands of Yahweh handed down in salvation history and from there proceeds to criticize the situation of the day.

His picture of the future (3: 6 ff., 19 ff.; 23: 6; 30 f.) is also determined by the idea of the renewal of the covenant and its sacral traditions. Yet it would be wrong to try and see in Jeremiah a reactionary or a cultic prophet who, in the face of mistaken developments, was striving to restore the past. His prophetic activity is not exhausted by his return to the tradition of the cult of Yahweh. By going back to its fundamental principles, and by proceeding from there to expand and at the same time to enlarge and to deepen it, he gives to this tradition an interpretation relevant to the present time, derived from the new perspective of his particular prophetic mission.

The reason for this lies beyond tradition in Jeremiah's personal experiences of God and in his own attitude towards them, which also takes him out further than the prophetic tradition. Thus one can discern in Jeremiah a certain turning point in the history of the OT prophetic movement.

The heritage of the early prophets is still alive in Jeremiah, but at the same time something new is fighting its way up in him which is leading out of the prophetic movement proper. Like his predecessors he stands as a prophet on the Godward side, forced into service by his personal experience of the power of God's otherness (20: 9; 6: 11; 23: 9, 29) so that he cannot pronounce the message as he wishes (42: 7; 18: 1 ff.; 13: 1 ff.; 28: 11). He is God's tool, his mouth, his slave, who with a certain passivity receives the revelation and hands it on obediently. But beside the knowledge concerning his existence on the Godward side, Jeremiah is conscious of his own human existence which is often in opposition to God. The tension between the prophet and the man Jeremiah continues from his call in 1: 6 throughout his whole prophetic life (15: 18; 20: 7, 9); and even when God and the man are in agreement, the man faces God with some kind of independence (15: 16). Thus Jeremiah's relationship to God becomes a mutual one, a dialogue, and it finds its typical expression in prayer (6: 9 f.; 7: 16; 12: 1 ff.; 15: 10 ff., etc.). His prayer does not, as with Amos, confine itself to intercession, and hence it becomes a new factor in his experience for his personal and prophetic certainty regarding God (see above). But thereby this certainty itself becomes on occasion a problem which gets acute especially in the controversies with the prophets of salvation and leads to a differentiation between the divine word and the prophet's own thoughts (23: 9–31; 28). By this route intellectual rational considerations find a wider entry into prophecy. The prophet is occupied with the idea of predestination in 1: 5, with the problem of theodicy in chapter 12: 1–5, with the question of solidarity in retribution in 31: 29. Again and again he is uneasy about his own relationship to the God who 'tries the reins and the heart' (11: 20; 17: 14 ff.). And yet in the last resort no intellectual solution is given. There is only *one* way out of the deepest despair, the way of obedience. Ultimate understanding is won in the process of living not *in intellectu*, but *in actu* (15: 19; 12: 5).

As regards his prophetic task also Jeremiah stands on the shoulders of the earlier prophets; he proclaims and delivers judgment and in doing so he stands completely on the Godward side. But this does not exhaust his task; in it too the human side is emphasized more strongly than by his predecessors. His duty is that of the 'metal refiner (6: 9, 10 ff., 27 ff.), he is the spiritual pastor and tutor for conversion. As intercessor he stands between God and people and must endure what is the worst form of isolation, namely, that intercession is forbidden him (7: 16, 11: 14; 14: 11, 15: 1). It is in this ambivalence that there lies the tension of his calling, the source of his inner suffering (cf. 1:10; 18: 7 ff.; 17: 15; 44: 4 ff.).

In his *conception of God* Jeremiah shows a close kinship with Hosea. In the foreground there stands first of all Yahweh's special relation to Israel, founded on God's original grace and love (2: 1 ff.; 3: 4 ff.; 31: 20 ff.) as exemplified in the covenant (11: 3 ff.; 31: 31 ff.). The rational conclusion drawn from God's absolute claim and

Jeremiah's religious experience at first hand of world history leads him to conceive of God as the universal God of the world, to whom as the creator of the world and lord of history (27: 5 f.; 31: 35 f.) all powers are subject and obedience is due (27: 6: Nebuchadnezzar is Yahweh's servant). It is this conception of God which supplies the explanation when Jeremiah counsels submission to the king of Babylon and summons the exiles to pray for Babylon and when, in this respect a forerunner of Deutero-Isaiah, he sets the crown on his hope for the future by looking forward to the recognition of Yahweh by all nations (31: 34).

Jeremiah sees *the relationship of man to God* to be based, from the point of view of man, on the inner surrender of the whole man to God (29: 12 ff.) in love and loyalty (2: 32; chapter 35). The immediacy of the relation to God thus excludes also the intervention of priests and cult and the mistaken trust in cultic methods (6: 20; 7: 1 ff.; 29: 12 ff.; 31: 34). Yet the duty of obedience is emphasized all the more strongly, especially with regard to social ethics in 2: 34; 6: 7; 21: 11 f.; 22: 3 ff.; 34: 8 ff. Although Jeremiah conscientiously examines the individual sins of the people, he recognizes sin not alone in the casual transgressions; he presses on to the recognition of the ingrained nature of sin which consists in a perverted basic attitude and in man's callousness with regard to God (4: 22; 5: 3; 6: 15; 13: 23). But whilst Jeremiah sees that it is impossible for man to overcome by his own efforts his habitual sinfulness, he maintains with undiminished earnestness his demand for conversion, that is the turning of the whole person to God (3: 1 ff.; 8: 4 f.; 15: 19; 36: 7). In this way he expresses the tension which is always the mark of the consciousness of reality in a living religion. For Jeremiah God himself relieves this tension. It is he who from the depths of his unfathomable love subdues his anger within himself (31: 20) and forgives human sin, who on his own initiative will make a new covenant on the foundation of the forgiveness of sins by giving man a new heart (31: 31 ff.; 24: 7). Thus in his hope for the future Jeremiah returns again to the starting-point of his whole prophetic work and reveals, as he exhibits his God-centredness, the deepest roots of a faith which has received the best of what it has to say as a gift from God himself.

26. Ezekiel

Commentaries: KeH: Smend², 1880. –SZ: Orelli², 1896.–KHC: Bertholet, 1897.–
HK: Kraetzschmar, 1900.–SBOT: Toy, 1904.–HSAT: Rothstein.–WC: Redpath,
1907.–SAT: H. Schmidt,² 1923.–HS: Heinisch, 1923.–KAT: Herrmann, 1924.–TU:
Troelstra, 1931.–HAT: Bertholet, Galling, 1936; Fohrer-Galling,² 1955.–ICC: Cooke,
2 vols. 1951.–Cornill, 1886.–James Smith, 1931.–Matthews, 1939.–R. Brunner
(Prophezei) 2 vols. 1944.–HBK: Schumpp, 1942.–LStB (Clamer): Dennefeld, 1947.
–LStB.: Auvray, 1949.–EB: Ziegler, 1948.–SBB: Fisch, 1950.–LSB: Spadafora, 1950.
–Bewer, 1954.–BOT: van den Born, 1954.–LSBR: Tondelli, 1955.–COT: Aalders,
1955.–BK: Zimmerli, 1955 ff.–IB: May, Allen, 1956.–Cornill, *Der Prophet Ezechiel*,
1882; idem, *Das Buch des Propheten Ezechiel*, 1886; Bertholet, *Hesekiels Verfassungs-
entwurf*, 1896; D. H. Müller, *Biblische Studien*, I, II, IV, 1904, 1907–8; Jahn, *Das
Buch Ezechiel auf Grund der LXX hergestellt*, 1905; Herrmann, 'Ezechielstudien',
BWAT 1908; Kuhl, *Die literarische Einheit des Buches Ezechiel*, Diss. 1917; Hölscher,
'Hesekiel, der Dichter und das Buch', BZAW 1924; Kessler, *Die innere Einheitlichkeit
des Buches Ezechiel* (Berichte d. theol. Seminars d. Brüdergemeinde) 1926; Sprank,
'Studien zu Ezechiel', BWAT 1926; Kittel, *Geschichte des Volkes Israel* III, 1, 1927,
144 ff.; Torrey, *Pseudo-Ezechiel and the original Prophecy*, 1930; Sellin, *Geschichte des
israelitisch-jüdischen Volkes* II, 1931, 32 ff.; Herntrich, 'Ezechiel-probleme', BZAW
1932; Kuhl, 'Zur Geschichte der Hesekielforschung', ThR 1933, 92 ff.; Spiegel,
'Ezekiel or Pseudo-Ezekiel', HThR 1931, 245 ff.; Torrey, 'Certainly Pseudo-Ezekiel',
JBL 1934, 291 ff.; Spiegel, 'Towards Certainty in Ezekiel', JBL 1935, 145 ff.; Battersby-Harford, *Studies in the Book of Ezekiel*, 1935; Bertholet, *Hesekiel-probleme, For-
schungen und Fortschritte*, 1936, 4 ff.; Berry, 'The composition of the book of Ezekiel',
JBL 1939, 163 ff.; Gaster, 'Ezekiel and the Mysteries', JBL 60 (1941), 289–310;
Irwin, *The Problem of Ezekiel*, 1943; Messel, *Ezechielfragen*, 1945; Van den Born,
De historische situatie van Ezechiels prophetie (Analecta Lovaniensia Biblica et Orien-
talia, Fasc. 2), 1947; Jaspers, 'Der Prophet Ezechiel. Eine pathologische Studie',
Festschr. f. Kurt Schneider, 1947, 77–85; H. W. Robinson, *Two Hebrew Prophets,
Studies in Hosea and Ezekiel*, London, 1948; Balla, 'Ez. 8 : 1–9 : 1 und 11 : 23–24',
Festschrift f. Bultmann, 1949, 1–11; Howie, 'The Date and Composition of Ezekiel',
JBL Monogr. Series, Vol. IV, 1950; Eissfeldt, OTMSt 1951, 153 ff.; Zimmerli, 'Das
Gotteswort in Ezechiel', ZThK 48 (1951), 17 ff.; Kuhl, 'Neuere Hesekiel-Literatur',
ThR 20 (1952); 1–26; Rowley, *The Book of Ezekiel in Modern Study*, 1953; Fohrer,
'Die Hauptprobleme des Buches Ezechiel', BZAW 72, 1952; Steinmann, *Le prophète
Ezéchiel et les débuts de l'exil*, 1953; Eichrodt, Krisis der Gemeinschaft in Israel,
Baseler Rektoratsrede, 1953; von Rabenau, 'Die Entstehung d. Buches Ezechiel in
formgeschichtlicher Sicht', *Wiss. Ztschr. d. Martin-Luther-Univ.* Halle–Wittenberg,
Jahrg. V (1955–56), vol. 4, Gesellsch. u. sprachwiss. Reihe, 659–694; Zimmerli,
Ezechiel, ein Zeuge der Gerechtigkeit Gottes, Das AT als Anrede, 1956, 37–61.–Biblio-
graphies also in Rowley and Kuhl; Gese, 'Der Verfassungsentwurf des Ezechiel
(Kp. 40–48) traditionsgeschichtlich untersucht' BHTh 25 (1957).

The prophet Ezekiel (in Hebrew Yᵉḥezk'=May God make
strong); in the LXX Yezekiel, in the Vulgate Ezechiel, in Luther
Hesechiel) is the son of a priest, Buzi (1: 3) and had no doubt
himself been a priest of the temple of Jerusalem, as we may conclude from his exact knowledge of the pre-exilic temple. In the
year 597 he was deported with other nobles to Babylon (1: 1;
33: 21; 40: 1) and lived there in Tel-Abib (3: 15) on the canal
Chebar (1: 1) near to Nippur where he had a house of his own
(3: 24; 8: 1). According to 24: 15 ff. he was married; his wife died

suddenly in exile. In the year 593 he was called to be a prophet and it is generally assumed that he seems to have exercised his ministry exclusively in Babylon and to have enjoyed special esteem as a prophet (8: 1; 14: 1) (Herntrich considers Jerusalem to be the only place of his ministry; Bertholet, Irwin and van den Born allow for a ministry in Jerusalem up to 586 which they think was followed from 585 onwards by his prophetic activity in the exile). Two periods may be distinguished in his ministry and these have also left clear traces of themselves in the book of Ezekiel: (1) from 593–587 the prophet destroys the frivolous and deceptive hopes for the inviolability of Jerusalem and speedy change of fortune and appears essentially as a preacher of repentance and an announcer of doom; chapters 1–24 contain in the main the written deposit of this period. (2) After the great revulsion of mood which the fall of Jerusalem brought about in the people, the function of the prophet changed also; now it was a question of raising up the despondent, of directing into the right channels the repentant disposition aroused by their shattered hopes, of preparing as a comforter and a 'watchman' (33: 1 ff.; 3: 16 ff.) for their renewal and to pave the way to reconstruction; Ezekiel becomes the prophet of the restoration, the pastor of souls and the one who prepares for it spiritually. The last dated prophecy in 29: 17 is from the year 571, so that Ezekiel's ministry may be assumed to have lasted roughly twenty years. A later legend gave him also the title of a martyr.

Ezekiel is the most individual figure amongst the prophets and the one who is psychologically the most remote from ourselves. His numerous visions, recalling most readily Zechariah and Daniel (1: 1 ff.; 3: 22 ff.; 8: 1 ff.; 11: 1 ff.; 37: 1 ff.; 40: 1 ff.) his states of ecstasy and trance (3: 10 ff.; 8: 1 ff.; 11: 1 ff.) and his symbolic actions show an inclination to the bizarre which is expressed in grotesque and in part repulsive forms bordering on the pathological. Consequently many scholars have wished to explain Ezekiel's deafness and paralysis and temporary dumbness (3: 15, 24 ff.; 4: 4 ff.; 24: 27; 33: 22) as a physical illness (catalepsy), which has, however, been rejected by medical men (see Dieckhoff, 'Der Prophet Ezechiel', *Ztschr. für Religionspsychologie*, 1907, pp. 193 ff.). As an explanation of his seeing things and actions at a distance (see especially chapters 8–11) Kittel has pointed to para-psychological analogies; Bertholet on the other hand tries to avoid these conclusions by assuming that Ezekiel had a double field of action. At any rate the customary standards of normal psychology are not adequate for understanding in Ezekiel's case the prophetic manifestations which overstep the limits of the normal. The conjecture of Reuss, Kuenen and others that Ezekiel was not a prophet at all in the real sense, but only an author, breaks down in face of the numerous passages indicating that his oracles were uttered by word of mouth, e.g. 2: 4 ff.; 3: 27; 11: 25; 20: 1 ff and *passim*.

The *book of Ezekiel* in its present form was for a long time considered to be the homogeneous work of Ezekiel owing to its apparently clear structure and the chronological order in which the dated passages succeed each other; it was also considered to have been preserved fairly undamaged apart from its very corrupt text. Cornill and Smend still supported vigorously the homogeneity of the whole book. But during the last decades a thorough change of opinion has taken place amongst scholars. In fact there are essentially three partly interlocking problems which are under discussion in the modern criticism of Ezekiel: (1) Is the book a homogeneous work? (2) when was it written? (3) where did Ezekiel exercise his ministry? The book falls into three sections: chapters 1–24 contain in the main prophecies of doom against Judah and Jerusalem; 25–32 oracles against foreign nations as a preparation for restoration; 33–48 prophecies of restoration, in which 33–39 describe the coming of the restoration, the new covenant, the resurrection of the people and the destruction of Gog of Magog, and 40–48 the great vision, followed by the programme for the new organization of the temple, the city and the land. But a closer examination shows that the dates, calculated from the year of Jehoiachin's exile (597), apply only to the passages which in each case follow them immediately, and that pieces having no relation to these dates have been inserted in between them. Moreover there are a considerable number of repetitions, inconsistencies and contradictions which exclude the possibility of a homogeneous book conceived by Ezekiel. Consequently Krätzschmar conjectured that the book of Ezekiel was put together by a redactor out of two different recensions in the first and third persons singular. But this distinction cannot be accepted

since it can only find support in 1: 2 f. and 24: 24; so Budde modified the conjecture and postulated that the book composed by
Ezekiel had existed in several editions differing from each other
before they were combined into one. Herrmann attempted to
cling to the authorship of Ezekiel, though at the expense of its
essential unity, by conjecturing that the book was put together
by Ezekiel gradually from separate pieces and that he himself
made corrections here and there. Yet there are far more later
additions than Herrmann is inclined to accept. Modern critics
did not stop short at denying that there was only one author.
Like Duhm in the case of Jeremiah, Hölscher assigns only the
poetic passages to Ezekiel whom he wants to explain as a poet
after the manner of the earlier prophets. He says that the authentic
passages which would comprise only about one-sixth of the
present book were subjected later to various revisions and expansions, of which the last in the fifth century was framed in the style
of the Deuteronomist. But as in the case of Duhm the criterion
is too subjective and arbitrary and limits Ezekiel's wide range far
too strictly; Hölscher has not solved the real problem, as Kittel
has perceived correctly, but has only shifted it on to the editorial
process. The same applies to the attempt of Irwin, who considers
a mere 250 verses to be genuine on the basis of another theory of
elimination. Torrey's criticism goes further still. After Zunz
(ZDMG 27, 1873, pp. 676 ff.) and Seinecke (*Geschichte d.V. Israel*
II, 1884, pp. 1 ff.) had made suggestions of this kind in earlier
days. Torrey has explained the whole book as a pseudepigraph,
based on the description of Manasseh in 2 Kgs. 21: 1–17 and
inserted as fiction into those times, but he thinks that in reality it
only came into existence about the year 230 and that later the
chronology calculated from Jehoiachin was added and the work
ascribed to Ezekiel. Messel also reaches similar conclusions. Apart
from the fact that this impossible conjecture does not reduce, but
increases the problems of the book of Ezekiel, the point of view
of the prophet in Babylon, which can be clearly recognized in
many passages, is left completely out of account. Torrey let himself be guided by the impression that Ezekiel's oracles addressed
to Jerusalem could be explained most readily by a ministry of the
prophet in that city, and this gave rise to the hypothesis of
Ezekiel's twofold ministry, put forward with various shades of

difference by James Smith, Oesterley-Robinson, Bertholet and others, who make use of Josephus' note (Ant. X 5: 1) stating that Ezekiel wrote two books about the destruction of Jerusalem. Either Ezekiel is thought of as a prophet in exile from the Northern Kingdom and afterwards in Jerusalem, thus a century earlier (Smith), or his ministry in Jerusalem is placed in 602–597 (Oesterley-Robinson) or in 593–586 (Bertholet, similarly Pfeiffer) and is followed by one in the Babylonian exile. Bentzen discusses the possibility that Ezekiel went at some time to Jerusalem with the knowledge and at the wish of the Babylonians and worked there in the interest of their policy. Herntrich, who holds to the customary date, denies altogether that Ezekiel exercised his ministry in the exile (similarly Matthews). All these attempts suffer from the objection that the dates and places assigned to Ezekiel's oracles are regarded as the inventions of redactors without a really convincing reason being brought forward for this assertion (cf. now also Howie and Fohrer). Besides no explanation is offered as to how a redactor, especially perhaps in chapters 8–11, could be thought to have made alterations and invented trances and things heard and seen from afar merely in order to stamp Ezekiel as an exilic prophet. By tracing the para-psychological phenomena back to the editor, the problem is only transferred, but its difficulty is not thereby reduced, still less solved.

It is hardly possible to call in question either the placing or the dating of Ezekiel's oracles on the whole and these may well go back to the prophet himself. This suggests that Ezekiel kept some kind of regular record of events in a continuous chronological order. It is true this does not yet render probable the homogeneity of the present book and of its arrangement. On the contrary, closer examination makes it clear that the oracles against foreign nations interrupt the continuity between 24: 26 f. and 33: 21 and so the order in which the sayings are placed cannot be that of Ezekiel. Yet on the other hand since authentic material doubtless lies hidden in the oracles against foreign nations (disputed by Berry) we must probably agree with Eissfeldt in distinguishing a double series of authentic dated passages which are now telescoped by editorial hands, i.e. a series of oracles concerning Judah and Jerusalem and another concerning foreign nations. But even these are not homogeneous in their present condition.

We must notice that in each case the dates only apply to the immediately succeeding passage and that other passages are inserted which do not fit into the context as regards either their period or their subject-matter and are framed on the whole in a more general and less concrete style than the dated descriptions. Therefore we shall credit not Ezekiel but rather a secondary redactor with joining the dates and the undated passages and interfering with the original arrangement. Now there is no reason to doubt that in the case of the oracles of doom and of restoration for Judah and Jerusalem, as well as of those against the foreign nations, even when the passages are undated, at least a kernel originated with Ezekiel, although here and there redactional expansions can be identified. We may quote as an example the poem about Tyre as a splendid ship (27: 2–9a, 25b–36), where the flat prosaic style in 27: 9b–25a reveals clearly that it is a later interpolation. But the separation of the authentic substratum from the expansions is not always so obvious; often it cannot be achieved at all with any certainty. In any case it can be carried out only by the exegesis of the passages individually. The prophecy against Gog which no doubt originally referred to Babylon also shows many traces of secondary revision, and so does the programme for the future in 40–48; recently Galling (Bertholet's commentary) has proved from the point of view of archaeology the possibility that these chapters might have originated with Ezekiel, as against Möhlenbrink ('Der Tempel Salomos', BWAT 1932, pp. 31 ff.) and this is an argument against Berry also.

The *origin and growth of the book of Ezekiel* may perhaps be seen in three stages: (1) Two different kinds of writings by the prophet himself: (a) a regularly kept diary of dated oracles concerning Judah and Jerusalem and a collection of oracles against foreign nations, also dated; (b) speeches and poems of a general nature, partly parallel too and connected with the material of the above-named passages, which explains some of the repetitions; details can no longer be given about its shape and the first amalgamation (by Ezekiel?). (2) The collection and arrangement by a redactor in order to place all the prophecies of Ezekiel into a chronological framework which included all the material; in doing this the insertion of the oracles against the foreign nations between those of doom and of restoration was intended as a preparation for the restoration of Jerusalem. The order that we now possess created a precedent, as shown by the arrangement of the collections of the Isaianic prophecies and of the book of Jeremiah in the LXX. (3) Later expansions and additions, for which the oracles against foreign nations in particular offered the occasion, as they did in other prophetic writings. In chapters 40 to 48 matters influenced by the priestly writings, related to the P of the Pentateuch, seem to have been introduced.

Next to the books of Samuel and the Psalms the text of the book of Ezekiel is amongst the worst preserved in the books of the OT. Yet it is possible to clear up many a difficulty with the help of the LXX, the text of which was highly esteemed above all by Cornill.

The significance of Ezekiel lies in the fact that he, like Jeremiah and yet in quite another way, was the connecting link between the pre-exilic prophetic movement and post-exilic Judaism. On the whole and particularly considering his direct influence he has more definite affinities with the latter, so that he has not without good reason been called the father of Judaism. This is partly connected with the peculiar two-sidedness of his nature which can also be detected throughout his writings. In Ezekiel the priest and the prophet are combined; he is an ecstatic and a theologian, God's witness and an organizer of the community at the same time; in transports of emotion he meets God and becomes directly aware of his majesty; and then again he is one who thinks coolly and broods almost over trifles.

As a *prophet* he received his call (1: 4 ff.) like Isaiah and knows by a special experience (3: 1 ff.) like Jeremiah that he is inspired by God. He realizes that his whole life and circumstances, even the sudden death of his wife, are intended to serve his prophetic task (24: 15 ff.). Actions which are both prophetic and symbolic and are the marks of divine activity in the prophetic profession, play in his case a special role in strikingly extravagant forms.

In connexion with his prophetic experience *Ezekiel* must also be considered *as a poet*, whose powerful vision, bold imagery and stirring language can show itself confidently beside the poetry of other prophets (cf., e.g. chapter 37; 27: 1–9a, 25–36; 28: 11–19). As an authentic prophet Ezekiel like all his predecessors, announces and brings to pass divine *judgment*; like them he attacks idolatry in 8: 10 ff., fornication in 16: 15, 25 f., like Jeremiah he denounces false prophets of deliverance in 12: 22 ff.; 13, and he inveighs especially against the mistaken reliance on the hope of protection and rescue and against the confidence in Egypt as in Is. 29: 6b ff. The ultimate theme and at the same time the ultimate aim of Ezekiel's message, and therefore also the pivot of all his prophecy, is God's holiness, and indeed in an intensified sense compared with Isaiah. The ever-recurring stereotyped phrase 'that ye may know that I am Yahweh' points in this direction. In fact God shows his holiness as much in judgment as in bringing deliverance (6: 9 f.; 28: 25 ff.; 36: 22 f.). The prophet is concerned to show that nothing can shake the power of God; therefore he presents a conception of God which is harshly theocentric and contains no comfort, but only deals destruction (20; 24 ff.). On the other side there corresponds with this stupendously powerful conception of God—and in this too Ezekiel is akin to Isaiah—the awareness that all mankind is helpless and transitory and this finds expression amongst other ways in the name, 'son of man', with which God addresses the prophet. Thus for Ezekiel Yahweh is the only one who acts both when he judges and also when he builds up. He himself brings about the resurrection of the people out of the exile, he gathers and unites Israel and Judah in chapter 37 and it is he who effects the change within men's hearts (11: 19 f.; 36: 24 ff.) (cf. Jer. 31: 33 f.).

But by the side of this authentically prophetic line and inter-twined with it there is another one which reveals *Ezekiel the priest and theologian*; this is the one which really made him the father of Judaism. His purely prophetic task does not exhaust his function. Especially after the fall of Jerusalem he received the office of 'watchman' and shepherd of souls. Seen from this angle, his task includes thinking with men and for them, working with them and for them, the meditation of a theologian and the organization of a priest; this implies at the same time the prosaic style which we find beside that of the poet and prophet. As an organizing priest and an authoritative theologian Ezekiel stands on the shoulders of the Deuteronomic thinkers. In his struggle with the idea of God's justice he directs the thought of retribution on to the in-dividual in order to arouse a sense of personal responsibility: each man pays the penalty for his own sin (14: 12 ff.; 18: 4–20 f.). This theology of retribution, that a man's lot in life corresponds with his conduct, opened up a new epoch in Judaism until, as a result of the experiences of others, this dogma broke down when faced with the actual facts. In his preparation for priestly government too, Ezekiel adheres closely to his prophetic conception of God. It is true that as a former priest he esteems cultic and ritual matters more highly and quite differently from the other prophets (4: 14; 22: 23 ff.; 24: 1); but in the elaborate programme for reconstructing the cult in 40–48 there stands in the background as the guiding principle the conception of God's holiness which is to be expressed for all to see in the distinction between the holy and the profane in the new community which is to be formed. In the organization which he planned, the segregation of Israel from the Gentiles and the different degrees of holiness within the community, in which certainly external physical matters were prominent, formed an essential part. On this point too Ezekiel showed the ways to later Judaism. This attitude enables us to understand that the outlook of the prophet is restricted to the relationship between Yahweh and Israel and that the world-wide breadth of a Deutero-Isaiah is sought in him in vain; here are the roots of Jewish particularism. And lastly this determined decisively the eschatological picture of the future. In his meditation on unfulfilled prophetic predictions in 38: 17; 39: 8 Ezekiel in the prophecy concerning Gog achieves the union of prophetic eschatology with theological learning and becomes by this route the father of Jewish apocalyptic. On an all-round view Ezekiel with his theories of a theocratic state prepared the ground on which later the reform of Judaism on the basis of the Priestly Book was accomplished. We are indebted to him that Israel did not succumb to the paganism of its surroundings, but preserved its faith in its restoration. Herein lies the historical importance of Ezekiel. What makes him in spite of all his peculiarities significant for the times beyond his own is the inflexible intensity and the towering height of his conception of God.

27. The Book of the Twelve Prophets

Commentaries: KeH: Hitzig–Steiner,[4] 1881.–SZ: Orelli,[3] 1908.–HK: Nowack,[3] 1922.–KHE: Marti, 1904.–KAT: Sellin,[2 3] 1929.–ICC: Harper, Amos Hosea; Smith, Ward, Bewer, Mi Zeph Nah Hab Ob Joel; Mitchell, Smith, Bewer, Hag Zech Mal Jon, 1948–1953.–WC: Edghill, Cooke, Amos, [2]1926; Wade, Mi Ob Joel Jon, 1925;

Stonehouse, Wade, Zeph Nah Hab, 1929; Brown, Hos., 1932.–CEB: van Hoon-
acker, 1908.–HSAT: Guthe, Marti, Rothstein, Kautzsch-Bertholet, 1922.–SAT:
Gressmann,[2] 1921; H. Schmidt,[2] 1923; Haller,[2] 1925; TU: Bleeker, Hos–Mi, 1932–
1934; Smit, Nah–Mal, 1926–1934.–HAT: Robinson, Hos–Mi, 1936; Horst, Nah–
Mal, 1938, [2]1954.–Duhm, 1910 (translation); idem, 'Anmerkungen zu den zwölf
Propheten', ZAW 1911, 1 ff.; 81 ff.; 161 ff. (and off-prints);–Riessler, 1911.–HS: Lippl,
Theis, Junker, 1937–38.–Procksch, I, 1910, II[2], 1929.–ATD: Weiser, Hos–Mi,
1949[2], 1956.–Elliger, Nah–Mal,[2] 1951.–Jepsen, 1938.–Frey, 1941.–Wellhausen,[3]
1898.–EB: Nötscher, 1948.–Bewer, 1949.–SBB: Lehrmann, Goldman, Cashdan,[2]
1952.–HBK: Schumpp, 1950.–LStB: Gelin, Hag Sach Mal, 1948.–Osty, Am Hos,
1952.–George, Mi Zeph Nah, 1952.–Trinquet, Hab Ob Joel, 1953.–BOT: Deden,
Hos–Mi, 1953.–LSB: Rinaldi, 1953.–LSBR: Vaccari, Bernini, 1955.–BK: H. W.
Wolff, 1956, ff.–COT: van Gelderen–Gispen, Hos, 1953.–IB:: Mauchline, Phillips,
Thomson, Langford, Fosbroke, Lovett, Smart, Scarlett, Wolfe, Bosley, Taylor,
Cleland, Thurman, Thomas, Sperry, Speers, Dentan, 1956.–Snaith, Am Hos Mi,
1956.–Budde: 'Eine folgenschwere Redaktion des Zwölfprophetenbuchs', ZAW
1921, 218 ff.; Wolfe, The editing of the Book of the Twelve', ZAW 1935, 90 ff.;
Jepsen, ZAW 1938, 85 ff.; Fohrer, 'Neuere Literatur zu atl. Prophetie', ThR 1951,
277 ff.; 1952, 193 ff.; 295 ff.

The books of the 'Major' Prophets are followed in the Hebrew
canon by the writings called by the Vulgate owing to their size
the book of the twelve 'Minor' Prophets which are put together
into *one* book. This collection, which includes a whole library of
various prophetic writings during a period of more than half a
millennium, was brought to a close as a complete book relatively
late. As Wolfe conjectures, it probably only came into being by a
gradual growth. In opposition to Budde who visualizes only *one*
editorial process, we must allow for different editings and stages
in the collection having had a share in the compilation and revision of the book. The *arrangement* of the separate books leads
us to the same conclusion. In the first half the LXX departs from
the customary sequence of the MT and places them probably
according to their size, thus: Hosea, Amos, Micah, Joel, Obadiah,
Jonah, putting the story of the prophet in the booklet of Jonah
at the end. This difference between the MT and the LXX is a
proof that when the LXX came into being the collection and the
principle governing it were not yet fixed in every respect. In the
arrangement of the MT also different view-points seem to have
played their part, which suggests that the book was assembled by
successive stages. The view-point of chronology can be recognized in the fact that the prophets Haggai, Zechariah and Malachi,
who at that time were considered post-exilic, were placed at the
end, and that the book of Jonah was inserted before that of Micah
as it was associated with the pre-exilic prophet Jonah in 2 Kgs.
14: 25. Joel and Obadiah seem to have been included with the

pre-exilic prophets owing to the similarity of subject-matter; in
Joel there are passages similar to Amos, e.g. with Joel 4: 16 ff.
compare Amos 1: 2, with the plague of the locusts in Joel 1 f.
compare Amos 7: 1 f. and with the day of Yahweh in Joel 3 compare Amos 5: 18 ff.; in the same way the day of Yahweh appears
to have been the connecting link for placing Obadiah after Amos.
Probably the size of the writings also played its part in their
grouping and the number twelve does not seem to have been
unintentional. If we must reckon with the fact that the Book of
the Twelve was gathered together by stages, the beginnings may
have been made in comparatively early days; the exile might be
suggested for the collection of the pre-exilic writings. Ecclesiasticus 49: 10, where Isaiah, Jeremiah and Ezekiel are followed by
'the twelve prophets', establishes the date before which the
collection was closed. Thus the writings which had been handed
down were put into *one* book in the third century. Whether preceding older partial collections were used, and if so of what kind
they were, can no longer be told. This does not mean that later on
some changes were not made in the form and content of the individual books, especially when it is remembered that this book
too was subjected in its practical religious use to ever new interpretations and reinterpretations to fit the circumstances of the day.

28. Hosea

Volz, *Die vorexilische Jahwe-Prophetie und der Messias*, 1897, 24 ff.; Valeton, *Amos
en Hosea*, in German by Echternacht, 1898; Öttli, 'Amos und Hosea', *Beitr. z. Förderung christl. Theologie*, 1901; Volz, 'Die Ehegeschichte Hoseas', ZWTh 1898, 321 ff.;
Riedel, *Alttestamentliche Untersuchungen*, Vol. I, 1902, 1 ff.; Meinhold, *Studien zur
israelitischen Religionsgeschichte* I, 1903; Baumgartner, *Kennen Amos und Hosea eine
Heilseschatologie?*, 1913; Alt, 'Hos 5 : 8-6 : 6', NKZ 1919, 537 ff.;=Alt II, 163 ff.;
Humbert, 'Osée le prophète bédouin', RHPhR 1921, 97 ff.; Heerman, 'Ehe und
Kinder des Hosea', ZAW 1922, 287 ff.; H. Schmidt, 'Die Ehe des Hosea', ZAW
1924, 245 ff.; Peters, *Osee und die Geschichte*, 1924; Budde, 'Der Abschnitt Hosea 1-3',
ThStKr 1925, 1 ff.; idem, 'Zu Text und Auslegung des Buches Hosea', JBL, 1926,
280 ff.; JPOS 1934, 1 ff.; JBL 1934, 118 ff.; Sellin, 'Die geschichtliche Orientierung
der Prophetie des Hosea', NKZ 1925, 607 ff.; H. Schmidt, 'Hos. 6 : 1-6', *Sellin-
Festschrift*, 1927, 111 ff.; Lindblom, *Hosea, literarisch untersucht*, 1927; Rieger, *Die
Bedeutung der Geschichte für die Verkündigung des Amos und Hosea*, 1929; Batten,
'Hosea's message and marriage', JBL 1929, 257 ff.; Nyberg, *Studien zum Hoseabuche*,
Uppsala, 1935; idem, *Hoseaboken*, 1941; T. H. Robinson, 'Die Ehe des Hosea',
ThStKr 1935, 301 ff.; Vriezen, *Hosea: profeet en cultuur*, 1941; H. W. Robinson, *Two
Hebrew Prophets, Studies in Hosea and Ezekiel*, London, 1948; Snaith, *Mercy and
Sacrifice: A Study of the Book of Hosea*, 1953; Bück, *Die Liebe Gottes beim Propheten
Osee*, 1953; Rowley, 'The Marriage of Hosea', BJRL, Vol. 39, No. 1 (1956), 200 ff.

The prophet Hosea (=may God help) appears to be a contemporary of Isaiah according to the title of the book by a later hand in 1: 1; which accounts for naming, in addition to the two contemporary kings of Judah and Israel, Uzziah and Jeroboam, three more kings of Judah, Jotham, Ahaz and Hezekiah (cf. Is. 1: 1). This statement is only partly correct. Hosea appeared during the period of Jehu's dynasty (1: 4), therefore before the murder of Zechariah, the son of Jeroboam II, in 746. According to 7: 16; 8: 4; 10: 3, 15 he witnessed the troubles over the succession after 746. There seem to be allusions in 5: 13; 7: 11 f.; 8: 9; 10: 5 f; 12: 2 to the tribute of Menahem to Tiglath-pileser in 738 and the relations with Assyria. 5: 8–6: 6 refers to the Syrian-Ephraimite war. The relations with Egypt mentioned in 7: 11; 9: 6; 12: 2 no doubt concern the doings of Hoshea, the last king of Israel. But we do not get the impression from any part of the book of Hosea that the prophet came forward after the fall of Samaria and the destruction of the Northern Kingdom. Thus we can assume the period of his ministry to have been during the quarter of the century between 750 and 725.

As the prophet has his eye almost always on the conditions in the Northern Kingdom, at least the sphere of his ministry and probably his home as well is to be sought there (cf. also 7: 8 ff. and 10: 3). It is evident that he belonged to the cultured class from the knowledge of history, the wide range and the ripe judgment on past and present events which he reveals, as well as from the elegant and well-chosen imagery of his language. That Hosea had been a priest (Duhm and others) cannot be deduced from his acquaintance with the conditions of the priesthood (4: 1 ff.; 5: 1 ff.); nor will it do to regard him as a member of the order of the Nebiim (Sellin, Eissfeldt, Rost and others) on the basis of the taunt in 9: 7 'the prophet is a fool, the man that hath the spirit is mad'; otherwise the same would be proved for Amos by Am. 7: 12 f., 16.

The only thing that we know about Hosea's personal circumstances apart from the name of his father, Beeri, is what is told in chapters 1 and 3 about *his marriage and his children*. The question has been much discussed whether these chapters contain poetical prophetic fiction intended to be allegorical (thus Reuss and recently Gressmann again) or whether they are based on an actual experience of the prophet (Wellhausen, Budde and others).

The latter must be the right answer, for the name of the wife, Gomer, as well as the weaning of the second child in 1: 8 and the mention of his wife's purchase-price are traits which forbid an allegorical interpretation; moreover the moral scandal would be just as great in the case of an allegory as in that of an actual happening. There is also the further question as to how the story in chapter 1 is related to that in chapter 3. Is the wife in chapter 3 the same as the one in chapter 1 or a different one (Duhm, Nyberg, Fohrer, Pfeiffer)? Is the account of the marriage in chapter 3 merely a repetition of 1: 2 f. (Robinson) or does it describe a re-marriage of Hosea with Gomer? Further, when Hosea first married (1: 2 f.), was he aware that he was marrying a prostitute, or did his wife's adultery only take place during their marriage, or at least only become known to Hosea then? The correct answer seems to be the last alternative, namely, that according to 1: 2 Hosea only came to know of his wife's faithlessness during their married life, and so his children may not have appeared to him to be his own. For if it had been a symbolic and prophetic action—for that must be the assumption in the first alternative—its motives and its effects would contradict all that we know elsewhere about the character of such actions. The realization that the inner failure of his marriage was the will of God, in order that this might reveal the relation of Israel to Yahweh, was intended first and foremost for the prophet himself, and not for the people; this is the indispensable presupposition of what is told in chapter 3. Therefore also chapter 3 must be concerned with the same wife whom Hosea had probably divorced after discovering her adultery. For it is only if Hosea *remarried* Gomer that there is any sense in interpreting this as Yahweh's loving acceptance for a second time of the faithless Israel. On the other hand the prophetically symbolic names of the children in 1: 3–9 are not connected in any way with their mother's adultery; therefore when the names were given at their birth, there was no reference to it and it probably took place without Hosea knowing about his wife's faithlessness. Consequently Hosea's children were born in wedlock, and since he gave them prophetic names he cannot have received the call to be a prophet through the adultery of his wife (against Wellhausen and others).

The *book of Hosea* has two parts: 1–3 grouped round the personal experiences of the prophet and 4–14, a compilation of sayings without any internal continuity. The coherence in 1–3 is due to its subject-matter and has not the significance of a primary literary continuity, as e.g. Budde (cf. Rost) assumes, who thinks that 1–3 is a consecutive narrative; for this could only be achieved if there were no scruples about changing the account in chapter 1 from the third to the first person, or alternatively the account in chapter 3 from the first to the third person. Probably only chapter 3 (in the first person) comes directly from Hosea himself and this is the one containing the prophet's experience which is decisive for his conception of God and for his message. On the other hand the account in chapter 1 (in the third person) as well probably as the putting together generally of those passages in chapters 1 to 3 which are related to the prophet's experiences are a subsequent literary composition from the hand of a close friend who was well informed by Hosea. Then the narrative about the birth and naming of the children in 1: 3–9, which was originally an independent piece of writing was prefaced with an explanation of Hosea's first marriage with Gomer which was necessary in order to understand chapter 3. That chapter 2 stands in close relationship with the biographical chapters 1 and 3 as regards subject-matter and style, ought not to have been denied. It is a grouping of oracles of God, no doubt by the same hand as the compilation of chapters 1 and 3, which take their origin and their meaning from the events described there. Thus Israel appears in 2: 4, 9, 18, as the wife of Yahweh who has broken faith with God; Yahweh's punishment, namely cutting her off from her lovers, is a measure of discipline, so that her former love may awake again, 2: 8–15 being parallel to 3: 4 f.; the fundamental motive of God's action is love which leads to a new betrothal in 2: 16–22, that is to say, the same fundamental idea which governs the action of the prophet in chapter 3; the change in 2: 23–25 of the symbolic names of ill omen into names of good omen, which from the literary point of view presupposes the connexion between chapters 1 and 3, depends on the success of God's disciplinary punishment and represents the rounding off in chapter 2 of the whole composition of which the theme was set out at the beginning in a parallel version in 2: 1–3 (by the same hand?). This close relationship of chapter 2 with the prophet's experiences, and also the fact that the conceptions and images agree with typical ideas of Hosea (e.g. return to the desert and a fresh start there in the relationship with God) are indications that chapter 2, apart from small alterations, goes back at least indirectly to Hosea. The form of the composition as we have it today is secondary; it is probably due to the intention to place the main feature of Hosea's prophecy and its connexion with his experience at the beginning of the book.

In *chapters* 4–14 there follow in the main rebukes and threats, especially against Israel's defection to the Canaanite agricultural civilization and its materialistic cult of Baal, against the monarchy and its policy, with allusions by the prophet to a series of historical events which unfortunately we can no longer always identify. A continuous arrangement cannot be discovered; occasionally individual sayings are linked together by catchwords or association of subject-matter, a proof that they were not combined by Hosea himself. The text of this section is particularly corrupt. This reminds us that North-Israelite prophecy has come down to us only through Judaean agency, which has led at least in some passages, such as 1: 7; 5: 5; 4: 15 and *passim*, to additions referring to Judah. But it is not feasible to cut out all mention of Judah in the book of Hosea (Valeton, Nowack, Marti); thus the section about the Syrian-Ephraimite war in 5: 8–6: 6 cannot be understood if the name of Judah is omitted. It is just as impossible to try with Volz, Marti and others to remove from Hosea all prophecies of salvation. The hope of salvation is linked in the case of this prophet so closely with his personal experience and his conception of God and has such a unique and strong stamp compared with the ideas of salvation in the other prophetic books that it cannot be dissociated from Hosea. It must also be distinguished from additions, made in the book of Hosea as in other prophetic books in course of time by their use in divine service. Thus amongst other items, for example, the lines of a hymn in 12: 6 taken from the liturgy and the final exhortation in 14: 10 to ponder what has been said come from later hands.

The religious significance of Hosea, whose particular kind of sensitive and deep feeling has much in common with Jeremiah, lies above all in the close connexion between the personal experience and conditions of his life with the content of his prophecy. The most secret stirrings of his being have shown him that what he experienced and felt in his marriage must be used in the service of divine revelation, and that he stands at the source of the deepest religious knowledge. The crucial and fundamental feature of his conception of God is the *love of God*, which never fails (2: 21 f.; 3: 1; 9: 15; 11: 1 ff.; 1 14: 5 ff.). It dominates the moving review of the past in the simile of father and son in chapter 11 and the prospect of the future in the simile of husband and wife in chapter 2. With this in mind Hosea sees *judgment* as the expression of the disappointed love of God, and this explains the occasional sheer cruel harshness of the oracles of judgment (5: 14; 13: 7 f.). At the same time judgment is the method of God's *disciplinary love*, which can be stern, but always aims at the restoration of the intimate relationship of the 'first love'. Thus there stands at the centre of his message the fundamental demand for love in return, which is man's complete surrender to God with all the impulses of his heart, his spirit and his will; this is what is meant when in 4: 1, 6: 6 Hosea demands *'emet, ḥesed* and *da'at 'elōhīm*. At the same time he assumes in 4: 2 that the basic ethical commandments, recalling the Decalogue, are known and binding; in doing so he takes his stand on the cultic tradition of the authentic covenant of Yahweh, which also provides the basis of his judgment (1: 1) and his hope for the future in his simile of the marriage bond (2: 18, 21 f.). Much space is occupied by fighting against *the fertility cult taken over from the Canaanite civilization* which Hosea rightly stigmatizes as apostasy from Yahweh (adultery, fornication) owing to its admixture of sensuality and materialism. When *reviewing the history* of the people in Canaan Hosea goes down to first principles. In chapter 12 he traces the development critically right back to the tradition concerning Jacob and considers that *the monarchy* and its policies were from the beginning developing on wrong lines which led away from Yahweh (cf. 9: 10 ff. with Num. 25; 9: 15 with 1 Sam. 11: 14 f.; 13: 7 ff.; 15: 10 ff.; and 10: 9 ff. with 1 Sam. 11: 4).

This drastic judgment on the whole of the history supplies an explanation of his characteristic *picture of the future*. There is only one way: back into the wilderness and thence a fresh start from the point where Israel's relationship to God was still unimpaired. But in Hosea these ideas for the future are not, it seems, a summons to a final human effort, but an announcement of a mighty act of *God* who manifests the unconceivable greatness of his divine nature just in this, that he does not give way to his wrath, like a man, but subdues it by compassion, in order to draw the people to himself by love (11: 7 ff.). Hosea's preaching was carried forward and given greater depth by Jeremiah; that is its historical significance. The pervasive key-note of divine love, drawing judgment and mercy together into an organic spiritual unity, rings out all through this original and imperishable prophecy.

29. Joel

Merx, *Die Prophetie des Joel and ihre Ausleger*, 1879; Holzinger, 'Sprachcharakter und Abfassungszeit des Buches Joel', ZAW 1889, 89 ff.; Stocks, 'Der "Nördliche" und die Komposition des Buches Joel', NKZ 1908, 725 ff.; Budde, 'Der von Norden', OLZ 1919, col. 1 ff.; idem, Der Umschwung in Joel 2, op. cit. col. 104 f.; Baumgartner, Joel 1 und 2, *Buddefestschrift*, 1920, 10 ff.; Dennefeld, 'Les problèmes du livre de Joël', *Rech. Science Rel.* 1925, 35 ff., 591 ff.; Kutal, *Liber prophetae Joëlis*, 1932; Kritzinger, 'De profesie van Joël', 1935; Rinaldi, *II libro di Joele*, 1938; Jepsen, ZAW 1938, 85 ff.; Kapelrud, 'Joelstudies', *Uppsala Univ. Årsskrift*, 1948.

Apart from the name of the prophet, Joel ben Pethuel, which occurs in the title of the book, we have no information about the personal or historical circumstances of his activity. The *book of Joel* falls into two sections: chapters 1–2 which deal with a plague of locusts and a drought as a sign that the day of Yahweh is at hand, whilst in chapters 3–4 the day of Yahweh is surveyed. The Septuagint and the Vulgate have made of chapters 2 and 3 one chapter, and Luther has done the same for chapters 3 and 4. Chapter 1: 2–12 contains the description of an extraordinary plague of locusts and its various consequences; verse 13 f. follows with a summons to a day of fasting, succeeded in verses 15–20 with a prayer of lamentation. In 2: 1–11 an alarm is sounded in Zion and the advance of the locusts is described like that of an army in battle array; verses 12–14 are a call to genuine heart-felt penitence. In verses 15–17 the summons to a day of fasting is repeated, followed by a supplication. In verses 18–20 this is granted and a promise is given that the distress shall be turned away; verses 21–27 contain a song of thanksgiving and more promises. The proclamation of the day of the Lord begins with the pouring out of the spirit on all flesh in 3: 1–2, signs in heaven and earth in verses 3–4 and deliverance for those who call on the name of the Lord in Jerusalem in 3: 5. Chapter 4 opens with the judgment of the nations in the valley of Jehoshaphat, verses 4–8 contain a rebuke and a threat to Tyre, Sidon and Philistia; verses 9–17 speak of the final decision in the valley of Jehoshaphat and the manifestation of Yahweh, whilst verse 18 promises fertility as in Paradise and verses 19–21 the destruction of Egypt and Edom, and verses 20 f. tell of an everlasting Jerusalem where God dwells.

The first part, chapters 1–2, still bears the clear marks of an experience, very frightening in itself, on which it looks back. An atmosphere of agitation, stirring language and imagery, alternations of fear and hope, a description passing by leaps from present distress to its eschatological interpretation, all this within a liturgical framework and in a liturgical style, such are the characteristics of these chapters. They also make up the particular problem of the book of Joel, namely the question whether an actual plague of locusts or an eschatological picture is to be understood. In the latter case all three chapters would have to be regarded as predictions of the future (Hengstenberg, Merx). But now it is generally thought to have been an actual plague, for 1: 2 ff. points to the experience of a present happening and the sudden change in 2: 18 can scarcely be interpreted in any other way than as a description of the turning point in the existing danger. Although there is agreement in the main that the plague of locusts refers to a past event, yet recently opinions have been diverging about the unity of the book of Joel. After Rothstein had already assigned the two parts to different authors and periods, Duhm has won recognition amongst various scholars (Sellin, Meinhold, Oesterley and Robinson and others) for the separation of chapters 1–2, a description of a plague of locusts, from chapters 3–4, an apocalypse added later. Now this interpretation assumes that the eschatological applications of this plague to the day of Yahweh in chapters 1–2 must be regarded as subsequent interpolations by the hand of the author of the apocalypse (1: 15; 2: 1b–2a (10a), 11b). But these passages bear no marks of being inserted afterwards and indeed fit smoothly into the whole both as regards style and subject-matter, therefore it may after all be understood as a literary unit (thus also Pfeiffer, Bentzen, Kapelrud and others). We might rather ask whether the rebuke and threat to the neighbouring nations in 4: 4–8 is not a subsequent addition, since it interrupts the train of thought. The composition of the book might then be thought of somewhat as follows, that Joel after the happy termination of the plague of locusts and of the drought (2: 18 ff.) wrote down the oracles pronounced on that occasion, and in order to supplement the allusions contained in them to the coming day of Yahweh added the more detailed apocalyptic prediction in chapters 3–4. Since in the second part too, the coming of the day of Yahweh represents for Israel an experience full of fear and terror in spite of the deliverance which it will finally bring to them (3: 3 ff.; 4: 9–12, 15 ff.), this does not supply any reason for ascribing chapters 1–2 and chapters 3–4 to different authors. From the point of view of the history of the form (*formgeschichtlich*) the first part at least can be claimed as a kind of 'prophetic liturgy', composed for the day of lamentation and penitence on the occasion of the plague of locusts and recited by the prophet in the course of the cult. In that case the second part would then be considered to be a subsequent interpretation and expansion in a general eschatological sense, which by employing traditional series of ideas made it possible to utilize the prophecy later on in divine worship. Kapelrud's conjecture that it is based on the ritual pattern of the Near-Eastern fertility cults goes too far and lacks compelling cogency.

Formerly, because nothing was said about the king and there was no mention of the Aramaeans and Assyrians in the book of Joel, the conclusion was drawn that it came into being during the minority of king Joash (about 840) (Hitzig, Ewald and others); König and Kapelrud wish to place Joel's activity round about 600; but today it is almost universally acknowledged to be post-exilic. In 3: 7 ff. the destruction of Jerusalem by Babylonia and the existence of a Jewish diaspora is pre-supposed; according to 1: 14; 2: 7 ff., 17; 3, 5 the temple and the wall of Jerusalem has been built and the worship of the community occupies the centre of interest. Consequently the book of Joel no doubt originated in the period after Nehemiah about 400. Since the Greeks are already known in Assyrian inscriptions of the eighth century, it is more than doubtful whether the mention of them in 4: 6, not as a world power, but as slave-dealers, suggests the period of Alexander's successors.

The book of Joel is an instructive example of the way post-exilic prophecy allies itself with cultic piety and takes over its liturgical forms and ideas, so as to produce that remarkable duality which characterizes the book. The prophet is intent on pointing to the terrible power, made known by the plague of locusts, of the God who must be taken seriously; yet in 1: 6 he speaks of Yahweh's pity for his people in the face of their distress. The prophet's concern to ward off the troubles of the present and the material damage is as deep as his desire to meet the living God in these troubles and to throw the light of eschatology on to the present moment. With the same breath he demands the genuine inner penitence of a broken heart (2: 12 f.) and issues a summons to cultic 'fasting, weeping and mourning'. He sees in God the guarantor of earthly blessings and at the same time knows also that the aim of all that happens is the manifestation of the divine power. His view of the future is dictated by a narrow Jewish particularism towards the nations and yet occasionally it reaches out to an almost cosmic breadth. Prophecy shows that its end is near by its use of prophetic, eschatological tradition in the interests of learning and by its desire to push on from a true eschatological faith to a knowledge of the details of the end in a way characteristic of apocalyptic. It is by this means, even though weakened and permeated by elements of a different kind, that authentic prophecy remained alive in post-exilic times.

30. Amos

Löhr, 'Untersuchungen zum Buch Amos', BZAW 1901; Baumann, Der Aufbau der Amosreden', BZAW 1903; Winter, 'Analyse des Buches Amos', ThStKr 1910, 323 ff.; Budde, 'Zur Geschichte des Buches Amos', Wellhausenfestschrift, 1914, 63 ff.; H. Schmidt, Der Prophet Amos, 1917; L. Köhler, Amos, 1917; Desnoyers, 'Le prophète Amos', RB 1917, 218 ff.; Budde, 'Zu Text und Auslegung des Buches Amos', JBL 1924, 46 ff., 1925, 63 ff.; Balla, Die Droh- und Scheltworte des Amos, 1926; Mowinckel, 'Amos Boken', Norsk theol. Tidsskrift, 1927, 1; Gwynn, The Book of Amos, 1927; Weiser, 'Zu Amos 4 : 6–13', ZAW 1928; 49 ff.; idem, 'Die Berufung des Amos', ThBl. 1928, col. 177 ff.; idem, 'Die Prophetie des Amos', BZAW 1929; Cripps, The Book of Amos (SPCK) 2, 1955; Cramer, 'Amos', BWAT 1930; Stephany, 'Charakter und zeitliche Aufeinanderfolge der Drohsprüche in der Prophetie des Amos', Christentum u. Wissenschaft, 1931, 281 ff.; Krause, 'Der Gerichtsprophet Amos, ein Vorläufer des Deuteronomiums', ZAW 1932, 221 ff.; L. Köhler, 'Amos-Forschung von 1917 bis 1932', ThR 1932, 195 ff.; Herntrich, 'Das Berufungsbewusstsein des Amos', Christentum u. Wissenschaft, 1933, 161 ff.; Kutal, Liber prophetarum Amos et Abdiae, 1938; Morgenstern, 'Amos Studies', Hebrew Union College Annual, Cincinnati, 1936, 19 ff.; 1937–38, 1 ff.; 1940, 59 ff. Herntrich, Amos, der Prophet Gottes, 1941; Hammershaimb, Amos, 1946; Würthwein, 'Amos 5 : 21–27',

ThLZ 1947, col. 143 ff.; Beeck, *Amos*, 1947; Rowley, 'Was Amos a Nabi?', *Fest-schrift*, O. Eissfeldt, 1947, 101 ff.; Neher, *Amos*, 1950; Würthwein, 'Amosstudien', ZAW 1950, 10 ff.; Maag, *Text, Wortschatz und Begriffswelt des Buches Amos*, 1951; Kapelrud, Central Ideas in Amos (Skriffer utgit av det Norske Videnskaps) Akademi i Oslo II Hist.-Filos. Klasse 1956, 4.

We learn from Amos himself in 7: 14 that he was a shepherd and a dresser of fig-mulberries before Yahweh 'took him from following the flock' and called him to be a prophet against the Northern Kingdom. According to the title in 1: 1 he was from Tekoa on the edge of the Judean desert and came forward during the reign of king Uzziah of Judah (784–746) and Jeroboam II of Israel (786–746). This is confirmed by the book itself in 7: 10 f. where Jeroboam is named. The political and intellectual exultation which the prophet scourges by his oracles (6: 1, 13; 3: 9 ff.; 4: 1 ff.) fits into the picture of the last period of prosperity of the Northern Kingdom during the era of Jeroboam II. Amos seems to have appeared as a prophet about the year 760 after he had had theophanies in visions (7: 1–9; 8: 1–3; 9: 1–4)—presumably already before his call—which were of crucial significance for his prophetic work. In obedience to the commission given him at his call to raise his voice against the Northern Kingdom (7: 15) Amos began his ministry no doubt in the capital, Samaria (cf. 3: 9 ff.; 4: 1 ff.; 6: 1 ff.) and then probably went to the autumn festival, where the Israelite community gathered at the national sanctuary at Bethel, in order to continue his activity there. Denounced to the king by the high priest of this sanctuary for creating a disturbance, he is told to leave the country (7: 10 ff.) and he returned to his home after what one must suppose to have been only a short ministry. Würthwein, who with many others places Amos's visions after his call, interprets 7: 15 as the call of Amos to be a cultic prophet, taking up a conjecture of Rowley. He divides Amos's ministry into two parts: the first was that of a cultic prophet with the task of bringing salvation to pass in Israel, and in this he wishes to include the poem about foreign nations in 1: 3–2: 4 and the two first visions; only at this point is there a change-over to a proclamation of doom. But apart from the difficulties which this creates for the exegesis of 7: 10–17, this result is only achieved by dubiously breaking up the obvious continuity as regards style and subject-matter of the poem concerning the nations and of the series of visions.

The *book of Amos* presents a variety of problems. Since the prophet was commissioned in the first place merely to proclaim his message by word of mouth, the reasons for writing down his oracles were by no means the same as the motives for their oral delivery. It must be made clear to begin with that the present arrangement of the prophet's oracles has been disturbed in several places. Thus the section describing in the third person the end of Amos's ministry in Bethel in 7: 10–17 clearly interrupts the continuity between the third and fourth vision; its natural and probably its original place was at the end of the book. In chapter 5 f. also the sequence of the oracles has got into rather serious disorder. Two groups can be recognized by their form as well as by their content: (1) the visions in the first person singular in 7: 1–9; 8: 1–3; 9: 1–4, and (2) the oracles, mainly in chapters 1–6 which no doubt ended originally with 7: 10–17.

(1) The five visions (of the locusts in 7: 1–3; of the fire in 7: 4–6; of the plumb-line in 7: 7–8; of the basket of summer fruit in 8: 1–2 and of Yahweh in the sanctuary in 9: 1–4 (7)) are proved by their construction, which rises rhetorically to a climax, and by their appositeness in form and subject-matter to be a literary homogeneous unit and belonged together already when proclaimed by word of mouth. They deal with the theophanies which the prophet had in his native land (it has indeed often been asserted, but cannot be deduced from the text that 9: 1 ff. is aimed at the sanctuary of Bethel and its destruction); the fifth vision which probably leads up to the threat of an earthquake and the inescapable destruction of the people was no doubt experienced at a Judean sanctuary (perhaps in Jerusalem). The fact that the first person singular is used for the visions points to Amos as the author. Presumably he wrote down the oracles concerning his visions, which indeed imply the prediction of an earthquake, on the occasion of the earthquake two years after his public appearance in the Northern Kingdom (1: 1) and sent them there, since he himself was denied access to Israel. This written account of the visions seems to have been supplemented later, especially in 8: 4–14, by other oracles, going back to genuine words of Amos, no doubt at a time when it was still circulating separately. On the other hand 9: 8–10 gives the impression of being later.

(2) After the title and a motto-like introduction in 1: 2, echoed

in Joel 4: 16 and Jer. 25: 30 f., the *collection of oracles* contained in chapters 1–6 begins with a long poem against the neighbouring nations divided into strophes and culminating in an oracle against Israel in 2: 6–16; it ends with a compilation of woes in 5: 7–6: 14 which were probably originally better arranged. Embedded in these larger groups there are at the beginning and at the end a number of independent oracles probably arranged with a chronological sequence in view, so that those oracles pronounced by Amos in Samaria and at the beginning precede those proclaimed later in Bethel. Originally this collection seems to have been brought to a close with the biographical account of the end of Amos's activity in 7: 10–17; and we cannot exclude the possibility that the well-informed author of 7: 10 ff. whom we expect to find in the circles close to the prophet compiled this collection of oracles in its first form after the death of Amos (cf. 1: 1). The incentive for this collection may have been the concern to preserve Amos's oracles, as contrasted with the account of the visions which subsequent events had brought into the realm of actuality.

Both parts of Amos's prophecies, the account of the visions and the collection of oracles, appear to have had a separate existence for a time; we can deduce this from the amplification of the account of the visions, especially 8: 4 ff. which show several allusions to Amos's oracles. Whoever it was who took 6: 14 out of the context of the woes and placed it at the end of Amos's oracles must have been thinking of the fall of the Northern Kingdom, so that the two collections could only have been put together after 721.

Because Amos's prophecies go down to first principles they have remained relevant long after their own time. The fact that they have engaged men's attention again and again has led to all kinds of *expansions*. In the poem about the nations in 1: 3 ff. the oracle concerning Judah in 2: 4 ff. with its Deuteronomic style and probably also those concerning Tyre and Edom are later supplements; in particular it is hardly possible to fit into Amos's prophetic message the prediction of salvation in 9: 11–15, which speaks of raising up again 'the tabernacle of David that is fallen', and of the fertility of the last days, as in Paradise, although various recent voices have claimed its authenticity. Sellin who alone has given serious attention to this matter wishes to attach this piece to the threat against Amaziah in 7: 17, so that the promise to raise up again the Southern Kingdom would at the same time intensify the threat against Amaziah. But quite apart from the fact that all we know elsewhere of Amos makes it hardly possible to attribute to him such an offensive expression of malicious duplicity, there is after all neither in the passage in 7: 10–17 which is complete in itself anything demanding a continuation, nor on the other hand is there in 9: 11 f. a hint that these words have any kind of relation to Amaziah. Since 9: 15 assumes that the nation has gone into exile and the whole passage stands in irreconcilable contrast to the rest of Amos's oracles, it must be understood as a later appendix originating in the need for a hopeful outlook in a cheerless present. The promise in 9: 13 of a fertility as in Paradise with its special introduction gives the impression of being a still later expansion taken from the eschatological material of the cultic tradition. As a consequence of adding a termination about salvation to Amos's prophecy, the biographical section in 7: 10–17 was transferred from the end to its present position after 7: 9, where it has a certain connexion with the subject-matter. During the exile or later the hymn-like passages in 4: 13; 5: 8; 9: 6, probably by the same hand, were inserted; perhaps they were intended to bring to a close the section read during the liturgy and to show how in those days men submitted themselves to God's judgment and honoured the prophet's oracles.

Amos is the earliest prophet of whose message we have direct evidence. At the same time he exhibits, better perhaps than any other, the essential characteristics of the prophetic movement with such definiteness and clarity, that he can be taken, so to speak, as a perfect example of it. The opinion prevailed for a long time that with the OT 'writing prophets' there had appeared a conception of God and man which was fundamentally new in every respect and was called 'ethical monotheism'. Recently by contrast we have learned to pay more attention again to the connexion of the prophets with the tradition which was centred in the genuine cult of Yahweh. Amos too takes his stand on this tradition; he adopts its cultic forms and conceptions, e.g. in 1: 2; 1: 3 ff. and in his moral demands, giving fresh life to them. Moreover the fact that he, as a man of Judah, comes forward in the Northern Kingdom shows that his prophetic message takes as its spiritual basis the old tradition that all Israel belongs together in the sacral union of Yahweh. Yet what is decisive for the particular stamp of his prophecy is his *personal meeting with God* in his experience of the visions and in his call. This means not only the intervention of the overwhelming power of God in the external circumstances of his life, but also a change in his inner self which submits unconditionally to God under the compulsion of the divine power and thus learns to see and to judge men and things from a new line of sight which both starts from God and turns towards him. This concentration on God in all he sees and thinks dominates his whole message; it convinces him that he is entirely on the side of God facing the people; from it he draws the inexorable conclusions for every sphere. For him *God* is the absolute personal power, free from all restrictive obligations to men and equally free from all fortuitousness and capricious demonic traits; he rules with imperturbable constancy and imposes his nature by his judgment on everything that attempts to exist and to assert itself beside him and against him.

Amos's *conception of Judgment* is correlated with his idea of God; as it is the manner whereby God imposes his nature, it does not mean only the occasional intervention in particular shortcomings, but it is fundamental and final; it is the necessary and complete annihilation of all that sets itself up against God. This prophet also presupposes that the demands of *ethics* and of *law* are known to the people, and his concentration on fundamentals gives to ethics and law the force of absolute validity, because in Amos's view there stands behind them the reality of God which must be taken unconditionally and seriously. This also explains *Amos's conflict with the cult.* He is not attacking idolatry, dubious morality or cultic abuses and excess of zeal in the cult, but the whole legitimate cultic system of sacrifices and festivals of his time with all its man-made institutions. The prophet sees in this cult the way men themselves have chosen to establish relationship with God and to take the initiative in it; in the conduct of the cult he feels the lack of the intense seriousness, of unquestioning response and of being seized directly by God's absolute power (cf. 5: 4 f.; 4: 6 ff.). It is also the consequence of Amos's conception of God that he attacks the *doctrine of election* when it is used to justify a special privilege for Israel above other men; for him 'election' is the 'free act of a free God' (9: 7) without any obligation on God towards Israel, but yet linked with God's right to make demands and to call to account (3: 2). In the presence of the transcendent power of God Israel's prerogatives collapse (2: 9 ff.); hence wherever men thrust themselves forward self-confidently, relying on their own strength—whether they feel themselves to be a great power (6: 1–13) or think that with their metropolitan manners they can hold their own with other great powers or in other large cities (3: 9 ff.)—Amos flagellates them for their unconcernedness and callousness toward God which shows itself in such behaviour, as it does in the unrestrained and unsocial life of luxury of a self-sufficient humanity (4: 1 ff.; 5: 1 ff.; 6: 1 b, 4 ff., 12). Everywhere the prophet utters his stern, pitiless No, derived from the full authority of his God, of whom his own personal experience has given him an assurance; thus he has become one of the most impressive witnesses to God's reality which no one is able to elude.

31. Obadiah

Peters, *Die Prophetie Obadjas*, 1892; Condamin, 'L'unité d'Abdias', RB 1900, 261 ff.; Bekel, 'Ein vorexilisches Orakel über Edom', ThStKr 1907; Beckhahm, An Introduction to the study of Obadiah, Diss, 1910; Th. H. Robinson, The Structure of the Book of Obadiah, JThSt. 1916, 402 ff.; Theiss, *Die Weissagung des Abdias*, 1917; Cannon, 'Israel and Edom. The Oracle of Obadiah', *Theology*, 1927, 129 ff.; 191 ff.; Rudolph, 'Obadja', ZAW, 1931, 222 ff., where further literature given; Masing, *Der Prophet Obadja*, 1937; Kutal, *Liber prophetarum Amos et Abdiae*, 1938; Gray, 'The Diaspora of Israel and Judah in Obadiah v. 20', ZAW 1953, 53 ff.; Biĉ, Zur Problematik des Buches Obadjah, *VT* Supp., I, 1953, 19 ff.

This, the smallest book in the Book of the Twelve Prophets, is called in v. 1 'The vision of Obadiah'. We are told nothing of the prophet himself. It has even been conjectured that the name Obadiah, =servant of Yahweh, was prefixed to an originally anonymous writing only by a later tradition, perhaps following the example of 1 Kgs. 18: 3 ff.; and was an invention. The title and introduction in v. 1 are followed in 2–9 by a prediction of the destruction of Edom, which in 10–14, 15b, appears to be the retribution for Edom's siding with the enemy at the fall of Jerusalem and gloating over Judah's misfortune. The allusion to the imminent day of Yahweh upon all the nations in 15a, introduces another prediction for Judah in 16–21 which speaks of the change in her circumstances, of deliverance and victory for the house of Jacob and Joseph over the house of Esau and announces that the possessions which had been lost will be reconquered and that Yahweh will reign.

The question whether 2–9 is intended to be a survey of the past (Wellhausen, Nowack, Baudissin and others) or a prediction of the future (Orelli, Sellin, Rudolph and others) must be answered in accordance with verse 1 which contains a summons to the battle; therefore it is a prediction. Another problem presented by the book is that of its *unity*. Usually the two parts 1–14, 15b and 15a, 16–21 are assigned to two different authors, as the second part is thought to have a wider horizon than the first oracle which is restricted to the punishment of Edom. Sellin considers the first part also as the combination of two different pieces and deduces from the use of Ob. 1–10 in Jer. 49: 7–22 that 1–10 came into existence before 605 (cf. Jer. 25: 1; 46: 2) (in his opinion in connexion with the revolt of Edom against Judah in the ninth century in 2 Kgs. 8: 20 f.), thus representing the earliest piece of written prophecy, whilst 11–14 clearly presupposes the events of 587 and must therefore be separated from 1–10 also from the literary point of view. Robinson goes even further and looks upon the book as a collection of different originally anonymous oracles against Edom. But 11–14 giving the reason for the judgment on Edom is connected so closely with 1–10 even in its details that it is not feasible to assign these verses to two authors; consequently, since verses 10 ff. have preserved fresh memories of the concrete events at the fall of Jerusalem, the whole cannot have originated very long after 587. The fact that Obadiah's oracle was utilized in Jer. 49 constitutes no objection to this, since there are good grounds for disputing both that the date of Jer. 49 was before 605 and also that the quotation of Obadiah under discussion originated with Jeremiah. Accordingly 1–14, 15 b must be claimed as a homogeneous oracle from the period after 587. As concerns the second part, 15a, 16–21, the position is not so clear. It is true that the fundamental idea of a change in the hitherto existing circumstances suggests the judgment upon all nations; but in verse 18 the whole ends up again in the judgment against Edom. This and the fact that in verse 16 Judah is addressed, leads to the conclusion that these oracles cannot have arisen out of the same situation as

1–14; but that is no compelling reason for denying the authorship of Obadiah altogether. Since even the saying in verse 1 about the ambassador has the nations in view, it is not possible to speak of a wider horizon in the second part. Yet things are certainly seen here from another point of view and focused on the idea of the day of Yahweh; this gives to the concrete punishment of Edom an eschatological colouring similar to that which can be noticed in the book of Joel. We are concerned here with ideas which seem to be familiar amongst the prophets of salvation and set a precedent, as is shown by the dependence on Obadiah of Jer. 49 and of Joel 3: 5; 4: 3, 9, 17, 19. It might indeed be asked whether verses 19–21, which speak of the recapture of other countries as well as of the conquest of the mount of Esau and are written in prose, also go back to Obadiah; but it does not seem to me that either of these two facts forces us to assume another author.

We may perhaps think of Obadiah as a prophet of salvation in the circles faithful to Yahweh which remained behind in Palestine and out of which the oldest lamentations have been handed down to us. His oracles give us a supplementary insight into the sufferings and hopes after the collapse of Judah and reveal the association of religion with national aspirations which was one of the characteristics of the prophecies of salvation in Israel. We cannot fail to recognize an earnest faith in God, which expresses itself in the conception of the eschatological reign of Yahweh as king and in the fact that the judgment on the other nations has both an ethical and a religious foundation. The message of Obadiah is dominated not by fanatical national hatred, but by the idea of divine retributive justice; yet at the same time the narrow particularism of the hope of salvation cannot be overlooked. It reveals neither the breadth of Deutero-Isaiah's idea of salvation nor the depth of the prophetic and the Deuteronomic idea of repentance addressed to their own people.

32. Jonah

Böhme, 'Die Komposition des Buches Jona', ZAW 1887, 224 ff.; H. Schmidt, 'Die Komposition des Buches Jona', ZAW 1905, 285 ff.; idem, 'Absicht und Entstehungszeit des Buches Jona', ThStKr 1906, 180 ff.; idem, 'Jona', FRLANT 1907; Stollberg, 'Jona' Diss. Halle, 1927; Dijkema, 'Het Boek Jona', Nieuw Theologisch Tidsskrift, 1936, 338 ff.; Boman, 'Jahve og Elohim Jonaboken, Norsk Teologisk

Tidsskrift, 1936, 159 ff.; Ronner, *Das Buch Jona*, 1947; Aalden, *The Problem of the Book of Jonah*, 1948; Johnson, 'Jonah 2 : 3–10, A Study in Cultic phantasy' (*Studies in OT Prophecy*, 1950), 82 ff.

The book of Jonah differs from all the other prophetic writings in that it does not contain a collection of a prophet's oracles, but a story about a prophet. This may be the reason why this writing which makes no claim at all to have been written by a prophet and from the literary aspect belongs to quite a different type, was admitted into the Book of the Twelve Prophets. Nor can it be said that this little book is a prophetic tale of a historical and bio-graphical nature (it contains none of the information required for this purpose). It is a didactic poem written in a stereotyped, instructive style (formalized and repetitive) in order to show that God has compassion also on the heathen when they repent (3: 10; 4: 10 f.).

Contents: in chapter 1 Jonah attempts to evade God's command to preach penitence to the city of Nineveh by fleeing to Tarshish; but whilst in the ship he is overtaken by a storm sent by Yahweh and is thrown into the sea by the mariners; whereupon the storm subsides and the heathen sailors make a thank-offering to Yah-weh. In chapter 2 God sends 'a great fish' which swallows the prophet. During the three days and nights which Jonah spends in the fish's belly he pours out a psalm of thanksgiving to God, by whose command he is spat out onto the dry land. In chapter 3 Jonah obeys God's second command to preach to Nineveh and brings the inhabitants to solemn penitence so that God refrains from carrying out the threatened calamity. In chapter 4 the prophet is angered by this and is rebuked by God; he has a per-sonal experience of suffering, caused by a miracle wrought on a gourd, and is forced to admit his own narrow-mindedness com-pared with the compassion of God. Thus the tale proves to be written with a moral directed against the intolerance of the Jews and their arrogance towards heathen peoples resulting from their doctrine of election misinterpreted in a particularist sense.

This moral alone would refer the little book to the post-exilic era. Its basic attitude takes for granted the influence of the idea of universal salvation of a Deutero-Isaiah. Besides, Nineveh is thought of in 3: 3 as a legendary city in the days of long ago. Moreover the language in which it is written with its Aramaeisms and the late Hebrew forms in its vocabulary and style (1: 6, 7; 2: 1; 3: 2, 7; 4: 6, 8 and *passim*) does not permit a date before the fifth century. There is a terminus ad quem in the fact that knowledge of this book is presupposed in the second century in Ecclesiasticus 49: 10 and Tobit 14: 4, 8.

Yet the subject-matter of the tale seems to reach back into far older times. It is linked with the historical figure of the prophet Jonah ben Amittai mentioned in 2 Kgs. 14: 25 in the time of Jeroboam II. Perhaps a prophetic legend had already arisen in early days in the schools of the prophets round this figure, influenced possibly by the story of Elijah's despair in 1 Kgs. 19, and had been embellished in the course of a long history with themes from folk-tales and mythology. The adventure with the fish for example is a mythical theme which recurs amongst the most various nations, and is best known in the Greek sagas of Hercules and Perseus. As regards the details, it is certainly no longer possible to distinguish between what was taken over from old legends, folk-tales and myths and what must be ascribed to the later revision. It is the amalgamation of these different literary types which explains the miraculous nature of the story.

Taken as whole the book is homogeneous. Attempts have been made to divide it into two sources on the basis of the as yet unexplained alternation of Yahweh and Elohim as the name for God (Böhme, H. Schmidt), but they cannot be considered successful. Apart from small additions in 1: 8, 10 and a transposition of 4: 5 from its original place after 3: 4, the only obvious insertion is Jonah's thanksgiving in 2: 3–10. This is composed all through in the style of a psalm; it makes no mention in 2: 6 f. of any time spent in the fish's belly, and as a thanksgiving for past experience it does not suit the circumstances for which merely a petition is required. Nothing can be determined about its age and origin and at all events it was inserted later.

Although this little book does not belong by its literary type to the prophetic literature, yet it was not wrong to include it in the Book of the Twelve Prophets. For it breathes the true prophetic spirit particularly in the general trend of thought given to it when it was put into shape in post-exilic times. As contrasted with the constriction of Judaism after the exile in its exclusive particularism and with the distortion of the doctrine of election imposed by religious egoism, this book testifies to the greatness of the prophetic conception of God and to the large-hearted tolerance implied by this conception; it has become by its far-flung religious horizon a lasting warning against all that narrows religion. Because it is intended to show that God's compassion is greater than the human heart, that his will to save reaches beyond the boundaries of his own people and therefore leads on to the missionary task, this book belongs to those in the OT which have prepared the way for the gospel.

33. Micah

Stade, 'Bemerkungen über das Buch Micha', ZAW 1881, 161 ff.; ZAW 1883, 1 ff.; ZAW 1884, 291 ff.; 1883, 1 ff.; ZAW 1884, 291 ff.; ZAW 1903, 163 ff.; Nowack, 'Bemerkungen über das Buch Micha', ZAW 1884, 277 ff.; Ryssel, *Untersuchungen über die Textgestalt und Echtheit des Buches Micha*, 1887; Budde, 'Das Rätsel von Mi I', ZAW 1917–18, 77 ff.; idem Mi 2 und 3', ZAW 1919–20, 2 ff.; Bruno, *Micha und der Herrscher aus der Vorzeit*, 1923; Gunkel, 'Der Micha-Schluss', ZS 1924, 145 ff.; Budde, 'Verfasser und Stelle von Micha 4 : 1–4', ZDMG 1927, 152 ff.; Mowinckel, 'Mikaboken' (*Norsk Teologisk Tidsskrift*, 1928), 13 ff.; Lindblom, *Micha, literarisch untersucht*, 1929; Jeremias, 'Moreseth-Gath, die Heimat des Propheten Micha', PJB 1923, 42 ff.; Elliger, 'Die Heimat des Propheten Micha', ZDPV 1934, 81 ff.; Copas and Carlson, *A Study of the Prophet Micah*, 1950; Smith, *The Book of Micah* (Interpretation 6, 1952), 210 ff.; Beyerlin, Die Kulttraditionen Israels in der Verkündigung des Propheten Micha, FRLANT 72, 1959.

The prophet Micah (the Hebrew abbreviation for mîk̲āyāhû = Who is like Yahweh?) came according to 1: 1, 14 from Moresheth, probably the offshoot of Gath, south-west of Jerusalem. According to the title he lived under Jotham, Ahaz and Hezekiah, and was therefore a contemporary of Isaiah; his ministry under Hezekiah is confirmed by Jer. 26: 18 f. It was a time of political troubles which stirred the people to the depths and thereby brought to the surface the scum of low instincts. We know nothing for certain about the personality of the prophet who comes forward only in 3: 1, 8, to speak in the first person singular. We may perhaps gather from his oracles against luxury and the decadence of the large city that he belonged to the class of oppressed peasants and cattle-breeders. His oracles create the impression that they were probably proclaimed in Jerusalem itself, so that we may assume that Micah, like Amos, passed from the position of a simple country man to that of a prophet. It is also a natural conjecture that he knew his contemporary, Isaiah; for his oracles occasionally reveal an affinity with those of Isaiah, cf.

1: 10–6 with Is. 10: 27 ff.; 2: 1–5 with Is. 5: 8 ff.; 5: 9–14 with Is. 2: 6 ff. This prophet's oracles are as hard and trenchant as Isaiah's criticisms when he attacks the rich in 2: 1 ff.; the prophets and priests, their greed and neglect of duty in 3: 5 ff.; heathen cultic customs in 5: 9 ff. and false religious security in 3: 1 f., 11.

We can distinguish in the *book of Micah* four groups of oracles: (1) Chapters 1–3 denunciations and threats (with one exception in 2: 12 f.); (2) chapters 4–5 promises with an eschatological tinge; (3) 6–7 denunciations and threats; (4) chapters 7: 7–20 a promise. After the title in 1: 1 there follow in verses 2–7 a rebuke and threat against the apostasy of the Northern Kingdom within the framework of a universal judgment. In verse 5 b the reference to Judah and Jerusalem was no doubt inserted later and harmonized with the title; 1: 8–16 is a lament over the destruction of the land of Judah. In chapters 2 and 3 the judgment is substantiated in separate oracles: 2: 1–5 a woe on the landed proprietors' greed for land; 6–11 on the prophet's opponents (in 2: 12 f. a promise is inserted that the remnant of Israel will be gathered together); 3: 1–4 an oracle against the unscrupulous judges; 3: 5–8 against the false prophets; 3: 9–12 against priests and prophets, ending up with the threat that Zion and the temple will be destroyed; 4: 1–5 = Is. 2: 2–4 the promise of Yahweh's kingdom of peace with Mount Zion as its centre; 4: 6–7 the return of the Dispersion and the reign of Yahweh as king in Jerusalem; 4: 8–14 the destruction of their enemies before Jerusalem; 5: 1–5 the Messiah to come out of Bethlehem; 5: 6–8 the promise of victory for the remnant of Jacob; 5: 9–14 the abolition of preparations for war, of witchcraft and heathen worship. The threats which follow lead up in 6: 1–8 to the magnificent picture of Yahweh's indictment passing into the prophet's fundamental demand for love, justice and humility; 6: 9–16 is a threat against covetousness and dishonesty in Jerusalem; 7: 1–7 a lament over the internal and external decadence of the people. A prophetic liturgy in 7: 8–20 which again leads into promises brings the book to a close.

The oracles contained in chapters 1–3 are universally regarded as genuine; since in 1: 6 Samaria also is threatened, the date at least of 1: 2–7 must be before 721. The lament over the destruction of his Judean home in 1: 8–16 probably springs out of Micah's own experience of the Assyrian military expedition in the year

701 (Elliger). It is not possible to fix exactly the date of the other oracles. Only the promise in 2: 12 f. which probably presupposes the dispersion of Israel in exile, is a later addition. In the case of 4: 6 f. and 5: 6–8 it is still most natural to think of the Diaspora and date these passages from the state of affairs after the exile. 4: 1–5 too contains post-exilic, eschatological ideas, namely the promise for the temple in the last days and the divine kingdom of peace, probably originally an anonymous oracle which was admitted later both into the book of Isaiah in Is. 2: 2–4 and into Micah; it was presumably inserted here in order to tone down the preceding harsh threat against the temple in 3: 12 when the passage was recited at the divine service of the Jewish community. Nor can 4: 6–8, 9–13 have originated in Micah's time, unless the mention of Babylon is to be regarded as a later interpolation, for the name of Babylon points to a later period and cannot be explained with Sellin from the situation in 701. On the other hand the eschatological imagery of the final assault of the nations on Jerusalem and their defeat which is particularly prominent in Isaiah (Is. 17: 12 ff.; 10: 24 ff.; 29: 1; 31: 4 f.; cf. Ps. 46: 5 ff.) might not be impossible in the mouth of Micah; so the question of its genuineness must remain in suspense. Our judgment on the prophecy of the Messiah out of Bethlehem, interpreted in the NT as referring to Jesus, will depend on our opinion regarding the corresponding passages in Is. 9: 1 ff. and 11: 1 ff. In view of the affinity between the two prophets in other respects, it is in itself not out of the question that Micah too had a conception of the Messiah similar to that of Isaiah, and the mention of Assyria in 5: 4 might well suit Micah's period. Nor is there in the case of 5: 9–14 any compelling reason to think of another author, except that the oracle against horses, chariots, strongholds, witchcraft and idolatry seems originally to have been a denunciation against his own people which was later turned into an oracle against foreign nations by verse 14. Yahweh's powerful indictment and the prophet's forceful summing up of his demands in 6: 1–8 can easily be imagined in Micah's mouth and so can the threat in 6: 9–16 and the lament in 7: 1–7. As it is not possible to offer a more precise date, no convincing proof can indeed be adduced either for or against the authenticity of the oracles in chapters 4–7. On the other hand the prophetic liturgy in 7: 8–20 must evidently be

taken out of Micah's time. Jerusalem has been destroyed, and reminiscences of Is. 56–66 assign to post-exilic times this passage which was intended to be an epilogue of promise when this book was used in the liturgy. We cannot decide whether Micah himself wrote anything down and if so, what it was; yet the present arrangement of the oracles, in which we cannot fail to recognize a certain attempt at order, can hardly go back to him himself. But if one or other of the promises in chapter 4 f. did not originate with Micah, it would be difficult to explain the double alternation of denunciation and promise.

It has been conjectured that Micah was a member of an order of Nebiim; that is unlikely, for in 3: 8 he contrasts himself sharply with them. He knows that he is 'full of power by the spirit of Yahweh, and of judgment, and of might' and has the charge to proclaim to Israel his sins. From this prophetic consciousness of mission is derived the harshness and sting of his oracles, the undismayed and unrelenting logic of his criticism, which distinguishes him from the other prophets. He confronts fearlessly the mighty men of property and influence, judges, prophets and priests, he stands up courageously for his oppressed fellow countrymen. But he is not driven to do so only by the hatred of the small man from the land, speaking out of his own experience, but by his knowledge of God's justice in the service of which he stands (3: 8). With clear insight he sees the underlying cause of the disintegration to be the false religious security which supposes that the presence of Yahweh in their midst will afford protection from misfortune (3: 11 f.). This security which verges on magical intuition destroys in the people the receptive feeling for the real divine demand. This demand the prophet formulates as a chord of three notes, like a catechism: 'to do justly, to love mercy and to walk humbly with thy God' (6: 8); thus he draws together to one point the different basic thoughts in the preaching of an Amos, a Hosea and an Isaiah. We cannot give the same confident answer to the question as to whether the hope of salvation fits into Micah's ideas, and if so in what way. It seems to move along the same lines as that of Isaiah, with this difference that Micah has given up the hope that Jerusalem will be saved. However, the greatness of Micah lies in the serious conviction underlying his courageous criticism and its religious background.

34. Nahum

Gunkel, 'Nahum 1', ZAW 1893, 223 ff.; Billerbeck u. A. Jeremias, 'Der Untergang Ninives und die Weissagungsschrift des Nahum', *Beitr. z. Assyriologie* III, 1895, 87 ff.; Happel, *Der Psalm des Nahum* (*Nahum* 1) 1900; idem, *Das Buch des Propheten Nahum erklärt*, 1902; Arnold, 'The Composition of Nah 1–2 : 3', ZAW 1901, 225 ff.; Haupt, 'Eine alttestamentliche Festliturgie für den Nikanortag', ZDMG 1907, 275; Kleinert, 'Nahum und der Fall Ninives', ThStKr 1910, 501 ff.; Humbert, 'Essai d'analyse de Nahoum 1 : 2–2 : 3', ZAW 1926, 266 ff.; idem, 'La vision de Nahoum 2 : 4–11', AfO 1928, 14 ff.; idem, Le problème du livre de Nahoum, RHPhR 1932, 1 ff.; Haldar, 'Studies in the book of Nahum', *Uppsala Universitets Årskrift*, 1947.

All that we know of Nahum (the abbreviated form of *naḥumyāh* —Yahweh has comforted) as a person is that he came from Elkosh 1: 1, although we cannot say where the home of the prophet is to be found. Different sites have been conjectured for his tomb (Capernaum since the fourteenth century; 'el kush near the old Nineveh since the sixteenth century), whilst Jerome supposed his home to be in Galilee and Epiphanius in Judea; this only shows the perplexity of tradition in face of the historical ignorance of the facts. The book of Nahum has as its title 'The burden (*maśśā'*) of Nineveh. The book of the vision of Nahum the Elkoshite'. It begins with an alphabetical hymn concerning Yahweh who appears in judgment and who brings vengeance on his enemies and protection to his worshippers; the alphabetical arrangement can be traced with certainty only from aleph to lamedh (by transferring verse 2 b after verse 9 and by rearranging verse 9); attempts to reconstruct an arrangement bringing in the whole alphabet cannot be considered successful. In 1: 10–2: 3 an oracle of salvation for Judah in 1: 12, 13; 2: 1, 3 and a threat against Nineveh in 1: 10, 11, 14; 2: 2 seem to have got mixed up together. In 2: 4–14 the threat against Nineveh is continued in a lively and impressive account, full of poetry, describing the enemy's attack. 3: 1–7 contains a second oracle of denunciation, introduced by a woe, dealing with the destruction of Nineveh, as the judgment on the harlotry, the witchcraft, the predatory and mercenary spirit of this metropolis. 3: 8–17 foretell for the city of Nineveh the same fate as befell No–Amon (the Egyptian Thebes) which was captured in 663. The prophecy closes with an ironical dirge about its condition after the catastrophe which causes the world to break out in songs of joy (3: 18–19).

It is possible to set limits to the period in which the threats against Nineveh originated because they refer to concrete historical events. The *terminus a quo* is the capture of Thebes in Upper Egypt by the Assyrians in the year 663, which is mentioned in 3: 8 f. as a memorable occurrence in the not too distant past. Since on the other hand the city of Nineveh is threatened with ruin, its fall in the year 612 is the *terminus ad quem* for the denunciations against it in chapters 2–3. In these passages the diction displays a compelling emotion and a most impressive kaleidoscopic agitation, so that it is not possible to doubt the authenticity of chapters 2–3. It is more difficult to say whether chapters 1: 1–2: 3 are genuine. The alphabetic hymn, although not without considerable pathos, does not exhibit the same depth of feeling as the denunciation of Nineveh; it has often been judged to be an eschatological psalm subsequently appointed to be read. It must remain an open question whether formerly all the letters of the alphabet had been utilized and then for unknown reasons its second part had been broken off, or whether it was of its present size to start with. Yet as its contents do not clash with the general attitude of Nahum's prophecy, the problem of its genuineness must be considered seriously. The difference in mood between the hymn and the denunciation of Nineveh may be explained by the fact that the hymn is tied to the liturgical tradition of the cult and probably did not arise out of the same situation as the main contents of chapters 2–3. Since the hymn deals with Yahweh's vengeance on his enemies as well as with his protection of his people, it seems to allude also to the oracle of salvation for Judah in 1: 12 f.; 2: 1–3, which, according to 2: 1 presupposes the fall of Assyria and must therefore have come into being after the capture of Nineveh; 3: 18 f. too which looks back on the catastrophe might have been written after 612. If this is so, Nahum's book would not all have been composed at the same time; the denunciations of Nineveh date from the time before its fall; the hymn, the oracle of salvation for Judah and the conclusion might well be deemed to be the accomplishment of these denunciations by the fall of Nineveh. This is also suggested by the remarkable fact of two titles in 1: 1; beside the particular theme 'the burden of Nineveh' which applies in the first instance only to the denunciations, the title is formulated in more general terms as 'the book of the vision of Nahum' which refers to the whole book, and especially to the Epiphany hymn in 1: 2 ff.; Perhaps 2: 1 enables us to recognize the special occasion at which Nahum's complete prophecy in its present form was recited. We may imagine this to have been the festal service held to offer thanks for the deliverance of Judah from the domination of Assyria brought about by the fall of Nineveh. Humbert and Sellin wish to consider Nahum's prophecy as a prophetic liturgy, not composed as a whole till after the downfall of Assyria; this view breaks down because the denunciations of Nineveh in 2: 4–3: 17 look forward genuinely to future events and not back on what is past. Elliger attempts to assign this book as a homogeneous composition to the period before the fall of Nineveh, by connecting 2: 1 with the death of Asshurbanipal, by interpreting 3: 18 f. as a prophetic anticipation of the destruction of the Assyrian capital in a taunt-song, and by explaining the introductory psalm as an 'eschatological exegesis' made by the exilic and post-exilic community. Whilst Elliger underrates the significance of the tradition of the cult in preserving and shaping the transmission of the prophets, it is emphasized in too one-sided a manner by Halder; he would like to use comparisons taken from the history of religion and to explain the struggle with Assyria against the mythological and cultic background of the primeval battle of the gods at the new year festival.

In Nahum we make the acquaintance of a representative of the national prophets of salvation with whose supporters the prophet Jeremiah engaged in an embittered controversy during the Babylonian era. We perceive here that not only did this kind of prophecy spring from a fanatical hatred which blinded them to God's will in history, but that they were inspired by a serious concern of faith, namely the idea of the power and justice of God in history. And it was just the thought that even the great world powers could not in their audacious arrogance evade the judgment of God, which is a genuine prophetic legacy, when this manifestation of God's greatness is recognized as in Nah. 1: 2 ff. to be the most important teaching of history. Herein lies the significance of the prophecy of Nahum which the all-too-human aspects of the political prophecy of salvation in the OT must not tempt us to overlook.

35. Habakkuk

Stade, 'Habakuk', ZAW 1884, 154 ff.; Giesebrecht, *Beiträge zur Jesajakritik*, 1890, 196 ff.; Rothstein, 'Über Habakuk Kap 1 u. 2', ThStKr 1894, 51 ff.; Böhmer,

'Habakuks Schrift im Feuer der neueren Kritik', NKZ 1899, 724 ff.; Duhm, *Das Buch Habakuk*, 1906; Caspari, 'Die Chaldäer bei Habakuk', NKZ 1907, 156 ff.; Cannon, 'The Integrity of Habakkuk, ch. 1, 2,' ZAW 1925, 62 ff.; Budde, 'Habakuk', ZDMG 1930, 139 ff.; idem, 'Zum Text von Habakuk Kap 1 und 2', OLZ 1931, 409 ff.; Staerk, 'Zu Habakuk 1 : 5–11, Geschichte oder Mythus', ZAW 1933, 1 ff.; Bévenot, 'Le cantique d'Habacuc', RB 1933, 499 ff., Walter and Lund, 'The literary structure of the book of Habakkuk', JBL 1934, 355 ff.; Torrey, 'The Prophecy of Habakkuk', *Jewish Studies in Memory of George A. Kohut*, 1935, 565 ff.; Humbert, *Problèmes du livre d'Habacuc*, 1944; Albright, 'The Psalm of Habakuk', *Studies in OT Prophecy*, 1950, 1 ff.; Mowinckel, 'Zum Psalm des Habakuk', ThZ 9 (1953), 1 ff.

We know nothing of the external personal circumstances of the prophet Habakkuk; not even his name has been handed down quite reliably (LXX ᾿Αμβακουμ). There is no historical value in the late legend of the dragon of Babylon which connects him with Daniel in the lions' den. Tradition calls Habakkuk a Nabi; in this it is correct in so far as Habakkuk belongs to the type of prophetic visionary. For he not only gives an account of what he saw in a vision of chapter 3, but in 2: 1 ff. he affords an insight into the way a vision comes to pass, describes his preparation to receive it and 3: 16 enables us to know something of the spiritual and physical symptoms accompanying it.

In its present form the *book of Habakkuk* falls into two parts each of which is marked by a special title: (a) chapter 1 to 2 and (b) chapter 3. After the first title 'the burden which Habakkuk the prophet did see' there follows in 1: 2–4 the lament of the prophet (hardly of the community as Sellin supposes) about the rule of the power of the wicked. 1: 5–11 contains the announcement that God allows the Chaldaeans to arise and the description of the irresistible might of their fierce onslaught. 1: 12–17 follows with a second lament that God, although he appointed the wicked man for judgment, watches his doings calmly whilst he destroys the righteous. 2: 1–3 speaks of the prophet's preparation for the revelation of the divine answer and of Yahweh's command to write the vision on tablets, with the comment that it will not occur at once, but will most certainly take place (therefore 2: 3 cannot already be the vision itself, against Duhm, Guthe and others). 2: 4–5 contains a rebuke (not a threat) to the wicked man in the form of a *māshāl* in which the well-known saying is embedded: 'the just shall live by his faith' (Rom. 1: 17; Gal. 3: 11). In 2: 6–20 five cries of woe are placed in the mouth of the oppressed peoples; against the plunderers of the nations in 2: 6–8, the braggart in 2: 9–11 who builds his town with blood in 2: 12–

14; against the shameful glutton in 2: 15–17 and idolater in 2: 18–19. The liturgical summons: 'Yahweh is in his holy temple, let all the earth keep silence before him', is intended for a transition to chapter 3. This is called in its special title 'a prayer of Habakkuk', it describes the vision of a theophany, in which Yahweh appears to fight against the enemy, and its imagery recalls Jgs. 5 and Deut. 33. The hymn is a forceful witness to the almighty power of God who hastens to help his people and destroys the wicked. It is supplied with the technical notes for the music, with which the psalms have made us acquainted.

Habakkuk's prophecy has been given the most varied interpretations, owing to the fact that the frequently mentioned wicked oppressor is not described so clearly as to enable the historical figure behind it to be definitely recognized. The purely literary problems mostly start from the observation that the announcement of the Chaldaeans in 1: 5–11 is felt as a disturbing interruption in the lament, since 1: 12–17 is thought to be the continuation of 1: 2–4. Thus Wellhausen, Nowack and others have considered 1: 5–11 to be a piece by another hand, whilst Budde and Eissfeldt place it after 2: 4 as God's original answer to be expected after 2: 1–3, in order in this way to achieve a continuous train of thought. Yet surely the first question to be asked is whether we have not in the case of Habakkuk as in that of the other prophecies a compilation of smaller units which certainly sprang from the same historical, religious and spiritual background, but need not on that account form an uninterrupted, consecutive train of thought. The text does not in any way force us to assume that the two separate laments in 1: 2–4 and in 1: 12–17 represent an original prophetic unit, and therefore also a literary one. On the contrary the prophet's first complaint in 1: 2–4 is followed by the announcement in 1: 5–11 of God's reply that he will allow the Chaldaeans to arise, no doubt in order to use them to bring the oppression to an end. In that case 1: 12–17 is a renewed lament making a fresh start formally too which in verse 12 presupposes the judgment announced against the wicked oppressor, such as is contained in 1: 5–11, and therefore it cannot be recited in the same breath as 1: 2–4. It springs from the prophet's impatience that the judgment which has been proclaimed still delays its appearance. For this reason it is also not necessary to interpret 1: 5–11 with

Duhm and Sellin as a present event which is already taking place, since the announcement is clearly a prediction of the future. Besides, the introduction to the 'vision' in 2: 1–3, which follows immediately and refers to the prophet's impatience, thus reverting to 1: 12 ff., leads us to conclude that the second lament in 1: 12 ff. has a more definite emphasis than the first one.

The next question is this: what is the vision which the prophet is ordered by divine command to write upon tablets. According to the context it would have to be an oracle in which the wicked are destroyed and the troubles are brought to an end. But 2: 4 f. does not say this, as it is often assumed. The form of 2: 4 f. is that of a rebuke, expressed in verse 4 clearly as a *māshāl*; and even if the saying 'the just shall live by his faith', is interpreted as a promise demanded by the context, yet 2: 3 has led us to expect an event which will 'take place' after a certain interval, and this could hardly be expressed in any other way than by a threat that the wicked will perish. Yet such a meaning cannot be gained from 2: 4 f. without daring alterations of the text, quite apart from the fact that the need for several tablets presupposes a longer denunciation. Neither can the woes owing to their whole construction be taken into account for this purpose. On the other hand chapter 3 seems to me to correspond most closely to what is to be expected from the context and from 2: 1–3 as the record of the 'vision' which contains the divine answer to the prophet's complaint. As a matter of fact not only is the introduction in 3: 2 connected closely with 2: 1–3, but the whole of the contents of chapter 3 culminates in verses 13–15 in Yahweh's help for his people and in the annihilation of the wicked; thus it includes the divine manifestation and the answer for which 2: 1–3 led us to look. The chapter is a unity and verses 18–19, about which doubts have often wrongly been expressed, relieves the tension with which the prophet has impatiently awaited in 2: 1 the answer of his God. Within the framework of a cultic theophany which is presented quite in the traditional colouring of the theophany at Sinai (cf. Jgs. 5: 4 ff.; Deut. 33: 2 ff.) the prophet receives the assurance that God assumes responsibility himself for the ultimate decision and thus the downfall of the wicked oppressor is sealed. In this way the presupposition and the basis have been created from which the laments receive their intrinsic justification and their meaning.

Another good reason is also provided for the conjecture that chapter 3 originally followed straight after 2: 1–3. Presumably 2: 4 f. too once belonged to the woes (read hôy hanne‘epāl) which is in any case suggested by its resemblance to a *māshāl* and by the form of the rebuke. Besides, we may perhaps infer the reason why chapter 3 was placed at the end of the book from the technical notes for the music. These point to the liturgical use of this chapter with musical accompaniment, when it was clearly intended as an impressive ending to the book of Habakkuk; for this purpose it was provided with a special title and musical notes and placed at the end. Hence the first cry of woe in 2: 4 f. came to stand directly after 2: 1–3 and was transformed into a reply to the prophet's complaint. The other cries of woe which must be imagined as being originally spoken by the prophet were turned into sayings of the oppressed peoples by adding the introduction in 2: 6. As the oracles against idolatry in 2:18 f. are framed in such general terms and have no direct relation to an enemy, their authenticity has often been disputed; for the same reason the liturgical formula in 2: 20, probably intended now as a transition to the recital of chapter 3 in the liturgy, only came into being later in connexion with the cultic re-editing of the book of Habakkuk. The remaining contents of the book go back no doubt to the prophet himself.

The only clue for *fixing the date* of Habakkuk's prophecy is the mention in 1: 6 of the Chaldaeans whom the prophet announces as the imminent scourge of God for the wicked. In that case, it would be best to understand the Assyrians (Budde and others) to be the wicked, since 1: 17; 2: 5, 8 have a foreign great power in mind (against Rothstein who supposes a conflict inside Israel between the wicked and the righteous at the time of Jehoiakim). The statements about the wicked, which in themselves could receive different interpretations, were applied by Duhm and many others to the Greeks, especially Alexander the Great; but in fact this is only possible by a thorough-going correction of the Kaśdîm in 1: 6 into Kittim and by a fresh interpretation of the prophecy in 1: 5–11 as the victorious march of Alexander which had already taken place; this has been rejected above. Sellin, who like Balla (RGG,[2] Vol. II, col. 1,556 f.) wishes to think of the book of Habakkuk as a prophetic liturgy (thus also

Humbert, who recently placed the 'liturgy' in the year 602–01)
transfers it to the Babylonian period by applying the judgment
and the woes to the Chaldaeans; this in its turn can only be
achieved by the questionable means of making 1: 5 ff. apply to an
event that is already past. Since it is the simplest and therefore
the most acceptable solution to interpret the wicked as the Assyrians, the date when Habakkuk's prophecy came into existence
must lie between 625, the revolt of Nabopolassar of Babylon
against Assyria, and 612, the destruction of Nineveh, the Assyrian
capital, by the Medes and the Babylonians. Elliger, who transfers
the origin of the book of Habakkuk to the period between the
death of Josiah in 609 and 598, allows for an alteration in the
figure of the wicked as a result of the whole domination having
changed hands during the last decade of the seventh century. He
thinks that the name of the Chaldaeans in 1: 6 was only added
later by the prophet, and that his prophecy, originally directed
against Egypt, in the end became an attack on Babylon. But if
it can be established that such a change in the actual object of the
prophecy took place, yet the question still remains open whether
it should not be traced back to its use in the worship of the
congregation rather than to the prophet himself.

The prophet Habakkuk stands close to the prophet Nahum, not
only in time, but also as regards his subject-matter; he belongs to
the prophets of salvation whose thoughts move along lines akin
to those of the Deuteronomic historians. For Habakkuk too the
idea of the justice of God forms the central problem in the understanding of history from the religious point of view. It is from
this that the prophet derives his right to intercede with God for
his people in laments and petitions. The fact that his activity
assumes the shape of a vision gives his prophecy a particular
stamp which distinguishes him from Jeremiah who is obliged to
wait for God's reply (Jer. 42: 7). Habakkuk emphasizes even more
strongly than Nahum the theological and theocentric impulse
which seeks the solution in the almighty power of God and is
linked with the old cultic tradition of the theophany at Sinai. This
prophet too, just like Nahum, fails to bring to bear God's justice
as a challenge to his own people; therein lies the limitation which
hinders him from grappling with the deepest aspects of the problem and from fighting his way through at the most profound level.

Even the well-known saying in 2: 4, 'the just shall live by his faith', did not receive the fullest meaning and its 'fulfilment' until it was taken up in Rom 1: 17; Gal. 3: 11 into the gospel of the New Testament.

36. Zephaniah

Schwally, 'Das Buch Sefanja', ZAW, 1890, 165 ff.; Budde, 'Die Bücher Habakuk und Sephania', ThStKr 1893, 393 ff.; Cornill, 'Die Prophetie Zephanias', ThStKr 1916, 297 ff.; Nicolsky, 'Pascha im Kulte des jerusalemischen Tempels', ZAW 1927, 171 ff.; Gerlemann, *Zephania (textkritisch u. literarisch untersucht)*, 1942; Kühner, *Zephania (Prophezei)*, 1943; Hyatt, 'The Date and Background of Zephaniah', JNESt 7 (1948), 25 ff.; Smith, Lacheman, 'The Authorship of the Book of Zephania', JNESt 9 (1950), 137 ff.

Contrary to the usual practice the title of the book of Zephaniah contains a genealogy of the prophet which is carried back to an ancestor of the fourth generation called Hezekiah. It has been inferred from this that Zephaniah came from princely stock, a collateral line of the Davidic dynasty, if the Hezekiah should be identical with the king of that name. Yet the Hezekiah named here is not called a king, and moreover chronological though not insuperable difficulties arise if Zephaniah were the great-great grandson of the king Hezekiah; thus this question, the significance of which ought not to be overrated, must remain undecided. It is not likely that Cushi, the name of his father, could be considered Ethiopian, thus giving rise to the idea that Zephaniah was a negro slave in the service of the temple (Bentzen). On the other hand it has been conjectured that the inclusion of several names in the list of ancestors is meant to prevent such a misunderstanding in view of Deut. 23: 8 f.. The title also refers Zephaniah's activity to the period of king Josiah, 639–609 which is no doubt correct. And indeed, since the Deuteronomic reform is nowhere presupposed, we must think of the time before 621. The fact that in 1: 8 only the royal princes, but not the king himself, are mentioned, has occasionally been explained as referring to the period of Josiah's minority.

The *book of Zephaniah* begins in 1: 2–18 with two denunciations now combined in the conception of the day of Yahweh. The first one in 1: 2–6, 8–13 speaks of the universal judgment which will overtake Judah and Jerusalem as a punishment for heathen cults in 1: 4–6, for the affectation of foreign ways and wrong-doing in 1: 8 f., for an unscrupulous mercenary and profiteering spirit in 1: 10 f. and for the callous self-confidence of those who are 'settled on their lees' in 1: 12. The second denunciation contained in 1: 7, 14–18, sketches a grim picture of the day of Yahweh and is the prototype of the well-known *Dies irae dies illa*. There follows in 2: 1–3 an exhortation to the meek and the righteous to seek Yahweh, so that this behaviour may perhaps preserve them in the day of Yahweh. 2: 4–15 contains a collection of threats of judgment on the Philistines, the Moabites, the Ammonites, the Ethiopians and the Assyrians. 3: 1–13 is a longer poem which combines in 3: 1–4 a cry of woe on disobedient Jerusalem and its ruling classes with Yahweh's fruitless warning of a judgment of the nations, verses 5–7. This leads up in verses 8–13 to the menace of a judgment which will purify and in which the presumptious will be annihilated and a meek remnant will be saved and live in peace and obedience. In the conclusion in 3: 14–20 Jerusalem is summoned to a song of rejoicing in Yahweh, the king, who will bring home those who have been dispersed.

The book shows the division into three parts, namely the threat of judgment, oracles against foreign nations and the announcement of salvation, familiar from other prophetic books. It was probably put together at a later revision which has left its traces in the gathering together in chapter 1 of material with a single train of thought and in the alteration of the position of 1: 7. It has been conjectured that the onrush of the Scythian bands of horsemen, which according to Herodotus swept across Palestine between 630 and 625, was the occasion of this prophecy, and especially of the announcement of the day of Yahweh. This would afford a historical explanation particularly of the conception of world judgment and of the menace to other nations as well as to Judah and is not impossible in itself. Yet we must remember that the irruption of the Scythians itself represents a historical problem and also that Zephaniah nowhere gives a hint which points directly to this explanation. The conception of the day of Yahweh, of the judgment of the world and of foreign nations, is already present in earlier prophets and might be due less to the themes of world politics than to intimate religious ones and above all to the traditions cherished in the cult. However this may be, we may without more ado assign chapters 1 and 2: 1–3 to the time of Josiah; in particular the influences of heathen cults (worship of Baal, adoration of the host of heaven) point to the period before the Deuteronomic reform. In the case of the oracles against foreign peoples in 2: 4–15 scarcely a doubt can be felt about the genuineness of this characteristic and impressive oracle against Assyria in 2: 13–15. The rest of the oracles against the neighbouring peoples are confined to such general terms that their contents do not enable us to decide whether they originated with Zephaniah or were introduced in the course of a later expansion, as has occurred partly with other prophetic books. Both in 2: 7 and in 2: 8–11 traces of a later revision can be noticed; but still this does mean that the whole of 2: 4–12 must also be later in date. Likewise no uncertainty can arise about the authenticity of the longer poem in 3: 1–13, even though we can detect in 3: 8 ff. some later touching-up. It is also worth while considering seriously whether in connection with the thought of the purifying judgment in 3: 8–13, the rejoicing of Jerusalem and the promise of salvation may not after all come from the prophet himself, without our being obliged here as in the case of other prophetic writings to assume an exilic or post-exilic eschatological supplement; for this passage could easily be explained by the prophet's dependence on the ideas of the festal cult (3: 15, 17). On the other hand 3: 20 with its partial repetition of 3: 19 seems a late addition.

The book of Zephaniah makes it evident how the prophetic movement became the forerunner of the Deuteronomic reform. This is shown in the first place by the fact that the prophets unflinchingly and with dauntless courage, unrestrained by considerations of any kind, emphasized the responsibility of the ruling class and thereby brought the leaders at last to act in a responsible manner. In the case of nearly all the ideas urged by Zephaniah he takes his stand on the older prophecies. In his conception of the day of Yahweh as an ominous day of judgment he carries on the line of thought to be observed in Amos 5: 18 f. and Is. 2: 7 ff.; thoughts of Amos, Isaiah and Micah are echoed also in the contrast of meekness and arrogance. The conception of the religious community growing out of the remnant which survived the judgment goes back to Isaiah. It is developed by Zephaniah in so far as he underlines still more firmly the distinction between the nation and the religious community. In the conception of the judgment which purifies, he like Isaiah combines the two different conceptions of his predecessors, Amos's judgment which annihilates and Hosea's which educates. In this way Zephaniah takes his place in the tradition of the great prophets and it is true to say of him something similar to what was said of Micah, namely that in him the lines of the earlier prophecies converge. Yet on the other hand we find in him a combination of cultic ideas and phrases with the specifically prophetic function and a denunciation of the foreign influences on the national and religious life supplemented by a corresponding promise of salvation; these bring Zephaniah's prophecies closer to the bearers of the Deuteronomic reform than are those of his predecessors.

37. Haggai

Budde, 'Zum Text der drei letzten kleinen Propheten', ZAW 1906, 1 ff.; Rothstein, 'Juden und Samaritaner', BWAT 1908; Bloomhardt, 'The Poems of Haggai', HUCA 1928, 153 ff.; Kittel, *Geschichte des Volkes Israel*, II, 2, 1929, 441 ff.; Bentzen, 'Quelques remarques sur le mouvement messianique parmi les Juifs aux environs de l'an 520 avant Jésus-Christ', RHPhR 1930, 483 ff.; North, 'Critical Analysis of the Book of Haggai', ZAW 68 (1956), 25 ff.

The oracles of the prophet Haggai which are all dated by the year, the month and the day, were each of them spoken in the last half of the second year of the Persian king Darius I (521–486), that is to say in the year 520. With 2: 3 in mind we like to imagine Haggai as an aged man who had seen the old temple and had shared in the exile; but there can be no definite proof of this.

The *book of Haggai* contains four oracles by the prophet, each provided with a special introduction: in 1: 1–11 the prophet summons the governor Zerubbabel and the high priest Joshua to rebuild the temple which he supports by interpreting their present distress (a drought) as God's punishment for their neglect to build it. Following on this in 1: 12–15 the success of his summons and the start of the building on the 24th of the 6th month is described. 2: 1–9 is addressed to the same people promising great glory for the second temple which will be more splendid than the first. In 2: 10–14 the prophet proves by means of two examples from the priests' torah which he has procured that the people and the sacrifices to Yahweh have up to now been unclean (presumably this is the reason for refusing to allow the Samaritans to share in the building and the cult of the temple); connected with this is the announcement in 2: 15-19 of the blessing which will attend the beginning of the building of the temple. The last oracle, of the same date as the preceding one, is a promise to Zerubbabel, whom Yahweh, after the destruction of the heathen empires, will make his 'signet', i.e. the messianic king.

As the book of Haggai speaks in the third person and in 1: 12-15 (2: 10-14) is written as a narrative it cannot have been composed in its present form by Haggai himself; yet it gives the impression of being close to the events and of going back to reliable sources. The promise of a blessing in 2: 15-19, which is attached to the beginning of the building of the temple, does not seem to stand in its original place; it belongs, as Rothstein has shown, after 1: 1-15 to the laying of the foundation stone of the temple (cf. 2: 18) and probably got into the wrong place by mixing up the dates (24. VI instead of 24. IX). There is no evidence for the conjecture which has occasionally been made that this writing of Haggai is a fragment of a larger book by the prophet or a compilation of two different writings (collection of oracles and narratives).

By urging the building of the temple, Haggai, like his somewhat younger contemporary Zechariah, takes up the position which Ezekiel has prepared with his sketch of a cultic programme. Thus the prophecy swings into the track of the Judaism which is developing. Moreover the connexion of the prophetic eschatology of salvation with the building of the temple, which gives this book its special character, reveals Haggai as an imitator of the prophets, one who stands closer to Judaism than to the old prophecies.

38. Zechariah 1-8

Van der Flier, 'Zacharja 1-8', ThStKr 1906, 30 ff.; Rothstein, 'Die Nachtgesichte des Sacharja', BWAT 1910; Möhlenbrink, 'Der Leuchter im fünften Nachtgesicht des Propheten Sacharja', ZDPV 1929, 257 ff.; Galling, 'Das vierte Nachtgesicht des Propheten Sacharja', ZMR 1931, 193 ff.; Sellin, 'Der Stein des Sacharja', JBL 1931, 242 ff.; idem, ZAW 1942-3, 59 ff.; Press, 'Das erste Nachtgesicht des Propheten Sacharja', ZAW 1936, 43 ff.; H. Schmidt, 'Das vierte Nachtgesicht des Propheten Sacharja', ZAW 1936, 48 ff.; Rost, 'Erwägungen zu Sacharjas 7. Nachtgesicht', ZAW 58 (1940-41), 223 ff.; Jepsen, 'Kleine Beiträge zum Zwölfprophetenbuch, III, Sacharja', ZAW 61 (1945-8), 95 ff.; Rignell, Die Nachtgesichte des Sacharja, 1950; Galling 'Die Exilswende in der Sicht des Propheten Sacharja', VT 1952, 18 ff.

It was one of the earliest facts ascertained by the literary criticism of the OT that the book of Zechariah as we have it today falls into two parts which must be kept separate from each other and that only chapters 1–8 can be ascribed to the prophet Zechariah. He is a younger contemporary of Haggai and in the difficult time when the post-exilic community was coming into being he took up the task, like Haggai, of building the temple and of giving spiritual support to the community. The pieces which he dated and handed down comprise the period from the eighth month of the second year of Darius I (520) to the fourth day of the ninth month of 518; yet he probably exercised his ministry as a prophet beyond this period. In 1: 1 he is described as the son of Berechiah and the grandson of Iddo; yet according to Ezra 5: 1; 6: 14 he is, no doubt correctly, the son of Iddo (presumably 'son of Berechiah' in 1: 1 should be crossed out; 1: 7 also belongs clearly to an interpolation, perhaps inserted because he was identified with Zechariah, the son of Jeberechia, mentioned in Is. 8: 2). Probably the prophet is the same as the Zechariah named in Neh. 12: 1 as the leader of a division of the priests; in that case he was no doubt called to be a prophet in his youth and presumably was active both as a prophet and a priest for a considerable time. This would be the easiest way of explaining the close association of prophetic and priestly interests which range him also beside Ezekiel.

The contents of the book of Proto-Zechariah fall into three parts: in 1: 2–6 an introduction; in 1: 7–6: 15 the eight night visions with an appendix concerning the coronation of Zerubbabel and in chapters 7–8 a series of isolated oracles of which the first and the last are concerned with fasting. The introduction in 1: 2–6 contains a call to repentance and a promise of God's mercy. Of the eight visions the first and last are independent, the middle ones being arranged in pairs; they describe in the first person singular the experiences of a night in February 519 which are explained by an angel-interpreter accompanying the prophet. The first vision in 1: 7–17 of the four horsemen and the promise that Yahweh will be jealous for Jerusalem in connexion with the building of the temple contains the announcement of salvation; the following pair of visions declares that external obstructions will be swept aside; the second vision in 2: 1–4 of four horns and four smiths=the hostile world-power and its destroyers; the third vision in 2: 5–17 the man with the measuring line=the immeasurable greatness of the future Jerusalem. There follows a summons to the Diaspora in Babylon to escape to Jerusalem, a threat to other nations and the conversion of the heathen to Yahweh. The next two visions deal with the removal of internal hindrances: in the fourth vision 3: 1–7 the high priest Joshua, accused by Satan, is pardoned; to this is attached in 3: 8–10 an oracle addressed to Joshua about the 'Branch' and the engraved 'stone'; the fifth vision in 4: 1–14 is of the candlestick and the two olive trees=Yahweh, Joshua and Zerubbabel; 4: 6b–10 treats of Zerubbabel as completing the building of the temple. In the third pair of visions the purging of the land is reported; in the sixth vision in 5: 1–4 the flying roll strikes thieves and perjurers; the seventh vision in 5: 5–11 concerns the woman (wickedness) in the ephah who is taken to Babylon; the last vision in 6: 1–8 speaks of the four chariots driving out to judge the nations. The appendix in 6: 9–15 describes as a symbolic act the coronation of Joshua (originally Zerubbabel) as the messianic king. The third part, chapters 7–8, begins with an inquiry addressed to the prophet concerning days of fasting in 7: 1–3; in the place of fasting Zechariah demands in 7: 4–14 love and justice; 8: 1–23 is a compilation of ten sayings. Only the one in 8: 18 f. in which days of fasting are turned into days of rejoicing bears any relation to the inquiry at the beginning and at the end, whilst in 8: 1–17 general statements are made about salvation for the Jews and in 8: 20–23 about the heathen journeying to Jerusalem to worship Yahweh there.

Looked at as a whole the night visions give the impression of being completely homogeneous and self-contained; from the literary aspect too they represent a definite unit with a well-planned internal construction. They are no doubt to be considered the core of the book of Zechariah which came into being at one time and perhaps, in addition to the visions, already contained at an early date the introduction in 1: 2–6 and the appendix in 6: 9–15. It is true that the clear continuity is interrupted in several places; thus the fourth vision in 3: 1–7 which differs from the night visions was probably added later (Jepsen); the word of God in 1: 16 f. was a new insertion; in 2: 6–13 the summons to escape, etc. breaks the thread of the third vision; 3: 8–10 seems to be an appendix to the fourth vision; the saying about Zerubbabel in

4: 6b–10a tears the fifth vision in two. There is no reason to deny
these interpolations without exception to Zechariah. But in
that case a special explanation is required for their remarkable
positions. Some scholars attempt to fit the pieces just mentioned
by a rearrangement into the prophet's account given in the
first person. Eissfeldt wishes to distinguish three different literary
elements: a dated record of Zechariah which can be recognized
by the introductory formulas in 1: 1, 7; 7: 1, next undated passages in this account, no doubt inserted by a late hand, and
thirdly, 'sayings' not in the first person. But the basis of this
merely external formal argument is too narrow to have power
to convince. We may rather imagine the process to have been
that Zechariah, when his predictions were not being fulfilled,
felt obliged to adapt the original account of the night visions
to the reality by subsequent additions. The allusions to the
former prophets in 1: 4 f.; 7: 7, 12 and the remark occurring
in the interpolations, 'ye shall know that Yahweh hath sent
me' in 2: 13, 15; 4: 9; 6: 15 sound like a justification of his
prophetic mission in view of the doubts arising from the non-
fulfilment of his earlier predictions. There is thus no need to
think of interpolations by another hand (against Elliger), not
even in the case of the appendix to the vision in 6: 9–15 which has
received the biggest alteration, for here the name of Zerubbabel
was replaced by that of Joshua and the royal crown was turned
into a votive offering for the temple where it is to be preserved
for the coming Messiah (the Branch). Chapters 7–8 too seem to
point to the prophet's later activity; the sayings in 8: 18 f.; 7: 4–14
form only a loose connexion with the introduction, and those in
8: 1–17, 20–23 on the other hand none at all; they may not have
been put together at one time; but this compilation may yet go
back in essentials to Zechariah himself or to the circles close to
him. Thus part of the prophet's struggles within his own breast
are reflected at the same time in the fate of his book. The form of
Zechariah's writing as we have it today nevertheless seems to
have been created by the hand of a redactor who had a share above
all in the new interpretations given in 4: 6–10 and 6: 9–15.

  In the case of Zechariah even more clearly than in that of
Haggai the mutual interaction of the experience of the prophet
and the meditation of the priest can be seen. Zechariah is a vision-

ary who consciously rests on the traditions of the old prophets and holds fast to all their serious moral demands; like Haggai he combines the building of the temple with the prophet's national and religious eschatology of salvation; by his own characteristic combination of visionary elements with these ideas he has been an influence in apocalyptic. The Jewish religion as it developed took the road from Ezekiel by way of Zechariah to the apocalyptic hope of Judaism.

39. Zechariah 9-14
(Deutero-Zechariah)

Stade, 'Deuterosacharja', ZAW 1881, 1 ff.; 1882, 151 ff., 275 ff.; Staerk, *Untersuchungen über die Komposition und Abfassungszeit von Zach 9–14*, 1891; Kraeling, 'The historical Situation in Zech 9 : 1–10', AJSL 1924–25, 24 ff.; Heller, 'Die letzten Kapitel des Buches Sacharja im Lichte des späteren Judentums', ZAW 1927, 151 ff.; Cannon, 'Some Notes on Zechariah, c. 11', AfO 1927, 139 ff.; Kremer, 'Die Hirtenallegorie im Buche Zacharias auf ihre Messianität untersucht', *Alttestamentliche Abhandlungen*, 1930; Jepsen, 'Der Aufbau des deuterosacharjanischen Buches', ZAW 57 (1939), 242 ff.; Elliger, 'Ein Zeugnis aus der jüdischen Gemeinde im Alexanderjahr 322 v. Chr. Eine territorial-geschichtliche Studie zu Sach. 9 : 1–8', ZAW 62 (1949–50) 63 ff.

Chapters 9–14 of the book of Zechariah make no further mention of the building of the temple of Zerubbabel and Joshua and, since they assume quite different circumstances to Zech. 1–8, must be treated separately. The contents can be grouped into three parts: (1) 9: 1–11: 3 the Jews and the heathen; (2) 11: 4–17 and 13: 7–9 the internal struggles of Judaism; (3) 12–14 with a new title, victory and splendour of Judaism in the last days. Taken in detail 9: 1–17 contains threats against Aram, Phoenicia and Philistia and the well-known promise of the king of peace in Zion as the bearer of world dominion (9: 6 ff. 'Rejoice greatly, O daughter of Zion'); 10: 1–11: 3 begins with a warning that Yahweh alone gives rain and not the teraphim or the diviners, and ends in a denunciation against the foreign shepherds and a promise that the people will return from Assyria and Egypt. The second part 11: 4–17 to which 13: 7–9 is held to be the conclusion is a symbolic and allegorical presentation of an action intended as a sign: the good shepherd who cut off 'the three shepherds' lays down his office as a shepherd and breaks his staves 'Union and Graciousness'. There follows the threat against the worthless shepherd and an oracle about the deliverance and purifying of one third of the people. In the third part an account is given in 12: 1–13: 6 of the deliverance of Jerusalem menaced by the heathen, of the outpouring of the spirit and of penitence; whilst chapter 14 in partly similar forms promises the deliverance of captured Jerusalem on the day of Yahweh, his reign as king, the destruction of the foes and the eschatological glorification of Jerusalem.

Chapters 9–14 were detached from Zechariah already at an early date, because the text about the thirty pieces of silver in Zech. 11: 12 f. is quoted in Matt. 27: 9 f. as a saying by Jeremiah and the tradition of the New Testament was considered more trustworthy than that of the Jews. But only since the end of the eighteenth century has the new criticism enlarged our scientific knowledge. In view of the peculiar nature of these chapters criticism has not even today reached a unanimous agreed conclusion as to their dating and their literary composition. A pre-exilic origin has again and again been deduced from the mention of Ephraim, Assyria and Egypt (Dillman, König and others); on the other hand Stade has placed chapters 9–14 in the early days of Alexander's successors; Duhm, Marti and others find their explanation in the period of the Maccabees. An attempt has been made to reconcile these views by the conjecture of a pre-exilic matrix, worked over in the Greek era (Kuenen, Baudissin, Steuernagel).

In particular the first part, 9: 1–11: 3, contains a series of archaic observations which might suggest that they came into being in pre-exilic times; thus 9: 1, 13; 10: 6 f. seem to assume the existence of the Northern Kingdom and the mention of Syria and Philistia in 9: 1 ff., of Assyria and Egypt in 10: 10 f. could point to the same period for their origin. Yet the naming of the Greeks as the enemies of Jerusalem in 9: 13, as well as the backward glance at Judah's exile in 9: 11 f., which cannot be explained as a later revision of older writings, places the passage in the Hellenistic period. In that case the archaisms must be explained as the conscious use of eschatological and apocalyptic expressions, in which, e.g. the kingdom of the Seleucids is concealed under the name of Assyria and the kingdom of the Ptolemies under that of Egypt. The warlike spirit of the passages, 9: 13 ff., 10: 3 ff., has led some scholars to the conclusion that they originated in the time of the Maccabean wars against the Seleucid domination in the second century; others think of the time of Alexander the Great; recently

K

especially Elliger explains that 9: 1–3 reflects Alexander's expedition to Syria and Phoenicia in the year 332 and refers 9: 11–17 and 10: 3–12 to the first decades of the wars of Alexander's successors.

Attempts have been made to find a solution of the second part (11: 4–17; 13: 7–9) too in the Maccabean period. Presumably the allegorical and symbolic narrative about the shepherds is to be understood unlike 9: 1–11: 3 not as a prediction but as a presentation of contemporary history with the last part only devoted to the future. It cannot be decided definitely who is meant by the shepherd: Sellin explains that the good shepherd refers to Onias III (2 Macc. 4 f.) and that the three shepherds who are cut off are the sons of Tobias, Simon, Lysimachus and Menelaus, and suggests that the last-named is at the same time also the worthless shepherd who caused Onias to be murdered. Marti thinks that the three shepherds are the disloyal high priests, Lysimachus, Jason and Menelaus, the good shepherd Onias IV and the worthless shepherd Alcimus (1 Macc. 7: 5 ff.; 9: 54); he dates the piece shortly before the death of Alcimus in 160, whilst Sellin considers it to be ten to twenty years later owing to its connexion with other passages. Elliger thinks that the core of the narrative in 11: 4–16, intended to be symbolic, was in his opinion distorted by a subsequent allegorical interpretation and represents the rise of the schism between the Jewish and the Samaritan communities in the last third of the fourth century; he considers 13: 7–9 to be the supplement to the preceding eschatological piece in 12: 1–13: 6.

The third part in chapters 12–14, uniting apocalyptics with eschatology, bears clear indications of a later origin. Earlier conceptions of prophetic eschatology are utilized in part like pieces in a mosaic (the idea of Jerusalem menaced by heathen peoples, its deliverance when at the last gasp, the wonderful changes in nature in the last days, the reign of God as king over the whole earth, etc.) and are sometimes inconsistent with each other, and a collection of oracles from different sources has been suggested; it is not absolutely necessary to conjecture this since the discrepancies can also be explained by the author being dependent on earlier materials. It seems to me open to question whether chapters 12–14 must be considered an independent booklet (Trito–Zechariah) because it has a special title in 12: 1 and lacks definite features. Assuming that 12: 10 alludes to a judicial murder of which the inhabitants of Jerusalem repented subsequently, Marti, Sellin and others have thought of the murder of Onias III in the year 170 (2 Macc. 4: 27 ff.). In that case there is nothing against the conjecture that the same author also wrote Zech. 9–14, and Deutero-Zechariah would be a somewhat younger contemporary of the author of the book of Daniel. Yet in view of the hypothetical nature of these allusions to contemporary events and of their interpretation it is perhaps going too far to fix such a date; we ought probably to allow for a considerably more complicated origin of the booklet in which several hands had a share.

This prophetic book does indeed revive the ancient warlike force of the OT faith in God and takes over from the old tradition the conception of the day of Yahweh and of his kingdom embracing the whole world; yet it reveals in its messianic picture in 9: 9ff., drawn from the circles of the 'meek' and the pious that the time of genuine prophecy is over. The late Jewish thinking in terms of ritual looks on the Kingdom of God as a 'Judaized world-kingdom' in which Jerusalem and its cult form the centre of an exclusively ritual holiness; this notion has combined with the eschatological hope which paints present happenings in eschatological colours and throws the light of the ceremonial life of the present on to the conceptions of the future. The colours and images in their manifold variety no longer grow out of the religious root of the prophet's experience of God, but they often stand side by side in almost embarrassing abundance, loosely associated and without being adapted or assimilated. And only in those passages still penetrated by the old tradition can something be felt of the vigorous throbbing of the heritage of the genuine prophetic vision of God which has been preserved even under the veil of another world of ideas and of history.

40. Malachi

Torrey, 'The Prophecy of Maleachi', JBL 1898, 1 ff.; Bulmerincq, *Der Prophet Maleachi*, Vol. I, 1926; Vol. II, 1932; Holtzmann, 'Der Prophet Maleachi und der Ursprung des Pharisäertums', ARW 1931, 1 ff.

The book of Malachi is an anonymous writing like Deutero-Zechariah. It derives its name from the statement in the title in

1: 1 the first part of which 'the burden of the word of Yahweh to Israel' is similar to the titles in Zech. 9: 1; 12: 1 and it was no doubt due to them that it was placed at the head of this prophecy. The second part of the title 'by *mal'ākî*' was originally not intended to be a proper name, but meant, as can still be seen in the LXX, 'by my messenger'. It probably became part of the title by applying 'My messenger' in 3: 1 to the writer of the book. It was only later on that *mal'ākî* was taken to be the name of an otherwise unknown author.

The book is in the form of dialogues between God or the prophet on the one hand and the listeners who are addressed on the other. It contains six sections clearly marked off from each other: 1: 2–5 Yahweh's love for Israel is proved by the fact that the kindred nation Edom (Esau) has been plunged into disaster whilst Jacob has been spared; 1: 6–2: 9 is a sermon calling the priests to penitence for sacrifices of poor quality; 2: 10–16 is a rebuke on the mixed and wanton marriages; 2: 17–3: 5 is directed to the pious who doubted that Yahweh's retribution is just, and the prophet refutes them by announcing an imminent judgment; 3: 6–12 traces the present distress to indifference towards religion (incomplete payment of tithes); 3: 13–23 turns once more to the pious doubters and proclaims the recompense of the righteous and the destruction of the wicked on the day of judgment as a demonstration of Yahweh's justice; the conclusion consists of an exhortation to keep the law of Moses and a declaration that Elijah will come as a herald of the day of Yahweh.

The arrangement of the separate parts seems to have been disturbed. Sellin pointed out no doubt correctly that 3: 6–12 is connected with 1: 2–5; for then the disasters of Israel which penitence can remove would be contrasted with the irrevocable misfortune of Edom and thus the present situation would illustrate rightly the train of thought in 1: 2–5. But in that case 2: 10–16 must also be brought into this context, so that a quite clear structure emerges in the prophet's sayings; (1) Preaching repentance to the people in 1: 2–5; 3: 6–12; 2: 10–16; (2) preaching repentance to the priests in 1: 6–2: 9; (3) preaching to the doubters in 2: 17–3: 5; 3: 13–21. Misgivings about authenticity are justified only in the case of 2: 11b–13a (Eissfeldt) and of the conclusion in 3: 22–23. This contrasts with the style of the whole and contains beside the exhortation to keep the law a later exegesis of the statement in 3: 1, in so far as it postpones to an indefinite date the day of Yahweh which according to 3: 1 is imminent. Therefore it must be an appendix which can hardly have come from the prophet himself.

There is general agreement as to *the time when the book came into being*. The existence of the post-exilic temple is taken for granted in 1: 10; 3: 1, 10, the cult plays an important part, the country is ruled by a governor (1: 8). On the other hand the reforms of Ezra and Nehemiah have not been carried out, for just those abuses on which the reform concentrated are still prevalent, namely mixed marriages, laxity in entering upon wedlock, negligence in performing cultic duties. Thus the book must have originated in the time between the completion of the building of the temple in 515 and Ezra's reforms in 458. The fact that in 1: 8; 2: 11; 3: 8 ff. some influence of Deuteronomic thought and modes of expression can be observed agrees with this.

The book of Malachi breathes the spirit of an original, genuinely prophetic personality. His awe and humility before the sublime God whose kingdom embraces the world (1: 14), his vigorous emphasis on the ethical demands for marriage and faithfulness and their basis in religion (2: 10, 13 f., 16), his seriousness about honest penitence and his broad outlook, which regards the heathen's religious sincerity in their cult as the worship of Yahweh, places the author amongst the great prophets who stand nearer to the NT than does particularist Judaism. Yet he is at the same time also a representative of this Judaism by the way he judges the Edomites, emphasizes the cultic requirements and endeavours to preserve the purity of the Jewish blood. In this respect in spite of his independence he must be considered a forerunner of the Judaism which issued from the reforms of Ezra and Nehemiah.

D. THE WRITINGS

41. The Psalms

Commentaries: KD: Delitzsch,[5] 1894.–KeH: Olshausen, 1853.–SZ: Kessler,[2] 1899.–HK: Baethgen,[3] 1904.–Gungel,[4] 1926.–KHC: Duhm,[2] 1922.–KAT: Kittel,[5][6] 1929.–HAT: H. Schmidt, 1934.–ICC: Briggs, 1951–2.–WC: Barnes, 1931.–HSAT: Bertholet, 1923.–SAT: Staerk,[2] 1920.–ATD: Weiser,[4] 1955, [5]1959.–TU: Böhl I, 1946, II, 1947: Gemser, III, 1949: Hupfeld–Nowack,[3] 1887–8.–Buhl,[2] 1918.–Wutz, 1935.–König, 1927.–Peters, 1930.–De Groot, 1932.–HS: Herkenne, 1936.–Calès, 1936.–HBK: Kalt,[2] 1937.–Fleming-James, Thirty Psalmists, 1938.–Buttenweiser, 1938.–Abramowski, 2 vols., 1938–9.–Oesterley,[2] 1953.–Bentzen, Fortolkning til de gammeltestamentlige Salmer, 1939; SBB: Cohen, 1945, [2]1950; Eerdmans, 'The hebrew Book of Psalms'. *Oudtestamentische Studien IV*, 1947.–EB: Nötscher, 1947.– Bonkamp, 1949, [2]1956.–Steinmann, 1951.–Podechard, I, 1949, II, 1954.–Leslie, 1949.–LStB (Clamer): Renard, 1950.–Zolli, 1951.–Kissane, I, 1953, II, 1954.–IB: Taylor, McCullough, Sclater, Poteat, Ballard, 1955.–LStB: Tournay, Schwab,[2] 1955. –LSB: Castellino, 1955.–Giesebrecht, 'Über die Abfassungszeit des Psalters, ZAW 1881, 176 ff.; Smend, Über das Ich der Psalmen', ZAW 1888, 49 ff.; Staerk, 'Zur Kritik der Psalmenüberschriften', ZAW 1892, 91 ff.; Beer, *Individual- und Gemeindepsalmen*, 1894; Jacob, 'Beiträge zu einer Einleitung in die Psalmen', ZAW 1896, 129 ff.; Köberle, *Die Tempelsänger im AT.*, 1899; Büchler, 'Zur Geschichte der Tempelmusik und der Tempelpsalmen', ZAW 1899, 96 ff., 329 ff., ZAW 1900, 97 ff.: Kautzsch, '*Die Poesie und die poetischen Bücher des AT*', 1907: König, *Die Poesie des AT*, 1907; Balla, 'Das Ich der Psalmen', 1912; Mowinckel, *Psalmenstudien*, *I–VI*, 1921–24; Löhr, 'Psalmenstudien', BWAT 1922; Quell, 'Das kultische Problem in den Psalmen', BWAT 1926; Welch, *The Psalter in Life, Worship and History*, 1926; H. Schmidt, 'Das Gebet des Angeklagten im AT', BZAW 1928; Haller, 'Ein Jahrzent Psalmenforschung', ThR 1929, 378 ff.; Bruno, *Der Rhythmus der atl. Dichtung*, 1930; Schulz, Kritisches zum Psalter, Atl. Abh., 1932; Gunkel-Begrich, *Einleitung in die Psalmen*, I, 1928; II, 1933; Birkeland, *Die Feinde des Individuums in der israelitschen Psalmenliteratur*, 1933; Begrich, 'Das priesterliche Heilsorakel', ZAW 1934, 81 ff.; Hylander, *Gamla Testaments Psalmbok*, Stockholm, 1937; Buttenwieser, *The Psalms chronologically treated with a new translation*, Chicago, 1938; Engnell, *Studies in Divine Kingship in the Ancient Near East*, Uppsala, 1943; Bentzen, *Det sakrale kongedφmme*, Copenhagen, 1945; Christoph Barth, *Die Errettung vom Tode in den individuellen Klage- und Dankliedern*, 1947; Bentzen, *Messias, Moses redivivus, Menschensohn*, 1948; Johnson, 'The Psalms', OTMSt. 1951, 162–209; Ridderbos, *Psalmen en Cultus*, 1950; Mowinckel, *Offersang og Sangoffer, Salmediktning i Bibelen*, 1951; Snaith, *Hymns of the Temple*, 1951; Westermann, *Das Loben Gottes in den Psalmen*, 1953; Mowinckel, Psalm-cricitism between 1900 and 1935, VT 5 (1955), 13–33; Stamm, 'Ein Vierteljahrhundert Psalmenforschung', ThR 23 (1955), 1–68; Johnson, *Sacral Kingship in Ancient Israel*, 1955. See also the bibliography to section 6b.

The name Psalter, derived from the Greek ψαλτήριον (stringed instrument) is used as the title in some MSS. of the Septuagint for the collection of the psalms and must be understood on the analogy of Körners 'Leyer und Schwert' ('the lyre and the sword'). In most Septuagint MSS. the title ψαλμοί=songs (for stringed music) is found; this corresponds with the name in the NT βίβλος ψαλμῶν in Luke 20: 42; Acts 1: 20, whence it was taken into our language. In the Hebrew canon there is no title for the book as a whole. The Jewish community calls it *t^ehillîm*=hymns, which occurs in the feminine as the individual title of Ps. 145. Apparently this masculine form is to designate 'the song book' as a whole in contrast with the feminine form in use elsewhere. According to Ps. 72: 20 the expression *t^epillôt*=prayers was employed at an earlier stage of the collection of the psalms; neither of these names include all the kinds of songs brought together in the Psalter; they are probably chosen *a parte potiori*.

The Psalter does not contain nearly all the psalms produced by the religious poets of the OT. Both within as well as outside the OT a number of psalms have been transmitted to us which were not taken into the book of Psalms, e.g. Ex. 15: 1–18; 1 Sam. 2: 1– 10; Is. 38: 10–20; Jonah, 2: 3–10. There are besides the hymns of Qumran and the 'Psalms of Solomon' from the time of Pompey. The OT Psalter numbers 150 songs. Sometimes several songs are combined into *one* psalm (e.g. Pss. 19, 24, 27); contrariwise occasionally one psalm is divided into two separate songs (e.g. Pss. 9+10, 42+43). The Septuagint reckons Pss. 9+10 and 114+115 as one psalm each, but divides Pss. 116 and 147 into two songs; thus the numbering of the psalms in the Septuagint from 9: 22– 146: 11 does not correspond with that of the MT. The 150 songs are arranged no doubt on the analogy of the Torah into five books which are concluded in each case with a liturgical doxology; in the last book the whole of Ps. 150 represents this final doxology. The first book contains Pss. 1–41, the second 42–73, the third 73–89, the fourth 90–106, the fifth 107–150.

The composition of psalms runs through the whole history of the people of Israel and has a copious story which cannot be surveyed in detail (cf. pp 32 ff.). The time when the individual psalms came into being can be determined only by the exegesis of each one and then only in part and approximately. It had been customary for many years to ascribe the majority of the psalms to post-exilic times, contrary to the Jewish tradition and to that of the Early Church to which the Catholic scholars stand the closest (cf. Herkenne, Bonkamp, Nötscher, Calès) and they had occasionally been regarded as the latest product of OT literature. But there is today an inclination to seek for the origin of a number of them in the period before the exile. The conjecture of Maccabean psalms, made particularly by Olshausen and Duhm, has been questioned after comparing them with the hymns of the Qumran and the Psalms of Solomon which are clearly distinguishable from the canonical songs as regards form and content; this conjecture is now shared only by a few scholars (e.g. Pfeiffer). Gunkel had already supported the pre-exilic origin of the royal psalms. In recent times the growing recognition, though in different forms, that most types of psalms were connected with the festival cult of Yahweh, has led to the deduction that the greater part of the psalms came into being before the exile and particularly that they were transmitted within the framework of the worship in Solomon's temple (Mowinckel, H. Schmidt, Bentzen, Weiser; with other presuppositions Eerdmans).

It would seem that we are well informed about the *authors* of the psalms by the titles of a large number of them; 73 psalms are ascribed to David, Pss. 72 and 127 to Solomon, Ps. 90 to Moses, 12 psalms to Asaph, 11 to the sons of Korah, also Ps. 88 to Heman, Ps. 89 to Ethan, Ps. 39 to Jeduthun. It appears from 2 Chron. 29, 30; 2 Macc. 2: 13; Mt. 22, 43 ff. that the later tradition considered such titles—especially *l^e dāwîd*—to indicate the name of the author. Although this tradition can hardly have been a complete fabrication, and we must allow for the possibility that one or other of the psalms (perhaps Ps. 18) may date from David's time, yet it is out of the question that all the 73 psalms ascribed to David were composed by him. That holds good especially of songs in which the temple on Mount Zion is mentioned or circumstances are presupposed which indicate the post-Davidic period. So we must ask whether these titles containing *l^e* did not originally mean something other than the name of the author— which is also linguistically not the most natural meaning—and whether they are not rather to be explained from the connexion of the psalms with the cult (see below). In the case of liturgies, congregational hymns and set forms of worship, members of the Temple staff might be thought of as the authors, but that the psalms in the OT were all of them hieratic poetry is unlikely (against Mowinckel), since a number of psalms contain quite individual features. Probably these personal songs of lament and thanksgiving were composed by individual poets and were recited at the cultic festival; by this means they found their way into the temple tradition and its archives where they were preserved for repeated use (cf. Ps. 102: 2, 19). The song for the King's marriage (Ps. 45) or the mirror of the ruler (Ps. 101), presumably also one or other of the royal psalms may have been composed by a court poet. But none of names appearing in the titles are those of the real authors; the psalms were originally anonymous and probably remained so for a long time.

The question of the origin of individual psalms must be kept separate from that of the *origin and use of the book of psalms*. Information as to how the psalms were performed at the cult as a musical liturgy is supplied by Ez. 3: 10 f.; Jer. 33: 11 (cf. Pss. 118, 136) and especially by 1 Chron. 16: 8 ff. Here a song of praise made up of different parts of psalms (Ps. 105, 1–15; 96, 1–13; 106, 1, 47, 48) is performed by a choir of temple-singers and the people respond with the acclamation, 'Amen, Alleluia'. In the Psalter itself some indications have also been preserved which point to cultic use in the Temple services and especially in the synagogue services of late Judaism. These are *the titles* which name particular occasions at which the psalms in question were sung: Ps. 30 at the dedication of the Temple, Ps. 100 as a thanksgiving, Ps. 92 for the sabbath day; according to the Septuagint Ps. 24 for Sunday, Ps. 48 for Monday, Ps. 94 for Wednesday, Ps. 93 for Friday; according to the Old Latin and Armenian versions, Ps. 81 for Thursday. These psalms were sung in turn at the regular morning burnt-sacrifice (*tāmîd*) and are therefore called *tāmîd* psalms. The Talmud, which in addition provides Ps. 82 for Tuesday, is acquainted with the custom at divine service to let the singing of particular verses from the psalms precede the prayers as hymns and also the practice attested in the NT (Mt. 26: 30) of reciting the Hallel-psalms (113–118) at the Passover and other great feasts. According to the prayer-book of the synagogue, definite psalms are recited by the congregation on the sabbath and on feast and ferial days.

The *liturgical notes* added to individual psalms also point to their use in the cult. The Alleluia-psalms (105, 106, 111, 112, 113, 146, 149, 150) belong to this group; they contain the liturgical response 'Alleluia' ('Praise ye the Lord') to mark their employment in divine service. The *musical notes*, also a later addition, indicate a similar use. Thus *lammᵉnaṣṣᵉaḥ* repeated fifty-five times in the titles, seems to be a *terminus technicus* probably related to the musical performance in the service. Its meaning is not clear and is usually interpreted on the basis of 2 Chron. 2: 1, 17 as 'for the Chief Musician' or 'for the musical performance (Luther: 'to lead the singing'). The fact that it is placed at the head of psalms, e.g. Pss. 51, 55, which probably originated independently of the cult shows that later on the cult took possession of songs originally outside its realm. The position is similar in the case of the expression *Selāh* which occurs 71 times in 39 psalms and is perhaps intended to indicate that after the performance of a section there should be a pause in the prayers marked by a musical interlude (LXX+διάψαλμα) for a refrain to be sung. The indication *mizmôr* (a song sung to a stringed instrument, Luther 'a psalm') which occurs in the titles of 57 psalms presumably suggests that psalms were used as choral anthems at the divine service. Fourteen psalms have the title *shîr* 'song', which points to their being sung; the meaning of other titles such as *miktām*, *maśkîl*, *shiggāyôn*, is quite uncertain. The added note 'on stringed instruments' which is found six times and 'with a flute accompaniment' (or with wind instruments R.V. margin) in Ps. 5 indicates cultic use. Perhaps the note added to the title, as e.g. Ps. 22: 1 'set to the hind of the morning', may be taken to refer to the tune to which the psalm was to be sung; this would presuppose a custom of singing psalms at divine service similar to the one for which we have evidence in the Reformation period and later, namely of singing hymns to secular tunes. But this late testimony to the use of various psalms in public worship does not justify the conclusion that the Psalter was from the outset the hymn-book of the congregation of the second temple. It is much more likely to be a question of continuing a cultic usage which can be shown to have existed in pre-exilic times. It is suggested in Ps. 102: 19 that private psalms too were written down to serve as set forms to be used again at a festival service, and this is clearly expressed in the title placed later at the beginning of this psalm. That titles of this kind were at times added to individual psalms points to an earlier stage in the collection when the psalms were preserved separately and had not yet been grouped in smaller or larger collections in a roll for which a general title at the beginning or the end such as Ps. 72: 20 would have sufficed.

This also throws light on the so-called *authors' titles*. It shows that the individual titles *l^edāwîd* are older than the collection of 'David's psalms' suggested by Ps. 72: 20 ('the prayers of David . . . are ended') and probably go back to the practice of grouping psalms already at the pre-exilic temple. But since the phrase *l^edāwîd* can hardly have been intended originally to denote the author (see above) the meaning 'for David' which is linguistically and, judging by the title of Ps. 102, the more natural one, will have indicated according to the analogy of Ugaritic parallels the Davidic King, to whom, in the role of the ancestor of the dynasty and as the representative for the promises to David and the recipient of the 'salvation of the King' (Ps. 18: 51; Ps. 20: 10; 21: 4, 6 ff.; 89, 2 ff., 25 ff., 50), the recital of the psalm in question at the festival service was addressed. It is uncertain how many of the psalms once bore this title and which these were. Even though under the influence of the Scandinavian scholars there is a tendency to claim as royal psalms a larger number of the psalms thought up till now to have been private songs, yet it is hardly likely that all the psalms ascribed to David were once intended for the King. The original significance of the *l^edāwîd* had lost its meaning when the monarchy came to an end. The fact that in the post-exilic time the designation was retained and extended to other than royal psalms points to a change in its significance. It was the staff in charge of the worship of the second temple who were mainly concerned to collect, preserve and give fresh life to the early stock of liturgical songs; and indeed it seems to have been above all the guilds of temple singers who besides singing and performing the *musica sacra* had the duty of collecting and arranging the psalms. The musical notes added to the titles probably go back to them, as do also the headings *l^e'āsāp* (Ps. 50, 73–83), *lib^enê kōrah* (Pss. 42–49, 84–88). It follows from Ps. 88, in the title of which Heman is named as the author, that at least the description *lib^enê kōrah* did not originally mean the author. According to 2 Chron. 20: 19 the 'children of the Korahites' were a guild of temple singers; something similar might be true of the families of singers of the second temple, Asaph, Heman, Ethan, Jeduthun, named after the singers of David as their ancestors (1 Chron. 6: 18 ff.; 16: 41 f.; 25: 1 ff. and *passim*). The fact that individual psalms were headed with the names of these singers as 'belonging to the children of the Korahites', etc. was probably intended at first to denote those psalms which had been transmitted by the individual guilds of singers and were intended by them for performance at divine service; thus in the above-mentioned groups remnants of the earlier collection of temple songs are indicated. Presumably the heading *lᵉḏāwîḏ* is to be understood in the same sense and the same connexion in the case of those psalms which were not destined for the use of the king, but came from the pre-exilic royal worship of the temple or were thought to have done so. At this stage of collecting the psalms the designation *lᵉḏāwîḏ* had the significance of a collective name, to distinguish the psalms concerned as belonging to the 'Davidic tradition' of the pre-exilic temple worship. Only in this way can it be explained that the general note 'The prayers of David . . . are ended' in Ps. 72: 20 stands at the end of a psalm attributed to Solomon.

Towards the end of the Persian period an attempt was made to legitimate the temple worship of Jerusalem through enhancing the authority of David in order to counteract the Samaritan claims to the tradition; in pursuance of this tendency which is strongly marked in the Chronicles David was considered in the levitical circles to be the ancestor of psalm-writing and thus the *lᵉḏāwîḏ* of the psalm-titles was interpreted as the Davidic authorship. In the course of this development those historical and biographical entries concerning the situations in which David is said to have written or sung the songs in question were placed at the head of thirteen psalms (3, 7, 18, 34, 51, 52, 54, 56, 57, 59, 60, 63, 142); this perhaps was suggested by the use of Ps. 18 in 2 Sam. 22. Since in the Septuagint other psalms also are provided with such editorial headings, it is likely that this process went on into the third century. This view, deriving the psalms from authoritative personalities in the history of OT worship, including Ps. 90 from Moses, Pss. 72 and 127 from Solomon, Ps. 88 from Heman, Ps. 89 from Etan, Ps. 39 from Jeduthun, sprang from a later apologetic trend; there is no need to prove that it has no direct historical value.

The collection of the psalms and the formation of the present book of psalms did not take place in *one* operation nor by the same hands. The Psalter itself still bears clear indications of its historical growth. It was a long process, which ran its course between the fourth and second centuries B.C.; but its individual stages are no

longer quite clear to us. The division into five books represents
the end of this process of assembling, in which the last collector
put together the present Psalter out of different earlier groupings
of psalms. For the presence in the Psalter of psalms transmitted
twice over (14=53; 40: 14 — 18=70; 57: 8 — 12+60: 7 — 14=108)
would hardly be possible if all the psalms had been gathered
together at the same time by the same hand. The fact that in the
group of psalms 42 to 83 the divine name Yahweh was replaced
by the general term for God 'elōhîm leads to the same conclusion.
If this elohistic editor had had the whole Psalter before him, it is
difficult to see why his alteration was confined to this group.
Consequently the 'elohistic psalter' (see below) is one of the earlier
independent collections out of which the complete Psalter gradually grew into one.

The Davidic Psalter 3-41. The psalms 3-41 represent another,
probably earlier collection which was intended to be a homogeneous Davidic Psalter owing to the title l'dāwîd prefixed to
nearly all of them. As no other principle of arrangement of the
varied songs gathered together here can be discovered, it may be
presumed that we are concerned with an earlier group of psalms
from the tradition of the first temple.

Another collection is represented by the elohistic psalter 42-89
which originally contained Pss. 42-83 and which seems to have
been enlarged later by a supplement 84-89. The reason why the
edition replaced the divine name Yahweh by Elohim in Pss. 42-83,
which a comparison of the doublets shows up, can be most
readily explained on the ground of their being read aloud at the
divine service in later Judaism, which refrained with reverent awe
from pronouncing the divine name and at the same time chose
the more general Elohim as the designation of the one true God
of its monotheistic religion. The elohistic Psalter is composed of
separate units which likewise bear the marks of cultic use. We
can first distinguish a group of psalms, 42-49 and in the supplement 84, 85, 87, 88, which are attributed to the Korahites. This
collection, arranged according to different kinds of songs, seems
to have been the choir-book of the sons of Korah, who worked
their way up in the fourth century from being a family of door-
keepers to a guild of temple singers (1 Chron. 15: 19; 2 Chron.
20: 19). Perhaps we may find amongst them the authors of one or

other of the psalms in this collection. The same can be said of the small collection of Asaph psalms, 50, 73–83, in which we see a choir-book of a respected guild of temple singers who returned from exile already with Zerubbabel and functioned from the beginning as a temple choir (Ezra 2: 41; 2 Chron. 35: 15 and elsewhere). A third early collection admitted by the collector of the elohistic psalter is a group of 'Davidic psalms', 51–65, 68–70 with 72 as a supplement arranged on similar principles as the Korah psalms; by the last words 'The prayers of David, the son of Jesse, are ended' these are proved to have been originally a unit and must have been brought together into one collection before the other Davidic psalms which follow them. Since these psalms almost without exception are headed with musical and liturgical notes, it seems safe to assume the cultic aim of this collection. Thus, seen as a whole, we have in the elohistic psalter a psalm book in which three different earlier cultic collections of psalms are combined, but their individual fortunes can no longer be discovered; the remarkable position of Ps. 50 (Asaph), the enlargement of the Korahite psalms by the supplement Pss. 84 to 88 (89 by Ethan) without the elohistic revision and the inclusion of Solomon's psalm 72 remain a mystery. The addition of the musical and liturgical notes will probably have taken place in those circles to whom we owe the collection of the choir books for the services. By their admission of personal songs into their collection they enabled the piety of individuals to find a place in their worship and by thus enriching and deepening it they have won for themselves lasting credit.

The rest of the psalms 90–150 no longer allow the story of their collection to be discerned. Amongst them is to be found the little 'book of pilgrim songs' 120–134, each with the title 'Song of Ascents' (Luther 'in the upper choir', according to others 'Song of Degrees' which are thought to have been sung on mounting one by one the steps up to the temple), yet apart from Ps. 122 it does not contain any real pilgrim song. It can no longer be definitely established whether the remaining psalms, besides a few, albeit not reliably attested, Davidic psalms (122, 124, 131, 133) belonged to older collections or, what seems to me more probable, were brought together before the whole Psalter was finally assembled. At any rate its division into five books on the analogy of the Torah comes from this last collector. It was he who put into their places Pss. 1 and 2 as an introduction and Ps. 150 as a doxological conclusion. As the doxologies at the ends of the individual books presumably go back to their use in divine service (1 Chron. 16: 8–36), it seems as if this last stage in the collection of the Psalter was also intended for the cult. The process of collecting the psalms had been brought to an end by the beginning of the first century B.C., for the so-called Psalms of Solomon of the time of Pompey were not admitted into the biblical psalter.

The composition of psalms accompanied the whole history of the people of Israel and the happenings in the life of devout individuals. Its forms adopted the heritage of millennial civilizations, came to terms with that heritage and gave it a new meaning of its own and a religious content. Thus there is reflected in the Psalter the history, filled with strong emotion, of at least seven centuries of religious activity. Consequently there is a great variety in the answers to the very diverse problems of life given by the many unknown poets who each in his own way sought the road to God. Although we cannot fail to recognize that the varied types of song are to a certain extent tied down to a common framework of cultic tradition, we may not on that account expect a homogeneous theological attitude or doctrine in the Psalter. But for that very reason the psalms stand closer to life and its realities than dogmatic reflexions. Here are mirrored in the most diverse forms and out of the most different situations in life some of the best things which the faith of the OT has to say to mankind. And Luther, although he did not possess the insight into the inner historical contexts which the new studies have given us, by his sensitive feeling for what is essential and decisive called the Psalter 'a Little Biblia', a 'proper school' in which 'the faith and a good conscience towards God is learned, practised and strengthened'.

42. The Book of Job

Commentaries: KeH: Hitzig, 1874.–Dillman,[4] 1891.–KD: Delitzsch,[2] 1876.–SZ: Volck, 1889.–KHC: Duhm, 1897.–HK: Budde,[2] 1913.–ICC: Driver–Gray, 1951. –WC: Gibson,[3] 1919.–SBOT: Siegfried, 1893.–EH: Peters, 1928.–CEB: Dhorme, 1926.–HSAT: Steuernagel, 1923.–SAT: Volz,[2] 1921.–HS: Szcygiel, 1931.–Ricciotti, 1924.–TV: Bleeker,[2] 1935.–HAT: Hölscher,[2] 1952.–Merx, 1871.–Buttenwieser, 1925. –König, 1929.–Wutz, 1939.–Lindblom, 1940.–SBB: Reichert, 1946.–Fohrer, 1948.– Hertzberg, 1949.–LStB (Clamer): Robin, 1939.–LStB: Larcher, 1950.–EB: Junker, 1951.–ATD: Weiser,[2] 1956.–TBC: Hanson, 1953.–IB: Terrien, Scherer,1954.–Stier,

1954.–Steinmann, 1955.–Torczyner, 1957.–Budde, *Beiträge zur Kritik des Buches Hiob*, 1876; Grill, *Zur Kritik der Komposition des Buches Hiob*, 1890; Laue, *Die Komposition des Buches Hiob*, 1895; Beer, *Der Text des Buches Hiob*, 1897; Kautzsch, *Das sog. Volksbuch von Hiob*, 1900; Sellin, *Das Problem des Hiobbuches*, 1919; Weiser; 'Das Problem der sittlichen Weltordnung in Buch Hiob', ThBl 1923, col. 157 ff.; Fullerton, 'The original Conclusion of Job', ZAW 1924, 116 ff.; Thilo, *Das Buch Hiob*, 1925: Torczyner, *Das Buch Hiob, eine krit. Analyse des Hiobtextes*, 1920; idem, 'Hiobdichtung und Hiobsage', MGWJ 1925, 234 ff.; H. Schmidt, *Hiob*, 1927; Richter, 'Textstudien zum Buch Hiob', BWAT 1927; Hempel, 'Das theologische Problem des Hiob', *Z. f. Syst. Theologie*, 1929, 621 ff.; Sellin, *Das Hiobsproblem*, 1931; Baumgärtel, 'Der Hiobdialog', BWAT 1933; Lods. 'Recherches récentes sur le livre de Job', RHPhR 1934, 501 ff.; Alt, 'Zur Vorgeschichte des Buches Hiob', ZAW 1937, 265 ff.; Kraeling, *The Book of the Ways of God*, SPCK, ix, 1939; Eerdmans, *Studies in Job*, 1939: Kroeze, 'Die Elihureden im Buch Hiob', *Oudtestamentische Studien II*, 1943, 156 ff.; Lindblom, *La composition du livre de Job*, 1945; Steinmann, *Job*, 1946; Stevenson, *The Poem of Job: A Literary Study with a New Translation*, London, 1947; Hertzberg, 'Der Aufbau des Buches Hiob'. *Bertholet-Festschrift*, 1950, 233 ff.; Baumgartner, OTMSt (1951), 216 ff.; Kuhl, 'Neuere Literarkritik d. Buches Hiob', ThR 21 (1953), 163–205, 257–317; idem, 'Vom Hiobbuch u. seiner Problemen', ThR 22 (1954), 261–316; T. H. Robinson, *Job and his Friends*, 1954; Möller, *Sinn und Aufbau d. Buches Hiob*, 1955; Knight, 'Job (considered as a Contribution to Hebrew Theology)', *Scottish Journ. of Theology*, 9 (1956), 63 ff.; Fohrer, Vorgeschichte u. Komposition d. Buches Hiob, *VT VI* (1956), 249–267; Westermann, 'Der Aufbau des Buches Hiob'. *Beitr. z. histor. Theologie*, 23, 1956.

The book of Job, named after its hero Job (Hebrew 'iyyôb; Greek and Latin Job), is one of the most significant productions of world literature. Not only its value as a work of art, displayed by the power of its language, by the depth of its feeling, by the grandeur of its structure, but also the subject with which it deals, the daring titanic struggle with the immemorial, yet ever new, questioning of mankind concerning the meaning of suffering, places this composition as regards its general significance beside Dante's *Divina Commedia* and Goethe's *Faust*.

The book of Job is composed of three parts: (I) *The Prologue* in chapters 1–2: a prose narrative which tells of Job's piety and good fortune in 1: 1–5, of the wager in heaven between Satan and God to test Job's piety in 1: 6–12, of Job's tribulation (loss of his possessions and his children) and of his standing firm in the test in 1: 13–22. There follows a second scene in heaven and another tribulation (boils) which ends again with Job's steadfastness in 2: 1–10. The visits of condolence from Job's friends Eliphaz, Bildad and Zophar form the transition to part II: *speeches* in poetic form in 3: 1–42: 6. The debate which begins with Job cursing himself contains a triple exchange of speeches between Job and his friends in 4–14; 15–21; 22–27 (the third speech of Zophar is lacking).

Chapter 28 follows with a poem about the inscrutability of the 'wisdom' belonging to God alone, in 29–31 Job looks back on then and now, clears himself with an oath and challenges God to answer him in 31: 35 ff. Chapters 32–37 contain the speeches of Elihu, a friend not mentioned so far. God's reply follows in chapter 38 f. When God appears in a whirlwind (38–39) Job humbles himself (40: 3–5) and a second speech by God (40: 6–41: 26) ends in Job's submission (42: 1–6). *Part III:* the Epilogue (42: 7–17) is again a prose-narrative; it contains (42: 7–9) Yahweh's condemnation of the friends, Job's intercession for them and in 10–17 his reinstatement and increased good fortune.

The difference between *the framework of narrative and the speeches* leaps to the eye at once and suggests a different origin for each of them. It is not only the difference between prose and poetry; the figure of Job too is dissimilar: in the narrative the submissive sufferer, in the poem the vehement, titanic struggler. The narrative has a practical instructive character; the pious sufferer is held up as an example; the poem is the confession of a fighter who treads a solitary and steep road and has given an account of his own battles in the description of Job and his friends. Therefore the frame of the narrative is not a free invention of the poet of Job; it is based on an old popular tradition about him, which assumes the knowledge of Ezek. 14: 14, 20 where Job is named beside Noah and Daniel as an example of an upright man. But it is not possible to prove, nor is it likely, that this narrative in the form of a folk-tale of job (Wellhausen, Budde, Duhm, Rost and others) once existed as an independent literary entity beside the poem of Job and was taken over by the poet without alteration, since the action in the surrounding narrative provides the foundation on which the speeches are built up. Consequently the poet has used this popular tradition and fitted the spiritual drama of the speeches into the framework of the narrative about Job. There are no means of ascertaining precisely how far he himself shaped the story. The two passages connecting the poem and the narrative, 2: 11–13, the introduction of the friends, and 42: 7, God's judgment on them, may have been given at least their present shape by the poet's hand; the two scenes in heaven (1: 6–12; 2: 1–6) which prepare for the problem presented in the poem, and by their greater wealth of detail and lively sense of drama form a contrast with the rest of the prose narrative, might also have been fashioned freely by the poet; on the other hand 42: 11-16 when compared with 42: 7-10 perhaps still bears traces of an earlier transmission of the Job narrative (Alt, Fohrer).

Thus the poet has made the folk-tale and the speeches into one work in spite of their different roots. But the following pieces do not fit into the context of the whole and must therefore be considered later additions; 1. *Chapter 28, the hymn to the hidden wisdom.* It is not possible for this hymn to be spoken by Job because it is based on a conception of wisdom different from that in the rest of the book; the fact that in it wisdom is recognized as being past understanding would make completely superfluous the contents of chapters 38 ff. in which Job is only brought to realize this by the appearance and speeches of God. 2. Chapters 32-37: *The speeches of Elihu.* Elihu is mentioned neither at the beginning nor at the end of the narrative where he could hardly have been overlooked in the comprehensive judgment on the friends in 42: 7 ff. His speeches interrupt the evident continuity which exists between the challenge to God for an answer at the end of chapter 31 and God's reply which follows in chapters 38 ff.; thus they prove themselves to be an interpolation. Moreover the language of these chapters is tinged with significantly more Aramaisms than the rest of the book. Besides the conception of suffering as seen in the speeches of Elihu is quite different in substance, they give the theological 'solution' that sufferings are intended to educate men by purging them of their pride. Thus in spite of the attempts of Budde, Cornill, Thilo, Hertzberg and Möller to find in the Elihu-speeches the only possible solution and the culmination of this problem, we are obliged to conclude that they are the later addition of a man who intended to tone down by his interpolation the shock given by the poem and for this purpose to bring it closer to the orthodox point of view; so we cannot agree with Sellin's view either, that the speeches of Elihu should be considered a later addition by the poet himself.

The authenticity of Yahweh's Speeches in Chapters 38-41 is disputed by some scholars, either altogether (Cheyne, Volz, Baumgärtel) or as regards their essential part (H. Schmidt). But surely Job's challenge in 31: 35 ff. and the connecting link with the final narrative in 42: 7 ff. which presupposes Job's humiliation, incorporates them organically both at the beginning and at the end; if they were removed, the whole poem without the episode of the divine speeches would remain a torso lacking an ultimate meaning. In the speeches of Yahweh themselves the sections about the Behemoth in 40: 15–24 and the Leviathan in 40: 25–41: 26 which are elaborated additions to the description of the animals in chapters 38 f., and linked with them the introduction to Yahweh's second speech in 40: 6–14 and one of the two answers of Job (40: 1–5) are judged frequently to be supplements by a later writer. Yet the assumption that only one speech of Yahweh and only one reply by Job to correspond with it is called for, is a postulate which would be justified only if both Yahweh's speeches and Job's replies were deemed to be parallels without any special development in the argument. Yet as a matter of fact God's first speech is directed to bringing Job to acknowledge his error and his helplessness in God's sight and to silence him (40: 4 f.). God's second speech with its gigantic mythological background occupies a peculiar position in relation to the description of animals in chapters 38 f.; it brings about Job's acknowledgment of guilt and his repentance (42: 6) and leads the internal dramatic movement of the poem up to the point at which his anguish of soul comes to rest in the theodicy (42: 5). In view of the special function of God's second speech which is not inferior to the first in poetic power, its original genuineness ought not to be doubted.

Several scholars go much further in their literary criticism and seek to reject as additions a greater or smaller number of passages which deal with more general subjects or seem to be loosely connected with the train of thought as it moves on. Amongst those making these attempts, Siegfried, Volz, Fullerton, Torczyner, Buttenwieser, Peters and Lindblom may be mentioned; the most radical action was taken by Baumgärtel, who chiefly by the use of form-critical analysis will admit only a skeleton of the first debate and a subsequent monologue of Job to be original. Kraeling follows partly in the footsteps of Baumgärtel by conjecturing that the dialogue has been re-edited several times. Lindblom tries to show the growth of the book; he says that the prologue and the epilogue developed out of a shorter Edomite primitive form and the debates out of an old simple dialogue, and that the book received its present form through several expansions and elaborations of an Israelite stamp (e.g. the figure of the Satan). But it is very largely on the basis of a subjective judgment that the work is broken up into various fragments, and this judgment overlooks the lively quality of the internal dramatic movement of the book by applying too strict a standard of a one-track logic and it usually arises from a definite general theological verdict on the whole. Moreover it does not do justice from the point of view of the history of types to the actual mixed character of the poem which in addition to the use of debate, has taken up into itself a variety of types (hymn, lament, thanksgiving, oath of purgation).*

It is not possible to discover with certainty when and where the book was written. An exact dating is impossible, owing to the lack of any allusions to historical events; this is not a matter for surprise since the wisdom-literature shows no interest in history. The conjecture that the author knew the historical work of the Pentateuch, when it had combined the Yahwist, Elohist and Priestly strands, and the chronological conclusions built up on it, do not stand up to a careful examination; nor is there any proof that Job 3: 3 depends on Jer. 20: 14 ff. or Job 13: 17 ff. on Is. 50: 4 ff., although this has often been asserted. Since Ecclesiasticus clearly takes the knowledge of the book of Job for granted, about the year 200 B.C. can be accepted as the lower limit of its origin. The upper limit should not be sought further back than the exile. To judge by its type the book of Job belongs to a form of Wisdom poetry already fashioned by a long process of development and the broad elaboration of its style and the Aramaic influence on its language reveal the marks of a later didactic poem. Moreover the general tenor of its thought assumes that the traditional doctrine of retribution has been shaken and that this doctrine has been applied to individuals also, as set forth in Ezek. 18, 33: 10 ff.; without claiming any dependence on Ezekiel, these facts point to the post-exilic period and moreover hardly to its early days. We may therefore place the book of Job between the fifth and third centuries.

On the other hand the *home* of the poet who wrote Job remains completely obscure. The fact that Job belongs to 'the children of the

* Westermann has applied the form-historical method in too one-sided a manner to the book of Job; he regards it as a 'dramatized lament' and tries to divide it up into its elements by their form, without paying sufficient attention to the peculiarities and differences in their subject matter.

east' (1: 3) and that the land of Uz (1: 1) and the home of the friends (2: 1) is to be found in the east of Palestine might be relevant at the most for the popular tradition of Job, but not for determining the home of the poet. Both the later tradition which places Job in the Hauran or in northern Syria and the attempts to use linguistic arguments for conjecturing Edom to be the home of the book (Yahuda, Eissfeldt, Pfeiffer) have no sufficient scientific foundation; nor are there enough allusions to Egyptian things (papyrus in 8: 11 f.; ships of reed in 9: 26; Behemoth in 40: 5 ff.; Leviathan in 40: 25 ff., etc.) to render probable the hypothesis put forward at different times that the book originated in Egypt, perhaps in the rich culture of Alexandria. A Palestinian author too might have learned about such things on his travels or by other cultural means.

The meaning of the poem. The problem of Job with which the poet deals, whilst using the old popular tradition of the long-suffering Job as a way of presenting it, is the problem of his own life. The speeches of his friends as well as his speeches to them and to God reflect the poet's own inner struggles, when the traditional doctrine of retribution, namely that suffering is the penalty for sin, is shattered by the actual facts of his own suffering. The poet presents these inner conflicts by making the friends advocates of the ethical rationalism of the doctrine of retribution, whilst in the speeches and experiences of Job he traces the dramatic road by which he himself was led by the various challenges of his sufferings to a deeper knowledge of himself and to a new relationship to God. Thus it is concerned neither with the theoretical problem of the meaning of evil, nor with practical guidance to others as to how to behave when suffering, nor yet with the problem of the theodicy, but with the personal confession of the poet whose actual fight against suffering has become the place where he meets God afresh. Standing on the firm ground of his pure conscience and his search for God, he finds himself misjudged by his friends. Since they do not comprehend the concern of his conscience and demand from him a humble confession of guilt to the God of the doctrine of retribution, he turns in repeated onsets and with passionate, titanic remonstrances to God himself, seeking to obtain from him the ultimate recognition of his innocence and his justification. That Job is breaking free in his heart from the

material goods of life and from the need for recognition by his
fellow-men can already be detected by the fact that he seeks his
sole and ultimate support in the approval of God, that is to say,
in the religious relationships of life. To meet with God himself
is now the goal of his longing. This is granted to him; he is
deemed worthy of a divine manifestation and in it he finds inner
peace (42: 5); but it is different from what he (and his friends too)
had imagined: the God who manifests himself in the whirlwind
is another God, is greater than the God of the doctrine. He is the
inscrutable Lord of creation, whose wisdom is unfathomable for
men, he is too lofty and too great for man to be able to remonstrate
with him about his fate. In his presence Job's complaint is reduced
to silence; in humility he bows down before the majesty of this
God, admitting that he spoke against him without understanding.
And after God has extorted from him even his right of moral
self-assertion to which he had clung to the last, he recognizes his
guilt and confessing his guilt, his penitence and his recantation
places himself under the judgment of God. Even now the divine
meaning of what had happened and thus of his suffering still
remains hidden from Job; it belongs to the inaccessible riddles of
the divine rule of the creator. But it is this mighty God, whose
unfathomable sublimity Job has perceived and whose judgment
he has acknowledged, who now in his turn acknowledges the
inner integrity of Job in his struggles; thus he takes from him the
sharpest sting of his unexplained suffering by letting him, the
sinner, participate in his ardently desired presence and thereby
himself removes the barrier which had separated him from God.
In this relationship between God and man, established by God
himself, the poet discovers the point where all the unsolved
riddles of his existence have come to rest; in his meeting with the
living God, who takes him at his word, he finds that peace for his
soul which quells all other torments of life. It is this which first
throws light on all that Job 'has spoken', which God in 42: 7
recognized as 'right'; it is God's grace which justifies the sinner.
For the poet the 'solution' lies not only in the one point of meeting
with God; it includes also all that took place in Job's soul and was
brought to light in the speeches showing his struggles to free
himself from a conception of God and a piety bound by human
limitations, from a worldly assessment of the goods of this life.

This motif runs all through the drama of Job's soul and issues in the one and only yearning for God which is satisfied by his meeting with Yahweh, after he has had to give up all the ties entangled in tradition and the human limitations of his piety. In the whole drama of Job's struggles to find God, God's judgment is being carried out up to the point where the sufferer on meeting God bows down before him as a sinner and in this judgment comes to know God's mercy; this raises him up and gives him as God's 'servant' the office of reconciliation with regard to his friends (42: 7 ff.) and thus bestows on the vindicated sinner a fresh meaning for his life. Consequently the restoration of his fortune means for the Job of the poet something different than it does in the old folk-tale. The blessing becomes here an additional gift of the mercy of the incomprehensible God. The book of Job, as a testimony of the intense struggles of a man with his God for the prize of God himself, is worthy to stand beside the most deeply felt confessions of OT piety: it is the illustration in the Old Testament of the promise in the New Testament so pregnant with meaning: Blessed are the pure in heart, for they shall see God.

43. The Proverbs

Commentaries: KD.: Delitzsch, 1873.–KeH: Nowack,[2] 1883.–KHC: Wildeboer, 1897.–HK: Frankenberg, 1898.–ICC: Toy, 1948.–SZ: Strack,[2] 1899.–SAT: Volz,[2] 1921.–HSAT: Steuernagel 1923.–HS: Wiesmann, 1923.–WC: Oesterley, 1929.–TU: Gemser, 1929, 1931.–HAT: Gemser, 1937.–SBB: Cohen,[2] 1952.–LStB (Clamer): Renard, Buzy, Weber, Spicq, 1946.–EB: Hamp, 1949.–HBK: Power, 1949.–HSC: Greenstone, 1950.–LStB: Duesberg, Auvray, 1951.–COT: Gispen, I, 1952.–BOT: van der Ploeg, 1952.–IB: Fritsch, Schloerb, 1955.–See literature for section 7. Frankenberg, 'Über Abfassungs-Ort und-Zeit sowie Art und Inhalt von Prov. I–IX', ZAW 1895, 104 ff; Erman, Eine ägyptische Quelle der 'Sprüche Salomos', Sitzg.-Ber. d. Pr. Akad. d. W. Phil. Kl, 1924, 86 ff; Gressmann, 'Die neugefundene Lehre des Amen-em-ope und die vorexilische Spruchdichtung Israels', ZAW 1924, 272 ff.; Oesterley, 'The Teaching of Amen-em-ope and the OT', ZAW 1927, 9 ff.; idem, The Wisdom of Egypt and the OT, 1927; Humbert, Recherches sur les sources égyptiennes de la littérature sapientale d'Israël, 1929; Ranston, The OT Wisdom Books and their Teaching, 1930; Kuhn, 'Beiträge zur Erklärung des Salomonischen Spruchbuchs', BWAT 1931; Fichtner, 'Die altorientalische Weisheit in ihrer israelitsch-jüdischen Ausprägung', BZAW 62, 1933; Zimmerli, 'Zur Struktur der alttestamentlichen Weisheit', ZAW 1933, 177 ff.; Dornseiff, 'Hesiods Werke und Tage und das alte Morgenland', Philologus, 1934, 397 ff.; Boström, Proverbiastudien. Die Weisheit und das fremde Weib in Spr 1–9, 1935; J. Schmidt, Studien zur Stilistik der alttestamentlichen Spruchliteratur, Atl. Abh 1936; Rankin, Israel's Wisdom Literature, 1936,[2] 1954; Dubarle, Les sages d'Israël, 1946; Ringgren, Word and Wisdom, 1947; Power, The Proverbs of Solomon, 1949; Alt, 'Die Weisheit Salomos', ThLZ 56 (1951), col. 139 ff. =Alt II, 90 ff.; Baumgartner, OTMSt (1951), 212 ff.; Brunner, 'Die Weisheitsliteratur', Hdb. d. Orientalistik (hrg. von Spuler, I Ägyptologie, 2 (1952), 90 ff.; Gese, Lehre und Wirklichkeit in der alten Weisheit, 1958.

The book derives its name from the title in 1: 1 'The proverbs (in Hebrew *mishᵉlê*, in Greek παροιμίαι, in Latin *proverbia*) of Solomon, the son of David, king of Israel.' Like the psalms, this book contains the deposit of the development and collection of wisdom-literature which went on for centuries. The book of Proverbs too, bears clear traces of its historical growth; it is true that tradition regards Solomon as its author, a view based on what is handed down in 1 Kgs. 5: 9–14; 10: 1 ff., where it is stated that Solomon was famous for his wisdom, had spoken 3,000 proverbs, and that wisdom was cultivated at his court (see above, section 7). The separate headings in 1: 1; 10: 1; 22: 17; 24: 23; 25: 1; 30: 1; 31: 1 already enable us to see that the book of Proverbs has grown together out of different collections. The fact that they appear in another order in the LXX proves that they introduced separate items. These titles distinguish at least seven individual collections amongst which three larger main ones can be discerned: I, 1–9 'The proverbs of Solomon'; II, 10–22: 16 more 'proverbs of Solomon' and III, 25–29 'These also are the proverbs of Solomon, which the men of Hezekiah king of Judah copied out.' Beside these there are four smaller collections of which two each are attached to the second and third main collections as appendices: 22: 17–24: 22 'the words of the wise' and 24: 23–34 'These also are the sayings of the wise', and at the end, chapter 30 'The words of Agur of Massa' and 31: 1–9 'The words of King Lemuel of Massa which his mother taught him.' The conclusion of the whole book is now formed by an alphabetic poem in praise of the virtuous housewife in 31: 10–31. Repetitions, doublets and variants within these groups, especially in 10–22: 16; 22: 17–24: 22; 25–29 point to older, smaller collections, which may be thought to have preceded the present ones, but their context and age can no more be clearly ascertained.

As regards *the age and formation of the individual collections*, this much may be said to begin with, namely that the first collection in 1–9 is the latest; as in the case of the pentateuchal revision and the collection of the psalms, here too the relatively late has been placed at the beginning (Gen. 1; Ps. 1). The history of forms and types shows already that the longer pieces with definite themes belong to a later stage in the development of Wisdom literature; the lengthy well-shaped sentences might be due to fresh stylistic influences, and indeed even the word 'etûn in 7: 16 seems to be a Hebrew version of a Greek word ὀθόνη, ὀθόνιοι. The effect too of the prophetic denunciations and rebukes and of the hymn-like style is seen in a change in the character of this type. To these causes must be added arguments based on the subject-matter; the prophets' teaching which connected wisdom and the fear of God, as well as the warning against the alien woman, are marks of a later origin. This collection as a whole, and therefore the book in its entirety, originated according to all the indications in the post-exilic time, probably hardly earlier than the fourth century. This does not exclude the possibility that here and there earlier material has been taken into the collection; thus for example the personification of wisdom in chapters 8 and 9, which as being a first stage in the speculation concerning the hypostasis has usually been considered more recent, must now, it seems, be referred to earlier Phoenician and Canaanite influence as a result of comparing its vocabulary and ideas with Ugaritic sources (see Albright, *From the Stone Age to Christianity*, 1940). But this fact is hardly sufficient to claim all the matter grouped together in chapters 1–9 as the earliest part of the book originating with Solomon (against Fritsch).

On the other hand 10–22: 16 with its appendices and also the third main collection give the impression of being older. They contain mostly isolated proverbs or sayings consisting of one verse each without internal coherence, probably the earlier and the original stylistic form of the wisdom saying. As the Israelite monarchy is taken for granted in 16: 12 ff.; 25: 2 ff., these sayings at least came into being in pre-exilic times, whilst its cultural background and its opinions also fit the period of the kings. With this in mind the question should be seriously considered, whether the statement in 25: 1 is not trustworthy, that the collection was formed under Hezekiah at the end of the eighth century. And it would not be impossible for older smaller collections, of which the traces are still visible, to reach back into a still earlier age and perhaps to have admitted with other sayings some material from Solomon. The appendix in 22: 17–24: 22, in which in 22: 17–23: 12 direct literary dependence on the Egyptian Book of Wisdom of Amen-em-ope (between the ninth and sixth centuries B.C.) can be proved (23: 13 is borrowed from the oriental Wisdom of the sayings of Aḥikar), must from the mention of the king in 22: 29 have originated in the pre-exilic period. On the other hand it is not possible to date the second appendix, 24: 23–34. To judge by their headings the last two appendices are no doubt also from another country, if Massa may be assumed from Gen. 25: 14; 1 Chron. 1: 30 to indicate a tribe or a district in northern Arabia. Evident reminiscences of Job 40: 4 f.; 42: 2 ff. suggesting a later origin can be observed especially in the first part of chapter 30; but the numerical sayings in 30: 15–33 probably represent older material. Further details as to the conditions in which these collections arose remain obscure. The alphabetical song in praise of the housewife was probably added to the rest at a later date, perhaps as an antithesis to the preceding warning against dangerous women who are to be contrasted with an ideal picture of womanhood.

The proverbial Wisdom of the OT includes in its wide survey every aspect of life. Its tone is predominantly practical, rational, sensible. Wisdom is above all sound common sense, useful worldly wisdom, but it includes the domain of ethics; thus wisdom and morality, folly and wickedness are treated as equivalent. Unlike the early oriental wisdom, the OT is concerned to cultivate wisdom not only in the matter of the morality to be expected of a particular cultured class; it addresses itself to men quite generally and has to do with all the people. This gives it its special breadth and depth. The relationship between children and parents, the high esteem shown to marriage and the consequent strictness in sexual morality, the responsibility felt for the needy, these are subjects which have received from the thought of the OT their particular stamp in its Wisdom maxims. The strong emphasis given by ethical rationalism has placed the idea of divine retribution at the centre of wisdom; since its thought is concerned with this world only, it often receives a utilitarian, eudaemonist colouring. For the same reason the idea of retribution in the next world has not been admitted into the wisdom teaching. But at the same time it must not be overlooked that, as contrasted with the rest of early oriental wisdom, under the influence of the prophets the permeation by religion is more strongly marked in the OT book of Proverbs; in 1: 7 'the fear of the Lord is the beginning =*principium*) of knowledge' it has been beautifully and profoundly expressed. 10: 22 also offers some evidence for the paramount reality of God by underlining that 'The blessing of the Lord, it maketh rich and toil addeth nothing thereto'. The characteristics of OT wisdom must be understood in the light of its practical educative aim; yet, for all its practical reasonableness, the OT declares the fear of God and righteousness to be the main pillars of this education.

44. The Song of Songs

Commentaries: KeH: Hitzig, 1855.–KD: Delitzsch, 1875.–SZ: Öttli, 1889.–HK: Siegfried, 1898.–KHC: Budde, 1898.–HSAT: Budde, 1923.–SAT: Staerk,[2] 1920.– HS: Miller, 1927.–TU: Gemser, 1931.–CEB: Pouget and Guitton,[2] 1948.–HAT: Haller, *Die fünf Megilloth (Ruth, Hoheslied, Klagelieder, Kohelet, Esther)*, 1940.– Hengstenberg, 1853.–Rothstein, 1893.–Kalt, 1933.–Wutz, 1940.–SBB: Cohen, Goldman, Lehrman, Reichert, Slotki, 'The Five Megilloth', 1946.–EB: Fischer, 1950. –LStB (Clamer): Buzy, 1950.–LStB: Robert, 1951.–Bea, 1953.–Chouraqui, 1953.– Feuillet, 1953.–Gordis, 1954.–TBC: Knight, 1955.–Herder, *Lieder der Liebe*, 1778; Budde, 'Was ist das Hohelied?', *Pr. Jahrb.*, 1894, 92 ff.; Haupt, *Biblische Liebeslieder*, 1907; Thilo, *Das Hohelied*, 1921; *The Song of Songs. A symposium*, by Margolis, Montgomery, Hyde, Edgerton, Meek, Schoff, 1924; Kuhn, *Erklärung des Hohen Liedes*, 1926; Wittekindt, *Das Hohe Lied und seine Beziehungen zum Istarkult*, 1927; Gebhardt, *Das Lied der Lieder*, 1931; Horst, 'Die Formen des althebräischen Liebesliedes', *Oriental: Studien, Festschrift für Littmann*, 1935, 43 ff.; Rowley, 'The interpretation of the Song of Songs', JThSt 1937, 137 ff.; idem, 'The Song of Songs: an examination of recent theory', *Journal of the Royal Asiatic Society*, 1938, 251 ff.; idem, AJSL 56, 1939, 84 ff.; Kuhl, 'Das Hohelied und seine Deutung', ThR 1937, 137 ff.; Baumgartner, ThR 1941, 178 f.; Rudolph, 'Das Hohe Lied im Kanon', ZAW 1942–43, 189 ff.; Baumgartner, OTMSt (1951), 230 ff.; Schmöckel, 'Zur kultischen Deutung des Hohenliedes', ZAW 64 (1952), 148 ff.; Linder, *Palästinische Volksgesänge* (ed. by Ringgren), Uppsala Univ. Årskrift, 1952, 5; Ringgren, 'Hohes Lied und *hieros gamos*', ZAW 65 (1953), 300 ff.; Schmöckel, *Heilige Hochzeit und Hohes Lied*, 1956.

In its title the book is called 'The Song of Songs, which is Solomon's'—'the sweetest of songs which is Solomon's'. The first reason for tracing it back to Solomon is no doubt because Solomon is mentioned in it in 1: 5; 3: 7 ff.; 8: 11 ff.; and next because according to 1 Kgs. 5: 12 Solomon was thought to have composed 1,005 songs of which the pick was to be found in the Song of Songs. In fact it is just the mention in it of Solomon which refutes his authorship and proves that this tradition was shaped subsequently according to external standpoints. Thus the character of this originally anonymous book must be determined by internal evidence. The attempts to explain it follow in the main two different courses: the whole is understood either as a homogeneous poetical work or as a loose collection of separate songs. If the first course is adopted, the attempt is made to explain the

Song of Songs as a drama; this has been supported in early days by Origen, and in the nineteenth century above all by Delitzsch, Rothstein and others, also by Gebhardt who referred to the Greek mime in which one actor plays the different parts by altering his voice (cf. also Pouget and Guitton). It has indeed been objected that there is a complete lack of any kind of dramatic development in a continuous plot and that the whole of the poetry is lyrical in character throughout. Recently Thilo has wished to explain the Song of Songs afresh as a homogeneous lyrical poem which advances in a well-arranged sequence from the first love-making to betrothal, wedding and marriage-state. But such a train of thought can be secured only by arbitrary distortions of the meaning and by neglecting the frequent changes in the characters, the moods and the ideas; the subject-matter too makes it hardly possible to maintain this conception, since a development in Thilo's sense is excluded by the fact that the yearning for a complete union in love has reached its goal already at the beginning.

All these observations leave open for serious consideration only the second possible way of explaining the form of the Song of Songs, namely that it is a collection of separate love-songs which cannot claim to be a single poem. Herder in particular, as well as Goethe, supported this understanding of them. The facts noticed by J. G. Wetzstein (*Zeitschrift für Ethnologie*, 1873, pp. 270 ff.) and their utilization by Budde not only supported this conception, but revealed their *Sitz im Leben* which makes the nature of the collection intelligible as the product of the life of the people. In the East weddings are celebrated by a succession of feasts, spiced with plentiful songs and lasting a whole week, called in some districts the week of the king; plays and dances are performed to honour the young couple as king and queen seated on a threshing board erected as a royal throne on the threshing floor, whilst the beauty of the bridal pair is praised in 'descriptive songs'. This situation throws an illuminating light on the component parts of the Song of Songs. In addition to the song which is sung whilst the royal throne is being put up (3: 6–11) there are 'descriptive songs' of the maiden by the man (4: 1–7), of the man by the maiden (5: 10–16) and of the maiden by those who are taking part (7: 1–6). This playing the part of royalty explains also why

the bridegroom is called Solomon, the most glorious king of the
Israelite past, and the bride the Shulammite, considered according
to 1 Kgs. 1: 3; 2: 17 the most beautiful maiden in Israel. Besides
these, other more general songs in praise of love will have been
introduced, for not all of the separate items in the Song of Songs,
about twenty-five in number, are directly connected with the
wedding festivities of the royal week. Some of them are simple
love-poems, such as are still found today in the East. There is
evidence that the Song of Songs was still recited in the second
century A.D. (cf. Tosef Sanhed. 12: 10 and Bab. Sanhed. fol. 101 a).

This conception of the Song of Songs as a collection of love-
lyrics to adorn a wedding celebration is the most satisfying one
and best explains all the facts; but another one may also be mentioned which aims at deriving it not from profane, but from
religious origins. Wittekindt in particular defended the hypothesis,
already suggested by others and supported recently by Ringgren
and Schmöckel, that the Song of Songs is a collection of cultic
myths taken from celebrations of the weddings of gods in the
Tammuz-Ishtar cycle; he conjectures that it was introduced into the
temple of Jerusalem in the time of Manasseh, and that it coloured
the Passover celebration, which would explain why the Song of
Songs was appointed to be read at the feast of Passover in the
Jewish ritual. But apart from the fact that much has been inferred
merely from questionable alterations of the text and frequently
ill-founded conjectures, it is in itself not probable that heathen
cultic songs were admitted without further ado into the religion
of Yahweh and its canon, especially as this religion provides no
points of contact from which to reinterpret the idea of divine
marriage in a Yahwist sense (for the refutation of this hypothesis
cf. above all Rowley, *The Song of Songs*, 1930). Certain echoes of
Sumerian and Assyrian hymns might be traced rather to the influence of the festivals of the gods' marriages on the secular wedding
songs; in that case an intelligible explanation would be given to
some remarkable features in the Song of Songs, such as the warlike manner of the bride in 6: 4 ff., 10 ff.; 7: 1 ff. from the cult of
Ishtar, the goddess of war, or the flight from Lebanon in 4: 8 from
the cult of Adonis (*Bertholet, Baudissin-Festschrift*, 1918, 47 ff.).
Conversely in some cases we might think of the influence of
profane lyrics on the mythological forms of the cult.

Love poetry is timeless. The origin of individual songs in the Song of Songs may reach back to quite old times, even though we may not perhaps infer from the mention in 6: 4 of Tirzah, once the capital of the Northern Kingdom (1 Kgs. 14: 17 and *passim*), that they came into being in the ninth century. Rudolph believes he can prove that a collection of love and wedding songs under the name of Solomon existed already about 500 B.C. But the present form in which the collection has been handed down is probably of later date; this can be deduced from its use at marriage festivities for which there is more recent evidence, as well as from the infusion of Aramaic words. Since the daughters of Jerusalem are addressed in 2: 7; 3: 5 and *passim*, we may think of that city as the place of its origin.

In this collection of profane love-lyrics we must not fail to appreciate its natural realistic style, adorned with oriental wealth of imagery and beauty of colour; we must not reinterpret its original meaning in the light of too narrow a puritanical ethic nor drag it down into the domain of the obscene. It has come down to us only because the secular love-songs received a fresh allegorical religious interpretation, relating them to the love between God and Israel, which made it possible to keep the book in the Hebrew canon in the face of the scruples of some rabbis of the second century A.D., and also because then the Christian Church applied its contents to the religious relationships between God or Christ and the community or individuals. The book, when understood in this sense, has played a not unimportant part particularly in the history of mysticism.

45. The Book of Ruth

Commentaries: KeH: Bertheau,[2] 1883.–SZ: Öttli, 1889.–KHC: Bertholet, 1898. –HK: Nowack, 1902.–HSAT: Kautzsch-Bertholet, 1923.–SAT: Gressmann,[2] 1922. –TU: Smit, 1930.–HS: Schulz, 1926.–KAT: Rudolph, 1939.–HAT: Haller, 1940.– LStB (Clamer): Tamisier, 1949.–TBC: Knight, 1950.–LStB: Vincent, 1952.–SBB: Slotki,[2] 1952.–ATD: Hertzberg, 1953.–Joüon, 1953.–IB.: Smith, Cleland, 1953.– EB: Fischer,[2] 1955.–BOT: de Fraine, 1956.–See the literature for section 44.–Gunkel, *Ruth, Reden und Aufsätze*, 1913, 65 ff.; L. Köhler, 'Ruth', *Schweiz. Theol. Zeitschr.*, 1920, 3 ff.; Cannon, 'The Book of Ruth', *Theology*, 1928, 310 ff.; W. E. Staples, 'The Book of Ruth', AJSL 1937, 145 ff.; Jepsen, 'Das Buch Ruth', ThStKr 1937-8, 416 ff.; Humbert, 'Art et leçon de l'histoire de Ruth', *Revue de Théologie et de Philosophie*, 1938, 257 ff.; David, 'The date of the Book of Ruth, *Oudtestamentische Studien I*, 1942, 55 ff.; Rowley, 'The marriage of Ruth', *The Harvard Theological Review*, Vol. XL, No. 2, 1947; Myers, *The linguistic and literary form of the Book of Ruth*, 1955; Fueter, *Das Buch Ruth*, 1955.

The little book of Ruth relates in an easy popular style a story which takes place in the time of the judges; for this reason it has been put after the book of Judges in the LXX and other versions. Its *contents* are as follows: in chapter 1: 1–6 a short concise introduction states that on the occasion of a famine a Judean family emigrated from Bethlehem to Moab; after the death of the father Elimelech, the two sons, Mahlon and Chilion, both marry Moabite women but die soon after, whereupon the mother Naomi wishes to return to her native land. In 1: 7–22 it is told in some detail how Naomi tries to persuade her two daughters-in-law who are escorting her to remain behind, how at last one of them, Orpah, returns, but the other, Ruth, accompanies her: 'whither thou goest, I will go' (1, 16 f.). In chapter 2 the narrative continues with pleasant prolixity to tell how the industrious and modest Ruth whilst gleaning pleases the rich Boaz, a kinsman of her husband. Chapter 3: In fulfilment of the levirate marriage custom, according to which the next of kin has the duty of marrying the widow of the dead man if he was childless in order to provide him with descendants, Ruth by the advice of her mother-in-law lays herself at Boaz' feet to await his decision in this matter. Chapter 4: After a nearer kinsman with a prior right to discharge this duty has renounced it in favour of Boaz, the latter takes Ruth to his home as his wife. She becomes the mother of a son who is adopted by Naomi and is called Obed; Obed is the grandfather of David. In 4: 18–22 a genealogy of David with a special heading is appended.

The narrative is similar to popular saga and no doubt grew out of one; owing to its detailed style its literary *type* is that of the short story and consequently from the point of view of the history of types it belongs to a later development of the literary form of narrative. The framework of time and place in which it is set, some particular features of the characters in it and their names, such as Elimelech, Naomi, Boaz, are probably based on a historical tradition. On the other hand the names of the sons, Mahlon = sickness and Chilion = vanishing, give the impression of being a poetic invention to illustrate symbolically the fate of those who bore them; this induced Herder to explain the whole tale as pure fiction. The names Orpah = she who turns her back, and Ruth = the companion, are also symbolic. That the names of the people and the place bear witness to an original cultic myth of a fertility-cult practised in Bethlehem (Staples) is mere conjecture without any reliable and convincing substance. Haller is much more restrained in assuming mythological themes. The loving description of the main characters, Naomi, Ruth, Boaz, as god-fearing, industrious, high-minded and faithful persons in the idyllic framework of rural life is due to the artistry of the poet and is intended to show how the good fortune of a family is built up on the magnanimous qualities of its members. Yet this is not the sole purpose of the booklet. A kind of protest against the ruthless policy of Ezra and Nehemiah in the matter of mixed marriages (Ezra 9 f.; Neh. 13: 1 ff., 23 ff.) has rightly been read into the circumstance that the Moabitess Ruth gives up her home and her religion in loyal devotion to the family of her husband. At any rate it is against this background that we can most easily understand the markedly benevolent judgment of Ruth, a stranger, who is depicted by the poet as a faithful adherent of Yahweh and is worthy to be the ancestress of David (against Gunkel, Eissfeldt, Rudolph, Haller and others).

This also defines more closely the *date* when this writing came into being in its Judean setting. Its position in the canon also suggests the period after the reform of Ezra and Nehemiah when a place could no longer be found for it in the second part and it was admitted amongst 'the writings'. The language too which reveals occasional Aramaisms brings us down to a relatively late period. Thus the end of the fifth or the beginning of the fourth century would be suggested; Rudolph and Haller mention the time of Jeremiah.

Considered as a whole the story is a self-contained unit. It is not possible to prove, nor is it likely, that Naomi was originally the chief character and the only woman in the narrative (Gunkel, Jepsen, Haller); the same must be said of the attempt to claim that the relationship of the tale to David was a secondary addition (Eissfeldt, Rost and others). It is only David's genealogy in 4: 18–22, similar to that in 1 Chron. 2: 4 ff., which must be considered a later appendix.

The little book of Ruth shows that even in the Judaism of the fifth and fourth centuries, whilst it was becoming increasingly narrow and particularist, there were not lacking those who spoke with refreshing broadmindedness combined with religious and ethical earnestness and sincere confidence in God's providence (the latter especially stressed by Rudolph). But it is not only on this account that the book has preserved its lasting value and power of attraction; its artistic qualities place it amongst the enduring monuments of OT literature. Goethe called it 'the loveliest complete work on a small scale, handed down to us as an ethical treatise and an idyll'. We may place beside this the verdict of Rud. Alexander Schröder: 'No poet in the world has written a more beautiful short story'.

46. The Book of Lamentations

Commentaries: KeH: Thenius, 1885.–SZ: Öttli, 1889.–HK: Löhr, ² 1906.–KHC: Budde, 1898.–HSAT: Löhr, 1923.–SAT: Staerk,² 1920 and H. Schmidt, 1923.–TU: Smit, 1930.–HS: Paffrath, 1932.–KAT: Rudolph, 1939.–HAT: Haller, 1940.–EB: Nötscher, 1947.–LStB: Gelin, 1951.–SBB: Goldman,² 1952.–LSBR: Vaccari, 1953. –LSB: Rinaldi, 1953.–HBK: Schneider, 1954.–Wiesmann, 1954.–TBC: Knight, 1955.–BK: Kraus, 1956.–IB: Meek, Merrill, 1956.–ATD: Weiser, 1957.–See literature for section 44.–Löhr, 'Der Sprachgebrauch des Buches der Klagelieder', ZAW 1894, 31 ff.; idem, 'Sind Thr IV und V makkabäisch?', ZAW 1894, 51 ff.; idem, 'Threni III und die jeremianische Autorschaft des Buches der Klagelieder', ZAW 1904, 1 ff.; Jahnow, 'Das hebräische Leichenlied im Rahmen der Völkerdichtung', BZAW 1923; Wiesmann, 'Die literarische Art der Klagelieder des Jeremias', Theol. Quartalschr., 1929, 381 ff.; idem, 'Der geschichtliche Hintergrund des Büchleins der Klagelieder', Bibl. Zeitschrift, 1934, 20 ff.; idem, 'Der Verfasser des Büchleins der Klagelieder ein Augenzeuge der behandelten Ereignisse?', Biblica, 1936, 71 ff.; Baumgartner, OTMSt 1951, 221 ff.; Gottwald, Studies in the Book of Lamentations (Studies in Bibl. Theology, 14, 1954).

The original name of this little book reads according to rabbinic tradition *kînôt* = dirges. The LXX and other versions ascribe it already in its title to Jeremiah and for this reason the Lamentations have been placed after the book of Jeremiah in the versions. This view is no doubt derived from the tradition in 2 Chron. 35: 25 which tells of the lamentations for Josiah and of Jeremiah having composed one of them; but these are not the same as those in our collection of laments. In the Hebrew manuscripts and printed books the lamentations now all contain the customary word *'kāh* = How? as a stereotyped opening. The little book contains five separate songs, the length of which coincides with the divisions into chapters. The first four are alphabetical songs with different forms of literary acrostic poetry. They are written in the 'qinah' metre, the rhythm for elegies. The fact that in the first song the usual order of the letters *'ayin* before *pe* is followed, whilst in

L

2, 3, 4 these letters are placed the other way round, might prove that they do not all come from the same author. As regards their type, in the main 1, 2, 4 are political laments, 3 an individual one and a thanksgiving, 5 a national lament with an irregular metre. But in all of them we can see a mixture of styles.

The *subject* of the laments 2, 4, 5 is the catastrophe which befell Jerusalem in 587 and the city's ensuing distress. Thus they must have come into existence at the time of or after the collapse of the year 587. The fresh colouring and concrete details of 2 and 4 give the impression that they stand nearest to the events and were no doubt composed soon after the disaster of 587. 5 also contains concrete details, whilst 1 and especially 3 keep to substantially more general forms. Rudolph perhaps justly considers chapter 1 to be the oldest song composed already in 597 under the influence of the siege and the first deportation of captives, whilst Kraus wishes to revert to explaining all five songs by the circumstances after 587. Chapter 3 occupies a special place because it is the lament of an individual concerning his own distress (sickness?) with occasional exhortations combined with reflexion, individual lament and thanksgiving; it is not until 3: 40 ff. that the poem passes over into a national lament, although there is no definite evidence that the background of this poem too is the fall of Jerusalem. It is not possible to determine with certainty whether the other laments came into existence during the exile. Even chapter 3 does not oblige us to think of a date later than 538. A certain affinity with Deutero-Isaiah would place it at the close of the exile. Yet the hopelessness of the situation suggests that it originated more probably before the exile ended.

It remains uncertain too whether *the place of origin* of the lamentations was in Palestine or Babylon. The fresh immediacy of the description in 2 and 4 and the allusion to Jerusalem as it lies there desolate is more intelligible in the mouth of a Palestinian poet, and it is hard to think of the sentence in 2: 9 'her prophets find no vision from the Lord', as spoken in Babylon where Ezekiel was carrying out his ministry. Not overmuch weight need be attached to the counter-argument of the relationship to Deutero-Isaiah and Ezekiel, since there was brisk traffic between the captivity and those who were left behind in Jerusalem. The *formation of the collection* of these laments which were composed at different times and, except for 3, are the songs of a congregation (in 3: 40 ff. too, reference is made to a community), presupposes no doubt a kind of cultic communal memorial celebration, at which the laments were recited and handed down (cf. Zech. 7: 1 f.; 8: 18 f.). Kraus suggests for this a liturgy performed on the ruins of the temple and would like to put the lamentations into a special type of 'lament for the destruction of the sanctuary' which he thinks he can deduce from a comparison with a Sumerian lament over the sacred site of Ur. But the basis on which his reasoning rests is not strong enough to bear its weight.

Seen in this light these testimonies to the people's distress are most moving and their solemn beauty is impressive. They afford an instructive insight into the inner life of the circles faithful to Yahweh after the national collapse. They are ready to learn from history and to bow in humility and shame before God's judgment. The depth of their penitence in 1: 3 f.; 5: 16–20 shows that in these circles the preaching of the prophets had not been in vain.

47. Ecclesiastes or the Preacher

Commentaries: KD: Delitzsch, 1875.–KeH: Hitzig–Nowack,³ 1883.–SZ: Volck, 1889.–HK: Siegfried, 1898.–KHC: Wildeboer, 1898.–ICC: Barton, 1948.–CEB: Podechard, 1912.–HSAT: Budde, 1923.–SAT.: Volz,² 1921.–HS. Allgeier, 1925.– TU: Gemser, 1931.–KAT: Hertzberg, 1932.–HAT: Galling, 1940.–Bickell, 1884, 86. –Paul Haupt, 1905.–Zapletal,² 1911.–Odeberg, 1929.–Bentzen, 1942.–EB: Nötscher, 1948.–COT: Aalders, 1948.–Bea 1950.–SBB: Reichert,² 1952.–Gordis,² 1955.– BOT: van der Ploeg, 1953.–LStB: Duesberg, Auvray, 1953.–Steinmann, 1955.–IB: Rankin, Atkins, 1956.–See literature for sections 43 and 44.–Kleinert, 'Sind im Buch Kohelet ausserhebräische Einflüsse anzuerkennen?', ThStKr 1883, 761 ff.; Friedländer, Griech. Philosophie im AT, 1904; Kleinert, 'Zur religions- und kultur-geschichtlichen Stellung des Buches Kohelet', ThStKr 1909, 493 ff.; Ebeling, Ein Babylonischer Kohelet, 1922, Thilo, Der Prediger Salomo, 1923; Ranston, Ecclesiastes and the Early Greek Wisdom Literature, 1923; Kuhn; 'Erklärung des Buches Kohelet', BZAW 1926; Humbert, Recherches sur les sources égyptiennes de la littérature sapientale d'Israël, 1929; Pedersen, 'Scepticisme Israélite', RHPhR 1930, 317 ff.; Galling, 'Kohelet-Studien', ZAW 1932, 276 ff.; idem, 'Stand und Aufgabe der Kohelet-forschung', ThR 1934, 355 ff.; Dornseiff, 'Das Buch Prediger', ZDMG 1935, 243 ff.; Zimmerli, Die Weisheit des Predigers Salomo, 1936; Gordis, The Wisdom of Ecclesiastes, 1945; Ginsberg, Studies in Koheleth, 1950, Baumgartner, OTMSt 1951, 221 ff.; Gordis, Koheleth, The man and his world, 1951; Lauha, 'Die Krise des religiösen Glaubens bei Kohelet', VT, Suppl. III (1955), 183 ff.

The book derives its *name* from the title 'The words of the Preacher, the son of David, King in Jerusalem' (Ecclesiastes being the translation adopted by the Septuagint for the Hebrew word kōhelet rendered 'The Preacher' in our version [translator's

note]). The striking feminine form kōhelet as the designation
of a masculine author has been explained, as in Ezra 2: 55, 57, as
the designation of an office or an activity and kōhelet='the
assembler' (קהל) as the leader or preacher of an assembly. The
same idea is seen in the translations (Greek *Ekklesiastes*; Latin
concionator, the preacher [of Solomon], these last words being
added as a correct interpretation of 'son of David' in the title).
Others consider kōhelet to be a pseudonym, the meaning of
which cannot now be determined. In that case of course it cannot
have been the author himself who named Solomon as the author,
for son of David here can only mean Solomon, and this name
must be considered a later literary disguise. In any case that is
merely a thinly veiled literary fiction, not worked out consistently,
as can be readily perceived in 1: 12 and the sayings about the
kingship. Clearly Solomon, the king who was famous for his
wisdom and his wealth and at the same time passed for the author
of part of the Wisdom literature appeared to be the most suitable
figure to confer a particularly impressive importance to the judgments of the Preacher.

For the *contents* of the book are summed up in the recognition
that the whole life is transitory, which is declared in the continu-
ally repeated phrase 'all is vanity'. It is not possible to trace in this
book a consecutive train of thought, complete in itself (Thilo).
It is a more or less loose compilation of personal confessions
written in an autobiographical manner (especially in chapters 1
and 2), of general reflexions and of individual wisdom sayings
and exhortations, culled from all realms of man's experience of
life. For this purpose the customary forms of the Wisdom literature are employed; the alternation of words 'I' and 'thou' is an
imitation of the usual style of wisdom writing, so that there is no
need to follow Herder and others in breaking up the book into
dialogues between different people. But the change which befell
the conception itself of wisdom through the Preacher's dialectical
criticism brought about a change also in its forms. The frequent
use of the first person singular in the confessions as well as the
genuine and rhetorical questions are proofs of an inner struggle
for self-knowledge. They are at the same time the indication,
given by the form, of the disintegration of 'Wisdom' wrought by
the problems posed by the author. The book bears witness to the

scepticism regarding the good things of life praised by wisdom and is also documentary evidence of a realism inclining to pessimism in contrast to the superficial optimism of the current wisdom of the schools.

The struggles of the author to reach truth are mirrored also in the fact that his conclusions contain inconsistences and contradictions. It is therefore not pertinent for literary and textual criticism to attempt to explain these irregularities by assuming for instance different authors or revisers (Haupt, Siegfried, Podechard and others) or by expansions in the transmission of the manuscript (Bickell). The uniform language too supports the literary unity of the book (thus also Gordis). Only the conclusion, 12: 9–14, or at least 12: 12–14 seems to have been added by a later hand; occasional qualifications and adjustments to the traditional faith, as for example in 2: 26; 3: 17; 5: 19; 7: 29; 8: 5; 11: 9; 12: 7, are also most easily understood as later additions, especially as we know that this book had to defend its canonical status up to the end of the second century A.D. against umbrage and doubts.

The *book of Ecclesiastes* belongs to the comparatively late products of the Wisdom literature of the OT. The softening of the old forms and the signs of disintegration in the dialectic of an enlightened scepticism suggest its place to be at the end of the development of OT Wisdom. The language which is late Hebrew and tending towards Aramaic in character and the foreign influence, especially of Greek thought (Allgeier thinks he can detect some connexions with Cynic and Stoic diatribes), brings its origin down into the third century whilst on the other hand the Maccabean rising does not seem to have made any impression on it. A definite opinion as to the *place of origin* cannot be gained. The views fluctuate between Jerusalem (recently especially Hertzberg and Galling) and Alexandria (Kleinert, Volz, Humbert and others). As the author is a man with a broad outlook and rich experience, there is no need to conclude from his imagery and turns of speech alone that he wrote in his native land. Although the intellectual culture of the Ptolemaic kingdom was not restricted to Egypt, yet Alexandria seems the more likely place; for the influence of Egypt on the individual conceptions and of Greece on the language as well as on the thought does not spring from a definite philosophic school, but approximates to a popular philosophy.

Through the impression made by Greek thought the spirit of the Enlightenment penetrated into the OT by means of the book of Ecclesiastes. Life with its experiences becomes a problem; its good things are of questionable value. Not that it is an atheistic scepticism; on the contrary it is just the thought of God's omnipotence which is the source of the pessimistic verdict on human life, since God has all the power and man has none (2: 24 ff. and *passim*). But the author has no personal relationship of faith in this God by whom he feels himself to be restricted and menaced rather than supported; nor is he able to fight his way through to such a faith. The wisdom of the Preacher who has grown weary of life and uncertain how to face it, spends itself in resignation, in passive acceptance of it and of its fleeting pleasures.

48. The Book of Esther

Commentaries: KeH: Bertheau-Ryssel,[2] 1887.–SZ: Öttli, 1889.–Scholz, 1892.–KHC: Wildeboer, 1898.–HK: Siegfried, 1901.–ICC: Paton, 1951.–HSAT: Steuernagel, 1923.–SAT: Haller,[2] 1925.–TU: Smit, 1930.–HAT: Haller 1940.–HS: Miller, Schildenberger, 1940–41.–COT: Aalders, 1947.–LStB (Clamer): Soubigou, 1949.–EB: Stummer, Hamp, 1950.–SBB: Goldman,[2] 1952.–LStB: Barucq, 1952.–HBK: Bückers, 1953.–IB: Anderson, Lichtenberger, 1954.–TBC: Knight, 1955.–ATD: Ringgren, 1957.–Erbt, *Die Purimsage in der Bibel*, 1900; Haupt, *Purim, Beitrag zur Assyriologie*, 1906; Jampel, *Das Buch Esther auf seine Geschichtlichkeit untersucht*, 1907; Gunkel, *Esther*, 1916; Hoschander, *The Book of Esther in the light of history*, 1923; Striedl, 'Untersuchungen zur Syntax und Stilistik des hebräischen Buches Esther', ZAW 1936, 73 ff.; Snaith, 'The Historical Books', OTMSt 1951, 105 ff.; see literature for section 44.

The book of Esther contains a narrative which takes place at the court of the Persian king Ahasuerus—Xerxes in Susa. In chapters 1–2 Esther, the adopted daughter of Mordecai, becomes queen in place of Vashti deposed for disobedience. In chapter 3 Haman, the enemy of the Jews, becomes grand vizier and succeeds in obtaining a decree to persecute them, the date of which was fixed by lot (*pûr*) for the 13th of Adar. Chapters 4: 1–8: 2 give a thrilling description of how Esther achieves the revocation of the murderous order and Haman is hanged on the gallows intended for Mordecai who in his turn is raised to high honours. At Esther's request the king allows the Jews to destroy their enemies. On the 13th of Adar 75,000 persons are killed in the provinces and 500 as well as the 10 sons of Haman in Susa, and on the 14th of Adar 300 more enemies of the Jews perish at Esther's special request; the 14th of Adar is fixed for the Jews in the provinces, the 15th for those in the capital, as a day of repose and rejoicing. 9: 20–32 reports Esther's and Mordecai's letters, and the celebration of the 14th and 15th of Adar as a feast day for all Jews; 10: 1–3 directs attention to further information about the king of Persia and Mordecai in the 'book of the chronicles of the kings of Media and Persia'.

In its present form the book of Esther is the *festival legend* of the Jewish feast of Purim, intended to describe the historical circumstances in which it came into existence. As the legend takes place at the court of the Persian king and is well acquainted with the circumstances there, the book seems to have originated in the eastern diaspora and to have served the purpose of the festival legend probably from the beginning. There is another question, namely, whether this story of the origin of the legend corresponds to the historical facts. That can hardly be supposed; for in this book the word *pûr* is considered to be a foreign one, which in 3: 7; 9: 24, 26 is translated by the Hebrew word *gôrāl*=lot. Moreover the days of Xerxes in 1: 1 are thought of as a long time ago, and the age of Mordecai, who is included among the exiles with Jehoiachin of the year 597 and would therefore at the time of the story be at least 120 years old, does not fit into the historical framework of the narrative, nor does the corresponding age of Esther. Moreover the general attitude expressed in the story can hardly be intended to describe the actual course of events leading up to this feast, nor if, as is probable, it is a question of the Jews having taken over what was once a foreign feast, then the events leading to its transference. It does indeed lay claim to depict historical facts by laying stress on names and exact numerical statements, by adducing royal decrees and by referring to public records; yet it is interspersed with poetic themes of sagas and tales, so that Gunkel and others call it a historical novel. As we can discover neither the source nor the original significance of the feast of Purim, the conjectures as to the history of the festival expressed by Jensen (*Wiener Zeitschr. f.d. Kunde des Morgenlandes,* 1892, 47 ff., 209 ff.) and Zimmern (*Die Keilinschriften u.d. AT.,* 1903, 515 ff.) are mere hypotheses. They see in the book of Esther

a connexion with mythical themes (Esther=Ishtar, Mordecai=
Marduk, Haman=the Elamite god Humman, Vashti=Elamite
Mashti); in this case we might have to do with themes concerning
a battle of the gods which reflect political struggles between Elam
and Assyria. If this is so, this material must have been subjected
to a not inconsiderable transformation and reinterpretation when
it was taken over by the Eastern diaspora. The present form of
this narrative, which can hardly be pure invention, perhaps goes
back to a persecution of the Jews; it is not possible to determine
whether this was in the Persian period or later. It was probably
handed down together with the festival of Purim at first in the
Jewish Dispersion of the East and was taken over at a late date,
possibly with various modifications, by the Palestinian Jewry, for
neither Jesus Sirach nor 1 Macc. 7: 49 know the feast of Purim;
not until 2 Macc. 15: 36 f. is a day of Mordecai first mentioned.
The contents offer no analogy or support to the attempt of Haupt,
Pfeiffer and others to connect the origin of the book of Esther
with the struggles of the Maccabees.

Later on, probably owing to an alteration in the arrangement
of the festival, the book received a supplement (9: 20–32; 10: 1–3),
which accepted the subsequent practice of the town and country
people to celebrate the feast on the 14th and 15th of Adar and
made it agree with the narrative from which in this respect it had
diverged. As a source for supplementary information about
Xerxes and Mordecai it refers to the book of the chronicles of the
kings of Media and Persia, but it is impossible to ascertain whether
this reference is based on a fictitious imitation of the style of the
Deuteronomic book of Kings or on an actually existing midrash-
like chronicle of the diaspora in Persia.

The book of Esther reaches a high artistic level by the exciting
build-up of its narrative and the characterization of its chief per-
sonages; it is a memorial to the nationalist spirit of Judaism which
had become fanatical, and as the result of Jew-baiting had lost all
touch with the great tasks which the prophets had placed before
their people. This trend was perceived also in Jewry itself, for
this entirely secular book did not make good its claim for a place
in the canon without various difficulties. And the additions to
Esther handed down by the Septuagint are conscious of this short-
coming and endeavour to remedy it by applying a religious

colouring to the narrative. The fact that Luther was 'an enemy' of
this book and felt a profound objection to it as having 'too much
of Judaism' with 'heathen naughtiness' is a testimony to the
impartial clarity of the Christian verdict.

49. Daniel

Commentaries: KeH: Hitzig, 1850.–SZ: Meinhold, 1889.–HK: Behrmann, 1894.
–KHC: Marti, 1901.–HSAT: Marti.–SAT: Haller,[2] 1925.–ICC: Montgomery, 1949.
–HS: Goettsberger, 1928.–TU Obbink, 1932.–Linder, 1939.–HAT: Bentzen,[2] 1952.
–Bevan, 1892.–Charles, 1929.–Lattey, 1948.–EB: Nötscher, 1948.–Young, 1949.–
Steinmann, 1950.–SBB: Slotki, 1951.–BOT: Nelis, 1954.–HBK: Schneider, 1954.
–LStB: de Menasce, 1954.–LSBR: Rinaldi, 1955.–Bewer, 1955.–TBC: Heaton, 1956.
–IB: Jeffery, Kennedy, 1956.–von Gall, *Die Einheitlichkeit des Buches Daniel*, 1895;
Hölscher, 'Die Entstehung des Buches Daniel', ThStKr 1919, 113 ff.; Haller, 'Das
Alter von Daniel 7', ThStKr 1920–21, 83 ff.; Thilo, *Die Chronologie des Danielbuches*,
1926; Noth, 'Zur Komposition des Buches Daniel', ThStKr 1926, 143 ff.; Baum-
gartner, *Das Buch Daniel*, 1926; idem, 'Neues keilinschriftliches Material zum Buche
Daniel?', ZAW 1926, 38 ff.; Rowley, 'Daniel, The Historicity of the fifth Chapter',
JThSt 1930–31, 12 ff.; idem, 'The Bilingual Problem of Daniel', ZAW 1932, 256 ff.;
Junker, *Untersuchungen über literarische und exegetische Probleme des Buches Daniel*, 1932;
Rowley, 'Aramaic dialect and the Book of Daniel', *Journal Royal Asiatic Society*,
1933, 777 ff.; idem, *Darius the Mede and the four World Empires in the Book of Daniel*,
1935; Beek, *Das Danielbuch, sein historischer Hintergrund und seine literarische Ent-
wicklung* (Diss. Leiden), 1935; Rowley, 'Some problems in the Book of Daniel',
Expository Times, 1935–6, 216 ff.; Bickermann, *Der Gott der Makkabäer*, 1937;
Baumgartner, ThR·1939, 59 ff., 125 ff., 201 ff.; Mariani, *Daniel 'il patriarca sapiente'
nella Biblia, nella tradizione, nella leggenda*, 1945; Baumgartner, 'Zu den vier Reichen
in Dan 2', ThZ 1945, 17 ff.; Rowley, 'The Unity of the Book of Daniel', HUCA,
XXIII, 1950–51, 223 ff.=*The Servant of the Lord*, 1952, 235 f.; Tatford, *The Climax
of the Ages: Studies in the Prophecy of Daniel*, 1953; Young, *The Messianic Prophecies of
Daniel*, 1954; Ginsberg, 'The Composition of the Book of Daniel', *VT* 4 (1954),
246 ff.; Rowley, 'The Composition of the Book of Daniel', *VT* 5 (1955), 272 ff.

The book of Daniel falls into two parts: I. Chapters 1–6 six
legends about Daniel and his three friends (narrative in the third
person singular; II. Chapters 7–12: four visions interpreted by
angels in the first person singular. In detail the *contents* are as
follows: Chapter 1: In the third year of Jehoiakim (605) Daniel is
taken into exile to Babylon and is brought up with his three
friends at the king's court, where they remained faithful to the
Jewish dietary laws. Chapter 2: By interpreting a dream of King
Nebuchadnezzar Daniel gives proof of his superior wisdom and is
honoured by the king who bows down before Daniel's God.
Chapter 3: 1–30 is a legend of martyrdom and tells how the three
friends, refusing to obey the royal command to do homage to an
idol, are thrown into a fiery furnace, but are rescued by an angel;
whereupon the king acknowledges the unique power of Yahweh.

3: 31–4: 34: Nebuchadnezzar's dream which Daniel had expounded becomes true: the king is bereft of his reason for seven years and on his recovery honours the God of the Jews. 5: 1–6: 1: Belshazzar's feast and the mysterious writing on the wall which Daniel interprets as foretelling the destruction of the Babylonian kingdom. 6: 2–29: Daniel, by adhering to his customary prayers, breaks the command of Darius 'the Mede'; he is thrown into the den of lions, but is miraculously preserved. The king issues an edict that the God of Daniel alone is to be honoured; a hymn follows. Chapter 7: The vision of the heavenly judgment on the four beasts (Babylonian, Median, Persian and Greek world kingdoms); appearance and dominion of the 'Son of man'. Chapter 8: The vision of the contest between the ram and the he-goat (the Medo-Persian empire and Alexander). Chapter 9: Daniel is instructed by the angel Gabriel concerning the prophecy in 'the Scriptures' in Jer. 25: 11; 29: 10 that the 70 years of exile mentioned there must be reinterpreted as 70 weeks of years=490 years. Chapters 10–12: An angel reveals the course of history from Cyrus to Antiochus; 11: 2–39 is a historical retrospect in the form of a prophecy, whilst 11: 40–12: 3 contains a genuine prediction of the future: overthrow of the heathen and deliverance of the godly; the resurrection of the godly to everlasting life and of the godless to everlasting shame. 12: 5–13: conclusion: Assurance is given that the prophecy will be fulfilled and the end will take place after 1,290 days (verse 11) or else 1,335 days (verse 12).

The book nowhere names its author; tradition considers him to be Daniel whom the legend describes as a seer at the royal court in Babylon. This has suggested the righteous and wise Daniel mentioned in Ezek. 14: 14, 20; 28: 3. But this can scarcely be correct, since Ezekiel places him beside Noah and Job and is probably thinking of figures known to popular tradition from remote antiquity. The Daniel with whom we have recently become acquainted through the Ras-Shamra texts also seems to belong to the early ages; so it is best to give up the attempt to identify him. As we know so little about the historical conditions during the exile, it is impossible to determine whether Daniel was an actual personage and, if so, what significance he possessed.

But quite apart from the question as to who was the author, the assumption that the book of Daniel came into existence during the exile is rendered impossible for a number of reasons. (1) Historical inaccuracies and impossibilities; no siege of Jerusalem in the third year of Jehoiakim in 605 (1: 1) took place; Belshazzar (5: 1 f.; 7: 1) is not the son and successor of Nebuchadnezzar, but the son of last king of Babylon, Nabonidus, and was never himself king; besides, there never was a 'Darius the Mede' who was the successor of Belshazzar (6: 1), son of Xerxes (9: 1) and predecessor of Cyrus (6: 29); the historical sequence of the Persian kings was in fact Cyrus, Cambyses, Darius, Xerxes. (2) The language has the characteristics of late Hebrew with linguistic influences from Persia and Greece. (3) Its theology which avoids the name of Yahweh and has a developed doctrine of angels and a belief in resurrection, points to a late post-exilic period. (4) The book of Daniel is first attested in late literature; it is not mentioned in the 'praise of our forefathers' in Ecclus. 44 ff., but first in the Sibylline Oracles III, 338 ff. (about the year 140 B.C.) and 1 Macc. 2: 59 f. (about 100 B.C.). (5) Finally its position in the canon, where it was not placed, as might be expected, amongst the prophets, but in the third part, supports the view that it came into existence at a late date.

The book itself contains clear indications of its origin during the religious distress of the Syrian era. It brings the interpretation of history down to Antiochus IV; whilst it is very imperfectly informed about the exile and the period immediately after it, it possesses accurate information about the details of Antiochus' times. It knows of his two Egyptian expeditions, his suppression of the Jewish religion and introduction of the Greek cult into Jerusalem in the year 168 (11: 21–39). It is open to question whether in 8: 14 the dedication of the temple by Judas Maccabaeus (December 164) had already taken place or was still to come, since the end of the religious emergency connected with the edict of the spring of 164 and mentioned in 2 Macc. 11: 30 seems still to be awaited (Bickermann). At any rate the author is writing before the death of Antiochus (164), since he was not killed in fighting against Jerusalem, as prophesied in 11: 40 ff., but died far away in the East. All this shows that the book of Daniel as we have it must have come into existence between 168 and 164.

The book in its present shape is conceived as a homogeneous whole. The object common to the legends and the visions is to comfort and encourage an undaunted faith in the God who controls all history, who brings his dominion to final victory and helps his own through all their troubles. The constancy of Daniel and his friends serves as an example of loyalty to their faith which stands firm till martyrdom. It is this and the emphasis on God's omnipotence which gives the old legends their significance for the later times in which the author of the book of Daniel is writing and for whose sake he sometimes brings the narrative right into his own times (e.g. 2: 41–43).

Yet the book is not all of a piece. This is shown first by the *change of language*. The fact that 2: 4b–7: 28 is written in Aramaic has been explained in different ways, but has not up to the present been accounted for satisfactorily. It seems simplest to assume for 1–7 that its author found older pieces already in existence in Aramaic and left them in their original form with the exception of 1: 1–2: 4a, where he reshaped what he had found and could thus consider it to be his own production (Rowley). His own composition he wrote in Hebrew, perhaps to mark his loyalty both to the religious and the national tradition, which is easily intelligible in the time of the religious persecution by Syria (Noth).

The distinction between the legends and the visions also points to the compilation of the book out of different component parts: The legends which keep to the style of oriental court stories came into being in other surroundings than the visions. They presuppose the conditions of the Eastern diaspora in which there is no hostility in principle against the heathen state and its king, as there is in the visions. In chapters 2 and 4 and again in chapters 3 and 6 parallel traditions appear and in 3: 1–30 Daniel plays no part at all, whilst some discrepancies can also be detected. All this points to a separate existence of the individual narratives to start with. These did not grow into a cycle of legends until later on and were taken by the author into his book as a cycle in the time of Antiochus. Nothing precise can be said about the age of the collection of legends nor of its individual elements. Since 2: 41 alludes to the death of Alexander the Great and use is made of words borrowed from Persian and especially from Greek (in chapter 3), the period between 323 and the persecution of the Jews by Antiochus Epiphanes, presumably the third century B.C. is the most likely time for the legends to have been collected.

On the other hand *the visions* no doubt came into being in Palestine which in 8: 9; 11: 16, 41 is called 'the glorious land'. They were composed by a contemporary of Antiochus, yet they were not entirely the creation of the author. The visions themselves, though they presuppose knowledge of visionary experiences, yet hardly rest on a personal experience, but are literary productions which imitate the forms of the prophets and make use of older traditional material derived from mythology and astronomy. The work of revising the legends and of bringing them up to date must also be placed to the account of the author who wrote under Antiochus. The conclusion in 12: 11 f. is presumably a later appendix which corrects the 1,150 days of 8: 14 and postpones twice over the date fixed for the end; it is therefore no doubt due to two hands. The prayer of Daniel in 9: 4–20 also gives the impression of a secondary interpolation.

As regards its nature the book of Daniel takes its place amongst the apocalypses. Whilst making use of the prophetic heritage and imitating the style of the prophets and the forms taken by their experiences, it combines the prophetic view of history with a learned interest in calculating and predicting precisely the details of the end. Moreover the book occupies itself with the writings of the earlier prophets which are treated as finished entities and sources of knowledge and are made serviceable to the interests of the writer by reinterpretation. These reasons set it amongst the apocalyptic literature just as definitely as does the attempt to hide its anonymity under a name of the past. As a result of the strong emphasis placed on knowing about the future the prophetic foundation of confident reliance on faith is abandoned and is propelled on to another track. Yet this must not let us overlook the traits of a genuine trust in God, with which the book champions the true heritage of the prophets, namely faith in the God who controls all history and whose kingdom will soon appear to save those who confess their loyalty to him and remain steadfast.

50. Ezra and Nehemiah

Commentaries: KeH: Bertheau-Ryssel,[2] 1887.–SZ: Öttli, 1889.–HK: Siegfried, 1091.–KHC: Bertholet, 1902.–ICC: Batten, 1952.–HSAT: Hölscher, 1923.–SAT: Haller,[2] 1925.–HAT: Rudolph, 1949. LStB (Clamer): Médebielle, 1949.–EB: Rehm, 1950.–SBB: Slotki, 1951.–LStB: Gellin, 1953.–HBK: Bückers, 1953.–IB: Bowman,

Gilkey, 1954.–ATD: Galling, 1954.–Smend, *Die Listen der Bücher Esra und Nehemia*, 1881; Kosters, *Het herstel van Israel in het perzische tijdvak*, 1894; in German by Basedow, 1895; Wellhausen, 'Die Rückkehr der Juden aus dem babylonischen Exil', *Nachr. d. Gesellschaft d. Wiss. zu Göttingen*, 1895, 166 ff.; Ed. Meyer, *Die Entstehung des Judentums*, 1896; and discussion by Wellhausen, *Gött. gel. Anz.*, 1896, 606 ff.; Torrey, 'The Composition and Historical Value of Ezra–Nehemiah', BZAW 1896; Geissler, *Die literarischen Beziehungen der Esramemoiren*, 1899; Torrey, *Ezra Studies*, 1920; Mowinckel, *Ezra den Skriftlärde*, 1916; idem, *Statholderen Nehemia*, 1916; R. Kittel, *Geschichte des Volkes Israel III*, 2, 1929, 330 ff., 519 ff.; Schäder, *Iranische Beiträge I*, 1930; idem, *Esra der Schreiber*, 1930; Sellin, *Geschichte des israelitisch-jüdischen Volkes II*, 1932, 134 ff.; Ahlemann, 'Zur Esra-Quelle', ZAW 1942–3, 77 ff.; Noth, *Überlieferungsgeschichtliche Studien I*, 1943, 110 ff.; Kapelrud, *The Question of Authorship in the Ezra-Narrative*, Oslo, 1944; Johannesen, *Studier over Esras og Nehemjas Historie*, 1946; Wright, *The Date of Ezra's Coming to Jerusalem*, London, 1947; Snaith, 'The Historical Books', OTMSt 1951, 107 ff.; Rowley, The Chronological Order of Ezra and Nehemiah, Ign. Goldziher Memorial, Vol. I (1948), 117 ff. =*The Servant of the Lord*, 1952, 129 ff.; Torrey, *The Chronicler's History of Israel*, *Chronicles—Ezra—Nehemiah Restored to its Original Form*, 1954; Rowley, 'Nehemiah's Mission and its Background'. BJRL, Vol 37, No. 2 (1954–55); Pawlovsky, 'Die Chronologie der Tätigkeit Esdras', *Biblica* 38 (1952), 275–305, 428–456.

The books of Ezra and Nehemiah were originally attached to the end of the Chronicles, as can be seen from the fact that the last verses of 2 Chronicles are identical with Ezra 1: 1–5 and formed with them one historical work, homogeneous in linguistic usage, style and in its world of ideas. Apparently on account of the importance of their contents, perhaps also because the Chronicles were analogous to the books of Samuel and Kings, they were cut off and inserted in the canon before the Chronicles. There they formed *one* book, called Ezra—and to begin with in the LXX too. Later on they were divided into two parts in the LXX and the Latin versions, as we learn first from Origen. This partition was then taken over since 1448 into the Hebrew Bible as well and the books were called Ezra and Nehemiah. The names in the LXX and the Vulgate are different: The book of Ezra=LXX *῎Εσδρας β'*, Vulg. Esdras I; the book of Nehemiah=LXX *῎Εσδρας γ*, Vulg. Esdras II, whilst *῎Εσδρας α'* (Vulg. Esdras III) is the name given to an apocryphal book of Ezra (see section 64), and *῎Εσδρας δ'*, (Vulg. Esdras IV) is that of the Ezra Apocalypse (see section 86).

The *subject* of the book is the history of the formation of the post-exilic religious community in Jerusalem. Ezra 1–6 deals with the first restoration in the time of Cyrus in 538 up to the building of the second temple in 516; Ezra 7–Neh. 13 with the second restoration, the reform of Ezra and Nehemiah from 458 (?)–433; the latter is considered the more important.

The books of Chronicles, Ezra and Nehemiah originally belonged to one historical composition comprising the whole history of Israel down to the time of Nehemiah. This can be inferred not only from their close relationship as regards subject matter, but also from their having a common author, the 'Chronicler', to whom these four books are due. The whole work is shown to be the homogeneous literary production of the Chronicler by the methods of its construction and its style and by its special interest in the temple and its cult, in the law and the affairs of the Levites; it is not likely to have come into existence in this form before the year 300 (see pp. 324 f. below). Just as in the Chronicles, the author presents us with extracts from sources which he shapes by means of contributions of his own and on to which he throws a light to suit his own purpose.

The sources. In the case of Ezra 1: 1–4: 5 we cannot be sure whether a source was used or whether we have the Chronicler's own narrative, based on Haggai and Zechariah and some special material (1: 9–11a, the inventory of the vessels of the temple given back by Cyrus; the list of those who returned). In 4: 6–6: 18 a fragment of an *Aramaic source* has been incorporated which Klostermann, Kittel and Schaeder regarded as a *written defence addressed by the Jews to Artaxerxes I* (465–424) to demonstrate their loyalty and as an account of the historical circumstances, utilizing documents from the days of Cyrus, Darius I and Artaxerxes I. They thought this might explain the fact that the chronological order of the events mentioned had not been observed, without the necessity of looking upon the passage 4: 7–23 as an appendix taken from the Memoir and inserted in the wrong place. But the actual concern of the postulated 'Memoir' is nowhere expressed, nor does the account of the Chronicler give us anywhere a hint to throw light on the hiatus between 4: 8, 23 and 4: 24 and on the contradiction between 4: 24 and 5: 16, if we can assume that the written defence was originally one homogeneous document. As against this Noth, referring to an earlier analysis of the Aramaic source of 4: 6–6: 18 wishes to consider it as a description from about 300 B.C. of the restoration of the city and the temple, which the Chronicler worked in. This account utilized for the building of the city an exchange of letters from the period of Artaxerxes I and for that of the temple a correspondence with that of Darius I (521–485). The long distance in time from the events described would then be the reason why this source looked upon the rebuilding of the temple and the city, two events which lay in fact nearly a century apart from each other, as *one* continuous undertaking and why it placed the exchange of letters which led to the interruption of the work (4: 8–23) in front of the correspondence resulting in the completion of the enterprise, without realizing that thereby the historical order of these events was inverted. By this means an explanation would also be provided for the contradiction between the setting of the narrative in 4: 24 and the document used for it in 5: 16 and for the confusion with regard to the Persian kings connected with it. Since there were three bearers of each of the names Artaxerxes and Darius, this is not really surprising in an author who wrote 200 years later. The idea of Rudolph seems more convincing: he considers 5: 1–6: 18; 4: 6–23 to be an Aramaic account used by the Chronicler who inverted their original chronological order. It describes the difficulties under which the temple and city wall were built (cf. Galling who places this document in the year 430); owing to Neh. 1 ff. it was abbreviated by the Chronicler by omitting the completion of the city wall and was brought to a conclusion with verse 4: 24 written originally in Hebrew. Rudolph deals with the chronological confusion by assuming a copyist's error at the beginning of 4: 24 (כְּדִנָ[ה] = 'in the same way', instead of בֵּאדַיִן = 'thereupon').

In 7: 12–9: 15 the Chronicler uses the *Memoirs of Ezra*, written in the first person singular and representing a historically valuable source. It is not certain whether chapter 10, which keeps to the third person singular, also belonged to 'Ezra's Memoirs' and was subsequently changed over from the first to the third person (Budde, Rudolph). On the other hand Neh. 8–9 is essentially a narrative about the introduction of 'the Book of the law of Moses' and should perhaps have been placed originally after Ezra 7–10; except for 8: 9, where Nehemiah seems to have been inserted later, it no doubt belonged to the 'Ezra source' and was probably put into the third person singular when it was transferred. Noth (cf. also Kapelrud's critical examination of the style) denies the existence of any 'Memoirs of Ezra' as a source of the Chronicler's account. He sees in Ezra 7–10 the 'history of Ezra', freshly created by the Chronicler himself and modelled by him on the style of Nehemiah's memoirs, with which he amalgamates them from the beginning (Neh. 8–10). This history he fashions on the basis of the royal edict in Aramaic in Ezra 7: 12–26 and the list of those who returned in 8: 1–14. But the explanation of the use of the first person singular, 7: 12–9: 15, as an imitation of Nehemiah's memoirs, and of the change of person in 7: 1, 6 ff.; 10 as an 'inconsistency' of the Chronicler, as well as the Babylonian place-names in 8: 15, 17, 21, 31, for which no reason is given in Noth's interpretation, do not support this thesis which over-simplifies the literary facts of the case and hardly does justice to the Chronicler's method of working. There is more probability in the assumption that he had before him memoirs composed by Ezra himself, which no doubt he supplemented in some places (e.g. Ezra 7: 1–11) and perhaps also abbreviated.

A further source are the *Memoirs of Nehemiah* marked by the Chronicler with a special title in Neh. 1: 1. They are to be found in Neh. 1–7, probably also in the account of the sealing of the covenant in Neh. 10. This chapter, according to 10: 3 and to the relation of the subject matter in 10: 31–40 with that of 13: 4–31, is not to be assigned to the reform of Ezra, who is missing amongst the signatories, but to that of Nehemiah. Moreover Neh. 12: 27–43, the narrative of the dedication of the walls, and chapter 13, the account of the measures for the reforms, are also taken from Nehemiah's memoirs. This document which the author considers to be a votive offering to God, as the style in 5: 19; 13: 14, 22, 31 indicates, is written by Nehemiah, the diplomatic courtier, not without a certain complacent vanity, but it is nevertheless an excellent source of information for the reform.

In addition to the main sources already mentioned there are a number of *lists*. Some of them may already have been available to the Chronicler as parts of the sources he was using: for example, this could be assumed in the case of those who returned with Ezra in Ezra 8: 1–14, which would thus be a component part of the Ezra source; others think it is a later appendix. Similarly the list in Neh. 3: 1–32 of those taking part in building the wall, is often considered to be secondary, but without compelling reasons, it is more probably to be reckoned as part of Nehemiah's memoirs. The fact too that the roll of the first exiles returning with Zerubbabel has been handed down twice (in Ezra 2 and Neh. 7: 6–72) would be most easily explained, if these lists had already stood in the two different sources which were both used by the author. The literary connexion in Neh. 7 is looser than in Ezra 2 and from this it might be concluded that the list in the book of Nehemiah was interpolated subsequently. Not all the lists included are derived from the old sources. Just in their case it is natural to think of *later insertions*, as for example, in Neh. 11: 3–19 the list of the inhabitants of Jerusalem and in Neh. 11: 20–36 that of the country dwellers. Here the use of older material as well as later amplifications must be allowed for. But Hölscher and Mowinckel are going too far when they declare that all the lists, except that in Neh. 3, are later fabrications.

The Chronicler has dealt rather freely with his sources. He has torn Nehemiah's Memoirs apart, combined the 'Memoirs of Ezra' with the account of the sealing of the covenant (Neh. 8–9 and 10), whilst perhaps leaving out the report to be expected on the introduction of the law which Ezra brought with him. This may have been because he intended to connect both reformers together with the decisive events (the carrying out of the legal reforms and the dedication of the walls of Jerusalem). At any rate this mis-representation of the history which we owe to him dominated the tradition and determined our studies for a long time. Recent research has indeed helped to throw light on the literary circum-stances, so that the activities of Ezra and Nehemiah in their relationship to each other can be kept apart more easily. Yet no agreement has been reached as to how the two reforms succeeded each other in time. The date of Ezra's mission was according to Ezra 7: 7 ff. the year 458 and on it the traditional sequence of events was based (thus also Johannesen, Rehm, Wright). But a number of scholars have for various reasons doubted whether it is the right one and have placed Ezra's mission after that of Ne-hemiah, either between Nehemiah's first and second sojourn in Jerusalem (445–433 and 433–430) (Rudolph) or in the last days of Artaxerxes I or in the first years of the reign of Artaxerxes III (404–359) (Rowley, Galling); these conjectures would remove many a literary and historical difficulty.

The books of Ezra and Nehemiah are a valuable historical source for our knowledge of the formation of the post-exilic

Jewish religious community; they are constructed in part from good source material; thus, when they are used critically, a more or less clear picture can be gained of the efforts at reform of the two personalities, to whose energy Judaism owes its restoration, whilst their characters too are distinctly and strikingly drawn.

51. The Books of the Chronicles

Commentaries: KeH: Bertheau,[2] 1873.–SZ: Öttli, 1889.–KHC: Benzinger, 1901.– HK: Kittel, 1902.–ICC: Curtis and Madsen, 1952.–HSAT: Rothstein, 1923.–SAT: Haller,[2] 1925.–KAT: Rothstein–Hänel I, 1927.–HS: Goettsberger, 1939.–TU: van Selms, I, 1939; II, 1947.–EB: Rehm, 1949.–LStB (Clamer): Marchal, 1949.–SBB: Slotki, 1951.–HBK: Bückers, 1952.–ATD: Galling, 1954.–LStB: Cazelles, 1954.– IB: Elmslie, 1954.–HAT: Rudolph, 1955; see literature for section 50.–Budde, 'Bemerkungen zum "Midrasch des Buches der Könige" ', ZAW 1892, 37 ff.; Wellhausen, *Prolegomena zur Geschichte Israels*[6], 1905, 165 ff.; Asmussen, 'Priesterkodex und Chronik', ThStKr 1906, 165 ff.; von Rad, 'Das Geschichtsbild des chronistischen Werkes', BWAT 1930; idem, 'Die levitische Predigt in den Büchern der Chronik'. *Prockschfestschrift*, 1934, 113 ff.; Junge, 'Der Wiederaufbau des Heerwesens des Reiches Juda unter Josia, BWAT 1937; Welch, *The Work of the Chronicler, its Purpose and its Date* (Schweich Lectures), 1939; Bea, 'Neuere Arbeiten zum Problem der biblischen Chronikbücher', *Biblica*, 1941, 46 ff.; Noth, *Überlieferungsgeschichtliche Studien I*, 1943, 152 ff.; van den Bussche, Het Problem van Kroniken, 1950; Rudolph, Problems of the Work of Chronicles, *VT* 1954, 401 ff.; Rowley, 'Sanballat and the Samaritan Temple', BJRL, Vol. 38, No. 1, 1955

Originally the books of the Chronicles formed the first part of the great continuous historical composition reaching from Adam to Nehemiah at the end of the canon. Even after Ezra and Nehemiah were cut off, they were reckoned as *one* book, as can be seen from the numbering of the biblical books and the position of the massoretic colophon at the end of 2 Chronicles. The Jews called the book (*sēp̱er*) *diḇerê hayyāmîm*=the book of the events of the day (=history), whilst the LXX, to which the division into two parts is due (in the Hebrew editions too since 1448) calls them *paraleipomena* (=passed over) α' + β' (in Latin *paralipomena liber I et II*). This expresses the idea that the Chronicles supplement the books of Samuel and Kings and gives us material 'passed over', 'omitted' in them. The name of Chronicles, in use in the German and English Bibles, is derived from Jerome who in the *prologus galeatus* recommends the name *chronicon totius divinae historiae* which is more correct from the point of view of the subject matter.

The *contents* may be divided into the following sections: (1) 1 Chron. 1–9, the time from Adam to David, consisting almost entirely of genealogies; (2) 1 Chron. 10–29 David; (3) 2 Chron.

1–9 Solomon; (4) 2 Chron. 10–36 from the division of the kingdom to the exile, in which the kings of Judah alone receive attention. A comparison with the books of Samuel and Kings, which
treat the same subject as the bulk of Chronicles, reveals marked
differences. Their dominant and basic purpose is the history of the
theocracy embodied in the Davidic monarchy and in the post-
exilic cultic community. The interest is focused on the temple of
Jerusalem and its worship. Consequently the history before
David, with the exception of Saul's death, and similarly the history of the Northern Kingdom is not dealt with. David himself is
presented essentially as the spiritual father of the building of the
temple, who prepares it down to the smallest detail and hands
over to Solomon money, building material, plans and models for
it. The organization too of that part of the temple worship concerned with music and singing is traced back to David, the
psalmist. In addition to David and to Solomon, the temple builder,
the chief figures in the history are Jehoshaphat, owing to his
labour on behalf of the law of Yahweh (2 Chron. 17: 7–9; 19: 4–11),
and Josiah and Hezekiah, the kings who reformed the worship
of Yahweh. They are portrayed in particular detail and as both
pious spiritual sovereigns and national saints. Anything that
might throw discredit upon these kings is expunged, as e.g.
David's family history and the scarcely happy manner in which
Solomon succeeded to the throne (2 Sam. 9–20); or these things
are replaced by more favourable accounts. Moreover in the presentation of the history God's behaviour in intervening directly
in the current of events is emphasized (cf. e.g. 2, 20: 1–30), a
method of presenting 'sacred history', the beginnings of which
appear already in the Elohist, in Deuteronomy, in the Deuteronomic writing of history, and above all in the priestly historical
work. The dominating view-point of the Chronicler's presentation
of history is the idea of retribution carried through mechanically
and, as regards each individual, down to the smallest details; when
history does not appear to fit in with it, it is suitably distorted.
Thus for example the reason given for the long reign of the godless
king Manasseh in 2 Chron. 33: 10 ff. is that he is thought to have
been converted in Babylon. The historical basis of this is Manasseh's summons to appear before the king of Assyria which the
Chronicler has misunderstood and reinterpreted according to his

own ideas. Above all in the Chronicler's account much is made of the cultic and particular levitical interests. Frequently the law of the Priestly Book is the accepted standard, as e.g. in the Passover celebrations of Hezekiah in 2 Chron. 30: 13–27 and of Josiah in 2, 35: 1–19. Against this von Rad has pointed out the fact that the whole Pentateuch and especially Deuteronomy has been taken into consideration by the Chronicler; but after all P predominates in the Chronicles just as much as in the Pentateuch. The preference given to the musicians of the temple, above all to the singers and their concerns, goes beyond the tradition of the Priestly Book. It must remain an open question whether the author is to be found for certain in these circles who might have developed their special tradition beside the Priestly Book and have influenced the formation of the Chronicler's production.

This also offers a clue by which to fix *the date* of Chronicles. The Priestly Book and the reform of Ezra and Nehemiah, the history of which the Chronicler has included in his book, constitute the *terminus a quo*; therefore Chronicles can in no case have come into existence before 430. The list of the sons of David in 1, 3: 19 ff. probably reckons five or six generations after Zerubbabel (in the present text eleven generations) and the list of the high priests in Neh. 12: 10 f. also five generations after Josiah. These statements have been quoted with a view to establishing a date. But even if it were certain that they had been accepted by the Chronicler, they would be of importance only for determining the *terminus a quo* already mentioned, but not for ascertaining the absolute time when Chronicles was written. The unmistakable propensity of this book to resist the pretensions of the Samaritans (see below) does not take us much further. Their opposition to the community of Yahweh in Jerusalem had already become keen owing to the reform of Ezra and Nehemiah, so that this again only provides us with the same upper limit for the origin of Chronicles. Galling assumes that the rival sanctuary on Gerizim had been founded; he dates this to have been between 350–330 and thereby arrives at the period of about 300 for the composition of Chronicles. But neither this conjecture nor the date for the formation of the Samaritan community based on the narrative of Josephus (Ant XI 7, 2; 8, 2.4) afford reliable support. As we must assume that a certain amount of time elapsed between the Chronicler and the reforms in Jerusalem, since he cannot keep them clearly apart, we may consider Chronicles to have come into being at the earliest at the beginning of the fourth century (Rudolph).

The author used *sources* for Chronicles just as he did in the case of the books of Ezra and Nehemiah. It is evident from the similarity in plan and especially from the partly verbal agreement in individual passages that he had before him the historical tradition of the books of Genesis to Kings. Just like the author of the books of the Kings the Chronicler repeatedly mentions his sources which will give further information about the individual kings. On the strength of a first impression, he might appear to be quoting a whole series of different sources, both historical and prophetic. The following are mentioned as historical sources: The book of the Kings of Israel and Judah in 1, 9: 1; 2, 27: 7 and *passim*; the book of the kings of Israel in 2, 20: 34; the acts of the kings of Israel in 2, 33: 18 and the midrash of the book of the Kings in 2, 24: 27. Yet probably these do not mean different works, but one and the same book, since those sources which mention only the kings of Israel (2, 20: 34 and 2, 22: 18) include also kings of Judah. It remains an open question whether the Chronicler's inaccuracies in quoting his sources should make us regard his statements simply as an imitation of the quotations in the book of Kings, giving us no special historical information from the literary point of view about what was available for his use (Noth), or whether further conclusions might be drawn from them concerning his literary sources. In any case the historical tradition of the books from Genesis to Kings in the canon was not the only source of the Chronicler's composition. This appears from the fact that he often supplies more and more pertinent matter than can be found in the book of Kings; e.g. in 2, 32: 30 the information about the tunnel of Siloam, in 2, 35: 20 ff. the description of Josiah's end; historical material taken from army statistics such as in 2, 14: 7; 17: 14 ff.; 26: 11 ff. (Junge, op. cit., 37 ff.) as well as details about buildings for defence, military preparations, and the wars of the kings of Judah (e.g. 2, 11: 5–12; 17: 2, 12–19; 26: 9, 11–15; 27: 3 f.; 33: 14), which force us to conjecture further sources no longer known to us. It is impossible to decide whether we may infer from the name Midrash that the old historical books have been painted over for purposes of edification and developed further by scholars, or whether we may gather from the additional matter in Chronicles that the Chronicler had still before him the old sources or a more extensive edition of the book of Kings. Moreover apart from the tendencies just mentioned, we cannot always distinguish clearly from the literary point of view between the Chronicler's own material and that which he has taken from his sources. The conjecture of Engnell and Bentzen that oral traditions have been utilized as well is less probable. The prophetic sources are quoted as 'Oracles, prophecies, visions, midrash' by prophets, all of whom are mentioned or occur in the books of Samuel and Kings (Samuel, Nathan, Gad, Ahijah, Iddo, Shemaiah, Isaiah). When it is said in 2, 20: 34 of the words of Jehu that they are inserted in the book of the kings of Israel, it is likely that, unless after all merely the narratives concerning the prophets in the books of the Kings are meant, at least a part of these prophetic sources are also components of the midrash of the book of Kings. In this matter the Chronicler no doubt shares the view of the later tradition according to which the historical literature of the 'Former Prophets' was written by prophets. But this does not exclude the possibility that the Chronicler had also other sources at his disposal.

The work of the Chronicler *was expanded* later on, as for example by 1, 12: 1–23 and parts of chapters 15 and 16, but especially by the genealogies in 1, 1–9 and the lists in 1, 23–27. In subsequent times (partly probably in the Maccabean period) these were adapted to the new circumstances and took account of the awakened national interests. Rothstein wishes to distinguish two revisions, the first (432) which conforms to the Priestly Book and the older material of the history of the Kings and a second one (c. 400) which is modelled on the Pentateuch as a whole. But this sharp division cannot be carried out with certainty, especially as we can trace a dependence on the entire Pentateuch also in passages considered to belong to the first stage of the revision (von Rad). The same objection applies to Galling too: he conjectures two different authors of Chronicles and places the second one at the beginning of the second century. The later additions do not make the impression of having been handled uniformly, but are rather to be attributed with Rudolph to various revisers who made use partly of earlier, partly of later material.

Chronicles is not strictly speaking a historical work, although we cannot fail to recognize the intention to write the history of the theocracy with the help of written sources. In it less significance is attached to profane history than in the older historical works, for the Chronicler's own tendentious interpretation and development of the material occupies much more space in Chronicles than in the older books. The aim of this composition is rather to demonstrate from history that the Judaism of the law of the post-exilic cultic community of the Jerusalem temple possesses a legitimate title. This explains the facts that his presentation of history starts with David, the spiritual founder of the temple building, that the history of the monarchy of Northern Israel is neglected by the Chronicler as being illegitimate, and that the centre of his historical picture is occupied by the history of the temple at Jerusalem. He looks upon history as a means of exhortation, and often elaborates and transforms the traditions very freely in order to display disobedience as misfortune and piety as a blessing. This comes out particularly clearly in the speeches composed by the Chronicler himself in the syle of a Levitical sermon (e.g. 1, 22: 7 ff.; 28: 2 ff.; 2, 13: 4 ff.) as well as in his assigning to the prophets whom he quotes copiously the role of preachers of repentance. For this reason Chronicles cannot be placed on the same level as the books of Samuel and Kings as a historical source. What lies behind this bias is the controversy with the cultic community of the Samaritans which sought recognition of its legitimacy by putting forward claims to the long-hallowed historical traditions of the people 'Israel'. Yet even for the earlier period careful criticism can learn many an item of historial value from Chronicles. They are a specially precious historical document for the era after the reform of Ezra and Nehemiah, which lies almost completely hidden from us. This work reveals clearly the intellectual and spiritual interests and forces, both of religion and of the cult, which contributed to the shaping of Judaism, and the remoteness from reality of a rational, theological dogmatism in which no longer much of the religious contact with history and the realistic outlook of earlier days can be recognized.

SECOND PART

The Collection of the Sacred Writings and the Formation of the Canon

Buhl, *Kanon und Text des AT*, 1891; Wildeboer, *Die Enstehung des alttestamentlichen Kanons*, in German by Risch, 1891; W. Robertson Smith, *The Old Testament in the Jewish Church*, 1881, [2]1892; Budde, *Der Kanon des AT*, 1900; Hölscher, *Kanonisch und Apokryph*, 1905; Duhm, *Die Entstehung des AT*,[2] 1909; Lofthouse, *The Making of the Old Testament*, 1915; König, 'Kanon und Apokryphen', *Beitr. zur Förderung christlicher Theologie*, 1917; Hänel, 'Der Schriftbegriff Jesu', *Beitr. zur Förderung christlicher Theologie*, 1919; Staerk, Der Schrift- und Kanonbegriff der jüdischen Bibel, ZSTh 1929, 101 ff.; Horst, 'Das AT als heilige Schrift und als Kanon', ThBl 1932, col. 161 ff.; Zeitlin, *An historical Study of the Canonization of the Hebrew Scriptures*, 1933; H. W. Robinson, 'Canonicity and Inspiration', *Expository Times*, 1935–6, 119 ff.; Beyer, Art. 'κανών', ThWB III, 1938, 600 ff.; R. Meyer, 'Art. χρύπτω', ThWB III, 1938, 979 ff.; Jepsen, 'Kanon und Text des AT', ThLZ 74 (1949), col. 65–74; Östborn, *Cult and Canon* (Uppsala Univ. Årsskrift) 1950; Koole, *Het Problem van de Canonisatie van het OT*, 1955, Jepsen, ZAW (1959), 194 ff.

52. The tradition concerning the formation of the Old Testament Canon

The *Word Canon* is derived from a Semitic root (Hebrew kāneh =reed) and means in classical Greek a straight rod, and when transferred to intellectual matters, especially in philosophy, the guiding principle, rule, norm. The word is used in this sense by Philo and in the NT in Gal. 6: 16; 2 Cor. 10: 13 ff. Whilst in these passages it has the meaning of a Christian standard, it is used in the third century in the sense of a guiding rule of the Church for ordinances of the Church and Conciliar decrees. Not until the fourth century is it transferred to the sacred writings (Canons of the Council of Laodicea 360 and Athanasius, *De decretis Nicaenae synodi* 18: 3); here it refers to the Church's message concerning the truth for faith of Holy Writ. It was the Latin Fathers who first made Canon and Bible synonymous.

The Jewish concept of the Canon presupposes the same idea of the binding nature of the contents of the holy scriptures of the OT; but the Pharisaic theory of it which we find in Josephus (Contra Apionem I, 8) (*c.* A.D. 100) indicates that its external character has been emphasized by attaching greater weight to its formal aspect. According to Josephus the *criteria of the nature of the Canon* are (1) it is inspired by God; the writings originate in a precisely defined era of revelation, i.e. from Moses to Artaxerxes (465–424); (2) it is marked off from profane literature by the sacred quality of its material which on being touched 'defiles the hands' so that ritual cleansing is required. (3) The number of the books is restricted

(Josephus reckons 22 books, elsewhere 24 are named); (4) the wording must not be touched.

According to Josephus and to the Jewish conception generally prevailing in the Judaism of that period it was believed that the divine authority of the Canon was guaranteed by the inspiration of the individual authors and it regarded the Canon as closed in the time of Artaxerxes. 4 Ezra 14: 18–48 (also *c*. A.D. 100, see below, section 86) presents us with another view of the origin of the Jewish Canon. This describes how the Canon came into being not gradually, but all at the same time in the days of Ezra who is described in this book as having visions thirty years after the fall of Jerusalem (557). In response to his prayer, Ezra was filled by God with the holy spirit and dictated the books of the OT, which had been destroyed by fire, to his five assistants who wrote down in forty days the 24 canonical books and the 70 to be kept secret. These last were intended for the 'wise' alone; that means the apocalypses. This idea of the way the Canon originated was accepted in the second century by Christians; it is found in Irenaeus, Tertullian, Clement of Alexandria and Origen. It was authoritative too in the mediaeval church. In the sixteenth century another idea, already hinted at by David Kimchi (*ob.* 1275), was advanced by the German Jew Elias Levita. In the preface of his book *Massoreth-ha-Massoreth*, which appeared in 1538, he says: the 24 books of the OT were already in existence at the time of Ezra, but were brought together by him and the men of the 'Great Synagogue' whose names are given already in the Talmud (*baba bathra*). To them is due the division of the Canon into three parts, the Torah, the Nebiim and the Kethubhim, but in the second and third parts they appear in a different order to that given in *baba bathra*. That the Canon was put together *simul et semel* at the time of Ezra remained the prevalent view in Judaism and Christendom and was taken over into Protestantism and developed further by Buxtorf the elder (*b.* 1629), Hottinger (*ob.* 1667), Leusden (*ob.* 1699) and Carpzov (*ob.* 1767).

This theory of the origin of the OT Canon in Ezra's time cannot be sustained. Apart from the fact that today we possess to a certain extent a more exact knowledge of the formation of the individual writings of the OT, the arrangement whereby the book of Daniel and Ezra—Nehemiah—Chronicles are placed in the third part of the Canon would be unintelligible according to this theory. The acceptance by the Samaritan community of the Torah alone and the differences in the Alexandrian collection of the scriptures in the LXX from the Palestinian Canon are additional objections to the Jewish tradition. Finally the 'Great Synagogue' as understood by the Talmud, is no historical entity; it is in fact a theory of a 'College', inferred from the assembly of the people in Neh. 8–10 (cf. Kuenen, *Over de mannen der groote Synagoge*, 1876, in German by Budde, *Gesammelte Abhandlungen zur Biblischen Wissenschaft von Dr. Abr. Kuenen*, 1894, pp. 125 ff.). These considerations compel us to conclude that the formation of the Canon is the result of a longer historical process, in which a distinction must be drawn between the collection of the Holy Scriptures of the OT and the development of the idea of the Jewish Canon.

53. The formation of the Old Testament as a collection of Holy Scriptures

In this section we will leave on one side the various purely literary, cultic and other motives which led to the formation of individual writings, and to different sources coalescing into the books of the OT; instead the OT will be considered as a whole, having regard to the processes and motives which determined its character as Holy Writ. It is divided as a whole into three parts: the Law (Torah), the Prophets (Nebiim) and the Writings (Kethubhim). This tripartite division which the Jews still use to designate the OT reflects the historical growth of its collection.

The presupposition of the collected sacred writings is the belief that God revealed himself in the word, to which is therefore due divine authority and respect for its standards. Although the expressions 'holy scriptures' and sacred writings are used first in 2 Macc. 8: 23, in Philo, in Josephus and in the NT in Rom. 1: 2; 2 Tim. 3: 15; Matt. 21, 42, the thing signified had already existed for a long time. The precept of the priest, the oracle of the prophet, and to a less extent the song also of the singer and the *māshāl* of the teacher of wisdom, all claim to be inspired by God and base their authority on this claim. The setting down in writing of God's living word is rooted in the very old and widespread occult conceptions of the magical power of the written word. Its remains can still be seen in Num. 5: 11 ff. where the woman accused of adultery must as an ordeal drink the water used to wash away a written curse, so that in a literal sense she drinks the curse to be worked out in her. Behind the symbolism in the case of Ezekiel (3: 1 ff.) who is required to eat the roll of the book, there still stand magical rudiments of this kind, though here they have, of course, become the expression of the idea of inspiration. It fits in with the conception in the OT religion of God as a person that the magical, mechanical form in which the holiness of the scriptures is conceived recedes before a more personal idea; thus in the popular tradition the commandments are regarded as being written down by God himself in Exod. 24: 12; 31: 18; 32: 16 (similarly in the case of the Egyptian God Thot and the Babylonian Ea) or as being dictated by God. In the OT it is especially the inspiration of the prophets which is presented in different forms (cf. Jer. 1: 9; Ezek, 3: 1 ff.; 1 Kgs. 22); right up to a late period it plays an important part in the development of the OT holy scriptures. For after all the written record of the prophecies came into existence in order to provide evidence for the truth and authority of the divine word (see section 30 on Amos, also Is. 8: 1 ff.; 30: 8; Jer. 36). Besides this the reading aloud of the written word in the cult gave a natural impetus to the collection of the OT as sacred writings. Here is the real setting (*Sitz im Leben*) for the OT as holy scripture. The general proposition that the word comes alive when it is being recited is true also of the word in the OT. God speaks to the congregation when the writings deposited in the sanctuary are read aloud (1 Sam. 10: 25; Deut. 31: 26; cf. Deut. 10: 1 ff.); he makes his demands known in the law (Exod. 20: 22 ff.; 24: 3); in the narratives of sacred history connected with it (J, E, D, P) God's dealings with his people come alive again for the present day. Thus the sacredness of the book consists in the dynamic effect of its contents, mediating a meeting between God and the people, which is *its proper function*, and not in the magical or literary quality of the books as such. The continuing life of the oral tradition and the OT faith in the God who was showing himself active in history resulted necessarily in the revelations by the word adopting ever fresh forms; thus old traditions had to give way to new ones, or became neutralized, reinterpreted or amplified. It is with these general considerations in mind that the formation of the separate parts of the OT must be understood.

The first place is occupied, in view of its growing importance, particularly in post-exilic Judaism, by *the law* (Torah), that interweaving of sacred history and sacred jurisprudence, so characteristic of the OT, as the expression of God's activity and of his will for the people (see above, section 13). As the Yahwist, Elohist, Deuteronomic and Priestly forms of the tradition became fused in the framework of the cultic recital, this amalgam acquired in the Pentateuch an importance showing an ever-increasing bias towards the law, which comes to light above all in the later strands. It was in particular two crucial events which brought about a general recognition of the special importance of the divine claims enshrined in the law and thereby procured for the Torah its dominating authority.

(1) *The Deuteronomic reform* of the year 621, by means of which Deuteronomy as the 'Mosaic tradition' was raised to a position of controlling significance and impressed itself definitely on the ordering of the political life of the state and of the cultic life of its religion. For the first time in Israel's history we see here how a book and the movement behind it, composed of a blend of prophetic and priestly mentality, acquires an influence on the shaping of the whole of life. The rationalizing of this event, whereby the 'law' was regarded as the basis of all ordinances, was extended in the Deuteronomic historical writings also to the presentation and interpretation of past happenings according to the standards set in this law. Although by ancient custom Deuteronomy was deposited in the sanctuary (Deut. 31: 26) and was thus intended to be preserved from being curtailed and amplified (Deut. 4: 2; 13: 1), these early attempts to obtain recognition for it alone did not succeed; the later laws of the 'Holiness Code', and of Ezekiel's draft in Ezek. 40–48, and the laws of the Priestly Book prove that active development had not come to an end. But by the reforms of Josiah, by its motives and its consequences, an important step had been taken in the direction of setting up the 'Mosaic Torah' as the standard and of attaching the fullest weight to it.

(2) It was *the reform of Ezra and Nehemiah*, basing itself on the Priestly Book incorporated in the Pentateuch, which first made this book the definitive foundation of the Jewish religious community and thereby gave the Torah that unique authoritative

position as Holy Writ, which Judaism continued to develop and has retained to this day.* This estimation of the Torah can be learned from the following facts: when the Samaritans broke away, they took over the Pentateuch alone as Holy Writ. In the Greek Diaspora at first only the five books of Moses were translated into Greek and recognized as the official version. In the NT the name of 'Law' is used for the whole of the OT in John 10: 34; 15: 25, where the Psalms are described as being 'in the Law', and in 1 Cor. 14: 21 where Is. 28: 11 ff. is spoken of in the same way. In spite of its fundamental importance, which can be seen also in its influence on Chronicles, the Torah did not at first possess a formal canonical character, in the sense of its contents, its extent and its text being regarded as completed and unassailable. It continued to receive further alterations and amplifications; thus for example, the form of Exod. 35–40 was not yet fixed at the time of the LXX, and later than that editorial changes were made in the text, as a comparison with the Septuagint will show.

The second part of the OT, the Prophets, has been divided only since the eighth century A.D. into the 'former' and the 'latter' prophets (נְבִיאִים רִאשׁוֹנִים and נ׳ אַחֲרוֹנִים); it is not possible to say whether these names indicate the position of the books in the Canon or the order in time of their formation. The 'historical' writings of the former prophets came into being during a long and varied literary process, no doubt contemporary with the Pentateuch and partly together with it, and were amalgamated and recast from different sources. When they had been woven into one whole, they were read as evidence for God's activity in history, and related to the contemporary events of the day; in this respect they were deemed holy scriptures. The Deuteronomic revision of the history, the recasting and supplementing of the book of Joshua by the priestly editors confirms this assessment of the historical literature. The fact that Chronicles was too late to be admitted into the second part of the OT writings indicates that by its time this collection was already in existence as a fixed completed entity. On the other hand we can see from the account

---

* Noth (*Geschichte Israels*, p. 302 ff.) disputes the fact that the 'law of the God of heaven', brought by Ezra from Babylon (Ezra 7 : 12–26) was the Priestly Code or the Pentateuch. But even if he were correct, it is indisputable that with Ezra's reform a decisive step had been taken in the direction of establishing the Torah in that dominant position for which there is evidence soon after.

in Chronicles which diverges from that given in the books of
Samuel and of Kings and from the partly important differences
between the LXX and the Hebrew text in the same books that
this collection too had not yet in the fourth and third centuries
possessed an unalterable formal canonical quality.

In the *'latter'* *prophets* the divine authority of their message is
given in a more direct manner than in the historical literature
owing to their personal meeting with God. Their witness to God's
wishes and operations at a particular moment of history claims to
be a word of God with direct bearing on the present. Their sayings when fixed in writing and collected either by the prophets
themselves or by their disciples or adherents served to keep alive
these divine oracles, which bear in themselves from the first the
stamp of holy scripture. Whatever might be the personal qualities
of the prophets' manner of thinking and expressing themselves,
something like a prophetic tradition developed resting on an
inter-relationship due to their subject matter between the individual writing prophets; this can be observed in the relationship of
the young Jeremiah with the prophecy of Hosea or of Micah with
that of Isaiah, and also in Jer. 26: 18; 28: 8 f. But this certainty of
the prophets, which was bound up with their personal experience
of God, necessitated at the same time a lively controversy with
other prophets who likewise claimed divine revelation, so that on
occasion prophets prophesied against each other. We may take
as examples the different verdicts of the prophets on Jehu's
revolution in 2 Kgs. 9: 1 ff. and Hos. 1: 4 f. and the conflict with
the nationalist prophecy of salvation, as we see it particularly in
the case of Micaiah son of Imlah in 1 Kgs. 22 and Jer. 23, 27–29;
or again the fact that representatives of the national prophecy of
salvation like Nahum and Obadiah are allowed their say in the
OT scriptures beside the writing prophets who hold the opposite
point of view. All these instances show us the difficulties which
stood in the way of the recognition of the prophetic scriptures as
the revelation of God so long as prophecy was engaged in active
warfare. It was not until the catastrophe of the exile which on the
one hand confirmed the authority and the truth of the pre-exilic
prophecy of judgment, and on the other opened the door through
penitence to a fresh hope of salvation, that these tensions were
adjusted. Exilic and post-exilic prophecy with this point of view

M

in mind is concerned more fully with the prophetic tradition and thereby contributes to enhancing the authority of the prophetic writings (e.g. Ezek. 38: 17, the 'proof from prophecy' in Deutero-Isaiah in Is. 40: 21; 41: 26; 43: 9; 45: 20 and *passim*; Zech. 1: 4; 7: 7 and *passim*, Dan. 9: 2). The doxologies in the book of Amos (cf. Horst, ZAW 1929, pp. 45 ff.) show how the congregation for its part recognized the prophetic writings as the word of God when recited in the liturgy. But when the priestly reforms of Ezra and Nehemiah organized the Jewish religious community, a development was initiated which was by its nature directed against the creative vitality of prophetic inspiration and brought it gradually to extinction (cf. Zech. 13: 2 ff.; Ps. 74: 9; 1 Macc. 4: 46). In course of time this led to the cessation of the collection of prophetic writings to which Is. 34: 16 seems to allude. At the time of Jesus ben Sirach (*c.* 200 B.C.) the second part of the Canon must also have been concluded; since in the 'praises of the fathers' in Ecclus. 48: 22–49: 12 he names Isaiah, Jeremiah, Ezekiel and the twelve prophets. The fact that the book of Daniel, written about 165, was not admitted into the Canon of the prophets points in the same direction. But its being closed did not yet imply canonization in the later sense; for even after this time fresh pieces, such as, e.g. the apocalypse in Zech. 12–14, were received into the collection of the prophets, no longer, it is true, as independent books, but as interpolations into prophetic writings already in existence. Yet this is done in a way which shows that there can be no question here of the sacred writings being valued as the sole standard of *faith*, which excludes all other religious literature.

The third part, the Writings (Kethubhim) no doubt derives its name from the fact that, unlike the books in the first and second part which were read aloud at the divine service, it contained writings which were not read aloud, but only written down. In addition, the more specific name of hagiographa is used. Very little that is certain can be discovered about the collection of this part which took place last of all; this is easy to understand since the literature gathered together here does not claim divine authority as directly and manifestly as the Torah and the prophetic oracles. The Psalter seems to have been the earliest to receive recognition as holy scripture; this was probably brought about in part by its use in the cult and by the interest of the Levites and singers who entered into the inheritage of the cultic prophecy. The description in Luke 24: 44 of the OT as 'the law of Moses, the prophets and the psalms' (cf. 2 Macc. 2: 13 'the writings of David') is a sign of the particular esteem in which the psalms were held. The Lamentations too may have gained special consideration from being employed in the cult at the memorial service for the destruction of Jerusalem, perhaps assisted by their attribution to Jeremiah. The cult lent support also to the book of Esther as being the festival legend of the feast of Purim. The work of the Chronicler, Ezra—Nehemiah—Chronicles, through its connexions with the cultic circles of the Levites and with the Torah was given at once a peculiar significance of its own as the salvation-history of the congregation of the second temple. Proverbs, Ecclesiastes and Job could claim divine inspiration as Wisdom literature. In the case of Proverbs in which older already existing collections were gathered together, and in that of Ecclesiastes and of the Song of Songs their derivation from Solomon may have been the basis of their reputation. Job and Ruth too were perhaps esteemed owing to the age of the traditions utilized in them. The admission of Daniel into the collection of the sacred 'writings' was also probably influenced by its use of older traditions as well as by the back-dating of the apocalyptic part.

However, in the pre-Christian era there was no question of the Canon being closed. We learn this from the preface in Ecclesiasticus by Jesus ben Sira who translated the work of his grandfather into Greek. He speaks there of the law, the prophets and 'other books of our fathers' and places his own and his. grandfather's work more or less on a level with those books, looking upon it as a continuation of the literary activity of their forefathers. It is evident from this that he did not know of a completed collection of 'writings' marked off from all other books, and that the third part of the Canon had not yet a proper name of its own.

The Septuagint reveals a similar state of affairs amongst the Hellenistic Jewry in Alexandria. In it the Torah indeed occupied the first and authoritative position and was recognized in an official translation; the other writings too were read and valued as holy scriptures for purposes of edification. But the LXX is not yet aware, like the later Jewish Canon, of a sharp line dividing off these writings. Both the fluid state of the text, to be observed in the LXX, e.g. in Jeremiah and the books of Kings, as well as the unhesitating acceptance of the Apocrypha and individual pseud-epigraphical books and their inclusion among the other writings of the OT go to show that the LXX knows nothing of being tied to a formal Canon. In the same way it has taken its own course in the matter of the arrangement of the OT writings (cf. on this last point Swete, *An Introduction to the OT in Greek*, 1914).

The *Apocrypha* has been understood since Jerome and in the Protestant Church since Karlstadt (*De canonicis scripturis*, 1520) and Luther to be the name for those books which the Church has taken over from the Greek OT for purposes of edification and are reckoned in a broad sense as part of the OT in the Greek and Latin Bible. These are 3 Ezra (1 Esdras), 1-3 Maccabees, Tobit, Judith, the Prayer of Manasses, the rest of Daniel, the rest of Esther, Baruch, the Epistle of Jeremiah, Ecclesiasticus, the Wisdom of Solomon. The Codex Alexandrinus contains in addition the fourth book of Maccabees from the Pseudepigrapha so that there is a case for its inclusion in the Apocrypha; some copies of the Septuagint contain other Pseudepigrapha. This circumstance, as well as the fact that the fourth book of Ezra (2 Esdras) which enjoys high, almost canonical esteem in the Roman Catholic Church and in a few sects, was admitted into the appendix of the official Vulgate, shows clearly that the border-line between Apocrypha and Pseudepigrapha cannot be drawn quite definitely.

Pseudepigrapha is the name given to those numerous books in the different Eastern churches (Syrian, Coptic, Ethiopic, etc.) which were written in the languages of these churches. Some of them are preserved only in fragments or are known only from their title, and with few exceptions they do not appear either in the Septuagint or in the Vulgate. The etymological meaning of the designation 'pseudepigrapha' really only indicates that these writings circulated under names other than those of their authors. This partly fictitious pseudonymity—a custom widespread in antiquity in order to enhance the authority of the writings concerned —appears in the canonical and apocryphal books also and is therefore not a material criterion peculiar to the pseudepigrapha. The demarcation as well as the arrangement of the individual writings is not constant in the different transmissions of the text in the case of the apocryphal books and this is true to a much greater extent still in that of the pseudepigrapha. The most important of them are: the Letter of Aristeas, the Book of Jubilees, the Martyrdom of Isaiah, the Psalms of Solomon, the Odes of Solomon, the fourth book of Maccabees, the Sibylline Odes, the book of Enoch, the Ascension of Moses, the fourth book of Ezra, the Apocalypse of Baruch, the Testaments of the Twelve Patriarchs, the Life of Adam and Eve (cf. for these Part IV, where the Apocrypha and the most important Pseudepigrapha are discussed in the selection and order of Kautzsch, *Die Apokryphen und Pseudepigraphen*, 1900).

Together with the Greek version of the OT the earliest Christian Church accepted also the Septuagintal conception of the scriptures. We learn from Matt. 23: 35, where 'the blood of Abel unto the blood of Zacharias, the son of Barachiah', is mentioned (cf. 2 Chron. 24: 20 f.) that the whole collection of the OT writings from Genesis to 2 Chronicles seems to have been known in NT times. 'The law and the prophets', the name given in the NT to the OT (Matt. 5: 17; Acts 28: 23) may hardly be taken as an indication that the collection of writings in the OT consisted of two parts only; neither does Matt. 23: 35 contain any judgment on the value and authority of the different books. Nevertheless it is striking that in addition to Ezra and Nehemiah, neither the Song of Songs, Ecclesiastes nor Esther are quoted in the NT (it is uncertain whether John 3: 8 looks back to Eccles. 11: 4 ff.), and these are books the assessment of which was under discussion amongst the Jews also. On the other hand the NT cites as quotations, with the same formula as in the case of canonical writings, passages and books which were not admitted into the Jewish Canon. In 1 Cor. 2: 9 a saying from an Apocalypse of Elijah is referred to, in Jude 15 Enoch 1: 9 is quoted. Luke 11: 49; John 7: 38; Eph. 5: 14 and James 4: 5 f. are quotations from unknown sources, whilst in the case of 2 Tim. 3: 8 and Hebr. 11: 37 it cannot be determined whether a written or an oral tradition underlies them. These facts prove that the NT too knew nothing of being tied exclusively to a formally limited Canon. The NT Christians were attached to the scriptures owing to the 'fulfilment' which Jesus accomplished with the freedom arising out of the fullness of his own authority. He effected this 'fulfilment' by tracing the revelation of God in the scriptures back to its ultimate purposes and by carrying it forward to its goal. For him too the scriptures, a witness to the living revelation of God's will and operations, are Holy Writ. He fulfilled them and at the same time abolished the bondage to the letter imposed by Pharisaic piety.

54. The development of the Jewish conception of the Canon and the closing of the Canon

The formation of the Jewish Canon was brought to a close when the OT had been collected and recognized as Holy Writ. In this process its practical use in the divine services in the temple and the synagogue played an important part. But the presuppositions and motives arising out of the general history and out of the intellectual trends of the times which led to the Canon being closed and to the Jewish conception of it being defined, must be distinguished from the reasons discussed in the preceding section for the collection of the OT as Holy Writ. In the days of the grandson of Jesus ben Sirach in c. 117 B.C. a completed canon was not yet in existence and in those of Josephus in c. A.D. 100 the rabbinic conception of a canon was clearly developed; it must therefore have been closed during the two centuries between 100 B.C. and A.D. 100. It was not a question of the sacred writings being collected or of a collection of them which had been started being continued and completed; but the holy scriptures already in existence were dogmatically fixed, cut down and defined in a particular historical situation. Apocalyptic writings in which the heritage of the OT and foreign syncretistic matter were combined and which presented themselves with a claim to prophetic inspiration, had spread as a result of the Maccabean revolt. This meant that the Judaism of the law was in danger of dissolution from within; indeed the danger was all the greater since the apocalyptic literature sought to outbid the Torah by tending to appear older than the latter, for Adam, Enoch, Noah, the Patriarchs were considered to be the authors of these books. According to 4 Ezra 14: 44 ff. the canonical books were intended for the mass of the 'worthy and unworthy', the apocalyptic books on the other hand for the 'wise', and Enoch in 104: 11–13 associates blessedness with reading and obeying his book. When the Messianic and apocalyptic hopes which had been transferred to the Maccabees were disappointed, the danger of the foreign influence from apocalyptic was recognized, and in consequence this type of literature was rejected. Thus Jewish theology turned back to the remembrance of its roots in the 'law and the prophets' and so the Jewish concept of the Canon was born. The fact that it did not gain general acceptance is proved by the fragments found in Qumran of the book of Jubilees, of 1 Enoch, the Testament of the Twelve Patriarchs, Tobit, the Apocalypse of Abraham, the Martyrdom of Isaiah and of other apocryphal and pseudepigraphal literature not yet known to us, which was evidently regarded with special favour by that sect. The details of the history describing how the Canon was formed and won recognition are still hidden from us; yet we can perceive the motives and trends leading to its delimitation.

According to the evidence of Josephus, who expounds the rabbinic concept of the Canon in Contra Apionem 1: 8, this was done by fixing the period when inspiration was thought to have been in operation as the time between Moses and Artaxerxes. Thus inspiration and literature before Moses and after the prophets were ruled out and thereby a blow was dealt at Apocalyptic as not having been inspired within the principal meaning of the Canon. All literature which came into being 'from then onwards and in the future' was reckoned, according to the expression used in the Talmud, as 'defiling the hands', i.e. the canonical books as such possessed a material quality of holiness, were to a certain extent *taboo*, so that whoever touched them must undergo a ritual cleansing. In this way a clear external line of demarcation was drawn between sacred and profane literature; the latter might be read 'as a letter is read'. A fixed formal concept of sanctity took the place of the functional, dynamic conception of the sacred writings; something of the old magical conception of the written word came to life again. By defining prophetic inspiration, presented by the rabbis in a variety of forms (in the case of the Torah, e.g. the old synagogue taught its creation by God and its pre-existence) its active life was *de facto* destroyed and transformed into a dead piece of machinery governed by the letter.

This demarcation of the concept of the Canon hit nearly all the apocalypses. Only the book of Daniel, attributed to a prophetic author of the exilic period, and the anonymous passages like Is. 24–27 and Zech. 12–14 could maintain their place in the Canon by being inserted amongst the recognized prophetic writings. Moreover their status as canonical books was secured for the approved books by giving them suitable dates. Thus, e.g. the book of Job, whose author was identified with the Edomite Jobab in Gen. 36: 33 ff. was saved for the Canon by ascribing it to Moses. The Psalter was considered to be the work of David, Proverbs, Ecclesiastes and the Song of Songs that of Solomon; the book of Ruth, and also that of Esther, like Joel and Jonah, were regarded as products of the time in which prophetic inspiration according to the dogma had not yet become extinct. On the other hand the limitation of the Canon resulted in Ecclesiasticus and the first book of Maccabees not being admitted, although the first named neither conflicted with the standard of the Torah nor differed materially from the canonical Wisdom literature.

The Sadducees did not recognize this Canon of the Pharisees; for them the Torah alone remained the authoritative book. But even in the circles of Pharisaic Judaism the canonical status of some of the writings was under discussion. Thus it was disputed whether or not the Song of Songs and Ecclesiastes 'defiled the hands'. They were both included in the Canon at the Synod of Jamnia (c. A.D. 100). Nevertheless the altercation about the Song of Songs and Ecclesiastes flared up again; in the Mishnah (Yadayim III, 5) Ecclesiastes is regarded as canonical. At the same time we learn of controversies amongst the Rabbis about Ezekiel, Proverbs and Esther, as to whether they should be 'hidden' or, in other words, excluded from the Canon or from being read aloud at the divine services. In the case of Ezekiel the exegesis of Hananiah ben Hezekiah succeeded in eliminating the discrepancies with the Torah and therewith also the scruples. But these disagreements between the different schools of learning hardly presented any serious danger to the canonical writings and it can be said that at about the year A.D. 100 the Canon was finally limited to a definite number of books (Josephus, Contra Apionem 1: 8 counts 22 books probably by including Ruth with Judges and Lamentations with Jeremiah, whilst 2 Esdras 14: 44 ff. mentions 24 canonical writings).

The *arrangement* of the books in the second and especially in the third part of the Canon varies in the old books which have been handed down. It is attested since the sixth century A.D. that the five *Megilloth* (=festival scrolls) were put together to be read aloud at the chief festivals of the Jewish cycle of feasts; thus the Song of Songs was recited at the Passover, Ruth at the feast of Weeks, Lamentations at the feast commemorating the destruction of Jerusalem, Ecclesiastes at the feast of Tabernacles and Esther at the feast of Purim.

It resulted from the conception of the material sacredness of the Canon that the Jewish theory declared the *wording* of the canonical writings to be inviolable, in order to protect it from alterations and expansions. By this action the distinctive quality of the OT as a standard because it was Holy Writ, a quality applied originally to its contents and showing itself in practical use to be dynamically alive, became a rigid formal principle, fixed and immutable, underpinned by a theological, dogmatic theory.

The closing of the Canon and the development of the Pharisaic concept of the Canon signified a victory for the legal trend of Judaism. The process of forming the Canon is a step taken by the Judaism of the law in order to grasp its own nature and to preserve itself; it was achieved by reducing and formally restricting the sacred writings to a rigid legal standard out of which issued Talmudic Judaism. By imposing this standard on the Canon, Judaism dissociated itself from heretics as well as from Christianity and sought to protect itself. Hellenistic Judaism followed the path in this direction consistently to the end; it gave up the Septuagint used by the Christians and replaced it with the literal translation of Aquila (see below, p. 371).

55. The Canon of the Old Testament in the Christian Church

Diestel, *Geschichte des AT in der christlichen Kirche*, 1869; Siegfried, *Die Aufgabe der Geschichte der alttestamentlichen Auslegung*, 1876; Gilbert, *Interpretation of the Bible, a short History*, 1907; Bonwetsch, 'Das AT in der Geschichte der Kirche', *Allgem. Evang.-Luth. Kirchenzeitung*, 56, 1923, No. 4f.; von Harnack, *Die Mission und Ausbreitung des Christentums in den ersten drei Jahrhunderten*,[4] 1924, I, 73 ff., 289 ff.; Koole, *De overname van het Oude Testament dor de Christelijke Kerk*, 1938; Philips, *The Old Testament in the World Church*, 1942; T. H. Robinson, 'The OT and the Modern World', OTMSt, 1951, 346 ff.; van Ruler, 'Die christliche Kirche und das AT' (*Beitr. zur ev. Theologie*, Vol. 23), 1955. On the history of criticism: Duff, *History of OT Criticism*, 1910: Gray, *OT Criticism, its Rise and Progress*, 1923; Kraeling, *The OT since the Reformation*, 1955; Kraus, *Geschichte der hist.-krit. Erforschung des AT von der Reformation bis zur Gegenwart*, 1956.

The history of the varying significance of the OT for the faith and the life of the Church can be understood only in connexion with the history of the Church, that is to say, of its beliefs and dogmas, and that is where it belongs. Similarly the history of the exegesis of the OT has its place in studies of the interpretation of the Bible. Since these comprehensive groups of questions cannot be treated in a mere paragraph, we will confine outselves to a short sketch of the attitude of the Christian Church to the Canon of the OT.

At the beginning Christianity regarded the OT from a point of view contrary to that of rabbinical Judaism. It read and made use of the holy scriptures as testimony to God's revelation, but it did not share the external and formal restrictions of the Jews' mechanical and literal theory of inspiration and of the Canon, as is shown by the free quotations (e.g. 1 Cor. 1: 19; Eph. 4: 8 and others). As it lacked knowledge of the original language, it followed the LXX and the Vulgate, which came into being under its influence, and in so doing it accepted a dynamic and functional conception of holy writ as the living revelation for salvation and edification. This led in individual churches to some increase in the holy scriptures. But the influence of the Jewish idea of the Canon can also be observed.

In theory the *Greek Church* made a distinction between the canonical writings and the 'reading-books' (Athanasius); some of the latter were even rejected as 'apocryphal'. But in the Church's practice little importance was attached to this distinction. The Synod of Jerusalem in 1672 recognized the Wisdom of Solomon, Ecclesiasticus, Tobit and Judith as canonical.

The practice of the *Western Church* followed the LXX. The *Church Fathers*, Irenaeus, Tertullian, Clement of Alexandria quote the apocryphal writings without distinguishing them from the canonical ones. Under the influence of Augustine, who rated the scriptures more highly as a means of edification than as evidence for the dogmas of the Church, the decrees of the Councils of Hippo in 393 and of Carthage in 397 raised the prestige of the Apocrypha; Jerome alone stood up for limiting canonicity to the *hebraica veritas* and he has again and again attracted supporters. The Council of Trent in 1546 for the first time sanctioned the canonical status of the books of the Vulgate and thereby the adhesion of the Roman Church to the Alexandrian collection of the LXX.

Unlike the Roman Catholic Church which gave equal rank to the holy scriptures *and* to tradition, the reformers provided the Protestant churches with a new and firm criterion, namely the principle that the scriptures stand higher than tradition of every kind. *Luther* judged the canonical value of the individual books of the Bible by the criterion: 'do they lead us to Christ?' Therefore with truly evangelical freedom he valued the apocryphal books differently according to their contents, judging the Wisdom of Solomon and Ecclesiasticus most favourably; but he did not refrain from giving a verdict on the canonical books as well. In his translation of the Bible of 1534 he calls the Apocrypha 'Books not on a level with Holy Writ and yet profitable and good to read'. He shows his inner freedom from the formal Hebrew Canon by altering the sequence of the books, introducing that of the Vulgate both for the OT and the NT. Luther's denominational writings contain no express declaration against the Apocrypha. It was the Old Protestant theology which first took over from the Jews their theory of the Canon and developed it further.

The early *Reformed* Church accepted the Apocrypha including 1 and 2 Esdras and 3 Maccabees, but valued them differently from the canonical books. The growing aversion to them which was expressed clearly at the Synods of Dordrecht in 1618 and of Westminster in 1643 led finally to the omission of the Apocrypha in the editions of the Bible of the Reformed Church.

THIRD PART

The Text of the Old Testament

56. The outward form in which the text was handed down (writing and books)

Buhl, *Kanon und Text des AT*, 1899, 197–209; Blau, *Studien zum althebräischen Buchwesen*, 1902; Schubart, *Das Buch bei den Griechen und Römern*, Hbb. d. Kgl. Museen Berlin,[2] 1921; Procksch, 'Der hebräische Schreiber und sein Buch, *Kuhnert-festschrift*, 1928, 1 ff.; H. H.Schaeder, *Esra der Schreiber*, 1930; Sethe, 'Der Ursprung des Alphabets', *Nachr. d. K. Ges. d. Wiss. zu Göttingen*, 1916, Vol. 2, 88 ff.; Grimme, 'Die altkanaanäische Buchstabenschrift zwischen 1500 und 1250 v. Chr', AfO 1935–36, 267 ff.; Galling, BRL, col. 460 ff.; H. Bauer, 'Der Ursprung des Alphabets', AO 1937; Böhl, 'Die Sichemplakette', ZDPV 1938, 1 ff.; 1939, 163; Torczyner, *The Lachish Letters*, 1938, Hempel, 'Die Ostraka von Lakis', ZAW 1938, 126 ff.; Elliger, 'Die Ostraka von Lachis', PJB 1938, 30 ff.; idem, 'Zu Text und Schrift der Ostraka von Lachis', ZDPV 1939, 89 ff.; Grimme, 'Altsinaitische Forschungen', *Studien zur Geschichte und Kultur des Altertums* XX, 3, 1937; also Dunand, RB 39, 1930, 321 ff.; Albright, BASOR 70, 1939, 11 ff.; 73, 16 ff.; 82, 1941, 18 ff.; 110, 1948, 6ff.; Jack, PEQ 70, 1938, 165 ff.; Vaccari, *Biblica* 20, 1939, 180 ff.; Thomas, JThSt 40, 1939, 1 ff.; de Vaux, RB 48, 1939, 180 ff.; Bea, 'Die Entstehung des Alphabets, eine kritische Übersicht', *Miscellanea Giovanni Mercati*, Vol. VI, 1946; Diringer, *The Alphabet, A key to the History of mankind*, London, 1948; Fr. Delitzsch, *Die Lese—und Schreibfehler im AT*, 1920; Geiger, *Urschrift und Übersetzungen der Bibel*,[2] 1928, ed. by Kahle; Ap–Thomas, *A Primer of Old Testament Text Criticism*, London; Joh. Fischer, *Das Alphabet der LXX–Vorlage im Pentateuch*, 1924; idem, 'In welcher Schrift lag das Buch Isaias den LXX vor?' BZAW 1903; Bonkamp, *Die Bibel im Lichte der Keilschriftforschung*, 1939, 6 ff.; Noth, *Die Welt des AT*,[2] 1953, 158 ff., 237 ff.; Paret, *Die Bibel: ihre Überlieferung in Druck und Schrift*,[2] 1950; Würthwein, *Der Text des AT*, 1952; Driver, *Semitic Writing*,[2] 1954. For the MSS. discovered in the Judean Desert cf. sections 91–94 and the bibliographies there.

We have no knowledge of the beginnings of Israelite literary activities, so that nothing definite can be said about the use of writing before the period of the entry into Canaan. At the most it might be concluded from the presumed connexion of Urim and Thummim, the tokens for the oracle, with the first and last letters of the alphabet that an alphabetic writing was known and used in the time of Moses; but this is only one of several possible explanations. After the conquest Israel came under the influence of the Canaanite civilization, including that of the writing in use there (see above pp. 14 f.). Two systems of writing were then being employed: (1) for official documents, such as laws and treaties, and in diplomatic intercourse the *Babylonian cuneiform script*, customary in all Near-eastern Asia, was current and remained in use right up to the last centuries B.C. (2) Beside this there existed an *alphabetic script*, the alphabetical elements of which appear to have been a cuneiform list of signs intended for school use from the fourteenth century, found in Ras Shamra.* It is a consonantal writing, the principle of which is borrowed from the Egyptian hieroglyphic script; at least this has perhaps been deduced from the 'pseudo-hieroglyphic' inscriptions of Byblos from the beginning of the second millennium and the 'Sinai inscriptions' of the fifteenth century B.C. The detailed development of this script has not yet been worked out. The following may be regarded as intermediate links: marks of writing on discoveries at Tell ed Duweir (the old Lachish) and on an ostracon of 'Ain Shems, a potsherd of Gezer, a plaque and a fragment from Shechem and a gold ring with illegible marks of writing from Megiddo, which belong in part to the pictorial type of the Sinaitic script and date from the last third of the second millennium, also the Old Phoenician inscription of king Jehimelech from Byblos, the inscription of the Ahiram sarcophagus and of Abibaal and Elibaal, the farmer's calendar of Gezer of the tenth century and the Siloam inscription of the eighth century. The type of Old-Canaanite and Old Hebrew script related to this Old Phoenician script is also found on about eighty Israelite ostraca of Samaria from the ninth century (receipts for deliveries of oil and wine to the royal court) on stone seals, of which the beautiful seal of the '*Shema‘*, of the servant of Jeroboam' from the eighth century is the most famous, on about 100 jar-handles of the eighth to seventh centuries and on the *ostraca* from Lachish of the sixth century. A similar type of script on the inscription of King Mesha of Moab, on the Kilamuwa writing of Zendjirli (ninth century) and on the Zakir writing of Hamath (eighth century) tells us that the Old Canaanite script was also in use with the Moabites and Aramaeans (for the script cf. also the books on biblical archaeology and Galling, BRL, col. 460 ff.).

It may be assumed that the books of the OT which came into being before the exile were written in this Old-Canaanite, Old Hebrew script. The Pentateuch seems in the post-exilic time also to have been written at first still in this script, for the Samaritan Pentateuch (see below) which the Samaritans adopted when they broke away from the Jews in the fourth or third century is written

* Gordon, The Ugaritic ABC. *Orientalia* 19 (1950), pp. 374 ff.

in the manner of the Old Hebrew (Samaritan) script. This type of script maintained itself until a late date, as we can see from its use in some of the fragments of the book of Leviticus and Numbers found in Qumran and in the manuscripts which give the divine name or the word 'God' in the Old Hebrew script.* This script was still employed archaistically on coins of the Maccabean period and of the revolt of Bar-Cochbah (132–135 A.D.).

After the exile under the influence of the Diaspora the *Aramaic cursive* script was adopted in Palestine for profane writings, for trade and diplomatic intercourse (jar handles of Jericho and Gezer); it was used also by Jews and non-Jews in Babylon and Egypt (Papyrus of Elephantine of the fourth century). Out of this there developed partly in association with the spoken dialects several separate alphabets. Amongst these the square script כְּתָב מְרֻבָּע, so called from its shape, acquired particular importance; owing to its coming from the area where Syrian was spoken it was called also כְּתָב אַשּׁוּרִי (Assyrian, better Syrian, script) and was utilized at first for ornamental purposes and for inscriptions on tombs and in synagogues. The oldest extant document in the square script is the inscription from 'Araq el-Emir in Transjordan from the third century B.C. and the one on the tomb of Jacob in the Kidron Valley near Jerusalem from the first century B.C. It is not possible to ascertain precisely when the square script came into use for the OT writings and when the holy scriptures were transcribed into the new script. According to the rabbinical tradition (bab. Sanhedrin 21b) Ezra is said to have introduced the square script for the sacred books, yet this remains uncertain, although Schaeder has recently again upheld this tradition. The hypothesis advanced by Fischer for the Torah and Isaiah is more likely, namely that the translators of the Septuagint found in their parent text a new Aramaic script approximating to the square script, so that the employment of this script for the OT books seems to have arisen gradually during the early Hellenistic period. In any case at the time of our Lord the Torah was in the square script, the only one in which the smallest letter of the alphabet is the iota or jot (Mt. 5: 18). The oldest manuscript of a biblical

---

* The palimpsest papyrus found in 1952 in the Wadi Murabba'at containing in Old Hebrew script a list of names and beneath it almost obliterated a letter, dates according to de Vaux and others, from the time before the exile.

text in the square script is the scroll of Isaiah found near the Dead Sea in the spring of 1947 (cf. sections 91 and 92). The first or second half of the second century B.C. is usually proposed as the time when it was written. The type of its script appears to approach the cursive style with ligatures, i.e. the joining of certain letters, whilst in later documents in the square script each letter stands by itself. As regards the general appearance of its script this scroll of Isaiah is nearest to the Nash papyrus, which has been known for some time and is called after its first purchaser. This payrus is now in the University Library of Cambridge; it is a liturgical text containing the decalogue in Exod. 20: 2–17 and the beginning of the Shᵉma' in Deut. 6: 4 with remarkable variants of the text and dates possibly from as early as the second century B.C.*

The Book. The oldest documents (laws, treaties, letters) were scratched on *tablets* of stone, clay, wood or metal with a hard, sharp stylus pen, a practice attested until late times in Exod. 31: 18, 34: 1; Is. 8: 1; 30: 8; Jer. 32: 10 f.; Hab. 2: 2; 1 Macc. 8: 22 and *passim*. The *ostraca* of Samaria and Lachish (see above) show that beside this the communications of everyday life in particular were written with ink on fired potsherds. But it is open to question whether the whole of Isaiah's prophetic compositions was written down on tablets, as Procksch has attempted to prove, since there is no mention of the production of complete books on tablets of wood and clay. At any rate it is certain in the case of the prophet Jeremiah that he used a *roll of a book* when writing down his oracles. In Jer. 36, the oldest passage to afford an insight into the nature of books in the OT, this roll of a book is called מְגִלַּת סֵפֶר, it is cut in pieces by the king and burned, so that we may conclude that it consisted of papyrus. This had no doubt been used as a writing material in Palestine for a long time. The import of papyrus from Egypt to Byblos (=the papyrus city) is attested as early as c. 1100 B.C. in the account of the travels of Wen-Amon. The pith of the stem of the papyrus plant was cut into thin strips, which were laid lengthwise and crosswise in layers, glued together, pressed, dried and then smoothed. By sticking several sheets together, the scroll needed for longer texts was produced. It was rolled on to *rods* in such a way that the

* cf. S. A. Cook, *Proceedings of the Society of Biblical Archaeology*, 25 (1903), pp. 34 ff.

beginning of the scroll was on the right and the end on the left.
A reed (עֵט) with ink (דְּיוֹ) was used for the writing which was
arranged in columns side by side (דֶּלֶת). Besides this, smoothed
skins of animals were employed, especially for written compositions which were handled frequently and had to last a long time.
Thus, for example, the first scroll of Isaiah from Qumran (1 Q Is[a])
was written on seventeen pieces of skin of different sizes, sewn
together at their edges, in one place glued together as well, and
when unrolled is 7.34 metres in length. Later the Torah-scrolls
were allowed to be written only on skins or parchment,* and even
the animals were prescribed whose hides were to be used for the
Torah. Up to the present day the scroll is the only form allowed
to be employed in the synagogue. The *book-form*, the 'Codex',
was introduced for private manuscripts in the second and third
centuries A.D. Most of the extant manuscripts of the OT are
codices of leather, parchment or papyrus.

There were different ways of dividing up the books of the Bible
on the scrolls; either a separate scroll was taken for each book
or several books were written on one scroll (for example the
twelve prophets or the Torah) so that in this way different books
could easily become merged into one (Is. 1–39 and Is. 40 ff.); and
there were scrolls containing the whole OT with correspondingly
small writing: Jerome complains in the preface to Ezek. 20 about
the difficulty of reading the small Hebrew letters, and this may
have caused many a mistake in copying.

In view of this physical process of handing down the actual
text it is easy to see that the form of the OT text was subjected
to many variations and mutilations resulting in *textual corruption*.
This necessitated the scientific work of *textual criticism* as the
fundamental requisite for *establishing the text*. With the pure consonantal text which especially in the early days made use very
sparingly of the consonants vaw, jod and aleph as makeshift vowel
signs there was already a risk of wrong readings. The *ostraca* of
Lachish from the beginning of the sixth century B.C. were certainly aware of the use of *matres lectionis*, but a systematic use of

---

* The use of leather for writing goes back a very long way in the East; in order
to make it durable, it was left unsplit and prepared with salt and flour. In the second
century B.C. in Pergamum in Asia Minor parchment (from Latin *pergamena*, hence
the name) came into use; the skin was split, treated with caustic lime and smoothed
to make it suitable for writing.

vowel points in the consonantal text was adopted only from the fifth century A.D. onwards. Added to this there was confusion between similar letters, which was very easily possible both in the Old Hebrew and in the square script. We must also take into consideration as a source of mistakes the transcription of the OT books from the Old Hebrew into the square script. It is comparatively easy to recognize the variants in the text when the OT books were handed on in the square text, in so far as they were scribal errors. Delitzsch in *Die Lese-und Schreibfehler im AT* drew up a classification and statistics of the possible mistakes. The following are particularly characteristic and frequent: (1) wrong division between words: e.g. Am. 6: 12 'will one plow there', בַּבְּקָרִים is read as בַּבָּקָר יָם 'will one plow the sea with oxen'; in Is. 2: 20 לַחְפֹּר פֵּרוֹת read with Theodotion לַחֲפַרְפָּרוֹת. (2) Owing to the carelessness of the copyists, the following are particularly frequent: (a) dittography, whereby a word or a letter is written twice over by mistake, e.g. in 1 Sam. 2: 3 cross out the one גְּבֹהָה with the LXX; in Ezek. 23: 14 כַּשְׂדִּיים read *Q°rê* כַּשְׂדִּים; (b) haplography; i.e. in the case of two words or syllables which are written alike or similarly, one of them is omitted by mistake; thus in 1 Sam. 4: 7 read with the LXX [אֲלֵיהֶם] בָּא אֱלֹהִים or in Gen. 12: 7 with the Samaritan Pent., LXX, Syr., Vulg. וַיִּצָּמֶר [לוֹ] לְזַרְעֶךָ. (3) Scribal errors due to influence of neighbouring words (a) Homoiarkton=assimilation at the beginning of a word, e.g. in Ezek. 45: 16 read כָּל־עַם הָאָרֶץ instead of כֹּל הָעָם הָאָרֶץ; (b) homoioteleuton=assimilation at the end of the word, e.g. in Num. 16: 1 read קֹרַח קֵרַד אִיקָם instead of וַיִּקַּח קֹרַח.

In addition to these unintentional errors, which led to textual variants, we must take note of conscious influences resulting from aesthetic or dogmatic considerations (cf. for this Geiger, *Urschrift und Übersetzungen der Bibel*). We may mention here particularly the variants connected with the reverence due to the divine name, the expression 'bless God' in Job 1: 11, 2: 5, 9 is a variant of 'renounce God' which was felt to be offensive. Dogmatic corrections such as these arose in the circles of the scribes (*sōp°rîm*) who were active mainly in the period after the reform of Ezra until NT times. The Talmud traces several variants back to the *sōp°rîm*: the *tiqqûnê sōp°rîm* (emendations of the scribes), e.g. 1 Sam. 3: 13 where אֱלֹהִים is altered to לָהֶם or Gen. 18: 22 where the sentence 'Yahweh remained standing before Abraham' was changed to 'Abraham stood yet before Yahweh', because 'to stand before' was understood to mean 'to serve' and thus the original wording gave offence. In later times eighteen of these 'emendations' were counted; yet originally there will no doubt have been a good many more. The 'omissions of the scribes' (*'ittûrê sōpᵉrîm*) are also traced back to these circles (*Nedarim* 37b); and so is the origin of the well-known *Qᵉrê and kᵉṯîb* (see below).

57. The Massoretic Text

(The abbreviations of the *Biblia Hebraica*² of Rud. Kittel (BH) are added in square brackets.)

See the literature for section 56. Lagarde, *Materialien zur Kritik und Geschichte de Pentateuchs* I, 1867, p. XII, 230 f.; ZAW 1884, 302 f.; 1889, 303; 1892, 309; Ginsburg, *Introduction to the Massoretico-Critical Edition of the Hebrew Bible*, 1897, Albrecht, 'Die sog. Sonderbarkeiten des masoretischen Textes'. ZAW 1921, 160 ff.; Ehrentreu, *Untersuchungen über die Massora, ihre geschichtliche Entwicklung und ihren Geist*, 1925; Kahle, 'Masoreten des Ostens', BWAT 1913; idem, Untersuchungen zur Geschichte des Pentateuchtextes, ThStKr 1915, 399 ff.; idem, sections 6–9 in *Bauer-Leander, Histor. Grammatik der hebräischen Sprache des AT*, 1922, 71 ff.; idem, 'Die Punktation der Masoreten', *Martifestschrift*, 1925, 167 ff.; idem, 'Masoreten des Westens' I, BWAT 1927, II, 1930; idem, 'Die hebräischen Bibelhandschriften aus Babylonien', ZAW 1928, 113 ff.; idem, 'Der Alttestamentliche Bibeltext', ThR 1933, 227 ff.; Joh. Fischer, 'Die hebräischen Bibelzitate des Scholastikers Odo', *Biblica*, 1934, 50 ff. and BZAW 66 (1936) 198 ff.; Lipschütz, *Ben Ascher–Ben Naphthali. Der Bibeltext der tiberischen Masoreten*, Diss. Bonn, 1935; Edelmann, 'Zur Geschichte der Masora', *Kahle-Festschrift*, 1935, 15 ff.; Kahle, *Vorwort zur Biblia Hebraica²*, ed. Rud. Kittel, 1937, VI ff.; Wutz, 'Beiträge zur Technik alttestamentlicher Textkritik', *Bibl. Zeitschr.*, 1934, 16 ff.; Nyberg, 'Das textkritische Problem des AT am Hoseabuche demonstriert', ZAW 1934, 241 ff.; Volz, Ein Arbeitsplan für die Textkritik des AT, ZAW 1936, 10 ff.; Noth, Die Welt des AT',² 1953, 239 ff.; Wheeler Robinson, *The Bible in its Ancient and English Versions*, 1941; Kahle, *The Cairo Geniza* (Schweich Lectures), 1947, 36 ff., ²1959; B. J. Roberts, *The OT Text and Versions*, 1951; Dhorme, 'Le texte hébreu de l'Ancien Testament', RHPhR 35 (1955), 129 ff.; Jeremias, 'Ein Anhalt für die Datierung der masoretischen Redaktion?' ZAW 67 (1955), 129 ff.

With the canonization of the OT is associated the theory that the sacred texts are inviolable. Amongst the *sōpᵉrîm* there was set on foot that labour devoted to establishing and safeguarding the OT text. The schools of the rabbis and later those of the Massoretes continued and completed the work of the scribes by definitely fixing a form of the text which is called the Massoretic text (𝓜).

מסרה, מסרת=transmission is used with reference only to the transmission of the form of the text to distinguish it from the tradition of the contents of the OT (*halakāh*); the pronunciation of the word is uncertain (either מְסֹרָה, or מַסֹּרָה). The Jewish scholars who occupied themselves with the transmission of the text were called Massoretes.

Their task was concerned with the consonantal text and its pronunciation. It consisted in determining in detail what was written in the manuscripts and in supervising the work on them by means of a large number of statistical data, such as counting the verses, words and letters, determining the middle of a book, counting how often individual words and forms occur, noting the peculiarities of the style, etc. In earlier times these were handed on orally, later they were written down in small notes in the side-margins (*massorah parva*) and in longer notes on the upper and lower margins of the manuscripts (*massorah magna*). These notes are called *massorah marginalis* to distinguish them from the concluding notes (*massorah finalis*) which brought together the Massoretic material in alphabetical order at the end of the books or of the OT. In the third edition of the BH the Massorah of Aaron ben Moshe ben Asher (see below) has been made comparatively easily accessible with the help of indices of the Massoretic technical terms; the *massorah magna* planned as an appendix to BH³ has not yet been published.

Some of the Massoretic notes which are important in the work of textual criticism may be mentioned here: (1) *kᵉtîb* [K] and *Qᵉrê* [Q]. The inviolability of the text demanded that in the case of obvious textual errors or of expressions giving offence (e.g. 1 Sam. 5: 6, 12; 2 Kgs. 18: 27) the amended text was written in the margin as *Qᵉrê* (=to be read) without altering the written text (*kᵉtîb*); in the case of the divine name Yahweh its pronunciation as *ᵃdônāy* was not noted (*qᵉrê perpetuum*) because this alteration had long become customary. The kᵉtîb יְהֹוָח, given by BH³ on the basis of old manuscripts, is either to be read as שְׁמָא (Aramaic=the name [in Hebrew=הַשֵּׁם]), one of the later substitutes for the tetragrammaton, or its remarkable pointing is to be derived from *ᵃdônāy* in order to indicate that the divine name cannot be expressed. Something similar must no doubt be understood in the Qumran manuscripts when the name of Yahweh is sometimes replaced by points or by writing the tetragrammaton or 'ēl, the designation of God, in Old Hebrew letters. The same explanation is given by Jerome in the *Prologus Galeatus* (see section 62) for writing the divine name in Hebrew script in the Greek versions, for which the papyrus Fouad 266 should be compared.* These corrections began already early and gradually grew to 1,300 in number. (2) Related to qᵉrê and kᵉtîb we find *Sebir* =it is to be expected; this is used where a reading is declared plainly to be incorrect and the one to be expected is placed beside it. (3) The *Puncta extraordinaria*, dots placed above individual letters (e.g. Gen. 16: 5) or words (e.g. Gen. 33: 44) to indicate that the text was faulty; the same function seems to be performed by the *nun inversum*, an inverted *nun*, which is perhaps also intended to show that the verse thus bracketed is not in its right place (e.g. Num. 10: 35 f.). (4) It is not clear in every case what is the purpose of the *literae suspensae*, letters placed above the line, and the *literae majusculae* and *minusculae*, enlarged and reduced letters; in Jgs. 18: 30 the *nun* placed above the line in מנשה is a sign for crossing out, משה is to be read instead of 'Manasseh'.

It was first through the investigations of Kahle that a clearer light has been thrown on the *history of the transmission of the text*. The consonantal text had consolidated different forms of the text at a comparatively early date and in fundamental matters it shows a definite consistency. For the fragments of OT texts from the second century A.D. which were found during the excavations in Wadi Muraba'at in the Judean desert and which agree with the MT, as well as the rabbinical literature and the versions of the second and third centuries of Aquila, Theodotion and Symmachus (see section 59) all presuppose a relatively uniform Hebrew text of the OT. The fragments of the Septuagint discovered in 1917 and published in 1936 as the *Rylands Greek Papyrus* 458 (see lit. for section 59) suggested the probability that already in the second century B.C. there was a Hebrew text constant in essentials. This fact and the remarkable agreement of the manusrcipts of the consonantal text down to numerous superficial matters had been explained up till then by assuming that in the first half of the fifth century, one manuscript of the OT had been accepted as a model and had in this way become the archetype for all subsequent copies. A whole series of variants in the consonantal

---

* cf. Wadell, JThSt 45 (1944), 158 ff. and Würthwein, *Der Text des AT*, 1952, 138 f.

text were indeed known, but they were explained as scribal errors
which in course of time had found their way into the originally
uniform text. This thesis of a uniform standard form of the text at
the beginning of the development was shaken by Kahle in certain
points, in others at least much modified. He showed that at the
beginning there was diversity in the transmission of the text and
that the trend of the Massorah was 'to advance from the multiplicity of what existed originally to an authoritative unity'. An
insight into the characteristics of these different pre-Massoretic
popular texts is afforded for instance by the first manuscript of
Isaiah (1 Q Is a) from Qumran (see sections 91 and 92). As it has a
pure consonantal text without any vowel pointing, the use of
matres lectionis to indicate the vowels in some cases, which is
strikingly frequent but not carried through consistently, must be
understood as a help to make a distinction from the Aramaic
pronunciation. But it was not yet the established practice to write
out the manuscript systematically in full; this was left rather to the
discretion of the scribe, as appears from the fact that in the second
half beginning with chapter 34 presumably a second scribe dealt
with it more consistently than was done in the first part. Thus a
fixed consonantal text does not yet seem to have existed. As
regards the type of the script, the first Isaianic scroll (1 Q Is a)
proves to be older, as it does not appear to know some of the
final letters, unlike the Nash Papyrus and other manuscripts from
the Qumran.

There are about 5,000 textual variations, of which according to
Kahle 3,500 are orthographical. We find cases of some of the other
1,500, both in the Nash Papyrus and in the scroll of Isaiah, which
give a text nearer to the parent text of the Septuagint than to that
of the MT. Yet we must not overlook the fact that in only a
third of the readings differing from the MT are the variants
superior to it. Nevertheless a comparison with the later additions
to the first scroll of Isaiah and with the text of the second manuscript of Isaiah (1 Q Is b), which stand nearer to the MT, teaches
us that much trouble was taken with the text not only in connexion with the internal reform of Judaism resulting from the
catastrophe of the year A.D. 70, but also considerably earlier.

It was at latest towards the end of the first century A.D. that the
main substance of the consonantal text seems to have become

fixed.* But this is only the beginning of the further history of the work on the text and of the harmonization of its different transmissions. After the final destruction of Jerusalem, the scholars continued their labours in the towns of Galilee; but that lasted only a short time, since the revolt of Bar-Cochbah in A.D. 132–5 and the spread of Christianity led to the emigration of many Jewish scholars to Babylon. This meant at the same time a decadence in the Palestinian Massoretic tradition which lasted during the period of the Byzantine rule. On the other hand the work of the Babylonian Massoretes (מָדִנְחָאֵי=Eastern [Or] flourished from the third to the 9th centuries. These were established mainly in two centres, in Nehardea and Sura (Sor)=Soraei; the school in Nehardea came to an end when that city was destroyed in the third century, the one in Sura continued up to the tenth century. It was not until the period of the tolerant Arabic rule that Massoretic studies began to develop again in Palestine also. The centre of the Massoretes of the West (מַעֲרְבָּאֵי=Western [Occ] was Tiberias. They flourished mainly in the eighth and ninth centuries. The work of the Palestinian Massoretes became authoritative for the text of our Bible.

At first the Massorah was transmitted by word of mouth. Moreover we do not possess old manuscripts from the early days when the text was first handed down, because copies no longer in use were kept in the Genizah (storeroom) of the synagogue and buried ceremonially from time to time, in order to guard against any profanation of the sacred scriptures. Thus only a little information is available about the variations between the schools in the transmission of the consonantal text. However, the contents of the Genizah of the synagogue of Old Cairo have been preserved because it was walled up and forgotten; when it was discovered they were given away or sold; to these happy circumstances we owe it that we have recently been able to distinguish more clearly the work of the Eastern and Western Massoretes. The keen detective ability of Kahle succeeded in discovering Hebrew manuscripts of the Bible including those from the Cairo synagogue, which had been scattered throughout the most varied

* The fact that the English Scholastic Odo in the twelfth century appears to have known a consonantal text diverging from the MT with pre-Massoretic pointing (Var °) can hardly invalidate the dating given above; for it is no doubt a case of a side shoot independent of the proper textual transmission.

places in Europe and America, and in winning from them an understanding of the mediaeval history of the text. In the course of his work he showed that the Babylonian Massoretes sometimes had another text and other forms, so that a Hebrew grammar of the Eastern Massoretes would look different from ours based on the Western transmission.

The efforts of the different Massoretic schools to fix the text and its pronunciation, had led since the sixth century to the custom of regulating and perpetuating the pronunciation by *pointing* and *accenting*. Here the divergencies between East and West can be clearly recognized. *The Massoretes of the East* had at first a simple supra-linear system of vocalization (the vowel signs are placed above the letters) with only six vowel signs; it had therefore only a limited means of expression. In the ninth century it was replaced by a more complicated system. The Massorah, which developed the Talmudic traditions, gradually came under Western influences and there emerged finally a mixed type which obliterated the characteristics of the Eastern Massorah. This was the reason why, although the Eastern Massorah was not unknown, it was not possible to interpret it fully; in the mixed types pointing and Massorah no longer agreed. When the Massoretic tradition came to an end in the twelfth century the Eastern School of Massoretes had long since ceased to exist. It was Kahle who was first able to create a clearer picture by collecting and interpreting more than 100 fragments of biblical manuscripts from Babylon which he has tabulated in the BH pp. XXX ff. (Here E denotes manuscripts with simple earlier pointing and K those with complicated later vocalization; a small *a* following indicates the Pentateuch, *b* the Prophets and *c* the Writings.) An example of the mixed type and of the way the Eastern Massorah was influenced from the West is seen in one of the oldest dated biblical manuscripts, still extant, namely the 'S. Petersburg Codex of the Prophets' of the year 916 edited by Strack in 1876 [Var$^\text{P}$]; it has Babylonian vowel markings but a Palestinian Massorah; even in its pointing an approximation to the Western transmission can be observed.

Amongst *the Massoretes of the West* too, Kahle has identified two different systems of pointing, an older supralinear one dating no doubt from the fifth century A.D. called 'the pointing of the land of Israel' and related to the Samaritan system. It is not only the older form of the Palestinian transmission, but the historical root of the Babylonian pointing as well. This older pointing attempts to retain the customary pronunciation without troubling about grammatical consistency. After the decline of the old Palestinian Massorah the influence of the sect of Qaraites, who in their reaction against the Talmud relied on the Bible alone, brought about in Palestine a revival of Massoretic studies, resulting in a fresh thoroughgoing regulation of the pronunciation on which the present form of the Hebrew grammar rests. This was done with the help of the 'Tiberian' pointing, still in use in our texts. In this system everything was thought out exhaustively down to the minutest detail and sometimes even the customary pronunciation was corrected according to its rules. In consequence of the concentrated labour and the gradually dominating authority of the Massoretes of Tiberias, this Tiberian vocalization and the Massorah belonging to it gradually displaced the Babylonian one and at last became supreme.

But the Massoretes of the West did not agree amongst themselves. The two most important branches of the transmission named after the most famous Massoretes, that of *Ben Asher* and that of *Ben Naphtali*, had long been known (see the Massoretic lists of the divergences between the texts of Ben Asher and Ben Naphtali in the text edited by Baer and Delitzsch). We have some accurate information about two members of the renowned Massoretic family of Ben Asher. Moshe ben Asher copied a codex of the Prophets in 895 and supplied it with pointing and a Massorah; this is in the Qaraite synagogue in Cairo [C]. His son Aaron ben Moshe ben Asher provided the pointing and a Massorah for a complete codex of the Bible written by another at the beginning of the tenth century; this model codex is preserved in the synagogue of the Sephardim at Aleppo. In face of the doubts held hitherto as to their authenticity Kahle has proved conclusively that the codices in Cairo and Aleppo, which had long been known, represent the original text of Ben Asher; he has also identified this text in other manuscripts of the tenth to twelfth centuries (see below pp. 364). Kahle has drawn on other manuscripts too to ascertain the type of the text of Ben Naphtali which is to be found, e.g. in the well-known codex of Reuchlin of the year 1105 at Karlsruhe. He has thus made possible a more exact comparison between the two chief forms of the Western transmission of the text. This shows that beside divergencies in pronunciation and accentuation Ben Naphtali goes further than Ben Asher in fixing the niceties of the pronunciation and especially in the placing of the *meteg*.

From the tenth century onwards the history of the text is characterized by the competition between the two types of text. The point to be noticed is that the Ben Asher type penetrates to an increasing extent into the Ben Naphtali text and thus robs it of its special character. No doubt owing to the authority of the philosopher Maimonides (*ob.* 1204) the decision was taken in favour of the Ben Asher text. But on the other hand this text, influenced by that of Ben Naphtali, fixed the pronunciation more and more exactly by extending its system of accentuation and its use of the *meteg*. The foreign influences found their way into the Massorah also; a compromise was reached, so that here too the pointing and the Massorah often no longer agree. It was not till the fourteenth century that the process of mutual assimilation was accomplished. Thus at the end of this long development there stands that uniform (mixed) text which is handed down as the *textus receptus* in most of the manuscripts of the Bible.

The *textus receptus* of the late Middle Ages is found in the 'Rabbinic Bibles' which contain in addition to the Hebrew text the Aramaic version (*Targum*) and the commentaries of authoritative rabbis (Rashi, Ibn Ezra, Kimchi and others). The first Rabbinic Bible was produced by Felix Pratensis and published by Daniel Bomberg in Venice in 1516–17. It served as the basis of the second Rabbinic Bible, the work of Jacob Ben Chayim in 1524–25, likewise printed by Bomberg in Venice (Bombergiana [*B*]). This Bible became almost at once of greater importance than its predecessor because it provided a revised text based on the comparison of several manuscripts or editions and on his own Massoretic studies and a Massorah in which these results are put together. For a long time it was considered the best transmission of the text and for this reason remained authoritative right into the twentieth century.

The judgment of the Christian Church on the text. The Roman Catholic Church at the Council of Trent in 1546 declared the text of the Vulgate to be authoritative and fixed it officially in 1590–98.

The Protestant Church considered as fundamental the original Hebrew text taken over from the Jews. As regards the pointing, it had at first shared the view of Elias Levita, who thought it had come into being in the Middle Ages. But soon the dogmatic concern of the Old-Protestant theology led to the pointing being declared to be of the same age as the consonantal text and, like it, to have been inspired. This produced lively discussion amongst scholars in which the Roman Catholic, Rich. Simon, submitted a coherent critical history of the text (*Histoire critique du VT*, 1678). In the end the authority of historical truth prevailed and textual criticism was generally recognized as right and necessary.

The most important editions. In 1477 the first editions of individual books began to appear, e.g. the Psalter in Bologna in 1477–78; in 1488 the whole Hebrew Bible, e.g. in 1488 in Soncino, in 1491–93 in Naples, in 1494 in Brescia; this last was the one used by Luther. Beside Bomberg's editions of 1524–5 already mentioned the Amsterdam edition of Joh. Leusden of 1661–67 acquired a special reputation.

For textual criticism the edition of Kennicott, *Vetus Testamentum Hebraicum cum variis lectionibus*, Oxford, 1776, ff. [Var^Ken] is of importance owing to its large collection of variants. An independent critical edition is that of Baer-Delitzsch, 1869, ff. [Var^B] which made use of several older manuscripts and information from the Massoretic tradition, but did not recognize the interweaving of the different Massoretic traditions and in consequence it incidentally reconstructed a text such as had never existed in reality. Two modern editions have taken the text of Jacob ben Chayim as their authority: The edition of Ginsburg in 1908 ff. (1926) [Var^G] which is distributed from England and offers still more variants to its text, and the *Biblia Hebraica*, the first and second editions by Rud. Kittel. This contains in its apparatus variants from De Rossi, *Variae lectiones V.T.* 1784–88 [MS.] and suggests amendments from the versions and the conjectures of modern scholars. Kittel struck out a new line in the third edition of his *Biblia Hebraica*: he presents the text of Ben Asher, and as the Codex of Aleppo was inaccessible, he used an exact copy of it, the Leningrad Codex B 19^a [L] of the year 1008; in the apparatus are entered the variants of the manuscripts and versions and the conjectures of the collaborators. Thus this edition offers a text

600 years older than that of previous editions; it has, moreover, the advantage that it prints also the homogeneous Massorah of Aaron ben Moshe belonging to the text, in the place of that collection of Massoretic elements of various origins often diverging from the text contained in the Ben Chayim text.

The division of the Hebrew Text. The division of the text into sections according to the sense (paragraphs) attested in the Mishnah (*c.* A.D. 200), was already in use at an early date. In the Qumran manuscript of Isaiah (1 Q Is a) in the case of long sections the remainder of the whole line is left blank; in the smaller ones a gap is left in the line. The former are called 'open' sections (=p^ctûhā), the latter 'closed' sections (=s^ctûmā). Later on (thus also in BH) instead of this, only a small gap was left in which was placed the first letter of the appropriate word (ם for 'open', ס for 'closed' sections). The division into verses is also known in the Talmud, although there is no uniform arrangement; in Babylon 5,888 verses were counted in the whole OT, in Palestine 15,842. For reading the law aloud in the synagogue for liturgical purposes it was divided in Palestine into 154 *sedarim* (*sĕder*= arrangement) and read through in a three-yearly rotation; in Babylon, where the whole law was read in one year, it was divided into fifty-four sections. The division into chapters was taken over in the fourteenth century from the Vulgate and was printed for the first time in the Bomberg Bibles. In the sixteenth century the numbering of the verses also penetrated into the Hebrew Bible.

58. The Samaritan Pentateuch

Gesenius, *De Pentateucho Samaritani origine, indole et auctoritate commentatio philologico critica*, 1815; Von Gall, *Der hebräische Pentateuch der Samaritaner*, 1914–1918; Kahle, 'Aus der Geschichte der ältesten hebräischen Bibelhandschrift', *Baudissinfestschrift*, 1918, 247ff.; Dugmore, 'Two Samaritan MSS. in the library of Queens' College, Cambridge', JThSt 1935, 131 ff.; Goldberg, 'Das samaritanische Pentateuchtargum, eine Untersuchung, seine handschriftlichen Quellen', *Bonner Orientalische Studien*, 1935; E. Robertson, *Catalogue of the Samaritan Manuscripts in the John Rylands Library*, Manchester 1938.

A special place in the transmission of the text is occupied by the Samaritan Pentateuch, namely the Torah in the Hebrew language, but in the Samaritan script [ɯ] which was taken over by the religious community of the Samaritans when they broke away from the Jews. The form of its text is several centuries older than the Massoretic text and has a history of its own, as the 6,000 variants from the MT show. The divergences are mainly ortho-graphical and grammatical (e.g. fuller use of vowel letters) and enable us to realize that the transcription was based on a populariz-ing pre-Massoretic text for the people and this has been confirmed by the fragments of the Pentateuch discovered in the Judean desert. In respect of the fuller use of vowel letters this text is later than the MT. But there are also material differences such as the abolition of the plural form of *'lōhîm*, the insertion after Exod. 20: 17 of the command to build a sanctuary on Mount Gerizim, and the new meaning given to the choice of Shechem for the sanctuary to be seen in several passages of Deuteronomy. On the other hand in Deut. 27: 4 it is not certain which of the designations (MT=Ebal; Sam=Gerizim) is the original one, since verses 12 f. and 11: 29 suggest a subsequent alteration in the Jewish text. Dogmatic alterations such as these are no doubt late, but in the case of other divergences, as e.g. in the system of calculation in Gen. 5 and 11, it cannot be decided whether the Samaritan text or the MT is to be preferred. Above all in those cases where the Samaritan text diverges and is supported by the LXX and the Greek text underlying some NT passages (Acts 7: 4, 32; Heb. 9: 3 f. ?) (about 1900) it is to be valued as important and early evidence of the text. The Samaritan Pentateuch is written in letters akin to the Old Hebrew script in style and it has a developed vocalization and a division of its own into para-graphs. There are in existence numerous manuscripts by which to ascertain its text, as well as another Greek translation (the 'Samaritikon'),* and Aramaic (the Samaritan Targum [ɯ]) and Arabic versions. The edition of the text by von Gall unfortunately drew on only a few late mediaeval manuscripts. E. Robertson has made fresh manuscripts of the book accessible and has published the most important ones. Some of the manuscripts in the posses-sion of the Samaritan community of Nablus (Shechem) are older than the earliest Massoretic ones, but are strictly guarded from publication by their owners.

* The discovery in Qumran of a fragment of Exodus, giving the Samaritan text in Hebrew script (cf. Skehan, JBL 74 (1955), 182 ff. has again raised the question of the purpose of such texts in an acute form.

59. The Greek versions

Swete, *An Introduction to the OT in Greek*, 1900; Rahlfs, 'Verzeichnis der griechischen Handschriften des AT', *Nachrichten von der Königl. Gesellschaft d. Wiss. zu Göttingen*, phil.-hist. Kl. extra vol. 1914; idem, 'Paul de Lagardes wissenschaftliches Lebenswerk, Die Septuagintaarbeit seit 1866'. *Mitt. d. Sept.-Unternehmens d. Ges. d. Wiss. zu Göttingen*, 1928, 66 ff.; Herrmann und Baumgärtel, 'Beiträge zur Entstehungsgeschichte der Septuaginta', BWAT 1923; C. Schmidt, 'Die neuesten Bibelfunde in Ägypten', ZNW 1931, 285 ff.; Bertram, 'Zur Septuagintaforschung', ThR 1931 283 ff.; 1933, 173 ff.; 1938, 69 ff.; 133 ff., with bibliographies; Pretzl, 'Die Aussprache des Hebräischen nach der zweiten Kolumne der Hexapla des Origenes', *Bibl. Zeitschr.*, 1932, 4 ff.; Wutz, Die Transscriptionen von der Septuaginta bis zu Hieronymus', BWAT 1933; Kenyon, *The Chester Beatty Biblical Papyri I–VII*, 1933–37; Sperber, 'The problem of the Septuagint recensions', JBL 1935, 73 ff.; Procksch, 'Tetraplarische Studien', ZAW 1935, 240 ff.; 1936, 61 ff.; Sperber, 'Probleme einer Edition der Septuaginta', *Kahlefestschrift*, 1935, 39 ff.; Procksch, 'Die Stuttgarter Septuaginta, *Lutbertum* 1935, 237 ff.; C. H. Roberts, *Two biblical papyri in the John Rylands Library, Manchester*, 1936; Opitz and H. H. Schaeder, 'Zum Septuagintapapyrus Rylands Greek 458', ZNW 1936, 115 ff.; Hempel, 'Zum griechischen Deuteronomiumtext des II. Jahrhunderts a. C.', ZAW 1937, 115 ff.; Rehm, 'Textkritische Untersuchungen zu den Parallelstellen der Samuel-Königsbücher und der Chronik', *Atl. Abh.* 1937; Allgeier, 'Die Chester Beatty-Papyri zum Pentateuch. Untersuchungen zur älteren Überlieferungsgeschichte der Septuaginta', *Studien zur Geschichte und Kultur des Altertums*, XXI, 2, 1938; Stegmüller, *Berliner Septuagintafragmente* (Berliner Klassikertexte aus dem staatl. Museum zu Berlin, Vol. VIII), 1939; Gerleman, *Studies in the Septuagint I, Book of Job*, 1946; II. *Chronicles*, 1946; Kahle, 'Die Septuaginta', *Festschrift für Eissfeldt*, 1947, 161 ff.; idem, *The Cairo Geniza (Schweich Lectures)*, 1947, 132 ff.; Mercati, *Il problema della Colonna II dell, Esapla*, 1947; Seeligmann, *The Septuagint version of Isaiah*. Diss. Leiden, 1948; Ziegler, *Der Bibeltext im Danielkommentar des Hippolyt von Rom* (Nachr. d. Akad. d. Wiss. in Göttingen. 1. Phil. Hist. Kl. No. 8 (1952); Wevers, 'Septuaginta-Forschungen', ThR 22 (1954), 85–138, 171–190; Gooding, *Recensions of the Septuagint Pentateuch*, 1955.

As the Massoretic text does not represent the original form of the OT text, we must draw upon other sources in addition to the Hebrew variants in order to ascertain what it was; for this purpose the first to be considered are the versions. Amongst these the most important is

The Septuagint

The story of its origin is told in the Letter of Aristeas, written no doubt in the second half of the second century B.C. (cf. section 77): we are told that Ptolemy II Philadelphus (285–247) was induced by his librarian to have a translation of the Jewish Law prepared for his library. He applied to the high priest Eleazer in Jerusalem who placed at his disposal for this work six men from each tribe, seventy-two in all. It is said that in seventy-two days they translated one section each from the scroll of the Torah procured from Jerusalem, and afterwards decided on the wording together. So the version was called Septuagint (the translation of the Seventy). This story was accepted also by the teachers in the Christian Church and elaborated, to the effect that the seventy-two had translated not only the Torah, but the whole OT, and indeed independently of each other, in complete seclusion; this was intended to prove the inspiration (thus Philo already) and reliability of the Christians' favourite version.

The whole is a legend to emphasize the importance of the LXX. Kahle supposes it to be a piece of propaganda on behalf of a translation of the Torah introduced at the time when the Letter of Aristeas was written and that it replaced as a standard text several different translations of the Torah, which had been current for some time. Kahle allows for the possibility that the first Greek translations of the Torah were made already in the fourth century. We might say as a matter of history that the Greek translation of the Torah originated in the middle of the third century and in Alexandria, the home of the largest community of the Dispersion in the area of Greek speech. There is a element of historical truth too in the features of the legend which tells that several hands shared the translation (though the number 72 bears on the face of it the stamp of invention), that the Torah was the first to be translated and that it enjoyed official authority; all this may be read between the lines of the legend. But there was a different motive behind it. In reality no doubt the LXX arose out of the need of the Greek-speaking Jewry of the Diaspora who wished to understand the OT in their own language. Presumably there were already in existence transliterations of the Hebrew OT into the Greek alphabet somewhat analogous to the Samaritan Pentateuch. This would be a first step for the Greek Jews, who could no longer read the Hebrew script, to make the sacred scripture intelligible when the original Hebrew text was read aloud in the synagogue. But it is unlikely that the LXX used such transcriptions almost exclusively (Wutz), although it employs transliteration occasionally, especially in the case of names. We may

N

conclude that the Septuagint had a complicated and long pre-history from a number of manuscript fragments from Cave 4 in Qumran,* which provide evidence for previous stages of the Hebrew text underlying the Septuagint; the same conclusion may be drawn from the fact that for the first time two Septuagint manuscripts have been found in pre-Christian Palestine. But before these finds have all been published and examined, these matters must be treated with reserve. After the Torah, the most important book, translations of the other OT books probably came into existence gradually and in fact by different hands. Jesus ben Sirach, the grandson, in 117 B.C. already knew Greek trans-lations of the law, the prophets and the other books. Indeed the fact that the translation of the LXX extended over a century (the translation of the latest OT writings were not made until about 100 years after that of the Torah) makes it impossible to avoid the assumption of several translators and translations. The same conclusion follows from the different treatment of the individual books. The Torah was translated with care, most of the books literally, Isaiah and the Psalms were less well done; Daniel is reproduced in a very free paraphrase. It is not possible to prove with certainty that several translators worked on individual books (Herrmann und Baumgärtel). Consequently the LXX as a whole is a collection of translations of the OT scriptures, which was produced, not by Palestinian Jews, but by those of the Diaspora and which does not repudiate the spirit of Hellenistic Judaism. It is not possible to give an answer in general terms to the question whether the LXX worked on the basis of Aramaic versions, and if so, to what extent; this might be indicated by a certain parallelism between Aramaic traditions and the LXX (cf. Rost, 'Die Vorstufen von Kirche und Synagoge in AT', BWAT 1938, pp. 95 f.). The translators did not refrain from interpreting the text frequently to suit themselves and to alter it where it disturbed their religious scruples. Thus for example, the juxta-position of God and man in the sentences in Jgs. 9: 9 'Should I leave my fatness wherewith by me they honour God and man?' seemed shocking to the translator and was changed in the LXX

---

* cf. Provisionally F. M. Cross, jr., 'A new Qumran Biblical fragment related to the original Hebrew underlying the Septuagint', BASOR 132 (1953) pp. 15 ff.; and idem, A report on the Biblical fragments of cave four of Wadi Qumran, BASOR 141 (1956), pp. 9 ff.

Codex B to ἐν ᾗ δοξάσουσι τον θεὸν ἄνδρες. The arrangement too of the individual books in the LXX according to the pattern: historical, poetical and prophetic books, differs from the Hebrew Canon and has been taken over into the Vulgate and Luther's Bible. This shows in spite of some variations in detail an independent and outspoken attitude of mind which is typical also of the 'theology' of the LXX and occasionally makes its value as a translation appear questionable. Hatch and Redpath's *Concordance to the Septuagint*, 2 vols., 1897, and *Supplement*, 1906, is an indispensable aid when studying the characteristics of the LXX translation.

The special value of the LXX for the missionary task of the Jewish Diaspora lay in the fact that it made the OT accessible to the non-Jew also; at the same time it acquired an unexpected importance, unwelcome to the Jews, by becoming the sacred scriptures of the Christians. In their discussions with Judaism the Christians appealed to the LXX; this and the fact observed by the Jews that the LXX often did not correspond accurately with the Hebrew text induced them finally to give it up and to replace it with other translations. Fragments of a Greek translation of the Minor Prophets were found by Bedouins in 1952 in the Judean desert. Until these finds have been examined further, it must remain an open question whether these fragments can be regarded as a rabbinical recension and a preliminary stage of the later versions of Aquila, Symmachus and Theodotion (see below) (thus Barthélemy, RB 60 [1953], pp. 18 ff.; cf. for this Kahle, ThLZ 79 [1954], col. 81 ff.).

The Version of Aquila

The *version of Aquila* [A,], a Greek converted to Judaism, satisfied by its extreme literalness the need of the Greek-speaking Jews for a new Greek version of their Bible and their concern for its wording. It was produced about A.D. 130 and soon came into favour with the Jews. The principle of translating the individual words with a mechanical accuracy led to a text which sounded completely unlike Greek; thus, e.g. the Hebrew אֶת is always reproduced by σύν without regard to the meaning, לֵאמֹר by τῷ λεγειν, לְמִן by εἰς ἀπό. Only a few pieces of Aquila's version have been preserved in fragments of Origen's Hexapla and in palimpsests from the Genizah of the synagogue of Old Cairo of the sixth century.*

The Version of Theodotion

Not much later, at about the middle of the second century A.D., a contemporary of Aquila, Theodotion, a proselyte of Asia Minor, prepared a second Greek version with the object of producing one in better Greek [Θ]. This work does not represent a completely new translation, but a correction of a Greek one according to the original Hebrew text. Rahlfs assumes that Theodotion used the Septuagint as the basis of his revision; but as readings quoted in Theodotion are found already in writings which are older than it is, the Greek version which he revised must be distinguished from the Septuagint (Kenyon, Kahle). This version was esteemed more highly by the Christians than by the Jews and in the case of the book of Daniel actually supplanted the old LXX version probably under the influence of Origen. Only fragments of this version are extant.

The Version of Symmachus

Mention must be made of a third Greek version from the beginning of the third century by Symmachus [Σ], who according to the early Christian tradition was a Jew converted to Ebionite Christianity, and produced a new translation of his own in good Greek. This one too is known only from a few fragments of the Hexapla. We learn from the Hexapla, the great work on the text by Origen, that beside these there were other Greek versions of which very little is known, namely the 'Quinta' [E'], the Sexta and the Septima, presumably versions deviating from the LXX and in use amongst the Jews already in pre-Christian times (Kahle).

The Work of Origen

Thus several Greek versions existed side by side, diverging frequently from the Hebrew text and from each other. The transmission of the LXX too displayed considerable variations, as

* Burkitt, *Fragments of the Books of Kings according to the translation of Aquila*, 1897; Taylor, *Hebrew-Greek Cairo Genizah palimpsests from the Taylor-Schechter Collections*, 1901; Rüger, 'Vier-Aquila–Glossen in einem hebräischen Proverbien-Fragment aus der Kairo–Geniza', ZNW 1959, 275 ff.

shown by quotations in the NT and the Apostolic Fathers, and it can be said frankly that it had run wild. Origen, the great theologian of antiquity, attempted to remedy this undesirable state of affairs by setting out clearly to start with, as Procksch has plausibly suggested, the relationship of the Greek translations to each other in a synopsis containing side by side the versions of Aquila, Symmachus, Theodotion and the LXX and usually called the *Tetrapla* (=the four-fold [version]). Later he added the Hebrew text as well for the purpose of comparison and produced during the years 240–245 in Caesarea the *Hexapla* (=the sixfold [version]) a work of great importance for the history of the text. In six parallel columns Origen placed side by side: (1) the Hebrew text in the square script, (2) the same text transcribed into the Greek script, (3) the version of Aquila, (4) that of Symmachus, (5) the Septuagint, (6) the version of Theodotion. For his work on the fifth column (the LXX) Origen employed the 'signs of Aristarchus' in use at that time; thus for example, the passages absent from the MT he marked at the beginning with an obelus (—, ÷, ÷) and at the end with a metabolos (:, /*, ɤ); in front of the passages missing in the LXX, which he mainly supplied from Theodotion, he placed an asterisk (*) and brought them to an end with a metabolus. Occasionally he altered the text of the Septuagint too, without noting it. In any case the fifth column of the Hexapla does not represent its original text, but a recension of it [G^h]. The original manuscripts of Origen's gigantic productions, which were seldom copied owing to their size, were kept in Caesarea and were probably lost when that city was conquered by the Arabs. On the other hand the fifth column was no doubt copied frequently; for since the beginning of the fourth century it was held in high esteem and circulated widely in Palestine through Eusebius and Pamphilus. The *Codex Colberto-Sarravianus* [G^G or G] from the fourth–fifth century, the parts of which are in Leyden, Paris and Leningrad, give the Hexaplaric text of Gen. 31–Jgs. 21 with the Aristarchean signs, though there are some gaps. Hexaplaric readings are recorded in the marginal notes of the *Codex Marchalianus* from the sixth century [G^Q] (in the Vatican Library), which includes all the prophetic writings, and of the *Codex Coislinianus* from the seventh century [G^M] which contains Gen. 1 to 1 Kgs. 8 with gaps. In several cursive manuscripts too some of the Hexaplaric text or of the Hexaplaric marginal readings have been preserved. The extant fragments were collected by Montfaucon in *Hexaplorum quae supersunt*, 1713, and by Field, *Hexaplorum quae supersunt*, 1875, and are easily accessible there. The Septuagint column was translated with slavish exactness into Syriac by Paul of Tella in 616–17 [S^h]; a manuscript about 200 years later was published by Ceriani in *Codex Syrohexaplaris Ambrosianus*, 1874. The only remnants of a transmission of the Hexapla in manuscript are the 'Mercati fragments' in a palimpsest discovered by Mercati in Milan at the end of the last century; this contains portions of the Psalms in the last five columns of the Hexapla in a cursive manuscript of the tenth century. A sample of these texts which have not yet been completely published was presented by Klostermann in ZAW 1896, pp. 334 ff. New fragments of the Syro-Hexapla were discovered by Gottstein amongst London manuscripts (*Biblica* 36 [1955], pp. 162 ff.).

But Origen's recension of the Septuagint was not able to drive out other forms of its text. In Syria and Asia Minor as far as Constantinople another recension was held in esteem, that of the presbyter, *Lucian* of Antioch (*ob.* 312). He seems to have made use of the Hexaplaric one; his emendations are mainly grammatical and stylistic. The few fragments of the OT in the Gothic translation of Ulfila preserved in the famous *Codex argenteus* are based on the Lucianic recension which was authoritative in Constantinople. In Egypt a third one, that of Hesychius (*ob.* 311) was in common use, as we learn from a remark of Jerome in his preface to the books of Chronicles. Nothing more is known of it. On the basis of quotations from the Church Fathers, collected by monks of the Greek Church since the sixth century in the 'catenae' (continuous 'chain'-like biblical texts supplied with the most important patristic comments) Rahlfs constructed an independent catena-recension of the LXX in addition to those already mentioned. The different recensions of the text have influenced and penetrated each other, which makes it difficult to determine the separate groups of texts. It has also frustrated Lagarde's attempt to publish the Lucianic text from Genesis to Ruth (*Librorum Veteris Testamenti canonicorum pars prior graece* (1883) [G^L]).

Finds of fresh papyri (called after their English owner Chester

Beatty papyri) have brought to light several fragments of the old LXX from the second to fourth century A.D. [G Beatty]. These have made it to some extent possible to get behind the various last-named recensions of the Septuagint text and closer to its original forms; they have also enhanced the value of the LXX for textual criticism. The *Rylands Greek papyrus* 458 (see above, p. 359) dating from the second century B.C. and containing some Septuagint fragments from Deuteronomy, and the *Fouad Papyrus* 266 with parts of the Greek translation of Deut. 31: 28–32: 7 from the same period, in the possession of the Société Royale de Papyrologie du Caire, have in fact brought within the bounds of possibility the thesis championed by Lagarde and his pupils that an original Septuagint was the foundation of all the other Greek text forms disseminated by the Christian Church; but recently Kahle has disputed this. He has put forward a fundamentally different opinion about the history of the formation of the Septuagint and about the method of investigating it. He starts from a new interpretation of the Letter of Aristeas which, he thinks, reveals very early traces reaching back into the third century of a multiplicity of different Greek translations. By the side of these a standard version was made in Alexandria towards the end of the second century for the Torah, but this was not accepted everywhere and was later given up by the Jews in their controversies with the Christians (see above). In his view it was in the Christian Church that a Greek version of the whole OT gradually developed in the second century A.D. out of different translations into a standard text to which the name Septuagint and the esteem it enjoyed was transferred. According to Kahle the task of science is to discover and collect the traces of older forms of the Greek translation, and not to reconstruct an imaginary original text of the Septuagint.

We possess a large number of complete *manuscripts of the Septuagint* (*c.* 600), of which some are older than those of the MT. They are divided into Uncials (written in Greek capital letters) from the fourth–tenth centuries and the cursives (in ordinary Greek script) from the ninth–sixteenth centuries. The most important Uncials, containing the OT and NT are: (1) Codex Vaticanus [G^B] from the fourth century in the Vatican library in Rome. Its text does not belong to the Hexaplaric recension, but in some passages has been influenced by it. Rahlfs conjectures that Codex B points to Egypt and must be classed as a Hesychian recension. (2) Codex Sinaiticus (G Aleph or Gℵ] also abbreviated to S), also from the fourth century, formerly in S. Petersburg, now in the British Museum in London; the first forty-three sheets to be discovered are in the possession of the University library in Leipzig. It derives its name from the fact that it was found by Tischendorf in 1844–59 in the monastery of St. Catherine on Mount Sinai. Perhaps it was written by a non-Greek, as it contains many mistakes in orthography and was subsequently corrected by several hands. Only a part of the OT is preserved in this Codex which probably originated in Egypt or Palestinian Caesarea. Its importance is not much less than that of Codex B. (3) The Codex Alexandrinus [GA] from the fifth century is also preserved in London. The manuscript is almost complete and has an independent type of text revised according to the Hexapla. Some scholars prefer it to Codex B, especially in the case of the prophetic books. For the other Codices occasionally quoted in BH, cf. Würthwein, *Der Text des AT*, 1952, pp. 58 f.; and Noth, *Die Welt des AT* (1953), pp. 258 ff. The rest of the Septuagint manuscripts (2,000 in number, including portions of translations and fragments) are quoted in Rahlfs, *Verzeichnis der griechischen Handschriften des AT*.

The *most important printed texts* of the *LXX*: The Complutensian Polyglot, 1514–17 (see below) and the Aldine, Venice, 1518, depend on cursive manuscripts. The Sistine, Rome, 1590 (see below) made use of Codex B and cursive manuscripts. On the latter was based the convenient edition of L. van Ess, 1824, and also the largest collection of LXX variants, that of *Holmes and Parsons, Vetus Testamentum Graecum cum variis lectionibus*, Oxford, 1798–1827, which contains variants from 300 manuscripts and draws on daughter-versions (see below) and quotations from the Church Fathers. Hence it still remains important today for Septuagintal studies. Amongst the scientific and critical editions of the Septuagint we must mention: (1) The English three-volume edition of *Swete*, 1887–1907 which presents the text of Codex B, supplying its lacunae mainly from Codex A. Its *apparatus criticus* contains variants from the most important uncial manuscripts. (2) The Cambridge edition of *Brooke, McLean, Thackeray* and *Manson*, based on the same principle, but offering a much larger *apparatus*, with all the variants of the uncials and a large part of those of the cursives and of the daughter versions; so far Genesis —Kings appeared in 1906 ff. and Esther, Judith and Tobit in 1940.

(3) In Germany under the auspices of the *Gesellschaft der Wissenschaften in Göttingen* Rahlfs has begun work on a large-scale edition of the Septuagint, estimated at sixteen volumes; *Vetus Testamentum Graecum. Auctoritate Societatis Litterarum Gottingensis ed.*; the following have appeared so far: Vol. X, *Psalmi cum Odis*, 1931 (Rahlfs), Vol. IX. 1 *Maccabaeorum liber* 1, 1936 (Kappler), Vol. XIV *Isaias*, 1939, Vol. XIII *Duodecim prophetae*, 1943, Vol. XVI I *Ezechiel*, 1952, II *Susanna, Daniel, Bel et Draco*, 1954; XV Jeremiah, Baruch, Threni, Epistola Jeremiae, 1957 (Ziegler), have been issued. These, unlike the English editions, are based on a study of all the texts in a new approach aiming at the reconstruction of the oldest attainable text of the Septuagint, that is to say, of a critical text. The *apparatus* gives the readings of the separate groups of texts from manuscripts and quotations of the Church Fathers.

(4) Shortly before his death Rahlfs published in 1935 a cheap pocket-edition, the *Stuttgarter Septuagint*; it was prepared on the same principles, used by Lagarde (see above), as the great Göttingen undertaking; but it relies in the main on the most important codices B, S and A and only occasionally makes use of other material.

The daughter translations of the Septuagint

In order to establish the text of the Septuagint those Christian translations also are of value which became necessary when Christianity spread to countries where Greek was not spoken. Amongst these the most important are:

I. The *Vetus Latina*

Rönsch, *Itala und Vulgata*, 1869; Burkitt, *The Old Latin and the Itala*, 1896; Denk, *Der Name Sabatier und sein wissenschaftliches Programm*, 1914; Stummer, 'Die lateinische Bibel von Hieronymus und das Judentum', *Theologie und Glaube*, 1927, 184 ff.; idem, *Einführung in die lateinische Bibel*, 1928; Allgeier, *Die altlateinischen Psalterien*, 1928; idem, 'Lehrreiche Fehler in den altlateinischen Psalterien', *Bibl. Zeitschr.*, 1929, 271 ff.; Lagrange, 'De quelques opinions sur l'ancien psautier latin', *Revue Biblique*, 1932, 161 ff.; Schildenberger, 'Arbeit an der lateinischen Bibel', *Benediktin. Monatsschrift*, 1935, Vol. 9–10, 1 ff.; H. Schneider, *Die altlateinischen biblischen Cantica*, *Texte und Arbeiten*, publ. by the Abbey of Beuron, Vol. 29–30, 1938; Dold, *Neue St. Galler vorhieronymianische Propheten-Fragmente*, op. cit., Vol. 31, 1938; Schildenberger, *Die altlateinischen Texte des Proverbienbuches untersucht und textgeschichtlich eingegliedert:*

Erster Teil: Die alte afrikanische Textgestalt. Texte und Arbeiten, publ. by the Abbey of Beuron. 1. Part 32–33, 1941; Weber, 'Les anciennes versions latines du deuxième livre des Paralipomènes' (*Collectanea Biblica Latina,* Vol. VIII, 1945); idem, 'Le Psautier Romain et les autres anciens Psautiers Latins' (*Collectanea Biblica Latina,* Vol. X), 1953: Kusch, 'Die Beuroner Vetus Latina und ihre Bedeutung für die Altertumswissenschaft', *Forschung u. Fortschritte* 29 (1955), 46–57; see literature for section 62.

The original home of the *Vetus Latina,* called also *Itala* from a note in Augustine, *De doctrina christiana* II, 22, was in North Africa (Carthage), where Latin first took the place of Greek as the language of the Church. Here there came into existence presumably already in the second half of the second century the first Latin translations of the LXX which go back to its text as it existed before the recension of the third and fourth centuries and therefore provide valuable textual evidence; there are quotations from them in Tertullian (*nat. c.* 160) and Cyprian (*ob.* 258). The later African translations show affinities with the recension of Lucian. In Europe too (Southern Gaul in the second century, Rome in the third) there appeared Latin translations which influenced each other and led to the text running wild, as in the case of the Greek LXX. In order to remedy this disorder Bishop Damasus in 383 commissioned the monk Jerome in Rome to revise the Latin text of the Bible. He began with a revision of the Psalter on the basis of the *Vetus Latina* (the *Psalterium Romanum,* so called from its use in the liturgy in the city of Rome. See De Bruyne, *Revue Bénédictine* 42, 1930, 101 ff. for objections to Jerome's authorship); next he prepared a second edition based on the Hexapla (*Psalterium Gallicanum,* so called because it was first adopted in Gaul) and he then revised the rest of the OT books; but apart from the Psalter and a recension of Job only passages from Proverbs, the Song of Songs and Ecclesiastes are still extant; the remaining books disappeared before their publication. The fragments and quotations of the Old Latin translations preserved in early ecclesiastical authors were collected by Sabatier, *Bibliorum sacrorum latinae versiones antiquae seu vetus italica* 1739,[2] 1751 [L]. Of the manuscripts named in Summer, *Einführung in die lateinische Bibel,* pp. 33 ff., the following used in BH[3] may be mentioned: Gothic L[D]=The Old Latin fragments of the Prophets and the Gospels from the fifth century from Constance, published by Dold in 1923; Gothic L[L]=Codex Lugdunensis (sixth century) now in Lyons, containing Numbers, Deuteronomy, Joshua and fragments of the rest of the Pentateuch and Judges and published 1881–1900 by Robert; Gothic L^h=the palimpsest manuscript of Würzburg (sixth century) published in 1871 by Ranke with fragments from the Pentateuch and the prophets; Gothic L^Vind=the Vienna palimpsest with fragments from Genesis and Samuel, published in 1885 by Belsheim. A new edition planned for 1915 ff. by Denk ('the new Sabatier') and based on his own comprehensive collections of Old Latin texts was prevented by the first World War. The collected material and the work on it is now in the hands of the Abbey of Beuron and is being published by Father Bonifatius Fischer as *Vetus Latina, die Reste der altlateinischen Bibel nach Petrus Sabatier neu gesammelt und herausgegeben von der Erzabtei Beuron*, 1949, ff.

II. *The Coptic Versions*

Leipoldt, *Geschichte der Koptischen Litteratur, Die Literaturen des Ostens* VII, 2, 1907, 131 ff.; Hallock, 'The Coptic OT', AJSL 1933, 325 ff.

From about the year 300 onwards translations of the LXX appeared in different vernacular dialects (Coptic) amongst the Christians in Egypt [K] and after the Coptic Church had separated from that of the Empire they became the official text of the Bible. Thus beside others there was in Upper Egypt the Sahidic version of about 300 [Sah], in Lower Egypt the later (seventh century?) Bohairic version. They agree with the Hesychian recension of the Septuagint, but occasionally show the influence of other text forms.

III. *The Ethiopic, Armenian and Arabic Versions*

Littmann, *Geschichte der äthiopischen Litteratur, Die Litteraturen des Ostens*, VII, 2, 1907, 223 ff.; Harden, *An Introduction to Ethiopic Christian Literature*, 1926, 37 ff.; Guidi, *Storia della letteratura etiopica*, 1932, 13 ff.

The Ethiopic version [Ä] came into existence in the fourth century soon after the introduction of Christianity by Syrian missionaries; for this reason the influence on it of the Lucianic recension has been conjectured. But it is difficult to form an opinion since the oldest manuscripts from the thirteenth century show a considerably damaged or revised text.

An *Armenian version* [Arm] begun in the course of the fifth century was recognized by the Armenian Church which was breaking away from the Church of the Empire at that time; it agrees with the hexaplaric recension of the Septuagint; perhaps it was preceded by an Armenian Bible from the beginning of the fifth century which was translated from the Syrian Peshitta (see section 61).

Besides these the *Arabic versions* [A] must be mentioned; they became necessary when the Jews and the Christians in the countries conquered by Islam adopted Arabic as the language of daily intercourse. Saadia ha-Gaon (tenth century) made a translation from the Hebrew of which parts are still extant. Several translations of the Psalms and the translations of the prophetic and poetical books of the OT printed in the Paris and London Polyglots (see section 63) were prepared from the Greek by different hands.

60. The Targumim

Lagarde, *Prophetae chaldaice*, 1872; idem, Hagiographa chaldaice, 1873,]TL[; Berliner, *Targum Onkelos*, 1884; Merx, *Chrestomathia Targumica*, 1888]TM]; Brederek, 'Bemerkungen über die Art der Übersetzungen im Targum Onkelos', ThStKr 1901, 351 ff.; Ginsburger, *Pseudo-Jonathan*, 1903, [TJ]; idem, *Das Fragmententargum*, 1899, [TJ II]; Kahle, 'Masoreten des Westens II', BWAT 1930, 1*–13*, 1–65; Marmorstein, 'Einige vorläufige Bemerkungen zu den neuentdeckten Fragmenten des jerusalemischen (palästinischen) Targums', ZAW 1931, 231 ff.; Louise P. Smith, 'The prophetic Targum as guide and defence for the higher critic', JBL 1933, 121 ff.; Churgin, 'The Targum and the Septuagint', AJSL 1934, 41 ff.; Wohl, *Das Palästinensische Pentateuchtargum. Untersuchungen zu den Geniza–Fragmenten und deren Verhältnis zu den übrigen Targumen und der Peschitta* (Diss. phil. Bonn) 1935; Stummer, Beiträge zu dem Problem 'Hieronymus und die Targumim', *Biblica*, 1936, 174 ff.; Churgin, *The Targum to the Hagiographa*, New York, 1945; Kahle, *The Cairo Geniza* (Schweich Lectures), 1947, 117 ff.

When in the last centuries B.C. Hebrew had been replaced by Aramaic as the vernacular, the need was felt in the synagogue for an Aramaic translation to be added when the Hebrew text was read aloud at the divine service. This translation (=*targûm*) which had to be supplied orally by the interpreter (*mᵉturgᵉmān* =dragoman) was in consequence naturally a more or less free paraphrase of an edifying kind.

Besides this, already in pre-Christian times written Targumim were composed. In view of the importance of the Torah, it can be taken for granted that to begin with one was produced for the Pentateuch. Fragments of a Targum of the Pentateuch from Palestine [TP] found in the Genizah of the Old Cairo synagogue was published by Kahle (*Die Masoreten des Westens* II, 1930, pp. 1–13, 1*-65*, plates 1–6). The age of the manuscripts suggests that it was still in use from the seventh–ninth centuries. Gradually Aramaic versions of nearly all the OT books came into existence, in the case of some, even several; but none exist for Daniel and Ezra—Nehemiah. The most important Targumim are (1) the Targum to the Pentateuch of Onqelos [T^O] who, according to rabbinic tradition, is said to have composed it in the second century, but it must be of later date. Subsequently it was declared to be the official Targum of the Pentateuch and after the addition of a Massorah it was treated as a sacred text. (2) The Targum Jonathan to the Prophets which, like the Targum Onqelos, originated in Palestine. Presumably several hands had a share in these, so that the names they bear are not correct. Perhaps the name Onqelos goes back to Aquila, and that of Jonathan, as a Hebrew translation of the name Theodotion, to a mistaken tradition about those translators of the OT into Greek. Both Targumim were revised in the fifth century in Babylon. Kahle takes the view that they originated in Babylon and ousted older Palestinian Targumim as official translations. (3) A second complete Targum of the Pentateuch is known; this is the Jerusalem Targum I, also called 'Pseudo-Jonathan' [T^J] owing to a wrong interpretation of the abbreviation יﬞﬧ. It is based on a mixture of the old Palestinian traditional Targum with that of Onqelos. The Jerusalem Targum II [T^J II] is extant merely in fragments and is therefore also known as the Fragment-Targum. It contains sermon-like expansions of an older Palestinian Targum of the Pentateuch, which was driven out later by the Targum of Onqelos. There are besides fragments of Targumim, containing only isolated verses or parts of verses. The most important editions are mentioned in the bibliography. Owing to their origin the Targumim are inclined in a greater or lesser degree to depart from the text, paraphrasing and explaining it; thus they can be used for text criticism only with great circumspection.

61. The Peshitta

Heller, *Untersuchungen über die Peschîtâ zur gesamten hebräischen Bibel*, I, 1911; Hänel, 'Die aussermasoretischen Übereinstimmungen zwischen der Septuaginta und der Peschitta in der Genesis', BZAW 1911; Haefeli, 'Die Peschitta des AT mit Rücksicht auf ihre textkritische Bearbeitung und Herausgabe', Atl. Abh. 1927; Baumstark, 'Pesitta und palästinensisches Targum', *Bibl. Zeitschr.*, 1931, 257 ff.; Peters, *Peschittha und Targumim des Pentateuch*, Diss. Münster, 1933; idem, 'Pešitta-Psalter und Psalmentargum', *Muséon* 52, 1939, 275 ff.; Kahle, *The Cairo Geniza* (Schweich Lectures), 1947, 179 ff.

Already very soon after the Syrian Church of Edessa was established in about 150, it possessed a Syriac Bible comprising the Old and New Testaments, which was probably the Peshitta. The name Peshitta, according to the Jacobite pronunciation peshitto (=the simple [translation]), perhaps in contrast to the Syrian Hexapla (the sixfold) (see above), arose comparatively late. Its origin is still unknown. It may be, but cannot be definitely proved, that some of the translation of the OT reaches back to pre-Christian times, since the Syrian Christian Church had many Jewish members and they might have already translated their sacred scriptures into Syriac; moreover parts of the translation agree closely with the Jewish exegesis. Kahle conjectures that in the middle of the first century A.D. the OT or portions of it were translated into Syriac for the Jewish royal family of Adiabene. The relationship of the Aramaic Peshitta of the East to the Aramaic Targumim of the West still needs to be elucidated. For the Pentateuch, the Psalms and other books Peters and Baumstark have made a connexion between the Peshitta and the Targum appear likely. The Peshitta is hardly a homogeneous piece of translation; sometimes it is quite literal, at others rather free. Only Job is translated from the original Hebrew; Isaiah, the Minor Prophets and the Psalms are strongly influenced by the LXX. Probably it was also revised subsequently in accordance with the Septuagint. Since Chronicles as well as the Apocrypha were lacking originally, being considered uncanonical, these books were added as a supplement in the third century from the Jewish Targum. The oldest extant manuscript of the Peshitta dates from as far back as the year 464; more recent manuscripts have been preserved from the period after the schism in the Church in the fifth century. We have the Syriac text transmitted in an Eastern (Nestorian) recension and in three Western ones (Jacobite, Melchite and Maronite). The most important manuscript of the Peshitta is the Codex Ambrosianus dating from the sixth or seventh century, presenting the Western Syriac transmission of the text (published in a photolithographic edition by Ceriani in 1874

[S^A]). The same text is contained in the Paris Polyglot and the London one which is based on it [S^W] and also in the edition of the British Bible Society by Lee of 1821 ff. [S^L]; the Bible of Urmia of 1852 [S^U] has the Eastern Syriac text. A scientific and critical edition of the Peshitta is still awaited.

62. The Vulgate

Berger, *Histoire de la Vulgata*, 1893; Aman, *Die Vulgata Sixtina von 1590, 1912*; Stummer, 'Die neue römische Ausgabe der Vulgata zur Genesis', ZAW 1927, 149 ff.; idem, 'Die lateinische Bibel vor Hieronymus und das Judentum', *Theologie und Glaube*, 1927, 184 ff.; idem, *Einführung in die lateinische Bibel*, 1928; idem, 'Einige Beobachtungen über die Arbeitsweise des Hieronymus bei der Übersetzung des AT aus des *Hebraica Veritas*', *Biblica* 1929, 3 ff.; idem, 'Hauptprobleme der Erforschung der alttestamentlichen Vulgata', BZAW 66, 1936, 233 ff.; 'De Bruyne, 'La critique de la Vulgate', *Revue Bénédictine*, 1924, 137 ff.; idem, 'La reconstruction du psautier latin', op. cit., 1929, 297 ff.; idem, Le problème du psautier romain, op. cit., 1930, 101 ff.; Allgeier, 'Die mittelalterliche Überlieferung des *Psalterium juxta Hebraeos* von Hieronymus und semitische Kenntnisse im Abendland' (*Oriens Christianus*) 1929–30, 200 ff.; idem, *Die Psalmen der Vulgata*, 1940 (see literature for section 59, I); Ziegler, 'Die jüngeren griechischen Übersetzungen als Vorlagen der Vulgata in den Prophetischen Schriften' (*Beilage zum Personal- und Vorlesungsverzeichnis der staatlichen Akademie zu Braunsberg*) 1943–44; Ziegler, 'Das neue lateinische Psalterium', ZAW 63 (1951), 1 ff.; Weber, 'Le Psautier Romain et les autres anciens Psautiers Latins', *Collectanea Biblica Latina*, Vol. X (1953); Marks, *Der textkritische Wert des Psalterium Hieronymi iuxta Hebraeos*, 1956.

When Jerome after his move to Bethlehem in 386 had learned the Hebrew language and completed the work of revising the Old Latin version mentioned on p. 378, he passed on to translating the whole OT from the original text into Latin. He began in 390 with the books Samuel–Kings and appended to them the *Prologus galeatus*. In 405 the task was finished.

Jerome expressed his views about his own labours in the prefaces to the individual books; his object was to produce a careful and faithful translation in good Latin whilst treating the *Vetus Latina* with as much consideration as possible. In addition to the Old Latin version, he drew for his work on the Greek translations of the Septuagint, of Aquila, Symmachus and Theodotion (see p. 372) as well as on rabbinic learning.

At first his translation met with opposition; but from the seventh century onwards it was recognized for use in the Church, with the exception of the Psalms, for which the *Psalterium Gallicanum* continued to be employed. The growing esteem in which

Jerome's version was held is seen in the fact that in the Middle Ages it could be designated as the Vulgate [V] (the one generally known). The text of the Vulgate soon became corrupt through copyists and had to be revised several times. The Council of Trent (1546) decided that this text should be the standard authority for the Roman Catholic Church, and in consequence in 1590 under Pope Sixtus V a new edition (Sixtina) was printed; at the instigation of the Jesuits it was withdrawn as unsatisfactory by Pope Clement VIII and replaced by a fresh edition (Clementina) which, after a threefold revision (1592 to 1599) has since then been accepted as the undisputed Bible of the Roman Church and is current in several editions. The most convenient pocket edition is that of Hetzenauer, Biblia sacra vulgatae editionis,[2] 1922;* the most complete collection of variants is in Vercellone, *Variae lectiones Vulgatae Latinae bibliorum editionis*, 2 Vols., 1861–64. Since 1907 the Benedictine Order has been entrusted with the preparation of a critical edition of the Vulgate. The papal Vulgate-commission was handed over in 1934 to the papal Abbey of S. Jerome in Rome and here the work has been proceeding since then under the title: *Biblia Sacra iuxta latinum Vulgatam versionem ad codicum fidem iussu Pii PP. XI cura et studio †Monachorum Sancti Benedicti Commissionis Pontificiae a Pio PP. X institutae sodalium praesido Aidano Gasquet S.R.E. Cardinale edita.* In this edition there have appeared Genesis 1926, Exodus and Leviticus 1929, Numbers and Deuteronomy 1930, Joshua, Judges and Ruth 1939, Samuel 1944 and Kings 1945, Chronicles 1948, Ezra, Tobit, Judith 1950, Esther, Job 1951, Psalms 1953. As compared with the Clementina, its purpose is to draw upon a much larger number of manuscripts, in fact about 8,000, in order to establish the text of Jerome. A fresh translation of the Psalms and Odes (=canticles which are given as an appendix to the Psalter in manuscripts of the Septuagint, cf. section 70) was introduced in 1955 into the Roman Catholic Church.

---

* Out of print at present. The *Biblia sacra iuxta Vulgatam Clementinam,* 1956 (a new edition published by the professors of the theological faculty in Paris and the Seminary Sancti Sulpitii) is on sale.

† From Vol. III. *Monarchorum Abbatiae Pontificiae S. Hieronymi in Urbe Ordinis Sancti Benedicti edita.*

63. The Polyglot Bibles

Kahle, The Hebrew text of the Complutensian Polyglot, Homenaja a Millas-Villacrosa I (1954) 743 ff.

Many of the texts and versions of the OT discussed in sections 57–62 have been assembled and printed together with various texts of the NT in the great polyglot productions (Bibles in several languages) of the sixteenth and seventeenth centuries. The most famous and important are the following:

(1) *The Complutensian Polyglot*. It was produced at the expense and under the direction of Cardinal Ximenes in Alcala in Spain (the Roman Complutum) in the years 1513–17 and published in 1520 in six folio volumes. It includes the OT in the Massoretic text revised independently on the basis of Ben-Asher and other old manuscripts, the Targum Onqelos of the Pentateuch, the Septuagint based on manuscripts of the Lucianic recension, the Vulgate and in addition Latin translations of the Targum and the Septuagint; a special volume contains: *Introductiones Artis grammaticae hebraicae*, a *Vocabularium chaldaicum atque hebraicum V.Ti* and *Interpretationes omnium hebr. chald. graec. nominum utriusque Ti* from the hand of Alphonse of Zamora, one of the most active scholars co-operating in the Polyglot.

(2) *The Antwerp Polyglot*. This was produced in Antwerp in 1569–72 at the expense of King Philip II and hence is also called *Biblia Regia*. Like the Complutensian Polyglot, on which it largely depends, it presents in eight folio volumes the Hebrew text, the Vulgate, the Septuagint with a Latin translation and, what the Complutensian Polyglot does not possess, Targumim to nearly all the OT books; besides this there are dictionaries, grammars and archaeological treatises.

(3) *The Paris Polyglot*, 1629–45 in ten volumes is externally the most splendid of the polyglots, but has not so great a scientific importance as the others. It offers first a copy of the Antwerp Polyglot, then the Samaritan Pentateuch with the Samaritan Targum, the Peshitta and an Arabic translation of the OT.

(4) The *London Polyglot* was prepared in the Protestant Church and illustrates the superiority of Protestant learning in the seventeenth century over that of Roman Catholicism, above all by the way it draws on a larger number of Eastern versions and by the

greater care and trustworthiness bestowed on the text. From the scientific point of view it is the most valuable and best known of the polyglot productions. It was completed in six volumes in 1657 by Walton with the collaboration of almost all the English scholars of the time. It contains the Massoretic text, the Samaritan Pentateuch with its Targum, the Septuagint with variants from Codex A, fragments of the Vetus Latina, the Vulgate, the Peshitta, an Arabic version, the Targumim to which the Targum Pseudo-Jonathan and the Fragment-Targum Jerusalem of the Pentateuch have been added, besides an Ethiopic version of the Psalter and of the Song of Songs and a Persian one of the Pentateuch. A critical introduction by Walton and a collection of variants were added. In 1669 there was appended the *Lexicon heptaglotton* by the Arabic scholar Castell, a dictionary of the Hebrew, Chaldaic (Aramaic), Samaritan, Ethiopic, Arabic and Persian languages.

The polyglots are a testimony to the industry of men of learning and command our respect. In some cases they still offer today the best edition of the texts. In many matters they have been superseded by the recent textual research and replaced by critical editions of the text and of the versions.

FOURTH PART

The Apocrypha and Pseudepigrapha of the Old Testament*

Texts

O. F. Fritzsche, *Libri Apocryphi Veteris Testamenti graece*, 1871 (Kritischer Text der griechischen Apokryphen); Swete, *The Old Testament in Greek according to the Septuagint*, 1899 (a reproduction of Codex B supplemented by A where necessary); Rahlfs, *Septuaginta*, 1935; cf. section 59.

Versions and Commentaries

Fritzsche and Grimm, *Kurzgefasstes exegetisches Handbuch zu den Apokryphen des AT* 1851–1860; Zöckler, *Die Apokryphen des AT nebst einem Anhang über die Pseudepigraphenliteratur*, 1891; De Faye, *Les apocalypses juives*, 1892; Kautzsch, *Die Apokryphen und Pseudepigraphen des AT in Verbindung mit anderen übersetzt und herausgegeben*, 1900, reprinted 1921; Charles, *The Apocrypha and Pseudepigrapha of the Old Testament*, 1913; Burkitt, *Jewish and Christian Apocalypses*, 1914; Riessler, *Altjüdisches Schrifttum ausserhalb der Bibel, übersetzt und erläutert*, 1928; *The Apocrypha (King James Version)* with an Introduction by R. H. Pfeiffer, 1954.

Introduction and History of the Literature

Hughes, *The Ethics of Jewish Apocryphal Literature*, 1909; Schürer, *Geschichte des jüdischen Volkes im Zeitalter Jesu Christi*, III⁴ 1909, 188–716; Bousset, *Die Religion des Judentums im späthellenistischen Zeitalter*, 3rd edition by Gressmann, 1926, 6–52; Stählin, *Die Hellenistisch-Jüdische Literatur* (an off-print from Christ, *Griechische Literaturgeschichte* II, 1,⁶ 1921, 535–658); Oesterley, *The Books of the Apocrypha, their Origin, Teaching and Contents*,³ 1916; Moore, *Judaism in the First Centuries of the Christian Era*, Vol. I, 1927, 125–216; Lagrange, *Le Judaïsme avant Jésus-Christ*, 1931; Volz, *Die Eschatologie der jüdischen Gemeinde im ntl.* Zeitalter, 1934; Oesterley, *An Introduction to the Books of the Apocrypha*, 1935; idem, *The Jews and Judaism during the Greek Period. The Background of Christianity*, SPCK, 1941; Rowley, *The Relevance of Apocalyptic*, ¹1944, ²1947; Torrey, *The Apocryphal Literature*, 1945; Beek, *Inleiding in de Jodse apokalyptiek van het O. en N.-Testamentisch tijdvak*, 1950; Frost, *Old Testament Apocalyptic; Its Origins and Growth*, 1952.

64. The First Book of Esdras

Fritzsche-Grimm: Fritzsche.–Zöckler, 155–61.–Kautzsch: Guthe I, 1–23.–Charles: S. A. Cook, I, 1–58.–HAT: Rudolph, 1949.–Torrey, 'The Nature and Origin of "First Esdras"', AJSL 1907, 116 ff.–idem, 'The Story of the three Youths', loc. cit., 197 ff.–Bayer, *Das III. Buch Esras und sein Verhältnis zu den Büchern Esra-Nehemia* (Bibl. Studien, XVI, 1), 1911.–Walde, *Die Esdrasbücher der Septuaginta* (Bibl. Studien, XVIII, 4), 1913.–Tedesche, *A Critical Edition of I Esdras* (Diss.) 1928. Cf. also literature on section 50.

The apocryphal book of Esdras is called 3 Ezra according to the Latin Bible, where the books of Ezra and Nehemiah are reckoned as 1 and 2 Ezra. In the LXX it is designated as Εσδρας a. The Greek text is the original one, it exists also in Latin, Syriac,

Ethiopic and Armenian versions. The book is a torso; the beginning, starting in the middle of the history of Josiah, appears abrupt; at the end it breaks off in the middle of a sentence. What we have is a history of the Jewish temple and its cult. It opens with Josiah's celebration of the Passover. After describing the last period of Jerusalem, its fall and the destruction of the temple, it passes on to the liberation edict of Cyrus and the first return under Sanabazar (chapters 1: 1–2: 14). The continuation in 2: 15–26 is intended to explain why the building of the temple was not resumed until the second year of Darius in spite of Cyrus's directions. The story of the contest between Darius's pages, which follows in 3: 1–4: 63, provides with full details the reasons for sending Zerubbabel to take up again the building of the temple. Next there come in chapters 5–7 the account of the return under Zerubbabel, the building of the altar, the laying of the foundation stone of the temple and its completion with a concluding celebration of the passover. Chapters 8–9 describe the arrival of Ezra, his measures against mixed marriages and his reading of the law to the people.

The book is not an independent literary production, but with the exception of 1: 21 f.; 3: 1–4: 63; 5: 1–6 a translation from the books of the Chronicler (cf. section 50 f.): chapter 1 = 2 Chron. 35–36; 2: 1–11 = Ezra 1: 1–11; 2: 16–26 = Ez. 4: 7–24; 5: 7–71 = Ezra 2: 1–4: 5; 6: 1–9: 36 = Ezra 5: 1–10: 44; 9: 37–55 = Neh. 7: 72–8: 13. The change in the arrangement of these passages from that in the books from which they were taken no doubt goes back to the author himself (against Hölscher, Mowinckel) who also inserted into the thread of his narrative the separate pieces listed as exceptions, taken probably from existing material. The story of the contest of Darius's pages in 3: 1–4: 63 is likely to be of Greek origin and was only transferred subsequently to Zerubbabel to sing his praise; it is to be classed with the 'deipnosophistic' type of literature (witty table-talk) (cf. on section 77). Rudolph has argued afresh for the natural assumption that this tale was first written in Greek against Torrey who considers it to be a translation from a Hebrew and Aramaic original. Since Josephus (Ant. XI: 1–5) makes use of 1 Esdras, it must have been produced between the work of the Chronicler (after 400 B.C.) and A.D. 90. The fact that the present form of the account of the pages' contest is dependent on Daniel (Bentzen, Rudolph) points to a date after 160 B.C. as the *terminus a quo*; since the whole of Southern Syria is called in 2: 16 Coele-syria, the period before the Roman epoch must be considered. In several places this book offers better readings than the MT and it is therefore of special importance for textual criticism.

65. The first book of Maccabees

Fritzsche–Grimm: Grimm.–Zöckler, 27 ff.–Kautzsch: Kautzsch I, 24 ff.–Charles: Oesterley, I, 59 ff.–HS: Bevenot, 1931.–Gutberlet (Alt. Abh. VIII, 3–4, 1920.–CEB:: Abel, 1949.–EB: Schötz, 1951.–LStB (Clamer): Grandelaudon, 1951–LSB: Penna, 1953–Niese, Kritik der beiden Makkabäerbücher, 1900.–Wellhausen, *Über den geschichtlichen Wert des zweiten Makkabäerbuchs im Verhältnis zum ersten* (Nachr. d. Ges. d. Wiss. zu Göttingen Phil. Hist. Kl., 1905, 117 ff.).–Ed. Meyer, *Ursprung und Anfänge des Christentums* II, 1921, 121 ff., 454 ff.–De Bruyne, 'Le Texte grec des deux livres des Machabées', RB 1922, 31 ff.–Willrich, 'Urkundenfälschung in der hellenistisch-jüdischen Literatur', FRLANT 1924.–Ettelson, The Integrity of I Maccabees, 1925.–Kolbe, 'Beiträge zur syrischen und jüdischen Geschichte', BWAT 1926.–Bevan, 'Syria and the Jews' (*Cambridge Ancient History*, VIII, 1930, 495 ff.–Momigliano, *Prime linee di storia della tradizione maccabaica*, 1930.–Bickermann, *Der Gott der Makkabäer*, 1934.–Fischel, *The First Book of Maccabees with Commentary*, 1948.–Tedesche, *The First Book of Maccabees: An English Translation, with Introduction and Commentary* by Salomon Zeitlin, 1950.–Dancy, *A Commentary on I Maccabees*, 1954.–Schunk, *Die Quellen des I. und II. Makkabäerbuches*, 1954.–Schaumberger, 'Die neue Seleukidenliste BM 35603 und die makkabäische Chronologie', *Biblica* 36 (1955), 423 ff.

The *text* of both books of Maccabees has been handed down in Greek, Latin and Syriac. Whilst the text of 2 Maccabees was first composed in Greek, the text of 1 Maccabees goes back to a no longer extant Hebrew original; this is confirmed by its language and by the evidence of Origen and Jerome.

The *name* Maccabee was first only the nickname of Judas (1 Macc. 2: 4) and its meaning is not certain (Hammer ?). It was then transferred to the whole family, whom the Jews usually called 'Hasmonaeans', and in the end to their adherents, the faithful Jews in the wars of independence against the Syrian rulers.

The history of these wars and the rise of the dynasty of the Hasmonaeans form the *subject* of this book. In chapter 1, after a short introductory mention of Alexander's expedition to the East and of the establishment of the kingdoms of his successors, it begins with the accession of Antiochus IV Epiphanes (176/75 B.C.) and his measures to suppress the Jewish religion. Chapter 2 records the start of the Maccabean revolt under the priest Mattathias in Modin. Chapters 3–16 describe the chequered conflict for liberation under his sons Judas (who fell in 160 B.C.), Jonathan (160–143) and Simon (143–135). These struggles led to the reconquest and the restoration of the temple in Jerusalem, to the attainment of political and religious freedom, and finally to the creation of an independent Jewish state recognized also by the Romans under the spiritual and political leadership of the Maccabees. Since at the end of the book Simon's son John Hyrcanus is brought in (16: 19 ff.) the author's survey extends as far as the last decades of the second century B.C.

The view of history taken in this book is pervaded by enthusiasm for the Maccabean dynasty and by a deep and earnest fidelity to religious convictions and to the tradition. Yet with it all the presentation of history in 1 Maccabees differs from the record of salvation history handed down in the OT. For the latter is connected with the cultic tradition, whilst in the former the springs of action controlling the natural human course of historical happenings are described as being predominantly within history itself. There is no question of God intervening directly in the march of events. Moreover the most important political episodes are dated according to the Syrian-Macedonian chronology, which begins with the autumn of the year 312 B.C.; this circumstance points to a Seleucid origin, as Bickermann has plausibly argued. The long, connected accounts as well as the details are told with an obvious sober simplicity and this makes the book a historical source of particular trustworthiness. Of course this judgment applies merely so far as Jewish history is concerned; the author is only imperfectly acquainted with the state of affairs in foreign countries, such as Rome and Sparta. Thus doubt has been thrown on the authenticity of the documents not only from the historical, but also from the literary point of view (chapter 8: Judas's treaty with Rome; in 10: 22–47 Demetrius's offer of a treaty to Jonathan; in 12: 1–23 the renewal of the treaty with Rome and Sparta and in 15: 15–24 the renewal of the treaty with Rome guaranteeing the Maccabean state). For they are only loosely connected as regards subject matter and literary construction with the composition as a whole and show some similarities to Hellenistic historical writing (against this Bickermann, p. 175, note 7). Caution is recommended too in the case of the exaggerated statements of numbers. The fact that Josephus in Bell. jud. I, 1: 1–2: 3; Ant. XII 5: 1–XIII 7: 4 uses the first book of Maccabees, chapters 1–13, but betrays no knowledge of chapters 14–16, can hardly be used as a proof that these last two chapters were added later, for the freedom with which he treats his sources is well known. When a historian goes into such great detail, we naturally ask about the sources he used. At any rate for the narrative up to the death of Judas (chapters 1–7, cf. 9: 22) with which the second book of Maccabees is also in the main concerned (2 Macc. 4: 7–15: 36) perhaps the historical work of Jason of Cyrene in five volumes, mentioned in 2 Macc. 2: 20 ff., was available to the author of 1 Maccabees as well (Kolbe). On the other hand Bickermann thinks he may have used the Maccabean archives (cf. the reference to the official chronicles of the priesthood of Hyrcanus in 16: 24). Schunk refers to Jewish sources those passages which are dated from the beginning of the Seleucid chronology in the spring of 312, whilst he considers the Jewish historian Eupolemos to be the author of the narrative concerning Judas Maccabaeus and the official records of the high priests to be the source for Jonathan and Simon.

The monument which Simon caused to be built in 141 over the graves of his father and his brothers seems to the author to have been erected some time ago (13: 30) and at the end there is an allusion to the annals of the high-priesthood of John Hyrcanus (135–104). Consequently we may place the *origin* of 1 Maccabees in the reign of John Hyrcanus during the last decades of the second century B.C. The author is an enthusiastic adherent of the Hasmoneans and desires to describe in his book the rise of their dynasty. It does not appear to me likely that it is actually a 'semi-official' account (Bickermann). On the other hand Bickermann is probably correct in considering the much-discussed question of its production amongst the Sadducees or Pharisees as irrelevant and impossible to answer; he divests it of the importance hitherto attributed to it and modifies it.

66. The second book of Maccabees

cf. the literature for section 65. Fritzsche–Grimm: Grimm.–Zöckler, 90 ff.–Kautzsch: Kamphausen, I, 81 ff. Charles: Moffatt, I, 125 ff.–HS: Bevenot, 1931.–Gutberlet, Atl. Abh, 1927.–Laqueur, *Kritische Untersuchungen zum zweiten Makkabäer-*

buch, 1904.–Kappler, *De memoria alterius libri Maccabaeorum* (Diss. Göttingen), 1929.–
De Bruyne, *Le Texte grec du deuxième livre des Machabées*.–RB 1930, 503 ff.–Mugler,
'Remarques sur le second livre des Machabées', RHPhR 1931, 419 ff.–Bickermann,
'Ein jüdischer Festbrief vom Jahre 124 v. Chr. II Makk 1. 1–9', ZNW 1933, 233 ff.–
Tedesche and Zeitlin, *The Second Book of Maccabees*, 1954. See literature, section 65.

Although the main part of the second book of Maccabees (4: 7–
15: 36) deals with the same subject as 1 Macc. 1–7, yet this book
has a materially different character, indeed a theological one. Its
author has been schooled in Greek rhetoric and his style shows
that he wrote his work in the Greek language. The book opens
with two letters from the Palestinian Jews to their fellow countrymen in Egypt exhorting them to celebrate the feast of the Dedication of the Temple as they themselves were doing (1: 1–10a;
1: 10b–2: 19). Since the preface starts at 2: 20 these letters have
been regarded rightly as a later addition. In his preface the author
explains that his book is an abridgment of the five-volume
historical work of Jason of Cyrene and he gives some indication
of his method. We have no other information about this source
or its author. Schunk sets out from the assumption that the
author of 2 Maccabees reckons the Seleucid era to have begun in
the autumn of 312; he then conjectures him to be the same man
who wrote 1 Maccabees (see section 65); but Schaumberger,
working on a new list of Seleucids has calculated that the second
book of Maccabees follows a chronology based on the spring of
311. The narrative itself starts from an earlier point of time than
1 Maccabees, namely with the last days of Seleucus IV Philopator
(187–176–5), the brother and predecessor of Antiochus IV Epiphanes. Heliodorus, the envoy of Antiochus, plunders the temple
treasure of which he had been informed by a Jew, but he is
miraculously punished by God (chapter 3). The priest Jason who
favours Greek ways succeeds by rich gifts and promises to Antiochus IV in ousting from his office his brother Onias, the High
Priest, who was faithful to the law, and in winning this honour
for himself. But after three years he is obliged to surrender it to
his brother Menelaus who had offered the king a bigger bribe.
Finally he causes Onias to be murdered (chapter 4). The remainder
of the narrative is on the whole similar to 1 Macc. 1–7, but ends
with Judas's victory over Nicanor (161 B.C.).

The narrative of this book regarded both in its entirety and in
its details has after all a different quality from that of 1 Maccabees.

Apart from the vigorous rhetorical display of emotion which betrays the Greek training of the author, occasional hints to the reader indicate clearly that the work was intended to be religious and edifying. The high esteem shown to the temple as the one and only legitimate place for the cult, the loyalty to the law which does not shrink from martyrdom itself, the strong faith in the resurrection (7: 14, 26–36; 14: 37–46), all these reveal at least clear affinities with the type of piety represented by the Pharisees, even if the author is not actually to be sought amongst them. As contrasted with 1 Maccabees the firm belief in miracles is striking. Yet if we take into account the characteristics of the 'pathetic' writing of history, we shall not assert as a matter of course that the book has no value as a historical source; neither may we, with Niese and others, overestimate its value. The home of the author cannot be definitely ascertained (Alexandria?). His work seems to be later than 1 Maccabees, but was produced before the destruction of Jerusalem in A.D. 70 (cf. 15: 37). Beside the two letters inserted before the preface in 1: 1–2: 18, the documents quoted in chapter 11 (11: 16 ff., 22 ff., 27 ff., 34 ff.) may be subsequent additions perhaps interpolated from older material by a redactor who placed the story of the death of Antiochus in chapter 9 before the account of the dedication of the temple in 10: 1–8; this is contrary to the order in which the events happened and also to the original arrangement given in 2 Maccabees; perhaps it was done in order that 10: 1–8 might chime in with the subject matter of 1: 1–2: 18 and chapter 11. This book is a valuable source of information about the religion of late Judaism, the history of its theology and its attitude towards the Hellenistic peril.

67. The third book of Maccabees

Fritzsche–Grimm: Grimm. Zöckler, 140 ff.–Kautzsch: Kautzsch, I, 119 ff.–Charles: Emmet, I, 155 ff.–Willrich, 'Der historische Kern des III. Makkabäerbuches', *Hermes*, 1904, 244 ff.–Cohen, *Iudaica et Aegyptiaca. De Maccabaeorum Liber III, Questiones Historicae*, 1941.–Hadas, *The Third and Fourth Books of the Maccabees*, 1953.

The third book of Maccabees bears its name in error. It has nothing to do with the Maccabean revolt, but describes how Ptolemy IV Philopator (222–205 B.C.) after his victory over Antiochus the Great at Raphia (217) visits Jerusalem and wishes to force his way into the Holy of holies of the temple. In answer to the prayer of the High Priest Simon he is punished by a stroke from God and falls to the ground in a swoon (1: 1–2: 24). On his return to Egypt he wishes to avenge himself for this on the Jews in Alexandria. Since they cannot be forced to worship Dionysus he has them imprisoned in the race-course to be trampled to death by elephants. But divine intervention three times thwarts the execution of this murderous command (2: 25–6: 21). Finally the king becomes the Jews' friend and benefactor and allows them to hold an annual festival of rejoicing at his expense on the 6th–14th of Epiph (July 3–9) and to destroy their renegade countrymen. A similar feast of commemoration is also instituted at Ptolemais (6: 22–7: 23).

This book, of which the beginning is mutilated, seems to have been composed as the 'festival legend' for a feast celebrated amongst the Egyptian Jewry. This was no doubt originally a heathen festival and was intended in its Judaized form to keep alive the memory of the deliverance of the Jewish community from a serious danger. In this respect it is comparable to the books of Esther and of Judith; Eissfeldt, Bentzen and others suggest a Feast of Purim adapted to Egyptian conditions. This interpretation derived from the history of the cult is supported by the fact that Josephus (Contra Apionem II, 5, section 53 ff.) tells the story of the elephants and the countermanding of the king's penal order about a later king, Ptolemy Physcon (146–177 B.C.) which eventuates similarly in the founding of a feast for Alexandrian Jews. The authenticity of the cultic background may therefore be accepted, even though the events described belong to the realm of legend with the exception of the information about the battle of Raphia in 1: 1–7. The rhetorical bombastic style and the belief in miracles which as in 2 Maccabees rises to the supernatural also points this way. This book affords a valuable insight into the external and internal situation of the Jews in the Greek Diaspora: the inviolable sanctity of the temple in Jerusalem, the loyalty to the law, the rejection of the reproach that they are hated, the resistance to the attempts of heathen despots to Hellenize them, all these are the fundamental ideas and concerns of the book. It was written originally in Greek, and has been handed down also in Syriac, but not in Latin. It originated presumably in Alexandria, no doubt in the first century B.C. since it seems to be still ignorant of the destruction of the temple.

68. The book of Tobit

Fritzsche=Grimm: Fritzsche.–Zöckler, 162 ff.–Kautzsch: Löhr I, 135 ff.–Charles: Simpson I, 174 ff.–EH: Schumpp, 1933.–HS: Miller–Schildenberger, 1940–41.– LStB (Clamer): Clamer, 1949.–EB: Stummer, Hamp, 1950.–LStB: Pautrel, 1951. –HBK: Bückers, 1953.–LSB: Priero, 1953.–Marg. Plath, 'Zum Buch Tobit', ThStKr 1901, 377 ff.–Joh. Müller, 'Beiträge zur Erklärung und Kritik des Buches Tobias', *Bibl. Studien* 1914.–Torrey, ' "Nineveh" in the Book of Tobit', JBL 1922, 237 ff.– Liljeblad, *Die Tobiasgeschichte und andere Märchen mit toten Helfern.* (Diss. Lund), 1927.

The book Tobit (Vulgate and Luther: Tobias) is named after its hero. In the form of a short family story it relates what happened to Tobit who was deported to Nineveh in 721 under the Assyrian king Shalmaneser. Tobit belongs to the tribe of Naphthali and from his youth up had distinguished himself by his fear of God and loyalty to the law. Even in the foreign land he keeps himself pure from heathen influences. He displays charity to the living and piety to his fellow countrymen murdered by order of Sennacherib by burying them reverently, although he is himself threatened with death for doing so. After early prosperity he becomes blind, but in spite of the taunts of his friends and his wife he does not give up his faith in God nor his upright conduct, but submits humbly to God's judgment with a prayer of penitence (1: 1–3: 6). The pious Jewess Sarah, the daughter of Raguel in Ecbatana in Media, fares no better. In spite of her having had seven husbands killed by the evil spirit Asmodaeus on her wedding night, she still praises God and prays to him for deliverance. (3: 7–15.) God grants their petitions. The angel Raphael is sent to deliver them both from their unmerited suffering and to accompany Tobias, the son of Tobit, to Media, in order that he may bring back Sarah as his wife. God's messenger and his commission remain at first unknown to father and son. On the advice of his companion Tobias burns the heart and liver of a fish and thereby drives away the dangerous demon from Sarah's bridal chamber. On his return to his home with his wife, he cures his father by means of the gall of the same fish (chapters 4–11). It is only when Tobit and Tobias wish to repay the travelling companion, that he makes himself known as the angel Raphael and reveals to them his divine mission to reward their piety which had stood the test of suffering and to grant their prayer (chapter 12). In a hymn and a song of thanksgiving Tobit foretells the destruction of Jersualem (587) and the restoration of its splendour (chapter 13) and he advises his son to move to Media, since the punishment threatened by the prophet Jonah will fall upon Nineveh. After the death of his father and mother the son follows Tobit's advice; he is allowed to close the eyes of his wife's parents in Media also and dies there at a great age, having become, owing to his devout life, the father of a 'race acceptable to God and man'.

This prose narrative is skilfully built up; it is carried out vividly with many lively details and embellished with poetic passages (psalms, hymns, prayers in 3: 1 ff., 11 ff.; 8: 7 ff.; 13; wise sayings in 4: 13 ff.; 12: 6 ff.); it has moreover a strong didactic and admonitory tinge. Thus the individual figures in this family idyll are drawn as models of Jewish piety and morality. By their reverence for God and trust in him, by their humble patience in suffering, by their obedience to the law and their respect for their parents and the dead, through their benevolent charity to the needy and the integrity and pureness of their disposition and conduct, they are intended to influence readers by their example, and they are allowed to be assured of the just rule of divine providence and to rejoice in it. Hence the book has been a favourite amongst Jews and Christians; this is vouched for by the three different Greek recensions (the oldest is probably that of Codex Sinaiticus) and by the translations, sometimes differing from each other, into Hebrew, Armenian, Latin, Syriac and Ethiopic. The original form of the text, no longer extant, may have been Aramaic. Aramaic and Hebrew fragments of this book have recently been found in Cave 4 of Qumran.

The narrator has made use of foreign traditions, but has made them serve his own ideas and purposes and assimilated their inner meaning. The name of the demon Asmodaeus is related to that of the Persian demon of lust, Daeva Aeshma, and indeed the angelology and demonology was probably taken over altogether from Parseeism. Simrock (*Der gute Gerhard und die dankbaren Toten*, 1856, pp. 131 f.) conjectured and Marg. Plath has proved that the basic theme of the Tobit story goes back to a folk-tale current also in Germany, Italy, France, Holland, Denmark (cf. Andersen's

Travelling Companion) and Armenia about the grateful corpse
and the bride under a curse; but in its biblical form it has received
several modifications. The Eastern story of Ahikar known to us
already from the fifth century papyrus of Elephantine has influenced the book of Tobit (cf. 1, 21 f.; 2: 10; 11: 17; 14: 10),
which is later and no doubt originated amongst the Eastern Diaspora of whose conditions it gives a striking picture. As regards
its date only this much may be said, that according to 14: 5 the
author does not seem to be acquainted with the magnificent rebuilding of the temple by Herod begun in 20 B.C.; thus the book
must have been written before then. This is confirmed by the
fragments from Qumran.

69. The book of Judith

Fritzsche–Grimm: Fritzsche.–Zöckler, 185 ff.–Kautzsch: Löhr I, 147 ff.–Charles:
Cowley, I, 242 ff.–Scholz, Kommentar über das Buch Judith und über Bel und
Drache, 1885, ²1896.–HS: Miller–Schildenberger. 1940–41.–LStB (Clamer): Sou-
bigou, 1949.–EB: Stummer, Hamp, 1950.–LStB: Barucq, 1950.–HBK: Bückers, 1953.
–Carl Meyer, 'Zur Entstehungsgeschichte des Buches Judith', *Biblica* 1922, 193 ff.–
De Vuippens, *Darius I, le Nabuchodonosor du livre de Judith*, 1927; Stummer, *Geographie
des Buches Judith* (Bibelwissenschaftliche Reihe, Heft 3) Stuttgart, 1947.–Steinmann,
Lecture de Judith, 1953.

It is evident from the style and the errors of translation that *the
text* of the book of Judith was originally composed in Hebrew,
but this form is no longer extant. It is the source of the Greek
translation which we have in three recensions and which in its
turn was translated into Latin, Syriac and Ethiopic. Its contents
are as follows: Chapters 1–3: After his victory over Arphaxad,
king of Media, Nebuchadnezzar, king of Assyria (!) sends his
commander-in-chief Holofernes against the peoples of the West
who had refused to take their part in the campaign against the
Medes. They are subdued and their cities and sanctuaries are
destroyed. Chapters 4–7: The people of Israel have just returned
from exile and rededicated their temple (!). Under the leadership
of the high priest Joakim and fearing the desecration of the temple
they determine to resist Holofernes to the uttermost. This general
scorns the advice of the Ammonite leader Achior whom he had
sent to gather information about the state of affairs and directs his
main attack against Bethulia, near Dothan (Gen. 37: 17) an otherwise unknown fortress. By cutting off their water supply he

reduces the besieged Israelites to the greatest distress. Chapters 8–13: At the last moment when the Israelites had already decided to surrender the city to the enemy within five days, Judith, a beautiful widow noted for her good reputation and her piety, comes forward. She encourages the people to fear and trust God and to be patient and she offers herself to effect their deliverance. She prepares herself by prayer and then succeeds by her beauty and cunning in arousing the confidence and affection of Holofernes; when he becomes drunk with wine and lust and desires to possess her, she slays him and brings back to Bethulia his head and the covering of his couch as proof of what she has done. Chapters 14–16: Achior is so impressed by her deed that he accepts the Jewish faith and is circumcised, whilst the Assyrian army, demoralized by the loss of its leader, is driven to flight by the Israelites. Judith is honoured by the high priest and all the people, sings a hymn of praise to God who has given the victory and at the feast of thanksgiving brings the arms of Holofernes as booty to the temple in Jerusalem. She remains unmarried and dies at the age of 105, held in high esteem and lamented. Her victory over Holofernes was celebrated regularly as a feast day.

This book probably served as the legend for the regular victory feast, which is mentioned at the end as an explanation. It has all the marks of a short story. The characters and their motives are skilfully worked up, there is great poetic power in their presentation, the interweaving of speeches and prayers gives it all a dramatic vivaciousness. There have been repeated attempts to consider the book of Judith as a reliable source for history. But it contains a number of historical impossibilities, such as that Nebuchadnezzar (604–562) was king of Assyria and lived at the time when the Jews returned from exile and restored their temple (520–516), whilst his residence is supposed to be Nineveh which was destroyed already in the year 612. These points are definite evidence that the author had no clear historical picture of the people and events he portrays. It is not out of the question that the individual names, such as Holofernes and Bagoas, and the lists might go back to the historical traditions of the campaigns of Artaxerxes III Ochus (359–338) against Phoenicia and Egypt in which according to Diodorus a satrap Orophernes and a eunuch Bagoas took part as generals. But it is unlikely that the Jewish tradition dates from this period. Perhaps the historical memory of a heroic act of deliverance by a Jewish woman lies behind the central figure of the narrative which is decked out poetically with themes from folk-tales. This memory may also lie behind the feast described at the end. It is not possible to detect mythological traits which as in the case of the figure of Esther might be explained by reference to the Myth of Ishtar. From its nationalist and warlike spirit and its propensity to urge by example and exhortation that loyalty to the law can rely on divine assistance, we may conjecture that this book originated in the period of the Maccabean struggles. The heroine of the story is the perfect type of the legalistic piety of those times: she observes strictly the laws concerning purity and food, she lives in intimate and confident communion with God by prayer which endows her with courage and a vigorous power of decision; she is morally unassailable and full of good deeds; these are the qualities which command for the figure of Judith that respect which such an exemplary character deserves.

70. The Prayer of Manasses

Fritzsche–Grimm: Fritzsche.–Zöckler, 236 ff.–Kautzsch: Ryssel, I, 165 ff.–Charles: Ryle, I, 612 ff.–Nau, 'Un Extrait de la Didascalie: La Prière de Manasse', *Revue de L'Orient Chrétien*, 1908, 134 ff.–Wilkins, 'The Prayer of Manasseh', *Hermathena*, 1911, 167 ff.

We are told in 2 Chron. 33: 11 ff. that Manasses, king of Judah, was bound by the captains of the Assyrian army and taken to Babylon. There he humbled himself before the God of his fathers, so that God granted his prayer and brought him back to Jerusalem. This prayer is mentioned by the Chronicler in 2, 33: 18 f. as being in his sources. Presumably it was this passage which gave rise to the apocryphal Prayer of Manasses, with which a later writer proposed to supply what was missing. It is recorded in the collection of hymns for public worship (canticles) which are placed as an appendix to the Psalms at the end of most Greek manuscripts of the OT, in the Codex Alexandrinus and some other manuscripts of the LXX. It is also preserved in the Syriac *Didascalia* (third century A.D.) and in the *Apostolic Constitutions*, a later recension. The frequently doubtful Greek text is the original one and is not to be regarded as a possible translation of an older

O

Hebrew prototype. In addition the prayer exists in Latin, Syriac, Arabic and Hebrew versions. As regards its form it is a personal lament, with a hymn-like invocation to God in verses 1–4a [1–7], a confession of sin in verses 4b–7 [7–12], a prayer for forgiveness in verse 8 [13], a vow, a song of praise and a doxology in verse 9 [14–15]. It is composed in the well-known usual style of a psalm and is distinguished by its simple sincerity and warmth. Beyond the *terminus a quo* which has been indicated, nothing definite can be said about its origin.

71. The Rest of Daniel

cf. literature for section 49. Fritzsche–Grimm: Fritzsche.–Zöckler, 214 ff.; 231 ff.– Kautzsch: Rothstein I, 172 ff.–Charles: Bennet, Kay, Davies, I, 625 ff.–Scholz, *Kommentar über das Buch Judith und über Bel und Drache*,[2] 1896.–BOT: Nelis, 1954.– Baumgartner, 'Susanna, die Geschichte einer Legende', ARW 1926, 259 ff.; 1929, 187 ff.–Kuhl, 'Die drei Männer im Feuer', BZAW 1930.

I. *The Prayer of Azariah and the Song of the Three Children in the Fiery Furnace*

In the legend of the martyrs in Dan. 3 the story is told of three friends, who are thrown into a fiery furnace because they refuse to worship the image of the king. In the LXX and in Theodotion (see section 59) a passage is inserted after Dan 3: 23 describing how one of the friends, Azariah, prays in the furnace to God for deliverance, and how when his prayer is granted they sing a song of praise together and remain untouched by the fire, whilst the Chaldeans standing by are burned. The prayer and the song are given here as they were said. They were not composed as an expansion of the legend in the canonical book of Daniel, but are inserted in this place by a redactor from another context. For the prayer of Azariah does not fit in the least into its present position. It is a collective prayer of penitence; it begins with a hymn-like invocation of God (verses 3–4 [25–28]) followed by a confession of sin (verses 5–10 [29–33] and a prayer for mercy and deliverance verses 11–22 [34–45]). It was originally part of a congregational service and is not a prayer spoken by a martyr suffering for his loyal observance of the law. The hymn of the three children after verses 54 f. might also have belonged to the festival cult of the temple and go back to old liturgical traditions. Its affinity to Psalm 148 and the use of liturgical forms points to this. The ending of the psalm adapts it to the circumstances of its present context. Thus both psalms probably go back to earlier Hebrew cultic poetry. As they are so general in form, their date cannot be determined more exactly.

II. *The History of Susanna and Daniel.*

This story is inserted in the LXX in a shorter form at the end of the book of Daniel as an appendix; in the version of Theodotion it is placed at the beginning of Daniel in a longer recension. It tells how the pious Jewess Susanna is accused of adultery with threats and violence by two Jewish elders who covet her for her beauty. She is condemned to death but is rescued by young Daniel, who unmasks the two false accusers by astute interrogation and hands them over to the legal punishment. The narrative is skilfully constructed and presented tersely and vividly. It treats in a restrained manner this spicy and ticklish theme, frequent in stories, of the innocent slandered woman and the clever, adroit judge. The originally profane matter is transferred to Jewish conditions and dominated by the spirit of Jewish religion and morality. The emphasis on chastity and the rescue of the pious woman by God have become the leading ideas of the tale. Thus the purpose has been changed from pure entertainment to religious instruction. The time and place of origin of this addition to the cycle of legends about Daniel (cf. Ezek. 14: 14, 20; 28: 3, also section 49) are hidden from us, and so is the original form of the narrative.

III. *The Story of Bel and the Dragon*

Like the tale of Susanna and Daniel, these stories too have been handed down in two recensions (LXX and Theodotion), both at the end of the book of Daniel. In the LXX they have the heading: 'from the prophecy of Habakkuk, the son of Jesus, of the tribe of Levi'. The object of both is to scoff at the ways of the heathen. In the first Daniel exposes by means of a ruse the fraud practised by the priests who themselves consume the sacrifice offered to the statue of Bel, but allow the king to suppose that it is the statue of the god which eats and drinks it daily. The story ends with the killing of the priests and the destruction of the statue and its temple by Daniel.

In the second story Daniel, without using a sword, kills a

dragon worshipped as a god by the inhabitants of Babylon by flinging into its mouth indigestible lumps of pitch and fat and hair. The people are enraged by the overthrow of their two divine images and cast Daniel, who is surrendered to them by the king, into a den of lions. Habakkuk, the Jewish prophet, is seized by the hair of his head by an angel of God, 'with the blast of his breath' he is set down in Babylon, and brings food to Daniel who remains untouched by the lions. The king is so impressed by this marvel that he gives glory to Daniel's God and orders his accusers to be hurled into the lions' den in place of Daniel.

As in the narrative of Susanna, so here also well-known folk-tales and themes of sagas are taken up and made to do duty in a popular attack on the heathen gods and their worship. It is interesting to note the fusion of the legends of Daniel and Habakkuk, even though we are not in a position to say anything more about their relationship as regards time, place or other matters.

72. The Rest of Esther

See literature for section 48.–Fritzsche–Grimm: Fritzsche.–Zöckler, 222 ff.–Kautzsch: Ryssel, I, 193ff.–Charles: Gregg I, 665 ff.–Scholz, *Commentary on Esther*, 1892.–Jacob, 'Das Buch Esther bei der LXX', ZAW 1890, 241 ff.

In the LXX version of the book of Esther, a number of pieces, beside smaller additions, have been interpolated. They are placed by Jerome and consequently also in the Vulgate at the end of the book of Esther (chapters 11–16), in the Lutheran Bible (and English Revised Version) in seven chapters ('Rest of the chapters of the Book of Esther') in the Apocrypha. In the Septuagint (Codex B) their position is as follows: Before Est. 1: 1 Mordecai's dream about the miraculous deliverance of the Jewish people; after Est. 3: 13 the wording of the first edict of Artaxerxes (in the book of Esther: Ahasuerus), who orders the annihilation of the Jews; after Est. 4: 17 the wording of the prayers of Mordecai and Esther for the deliverance of their nation in the style of the psalms of lamentation and penitence, and in place of Est. 5: 1 f. Esther's reception by the king; after Est. 8: 12 in place of 8: 13 the wording of Artaxerxes' second edict which revokes the first and gives the Jews protection; after Est. 10: 3 the interpretation of Mordecai's dream, followed by the tail-piece for the whole book according to which Dositheus and his son Ptolemy brought the Greek version of the book of Esther to Egypt in the fourth year of king Ptolemy and his consort Cleopatra.

The additions to the book of Esther are of different kinds. The wording of the prayers, in accordance with a device used elsewhere also, is meant to give an added enrichment and a deeper religious note; the quotation of the royal edicts serves to make the history appear more concrete and thereby to rest on more reliable foundations; the description of Mordecai's dream and its interpretation must be considered as a poetical and religious embellishment by bringing in a new theme. These additions to the book of Esther are by no means the final stage in the process of its expansion. All that can be said about the time of their composition is the fact that Josephus (Ant. XI 6: 6 ff.) knew them and made use of them. It is open to question whether the tail-piece referring to the whole Greek book of Esther can be applied also to the origin of these additions. Nor can it be said which of the several Ptolemies whose wife was called Cleopatra is intended. Both Ptolemy VIII and the year 114 B.C. as well as Ptolemy XIV and the year 48 B.C. have been suggested.

73. The book of Baruch

Fritzsche–Grimm: Fritzsche.–Zöckler, 239 ff.–Kautzsch: Rothstein, I, 213 ff.–Charles: Whitehouse, I, 569 ff.–HS: Kalt, 1932.–Kneucker, Das Buch Baruch, 1879.–EB: Stummer, Hamp, 1950.–LStB: Gelin, 1951.–LSB: Penna, 1953.–HBK: Schneider, 1954.–Herbst, Das apokryphische Buch Baruch aus dem Griechischen ins Hebräische übertragen, 1886.–Harwell, The principal Versions of Baruch (Diss. Yale Univ.) 1915.–Stoderl, Zur Echtheitsfrage von Baruch, 1–3a, 1922.–Thackeray, The Septuagint and Jewish Worship (Schweich Lectures),[2] 1923.

The book opens (1: 1–2) with statements concerning its author, namely Baruch, son of Nerias, its place of origin (Babylon) and its date (582 B.C.). This is followed by an introduction in 1: 3–14 which dates the book earlier than 1: 2 (i.e. the reign of Jechonias after the deportation of 598). It relates how Jechonias and his Jewish fellow prisoners, after hearing the book read aloud to them by Baruch sent it with money they had collected to Jerusalem. They added the request to use the money to institute sacrifices for Nabuchodonosor and his son Baltasar (Belshazzar) and for the Jewish prisoners, and to read the book aloud in the temple on feast days. The actual substance of Baruch's book does not begin till 1: 15. It is made up of a national prayer of penitence (1: 15–3: 8), a didactic poem in the form of a hymn (3: 9–4: 4) and a collection of songs of lament and consolation for the disheartened people. The *penitential prayer* has its partly verbatim counterpart in the prayer in Dan. 9: 4 ff. where it is probably a secondary addition. This suggests a comparatively late origin from a Hebrew prototype. The *didactic poem* belongs to the sapiential poetry and echoes passages from the Wisdom literature, such as Prov. 8 and Job 28 f. The *laments* in 4: 9b–16, 17–29 and the *songs of consolation* in 4: 5–9; 4: 30–35; 4: 36–5: 4; 5: 5–9 recall the poetry of Deutero-Isaiah. Presumably they too go back to Hebrew originals. As 5: 5–9 is found almost verbatim in the Psalms of Solomon 11: 2–7, literary dependence has been assumed and it has been conjectured that the poems in the book of Baruch (3: 9–5: 9) came into existence in the second half of the first century B.C.; others have the first century A.D. in mind. At any rate the penitential prayer in 1: 15–3: 8 and the poems had in the first place nothing to do with each other. The introduction in 1: 3–14 is a later interpolation and disturbs the continuity both as regards form and subject-matter (see above). The book cannot be due to Baruch, the friend and assistant of Jeremiah, since he was never in Babylon. This and other writings are attributed to him because he experienced the catastrophe of 587 with his master and tradition could easily have placed him beside Jeremiah as the author of writings which in any way referred to this event.

74. The Epistle of Jeremy

Fritzsche–Grimm: Fritzsche.–Zöckler, 250 ff.–Kautzsch: Rothstein, I, 226 ff.–Charles: Ball, I, 596 ff.–HS: Kalt, 1932.–Naumann, 'Untersuchungen über den apokryphen Jeremiasbrief', BZAW 1913.–Thackeray, *Some Aspects of the Greek Old Testament*, 1927, 53 ff. cf. literature for section 73.

In the Vulgate and Luther's Bible (also in the English Revised Version) the 'Epistle of Jeremy' is appended to the book of Baruch as chapter 6. In the Septuagint, especially in old manuscripts, it stands by itself after the Lamentations of Jeremiah. According to its heading it professes to have been sent by Jeremiah to the Jews destined for deportation to Babylon. It contains a warning, worked out in full detail and composed in good Greek, against the worship of heathen idols, which are derided in the manner of Is. 44: 9 ff. (cf. Jer. 10: 1–16) as mere lifeless and powerless matter. The form of this combined pastoral and prophetic missive seems to be modelled on the genuine letter of Jeremiah to the Jews in captivity in Jer. 29. It is impossible to decide with certainty whether we have to do with a version from the Hebrew or with a Greek original. The knowledge of cultic customs in Babylon suggests that the author was a Jew of the Eastern Diaspora. In 2 Macc. 2: 1 ff. mention is made of instructions given by the prophet Jeremiah to the deported Jews and some have wished to use this as evidence for dating the apocryphal Epistle of Jeremy. It is said that it must have been in existence in the middle of the first century B.C. But it is altogether uncertain and not even likely that 2 Macc. 2: 1 ff. is referring to our Epistle of Jeremy. We must therefore give up the idea of fixing a precise date.

75. Ecclesiasticus

The Hebrew text.

Strack, 1903.–Peters, 1902, 1905.–Smend, 1906.–Marcus, *The newly discovered original Hebrew of Ben Sira*, 1931. Segal, *Sefer ben Sira haschalem*, 1953.

Versions and Commentaries

Fritzsche–Grimm: Fritzsche.–Zöckler, 255 ff.–Kautzsch: Ryssel, I, 230 ff.–Charles: Box and Oesterley, I, 268 ff.–EH: Peters, 1913.–SAT: Volz,[2] 1921.–HS: Eberharter, 1925.–Smend, 1906.–EB: Hamp, 1951.–LStB and LStB (Clamer) see lit. for section 43.–HBK: Schilling, 1956.–Baumgartner, 'Die literarischen Gattungen in der Weisheit des Jesus Sirach', ZAW 1914, 161 ff.–De Bruyne, 100 ff. cf. literature for sections 7 and 43.

The book of Ecclesiasticus belongs to the type of Wisdom literature, like the book of Proverbs, which it resembles. It is a collection of practical precepts dealing with daily life and has a definitely rational character. Questions concerning right conduct in general, the family, marriage, friendship, etc. are treated by means of commands, exhortations, warnings, promises and proverbs which reflect a rich experience of life and an educational tradition drawn from different periods and countries. It is impossible to detect a comprehensive plan covering the motley profusion of the material—the sign of a collective production.

Yet frequently sayings about the same subject are brought together: e.g. in 2: 1–18 exhortations to be patient in affliction; in 3: 1–16 admonitions to be obedient and submissive to parents and promises of the blessing which will follow; in 4: 1–10 encouragement of helpfulness and beneficence towards the poor and the oppressed; 6: 1–17 deals with friendship, 9: 1–13 with conduct towards women; 11: 29–34 with hospitality; 20: 1–8 with silence; 30: 33–40 with the treatment of slaves; 34: 1–7 with dreams; 34: 12–35: 13 with correct behaviour at a feast; 38: 24–39: 11 with scribes and teachers of wisdom and so forth. Occasionally as in the book of Proverbs and in Job there are *didactic poems* concerning wisdom, as in 1: 1–20; 4: 11–19; 14: 20–15: 8 and in the appendix in 51: 13–29 an alphabetic song of this type. The fact that strict adherence to form has been relaxed must be regarded as a sign of a late development in literary history; this comes out in the admission of *hymns* in 39: 12–35; 42: 15–43: 33; *prayers* in the style of a national lament in 33: 1–13; 36: 16–22; thanksgivings in 51: 1–12 as well as in the well-known and comprehensive 'Praise of the Fathers of old' in 44: 1–49: 16, a kind of poetic gallery of ancestors with the qualities both of an epic and a hymn; strange to say it begins with Enoch in 44: 16, goes down as far as Nehemiah, and then returns once more to the figures of primeval history (Seth, Shem) and finally to Adam. There has been attached to this section chapter 50, containing a panegyric on the high priest Simeon, with a description of his ministry as a priest on the day of atonement (50: 24 is the biblical germ out of which has grown the hymn 'Now thank we all our God').

As we are told expressly in the preface the Greek text is a translation from the Hebrew. The Hebrew original is derived from the grandfather of the translator, *Yeshua' ben Eleazar ben Sira'* of Jerusalem, who is named at the end of the book in 50: 27 ff. (cf. also the signature in 51: 1 ff. in the Appendix). According to the preface he came to Egypt in the thirty-eighth year of king Euergetes (132 B.C.) and there translated his grandfather's book into Greek for the Jewish Diaspora in Egypt. Thus the Hebrew book of Ecclesiasticus must have been composed in Palestine at the beginning of the second century B.C. The panegyric on the high priest Simeon in chapter 50 would agree with this. (According to Josephus. Ant. XII, 4: 10, section 223 ff. he is no doubt Simeon II, the father of Onias III who was deposed by Antiochus IV.)

Jerome still knew the Hebrew text under the title *mešhālīm* (=proverbs). In the year 1896 fragments of it were found in the *genizah* of the synagogue in Cairo. Since then about three-fifths of the Hebrew text have become known from five different manuscripts. The Syriac version also goes back directly, like the text of the Septuagint, to the Hebrew text. On the other hand the Latin, Arabic, Coptic, Ethiopic and Armenian versions have used the LXX as the parent text. Whether there is any connexion between the fragments from Cairo and those in Cave 2 at Qumran, and if so what it is, can be decided only when the latter have been published.

The statements in the preface are borne out in the contents of the book, namely, that it came into being as a result of the study of Holy Writ and that the writer neither can nor wishes to deny its dependence on the traditions, in part very old, of the Wisdom literature, and of the Psalms, etc. References can also be detected to the proverbial wisdom of Egypt, Syria (Aḥikar) and the Greeks. Yet a difference is perceptible from the canonical Wisdom books —this too is a sign of a later stage of development. The late Jewish legalistic piety and the emphasis placed on cultic and ritual forms in their lives are brought out more strongly. The much-travelled author has by no means refused to be influenced by Greek culture. In view of this fact his apologetic attitude is all the more remarkable, for he holds firmly to the tradition of his fathers. He concentrates and reflects on the heritage of his ancestors in order to counter the danger of the Hellenization of Judaism, thus revealing the contemporary background of the book. Although it does not conceal a certain openness to worldly influence, yet in the last resort, it must be understood in the light of the spirit of the Maccabean revolt. Amongst Jews and Christians this book has been a great favourite and at times has achieved almost canonical rank. The author of the Epistle of James seems to have known and used it (cf. Jas. 1: 19 with Ecclus. 5: 11).

76. The Wisdom of Solomon

Fritzsche–Grimm: Grimm.–Zöckler, 355 ff.–Kautzsch: Siegfried, I, 467 ff.–

Charles: Holmes, I, 518 ff.–EH Heinisch, 1912.–HS: Feldmann, 1926.–HAT:
Fichtner, 1938.–Peters, *Weisheitsbücher des AT*, 1914, 233 ff.–HBK: Kalt, 1938.–EB:
Fischer, 1950.–LStB: Osty, 1950.–LStB (Clamer):see lit. for section 43.–Weber, 'Die
Composition der Weisheit Salomos', ZWTh 1904, 145 ff.–idem, 'Aufsätze über die
Unsterblichkeit, die Seelenlehre, die Heimat und das Zeitalter, den Auferstehungs-
glauben der Weisheit Salomos; ZWTh 1905, 409 ff.; 1909, 314 ff.; 1911, 322 ff.; 1912,
205 ff.–Focke, 'Die Entstehung der Weisheit Salomos', FRLANT 1913.–Speiser,
'The Hebrew Origin of the first Part of the Book of Wisdom', *Jewish Quarterly
Review*, 1923-4, 455 ff.–Purinton, 'Translation Greek in the Wisdom of Solomon',
JBL 1928, 276 ff.–Kuhn, 'Beiträge zur Erklärung der Weisheit', ZNW 1929, 334 ff.–
Lange, 'The Wisdom of Solomon and Plato', JBL 1936, 293 ff.–Schütz, Les Idées
eschatologiques du livre de la Sagesse, 1935.–Fichtner, 'Die Stellung der Sapientia
Salomonis in der Literatur=und Geistesgeschichte ihrer Zeit', ZNW 1937, 113 ff.
–idem, 'Der AT-Text der Sapientia Salomonis', ZAW 1939, 155 ff.–Jansen, *Die
spätjüdische Psalmendichtung, ihr Entstehungskreis und ihr 'Sitz im Leben'*, 1937; Bückers,
'Die Unsterblichkeitslehre des Weisheitsbuches', Atl. Abh. 1938.–Till, 'Die Koptischen Versionen der Sapientia Salomonis', *Biblica* 36 (1955), 51 ff.

The tendency towards apologetics and polemics shows itself much more definitely than in Ecclesiasticus in the book of the Wisdom of Solomon. This book must be reckoned also as a late offshoot of the Jewish Wisdom literature, but it is much further removed than the former from the original types. Like the book of Proverbs and Ecclesiastes, this writing is attributed to Solomon, the father of wisdom and is composed fictitiously under his name like 'the Preacher' (8: 10 f.; 9: 7 f., 12) even though this fiction often seems to recede into the background.

Part I, chapters 1–5, deals in poetical form (*parallelismus membrorum*) with the contrast between the 'righteous' and wise on the one hand and the ungodly and their worship of idols on the other. Thus piety is presented as wisdom and ungodliness on the contrary as foolishness.

Part II, chapters 6–9, has intermingled prose passages. It addresses itself in the first instance to the kings and judges of the earth and recommends and extols wisdom. It closes with a prayer in the form of a psalm, asking that wisdom may be bestowed.

Part III, chapters 10–19 is mainly in prose with a marked tendency to apocalyptic. In a meditation on salvation-history it speaks of the wonderful things wrought by wisdom in the history of Israel from Adam up to the Conquest. Chapters 13–15 is a denunciation of idolatry interpolated into this context.

The book of the Wisdom of Solomon proves already by its form that it is a late product of Wisdom literature. The line of development traced from the Proverbs to Ecclesiasticus is continued further here. The original form of the concise proverbial wise-saw is used no longer. Its place has been taken by a more elaborate didactic poem and a 'treatise' in prose of a philosophical character. Its form, as Jerome pointed out ('ipse stilus Graecam eloquentiam redolet') exhibits the bombastic emotional appeal of the rhetorical style, which is a mark of Hellenistic workmanship. One cannot fail to be aware that the author knew the world of the Hellenistic genius and is influenced by it in spite of his Jewish standpoint from which he launches his attacks and on which he bases his apologetics. The book contains typically Greek forms of choice language and cultured modes of expression which support the view that it was originally composed in Greek, in spite of repeated attempts to trace a Hebrew parent text for at least some parts of it. The use of the 'chain-syllogism' in 6: 17 ff., of the 'definition' in 17: 11, the imitation of the language of the mysteries in 2: 22; 8: 4 are evidence that the writer was well acquainted with the world of Greek culture. He displays a strongly marked tendency to philosophical speculation and combines human and divine wisdom into *one* concept, indeed he almost identifies them. He makes the closest possible connexion between God and Wisdom (συμβίωσιν ἔχουσα Θεοῦ 8: 3 f.). He honours wisdom as the teacher of the four cardinal virtues (σωφροσύνη, φρόνησις, δικαιοσύνη, ἀνδρεία). In 8: 20 he expresses belief in the pre-existence of the soul which feels the bodily frame to be an oppressive burden and is more attuned to the beyond than to life in this world. All these points show that the author adopted not only Greek forms, but also certain ideas of Platonic and Stoic philosophy (perhaps mediated by Posidonius?) and that he blended them with his faith derived from the revelation of the Old Testament.

For this reason even in olden times, as Jerome tells us, the Alexandrian Jew Philo was thought to be the author and this has been accepted by Luther and many others. Yet in spite of great similarity to this typical representative of a Jewish philosopher trained in Greek thought in the era of our Lord, the differences are too great for Philo's authorship to be considered. For instance, the Wisdom of Solomon lacks the allegorical exegesis of the scriptures, the philosophical speculations concerning the *logos* and the systematic foundation of Philo's thought. The place of this book in the history of ideas may lie between Ben Sira and Philo. Its *date of origin* can also probably be assumed between these two men, although of course it is not essential to draw conclusions as to the time of its composition without further ado from its position in the history of ideas. Thus we may suppose the author to have been a cultured Jew of the Diaspora no doubt in the Alexandria of the last century B.C. He is endeavouring to defend his inherited religion against apostate co-religionists, and against the heathen as well, by means of ideas and opinions acquired from his Hellenistic training. This conclusion gives no support to the conjecture that the author belonged to the party of the Pharisees and meant by the ungodly the Sadducees or the Epicureans.

It is noteworthy that there are echoes of the Wisdom of Solomon in the NT and especially in Paul (cf. e.g. Rom. 9: 19-23 with Wisd. 11: 22; 12: 12-18; 1 Cor. 6: 2 with Wisd. 3: 8). Yet such passages are not sufficient evidence that Paul knew and made use of this book. It may equally well be that they both shared in the same stock of educational material or used a fixed tradition of apologetics.

B. PSEUDEPIGRAPHA

77. The Letter of Aristeas

Text: Aristeae Epistula, ed. Wendland, 1900.–Thackeray in Swete, *Introduction to the Old Testament,*[2] 1914, 153 ff.
Translations: Kautzsch: Wendland, II, 1 ff.–Charles: Andrews, II, 83 ff.–Hermann und Baumgärtel, 'Beiträge zur Entstehungsgeschichte der Septuaginta', BWAT 1923, 39 ff.–Willrich, Urkundenfälschung in der hellenistisch–jüdischen Literatur, FRLANT 1924, 86 ff.–Thackeray, *Some Aspects of the Greek Old Testament,* 1927, 17 ff. –Bickermann, Zur Datierung des Pseudo-Aristeas, ZNW 1930, 280 ff.–Stählin, 'Josephus und der Aristeasbrief', ThStKr 1930, 324 ff.–Tramontano, *La lettera di Aristea al Filocrate,* 1931–Momigliano, 'Per la data e la caratteristica della lettera di Aristea', *Aegyptus,* 1932, 161 ff.–Meecham, *The oldest Version of the Bible,* 1932; Kahle, *The Cairo Geniza* (Schweich Lectures) 1947, 132 ff.; idem, 'Die Septuaginta', *Festschrift für Eissfeldt,* 1947, 161 ff.; Stricker, *De Brief van Aristeas,* 1956.

The Letter of Aristeas is a narrative in the form of a letter in which a certain Aristeas gives an account to his brother Philocrates about the origin of the Greek version of the Torah (the Septuagint). The gist of the story which is adorned with extensive additions tells how King Ptolemy II Philadelphus (285–247 B.C.) at the suggestion of Demetrius of Phaleron, the head of the royal library at Alexandria, addresses himself first in writing and then by sending Aristeas and Andrew to the Jewish high priest Eleazar. The king asks him to send a roll of the Torah with suitable translators to prepare a Greek version of the Jewish Torah for his library: 72 men (6 from each tribe) are selected and come to Alexandria. They translate the Torah in 72 days and agree together upon the wording of the sections prepared by each of them. This is written down by Demetrius. The translation is confirmed by the priests and elders of the Jewish congregation in Alexandria and declared inviolable. On the king's orders it is carefully preserved and held in high honour. This framework which holds the story together is filled out and embellished at various points with excursuses which are mostly very long-winded: sections 12–27 the manumission of the Jewish slaves in Egypt; sections 51–82 a description of the gifts sent by the king to Eleazar; sections 83–120 a description of Jerusalem and the ministry of the priests there: sections 121–171 the conversation of Aristeas and Andrew on the deeper significance of the laws of food and cleanness; sections

413

187–300 table-talk of the king with the seventy-two translators on religious and philosophical questions and the principles of government with the intention of demonstrating the superiority of Jewish wisdom over Greek philosophy.

The letter of Aristeas is one of the Pseudepigrapha not only in the sense that the author writes under a name not his own, but also because he borrows or invents the whole historical framework of his narrative, as well as the characters and the events, in order to produce an account which bears on the face of it the stamp of a tendentious legend. According to his own statements in section 41 and section 43 the author is a high official at the king's court, and according to section 16 he is a Gentile. Yet the basic trend of the book which exalts Jewish customs and beliefs in every way as against the Greeks leaves us in no doubt that he is an adherent of Judaism. To this must be added a number of impossible statements: for example Demetrius of Phaleron appears no doubt under Ptolemy I to have earned merit for his services to the royal library, but under his successor he plays no part at all; again the defeat of Ptolemy II at Cos is turned into a victory in section 180, and there are similar instances. Yet this is not to say that the author had no historical sources at his disposal (among others there was the history of Hecataeus of Abdera who wrote in the reign of Ptolemy I (see section 31; Wendland). Moreover this account of the origin of the Septuagint, in spite of its strongly marked legendary character, is not quite without a historical background (on this see section 59 above). But it is impossible to ascertain how far the details of the tradition used concerning the Septuagint are founded on history. The author seems also to have used or copied contemporary descriptions of travel which he has stamped in the same way with propagandist exaggeration—here too in favour of Judaism (sections 83–120). He has also used the literary type of 'table-talk' in sections 187 ff., but in comparison with the pages' contest in 1 Esd. 3: 1 ff. he has drawn it out monotonously to a wearisome length (cf. section 64 above).

The author is as familiar with Greek culture as he is with life at the court, with the administration and with the official language of the Ptolemies. He must therefore have still written under their rule in Alexandria. Definite forms of this official style which we can date indicate that the Letter of Aristeas was composed at the end of the second century B.C. The territorial conditions which he takes for granted in sections 107, 115, fit in with this date.

It is easy to understand that an account of the origin of the Greek version of the Torah was popular both with the Jews and later on with the Christians as well, especially as it provided evidence for the reliability of the Septuagint and enhanced its authority. Josephus in Ant. XII, 2 refers in detail to the Letter of Aristeas. The Christian Church Fathers also took up the narrative and developed it to the effect that the seventy-two men had translated not only the Torah, but the whole OT and had done so independently of each other. This was intended to substantiate the inspiration of the translation. This interest in the Letter of Aristeas is also shown by the fact that it is preserved in a number of Greek manuscripts.

78. The book of Jubilees

Text: Ethiopic: Dillman, *Liber Jubilaeorum, aethiopice*, 1859.–Charles: *The Ethiopic Version of the Hebrew Book of Jubilees*, 1895.–Latin: Ceriani, *Monumenta Sacra et Profana I*, 1, 1861.–Rönsch, *Das Buch der Jubiläen oder die Kleine Genesis*, 1874.

Versions: Kautzsch: Littmann, II, 31 ff.–Charles: Charles II, 1 ff.–Bohn: 'Die Bedeutung des Buches der Jubiläen', ThStKr 1900, 167 ff.–Martin: Le livre des Jubilés, RB 1911, 321 ff.; Finkelstein, 'The Book of Jubilees and the Rabbinic Halaka', HThR 1923, 39 ff.; Zeitlin, 'The Book of Jubilees, its Character and Significance', JQR 30, 1939–40, 1 ff.; loc. cit., 35, 1944–45, 12 ff.; 36, 1845/46, 187ff.–Finkelstein, 'The Date of the Book of Jubilees', HThR 1943, 19 ff.–Rowley, *The Relevance of Apocalyptic*,[2] 1947, 60 ff.; 84 ff.–idem, 'Criteria for the Dating of Jubilees', JQR 36, 1945–46, 184 ff. –Finkelstein, 'Criteria for the Dating of Jubilees', JQR 36, 1945–46, 187 ff.–Kahle, *The Cairo Geniza* (Schweich Lectures) 1947, 12 note 3.–Torrey, *The Apocryphal Literature*, 1945, 126 ff.; Jaubert, 'Le calendrier des Jubilés et la secte de Qumran. Ses origines bibliques, VT 3 (1953), 250ff.–Morgenstern, 'The Calendar of the Book of Jubilees, its origin and its character., VT 5 (1955), 34–76.

The book of Jubilees derives its *name* from the fact that it is based on a division of time into periods of 49 years (=the jubilee period, cf. Lev. 25) which are themselves again subdivided into 7 weeks of years of 7 years and serve to date the individual events. From its contents it is also called the Little Genesis because it runs parallel to Genesis, but is considered less important than the canonical book. Sometimes it is also called from its form the Apocalypse of Moses, since the whole of it is set in the framework of a divine 'revelation' at Sinai, imparted to Moses by an angel at God's command for him to write down. By this means it is intended to give the writing an authority similar to that possessed by the biblical book. Its *text*, which was known to the early Church Fathers but had been lost since the thirteenth century, was discovered in the middle of the nineteenth century in Abyssinia in an Ethiopic version. This version, together with fragments of a Latin text found by Ceriani in 1861, goes back to a Greek version of an original Hebrew text of which fragments have recently been brought to light in Cave 1 at Qumran.

Contents. The presentation follows a strict chronology. It begins with the creation and goes as far as the institution of the feast of Passover at the Exodus from Egypt (Gen. 1–Exod. 12). It contains to a considerable extent simply repetitions of the old narratives of the Pentateuch. In between these there are amplifications and interpretations in the style of the midrash. Some are in the form of the *haggadah*, i.e. with the object of deepening the knowledge of God by means of the story-telling parts of salvation history, and some in that of the *halakah*, i.e. the expansion of the tradition of the law by individual precepts, by regulations for carrying them out and by giving more detailed reasons for them. The patriarchs are described in this context as patterns of the strictest performance of the law who even observed its rabbinic extensions (16: 31). What might give offence is passed over in silence, as, e.g. the white lie of Abraham (Gen. 12: 11 ff.) or it is altered, as, e.g. in 17: 16 where it is Mastema (the tempter=Satan) who induces God to test Abraham by ordering him to sacrifice Isaac. The central position in the whole book is occupied by the Mosaic law which is nothing but the unveiling by stages during the years of what had been inscribed on the heavenly tablets since time was (3: 8 ff., 30 ff.). The book of Jubilees itself purports to belong to the class of esoteric tradition, which was handed down by the patriarchs and finally entrusted to Levi to be kept in safe hands (45: 16).

Segregation from the Gentiles stands out as the particular concern of the book. Not only are mixed marriages forbidden (22: 20; 30: 7 ff.) but also meals shared with Gentiles (22: 16) and of course the worship of idols (11: 4) and other heathen customs (22: 17). In fact special emphasis is laid on avoiding contact with all that is 'unclean' and on preserving the purity of Judaism on the foundation of a strict observance of cultic and ritual regulations (the Sabbath in 2: 17 ff.; 50: 6 ff., circumcision in 15: 11 ff., 26, 33 f.;

the Feast of Weeks in 6: 17 ff.; new moons in 6: 23 ff.; the Feast of Tabernacles in 16: 20 ff.; the Day of Atonement in 34: 18 ff.; Passover in 49: 1 ff.; food laws in 6: 7 ff.; 7: 31 ff.; 21: 18).

The eschatological outlook in 23: 11 ff., which brings the narrative of Abraham to a close, pictures a time in which 'law and covenant, feasts and months, sabbath and Jubilees and all judgments' are forgotten. As against Zeitlin and Albright (*From the Stone Age to Christianity*, 1940, pp. 266 ff.) who place the book of Jubilees in the early post-exilic days or at the end of the fourth or the beginning of the third century B.C., this outlook, as Rowley has rightly emphasized again, points to conditions which have behind them the controversies of the Maccabean period (for the Sabbath cf. 1 Macc. 1: 45; 2 Macc. 6: 6; for idolatry cf. 1 Macc 1:47; for circumcision cf. 1 Macc. 1: 15, 48, 60 f.; 2: 46; 2 Macc. 4: 7 ff.; for the food rules cf. 2 Macc. 6: 7). In the meditation of Judaism on the heritage of its ancestors the book of Jubilees is attacking the danger of acute Hellenization and seems to be aimed at the conditions prevailing during the rule of Antiochus Epiphanes (175–164). The case for placing its date in the Maccabean period may claim therefore to be the most probable in spite of recent attempts to oppose it (Zeitlin, Kahle). Its relationship to the Pharisaic type of piety enjoining strict observance of the law has often lent support to the view that the book is of Pharisaic origin (Dillmann, Rönsch, Schürer, Bentzen). But the chronology and the rejection of the Pharisaic calendar in 6: 29 ff., the special prominence given to the Sabbath in 1: 17 ff., the doctrine of angels in 1: 18; 5: 1 ff. and *passim*, the conception of predestination in 1: 4, 26 and of immortality without resurrection in 23: 30 f., finally the importance of secret doctrines, all suggest an author from amongst the Essenes. This is also made probable by the discovery of fragments of this book in Qumran. Perhaps more light will be thrown on these questions when the 'Lamech' scroll from Qumran, in which can be seen a certain resemblance in the treatment of Genesis, has been deciphered. (See section 94 below.)

The book of Jubilees provides evidence for the continuing influence in late Judaism of the old cultic traditions of the Pentateuch concerning salvation-history. We can understand with what eyes and for what purposes they were read, how they formed Judaism and were in their turn shaped by it. Thus this book has a significance not only for the history of religion, but also for theology, a significance which will become clearer when its connexion with the literature of the sect at Qumran has been investigated more closely.

79. The Martyrdom and Ascension of Isaiah (Martyrium et ascensio Isaiae)

Text and Versions: Ethiopic and Latin: Dillmann, *Ascensio Isaiae Aethiopice et Latine*, 1877; Ethiopic, Latin, Greek, Slavonic: Charles, *The Ascension of Isaiah translated from the Ethiopic Version, which together with the new Greek fragment, the Latin Versions, and the Latin translation of the Slavonic, is there published in full.* 1900.– Kautzsch: Beer, II, 119 ff.–Charles: Charles II, 155 ff.–Hennecke, Neutestamentliche Apokryphen,[2] 1924: Flemming-Duensing, 303 ff.–Burkitt, *Jewish and Christian Apocalypses*, 1914, 45 ff.–Burch, 'The Literary Unity of the Ascensio Isaiae', JThSt 1919, 17 ff.–idem, 'Material for the Interpretation of the Ascensio Isaiae', loc. cit., 1920, 249 ff.–Galling, 'Jesaja-Adonis', OLZ 1930, col. 99 f.–Rowley, *The Relevance of Apocalyptic*,[2] 1947, 108 ff.; 144 ff.

In the early Church two apocryphal Isaianic writings were known. Origen mentions several times a Jewish writing about the martyrdom of Isaiah. Jerome is aware of an *Ascensio Isaiae*, with which Epiphanius also seems to have been acquainted as a book current amongst the sects, and which turned up again in the Middle Ages. In the list of the Canon published by Montfaucon, a 'Ησαίου ὄρασις is named and a Latin version of it under the name of *visio Isaiae* was known in the sixteenth century. So there were probably at least two different pseudo-Isaianic writings which we have known only in an Ethiopic version of the Greek dating from the fifth to the seventh century A.D. and in fragments in the Greek, Latin and Slavonic languages, since they were published at the beginning and towards the end of the nineteenth century respectively.

The Ethiopic text on which we must rely contains the following: Chapter 1. As a sequel to 2 Kgs. 20: 16 Isaiah foretells to Hezekiah in the twenty-sixth year of his reign the wickedness of king Manasseh and his own martyrdom. In chapters 2: 1–3: 12: after Hezekiah's death Manasseh departs from God and serves Satan, his angels and his powers. Isaiah, who had fled with his friends into the desert, is denounced to Manasseh by the Samaritan Balchira as a lying prophet, is accused as a rebel and arrested. In chapters 3: 13–5: 1 the reason given for this slanderous denunciation is that Satan (Belial) incited Balchira to it because Isaiah had prophesied the coming of Christ, the establishment of the Christian Church, the appearance of the Antichrist and the end of the world. Chapter 5: 2–14 tells of Isaiah's death as a martyr; he was sawn asunder with a wood-saw enduring his fate in silence whilst 'his lips spake with the Holy Spirit'. This is followed in chapters 6–11 by the vision of Isaiah in the twentieth year of Hezekiah. The prophet is taken up by an angel into the seventh heaven, where he beholds God himself and learns that Christ will descend to the earth. After he has seen the future birth, life and passion of Jesus, his resurrection and ascent into heaven, Isaiah's spirit returns again to his earthly body. It is for this vision that Manasseh causes him to be sawn asunder.

Even this synopsis enables us to realize that we have to do with at least two different narratives which are only with difficulty brought into connexion with each other (against Burkitt and Burch who maintain the literary unity of the book):1. A Jewish writing about the martyrdom of Isaiah comprising parts of chapters 1; 2: 1–3: 12 and 5: 2–14 which was presumably written originally in Hebrew. This book or the oral tradition of Isaiah's martyrdom which underlies it seems to have been known to the author of the epistle to the Hebrews (cf. Heb. 11: 37), to Justin Martyr (*Dial. cum Tryphone* 120) and to Tertullian (*de patientia*, chapter 14). This would provide the *terminus ad quem* of its composition. It is a prophetic midrash in which perhaps an Iranian legendary theme or a feature from the Adonis myth has been incorporated. It is written as a martyr's saga in a style which reached a high degree of development in Christian antiquity and in the Middle Ages. It has been conjectured with good reason that this type of legend reaches back to the period of religious persecution which led to the Maccabean revolt. This would give us the *terminus a quo* for the origin of the book. In such times of persecution narratives of this kind (cf. 2 Macc. 6: 18–7: 42) were relevant to the circumstances of the day and effective as an example and an encouragement to be loyal to the faith. The sphere of conceptions and ideas of this work suggest a comparison with that of the Essenes, so that we may perhaps look for its composition in this sect.

The second part, the *ascensio* or *visio* in chapters 6–11 is a Christian writing (on a Jewish foundation? Bousset) belonging to the widespread type of literature concerned with visions which reached its zenith in Dante's *Divina Comedia*. It arose perhaps in the second century A.D. (false prophets in the Christian community, the Antichrist described in the figure of Nero, etc.).

It remains an open question whether the *passage in the middle*, in 3: 13–4: 18, which interrupts the continuity and is an obvious interpolation, was originally an earlier independent Christian narrative (Eissfeldt and others; yet it can hardly be the same as the Testament of Hezekiah mentioned by Credenus at the beginning of the twelfth century. [Thus Charles, recently opposed by Rowley.]). On the other hand it may be attributed like the other connecting links (1: 3 f.; 11: 2–22) to the Christian work of revision which must be placed in the third or fourth centuries.

80. The Psalms of Solomon

Text and Versions: Fritzsche, *Libri apocryphi Vet. Testamenti*, 1871, 569 ff.–Swete, The OT in Greek,[2] III, 765 ff.–Rahlfs, Septuaginta, 1935, II, 471 ff.–von Gebhardt, *Texte und Untersuchungen*, 13, Vol. 2, 1895.–Syriac: Harris and Mingana, *The Odes and Psalms of Solomon*, 2 vols., 1916, 1920.–Retranslations into Hebrew: Frankenberg, 'Die Datierung der Psalmen Salomos', BZAW 1896, 66 ff.–Kautzsch: Kittel, II, 127 ff.–Charles: Gray, II, 625 ff.–K. G. Kuhn, 'Die älteste Textgestalt der Psalmen Salomos, insbesondere auf Grund der syrischen Übersetzung neu untersucht', BWAT 1937.–Wellhausen, *Die Pharisäer und Sadduzäer*, 1874, 131 ff.–Ryle and James, ψαλμοὶ Σολομῶντος: *Psalms of the Pharisees, commonly called the Psalms of Solomon*, 1891. –Gry, Le Messie des Psalmes de Salomon', *Le Muséon*, 1905, 129 ff.–Ed. Meyer, *Ursprung und Anfänge des Christentums II*, 1921, 315 ff.–Lietzmann, *Geschichte der alten Kirche*, I, 1932, 12 ff.–Begrich, 'Der Text der Psalmen Salomos', ZNW 1939, 131 ff.–Rowley, *The Relevance of Apocalyptic*,[2] 1947, 71 ff.

The eighteen ψαλμοὶ Σολομῶντος are mentioned in several early Christian lists of the Canon and are sometimes classed with the apocryphal books, sometimes with the antilegomena (the books rejected from the sacred scriptures). They were not rediscovered until the seventeenth century. Since then they have been published several times in different Greek versions derived from the original Hebrew text and in a Syriac transcription from Greek (Begrich against Kuhn) which puts the Psalms of Solomon after the Odes of Solomon (songs from Christian circles of the second century). The best edition, on which the translation in Kautzsch also is based, is that of Gebhardt.

Just as most of the canonical psalms were attributed to David, so these psalms were ascribed in their titles after his time to Solomon, perhaps because by then the canonical Psalter had already been closed. There is no reference at all to Solomon in the text. In fact it may be concluded with some certainty from Ps. Sol. 2, 8 and no doubt also from the well-known messianic psalm 17 that the overthrow of the Hasmonaeans by Pompey (63 B.C.) was the occasion for and the subject of these songs. (Others think that Herod (37–4 B.C.) is meant by 'the man that is alien to our race' in 17: 7.) We shall not be mistaken if we assign to the same period the other songs which are expressed in more general terms and are less suggestive of historical events. In that case the collection may have been made between 63 B.C. and the reign of Herod. Nothing more precise can be gleaned about the origin and the authors (there were probably several) of the individual songs. The old *types* can be identified in these psalms also, such as the hymn, e.g. 2: 30, 33 ff.; 3: 1 f., the private and the national lament in 2: 15 ff., 22 ff., 8: 1 ff.; 7; 8: 22 ff.; thanksgiving in 13: 1 ff. (16 is combined with a lament) and the notes for the music (8: 1 εἰς νῖκος=*lammᵉnaṣṣēᵃḥ*; 17: 31; 18: 10 διάψαλμα=*selāh*) which is an indication of their use in the cult. Compared with the canonical psalms it is noticeable that the forms are less strictly observed and that the original types are intermingled, a sign of decadence in the history of literature, to be seen also in the prevalence of reflexions (8, 15). Most of the songs are based on the opposition of the godly to the ungodly. This is usually explained as alluding to the struggles between Pharisees and Sadducees (Wellhausen, Ed. Meyer, Kittel and others) and is probably correct up to a point. For in those psalms which enable the conditions of the day to be discerned this opposition lies in the background, and the collection as such may have originated amongst the Pharisees (Eissfeldt). But it would be going too far to regard the Psalms of Solomon merely as the expression of Pharisaic piety. Certain fundamental ideas such as the hope of resurrection (3, 12; 13: 11; 14: 9 f.) the freedom of the will (9: 4) and the pronounced expectation of the Messiah (17, 18) were cherished not only amongst the Pharisees. This should put us on our guard against the attempts, especially in the case of the form of the messianic hopes, to refer and to limit the detailed exegesis only to the controversy between the Pharisees and the Sadducees. These Psalms have a larger background and enable us to see how far the tradition of the early piety of the psalms with its moral seriousness was preserved in broad sections of late Judaism and indeed shaped it in spite of its special peculiarity. Something similar may also be said of the five apocryphal psalms of David in Syriac recently published by Noth (ZAW 1930, pp. 1 ff.) which have been transmitted in some manuscripts together with a didactic poem by the Nestorian bishop Elijah of Anbar (tenth century).

81. The fourth book of Maccabees

Fritzsche, *Libri apocryphi Vet. Testamenti*, 1871, 351 ff.–Swete, *The OT in Greek*,[2] 1899, III, 729 ff.–Rahlfs, *Septuaginta*, 1935, I, 1175 ff.–Kautzsch: Deissmann, II, 149 ff. –Charles: Townshend, II, 653 ff.–Hadas, 1953.–Freudenthal, *Die Flavius Josephus beigelegte Schrift über die Herrschaft der Vernunft, eine Predigt aus dem ersten nachchristlichen Jahrhundert*, 1869.–Norden, *Die antike Kunstprosa*, I, 1898,[2] 1915, 416 ff.–Winckler, 'Das vierte Makkabäerbuch', *Altoriental. Forschungen*, 3rd series, I, 1, 1902, 79 ff.–Dupont=Sommer, *Le quatrième livre des Machabées*, 1939.

The IV Book of Maccabees, which has been handed down in several manuscripts of the Septuagint (in particular in the Cod. Alexandrinus and Sinaiticus) and in numerous manuscripts of Josephus, does not belong like the three first books of the Maccabees to narrative literature. It is a philosophical treatise (a diatribe [Norden]) in the form of a speech ($\lambda o \gamma o s$ $\phi \iota \lambda o \sigma o \phi \acute{\omega} \tau a \tau o s$) made either in fact or fiction on the Stoic theme that reason is the mistress of the emotions. Amongst the different titles transmitted with the book the one 'On the supremacy of reason' ($\pi \epsilon \rho \acute{\iota}$ $a \mathring{\upsilon} \tau o \kappa \rho \acute{a} \tau o \rho o s$ $\lambda o \gamma \iota \sigma \mu o \hat{\upsilon}$) is the best description of the subject matter and is no doubt the original one. The name 'IV Book of Maccabees' arises from the fact that the author has selected some narratives of martyrs from the Maccabean period as examples to prove his philosophical proposition.

The treatise is well arranged; the *prologue*, 1: 1–12, outlining the purpose and plan of the book, is followed in 1: 13–3: 18 by the *first philosophical and didactic part* which contains some references to Joseph, Moses, Jacob and David as historical examples to corroborate the thesis. The *second part* (3:19–17: 6) brings forward as evidence for the same purpose the traditions of the martyrs of the Maccabean period (Eleazer, cf. 2 Macc. 6: 18 ff.; the mother and the seven brothers, cf. 2 Macc. 7). Next comes a meditation summing up the significance of such testimony to their faith and a proposal for an inscription on the graves of the martyrs in 17: 7–18: 24; an additional speech by the mother to her sons (18: 6–19) ends up in a doxology.

The author, who especially since the fourth century has been wrongly thought to be Josephus, used his Greek training in order to lay stress on the significance and strength of the Jewish faith in God and of its obedience to the law by means of the philosophical terms of Greek thought. Stoic philosophy not only provides his theme, 'The supremacy of reason over the passions', but he mentions also the four cardinal virtues φρόνησις, δικαιοσύνη, ἀνδρεία σωφροσύνη in 1:18 (cf. Wisd. 8: 7) and the ἀπάθεια of the martyrs. But these Stoic ideas and concepts are only borrowed forms which are made to convey typically Jewish ideas about their faith. 'Reason' and 'virtue' are basically for the author faith in God and obedience to his will as revealed in the law of Moses. The book contains profound thoughts about the vicarious suffering of the righteous for the atonement and purification of the sinful nation (1: 11, 6: 29; 17: 21 f.). These as well as the manner in which the Greek conception of immortality has been fitted into genuinely Jewish ideas make it clear that contact between Hellenism and Judaism has not been achieved at the expense of the latter.

4 Maccabees addresses itself to readers (and hearers) in whom, as well as in the author, it must be taken for granted that West and East have met. Its home will therefore be in a place like Alexandria or Antioch. Since it uses the traditions of the second book of Maccabees, the *terminus a quo* of its origin is given. Usually the period between the middle of the first century B.C. and that of the first century A.D. is suggested. Dupont-Sommer who fixes its date in the year 117–18 B.C. thinks it was an actual synagogue sermon preached in Antioch at the tombs of the Maccabean martyrs. But against this there is the objection that its theme is not a text from Holy Writ, but a philosophical doctrine.

82. The Sibylline Oracles

Text and Versions: Alexandre, ΧΡΗΣΜΟΙ ΣΙΒΥΛΛΙΑΚΟΙ, 2 vols., 1841–1856.–Rzach, Oracula Sibyllina, 1891.–Kautzsch: Blass, II, 177 ff.–Charles: Lanchester, II, 368 ff.–Geffken in Hennecke, Neutestamentl. Apokryphen,² 1924, 399 ff.–Bouche=Leclercq, 'Les oracles sibyllins', RHR 1883, 236 ff.; 619 ff.; 1884, 220 ff.–Geffken, *Komposition und Entstehungszeit der Oracula Sibyllina, Texte und Untersuchungen*, 23, 1, 1902.–Bate, *Sibylline Oracles*, Books III–V, 1918.–Causse, 'Le mythe

de la nouvelle Jérusalem du Deutéro–Esaïe à la IIIᵉ Sibylle', RHPhR 1938, 377 ff.–
Rowley, The Relevance of Apocalyptic,[2] 1947, 68 ff.

Graeco-Roman antiquity possessed a voluminous Sibylline
literature, originally actual oracles associated with mantic sayings,
both ecstatic and charismatic, pronounced by word of mouth.
Prophetic sayings of this kind in hexameters were recorded in
writing and collected at a time when the old homes of the oracles,
e.g. Delphi, had fallen into disrepute and ruin. Tradition, already
discernible in Heraclitus, Euripides, Aristophanes and Plato,
traces them back to legendary prophetesses, Sibylla, who are said
to have spoken prophecies about the history of the dim past
which were to be fulfilled in the present or the future. The Sibylline oracles in Rome gained a particular importance. Frequently
these oracles are specimens of the literary type of *vaticinia ex eventu*
which was admitted also into Jewish apocalyptic literature (cf.
Dan. 10–12). Jewish and later Christian propaganda made use of
this literature in order to express under the name of a heathen
prophetess who was later transformed into a Jewish Sibylla its own
concern particularly in regard to polytheism and idolatry. To the
unrepentant Gentile the coming last judgment is foretold. Often
pagan models are used and modified to a greater or lesser extent
to suit Jewish purposes; frequently new Sibylline oracles are
produced and their subject matter is taken from Jewish history
with its messianic outlook, instead from that of Greece. Consequently in the collection, presumably made in the sixth century
A.D., pagan, Jewish and Christian traditional material was gathered
together in hopeless confusion. Of the twelve books still extant,
Books III–V contain the largest amount of Jewish elements,
whilst Books VI–VIII and XIII have a Christian stamp.

Book III, in which no Christian revision can be identified,
contains earlier Sibylline oracles of Greek, Babylonian or Persian
origin intermingled with a Jewish recension foretelling in narrative form the history of the world from the flood up to the
messianic kingdom. In other ways too it combines the praise of
Judaism with attacks on idolatry and with eschatological prophecies. From the allusion in verse 318 to the undivided rule of
Ptolemy VII Physcon (177–145 B.C.), the Greek king, the conclusion has been drawn that the author was an Egyptian Jew writing
at about 140 B.C. Later expansions have been conjectured, since

verses 46 ff. seem to refer to the second triumvirate of Antony, Octavius and Lepidus (43 B.C.) and verses 75 ff. points perhaps to Cleopatra to whom world dominion is foretold.

The short book IV had probably simply a Jewish revision. Here too a pagan foundation must be assumed, for in the observations on history the campaign of Xerxes, the Peloponnesian War and the deeds of Alexander the Great are brought in. At the beginning indications of a Jewish redaction are found in the prophecy of the destruction of Jerusalem by the Romans, in the flight of Nero across the Euphrates and his return, as well as in the promises to the Jews. They can be seen also at the end in a penitential sermon on an eschatological foundation. The mention of the eruption of Vesuvius (A.D. 79) affords a clue for its date.

Book V is a *mixtum compositum*. The Roman history at the beginning in 1–51, which is taken down as far as Hadrian (117–138) and his three successors (Antoninus Pius, 138–161; Lucius Verus, 161–169; Marcus Aurelius, 161–180), no doubt comes from a Roman hand in the time of the Antonines. This is followed by the outpourings of an Egyptian Jew against Egypt and its idolatry. The reference to the destruction of the temple and to the returning Nero as well as bitter denunciations against Rome are of earlier Jewish origin from the period after A.D. 70. The grotesque prophecy at the end about the battle of the stars amongst themselves, is no doubt derived from a pagan model.

83. The Ethiopic Book of Enoch

Text and Versions: Greek: Radermacher, *Das Buch Henoch*, ed. by Fleming and Radermacher, 1901, 18 ff., 113 ff.–Swete, The OT in Greek,² 1899, III, 789 ff.–Ethiopic: Dillmann, *Liber Henoch aethiopice*, 1851.–Flemming, *Das Buch Henoch, Äthiopischer Text* (Texte und Untersuchungen, 2 1), 1902.–Charles: *The Ethiopic Version of the Book of Enoch (with Greek and Latin Versions)*, 1906.–Kautzsch: Beer, II, 217 ff.–Charles: Charles II, 163 ff.–Martin, *Le Livre d' Hénoch*, 1906.–Förster, 'Adams Erschaffung und Namengebung', ARW 1908, 477 ff.–Kuhn, 'Beiträge zur Erklärung des Buches Henoch', ZAW 1921, 240 ff.–Messel, 'Der Menschensohn in den Bilderreden des Henoch', BZAW 1922.–Pedersen, 'Zur Erklärung der eschatologischen Visionen Henochs', *Islamica* II, 3, 1926, 416 ff.–N. Schmidt, 'The Apocalypse of Noah and the Parables of Enoch', *Oriental Studies for Paul Haupt*, 1926, 111 ff.–Lods, La chute des anges, RHPhR 1927, 295 ff.–Vitti, 'Ultime critiche su Enoc etiopico', *Biblica*, 1931, 316 ff.–Mowinckel, 'Henokskikkelsen i senjødisk apokalyptikk', *Norsk Teologisk Tidsskrift*, 1940, 206 ff.–idem, Henok og Menneskesønnen, loc. cit., 1944, 57.–Glasson, The Second Advent, 1945.–Sjöberg, *Der Menschensohn im Äthiopischen Henochbuch* (Acta reg. societatis humaniorum litterarum lundensis XLI) Lund, 1946.–Rowley, *The Relevance of Apocalyptic*,² 1947, 54 ff.; 77 ff.–van Andel, *De structur van de Henoch–Traditie en het Nieuwe Testament*, 1955.

The Ethiopic Book of Enoch derives its name from the fact that it has been transmitted to us in a complete form only in an Ethiopic version of the Abyssinian Church which had admitted it into its OT canon. This version only became known again in the eighteenth century, but numerous manuscripts of it have been found since then. It goes back to a Greek version of an original Hebrew, or more likely an Aramaic text (Schürer, Torrey). Partial Latin and Greek versions are also in existence. The book is a whole collection of apocalyptic literature of different kinds and different ages gathered together under the name of Enoch. In late Judaism Enoch was considered to be the inventor of arithmetic, astronomy, writing and other secret branches of learning. He was held in high esteem as a seer of apocalyptic visions, presumably because the tradition embodied in Gen. 5: 18 ff. was connected with him and was amplified. Moreover this tradition has behind it the Babylonian influence of the figure of the seventh primeval king Enmeduranki who was regarded as the father of divination and prophecy and the recipient of revelations from the sun-god. The book is composed of several separate writings which were originally independent. This is evident from the fact that in some passages not Enoch but Noah is the chief character (e.g. chapters 6–11, 54, 60, 106 f.) and the several parts are marked off from each other by special titles (cf. 37: 1 f.; 72: 1; 108: 1) or must be kept apart because different eras are presupposed in them.

Since the book is a compilation, no clear arrangement can be expected in it. Yet the contents may be divided into the following sections: chapters 1–5 *an introductory discourse* by Enoch, partly in poetic form, announcing the imminent judgment of the world. Chapters 6–36, *the book concerning the angels*, starting with the old myth of their fall (cf. Gen. 6: 1 ff.) and their punishment, with a description in a double parallel account of a journey made by Enoch in the company of angels through the earth and the underworld (17–19 and 20–36). Chapters 37–71: the *Similitudes of Enoch*, in which special mention must be made of the judgment by the Messiah (45–57) and by the Son of Man (58–69), the Ascension of Enoch and his installation as the Son of Man (70 f.). Chapters 72–82: the book of the stars, with astronomical discourses on the sun, the moon, the stars and on matters of the calendar, such as the division into years and months and leap years, the points of the compass, etc. This section ends with the return of Enoch to his home on earth. Chapters 83–90, *the book of history*, with two visions concerning the flood and the history of mankind from Adam to the coming of the messianic kingdom. Chapters 91–105, the *book of the instruction and exhortation of Enoch* with the *Apocalypse of Weeks* (93: 1–14 and 91: 12–17 [*sic*]) in which universal history is seen in a frame of ten weeks. Chapters 106–108 brings us to *the end* with a description of the signs and wonders at the birth of Noah and exhortations to his son and his descendants, who 'hold fast to the law in the last days'.

In view of the various items which have come together in the book of Enoch, it can easily be understood that no complete description of its literary formation is possible and that opinions on it diverge in many details. It is unlikely that pre-Maccabean collections have been admitted (against Charles, Glasson and others who conjecture that chapters 6–36 were known to the author of the book of Daniel). It cannot be proved that the Apocalypse of Weeks (93: 1–14: 91: 12–17) was ignorant of the persecution under Antiochus IV Epiphanes and must therefore be given an earlier date (Rowley against Charles, Martin, Eissfeldt). It is possible that chapters 6–36 as well as the short Apocalypse of Weeks came into existence in the Maccabean period. In the vision of the seventy shepherds in the History (chapters 85–90) the lambs with horns are probably to be interpreted as symbolic animals representing the Maccabees (90: 9 f.); it has been suggested that the lamb with the great horn should be interpreted as Judas (*ob.* 160 B.C.) or John Hyrcanus (134–104 B.C.). A *terminus ad quem* would then be provided by the year 160 or—in view of the author's friendly attitude to the Maccabees—by the breach of John Hyrcanus with the Pharisees. The hortatory book, chapters 91–105 (without 93; 91: 12–17), like the Similitudes (chapters 37–71) reflects the struggles between the Pharisees and the Sadducees, which had evidently lasted already a long time and had brought oppression and persecution to the Pharisees (103: 9, 15). This might suggest the period of Alexander Jannaeus (102–76 B.C.). As the final attack on Jerusalem by the power opposed to God is expected from the Parthians and Medes, and not from Rome, the conquest of Jerusalem by Pompey (63 B.C.) might be thought the latest limit for the writing of the Similitudes. It is not

possible to determine exactly when the rest of the book of
Enoch came into being. Perhaps the introduction, chapters 1–5,
the vision of the flood, chapters 83 f. and the last warning speech
of Enoch may be assigned to the time immediately preceding the
Romans. On the other hand, for the astronominal book, chapters
72–82, about the middle of the second century B.C. seems possible,
if it may be assumed that Jub. 4: 17 ff. depends on these passages
of Enoch. An earlier origin (first half of the second century) has
been conjectured also for the cycle of the Noah-tradition (chapters
6–11; 39: 1 f.; 54: 7–55: 2; 60; 65: 1–69: 25; 106–107) on the
assumption that in its essentials it is derived from the book of
Noah mentioned in Jub. 13; 21: 10; we must therefore allow for its
subsequent insertion into this book. It is an open question
whether this redaction was the work of one individual or the
result of a longer process of literary history, in which several
hands had a share. This latter is the more probable.

The place where the book of Enoch came into being is likely
to have been Palestine. The spiritual home of the collection is the
world of Pharisaic piety. So its author or redactor must be sought
amongst the Pharisees or in the circles closely connected with
them. The particular details of its doctrine as to angels, its emphasis on divine providence, its great regard for asceticism and
its rejection of riches, its defence of the solar year, the absence of
any mention of the resurrection of the body, all these points had
already earlier led to the conclusion that most of this book
originated in the sect of the Essenes (Riessler). Now the writings
of the sect of Qumran seem to throw fresh light on the conditions
under which it arose, since these display a striking similarity to
the first part of the book of Enoch and to the Noah tradition.
Van Aalders points to the parallel between the leading personage
in this sect, the Teacher of Righteousness, and the figure of Enoch
and would like to deduce from the different sections of Enoch the
different stages in the development of the sect or of its groups. If
we may assume that the Essenes introduced a calendar of 364 days*
for the sake of keeping the sabbath holy and for that reason dissociated themselves from the Pharisees and the temple feasts in
Jerusalem, we could explain 'the shortening of the years' and its
consequence for agriculture in 80: 2 ff. as the working out of this

* cf. Vogt, Antiquum Kalendarium Sacerdotale. *Biblica* 36 (1955), p. 403 ff.

new arrangement of the calendar. For after some decades it must have led to a displacement of the seasons of this kind and was no doubt given up. The fact that the 'retardation' of the seasons is presented here as the consequence of sin, would then be explained by its origin after the failure of the rearrangement of the calendar. But further research is needed before we can unravel the relationship of the book of Enoch to the sect at Qumran, together with the fragments found there, and to its use in the book of Jubilees, the Testament of the Twelve Patriarchs and the Zadokite Work.

The alternation of poetry and prose, the different literary types which are partly imitations of older forms (accounts of visions, prophecies, travel reports, prayers, hymns, denunciations and exhortations expanded into 'speeches', mythological stories, oracles of God, utterances of angels, apocalyptical and allegorical presentation and exegesis of history in the form of prophecy) already give a mere external picture of the different streams which are united here as in a reservoir. It is, however, not possible in every case to work up to the individual sources, to make one's way through to the origin of the abundant and variegated material and to pursue its history in the oral and written formation of the tradition. Babylonian, Persian, Egyptian and Greek learning and traditional material have been combined with specifically Jewish traditions into a motley gallimaufry which can be called an actual compendium of the apocalyptic esoteric learning of late Judaism.

Yet this sometimes grotesque abundance of images or similes and of ideas must not make us forget the vigour of the prophetic heritage which is evident in the unbroken reliance on salvation and loyalty to the faith and in the stern morality of this book, qualities which helped to prevail over the perils of persecution and oppression within and without. It is no wonder that this book exercised a strong and far-reaching influence. It is mentioned or utilized in several pseudepigrapha (Jubilees, Testaments of the Twelve Patriarchs, Apocalypses of Ezra and Baruch, the Zadokite Work, the Lamech scroll); the young Christian community could not escape from its influence (cf. the quotation in the Epistle of Jude 14 f.). For a long time it was prized very highly, especially in the Alexandrian Church, but later it was preserved in the Abyssinian Church alone.

84. The Slavonic book of Enoch

Slavonic: Popov, 1880–Novaković, 1884.–German Version: Bonwetsch, *Die Bücher der Geheimnisse Henochs, Texte und Übersetzungen*, 44, 2, 1922.–Kautzsch: Littmann, II, 218, note a.–Morfill and Charles, *The Book of the Secrets of Enoch*, 1896. –Charles: Forbes and Charles, II, 425 ff.–Förster, 'Adams Erschaffung und Namengebung, ein lateinisches Fragment des sog. slavischen Henoch', ARW 1908, 477 ff.– N. Schmidt, 'The Two Recensions of Slavonic Enoch', JAOS 1921, 307 ff.–Lake, 'The Date of the Slavonic Enoch', HThR 1923, 397 f.–Rowley, *The Relevance of Apocalyptic*,[2] 1947, 95 ff.–Vaillant, *Le Livre des Secrets d' Hénoch*, 1952.

In addition to the Ethiopic book of Enoch, further literary evidence of the extensive Enoch tradition has been preserved in a Slavonic translation from Greek, known since 1880 under the title of the Book of the Secrets of Enoch, the Slavonic Enoch or 2 Enoch. We have this book in two recensions, a longer one published by Popov and a shorter one edited by Novaković; both are available in the translation of Bonwetsch. Opinions differ as to their relationship. The shorter text used to be considered almost universally as an extract or summary of the more comprehensive one. But Schmidt and Vaillant regard it as the earlier original one which Vaillant wishes to trace back to a Christian book of Enoch known still to Origen and lost since then. It is doubtful whether we can accept Vaillant's view that the longer text is due to the imagination of fifteenth- or sixteenth-century Slavonic editors. The Slavonic book is indeed dependent on the Ethiopic one as regards its subject matter and its form. Yet it must be considered as an independent literary production within the framework of the Jewish–Hellenistic–Christian development of the Enoch tradition.

Contents. The *introduction* in chapters 1–2 gives an account in the first person singular of two visions of angels and Enoch's farewell to his children. Chapters 3–21 describes how Enoch was carried away and travelled through the seven heavens, on the pattern of the Ethiopic Enoch. The *second part* in chapters 22–38 contains God's revelation of the creation and the history of mankind from Adam to Enoch and the flood. This is followed in chapters 39–66 by Enoch's exhortation and teaching to his children. The *final chapters* give an account of his ascension and a retrospect of his life.

As compared with the Ethiopic Enoch, this book is more homogeneous, but also more monotonous. There are no messianic allusions, on the other hand the doctrine as to angels is expanded, and the account of the creation has a thoroughly individual stamp, which recalls the 'Hermetic' literature. This book too is characterized by the seriousness and high level of its religious and moral demands, especially those of social ethics. It may have come into being amongst the Greek-speaking Jews of the Diaspora probably in Egypt. Later it was worked over from the Christian point of view. In 51: 4 the visit three times a year to the temple is recommended, and in 59: 1 f.; 61: 4; 62: 1 the existence of a cult with sacrifices is taken for granted. These facts have led to what is no doubt the correct inference that the basic Jewish substance of the book must have come into existence before the destruction of the temple in A.D. 70, though this is occasionally disputed.

85. The Assumption of Moses (Assumptio Mosis)

In Latin: Ceriani, *Monumenta Sacra et Profana* I, 1, 1861.–Fritzsche, *Libri apocryphi Vet. Testamenti*, 1871, 700 ff.–Clemen, *Die Himmelfahrt des Mose*, Kleine Texte 10, 1904.–Hilgenfeld, *Messias Judaeorum*, 1869, 435 ff. (a translation back into Greek).–Kautzsch: Clemen, II, 311 ff.–Schmidt and Merx, *Die assumptio Mosis*, 1868.–Charles: Charles II, 407 ff.–Rosenthal, *Vier apokryphische Bücher aus der Zeit und Schule R. Akibas*, 1885, 104 ff.–Hölscher, 'Über die Entstehungszeit der "Himmelfahrt Moses" ', ZNW 1916, 108 ff.–Ferrar, *The Assumption of Moses*, 1918.–Kuhn, 'Zur Assumptio Moses', ZAW 1925, 124 ff.–Lattey, 'The Messianic Expectation in "The Assumption of Moses" ', *The Catholic Biblical Quarterly* 1942, 11 ff.–Torrey, ' "Taxo" in the Assumption of Moses', JBL 1943, 1 ff; 1945, 395 ff.–Rowley.–'The figure of "Taxo" in the Assumption of Moses', JBL 64, 1945, 141 ff.–idem, *The Relevance of Apocalyptic*,[2] 1947, 91 ff; 134 ff.–Mowinckel, The Hebrew Equivalent of Taxo in Ass. Mos. IX. *VT Suppl.*, Vol. I (1953), 88 ff.–Wallace, 'The Semitic origin of the Assumption of Moses', ThZ 11 (1955) 321 ff.

This book came to light again in 1861 by its discovery through Ceriani in the Ambrosiana in Milan. It is a Latin version from Greek which itself seems to go back further to an original text in Hebrew or Aramaic. Origen knew it. It is mentioned also in the records of the Council of Nicea. There is probably an allusion to it in the Epistle of Jude, verse 9, where he speaks of the archangel Michael disputing with Satan about the body of Moses. Although this story is not preserved in the Latin text, it must once have been included in it. For this is implied by the fact that the narrative breaks off at 12: 13 in the middle of a sentence, and that the name of the book requires a narrative about Moses' ascent to heaven. In the early lists of apocryphal books a διαθήκη Μωυσέως and a ἀνάλημψις, Μωυσέως are distinguished as being no doubt the names for the two parts of the book of which possibly the first one is preserved in the text we know. This might actually be Moses' 'testament' to Joshua (chapters 1 and 11 f.). But it consists in the main of an apocalypse in the form of a prophecy concerning the history of Israel from the conquest of Palestine to the dawn of the kingdom of God on the last day which will bring with it the end of Satan, the judgment of the Gentiles and the exaltation of Israel to heaven. The question has been raised whether the fragment of a farewell speech by Moses which has been found at Qumran and which contains a paraphrase of the establishment of the covenant should not be claimed as part of the Testament of Moses or at least as belonging to this apocryphal Mosaic literature.

It is fairly generally admitted that by the ungodly kings who are also high priests the Hasmonaeans are meant, and that the king who will reign for thirty-four years and who, not being of the priestly race, will punish them (6: 2 ff.) is intended to be Herod who was king for thirty-four years (37–4 B.C.). Since in 6: 7 f. the author expects Herod's sons to have shorter periods of authority, he cannot have witnessed the end of what was in fact the long rule of Philip (4 B.C.–A.D. 34) and of Antipas (4 B.C.–A.D. 39). In 6: 8 f., the conquest of the land by the cohorts of the mighty king of the West is mentioned. This obviously refers to the measures taken by Augustus when in 4 B.C. he sent the legate of Syria, Quintilius Varus, to Palestine to suppress the Jewish revolt. Moreover it is stated in 7: 1 that 'when this is done the times shall be ended' and in the rest of the account the historical details fade out. So we may conjecture that the book came into being not very long after the year 4 B.C. in spite of isolated attempts to fix a later date for it (Burkitt, Lattey, Rowley). In the prophecies concerning the persecutions of the Jews in chapters 8 f. an account is given of a member of the tribe of Levi called Taxo who with his seven sons prefers to die rather than to transgress the commands of the God of his fathers. This figure is still a mysterious one. It has been variously identified with Eleazar (2 Macc. 6: 18 ff., Charles) or the Messiah (Lattey) or Mattathias (Torrey) or Eleazar, a contemporary of Bar Cochbah (c. A.D. 130) (Hölscher), thus showing the uncertainty of scholars on this point. Only this much can be said that it is more likely to refer to a historical person than to an imaginary figure. Riessler connected the name Taxo=organizer, overseer or director with the office of the Essenes 'controller of the communal affairs'. More recently Mowinckel considers the Latinized Greek word Taxo (n) to be the translation of the Hebrew from Num. 21: 18 and interprets it as the title of the man who reorganized the Damascus sect after the death of the 'Teacher of Righteousness' and introduced its new system.

The hostility to the Hasmonaeans and their party, the Sadducees (cf. e.g. 5: 1 ff.), suggests that the book originated in Pharisaic or kindred circles in Palestine. It is impossible to say whether the Pharisees were the models for the character sketches of the pious hypocrite or the selfish glutton. If this should be the case, the author might more easily be found in the sect of the Essenes which had split off from the Pharisees (Merx, Riessler, Eissfeldt, Mowinckel and others) than amongst the Zealots (Ewald, Schürer and others). For the book does not anywhere exhibit features which would be characteristic of this last group; but it does contain some which have become more familiar to us through the manuscripts discovered in Qumran. The book breathes in all seriousness a spirit of penitent, humble piety and loyalty to the law. This would definitely leave open the possibility that it is a criticism of the backslidings and demoralization of certain circles within their own ranks, especially since we must not think of the sphere of influence of the Pharisaic type of piety as being too narrowly restricted. It will require more research into the literature and history of the Qumran sect and its relationship to the Damascus community before a definite decision on these questions can be made.

86. 2 Esdras (4 Ezra)

Text and Versions: Latin: Fritzsch, *Libri apocryphi Vet. Testamenti*, 1871.–Hilgenfeld. *Messias Judaeorum*, 1896, 36 ff. (Re-translation into the Greek).–Violet, *Die Esra –Apokalypse*, I, 1910 (all the texts, the eastern ones in translation).–idem, *Die Apokalypsen des Esra und des Baruch in deutscher Gestalt*, 1924.–Kautzsch, Gunkel, II, 331 ff.–Charles: Box, II, 542 ff.–WC: Oesterley, 1933.–Rosenthal, *Vier apokryphische Bücher aus der Zeit und Schule R. Akibas*, 1885, 39 ff.–Kabisch, *Das Vierte Buch Esra auf seine Quellen untersucht*, 1889.–Wellhausen, *Zur apokalyptischen Literatur, Skizzen und Vorarbeiten*, 6, 1899, 215 ff.–Vagany, *Le problème eschatologique dans le IVe livre d' Esdras*, 1906.–Sigwalt, 'Die Chronologie des 4. Buches Esdras', BZ 1911, 146 ff. –Box, *The Ezra–Apocalypse*, 1912.–Keulers, 'Die eschatologische Lehre des vierten Esrabuches', *Bibl. Studien*, 1922.–Mundle, 'Das religiöse Problem des IV. Esrabuches', ZAW 1929, 222 ff.–Schütz, 'Die Offenbarung des Johannes und Kaiser Domitian', FRLANT 1933, 40 ff.–Gry, *Les dires prophétiques d'Esdras*, 2 vols., 1938.–Rowley, *The Relevance of Apocalyptic*, ²1947, 99ff. 141 ff.

P

The name '4 Ezra' comes from the Latin Church where the books of Ezra and Nehemiah were usually called 1 and 2 Ezra (see section 50), the apocryphal book of Ezra was 3 Ezra (see section 64) and the pseudepigraphical apocalypse was 4 Ezra. The Latin version which has preserved most faithfully the text handed down to us is derived from a Greek one which itself originated in a lost Hebrew original. The other extant versions in Syriac, Ethiopic, Arabic, Armenian, Sahidic and Georgian are also from Greek (Gunkel). The numerous translations and quotations from this book by church writers prove the popularity of this apocalyptic book. Although it was excluded from the Canon, it was used and cited, it was printed in the Vulgate as an appendix, and is found too in German editions of the Bible for Roman Catholics, Lutherans and the Reformed Church. In some sects it still plays a not unimportant part at the present day. To judge both by its form and its contents it is one of the most outstanding and profound books of the later apocalyptic literature.

Contents. The author gives himself in 3: 1 ff. the name 'Salathiel, also called Ezra', a literary, historically indefensible, fiction. He purports to have seen his visions in the thirtieth year after the destruction of Jerusalem by the Babylonians (587 B.C.). Actually his starting point is the catastrophe of the fall of the city in A.D. 70 (10: 20 ff.) and his concern is the problem of the justice of God in history. This problem lies more or less plainly as a *leitmotif* behind each of the seven visions forming the framework of the book which at times rises to great poetic heights. Chapters 1–2, as well as 15–16 as numbered in the Vulgate (now called 5 and 6 Ezra), are presumably of Christian origin (second–third century A.D.). They are not found in the Eastern texts and will not be dealt with here (cf. Weinel in Hennecke, *Neutestamentliche Apokryphen*, 1904, pp. 305 ff., 311 ff.).

In the first three visions religious perplexities and speculations are placed in the foreground; in the four following ones it is the problems of eschatology and apocalyptic. In the *first vision*, chapters 3: 1–5: 19 these two questions are raised: whence does the sin and misery of this world spring? and How can Israel's sin and distress be explained in view of the fact that his oppressor ('Babylon') is not better than the chosen and rejected people of God? The answer given by the archangel Uriel in three poetic similes is that the spirit of mortal man cannot understand the ways of the eternal, but that the coming aeon will bring the solution when the number of the righteous has been completed.

The *second vision*, chapters 5: 20–6: 34 is based on the problem why God has abandoned his only chosen people to the mercy of the Gentiles. Here again the answer is that the problem is insoluble for man. There follows a further reference to the world approaching the end of its history and to the consummation which God alone will bring about, with its premonitory signs.

In the *third vision*, chapters 6: 35–9: 25, the problem is raised why Israel does not possess the world since it was after all created for Israel's sake. The angel points out to the author that the present world in its evil plight is the necessary approach to the coming good aeon which God has reserved for his people. There follow thoughts about the world judgment and about the question why the number of the saved is so small compared with the multitude of sinners who although created by God will be lost. In the end the answer is given that the sinners deserved their fate, and that Ezra should forget them and be satisfied that he himself belongs to the blessed.

In the *fourth vision*, chapters 9: 26–10: 59 Ezra beholds a woman in grief, bewailing the death of her son on his wedding night. Suddenly the woman disappears and in her place Ezra perceives a city built on a mighty foundation. He is told the meaning of this allegorical vision, namely that Zion's present sorrow will soon come to an end and that then Jerusalem will be built anew.

In a *fifth vision, a dream by night*, in chapters 10: 60–12: 50 Ezra sees an eagle with twelve wings, three heads and eight little wings rising from the sea and flying away over the earth. After the twelve wings and the six little wings have ruled and disappeared and finally only one head and two little wings are left, a roaring lion appears. He announces to the eagle that he is condemned to perish, whereupon the head of the eagle and his two wings disappear. According to the interpretation the eagle is the last of the four world empires described in Dan. 7 and the lion is the Messiah out of the house of David (cf. Gen. 49: 9 f.) who will break the world power and deliver the remnant of God's people.

The *sixth vision* too in chapter 13: 1–58 Ezra sees by night in a dream. In a storm there appears out of the sea 'as it were the likeness of a man' (cf. Dan. 7: 13 ff.) who flies on the clouds of heaven. Many people prepare to make war against him, but he flies on to a high mountain and burns up his enemies by the fiery breath of his mouth. Thereupon the man flies down from the mountain and gathers a peaceful army round him. The man is the son of God, the redeemer of the world, who destroys his enemies by his word and protects the ten dispersed tribes of Israel and 'those who remain' of the people of Israel.

In the *seventh vision* in chapter 14: 1–48 Ezra receives the commission to 'lay up in his heart' these visions and to prepare for his end, for he is to be carried away from the earth. Filled with the spirit of God, he dictates in forty days at the divine command the sacred books which had perished when Jerusalem was destroyed. These are the twenty-four canonical books which he is to publish openly and 'let the worthy and the unworthy read' them, and the remaining seventy books which are to be kept secret and are only intended for 'the wise among the people'. In conclusion Ezra, 'the writer of the knowledge of the Most High', is carried away.

In view of a number of unevennesses, of certain repetitions, and of the changes of emphasis in the presentation, the question of the literary unity of this book has been raised again and again. Different answers are still given today. Kabisch especially, then Charles, de Faye and Box advocated its division into several apocalypses. Amongst the more recent researches Torrey thinks he must distinguish an apocalypse of Salathiel which he places before A.D. 70 from an Ezra apocalypse of the time of Domitian (A.D. 81–96). Yet most scholars maintain no doubt correctly the unity of the book. The inconsistencies and the impression at times of a certain mosaic, especially when apocalyptic conceptions are described, are due to the fact that the author has used current and in part written traditions. But he has fitted them into his own framework, transformed and interpreted them. On the other hand he has shaped and decked out according to existing patterns his own visionary experiences about which we can hardly have any real doubts. The legend as to the way Ezra reproduced the sacred books (cf. Slav. Enoch 23: 4 ff.) is not likely to be the original handiwork of the author of 4 Ezra.

Beside the personal spiritual experiences of the writer it is above all his profoundly sincere piety, brooding in melancholy with religious and moral earnestness, which invests his book with a particular quality and, in spite of the tenacity with which he clings to the Jewish piety of the law, with a value reaching out beyond these barriers. For he knows how to extract from the questions arising out of the problem of theodicy, which confronts him as a result of the hard fate of his people, a universally human aspect which suggests a comparison with the book of Job. There is indeed this material difference that in 4 Ezra its solution is given in terms of apocalyptic eschatology, a sign that in the interval Judaism had changed radically from a religion of this world to one of the next (Eissfeldt). All this and the remarkable restraint in comparison with the other apocalypses and their inextricable tangle of fantastic mythological conceptions may have been the reason for the strong and far-reaching influence emanating from this book and raising it into the ranks of world literature.

The author seems himself to have witnessed the destruction of Jerusalem in A.D. 70 (5: 35; 10: 45); he wrote his book after this date. The three heads in the vision in 12: 35 are probably the three Flavians, Vespasian (69–79), Titus (79–81) and Domitian (81–96). The death of Titus is no doubt assumed in 11: 35; that of Domitian according to 12: 2, 28 is still to come. This leads to the conclusion that the book was presumably composed in the last decade of the first century A.D. We cannot be sure where it was written. The fact that it was originally in the Hebrew language might indicate Palestine; Rome has also been suggested, because the name 'Babylon' as in the Revelation of St. John might be used intentionally as a pseudonym for Rome.

87. The Syriac Apocalypse of Baruch

Text and versions: Syriac: Ceriani, *Monumenta Sacra et Profana*, V, 2, 1871.–Kmosko, *Patrologia Syriaca accur.* Graffin, I, 2, 1907, col. 1056 ff.–Latin: Fritzsche, *Libri apocryphi Vet. Testamenti*, 1871, 654 ff.–Greek: Charles, II, 487 ff.–German: Violet, *Die Apokalypsen des Esra und des Baruch in deutscher Gestalt*, 1924.–Kautzsch: Ryssel, II, 404 ff.–Charles: Charles, II, 470.–Rosenthal, *Vier apokryphische Bücher aus der Zeit und Schule R. Akibas*, 1885, 72 ff.–Kabisch, 'Die Quellen der Apokalypse Baruchs', JpTh 1892, 66 ff.–Sigwalt, 'Die Chronologie der syrischen Baruchapokalypse', BZ 1911, 397 ff.–James, *The Biblical Antiquities of Philo*, 1917.–Gry, 'La date de la fin des temps selon les révélations ou les calculs du pseudo-Philon et de Baruch', RB 1939, 337 ff.–Rowley, *The Relevance of Apocalyptic*, ²1947, 103 ff.; 142f.

The Syriac Apocalypse of Baruch was discovered in a manuscript of the Peshitta in Milan by Ceriani who published it. It is a translation of a Greek text of which small fragments are known and is itself derived from a Hebrew or Aramaic original. In its construction and subject matter it is close to 4 Ezra (cf. their collation in Ryssel) and might, according to the opinion of most recent scholars, be dependent on it as regards its style (against Kabisch, Charles, Ryssel and others). For the matter, the forms and the trains of thought in 4 Ezra are gathered together in much more homogeneous passages than in the Apocalypse of Baruch.

As in the case of 4 Ezra the *contents* of this book are divided into seven sections.

I. Chapters 1–12. In the twenty-fifth year of Jeconiah (591 B.C.) God announces to Baruch the imminent destruction of Jerusalem. The Chaldaeans appear and march into the city, after angels have hidden the vessels of the temple and laid down the walls. Whilst Jeremiah accompanies the exiles to Babylon, Baruch remains by God's command in Jerusalem in order to receive fresh revelations there (contrary to the historical facts!).

II. Chapters 13–20. In a dialogue with God Baruch learns that disaster has befallen the people in order to purify it, so that the end of the world may come more quickly. Then judgment will come upon the Gentiles now living in happiness and a just balance will be struck between the fate of the wicked and the godly.

III. Chapters 21–34. Baruch is rebuked for his doubts and is instructed concerning the judgment of the wicked, when it will begin and how long it will last, and the sequence of the eras: twelve periods of distress will befall the whole world, but when the Messiah appears a season of radiant joy will begin. Jerusalem will be rebuilt and then destroyed a second time; but after that it will be restored in glory to last for ever.

IV. Chapters 35–46. In the visions which follow next Baruch sees in the night a large wood (= the four world empires of the Babylonians, the Persians, the Greeks and the Romans) and a vine. Beneath the vine a spring gushes out which in its flood destroys the whole world except for one cedar (=the empire of the Messiah which brings the world empires to an end). After the cedar has been told by the vine that it will perish, it is thrown down and burnt. This is interpreted to mean that the last ruler of the fourth world empire will be killed by the Messiah on Zion whose dominion will endure till the end of the world. Lastly the elders are exhorted to be patient and faithful to the law.

V. Chapters 47–52. Baruch receives fresh disclosures about the last awful calamity, about the new corporeal state of the righteous at the resurrection and about the ultimate fate of the blessed and of the damned.

VI. Chapters 53–76. In another vision Baruch sees a cloud coming up from the sea and passing over the earth. Six times in succession it pours out alternately bright and dark water mingled with fire. Then it is hurled by lightning down to the earth. A flash of lightning which had appeared on the upper edge of the cloud, seizes power over the earth and subdues twelve streams which had surged up from the sea. Baruch begs the angel Ramael to give him the interpretation. The cloud is the created world and its duration. The first dark water is Adam's sin, the fall of the angels and the flood, the first bright water is the obedience to the law and the faith of the patriarchs. The rest of the dark rains are the sins and periods of oppression of the people of God brought about by enemies and by ungodly rulers from their own ranks (e.g. Egyptians, Jeroboam I, Manasseh), the bright waters are the periods and figures of righteousness (e.g. Moses, David, Josiah). The twelfth bright water is the rebuilding of Jerusalem; the last black water is the terrible ultimate world catastrophe, in which only the holy land will be spared. In the interpretation a fourteenth bright water is mentioned, which does not occur in the vision; it signifies the Messiah who brings salvation in the final period. After this Baruch is commissioned to instruct the people about the last days and then to await the arrival of the Messiah on a mountain peak.

VII. Chapters 77–87. The Jews who remained behind in Jerusalem are admonished to remain faithful to the law and a letter sent to the 9½ tribes in the Assyrian captivity is given verbatim. A second letter to the 2½ tribes in exile in Babylon is mentioned, but its contents are not told; obviously this closing section has been lost.

As in the case of 4 Ezra the questionings which became acute in Judaism after the destruction of Jerusalem in A.D. 70 were the occasion for the Apocalypse of Baruch. Here too they were raised to the universal human problem of how the suffering of the godly can be reconciled with faith in God's justice. But there is not in their treatment the same depth of personal suffering and of meditation as in 4 Ezra. In this book the severity of the afflictions in this world fades into insignificance compared with the consolations of the glory in the next. Beside the dissimilarity between the two authors we must take into account the fact that the literary dependence felt by the author of the Apocalypse of Baruch may have contributed to a certain defensive attitude towards the self-tormenting earnestness of 4 Ezra. We cannot indeed always decide how far this dependence goes in detail, especially as we must allow for the fact that both authors have made use of common traditional material, as e.g. the *Antiquitates Biblicae* of pseudo-Philo of the first or second (Gry) century A.D. For this reason too, as in the case of 4 Ezra, it is not necessary to analyse this book into various strands, nor could these be convincingly substantiated (against Kabisch, Charles).

This book belongs from the point of view of the history of thought to the same circles of 4 Ezra. Thus its dependence on it fixes its date (shortly before A.D. 100) on the one hand. It is determined on the other by the fact that it is quoted in the Epistle of Barnabas (Barn. XI, 9) which was written between A.D. 130 and 140 (cf. also the dependence of Papias on Apoc. Bar., 29: 5 in Irenaeus [*adv. haereses*, V 33: 3 f.]). The Jewish revolt of Bar-Cochbah (A.D. 132–135) and its ending does not seem to have been known to the author.

88. The Greek Apocalypse of Baruch

Text and Versions: Greek: James, *Apocrypha anecdota*, II, 1897, LI ff.; 84 ff.–Slavonic: Novaković, 1886.–German: Bonwetsch, *Das slavisch erhaltene Baruch Buch*, Nachr. d. Gött. Ges. d. Wiss., Phil.-hist. Kl. 1896, 91 ff.–Kautzsch: Ryssel, II, 446 ff.–Charles: Hughes, II, 527 f.–Lüdtke, 'Apokalypse des Baruch', ZAW 1911, 219 ff.

Amongst the various writings which were in circulation under the name of Baruch, Origen (de *princ.* II, 3: 6) mentions a book with an account of 'the seven worlds or heavens'. This was discovered and published towards the end of the nineteenth century, first in a Slavonic excerpt, then in a Greek version. This 'Greek Apocalypse of Baruch' is itself only an extract from the work known to Origen, for it represents an account of only five of the different heavens (the Slavonic version has but two) through which Baruch is said to have been conducted.

The *contents* are as follows: Chapter 1. In reply to his complaint that God had allowed Nebuchadnezzar and the heathen to destroy Jerusalem, Baruch is informed by an angel that he must not concern himself with the deliverance of Jerusalem, for God will show him now more and quite different secrets. Chapters 2–16. Baruch is led by the angel through five different heavens where he sees the marvels of God and is given an explanation of what he has seen in which there is no further mention of the destruction of Jerusalem. Chapter 17. The narrative ends with the return of Baruch to the place from which he started and an exhortation to the brethren who had shared in such a revelation to glorify God.

The 'historical' introduction which recalls the Syriac Apocalypse of Baruch is inserted without any reference to the whole, no doubt in conscious imitation of a tradition common to Jewish apocalyptic. But the main part of the book is cosmological in character and belongs to the type of 'heavenly journeys' which we know from the book of Enoch. In its details it is akin particularly to the Slavonic book of Enoch. Although it is written in prose, this book is distinguished by the delicacy of its poetical feeling and by the artistic restraint in its presentation. It is of Jewish origin which is shown also by its affinity with the Syriac Apocalypse of Baruch. On the other hand there is no mistaking the influence of the Greek spirit, as demonstrated by a strong Gnostic bias and particularly by the use of conceptions taken from Greek mythology. Thus, for example, there is a description in Chapters 6 ff. of the journey of the man (=the sun!) in the chariot of the sun to which forty angels are harnessed and which is accompanied by the bird, the phoenix, 'the guardian of the earth'; again in chapter 9 the moon appears as a woman in a car drawn by oxen and lambs. These references to the world of Greek conceptions and ideas suggest that the book came into existence in the Diaspora under the influence of the Hellenistic spirit. The period in which it was written is limited on the one side by its acquaintance with the Syriac Apocalypse of Baruch (*c.* A.D. 130) on the other by the fact that it is cited by Origen (*ob.* 254). Later, at a time which we cannot fix with any certainty, it was worked over and transformed into a Christian Apocalypse. This can be perceived in chapter 4 in the allusion to the wine as the 'blood of God' at the Lord's supper and to Jesus Christ as the vine, and again in chapter 12 in references to the apocalypse of Paul.

89. The Testaments of the 12 Patriarchs

Text and Versions: Greek: Charles, *The Greek Versions of the Twelve Patriarchs*, 1908.–Armenian: '*Schatz alter und neuer Väter*', *I, Nichtkanonische Schriften des AT*, ed. by Sargis Josepheanz, 1896.–Slavonic: Tichonravov, *Pamjatniki otretschennoi russkoi literatury I*, 1863, 96 ff.–Kautzsch: Schnapp, II, 458 ff.; 492 ff.–Kautzsch: 489 ff. (*Test. Naphthali aus der Chronik Jerachmeels*).–Charles: Charles, II, 282 ff.– Gaster, *Studies and Texts*, I, 1925–1928, 69 ff. (Hebr. Testament Naphthali).– Schnapp, *Die Testamente der zwölf Patriarchen untersucht*, 1884.–Preuschen, 'Die armenische Übersetzung der zwölf Patriarchen', ZNW 1900, 106 ff.–Bousset, Die Testamente der 12 Patriarchen, ZNW 1900, 141 ff.; 187 ff.–Hunkin, 'The Testaments of the Twelve Patriarchs', JThSt 16, 1914–15, 80 ff.–Eppel, *Le Piétisme juif dans les Testaments des douzes Patriarches*, 1930.–Munch, 'The Spirits in the Testaments of the Twelve Patriarchs', *Acta Orientalia*, 13, 1935, 257 ff.–Rowley, *The Relevance of Apocalyptic*,[2] 1947, 63 ff.–de Jonge, *The Testaments of the Twelve Patriarchs*, 1953.–Schubert, 'Testamentum Juda 24 im Lichte der Texte von Chirbet Qumran', WZKM 53 (1957), 227–236.

This book which Origen mentions has been preserved in a Greek version of a Hebrew or Aramaic original and was first published by Grabe in the year 1698. An Armenian version is also extant in which, as in several Greek manuscripts, some of the later Christian additions are lacking.

It is modelled on the form of Jacob's blessing (Gen. 49) and is a collection of the last words of each of Jacob's sons which they are supposed to have addressed to their sons assembled round their death-bed. But unlike Jacob's blessing these are exhortations in which the patriarchs hold up as examples to their descendants their own virtues to be copied and their vices to be shunned. At the same time the OT tradition concerning them is spun out further with features from the *Haggadah* and expanded with legends in the same way as in the book of Jubilees. Beside the special attention given to loyalty to the law, the main emphasis is placed on admonitions to love God and one's neighbour and to keep oneself morally pure and chaste. Visions and prophecies for the future are also told. Thus, for example, *Reuben*, remembering his misconduct with Bilhah, his father's concubine (Gen. 35: 22; 49: 4), issues a warning against unchastity and the dangers of intimacy with women. *Simeon's* Testament is an explanation of Gen. 42: 24 and cautions against jealousy and envy. Beside the Testament of

Judah and Joseph there is a specially elaborate one of *Levi* who narrates his being carried up to the seventh heaven; there he sees God in the 'holy temple' on the 'throne of glory', who endows him with the priesthood (5); it also tells of another 'vision', in which he is invested with the insignia of priesthood and he and his descendants are appointed 'priests of the Lord for ever' (8). He is instructed by his father Isaac concerning the law of the priests (sacrifices, etc.); after an exhortation to fear God, to be loyal to the law, and to cherish justice and wisdom, he imparts the fact, 'as is contained' in a book of Enoch, that his descendants through their sin will be derided by the Gentiles, until after their punishment God awakens a new priest who will sit in judgment and bring to the whole world the peace of the last days. The last words of *Judah* based partly on traditions known only from Jub. 34 describe Judah's bravery (1–8) and recalling Gen. 38 warn against the thoughtlessness of youth, the pleasures of wine, harlotry and covetousness (9–20). The admonition to submit to the priesthood of Levi (21) is followed by a foretelling of the future until the appearance of the messianic ruler ('star out of Jacob') and the resurrection of the patriarchs with Levi as the first. The testament of *Issachar*, in view of Gen. 49: 15 (LXX), urges that the simple pious life of the 'countryman' should be imitated; that of *Zebulun* encourages sympathy and compassion. *Dan* warns his sons against anger and lying. The traditions to which the Testaments of Zebulun and Dan refer are no longer known. *Naphtali's* last words exhort to natural kindness and purity corresponding to the divine ordering of creation, an interpretation of Gen. 49: 21. According to a tradition which has not been transmitted, the author thinks of *Gad* as a man of wrath and of hate; he warns against these passions and incites to love of the brethren and neighbours. *Asher's* summons to tread the path of goodness and to avoid the way of evil is no doubt derived from the meaning of his name (=straight, undefiled). The testament of *Joseph* connects its exhortations to chastity with the story of Potiphar's wife and its amplifications in the *Haggadah*. The testament of *Benjamin* points to Joseph as an example of a pure disposition. Benjamin himself is called no longer a 'wolf that ravineth' but a 'labourer for the Lord' who 'divides the spoil' (Gen. 49: 27) to those who do good.

For a long time the book was considered to be a Christian work owing to its various allusions to Jesus. Now the view, first suggested by Grabe, has been brought into prominence again by Schnapp, according to which we have to do with a Jewish production which was vigorously recast at different times by Christian hands. It is only its Jewish origin which renders intelligible the fact that salvation is confined to Shem (Simeon 6) and that the position of Levi and Judah is raised above that of the other tribes. This and the circumstance that fragments of the book have been found in Qumran contradict the opinion of de Jonge as well; he explains the Testaments of the Twelve Patriarchs again as a Christian work which, utilizing earlier Jewish material, came into existence in the second century A.D.

To judge by their form and content the individual Testaments of the sons of Jacob are in the nature of sermons. Thus the conjecture that their primary Jewish element goes back to synagogue sermons on the patriarchs cannot be simply rejected out of hand (Eissfeldt, cf. *Arnold Meyer, Das Rätsel des Jakobusbriefs,* 1930). The exhortation to be loyal to the law, the stern feeling for purity in inward and outward conduct which sometimes approaches asceticism, the emphasis on the love of God and of one's neighbour, all these bring the book near to those Jewish puritanical circles which at several points show certain similarities to Christian ways of living and thinking. In view of the connexions between this work and the books of Jubilees and Enoch (see above, sections 78 and 83) and owing to the discovery of fragments of it in Qumran, the earlier view of Nitzsch and Riessler that it is derived from the sect of the Essenes has now become more probable. In its messianic eschatology with the account of the struggle of the Messiah against Belial and the bad spirits subject to him the influence of the Persian and Iranian dualism can be detected here even more clearly than in the canonical book of Daniel. At the same time the doctrine of the twofold resurrection of the dead (some to eternal glory, the others to eternal shame) enables us to see its inner relationship to the apocalyptic conceptions of the book of Daniel (cf. Dan. 12: 2). But the alien material has been fitted into its own traditions and made to serve the genuinely Jewish fundamental purpose of the book in a way which suggests a comparison with the conceptions actively held by the Qumran sect.

The Jewish basis is not homogeneous. The history of its form (*formgeschichtlich*) would most readily be explained as having originated in the setting (*Sitz im Leben*) of the synagogue worship. The sections about Levi's priesthood and kingship and his predominance over Judah and the other tribes (Levi 8, Napht. 5 f., Reub. 6) have been regarded as evidence of the high esteem shown to the Maccabeans who were both priests and kings, and especially to John Hyrcanus (134–103 B.C.) in the time before his break with the Pharisees. They might therefore date from the end of the second century B.C. On the other hand those parts which relate how Levi's descendants lead all Israel astray by their sins (Levi 10, 14 ff.; Dan. 5; Judah 21 f.) cannot be placed before the decline of the Hasmonaean rule which began with Alexander Jannaeus (102–76 B.C.). They would reveal the verdict of the legalistic circles on the moral decay and worldliness of the royal race of priests. Other passages such as Judah 22, Zebulun 9 which allude to dissensions, to quarrels between two kings and to the government passing to strangers have been interpreted as the strife between Aristobulus II and Hyrcanus II (64 B.C.) and the Roman or Herodian rule. But there is no clue which would permit us to fix a date for the last passages of the Jewish book earlier than the year of the destruction of the temple (A.D. 70).

Two notes must be added. The Hebrew Testament of Naphtali published by Gaster from the Chronicle of Jerachmeel is probably not to be regarded as part of the original text, but as a later Jewish re-translation of the existing Greek version. The Aramaic and Greek fragments of a Testament of Levi included in the edition of Charles are certainly related to the Testament of Levi discussed here, yet they must be considered as parts of a separate more detailed book. As the temple worship is mentioned in them they are probably to be dated before A.D. 70.

It would be wise to reserve judgment both on general questions and on the details until a thorough study of the discoveries at Qumran has enabled a clearer light to be thrown backwards and forwards on the characteristics and history of the religious group living there and of its relationships.

90. The life of Adam and Eve (Vita Adae et Evae. Apocalypsis Mosis)

Text and Versions: Latin: Wilhelm Meyer, *Vita Adae et Evae*, Abh. d. Münch

Akademie, Philos. philol. Kl., 1878, 185 ff.–Greek: Tischendorf, *Apocalypsis Mosis* (*Apocalypses Apocryphae*), 1866, X ff.; 1 ff.–Ceriani, *Monumenta Sacra et Profana* V I, 1868, 21 ff.–Armenian: Jagič, *Denkschrift d. Wiener Akademie d. Wiss., Phil.-hist. Kl.*, 1893, 1 ff.–Conybeare, QJR 7, 1895, 216 ff.–Preuschen, *Die apokryphen gnostischen Adamsschriften aus dem Armenischen übersetzt und untersucht*, 1900.–Kautzsch: Fuchs, II, 506 ff.–Charles: Wells, II, 123 ff.–James, The Lost Apocrypha of the OT, 1920, 1 ff.–Rowley, *The Relevance of Apocalyptic*, [2] 1947, 98 f.

Speculation about the first man began already in the OT itself (cf. Ezek. 28: 12 ff.; Job 15: 7 f.; Prov. 30: 4) and was continued in the NT too (cf. Rom. 5: 12 ff.; 1 Cor. 15: 46). It became associated with the biblical figures of the first human couple, but features from other traditions were also brought in. Thus there arose an extensive literature of 'Books of Adam', mainly of Christian origin. A Jewish Book of Adam is known to the Talmud. Jewish *Haggadah* also form the basis of the two books, the *Vita Adae et Evae* and the *Apocalypsis Mosis*, which are in part identical in their wording and are therefore placed in parallel columns in the German translation of Kautzsch. The *Vita Adae et Evae* is a Latin version of a Greek text which is perhaps itself derived from a Hebrew original; it was first published by Meyer in 1878. The book of Adam published by Tischendorf in 1866 and wrongly named by him *Apocalypsis Mosis* is composed in Greek, but might presumably have also come from a Hebrew text. Beside the passages in the two books corresponding precisely to each other there are sections in each of them, which are lacking in the other.

The *contents* are as follows: After the fall Adam and Eve do penance (Vita 1–17 alone); the birth of Cain and Abel, Eve's dream and Abel's death, the birth of Seth and the other children are told in both books (Vita 18–24; Apoc. 1–5). Adam tells Seth that he was carried up into the 'Paradise of Righteousness' where his death was foretold him and he intends to impart to him 'still more future secrets' (Vita 25–29 alone). Next comes the sickness of Adam and an account of the fall; Eve and Seth are sent into Paradise to fetch healing oil, they meet a wild animal and return (Vita 30–44; Apoc. 5–15); Eve's narrative of the fall is contained in Apoc. 15–30 alone, whilst Adam's last will and death is found in both (Vita 45–46: Apoc. 31–32). Apoc. 33–36 alone has the petition of the whole angelic host for Adam's forgiveness. God grants it and shows mercy to Adam (Vita 46–47; Apoc. 37). The angels' prayer for the burial of Adam's body occurs only in Apoc. 38–39, the funeral of Adam and Abel in Paradise is in Vita 48;

Apoc. 40–42; Eve's death and burial is in Vita 49–51; Apoc. 42–43.

The *haggadah*-like elaboration of the narratives shows evidence of a lively, poetical imagination, a high artistic quality and a sensitive, delicate gift for colour. The whole is pervaded by a stern ascetic mood of penitence. Beside other current apocalyptic conceptions, as for example, that of the two-fold last judgment, we may notice the funeral of the bodies of Adam and Abel in Paradise containing the promise of 'the resurrection of all mankind' (an intermediate state!). In Vita 29 there seem to be allusions to the temple of Herod, but nowhere is there any thought of its destruction. Thus both books must have come into existence at some time during the period between Herod's building of the temple (20 B.C.) and its destruction (A.D. 70). It is impossible to determine their home. The old Slavonic Book of Adam published by Jagič in 1893 follows the *Apocalypse*, but has taken from the *Vita* the narrative of Adam's and Eve's penance, which is interpolated after Apoc. 29. An Armenian text, translated into English by Conybeare and into German by Preuschen, is a version from Arabic or Syriac, itself derived from a Greek text, a sign of the popularity of the literary type of Books of Adam.

C. THE MANUSCRIPTS DISCOVERED IN THE JUDEAN DESERT

Abbreviations*

1 Q Is a	=complete scroll of Isaiah. See section 92 I.
1 Q Is b	=fragmentary scroll of Isaiah. See section 92 I.
1 Qp Hab	=commentary on Habakkuk. See section 92 II.
1 QS	=Manual of Discipline. See section 93 I.
1 Q Sᵃ	=Fragment of a rule. See section 93 I.
1 Q Sᵇ	=Blessings. See sections 91 and 93 I.
1 Q M	=The War of the Sons of Light and the Sons of Darkness. See section 93 III.
1 Q H	=Hymns (Hôdāyôt: Psalms of Thanksgiving). See section 93 IV.
1 Q Lamech	=the 'scroll of Lamech' (now 'Genesis Apocryphon') See sections 91 and 94.
1 QDM	=the oration of Moses (*dibʰrê mōsheh*). See sections 85 and 91.

Literature

A. Texts

Sukenik, Megillôth genûzôth, I, 1948; II, 1950 (1 QM; 1 QH; 1 Q Is b, selections) in Hebrew; Burrows, Trever, Brownlee, *The Dead Sea Scrolls of St. Mark's Monastery*, Vol. I, 1950 (1 Q Is a; 1 Qp Hab); Vol. II, 1951 (1 QS); Sukenik, Ôsar hammegillôth haggenûzôth, 1954 (1 Q Is b; 1 QM; 1 QH) in Hebrew; English edition 1955; Barthélemy, Milik, *Discoveries in the Judean Desert I.: Qumran Cave I*, 1955 (fragments from Cave I at Qumran) (see section 91); Hospers and Vriezen; *Semietische Teksten met Vertaling*, pub. by Van t' Land, 1954 (1 Qp Hab). Avigad, Yadin, *A Genesis Apocryphon*, 1956 (1 Q Lamech).

* A complete list of abbreviations is to be found in Barthélemy and Milik, *Discoveries in the Judean Desert I: Qumran Cave I*, 1955, 46 f.

In the abbreviations the prefixed figure indicates the number of the cave where the MS. was found, Q=Qumran; this is followed by an abbreviation of the title or contents of the manuscript concerned. The 'commentaries' are denoted by p (*pesher* =interpretation); in the titles of the books, the Manual of Discipline is denoted by S (=*serek*=rules), the War of the Sons of Light by M (*milḥāmôt*), the hymns by H (*hôdāyôt*=Psalms of Thanksgiving). For the sigla of the Zadokite Work see section 93 II.

The earlier (English) abbreviations were made up with DS (Dead Sea) followed by the abbreviated title of the MS concerned: DSD=(the Manual of) Discipline, DSW=the War (of the Sons of Light).

B. Translations

Bardtke, *Die Handschriftenfunde am Toten Meer*,[2] 1954 (1 Qp Hab; 1 QS; fragments from 1 QM and 1 QH); van der Ploeg, Bibliotheca Orientalis VIII (1951), 2 ff. (1 Qp Hab); Elliger, 'Studien zum Habakuk-Kommentar vom Toten Meer', *Beiträge zur historischen Theologie* 15 (1953) (1 Qp Hab); Brownlee, BASOR No. 112 (1948) 8 ff. (1 Qp Hab); Brownlee, BASOR 121 (1951), 8 ff. (1 QS); Edelkoort, *De handschriften van de Dode Zee*, 1952; Vermès, *Les Manuscrits du Désert de Juda*, 1953,[2] 1954; Molin, *Die Söhne des Lichts: Zeit und Stellung der Handschriften vom Toten Meer*, 1954 (with the translation of the Zadokite work); Vincent, *Les Manuscrits hébreux du Désert de Juda*, 1955; Delcor, 'La guerre des fils de lumière contre les fils de ténèbres ou le "Manuel du parfait combattant"', *Nouvelle Revue Théologique* 77 (1955) 372 ff.; van der Ploeg, *VT* I (1955) 373 ff. (1 QM); Bardtke, ThLZ 80 (1955), col. 401 ff. (1 QM); Burrows, *The Dead Sea Scrolls*, 1955 (1Q Hab; 1 QS; 1 QM and 1 QH); Gaster, *The Dead Sea Scriptures in English Translation*, 1956 (1 QS; the Zadokite Document, the Blessings [1 QS b]; 1 QH; the Oration of Moses; 1 Qp Hab; fragments of the commentaries on Micah, Nahum, Psalm 37; 1 QM; 1 QSª!). Avigad, Yadin, *A Genesis Apocryphon*, 1956 (1 Q Lamech) Hebrew and English.

C. Selected Literature

Baumgartner, 'Der palästinische Handschriftenfund', ThR NF. XVII (1948–49), 329–346; XIX (1951), 97–154 (more literature there); Dupont-Sommer, *Aperçus préliminaires sur les manuscrits de la Mer Morte*, 1950, English translation by Marg. Rowley, 1952; Kahle, *Die hebräischen Handschriften aus der Höhle*, 1951; Rowley, *The Zadokite Fragments and the Dead Sea Scrolls*, 1952; van der Ploeg, Art. 'Totes Meer', *Bibellexikon*, ed. by Haag, 1951 ff., cols. 1637–1644; Fritsch, *The Qumran community, its history and scrolls*, 1955; Nötscher, 'Zur theologischen Terminologie der Qumran –Texte', *Bonner Biblische Beiträge* 10 (1956); Milik, Dix ans de découverts dans le désert de Juda, 1957.

In addition reference may be made to the reports and articles from the year 1948 onwards in the folllowing: BASOR, the Biblical Archaeologist, RB, ThLZ, ZAW, VT and Revue de Qumran.

In the spring of 1947 some Bedouin shepherds found in a cave at Khirbet Qumran on the north-western shore of the Dead Sea, about ten miles south of Jericho, several leathern scrolls covered with writing which had been wrapped in linen and stored in earthenware jars closed with lids. A part of these scrolls (a scroll of Isaiah with its text complete (1 Q Is a), a scroll with the text of Hab. 1–2 and an explanatory commentary (1 Qp Hab), a scroll of the 'Manual of Discipline' (1 QS) and the 'Lamech' scroll (1 Q Lamech)) came into the possession of the Syrian Convent of St. Mark by means which can no longer be completely ascertained. Other scrolls (another scroll of Isaiah with a fragmentary text (1 Q Is b), the scroll of the 'War of the Sons of Light and the Sons of Darkness' (1 QM) and three sheets with hymns (Hôdāyôt) (1 QH)) were bought up by Professor Sukenik of the Hebrew

University of Jerusalem. Since 1954 all the material is the property of the Museum for Jewish Antiquities in Jerusalem.

The significance of the discoveries for Old and New Testament studies was soon recognized, although at first voices were not lacking which declared them to be forgeries. Since then the literature about these finds and their interpretation has grown to such an extent that it is impossible to list it all within the limits of this textbook, and even more impossible to discuss in detail the abundant interpretations which often diverge widely.*

In what follows we shall therefore only give a summary survey of the most important results of the researches; this will serve at the same time as an introduction to the various problems raised by the discoveries. The discussion of the scholars on the documents published so far is still in full swing and a large number of small and tiny fragments await classification and thorough examination. This will presumably last for several decades more; besides we must allow for the possibility of fresh discoveries. It seems to me therefore to be fitting to observe a certain reserve as regards hasty surmises and hypotheses.

91. Sites and Discoveries. The archaeological exploration

The Archaeological Exploration

The archaeological exploration of the sites of the discoveries was carried on side by side with the deciphering of the above-named manuscripts. An examination of the cave (1 Q) in which the manuscripts had been found was begun in the spring of 1949 under the leadership of Father de Vaux, director of the École Biblique et Archéologique in Jerusalem, and G. L. Harding, in charge at Amman of antiquities in the area. As it had already been ransacked by others in the autumn of 1948, the yield proved slight. But still, in addition to some Roman remains, fragments of about fifty jars were discovered which the archaeologists considered at first to be late Hellenistic (second–first century B.C.) and they

---

* cf. Chr. Burchard, Bibliographie zu den Handschriften vom Toten Meer, BZAW 76 (1957)[2] 78 (1959). In addition to the first announcements of the discoveries in the daily press and learned periodicals, see *Baumgartner* (ThR), and also Rowley, *The Zadokite Fragments and the Dead Sea Scrolls*, 3 ff., note 6 and Eissfeldt, *Einleitung in das AT*[2] (1956), sections 101–112.

deduced from them a library of at least 150–200 scrolls, of which about 600 scraps of texts were found. Meanwhile work proceeded on the fragments jointly by the Jordan Department of Antiquities, the École Biblique et Archéologique Française and the Palestine Archaeological Museum. These were published by Barthélemy and Milik in *Discoveries in the Judean Desert I: Qumran Cave I*, 1955, with a report on the discoveries by Harding and a fresh scrutiny of the pottery by de Vaux who now assigns the jars to the first century A.D. and abandons the conclusion about the size of the library. Amongst the fragments of biblical texts the following are represented: the Pentateuch (the pieces from Lev. and Num. in a proto-hebraic script) Jgs., Sam., Is. (belonging to 1 Q Is b), Ezek., Ps. and Dan.; in addition parts of commentaries on Gen. 49, Is. 10, Mic., Zeph., Nah. and the Psalms; amongst non-canonical texts there are two fragments of the Book of Jubilees, scraps of the book of Noah used in the book of Enoch, and small pieces of an Aramaic text of the Testament of Levi and of some not yet identified apocryphal and pseudepigraphical writings, including a farewell oration of Moses (1 Q D M); there were also more fragments of the Manual of Discipline, of the scroll of the War, of the Hymns and the 'Blessings' (1 Q S^b).*

In the winter of 1951 spadework was begun on the ruined site at Khirbet Qumran about 1,000 yards to the south and annual excavations were continued until 1956. Here a building (100 x 122 ft.) was laid bare, which contained a chamber with a bench running round the walls and broken pieces of plaster tables and inkwells. This building seems to have been the meeting (and writing) place of a community, the members of which presumably lived in the neighbourhood of Qumran in caves, huts or tents, as traces of domestic life in the surrounding caves indicate. There were also found remains of other buildings, a large cistern, which has been connected with the water-purification rites of the community, and a cemetery with over 1,000 graves of men and women, oriented south and north, arranged in rows without accompanying gifts of any kind. They are neither of Christian nor Mohammedan origin and prove that Qumran was the centre of the Jewish settlement lying nearby.

* Translation in M. Burrows, *More Light on the Dead Sea Scrolls*. Regular reports are to be found in the Revue Biblique and BASOR.

The discovery of coins from the period of the Hasmonaeans, from the reign of Titus and Agrippa II (A.D. 86) and from the revolt of Bar Cochbah (A.D. 132–135) provided clues for fixing the dates. Thus as the work continued the following picture of the history of the buildings revealed itself to the excavators. Three periods of occupation are now distinguished: the first from the time of the Hasmonaeans to the reign of Herod the Great (32–4 B.C.), this was brought to an end by an earthquake;* the second from the beginning of the first century A.D. after the settlement had been built up again until its destruction by a great fire which has been connected with the crushing of the Jewish revolt by the Romans (A.D. 66–70); later the place seems to have been inhabited again and to have served as a strong point for the rebels in the second Jewish revolt (A.D. 132–135). The manner in which the manuscripts were stored had already led to the rejection of Sukenik's comparison with a Genizah in which discarded scrolls were put aside; it shows rather that their owners had been forced by an emergency to place their precious religious literature in safety to await quieter times. Consequently the history of the buildings of the settlement suggests that we should think of the Roman menace in the second half of the first century or at latest in the first half of the second century as the time when the cache was deposited in the caves. So we may leave out of account later estimates of the third or fourth centuries. (Kahle†, Driver‡), or the end of the first millennium (Zeitlin§, Lacheman‖ or in the time of the crusades (Weis¶). Nevertheless these conclusions establish only a lower limit for dating the manuscripts themselves and the texts from which they were copied.

The archaeologists did not restrict their work to Khirbet Qumran and Cave 1. In the spring of 1952 they searched systematically fifty caves within a radius of five miles from Qumran and found remains of articles of daily use and of pottery like the jars found in Cave 1 and Khirbet Qumran. These enable the picture of the extent and the characteristics of the Qumran settlement to be com-

---

* De Vaux suggests the earthquake in the seventh year of Herod (31 B.C.) mentioned by Josephus.

† ThLZ 75, 1950, col. 537 ff.

‡ *The Hebrew Scrolls from the Neighbourhood of Jericho and the Dead Sea.* 1951.

§ JQR N.S. 41, 1950–1, 1 ff.

‖ JQR N.S. 40, 1949, 15 ff.

¶ JQR N.S. 41, 1950–51, 125 ff.

pleted. From four caves numerous fragments of manuscripts, provisionally estimated at more than seventy scrolls, were collected. Thus nearly all the books of the OT are now represented; also 'commentaries' on Isaiah, some Minor Prophets and the Psalms, Hebrew and Aramaic fragments of the book of Tobit known hitherto only in a Greek wording, fragments of the Manual of Discipline, the War Scroll, more hymns, several fragments of the Zadokite Work and scraps of known and unknown apocryphal literature. Already these facts make it likely that we have to do with a whole library of religious writings which the folk of Qumran concealed in these caves. More can be said only when the different fragments have been pieced together and published.* We still do not know the contents of two copper scrolls belonging together, 12 inches wide and about 8 feet long in all, with an indented square script in Hebrew or Aramaic, since for some time it had proved impossible to unroll the heavily oxydized scroll.†

The archaeologists extended their explorations to some places rather farther away from Qumran. As early as January 1952 an expedition was sent to Wadi Murabba'at, eleven miles south of Khirbet Qumran, where Bedouins had been ferreting out antiquities on their own account. The caves investigated there produced traces of occupation from the fourth millennium, the eighteenth–seventeenth century, the ninth–eighth century B.C. and above all from the second century A.D. and the Arabic period. They contained Hebrew fragments of Gen., Exod., Deut., Is. with the Massoretic text, a phylactery with Exod. 13: 1–10, 11–16; Deut. 6: 4–9; 11: 13–21, another piece with Deut. 6: 4–9, parts of older phylacteries including the decalogue as well, also in the Massoretic text, a palimpsest papyrus in a very ancient Hebrew script, two Greek marriage contracts, one of which is from the year A.D. 127. Beside a few papyri from the time of the revolt of Bar Cochbah (=Son of the star, cf. Num. 24: 17) there are two

* Such a publication which demands laborious and time-consuming toil is planned on lines similar to these employed for the discoveries in cave 1Q by Barthélemy and Milik.

† Kuhn (RB 61 (1954) p. 193 f. and ThLZ 79 (1954) col. 303 f.; 81 (1956) col. 541 ff.) conjectured on the basis of his attempt to decipher a few words visible from outside that the frequent occurrence of measurements might indicate an inventory of property. Professor H. Wright-Baker of the Manchester School of Technology has opened up the scroll by cutting it into separate strips. For this cf. Eissfeldt, *Die Handschriftenfunde in der Wüste Juda*, 1956, illustrations 43–47, and Burrows, *More Light on the Dead Sea Scrolls*, 1958.

letters from the man himself who here uses the name Bar (or Ben) Kosebah (=Son of the Lion, cf. Gen. 49: 9).* There are also fragments of private and administrative documents in Hebrew, Aramaic and Latin. Pieces of Roman weapons too were among the finds. But it seems as though these discoveries, mainly of later times, had no direct connexion with the settlement at Qumran.

The same may be said of what was brought to light in the *Wadi en-Nar* (the old Kidron valley) and in the ruins of *Khirbet Mird* between Qumran and *Wadi Murabba'at*. A Belgian expedition under the scientific leadership of De Langhe discovered there in the spring of 1953 in the ruins of a monastery some hermits' cells, an aqueduct, the mosaic floor of a church, and graves; in the matter of manuscripts they found remains of Greek uncial codices of Mk., Jn., Acts, Wisd. of the fifth–eighth centuries A.D., Christian ritual texts, fragments of papyrus in Syriac and Arabic, a Greek fragment of the Andromache of Euripides and Syriac letters of a monk. No connexions with the discoveries at Qumran were established, nor are they likely, according to what we know at present.

Moreover, the Bedouins have combed the area and have discovered in places unknown to us beside documents from the second Jewish revolt, fragments from Gen., Num., the Psalms, and columns of a Greek version of the Minor Prophets.† Individual fragments have been purchased by the Universities of Montreal, Manchester and Heidelberg. Something may still be in the hands of the Bedouins.

92. Biblical Manuscripts and Commentaries

I. *Biblical Manuscripts*

The biblical manuscripts which have been discovered have a direct importance for introductory studies of the OT first of all in so far as they are able to enlarge and to deepen our knowledge of the history of the *script*, the *language* and the *transmission of the text*. The prerequisite for this is to *ascertain their age*. Various means have been used to achieve this: (1) archaeological classification (of pottery, coins, history of the building), (2) a palaeo-

---

* Text and translation by Milik in RB 50 (1953), pp. 276 ff.
† See Barthélemy, RB 60 (1953), pp. 18 ff.

graphic comparison of the manuscripts with each other and with known documents (Siloam inscription, the tombstone of Uzziah, the Lachish letters, Aramaic papyri of the fifth century, the papyri of Edfu and the Nash papyrus), (3) the examination of the linen wrappings of the scrolls by radio-carbon, (4) inferences from the contents chiefly of the non-canonical writings about contemporary persons and events. The presupposition for the use of these methods, which has not always been sufficiently borne in mind, is that the strength of the different arguments should be correctly assessed and that the formulation of the various problems which arise should be kept separate. Archaeology can provide the material for demonstrating when the scrolls were deposited in the caves. Yet the date of the jars originally thought to be late Hellenistic had to be brought down by at least a century (see section 91) and it was observed that jars such as these were not made merely to store the scrolls, but were also used for domestic purposes. These facts leave a wide margin in fixing the date of the cache, which is limited by the coins discovered and the history of the building. Discussions regarding the occasion for concealing the manuscripts range mainly round the Roman menace during the first or second Jewish revolt (A.D. 66 or A.D. 132).

Another question concerns *the time when the manuscripts themselves were written*. Both in the case of the biblical texts as well probably as of the non-canonical ones too, it follows from the different kinds of fragments of the Manual of Discipline, the War Scroll and the Zadokite Document that we have to do, not with original texts, but with copies. Therefore palaeographic examination can claim to be valid only for the time when these copies were written. Apart from the documents in protohebraic script which there is an inclination to place at the end of the pre-exilic period, the manuscripts are conjectured for reasons of palaeography to have been produced mainly in the second and first centuries B.C. The complete scroll of Isaiah (1 Q Is a) is considered to be the oldest text in the Hebrew square script. The type of its script approaches most closely to that of the Nash Papyrus (see section 56), but as the date of this document itself cannot be fixed with certainty,* it provides no fixed point from which to

* The dates proposed vary between the second century B.C. and the first century A.D.

start. The attempt has also been made to fit the peculiar use of
the vowels and final letters into the picture of the historical
development of the script and the language from the pre-Massoretic up to the Massoretic text. But these criteria cannot be established in the earlier texts, nor are they employed consistently in
the same scroll. Thus it is as difficult to fit them into this picture
as it is to fit the use of the full and the modified writing into the
MT. It is more pertinent to consider the question whether the
singular spelling and pronunciation did not arise from the quite
practical purpose of the manuscript, namely to facilitate the pronunciation of the Hebrew text for the Aramaic-speaking reader.
The fact that the fragmentary Isaianic scroll (1 Q Is b) is closer
to the style of writing of the MT has been regarded as evidence
for its later age. But here too we may ask whether the difference
between it and 1 Q Is a, may not be explained by the use of the
former scroll for liturgical purposes by a more experienced staff.
The traces of heavier wear in 1 Q Is a, which perhaps indicate its
more general use, and the additions by a later hand might be
interpreted, even though not conclusively, as indications of a
greater age.*

The *radio-carbon examination*, which is limited to the age of the
linen wrappings, produced as the point of departure the year
A.D. 33 with a margin of error of 200 years on either side. The
period between 168 B.C. and A.D. 233 to be allowed for dating the
scrolls is indeed stretched very wide, but at any rate it excludes
their being placed in the eighth–eleventh century A.D. (see above).

No clear and homogeneous picture of the precise dating of the
manuscripts has so far been obtained. Nevertheless this much can
be said about the value of the biblical texts which have been
discovered, namely that they are of great significance not only for
our knowledge of the script, the grammar and the vocabulary,
but above all for the history of the text and for textual criticism. †
As a result of the custom of the synagogue to store worn-out
manuscripts of the Bible in the Genizah and from time to time
to bury them ceremonially, we have had to rely hitherto on com-

---

* Perhaps we may connect with this the spelling, diverging from the MT, of
certain forms of pronouns (e.g. הוּאָה, הִיאָה) as an indication of an earlier form,
in use by the Samaritans, in which the final vowel was pronounced.

† The variants in 1 Q Is a and 1 Qp Hab have been incorporated for the most
part since 1951 into Eissfeldt's Biblica Hebraica.

paratively late complete manuscripts from the ninth–tenth centuries. The fact that the Qumran texts are roughly 1,000 years older is remarkable in itself, and the more so because these texts are much closer to the MT than had been expected. It is another question whether it follows from this that the MT is older; at any rate it seems that efforts to mould the text began already rather early. The two Isaianic texts must be regarded as popular texts by an independent editor, representing a pre-Massoretic stage in the history of the text. In those cases where they approach the LXX, they are significant also for the early history of the Greek version. In this connexion the fragments of Samuel from Cave 4 must be mentioned, for they seem to belong to another branch of the transmitted text, which presumably served as the parent copy of the LXX.*

It is still an open question how far the fragments of a Greek translation of the Minor Prophets can be utilized for the history of the later Greek versions (see section 59). Penetrating and detailed investigations and a thorough study of the numerous texts which have not yet been published are required before it can be clearly seen how the individual biblical manuscripts fit into the historical framework and how they are related to each other and before full use can be made of these discoveries.

II. *Commentaries*

Beside the actual biblical manuscripts we must mention the commentaries which, like them, are important for the history of the transmission of the text in so far as they contain biblical quotations. † From the point of view of the history of literature, we are concerned with a literary type of a special kind which lays stress mainly on exegesis. Since in addition to the Habakkuk commentary (1 Qp Hab) fragments of commentaries on other biblical books with different types of script have been found (see above), this literature of commentaries seems to have been a branch of the exposition of scripture in common use amongst the Qumran

---

* cf. F. M. Cross, jr., BASOR 132 (1953) pp. 15 ff. and BASOR 141 (1956) pp. 9 ff.
† In the Habakkuk commentary, Hab. 3 is lacking, but we should not conclude that this chapter was therefore a subsequent addition to the other two. The reason for its omission was probably the particular nature of the psalm which was less suitable for the kind of interpretation given in the commentary.

community. No objection can be raised to the much-discussed designation of 'commentary', if the difference on the one hand from the Targum, the Midrash and the rabbinical exegesis, on the other from our own scientific commentaries is borne in mind. The commentary of Habakkuk could best be compared with Dan. 9: 1 ff. both as regards its literary form as also its method of exegesis. It has been submitted by Elliger to a thorough and discriminating examination and displays the following characteristics: Into the middle of a continuous text and without any regard to the general context there is inserted an interpretation (*pēsher*=a disclosure of something that had not been understood hitherto)* of a statement or even of one word which relates the prophetic saying to contemporary events and persons. Thus, for example, 'the wicked' in 1: 4 becomes 'the wicked priest' and 'the righteous' 'the teacher of righteousness'. Both interpretations are conjectured to allude to two personalities of the day and the clash between them dominates the whole exposition. The Chaldeans in 1: 6 become the Kittim, presumably an expression in use at that time for the alien rulers. The right to such an interpretation which grows out of the text and stands beside it independently is derived by the author from the divine inspiration of 'the Teacher of Righteousness', for he, even if he is not the author himself, possesses for the author the authority of a new revelation. Perhaps we may find here the cause of the above-mentioned discord between the teacher of righteousness as the spiritual leader of the separate group (*yaḥad*) for whom the Habakkuk commentary was written, and the wicked priest, who has been presumed to represent the high priest of Jerusalem. The commentary contains a number of allusions to the fate of these two opponents and their followers. These could be understood at once at the time, but are largely incomprehensible to us. Thus it is easy to see why they have stimulated scholars to bring to light the contemporary background, and thereby also the circumstances which produced the commentary and the group behind it, who are called 'the Elect' or 'the Poor'. The most varied dates have been proposed, ranging from the pre-Maccabean era to the period of the Crusaders and corresponding attempts have been made to identify the persons

---

* In the fragments of the commentaries on Ps. 68 and Zephaniah, the designation *pesher* is used as a sort of technical term.

and the groups.* This is due to the ambiguity of the subject-matter, but occasionally also to the fact that a dominant picture has been constructed without a sufficiently critical testing of the data and by the use of hasty associations and roundabout con-nexions with individual statements in other documents; and this picture has reacted again upon the interpretation of ambiguous passages.† Prolonged and thorough study of the various manu-scripts discovered will be required until the present controversy can be brought back on to sound foundations and reliable con-clusions on individual subjects can be built up into a convincing picture of the whole.‡ The main concern of the Habakkuk com-mentary is to grasp its contemporary eschatological significance which has been extracted from the prophetic writings in virtue of their special inspiration and which is intended to strengthen the faith and bearing of the 'Community of the New Covenant' in expectation of 'the end'. Possibly these commentaries were used when the scriptures were read and expounded at the regular gatherings of the Qumran community.

93. Non-biblical manuscripts

An insight into the nature of the religious group to which the community of Qumran belonged is afforded by the *Rules* governing their lives. They represent a literary type of their own, comparable with the later rules of the monastic orders.§ This type is repre-

* Amongst others as the 'Teacher of Righteousness': the High Priest Onias III, one or more unknown leaders of the group, an eschatological figure, John the Baptist, Jesus, or a leader of the Jewish sect of the Isavites in the eleventh century A.D., or the name of an official position within the sect; as the wicked priest: Alex-ander Jannaeus, the Hasmonaean Aristobulus II, the high priest Hyrcanus, Paul, Bar-Cochbah, etc.; as the Kittim: the Macedonian Greeks, the Seleucids, the Romans or the Crusaders.

† Elliger has gone into these premature attempts critically and has rightly de-manded that the explanation of the texts must first be sought in the texts themselves. He has himself set a perfect example of the use of this basic principle and has arrived thereby at much more guarded results.

‡ The historical allusion of the Nahum Commentary on Nah. 2 : 11, referring the passage to Demetrius III Eucaerus and his campaign against Alexander Jannaeus in the year 88 B.C. (cf. Josephus. Ant. XIII 14, 1–2) and looking back to the period between Antiochus IV and the Kittim (here=the Romans) might give a clue for dating the Nahum commentary, though this is not undisputed. It could not be used without qualification for all the other literature of Qumran, cf. Rowley, JBL 75 (1956) pp. 188 ff.

§ From Jer. 35 we learn about the rules by which the community of the Rechabites lived; but we cannot ascertain whether their tradition had already become embodied in a particular literary form.

sented in the 'Manual of Discipline' and in a certain sense in the
Zadokite Document as well.

I. *The Manual of Discipline*

In addition to the manuscript discovered in 1947 (1 QS)* there
are also remains of more columns (1 Qsᵃ)† with partly divergent
terminology and contents and of more fragments not yet published. Whether we have to do with copies of the fundamental
rules, which were subject in course of time to various alterations,
or with rules with different characteristics, distinguishing individual groups, is a point which cannot be settled for the time
being. The same applies to the question of the literary homogeneity and the purpose of the rule (or rules). But in view of the
literary beginning and the hymn-like vow at the end of 1 QS, it
is not impossible to think of this document being read aloud in
connexion with the celebration of the renewal of the covenant
and the admission of novices.

After an introductory pledge to be faithful to the covenant and the law, there follows the ritual of initiation into the
annual celebration of the covenant in the manner of old cultic
traditions. A piece provided with the special title 'for the *maśkîl*'
(=instructor?) deals with the contrast between the two spirits of
light and darkness which in the present world are at war with
each other, but are created by God, who in the day of judgment,
will bring the power of evil to an end (cols. III, 13–IV, 26); this is
frequently considered an interpolation. Yet in its present context
it might be understood as the instruction in the fundamental
doctrines of the community, on which their faith and life is built
up and which the teacher uses when he begins to expound the
way of life and the organization of the community. To this the
next sections are devoted. There follow rules for the admission
of novices and for the annual examination of the members in their
understanding of their faith and as to their deeds, the fixing of
penalties in the usual terminology for case-law, namely, mulcting
of rations, expulsion for a definite period and permanently, up to

---

* Published by Burrows, *The Dead Sea Scrolls of St. Mark's Monastery*, Vol. II,
1951 and called by the editor 'The Manual of Discipline'. The title discovered
subsequently, is to be read as *serek ḥayyaḥad* (=regulations of the united ones).

† Published by Barthélemy and Milik, Discoveries in the Judean Desert I Qumran
Cave 1, 1955.

the death penalty; more instructions about their behaviour amongst each other and towards outsiders (they are to hold themselves apart and to keep the Torah secret). In conclusion there are vows in the form of a hymn (no doubt to be spoken by those entering into the covenant) which refer at different points to the preceding regulations.

In the fragments of the Manual of Discipline 1 QSª it is called 'the Rule for the whole community (*'ēdāh*) of Israel at the end of the days'. Unlike 1 QS women and children are also included in the community and exact regulations are prescribed for the order of precedence at the assemblies and for the ritual at the communal meals. Nothing is said here about a novitiate; but a training is mentioned lasting for decades in the service of the community and for leading civil and military positions on the lines of the *sēper ha-hagû* (or *ha-hegî*)* named also in the Zadokite Document.

A Formulary of Blessings (1 QSᵇ) for the community, the priests and the president of the community has been preserved in fragments of five columns (*dibᵉrê bᵉrāk* [āh]). At present nothing definite can be discovered about its original place and its context.

The Manual of Discipline makes it clear that it is composed for a Jewish 'sect', rooted in a high regard for the Torah and marked by communal ritual meals, prayers and assemblies, by rules of conduct and communal management of property. It banded itself together to live in cultic and ethical purity in view of the imminent end and to cut itself off from outsiders ('men of ill-repute'). In addition to their organization into four classes (priests, levites, members and novices) we can perhaps detect another one, of military origin, into groups of 10, 50, 100 and 1,000. There is a striking rule that in every place where there are ten men of the community one of them must be a priest, and indeed on the most varied occasions (legal proceedings, administration of property, meal-times and assemblies) the position and authority of the priests is particularly emphasized. It remains an open question

* This book seems to have been of fundamental importance for the community. Its name is no doubt connected with hgh=to read in an undertone, to meditate (cf. Ps 1 : 2) (or to moan) and should perhaps be rendered 'Book of Study', or 'Book of Moaning'. Its contents are unknown. Some have tried to recognize parts of it in the Manual of Discipline, the Zadokite Document or in the Book of Hymns (see also North, *Orientalia* 25 (1956), pp. 90 ff.).

whether we may conclude from this that the sect arose by splitting off from priestly circles. In this connexion the lack of any reference to the temple services has been regarded as evidence that the temple priesthood and its ministry were rejected. Beside the committee of management consisting of three priests and twelve laymen, stands the council of the 'the many'; there is also the office of 'superintendent', or several of them, about whose appointment nothing more can be learned. Nor do we know anything about the 'Anointed of Aaron and Israel' whose coming in the company of a prophet is awaited in the future. Fresh questions have been raised by the discovery of the fragment 1 QSᵃ: What is the relationship of this rule to 1 QS as regards date and subject matter? Have we to do with the regulations of various groups each with its own organization or do the differences reflect a piece of the history of the sect, so that 1 QSᵃ could be understood as a bridge between an active military organization as it is seen in the scroll of the War and the self-sufficing sect of 1 QS isolated from the outside world?

Several features of this sect correspond in a remarkable way to what we learn from Philo, Pliny and Josephus about the Essenes (see section 94) and lead to the conclusion that there must be some kind of relationship here. But it will not do to remain satisfied with merely placing them side by side without taking into account the not unimportant matters in which their descriptions differ. But this means submitting the whole question of the Essenes to a fresh examination from this point of view. For this purpose the study of the Qumran literature must first be pushed on so far that we can see the historical relationships of this and other religious groups of later Judaism in a clearer light.

II. *The Zadokite Document*

The Manual of Discipline displays a certain relationship with the Zadokite Document of which fragments have been found recently in the caves of Qumran (4 QD, 6 QD). Two not quite complete Hebrew manuscripts of this containing partly parallel recensions have been known for some time. They were found in the winter of 1896–97 by Solomon Schechter, Reader in the Talmud at Cambridge University, in the Genizah of the Ezra synagogue at Cairo, together with writings of the Qaraite sect and were published in 1910.* The name 'Damascus Document' in use in the German literature has been chosen owing to the name given to themselves by the Jewish sect, in and for which this document was composed and which called itself 'the Community of the New Covenant in the Land of Damascus'; in the Anglo-Saxon literature the name used is 'the Zadokite Work' derived from the 'Sons of Zadok', the name they gave themselves. The old dispute about the date of this document which ranged from the second century B.C. to the 11th century A.D., has been brought to an end by the appearance of fragments of this document amongst the discoveries in the caves of Qumran, at any rate in so far as the limits are now connected with the whole question of the dating of the Qumran documents and can be drawn more narrowly (see above). Nothing definite can be said about a more precise dating within this framework, since these questions are still in the melting pot and the quotation from the Book of Jubilees in the Zadokite Document can at best be assessed as a relative *terminus a quo*.

But if the Zadokite Document has a connexion as regards date and subject with the rules of the Qumran sect, then the further question is raised as to its relationship to the sect of the Qaraites of the tenth century A.D. For the two manuscripts of this document were found in Cairo amongst Qaraite writings which contain views resembling in some ways those known from the Qumran texts. Thus scholars at one time conjectured that the Zadokite Document arose amongst the Qaraites. The solution of this problem is today sought from the opposite direction. A letter from the Nestorian Patriarch Timotheus (*c.* A.D. 800) about the discovery of manuscripts in a cave near the Dead Sea has been connected with the information given by the Qaraite Kirkisani (tenth century A.D.) about a Jewish sect, called the 'cave-sect,

* Abbreviation formerly CDC (Cairo Damascus Covenant), now CD (Cairo Document). Text: Schechter, *Documents of Jewish Sectaries*, Vol. I, *Fragments of a Zadokite Work*, 1910; Rost, *Die Damaskusschrift (Kl. Texte*, ed. by Lietzmann, 167) 1933; Zeitlin, *The Zadokite Fragments: Facsimile of the Manuscripts in the Cairo Genizah*. Collection in the possession of the University Library, Cambridge, JQR Monograph-Series No. 1, 1952; Habermann, '*Edah we-'Eduth*, 1952 (with vocalized text); Rabin, *The Zadokite Documents*, 1953 (with translation and notes). Translations: Staerk, 'Die jüdische Gemeinde des Neuen Bundes in Damaskus', *Beiträge z. Förderung christl. Theologie*, 1922; Charles, *Apocrypha and Pseudepigrapha* II, 1913, 785 ff.; Riessler, *Altjüdisches Schrifttum ausserhalb der Bibel*, 1928, 92 ff.; also in Molin, Vermès, Vincent, Burrows, Gaster.

because their writings were discovered in a cave. It has been thought that this was the way by which the Zadokite Document, amongst others, came into the possession of the Qaraite sect which was interested in its contents and its transmission and whose teaching it influenced.* But we must not forget that this is only a possibility, in which several doubtful points are involved and which is consequently not valid evidence.

The beginning of the Zadokite Document both in form and content is an exhortation to 'all who have entered the Covenant'. It describes the history of the sect, especially the fight with its enemies and their leader 'the man of derision' who is charged with tempting the people to fornication, covetousness and dese-cration of the sanctuary. The community is instructed in the obligations of the Covenant during the 'period of sin' which is now under the domination of Belial, but will end in the immediate future when God will appear in judgment and it is urged to reform its ways in time. All this is expressed in the secret method used for 'expounding the law' which presupposes an intensive study of the books of the Torah and the prophets and like the Habakkuk commentary, applies the statements of the scriptures to the con-temporary external and internal circumstances of the community. Those who turn away from 'the children of perdition' and hold fast to the new Covenant, belong to the remnant which will be saved, designated by God to live for ever (there is no idea here of the resurrection of the dead). The expectation of the end includes also 'the coming of the Teacher of Righteousness at the end of the days' and at the same time (or afterwards?) the arrival of the 'Anointed of Aaron and Israel'. The exhortation, which could be imagined as being delivered at gatherings of the com-munity, is interspersed with a number of legal ordinances for the organization of the sect, for the administration of justice and for the personal behaviour of the members; amongst these special mention must be made of regulations for cleanness (the avoidance of uncleanness from intercourse with outsiders, from the enjoy-ment of forbidden food and from fornication), and for the observance of the Sabbath. Some of the phrases, ideas and con-cepts with which the other Qumran documents have made us

* cf. Kahle, VT I (1951), pp. 44 ff., a Qaraite catechism which appeared in 1948 has the significant title of *môreh ṣedek*!

acquainted reappear, so that there can hardly be a doubt that the Damascus sect is connected with the Qumran community (*serek*, 'to enter the Covenant', 'sons of Zadok', 'fall of the angels', 'teacher of righteousness', 'prophet of falsehood', *mᵉbaqqēr*=overseer, *sēper ha-hagŭ*, etc.). The division of the community into four classes (here priests, levites, 'sons of Israel' and *gērîm*=proselytes) might correspond with that in 1 QS as well as the arrangement into groups of 10, 50, 100 and 1,000 men. On the other hand the body of judges in this document, unlike that in 1 QS, is composed of four members of 'Levi and Aaron' and ten laymen, and special rules are given for communities in cities and in 'camps'. Further, the families and the wives are included in the regulations by which they are to live, again unlike 1 QS. Both the nature and the number of these differences forbid the idea of direct literary dependence. In this respect the Zadokite Document must be regarded as an independent record and to begin with must supply its own explanation.

At the same time the problems have not grown less, but have rather increased. The interpretations of the passages of scripture by the present and the allusions to the fate of the community of the New Covenant are ambiguous and obscure, so that often one cannot decide what should be understood as future and eschatological and what as referring to the present day, what may be symbolic in the esoteric manner and what contemporary and actual. Thus for example the emigration of the community to the land of Damascus has been explained to mean that the sect founded by the 'Teacher of Righteousness' emigrated from Jerusalem under the leadership of the 'unique teacher' (*mōreh hayyaḥîd*) to the city of Damascus where after the death of this teacher, they awaited the end. Yet it is not easy to see the relationship of this teacher with the above-mentioned 'teacher of righteousness' awaited in the future. It is an equally open question at what date this emigration took place and what is its connexion with what we know of the Qumran sect, in spite of several hypotheses (an earlier or later stage in the growth of the sect?). Another suggestion has been to explain the emigration, because of its context, symbolically as the interpretation of Am. 5: 26 f. in the manner of that exegesis and to apply it to the priests ('Sons of Zadok') and their followers separating themselves from the

Q

Jerusalem priesthood and moving out to the Judean desert. A chronology hinted at in the Zadokite Document (1: 5 ff.) does not take us any further either, since it is based on Ezek 4: 5 and not on a true historical reminiscence. In the same way the reference of Deut. 32: 33 to 'the kings of the nations' or 'the chief of the kings of Javan' is so general and ambiguous that even if the latter is thought to be the Seleucid Antiochus IV, we are not much nearer except for a *terminus a quo* to a more precise date for this Document. In order to make some progress with these problems we need a thorough examination of each of the different versions of the Zadokite document itself, of its literary nature, of its relationship to the other Qumran documents and of its differences from them, its association with the Testaments of the Twelve Patriarchs, and with the older parts of the Books of Enoch and of Jubilees; several places in this work show that these were known to it.

III. *The War of the Sons of Light and the Sons of Darkness*

It is even harder to form an opinion of this scroll which its editor, the late Professor Sukenik, called 'the War of the Sons of Light and the Sons of Darkness'. As regards its literary form it must be classified with the 'Rules'; *serek* (=usage, ordinance), the customary name for rules made familiar by the Manual of Discipline, is employed also in this scroll as the title of some of the sections. But as regards its contents, it is completely different. The concern with military and warlike matters is so much to the fore that the scroll has actually been pronounced to be the 'regulations for the parade ground' or 'the G.H.Q.-manual' for the group describing itself as Sons of Light. Yet on the other hand we cannot fail to recognize the religious framework in which the military orders are embedded. This framework dominates all the details with its ideology to such an extent that the whole has acquired an eschatological and utopian stamp which can hardly be reconciled with the idea of actual rules for men on active service.

The scroll was discovered in 1947. It has a gap at the beginning and contains two different recensions of the text. Columns XV–XIX give us another version, parallel to the preceding rule, of which the beginning and the end have not been preserved. The introduction presents a general survey of the War of the sons of

Light, consisting of the tribes of Levi, Judah and Benjamin, against 'the army of Belial', composed of the troops of Edom, Moab, Ammon, Philistia, the 'Kittim of Assyria' and those who have violated the Covenant. This war ends with the defeat of the army of Belial and its annihilation on the day for which God has prepared and on which he appears to deliver his people out of their distress and to bring them to everlasting salvation. The forty years' war is divided into campaigns arranged to last mostly for one year against the individual foes, whose names are taken from the register of nations in Gen. 10 and the family tree of Keturah in Gen. 25. Both sides observe the Sabbatical year. The different trumpets and standards are to be supplied with longer or shorter inscriptions (e.g. 'Levy of God', 'Princes of God', 'God has smitten all the sons of darkness and he will not turn back his anger until he has destroyed them'; or 'Aaron, Israel and the names of the twelve tribes'). There follows the arrangement of the battle-order with a detailed description of their varied, richly ornamented equipment. The army is to be composed of 6,000 men on horseback aged 35–40 years and 29,000 men on foot. The reasons for disqualifying men for military service are listed and special emphasis is laid on keeping the camp clean from the religious point of view. Next the battle itself is described, led by the priests who direct its different phases by trumpet signals. They kindle the soldiers' ardour by exhortations and support them with set prayers. Special attention is paid to tactics in disposing the troops in line, circle and square and in directing their movements during the battle. Their success is sealed by a curse on the enemy spoken by the priests, levites and elders and by a hymn of victory to Yahweh who has maintained and renewed the covenant for the everlasting salvation of the sons of light.

It is easy to understand how widely divergent are the interpretations given to this strange document, of which other fragments have meanwhile been found. Some consider it to be an actual manual for active service and appeal to the purely military features which would be a copy of the battle array, weapons and tactics of Hellenistic or Roman methods of warfare; the unmistakable religious tinge is explained as the adoption of old traditions of the holy war when the group of the sons of light waged war against the foreign nations. But this realistic, historical interpretation which it is attempted to support by parallels from the books of Maccabees, does not do justice to the eschatological, utopian quality which comes through again and again in this book. The fact that both sides observe the Sabbatical year, the whole conduct and technique of the fighting according to a fixed and detailed scheme as well as other factors bear the stamp not only of improbability, but actually of unreality, so that a different kind of interpretation of this War scroll also deserves serious consideration. There is a pervasive liturgical note in the military regulations in which the renewal of the covenant, the theophany of Yahweh in the day of his judgment on the nations and the dawn of the time of salvation for his people are seen at the vanishing point. This might point back to a cultic origin, and the cultic tradition of the destruction of their enemies, which reached back into the far past and in which Yahweh appeared as the victorious lord of battles, might be brought back to life with the vividness of a dramatic style decked out with military details. We can observe again and again references to the salvation history of the OT, and its revival in the present; the divine judgment is extended to embrace the universal and the cosmic. These features could be better understood in the framework of a cultic festival than in the regulations for active service worked out for a particular historical campaign. Yet both these attempts at interpretation are no more than two different methods of approach to the riddle of the War scroll and its solution.

To *fix its date* the statements about the foes have been chiefly brought into play and the 'Kittim of Assyria' have been interpreted as the Seleucids and the 'Kittim of Egypt' as the Ptolemies. This would place it in the pre-Maccabean period. Yet we cannot see the role of the 'Kittim of Egypt' clearly enough to use it as a reliable point of departure for dating the book. The nature of the weapons and the method of warfare have been used in an attempt to deduce from them the contemporary background. This approach might be best suited to yield a *terminus a quo*. Yet here too the interpretations vary between Hellenistic and Roman tactics as the model, with corresponding dates in the period of the Maccabees, the Hasmonaeans and the Romans. The fact that the Edomites are mentioned amongst the foes would fix the last century B.C. as the *terminus a quo*—before the Idumaeans were admitted into alliance with Judaism. But this fact would carry weight only if it were certain that the names of the enemies were taken from the actual political circumstances of the day. But the names of the hostile nations are taken from Gen. 10 and 25 and this weakens the strength of the historical argument. For the time being the War scroll considered by itself does not yet supply us with enough material to classify it as literature, as a literary type, or historically.

A number of other questions arise regarding the relationship of this scroll to the other Qumran documents and to the group or groups of sects behind them. The mere fact that different versions and fragments of this scroll have been found in the library of the Qumran folk makes it impossible to avoid this problem and suggests a comparison with the rest of the Qumran literature. In fact several phrases, ideas and concepts can be named which appear to point to the same native soil. This scroll shares with both versions of the Manual of Discipline and with the Zadokite Document the use of the word *serek* (ordering). Again in all of them is found the dualism between the 'Sons of light and of darkness' (this designation is not itself contained in the War scroll) and the contrast between them dominates all the rules, although not in the same way. Reference has already been made to the special significance of the names 'Aaron and Israel'. Other matters to be noted are the controlling position of the priests and the pivotal importance of the idea of the covenant, the imminent expectation of the final judgment on their enemies, combined with the hope of the attainment of everlasting salvation for the sons of light, the emphasis on ritual cleanness, the liturgical quality of the regulations together with an individual poetry of its own in the hymn, the division into groups of 1,000, 100, 50 and 10 men, indicating a military origin, as well as the mention of 'camps' (1 QSa and the Zadokite Document). All these points might be used to argue that the documents and those who handed them down had a common basis. But several of these factors prove in no way that this conclusion *must* be drawn. Moreover apart from this, there are differences in the organization and manner of life in the War scroll, itself not free from contradictions in several matters, from the other Rules and these are of such a kind that it would not be advisable as yet to identify the sons of light prematurely, by smoothing out the differences, with the group in Qumran or with one of the earlier or later stages in its development. The disparity between the military and warlike spirit of the War scroll, traces of which might perhaps be discovered in the organization described in 1 QS^a (see above) and the peaceful way of life of the sect revealed in 1 QS and the Zadokite document, need to be elucidated. The same applies to the fact that the War scroll is silent with regard to questions which are distinctive and have a crucial significance in the case of the other documents of the sect (e.g. *sēper ha-hagû*, the person and the fate of the Teacher of Righteousness, the messianic expectations, etc.).

IV. *Hymns*

The scrolls discovered in 1947 included also a collection of psalms which the editor called *hôdāyôt*=songs of praise.* The bad state of its preservation makes it impossible to ascertain the precise number of the songs which are written in eighteen columns and on fragments presumably by different hands. Titles and indications of the kind of song or of the author, such as we know them from the canonical psalms, are lacking as well as notes for the music. The name *hôdāyôt* has been chosen to denote the contents, since most of these personal psalms begin with the self-invocation '*ôdkāh* '*adônāy*† which marks them out as 'religious songs' or hymns. ‡ The forms and types which we know from the biblical Psalms, such as the hymn, the thanksgiving (X, 14–XI, 2), also a combination of a lament with a thanksgiving (IX, 2–X, 12), a song expressing trust (VII, 34–VIII, 3) are all represented here, as well as the characteristic components belonging to these types,

* The document was difficult to unroll; at first five songs were made known: Sukenik, *Megilloth genûzôth*, 1948, in Hebrew; versions: Bardtke, Dupont-Sommer, Edelkoort, Molin, Vermès, Vincent, Hempel, ZAW 62 (1950) 257 ff. Now the scroll has been published in facsimile and in a transcription by Sukenik, '*Osar hammegilloth haggenûzôth*, 1954 (Plates 35–38). (This edition will be quoted in what follows, and because the quotations will be easier to trace, the transcription will be used in which the Roman numerals indicate the columns, the Arabic figures the lines.) Translations in Burrows (a selection) and in Gaster; cf. Wallenstein, Hymns from the Judean Scrolls, 1950, and BJRL XXXVIII, No. 1, 1955; Bardtke, ThLZ 81 (1956), col. 149 ff. (column I).

† Some of the songs begin with the formula: 'Blessed (*bārûk*) art thou, Lord', XI, 27ff.

‡ The name frequently used, 'Psalms of Thanksgiving', is not appropriate in every case.

such as narrative, confession of sin, vows, etc. (see above, section 6b). Yet we find these in a strange medley or with individual parts puffed out, a sign that attention to form is being relaxed and that hand in hand with this the strict train of thought is no longer consistently carried through. The *parallelismus membrorum* is observed in the outward form, but regular formation of stanzas and precise rhythmical scansion cannot be detected. A general survey of these psalms places them nearer to the psalms of Solomon than to those in the Canon.

It is a characteristic of the contents of these hymns that they make frequent use of OT phrases, similes and statements, both in what they affirm as in the temptations and deliverance from distress they describe. Thus occasionally we get the impression of a mosaic of biblical quotations from which we can at any rate conclude that much time has been spent in a thorough study of the OT scriptures. At the same time we cannot miss seeing that they have their own stock of ideas and particular conceptions of life to which the interpretation of the OT quotations is directed. To a large extent this fits in with what we learn from the other Qumran documents about the peculiarities of the sect there. It is a distinctive feature of most of the psalms to contrast those who were chosen by Yahweh and who, having renounced private property and wealth (X, 20 ff.), confess themselves loyal to his covenant with the 'men of Belial' from whom they hold aloof and who therefore bear them ill-will. The ideas which constantly recur in the songs in a frankly stereotyped manner include the following: the inner enlightenment and understanding of the secrets of divine creation and guidance and of the nature of man, through which God gives to his worshippers the right self-knowledge in their penitence and the strength to overcome temptation and to keep his commandments; the hope that they are predestined by God for everlasting salvation in the community of the covenant, whilst in the imminent last judgment the wicked with their 'lying prophets' and the whole 'army of Belial' will be annihilated. The singular doctrine set out in 1 QS (III, 13–IV, 26) about the antithesis between the two spirits created by God in the world and in man underlies the psalms XV, 9–12 and XVII, 1–XVIII, 30. The consonance of XII, 3 ff. and XIV 1 ff. with the confessional vows at the end of the Manual of Discipline is unmistakable. These and

other observations (e.g. with regard to the doctrine of angels*)
lead to the conclusion that we have here a collection of psalms
composed within the sect.†

The psalms also contain some clues as to their *Sitz im Leben*
(setting or use) in this community. For example, when the worshipper speaks in III, 22 ff. of being given a place in the host of
holy beings and 'brought into communion (*yaḥad*) with the sons
of heaven . . . in order to praise God's name and deeds in the
community (*yaḥad*)' (similarly XI, 6 and XII, 3), we may imagine
such psalms being sung at the divine service during the festivals
of that community. When God is implored in XVIII, 9 ff. not to
withdraw his hand from these who hold firm to his covenant and
who stand blameless before him, this might be used at the annual
festival of the renewal of the covenant at which God is present
in his self-manifestation.‡ Perhaps the much-discussed sudden
changes of mood familiar from the biblical psalms, when lament
turns into certainty that the prayer will be granted in XI, 21 ff.,
come into this context, and the term used in XI, 26 seem to
suggest this. The confessions of sin might also have had their
place in the same cultic framework.§

There is a certain uniformity in the vocabulary and stock of
ideas which no doubt reveals the influence of a rigid ritual
organization and training. Nevertheless it can hardly be said that
the hymns are due to a single author. For the state of mind and
the external circumstances of the worshippers which we can still
detect in the individual psalms are too different from each other,
and so are the figures of their enemies. XVIII, 10 ff. and especially
IV, 5–40 give the impression of being the words of a 'teacher' or
'overseer', on whom rests the responsibility for the members of
the covenant entrusted to him and for their 'illumination' (IV, 20).
Yet it is not possible to prove with certainty that the man who
speaks here is the 'Teacher of Righteousness', as some have conjectured from the allusions to the conduct of the opponents.

We can hardly doubt that these confessional hymns to which a

* Especially in I, 10 ff.
† In this connexion and in view of the discovery of more fragments of psalms,
it is interesting to note the remark in the letter of the Patriarch Timotheus, mentioned above, that in the cave of which he spoke more than 200 psalms of David
had been found.
‡ cf. for this 1 QS I, 16 ff.
§ cf. 1 QS I, 20 ff. and also 1 QS II, 19–25.

number of unpublished songs must be added are connected with the life and cult of the Qumran sect. This determines also the question of their date, which is closely bound up with the total picture resulting from a study of the Qumran discoveries and of the history of its sect. We shall have to be satisfied provisionally with holding fast to the limits indicated by the discoveries as a relative historical framework in which the collection of psalms of the Qumran community also have their place. We must be content to hope that a further examination of the individual documents will enable us to obtain from the present discussion of the various possibilities a clearer outline of the whole historical picture.

Nevertheless the psalms convey a general impression of the theological position on which the community stands: God is the all-powerful creator, exalted above all the world and its spirits; he has made the good and the bad and predetermined their fate. Man, who spends himself in the conflict between the spirits of good and evil, is powerless in face of him. But God in his mercy has given his elect the covenant and the strength to overcome their trials. He has done this by revealing to them his secrets of the past, the present and the future and by granting to them the hope of an everlasting life in the divine light. In this light they can confidently and joyfully await the imminent final judgment on the powers of darkness. But everything that happens, happens for the sake of God, for his glory, and his praise is the real and deepest purpose of these hymns.

94. The Sect of Qumran

The documents discussed in the preceding paragraphs belonged to the library of a settlement with rather narrow geographical limits and with a history from the second century B.C. to the first century A.D. of which at least the archaeological outlines have been laid bare. This fact compels us to consider the further question as to the nature of the community which lived there and hid their documents away in safety. From the individual documents themselves we can form a vivid picture of these people's lives, their organization and the ideas and beliefs which they held. So it is easy to understand that, by comparing these documents with each other, attempts have been made to reconstruct a general picture of the community and that in the discoverers' first thrill of delight the common features received more attention than the differences. However the tacit presupposition, namely, that the documents originated in the same circle, is more than doubtful. If that is so, the last task of those who study the manuscripts of the Judean Desert will be to clear up the problem of fitting the Qumran sect into the history of the religious movements of late Judaism and of finding its place amongst them. Its final solution will be reached only when all the material is known and assimilated.

In view of this situation it is not surprising that the first attempts to identify the Qumran sect have gone out in quite different directions: as in the earlier case of the Zadokite document the Pharisees, the Sadducees, the Essenes, the Zealots, the Therapeutes, the Dositheans, the disciples of John the Baptist, the Ebionites and the Qaraites have been proposed, a sign that the manuscripts by themselves convey no unequivocal picture.

The majority of scholars are today inclined to connect the sect of Qumran with the Essenes. For this we have indirect information from what Philo* in the first half, and Pliny the Elder† and Josephus‡ in the second half of the first century A.D., tell us about the Essenes. Pliny's account of where they lived on the western shores of the Dead Sea and of their mode of life could apply without alteration to the Qumran sect, as we meet it, especially in the Manual of Discipline. The descriptions in Philo and Josephus coincide in the same way with many details of which we read in the Qumran manuscripts (special dwellings for the order, organization into four classes, the novitiate, communal meals and assemblies with characteristic arrangements, property held and administered in common, isolation from outsiders, secrecy with regard to their writings and doctrines, study and exegesis of the law, ritual and ethical purity, observance of the sabbath, periods of prayer, teaching concerning predestination and angels, their eschatology, etc.); thus it is hard to deny the validity of these parallels. Josephus knows about the Essenes in the days of Jonathan the Maccabee (c. 150 B.C.) and of Aristobulus I (105–104), and of their steadfastness in the persecutions

---

* Quod omnis probus liber sit, 75 ff.   † Naturalis historiae lib., V 17.
‡ Bell. Jud. II, 8, 2–14; Ant. XIII 5, 9; XV 10, 5 and XVIII 1, 5.

during the Jewish–Roman war. This too would fit into the period
which has been discussed for the Qumran documents. Nevertheless there remain a number of obscure points: according to Philo
the Essenes lived in villages, because they wished to escape from
the immorality of the cities; Josephus tells of Essenes in every
Palestinian town. Moreover the statements in Philo and Josephus
about the celibacy of the Essenes are as difficult to reconcile with
each other as those about the position of women within the
various Qumran writings.* We learn nothing from these descriptions of the Essenes about the significance of the covenant and its
renewal, about the Teacher of Righteousness, about the special
position of the priests and the different forms of Messianism. The
reason for this may indeed lie partly in the fact that those accounts
were written for non-Jews;† still these points cannot be simply
pushed aside as of no consequence, but together with other
differences they require the most careful scrutiny.

The comparison of the evidence of Philo, Pliny and Josephus
with the Qumran documents has made the relationship of this
sect with the Essenes, or perhaps even its identification with them,
highly probable. So now these documents have for their part
again raised the problem of the Essenes themselves and new
answers are demanded for the questions cropping up in them.
For instance, in the case of the obvious diversities, have we to do
with the deposit of stages of development in one and the same
sect, to be kept apart historically, which it has not yet been
possible so far to place more precisely in an unquestioned order;
or have we to do with the traditions of several religious groups in
late Judaism of a more or less similar character which are distinguishable even as regards their designation of themselves (see
above?‡ Nor has the answer yet been found to the question concerning the origin of those views which cannot be derived from
the OT.§ But even amongst concepts and ideas which have their

* In this connexion the burials also of women in the cemetery at Khirbet Qumran
should be noted.

† For example this may explain what Josephus says about the doctrine of the
Essenes concerning the immortality of the soul and its relationship to the conceptions of the Greeks.

‡ The designation 'Essenes' used by Pliny and Josephus, or 'Essaeans' (Philo and
Josephus) has up till now not appeared in the Qumran documents. Its origin and
meaning is today still not explained.

§ It has been conjectured that the dualism 'light–darkness' came from Parseeism.

roots in the OT so much variety in the terminology of the individual documents can be observed that in view of the mass of as yet unpublished material premature associations and conjectures are more likely to obscure the problems than to throw light on them. The thorough and detailed exegesis of most of the Qumran documents has hardly yet begun. This work and a renewed study of the apocryphal and pseudepigraphal literature used by the sect* with the Qumran documents in mind will put us in a better position to approach the old and new problems which they have opened up.

From such a scrutiny we may expect to gain a clearer knowledge of the religious currents in late Judaism. It is this which gives to the Qumran documents their *significance* in the studies of the OT, in so far as the history of its text, the after-effect of its institutions and traditions receives fresh light from them. Their significance is no less for research into the NT† and primitive Christianity, since they supply fresh points of contact in addition to those of the rabbinic sources. But in this field too we should be going to work the wrong way if, when considering what they have in common, we overlooked the differences and if we failed to appreciate the point of departure, which is decisive in the history of the Christian faith and life, namely the person of Jesus Christ, since here no comparison is possible. A publicity delighting in sensations has occasionally seized upon these questions and produced hasty comparisons and opinions. In view of this, we can only emphasize that here too the problems must first of all be correctly stated, carefully examined by reference to the texts and pondered. Then only will there be a sound foundation for what may be said about the relationship of the NT and of the formation of the primitive Christian community to the sect of Qumran and its documents.

* See above. Since then Avigad and Yadin have succeeded in unrolling five pages of the 'Lamech scroll' with the provisional outcome that it is seen to contain an Aramaic version of some chapters of Genesis (chapters 12-15), approximating palaeographically to the War scroll, and recalling the Book of Jubilees as regards its contents; these serve as the basis of various expansions in the style of the *Haggadah* (cf. *The Biblical Archaeologist*, XIX (1956) pp. 22 ff.). See also Avigad, Yadin, *A Genesis Apocryphon*, 1956, columns XIX–XXII; column II with a speech by Lamech (hence the original name, 'the Lamech scroll') which has also been published, has certain similarities to the book of Enoch. The editors hold out the prospect of publishing the whole scroll so far as its damaged condition permits.

† cf. Rowley, *The Dead Sea Scrolls and the New Testament*, SPCK, 1957.

INDEX OF BIBLICAL AND POST-BIBLICAL PASSAGES

(The passages in the books treated in their respective sections are easy to find there and are therefore not included here.)

Genesis
1–11, 71, 100
1–Ex. 12, 416
1, 73, 120, 296
1: 27, 73
2, 16, 73
2: 4ff., 73, 103
2: 25, 73
3: 1, 58
4, 60
4: 23f., 44, 103
5, 367
6, 103
6: 1–4, 58
6: 19, 73
7: 2, 73
7: 11–13, 73
7: 12, 73
8: 6–13, 14, 73
9: 6, 52
9: 25ff., 43, 103
10, 467
11, 60, 367
12–25, 71
12–50, 71, 101
12, 73, 107
12: 2ff., 107
12: 6, 72, 74, 107, 109, 110
12: 7, 109, 356
12: 8, 107, 110
12: 10ff., 109, 114
12: 11ff., 416
13: 7, 72
14, 103
14: 14, 72
15, 96, 109
15: 6, 114
15: 16, 74, 115
15: 18, 74
16, 16, 73, 109
16: 4ff., 60
16: 5, 359
16: 10f., 44
17, 61, 96
17: 7, 74
18: 25, 107
19, 60, 103
20, 73, 115
21, 16, 73, 109

21: 8ff., 60
21: 22ff., 73, 124
22, 60, 110, 114, 115, 124
22: 14, 60
23, 55
24: 60, 43
25–36, 71
25, 71, 467
25: 14, 298
25: 23, 51
26, 71, 73, 109
26: 26ff., 73
27: 27ff., 42
27: 37, 43
27: 40, 108
28, 60, 107, 115
28: 10ff., 109, 110
28: 18, 115
29: 31–30: 24, 43
30: 37ff., 107
31: 44f., 96
32, 16
32: 29, 107
32: 33, 72
33, 104, 107
33: 20, 109, 110
34–36, 103
34, 109
34: 38, 19
35, 107
35: 1, 115
35: 1ff., 109, 110
35: 8, 116, 124
35: 10, 107
35: 16ff., 124
35: 20, 115
35: 22, 442
36: 31, 72
36: 33ff., 344
37–9, 73
37–50, 71
37: 1, 74
37: 3, 74
37: 8, 124
37: 13, 74
37: 17, 399
37: 34, 74
38, 103, 109, 113
40: 15, 72

42: 24, 442
48: 14ff., 42
48: 22, 74
49, 44, 91, 104, 113, 117, 118, 442, 451
49: 4, 442
49: 7, 44, 117
49: 8ff., 44, 109
49: 9, 454
49: 9f., 435
49: 12, 117
49: 14f., 44
49: 15, 443
49: 21, 443
49: 22, 44, 117
49: 27, 443
50: 10f., 72
50: 11, 74

Exodus
1–19, 71
2–5, 102
1: 11, 116
3, 73, 74, 113
3: 1, 74
3: 18, 89
4: 21, 114
4: 24ff., 61
6, 73, 74
12: 1–17, 60
12: 2ff., 92
13: 1–10, 453
13: 11–16, 453
13: 18, 116
13: 19, 144
14: 13f., 108
15, 86, 87
15: 1–18, 106, 279
15: 15ff., 72
15: 20f., 18, 30, 32
15: 21, 30, 31, 106, 116
15: 22f., 60
15: 30f., 24
17: 6, 74
17: 7, 60
17: 8ff., 145
17: 14, 71, 116
17: 16, 18, 29, 116
19, 71, 83

477

Exodus
19: 3ff., 89
19: 6, 115
19: 11, 74
19: 18, 74
20, 105, 120
20: 1–17, 119
20: 2ff., 51
20: 2–17, 354
20: 17, 367
20: 18–21, 119
20: 22ff., 334
20: 22–23: 33, 121
20: 23–6, 122
21: 2ff., 131
21: 2–11, 127
21: 1–22: 16, 54, 122
21: 12, 51, 52, 53
21: 12ff., 120, 122
21: 15, 53
21: 15–17, 51
21: 17, 53
21: 18f., 54
22: 17–23: 19, 122
22: 18f., 53
22: 20–7, 122
23: 10ff., 94, 122
23: 17, 38
23: 19, 84
23: 20ff., 122, 181
24: 3, 334
24: 3f., 119
24: 4, 72, 115
24: 7, 121
24: 10–26, 105
24: 12, 334
24: 13, 145
25–31, 71
31: 14f., 53
31: 18, 14, 334, 354
32–4, 71
32: 16, 14, 334
32: 17f., 145
33:11, 114
33: 19, 51
33: 19ff., 58
34: 1, 105, 354
34: 6f., 51
34: 10ff., 181
34: 23, 38
34: 26, 84
34: 27, 72
34: 28, 105
35–40, 71, 336
35: 21ff., 56

Leviticus
1–7, 71, 140
6: 2, 52
6: 7, 52
6: 18, 52
7: 1, 52
7: 11, 52
8–10, 71
11–15, 71, 140
16, 138
17–26, 71, 138, 140
18: 7–17, 51, 53
18: 24ff., 72
19: 2, 51, 140
20: 2, 53
20: 7f., 140
20: 27, 53
24: 16, 53
25, 415
25: 1ff., 94
27, 53

Numbers
1–9, 71
5: 11ff., 334
6: 23ff., 42
6: 24–6, 43
10–20, 71
9: 15, 237
10: 35, 18, 30
10: 35f., 116
12: 6ff., 114
13f., 94
16: 1, 356
20–36, 71
21: 4ff., 114
21: 14, 31
21: 14f., 30, 116
21: 17f., 27, 116
21: 27–30, 27, 117
22: 1, 72
22: 6, 42
22: 22ff., 117
22: 28, 63
23: 7–10, 117
23: 18–24, 117
23: 21f., 117, 124
24: 3–9, 44, 104
24: 7, 105, 117
24: 15–19, 44
24: 16ff., 108
24: 16–19, 104
24: 17, 105, 453
24: 20–4, 105
25, 237
25: 1ff., 115
27: 1ff., 144
31: 32ff., 56

33: 2, 72

Deuteronomy
1–4, 71, 128, 130, 134
1–11, 126
1, 181
1: 1, 72
1:5, 72
1: 22ff., 94
2: 12, 72
3: 14, 72
4: 2, 335
4: 45, 72
5–11, 71, 128, 130
5, 120, 131
5: 6ff., 51
5: 6–18, 119
6: 4, 354
6: 4–9, 453
6: 20–5, 89
10: 1ff., 334
11: 13–21, 453
11: 29, 144
11: 29f., 144
12–26, 71, 122, 126, 130
13: 1, 335
15: 1ff., 94
15: 12–18, 54, 127, 131
16: 16, 38
17: 14ff., 72
17: 18, 126
18: 6ff., 128
19: 1–13, 131
22: 18–29, 54
23: 8f., 264
26, 88
26: 1ff., 84
26: 5ff., 83, 84, 85, 86, 99
27–30, 71, 126
27, 83, 94
27: 2ff., 94
27: 2–8, 122
27: 4, 367
27: 9
27: 11ff., 43, 144
27: 12f., 128
27: 15ff., 120
27: 15–26, 51, 53
31–4, 71, 126
31: 9, 72
31: 9f., 94
31: 9ff., 94, 119, 134
31: 11, 94
31: 19, 72
31: 24, 72
31: 26, 14, 134, 334, 335

Deuteronomy
31: 30, 72
32, 71
32: 1–43, 118
32: 33, 466
33, 44, 52, 71, 98, 104,
  117, 118
33: 2ff., 261
33: 5, 91
33: 7, 124
34, 71
34: 1, 72
34: 6, 72
34: 10ff., 114

Joshua
1–11, 19
5: 2f., 61
8: 30ff., 94
8: 34, 83
10: 12ff., 30
10: 13, 31
11: 1ff., 151
14: 6ff., 94
15–19, 56
15: 13ff., 145
15: 15f., 15
15: 63, 149
16: 10, 145, 149
17: 12ff., 145, 149
24, 50, 67, 83, 87, 88, 89,
  92, 93, 96, 97, 115, 149
24: 2ff., 113
24: 2–13, 87
24: 14ff., 115
24: 14–26, 87
24: 25, 121
24: 27, 94
24: 30, 124
24: 32, 124
24: 33, 124

Judges
1: 3, 144
1: 10–15, 145
1: 11f., 15
1: 27ff., 94
1: 27–9, 145
5, 30, 104, 260
5: 3f., 32
5: 4f., 58
5: 4ff., 98, 261
5: 8, 94
5: 11, 91
5: 12, 44
5: 15ff., 104
5: 15–18, 44
5: 23, 44

5: 23f., 43
5: 28ff., 104
9, 65
9: 8ff., 63
9: 9, 370
9: 27, 26
10: 1–5, 56
11:34, 30
12: 7–15, 56
14: 12–18, 40
18: 20, 155
18: 29, 72
20: 28f., 51
21: 21, 26

1 Samuel
1: 10ff., 34
1: 17, 51
1: 27f., 61
2: 1–10, 168, 279
2: 3, 356
3: 13, 356
4–6, 61
4: 7, 356
5: 6, 358
5: 12, 358
7, 67
9: 1ff., 63
9: 6ff., 45
9: 9, 46
9: 13, 42
10: 5ff., 45
10: 11, 45
10: 25, 14, 134, 334
11, 65
11: 4, 237
11: 6ff., 45
11: 14f., 237
12, 50, 67, 87, 97
12: 7, 89
12: 8ff., 86, 92
12: 14ff., 89
13, 65
13: 7ff., 237
14, 65
14: 18f., 50
14: 41, 50
15, 62, 105
15: 10ff., 237
16: 1ff., 63
16: 4–2 Sam. 5: 25, 65
16: 7, 40
17, 61
17: 42ff., 43
18: 6f., 24, 30
18: 7, 30
18: 17, 31
19: 24, 45

23: 9ff., 51
25: 28, 31
30: 7, 51
31: 11f., 155

2 Samuel
1: 18, 31
1: 19–27, 28
2: 5ff., 155
3: 33ff., 28
5: 3, 55
6, 61, 108
6: 18, 42
7, 108, 110
7: 9–20, 65
8: 17, 17
9–20, 324
11: 15, 56
11: 27, 66
12, 62
12: 24, 66
14: 1ff., 55
15: 2ff., 55
15: 25f., 66
17: 14, 66
19: 36, 28
22, 168, 284
23, 41
23: 1, 28
23: 24ff., 56
24, 60, 110

1 Kings
1–2, 65, 164, 166
1: 3, 301
2:17, 301
2: 44f., 66
3–11, 66
4: 7–19, 56
5: 2f., 55
5: 9ff., 40
5: 9–14, 296
5: 12, 299
5: 13, 41
5: 16ff., 296
6–8, 65, 108
6: 1, 150
8: 2, 94
8: 14, 42
8: 53, 31
8: 55, 42
10: 1ff., 41, 296
11: 14–22, 108
11: 41, 65
12: 19, 108
12: 26ff., 124

1 Kings
12: 32, 94
14: 17, 302
14: 19, 65
14: 25, 56
14: 29, 65
17: 7ff., 63
17: 17ff., 62
18, 62
18: 3ff., 247
19, 251
20: 11, 40
22, 334, 337
22: 10, 45

2 Kings
4: 8ff., 62
8: 20, 108
8: 20f., 248
9: 1ff., 337
9: 11, 45
10: 1ff., 56
14: 6, 70
14: 9, 63
14: 25, 231, 251
18: 4, 61
18: 14–16, 193
18: 27, 358
20: 16, 418
21: 1–17, 225
21: 24, 133
22, 134
22f., 65, 127, 129, 133
22: 11, 129
22: 19, 129
23: 4, 128
23: 6ff., 128
23: 7, 127
23: 8f., 127, 128
23: 10, 128
23: 11f., 127, 128
23: 15ff., 133
23: 21ff., 128
23: 24, 128
24: 18–25: 30, 217
25, 181

Isaiah
1–35, 186, 213
1–39, 183–97, 355
1: 1, 186, 187, 233
1: 2, 49
1: 10ff., 49, 52
1: 16f., 48
1: 17, 49
2: 1ff., 59
2: 2–4, 253, 254
2: 3, 38

2: 4, 59
2: 6ff., 253
2: 7ff., 49, 266
2: 20, 188
5: 1ff., 49, 63
5: 1–7, 27
5: 8ff., 49, 253
5: 11f., 26
6–9, 50
6, 50
6: 1ff., 46
7: 10ff., 48
8: 1ff., 50, 334
8: 2, 269
9: 1ff., 254
9: 7ff., 49
10: 15, 40
10: 24ff., 254
10: 27ff., 253
11:1ff., 254
11: 6ff., 59
13f., 190
14: 4–21, 28
14: 4–23, 49
14: 13f., 59
16: 10, 26, 27
17: 12ff., 59, 254
21: 11f., 27
22: 13, 26, 49
23: 15, 26
24–7, 343
27:1, 59
28: 11ff., 336
29: 1, 254
29: 6ff., 229
29: 14, 41
29: 16, 40
30: 7, 59
30: 8, 334, 354
30: 8f., 50
31: 4f., 254
33, 49
33: 14ff., 52
34: 16, 338
36–9, 178
37: 14, 134
37: 22ff., 49
37: 22–9, 26
38: 10–20, 279
40–55, 197–205
40ff., 355
40: 21, 338
41: 1ff., 49
41: 26, 338
42: 10ff., 49
43: 9, 338
44: 6ff., 44
44: 9ff., 407

44: 27, 59
44: 28, 186
45: 9, 40
45: 20, 338
47, 26
50: 2, 59
50: 4ff., 292
51: 6, 59
51: 9f., 59
55: 11, 48
55: 13, 59
56–66, 205–8, 255
56: 12, 26
63: 7–65: 25, 118
65: 17, 59

Jeremiah
1: 4ff., 46
1: 9, 334
2: 1ff., 67
7: 1ff., 67
7: 22ff., 89
8: 4ff., 67
8: 8f., 41
9: 10ff., 28
9: 16, 27
10: 1ff., 67
10: 1–16, 407
11:1ff., 67
11: 18–23, 34
12: 1–6, 34
14: 7–10, 35
14: 19–15: 4, 35
15: 10ff., 49
15: 10–12, 34
15: 15–21, 34
16: 1ff., 46, 67
17: 14–18, 34
17: 19ff., 67
18: 1ff., 40, 67
18: 18, 41
18: 18–23, 34
19, 46
19: 4–20: 6, 66
20: 7, 34
20: 9, 34, 46
20: 10–12, 34
20: 14ff., 292
20: 14–18, 34
22: 14f., 26
23, 337
23: 25ff., 47
23: 28, 40
23: 29, 48
24: 9, 43
25: 1, 248
25: 11, 314
25: 30, 26, 27

Jeremiah
25: 30f., 244
26, 66
26: 18, 337
26: 18f., 252
27–9, 66, 337
27: 2ff., 48
28: 8, 48
28: 8f., 337
29, 407
29: 1–23, 56
29: 10, 314
31: 6, 38
31: 31ff., 7, 89
31: 33f., 229
32, 55
32: 10f., 354
33: 11, 281
34, 66
36–45, 66
36, 334
36: 1ff., 50
42: 7, 263
44: 29f., 48
46: 2, 248
48: 29ff., 191
48: 33, 27
49, 248, 249
49: 7–22, 248
51: 14, 27
51: 59ff., 66

Ezekiel
1: 4ff., 46
3: 1ff., 334
4: 5, 56, 466
14, 314
14: 14, 289, 314, 403
14: 20, 289, 403
17: 3ff., 64
19: 2–14, 28
20, 314, 355
23: 14, 356
27: 2ff., 28
28: 3, 314, 403
28: 11ff., 28
28: 12ff., 446
28: 14ff., 59
31, 64
32: 2–16, 28
38: 17, 338
40–8, 335
45: 16, 356

Hosea
1: 4f., 337
2: 7, 84
2: 10, 84

2: 20, 59
4: 1ff., 48, 49
6: 1ff., 49
6: 1–6, 35
9: 7, 45
11: 1ff., 67
12, 16
12: 1ff., 67
14: 3–9, 35

Joel
1–2, 35
3: 5, 249
4: 3, 249
4: 9 249
4: 16, 244
4: 16ff., 232
4: 17, 249
4:18, 59
4: 19, 249

Amos
1: 3ff., 107
1: 3–2: 16, 49
2: 6ff., 244
3: 3–8, 49
3: 8, 46
3: 9, 49
3: 12, 49
4: 4f., 38, 49
4: 6ff., 67
4: 6–12, 49, 189
5: 1f., 49
5: 2, 25, 28
5: 5, 124
5: 7ff., 49
5: 16, 27
5: 18f., 266
5: 23, 26
5: 26f., 465
6: 4ff., 26
6: 12, 49, 356
7–9, 46, 49
7: 10–17, 66
7: 12f., 233
7: 16, 233
8: 14, 124
9: 13, 59

Jonah
2: 3–10, 279

Micah
1: 2ff., 107
3: 12, 210
4: 1ff., 59
4: 1–4, 188
6: 1ff., 49

6: 6f., 49
6: 6ff., 52
7: 7–20, 49

Nahum
1: 2ff., 258
2: 11, 256
3: 7, 28
3: 18f., 28

Habakkuk
1–2, 259
1–3, 49
1: 6, 262
2: 2, 50, 354
2: 6ff., 28
3, 98
3: 2ff., 107

Haggai
2: 10ff., 52

Zechariah
1–8, 50, 272
1: 4, 338
7: 1f., 307
7: 7, 338
8: 18f., 307
9: 1, 276
12–14, 338, 343
12: 1, 276
12: 10ff., 27
13: 2ff., 338

Malachi
3: 22, 72

Psalms
1, 41, 296
1: 2, 461
2, 28
3: 5ff., 36
4, 37
5: 13, 36
6: 13, 38
9f., 25
9: 8f., 17ff., 107
10: 7, 43
11, 37
12: 6, 36
13, 421
15, 52
16, 37
16: 5f., 94
16: 10f., 36
17, 93
18, 168
18: 8ff., 98

Psalms
18: 8–16, 52
18: 20f., 29
20, 29
22: 23ff., 38
23, 37
24: 3–6, 52
25, 25
27: 1–6, 37
27: 13, 36
28, 93
30, 281
31, 67
37, 25, 42
40: 2ff., 37
41, 279
42: 5, 36
42: 6, 25, 36
42: 12, 25, 36
43: 4, 37
43: 5, 25
44, 93
44: 2ff., 33, 87, 89
45, 29
46, 33
46: 3ff., 59
46: 4ff., 93
46: 5ff., 254
46: 8, 25
46: 12, 25
47, 34
47: 4, 59, 107
48, 33
49, 42
50: 2ff., 52
50: 14f., 37
51, 36, 37
54, 284
56, 284
60: 8ff., 94
65, 27
67, 27
68, 458
68: 2ff., 52
68: 25, 98
69, 285
69: 31f., 37
72, 29
72: 20, 279
73, 42
73: 23ff., 36
74: 9, 338
74: 13ff., 59
76, 33
77: 12ff., 82
77: 17ff., 52, 98
78, 67, 87, 93
78: 2ff., 87

78: 5, 97
81, 93
81: 6ff., 89, 97
81: 9ff., 88
84: 3ff., 38
87: 4, 59
89: 10ff., 59
93, 34
94: 2, 107
95, 93
95: 7ff., 98
96–9, 34
96: 6, 98
97: 2ff., 107
97: 3–6, 52
97: 10ff., 89
98: 9, 107
101, 29, 169
102: 1, 38
102: 19, 38
103, 33
104, 17
105, 67, 87, 93
105: 5ff., 97
106, 67, 87, 93
110, 28
111, 25
111: 4, 6, 87, 89
111: 10, 42
112, 25
114, 59
118, 37
119, 25
121, 37
122: 1, 38
122: 8f., 38
125, 37
127, 41
128, 41
130: 5, 7, 36
131, 37
132, 28
133, 41
135, 67, 93
135f., 93, 107
136, 67, 86, 87, 93
145, 25, 279
148, 41, 402

Job
1: 11, 356
2: 5, 356
2: 9, 356
4: 12ff., 47
15: 7f., 446
28f., 406
28: 28, 42
38ff., 41

40: 4f., 298
40: 15–41: 26, 58
42: 2ff., 298

Proverbs
1: 6, 40
8, 406
16: 10, 40
22: 17–23: 12, 41
22: 29, 40
25: 1, 2, 4f., 40
30: 1, 41
30: 4, 446
30: 15f., 18ff., 24ff., 29ff., 41
31: 1, 10–31, 41

Lamentations
1, 28
2, 28
3, 306
4, 28
5, 35

Ecclesiastes
11: 4ff., 341

Esther
1: 1, 404
3: 13, 404
4: 17, 404
5: 1f., 404
8: 12, 13, 404
10: 3, 404

Daniel
1: 5ff., 445
3, 62
3: 31, 62
6, 62
6: 1, 26ff., 29, 62
7–12, 50
7: 13ff., 436
9: 1ff., 458
9: 2, 338
9: 4ff., 406
10–12, 314
12: 2, 444

Ezra
1: 1ff., 186
1: 1–11, 390
1: 2ff., 56
1: 1–4: 5, 319
2: 1–4: 5, 390
2: 41, 286
2: 55, 57, 308
3: 2, 72

Ezra
3: 10f., 281
4ff., 56
4: 7–24, 390
5: 1, 269
5: 1–10: 44, 390
6: 3ff., 56
6: 14, 269
6: 18, 70
7: 1ff., 138, 145
7: 6, 72
9f., 304
10: 3, 70

Nehemiah
4: 4, 27
5: 19, 67
7: 72–8: 13, 390
8–10, 321, 333
8: 13ff., 18, 138
9: 1ff., 138
10, 138
10: 31, 32, 30ff., 139
12: 1, 269
13: 1ff., 138, 139, 304
13: 14, 22, 67
13: 23ff., 304
13: 29, 31, 67

1 Chronicles
1–9, 56
1: 30, 298
2: 4ff., 304
6: 18ff., 283
15: 19, 285
16: 8ff., 281
16: 8–36, 287
16: 41f., 283
25: 1ff., 283
29: 29f., 158

2 Chronicles
2: 1, 282
2: 17, 282
20: 19, 283, 285
24: 20f., 341
25: 4, 72
29: 30, 280
30: 16, 70
32: 32, 194
33: 11ff., 18f., 401
35–6, 390
35: 12, 72
35: 15, 286
35: 25, 305
36: 22ff., 186

1 Esdras
3: 1ff., 390, 414

1 Maccabees
1: 15, 45, 47, 48, 60f., 417
2: 59f., 315
4: 46, 338
7: 5ff., 274
7: 49, 312
8: 22, 354
8: 22ff., 55
9: 54, 274
11: 46, 393

2 Maccabees
2: 1ff., 407
2: 13, 280, 339
2: 20ff., 393
3, 395
4f., 274
4: 7ff., 417
4: 27ff., 275
6, 62
6: 6, 7, 417
6: 18–7: 42, 419
6: 18ff., 422, 432
7, 62, 422
8: 23, 333
11: 30, 315
15: 36f., 312

Tobit
14: 4, 8, 251

Ecclesiasticus
5: 11, 409
38: 25, 26
44ff., 315
48: 22–49: 12, 338
49: 9, 408
49: 10, 251

Wisdom of Solomon
8: 7, 423

Jubilees
4: 17ff., 428
13, 428
21: 10, 428
34, 443

Ascensio Isaiae
5: 11–14, 185

Psalms of Solomon
11: 2–7, 406

Sibyllines
III 338ff., 315, 424

Ethiopic Enoch
1: 9, 341, 426
104: 11–13, 429

Slavonic Enoch
23: 4ff., 430

2 Esdras
14: 1–48, 436
14: 44ff., 436

Manual of Discipline
III, 13–IV, 26, 460

Matthew
5: 17, 70, 341
5: 18, 353
19: 7f., 72
21: 42, 333
22: 37, 135
22: 43ff., 280
23: 35, 341
26: 30, 281
27: 9f., 273

Mark
12: 26, 70, 72

Luke
1: 46ff., 68ff., 32
11: 49, 341
20: 42, 279
24: 44, 339

John
3: 8, 341
5: 46f., 72
7: 38, 341
10: 34, 336
15: 25, 336

Acts
1: 20, 279
7: 4, 32, 367
8: 34, 201
15: 21, 72
28: 23, 341

Romans
1: 2, 333
1: 17, 259, 264
5: 12ff., 446
9: 19–23, 412
9: 20f., 40
10: 5, 72

1 Corinthians
1: 19, 346
2: 9, 341
6: 2, 412
14: 21, 336
15: 46, 446

2 Corinthians
3: 6–18, 7
10: 13ff., 331

Galatians
3: 11, 259, 264
6: 16, 331

Ephesians
4: 8, 346
5: 14, 341

2 Timothy
3: 8, 341
3: 15, 333

Hebrews
9: 1–14, 7
9: 3f., 367
11: 37, 185, 341, 419

James
1: 19, 409
4: 5f., 341

Jude
14f., 429
15, 341

GENERAL INDEX

Adam and Eve, life of, 445–7
Adapa, myth of, 17
Adrianus, 1
Akhnaton, hymn to sun and Ps. 104, 17
Alphabet, origin of, 15
Alphabetic script, 352; invention of, 14–15
Amarna, letters of, 12
Amen-em-ope, Wisdom of, 17, 41
Amos, 242, 245–6; and judgment, 246–7
Amos, book of, 232, 243–7
Antwerp Polyglot, 385
Apocalypse of Weeks, 427
Apocrypha, 340, 389–412; Reformed Church and, 347
Apostolic Constitutions, 401
Aquila, and version of Old Testament, 371–2
Arabic versions, 380
Aramaic migration, 12
Archaeological exploration, 450–4
Aristeas, Letter of, 413–15
Ark, the, Books of Samuel and, 162
Ark oracles, 116
Armenian version, 379–80
Assyrian cycle, Isaiah and, 192–3
Atanachli, signet-cylinder of, 13
Augustine, 1
Azariah, Prayer of, 402–3

Balaam, Oracles of, 104–5; saga of, 117
Baruch, book of, 405–6; Syriac Apocalypse of, 437–40; Greek Apocalypse of, 440–2
Beersheba, 16
Bel, and dragon, 403–4
Bethel, 16
Blessings and curses, 42–4
Book, The, 354–7

Canaan, culture and civilization, 13; Babylonian influence on, 14; tradition of, 19
Canon (of Old Testament), formation of, 1, 331–3; Jewish concept of, 331–3, 342–5; in Christian Church, 345–7
Chronicles, books of, 319, 323–8; contents, 323–5; date of, 325–6; sources, 326–8
Clement of Alexandria, and Canon of Old Testament, 346
Codex Alexandrinus, 340
Codex argenteus, 374

Codex Coislinianus, 373
Codex Colberto-Sarravianus, 373
Codex Marchalianus, 373
Codex Sinaiticus, 376, 398
Codex Syrohexaplaris Ambrosianus, 374
Codex Vaticanus, 375
Commentaries, 457–9
Complutensian Polyglot, 385–6
Conquest tradition, 83
Covenant, Book of the, 95, 121–5
Cultic sayings, 50–2
Cuneiform script, 351
Cursive script, 353

Damascus, Isaiah and fall of, 185
Daniel, 314
Daniel, book of, 313–7; contents, 313–5; author of, 314; origin, 315
David, Books of Samuel and rise of, 163–4; court history of, 164–5
Deborah, Song of, 52, 96
Decalogue, 119–21; Mosaic origin of, 120–1
Delitzsch, and Song of Songs, 300
Deuteronomy, 125–35; origin, 127; as 'Mosaic tradition', 335
Deutero-Isaiah, 194, 197–205; significance of, 204–5
Deutero-Zechariah, 272–5
Deuteronomistic writing of history, 67–8, 180–2
Diaspora, 254
Didactic poem, 42
Didascalia, 401
Dinah and Tamar, legend of, 19
Dirge, 34–7
Discipline, Manual of, 460–2

Ecclesiastes, 307–10; origin of name, 307–8; contents, 308; date, 309–10
Ecclesiasticus, 407–9
Edessa, Church of, 382
Elihu, 290
Elijah, book of Kings and, 175–7
Elohist, strand, 111–25
Enoch, Ethiopic book of, 425–9; origin of name, 426; Slavonic book of, 430–31
Esdras, First Book of, 389–91
Esdras, Second Book of, 433–7; contents, 434
Essenes, and book of Enoch, 428; and sect of Qumran, 474–6

485

Esther, book of, 310–12; Septuagint version of, 404
Ethiopic version, 379
Ewald, and Supplementary Hypothesis, 76
Ezekiel, 222–4; significance of, 228; as prophet, 228–9; as priest and theologian, 229–30
Ezekiel, book of, 224–8; origin and growth of, 227–8
Ezra, book of, 318–21; subject of, 318; sources, 319

Fable, 63
Flood, The, Babylonian story of, 17
Folk tales, 62

Gebhardt, and Song of Songs, 300

Habakkuk, 259; vision of, 261–2; and Nahum, 263–4
Habakkuk, book of, 259–64; date of, 262–3
Haggai, 231, 268
Haggai, book of, 267–8
Hebrew text, of Old Testament, 351–67; outward form of, 351–7
Hexapla, 373
Hobbes, Thomas, and Old Testament books, 2
Holiness, Law of, 140
Hosea, 233–4; religious significance of, 236–8; and love of God, 237; and judgment, 237; and future, 237–8
Hosea, book of, 234–8
Humanism, 1
Hupfeld, and New Documentary hypothesis, 76
Hykos, invasion of Egypt, 11–12
Hymns, 470–3; composition of, 32–4

Ibn Ezra, 1
Irenaeus, and Canon of Old Testament, 346
Isaiah, life of, 184–6; and fall of Damascus, 185; as prophet, 185–6; significance of, 195–7; martyrdom and ascension, 418–20
Isaiah, book of, 177–8, 183–6, 194–5; contents, 186–94

Jacob, blessing of, 104
Jeremiah, life and ministry, 209–12; religious significance of, 218–20; conception of God, 220–1; and relationship of man to God, 221

Jeremiah, book of, 212–18; contents, 213–17; origin and growth of, 217–18
Jeremy, Epistle of, 406–7
Jerome, 1
Job, 288, 289; home of, 292–3
Job, book of, 287–95; scholars and, 291–2; origin of, 292; meaning of, 293–5
Joel ben Petuel, 238
Joel, book of, 231–2, 238–41
Jonah, 251
Jonah, book of, 249–52; contents, 250–2
Joshua, book of, 143–7; Deuteronomic revision of, 146–7
Josiah's law-book, discovery of, 133–4
Jubilees, book of, 415–18; origin of name, 415–16; contents, 416–18; and Pentateuch, 417
Judges, book of, 147–57; origin of name, 147–8; author of, 148; contents, 148–51; and stories of heroes, 151
Judith, book of, 399–401; text of, 399
Junilius Africanus, 1

Kethubhim, see Writings
Kings, books of, 170–82; contents, 171; sources, 173–4
Kiriathsepher, 15

Lamech, Song of, 103
Lamentations, book of, 305–7; subject of, 306; origin of, 306; formation of, 306–7
Laws, 54–5
Legends, 61; of martyrs, 62
Liturgical speech, 76–8
London Polyglot, 385–6

Maccabees, First Book of, 391–3; text of, 391; meaning of name, 391
Maccabees, Second Book of, 393–5
Maccabees, Third Book of, 395–7
Maccabees, Fourth Book of, 422–3
Malachi, 231, 277
Malachi, book of, 275–7
Mamre, 16
Manasses, Prayer of, 401–2
Manuscripts, biblical, 454–7; non-biblical, 459–73
Massoretes, 358–66
Massoretic Text, 357–66; Roman Catholic Church and, 364; Protestant Church and, 365; editions of, 365; division of Hebrew Text, 366
Micah, 252–3; and Nabis, 255
Micah, book of, 252–5
Miriam's Song of the Sea, 116
Mosaic tradition, 18–19

Moses, blessing of, 117–18; Song of, 118–19; law of, 276, 339; assumption of, 431–3; Apocalypse of, 445–7
Myth, Old Testament and, 57–9

Nabis, Micah and, 255
Nahum, 256; Habakkuk and, 263–4
Nahum, book of, 256
Narratives, poetic, 57–64; in prose, 64–8
Nehemiah, book of, 319, 321
Nicholas of Lyra, 1
Noah, Oracles of, 103–4

Obadiah, 247–8; as prophet of salvation, 249
Obadiah, book of, 231–2; 247–9; authorship of, 248–9
Old Testament, formation of, 1, 6, 333–42; historical and cultural background, 11–16; literary tradition of, 16–20; pre-literary development, 21–2; poetic structure, 23–5; rhythmic arrangement, 24; canon of, 331–3, 345–7; text of, 351–86; Greek versions, 368–80; version of Aquila, 371–2; version of Theodotion, 372; version of Symmachus, 372; Ethiopic version, 379; Armenian version, 379–80; Arabic versions, 380
Oracles of Baalam and Job, 47
Origen, and Song of Songs, 300; and Greek versions of Old Testament, 372–3; and Assumption of Moses, 431; and Testament of Twelve Patriarchs, 442–5

Palestine, history and civilization of, 11
Papyrus, Fouad, 375
Papyrus, Rylands Greek, 375
Parallelismus membrorum, 23, 40
Paris Polyglot, 385
Paul, and old covenant, 7
Pentateuch, The, contents, 70–1; authorship of, 71–4; criticism of, 74–81; sources, how formed, 81–99; and salvation history 85, 90, 92; narrative form of, 92; Samaritan, 366–7, 369
Penuel, legend of, 16
Peshitta, The, 381–3
Pilgrimage songs, 38–9
Polyglot Bibles, 385–6
Priestly Book, the, 135–42; origin and growth of, 138–42
Priest's torah, 52
Prophetic Saying, the, 44–50
Prophets, book of Kings and, 175, 178
Prophets, Former, 143–82, 336–7
Prophets, Latter, 183–277, 336–7

Prophets, Twelve, Book of, 230–2; arrangement of, 231–2
Proto-Isaiah, formation of book, 194
Proverb, 40
Proverbs, 295–9; origin of name, 296; age of, 296–9
Psalms, 278–87; composition of, 279–80, 287; authors of, 280–1; origin and use of book of, 281; liturgical notes added to, 281–2; authors' titles for, 283; formation of book of, 284–5; Davidic Psalter, 285; elohistic psalter, 285–6
Psalter, 278–9; Davidic, 285; elohistic, 285–6
Pseudepigrapha, 340–1, 413–76

Qumran, hymns of, 280; Septuagint fragments at, 370; and book of Enoch, 428; sect of, 473–6

Rad, von, and Conquest tradition, 83; and Pentateuch, 83–90
Rashi, 1
Ras Shamra, 14, 17, 27
Rationalism, 2
Records, 55–6
Red Sea Song, 106–7
Reformation, The, and Scriptures, 1
Reformed Church, and Apocrypha, 347
Rothstein, and Song of Songs, 300
Ruth, book of, 302–5; contents of, 303; date of, 304

Sagas, 59–64
Salvation history, 85, 90, 92
Samuel, Books of, 157–70; origin of, 158; contents, 158–62; and rise of Saul, 162–3; formation of, 165–70; Deuteronomic revision, 168–70
Saul, Books of Samuel and rise of, 162–3
Sayings, 39–53
Scripts, cuneiform, 351; alphabetic, 352; cursive, 353
Septuagint, 339–40, 368–71, 375; printed texts of, 376–7; translations of, 377–80; Coptic versions, 379; and book of Esther, 404–5
'Servant Songs', Isaiah and, 200–4
Shechem, 16
Sibylline Oracles, 423–5
Sihon, taunt-song against, 117
Sites, archaeological exploration of, 450–4
Solomon, and Song of Songs, 299
Solomon, Psalms of, 280, 420–2
Solomon, Wisdom of, 409–12

Song of Songs, 299–302
Song of thanksgiving, 37–8
Song of the Wall, 116
Songs: profane, 26–31; cultic, 32
Statutes, 52–3
Susanna and Daniel, History of, 403
Symmachus, and version of Old Testament, 372

Talmud, and book of Joshua, 143
Targums, The, 380–1
Tertullian, and Canon of Old Testament, 346
Tetrapla, 373
Theodotion, and version of Old Testament, 372
Theophany, 88
Three Children, Song of, 402–3
Tobit, book of, 397–9
Torah, priest's, 52
Torah, The, 69–142, 335, 339, 366–7
Trent, Council of, 364
Tribal sayings, 44
Trito-Isaiah, 205–8
Twelve Patriarchs, Testaments of, 442–5

Vatke, and Biblical Theology, 2
Verval inspiration, from Judaism, 1

Vetus Latina, 377–9, 383
Vulgate, The, 383–4

'War of Sons of Light and Sons of Darkness', 466–70
Weeks, festival of, 83
Wellhausen, and modern school of criticism, 3
Wen Amon, 15
Wisdom, *see* Solomon, Wisdom of
Wisdom saying, the, 40–2
Writing, art of, 14
Writings, The (Kethubhim), 338–9

Yahweh, oath at throne of, 116; book of wars of, 116
Yahweh cult, 49
Yahwistic decalogue, 105
Yahwist source-strand, 99–111; origins of, 102–111; place of origin, 109

Zadokite Document, The, 462–6
Zechariah, 231, 269, 271–2
Zechariah, book of, 269–75; contents of, 269–71, 272–5
Zephaniah, 264, 267
Zephaniah, book of, 264–7
Zion, Songs of, 33

ABBREVIATIONS

1. BIBLICAL BOOKS
(including the Apocrypha)

Am.	= Amos	Lk.	= Luke
Bar.	= Baruch	Macc.	= Maccabees
Bel.	= Bel and the Dragon	Mal.	= Malachi
Chron.	= Chronicles	Mic.	= Micah
Col.	= Colossians	Mk.	= Mark
Cor.	= Corinthians	Mt.	= Matthew
Dan.	= Daniel	Nah.	= Nahum
Deut.	= Deuteronomy	Neh.	= Nehemiah
Eccles.	= Ecclesiastes	Num.	= Numbers
Ecclus.	= Ecclesiasticus (Ben Sira)	Ob.	= Obadiah
Eph.	= Ephesians	Pet.	= Peter
Esd.	= Esdras	Phil.	= Philippians
Est.	= Esther and Rest of Esther	Philem.	= Philemon
Exod.	= Exodus	Pr. Man.	= Prayer of Manasses
Ezr.	= Ezra	Prov.	= Proverbs
Ezek.	= Ezekiel	Ps.	= Psalms
Gal.	= Galatians	Rev.	= Revelations
Gen.	= Genesis	Rom.	= Romans
Hab.	= Habakkuk	Sam.	= Samuel
Hag.	= Haggai	S. of S.	= Song of Songs
Heb.	= Hebrews	S. of III	
Hos.	= Hosea	Ch.	= Song of the Three Holy
Is.	= Isaiah		Children
Jas.	= James	Sus.	= History of Susanna
Jer.	= Jeremiah	Thess.	= Thessalonians
Jgs.	= Judges	Tim.	= Timothy
Jn.	= John	Tit.	= Titus
Jon.	= Jonah	Tob.	= Tobit
Jos.	= Joshua	Wisd.	= Wisdom of Solomon
Kgs.	= Kings	Zech.	= Zechariah
Lam.	= Lamentations	Zeph.	= Zephaniah
Lev.	= Leviticus		

2. COMMENTARIES

ATD	= Das Alte Testament Deutsch, ed. by Herntrich and Weiser, Göttingen.
BK	= Biblischer Kommentar, AT; ed. by Noth, Neukirchen.
BOT	= De Boeken van het Oude Testament; ed. by Grossouw, van der Ploeg, van Dodewaard, Roermond en Maaseik (R.C.)
CEB	= Études Bibliques, Paris (R.C.).
COT	= Commentaar op het O.T.; ed. by Aalders, Gispen, Ridderbos, Kampen.
EB	= Echter Bibel; ed. by Nötscher, Würzburg (R.C.).
EH	= Exegetisches Handbuch zum AT; ed. by Nikel and Schulz, Münster (R.C.).
HAT	= Handbuch zum AT; ed. by Eissfeldt, Tübingen.
HBK	= Herders Bibelkommentar, Freiburg (R.C.).
HK	= Handkommentar zum AT; ed. by Nowack, Göttingen.
HS	= Die Heilige Schrift des AT; ed. by Feldmann and Herkenne, Bonn (R.C.).

HSAT   = Die Heilige Schrift des AT; ed. by Kautzsch; 4th ed. by Bertholet, Tübingen, 1922 f.
HSC   = The Holy Scripture with Commentary, Philadelphia (Jewish).
IB   = Interpreter's Bible; ed. by Buttrick, New York.
ICC   = The International Critical Commentary, Edinburgh.
KAT   = Kommentar zum AT; ed. by Sellin, Leipzig.
KD   = Biblischer Kommentar über das AT; ed. by Keil and Delitzsch, Leipzig.
KeH   = Kurzgefasstes exegetisches Handbuch zum AT, Leipzig.
KHC   = Kurzer Hand-Commentar zum AT; ed. by Marti, Freiburg, Leipzig, Tübingen.
LSB   = La Sacra Biblia; ed. by Garofalo, Turin and Rome (R.C.).
LSBR   = La Sacra Biblia tradotta dai testi originali con note e cura del Pontificio Istituto Biblico di Roma, Florence (R.C.).
LStB   = La Sainte Bible de Jérusalem (Les Editions du Cerf), Paris (R.C.).
LStB
(Clamer) = La Sainte Bible, texte latin et traduction française avec un commentaire exégétique et théologique; ed. by Clamer, Paris (R.C.).
SAT   = Die Schriften des AT; by Gunkel, Gressmann a.o., Göttingen.
SBB   = The Soncino Books of the Bible; ed. by Cohen, London, Bournemouth (Jew.).
SBOT   = The Sacred Books of the OT, ed. by Paul Haupt, Leipzig, Baltimore.
SZ   = Kurzgefasster Kommentar zu den heiligen Schriften Alten und Neuen Testaments; ed. by Strack and Zöckler, Munich.
TBC   = The Torch Bible Commentaries, London.
TU   = Tekst en Uitleg, Praktische Bijbelverklaring; ed by Böhl and van Veldhuizen, Groningen, den Haag.
WC   = Westminster Commentaries; ed. by Lock and Simpson, London.

3. PERIODICALS, ETC.

AfO   = Archiv für Orientforschung, Berlin.
AJSL   = American Journal of Semitic Languages and Literatures, Chicago.
Alt I   = Alt, Kleine Schriften zur Geschichte des Volkes Israel, Vol. I, 1953
Alt II   = Alt, Kleine Schriften zur Geschichte des Volkes Israel, Vol. II, 1953.
ANET   = Ancient Near Eastern Texts Relating to the Old Testament, ed. by Pritchard, 1955.
AO   = Der alte Orient, Leipzig.
AOB   = Altorientalische Bilder zum Alten Testament; ed. by Gressmann, 2nd ed., Berlin, 1926.
AOT   = Altorientalische Texte zum Alten Testament; ed. by Gressmann, 2nd ed., Berlin, 1926.
ATAO   = A. Jeremias, Das Alte Testament im Lichte des alten Orients, 4th ed., 1930.
ARW   = Archiv für Religionswissenschaft, Leipzig and Berlin.
BASOR   = Bulletin of the American Schools of Oriental Research, New Haven (Conn.).
BJRL   = Bulletin of the John Ryland's Library, Manchester.
BRL   = Biblisches Reallexikon by K. Galling, Tübingen, 1937.
BWAT   = Beiträge zur Wissenschaft vom Alten Testament; ed. by R. Kittel, Alt and G. Kittel, Leipzig, Stuttgart.
BZ   = Biblische Zeitschrift, Paderborn.
BZAW   = Beihefte zur Zeitschrift für die altestamentliche Wissenschaft, Giessen.
FRLANT = Forschung zur Religion und Literatur des Alten und Neuen Testaments; ed. by Bousset, Gunkel, Bultmann, Göttingen.
HThR   = The Harvard Theological Review, Cambridge (Mass.).
HUCA   = Hebrew Union College Annual, Cincinnati (Ohio).

JAOS	= Journal of American Oriental Society, New Haven (Conn.).
JBL	= Journal of Biblical Literature, New Haven (Conn.).
JNESt	= Journal of Near Eastern Studies, Chicago.
JPOS	= Journal of the Palestine Oriental Society, Jerusalem.
JpTh	= Jahrbücher für protestantische Theologie, Braunschweig.
JQR	= Jewish Quarterly Review, Philadelphia.
JSS	= Journal of Semitic Studies, Manchester.
JThSt	= Journal of Theological Studies, Oxford.
MGWJ	= Monatsschrift für Geschichte und Wissenschaft des Judentums, Breslau.
NKZ	= Neue kirchliche Zeitschrift, Erlangen and Leipzig.
OLZ	= Orientalistische Literaturzeitung, Leipzig.
OSt	= Oudtestamentische Studien, Leiden.
OTMSt	= Old Testament and Modern Study, ed. by Rowley, 1951.
PEFQSt	= Palestine Exploration Fund, Quarterly Statements, London.
PJB	= Palästina-Jahrbuch, Berlin.
RB	= Revue Biblique, Paris and Rome.
RHPhR	= Revue d'histoire et de philosophie religieuses, Strassburg, Paris.
RHR	= Revue de l'histoire des Religions, Paris.
RVB	= Religionsgeschichtliche Volksbücher, Tübingen.
SPCK	= Society for Promoting Christian Knowledge, London.
ThBl	= Theologische Blätter, Leipzig.
ThLZ	= Theologische Literatur-Zeitung, Leipzig.
ThR	= Theologische Rundschau, Tübingen.
ThStKr	= Theologische Studien und Kritiken, Stuttgart and Gotha.
ThWB	= Theologisches Wörterbuch zum Neuen Testament; founded by G. Kittel; ed. by G. Friedrich, Stuttgart.
ThZ	= Theologische Zeitschrift; ed. by the Theol. Faculty Basel, Basel.
TThQ	= Tübinger Theologische Quartalschrift.
VT	= Vetus Testamentum, Leiden
WZKM	= Wiener Zeitschrift für die Kunde des Morgenlandes.
ZAW	= Zeitschrift für die alttestamentliche Wissenschaft, Giessen, Berlin.
ZDMG	= Zeitschrift der Deutschen Morgenländischen Gesellschaft, Leipzig.
ZDPV	= Zeitschrift des Deutschen Palästina-Vereins, Leipzig.
ZKWL	= Zeitschrift für kirchliche Wissenschaft und kirchliches Leben, Leipzig.
ZMR	= Zeitschrift für Missionskunde und Religionswissenschaft, Berlin.
ZNW	= Zeitschrift für die neutestamentliche Wissenschaft und die Kunde der älteren Kirche, Giessen, Berlin.
ZS	= Zeitschrift für Semitistik und verwandte Gebiete, Leipzig.
ZSTh	= Zeitschrift für Systematische Theologie, Gütersloh, Berlin.
ZThK	= Zeitschrift für Theologie und Kirche, Tübingen.
ZWTh	= Zeitschrift für wissenschaftliche Theologie, Jena, Halle, Leipzig.

4. DICTIONARIES AND ENCYCLOPEDIAS
(See the relevant articles)

(a) Protestant

PRE	= Realenzyklopädie für prot. Theologie und Kirche, 3rd ed., Leipzig, 1896–1913.
RGG	= Die Religion in Geschichte und Gegenwart; 2nd ed., Tübingen, 1927–32. 3rd ed., 1956 ff.
BRL	= Galling, Biblisches Reallexikon (HAT), 1937.
	Evang. Kirchenlexikon, ed. by Brunotte and Weber, Göttingen, 1955, ff.
	Hastings-Selbie, Dictionary of the Bible, Edinburgh, 1898–1907.
	Cheyne-Black, Encyclopaedia Biblica, London, 1899–1903.
	Jackson, The new Schaff-Herzog Encyclopaedia of Religious Knowledge, New York-London, 1908–1912.
	Hastings, Encyclopaedia of Religion and Ethics, 1908–1926.

(b) Roman Catholic

Vigouroux, Dictionaire de la Bible, Paris, 1905–1912; Supplement, 1926–1932.
Buchberger, Lexikon für Theologie und Kirche, 1930 ff.
Bibellexikon, ed. by Haag, Einsiedeln, Zürich, Köln, 1951 ff.

(c) Jewish

Encyclopaedia Judaica, Berlin, 1928, ff.

(d) General

Pauly-Wissowa, Kroll-Ziegler, Realenzyklopädie der klassischen Altertumswissenschaft, revised, Leipzig, 1893 ff.

These titles refer to the bibliographies for each section or to the books mentioned in section 1.